Fodor's
Portugal

SO-ATA-815

Fodor's Travel Publications, Inc.
New York • Toronto • London • Sydney • Auckland

Fodor's Portugal

Editor: Alison Hoffman
Researcher: Mary Ellen Schultz
Contributors: Jules Brown, Robert Blake, Dennis Jaffe, David Ing, Andrea Lehman, Deborah Luhrman, Larry Peterson, Linda K. Schmidt
Creative Director: Fabrizio La Rocca
Cartographer: David Lindroth
Illustrator: Kark Tanner
Cover Photograph: Owen Franken

Design: Vignelli Associates

Special Sales

Contents

Maps

Foreword

While every care has been taken to ensure the accuracy of the information in this guide, the passage of time will always bring change, and consequently, the publisher cannot accept responsibility for errors that may occur.

All prices and opening times quoted here are based on information supplied to us at press time. Hours and admission fees may change, however, and the prudent traveler will avoid inconvenience by calling ahead.

Fodor's wants to hear about your travel experiences, both pleasant and unpleasant. When a hotel or restaurant fails to live up to its billing, let us know and we will investigate the complaint and revise our entries where the facts warrant it.

Send your letters to the editors of Fodor's Travel Publications, 201 E. 50th Street, New York, NY 10022.

Special thanks to Ana Marie Osório and Carlos Lameiro with the Portuguese National Tourist Office in New York; Gloria Melo at TAP Air Portugal; Pilar Pereira at the Portuguese National Tourist Office in London; Fátima Santana at the Portuguese Tourism Promotion Board in Lisbon; Manuel Nascimento and Maria Fernanda Rocha Ribeira at Portuguese Railways; Elisabeth Santos with the Algarve Tourist Board; Luisa Mendoca with the Portuguese Promotion Board in Oporto; José Martins dos Santos; and John Pare. And most greatly appreciated was the assistance of Mary Ellen Schultz, without whose translation *and* patience *Fodor's Portugal* would not have been possible.

Highlights and Fodor's Choice

Highlights

Portugal is a rapidly changing country. Since its entry into the European Community (EC) in 1986, it's seen a deluge of high-rise office buildings and apartment complexes, twisting superhighways where men with oxcarts used to dominate brick-paved lanes, and an influx of scantily clad sunbathers who frolic with their blaring boom boxes along once-secluded stretches of beach.

However, this is not to suggest that Portugal has become one huge shopping mall surrounded by asphalt. The country is proud and respectful of its history, and it understands the necessity of preserving the past. A walk through almost any town or village here reveals Portugal's tradition: *Fado* (traditional Portuguese music, with a soulful blues sound) drifts into the alleys from neighborhood cafés, and smells of fresh grilled sardines—a longtime favorite—permeate the air.

The Portuguese Office of Tourism has earmarked considerable amounts of money to promote its country around the world. Hence, tourism has increased 900% between 1976 and 1992—to 18 million visitors from 2 million. This is good and bad news for the overseas traveler. No longer is Portugal the inexpensive destination it once was, both because of its increasing popularity and because the dollar has been weak throughout Europe. On the up side, however, Portuguese tourist offices inside and outside the country have become genuinely enthusiastic and are well stocked with literature, itineraries, and maps.

The next several years will be especially good ones for visiting Portugal. In 1992 the country began celebrating the **500-year anniversary of the "Discoveries,"** which commemorates valorous mariners who unlocked sea routes to Africa, India, the Far East, and the Americas. Events throughout the country hail great explorations that surpassed even those of the Dutch and the Spanish. Museum exhibits, concerts, and cultural events throughout the country are scheduled for the next few years.

No one can say, however, that Portugal lives in the past: With an eye toward the future, Lisbon has just been named to host **EXPO '98** (the last EXPO of the century); it will host multimillion-dollar exhibits that are expected to attract at least 9 million visitors over a three-month period. The theme of EXPO '98 will be "The Oceans, A Legacy for the Future," which will spotlight the key role the seas have played in world history and their vital importance in the coming century.

In preparation for all of its visitors Portugal is building and renovating a variety of hotels. Sizes and styles range from the **Venezia in Lisbon** (a 19th-century mansion reborn as a 38-room bed-and-breakfast) to the new **Sheraton Algarve Hotel & Resort** (a 183-room all-inclusive resort that opened in August 1992). One of the most eagerly awaited, however, is the luxurious new **Tivoli** (located near the banks of the Rio Tejo), scheduled to open in early 1993.

Another lodging option, and one that should be included on every itinerary, is the *pousada* (government-run inn). Presently there are 30 situated in converted castles, convents, and national monuments throughout the country. Portugal recently celebrated its 50th anniversary of the opening of its first pousada, which means "resting place." Visiting these small, elegant hostelries that are located mostly in rural areas has been itinerary enough for more than a few travelers, and now the national network proudly and eagerly awaits more prospective openings, in Queluz Palace in Lisbon, a convent in Beja, and a castle in the town of Alvito.

To make travel in Portugal easier, a major overhaul of roadways has begun, as the country literally paves its way to the future. A new **superhighway** between Lisbon and Oporto cuts driving time to just over three hours, with connecting highways farther north and west. There are better roads now between Lisbon and Fátima, between Fátima and Oporto, and along the Estoril Coast, site of the annual Grand Prix Formula One World Championship.

The important thing to remember when visiting Portugal is that no matter how much time you have to explore, the country is both small enough to cover a lot of territory in a few days and large enough to hold out the promise of more to discover the next time.

Fodor's Choice

No two people will agree on what makes a perfect vacation, but it can be fun and helpful to know what others think. We hope you'll have a chance to experience some of Fodor's choices yourself while visiting Portugal. For detailed information of individual entries, see the relevant sections of this guidebook.

Castles and Palaces

Castelo de Bragança (Bragança)

Castelo de São Felipe (Setúbal)

Castelo de São Jorge (Lisbon)

Fortaleza de Sagres (Sagres)

Palácio dos Biscainhos (Braga)

Palácio Nacional de Pena (Sintra)

Palácio Nacional de Queluz (Queluz)

Towns and Villages

Arraiolas

Batalha

Câmara de Lobos (Madeira)

Cascais

Coimbra

Évora

Funchal (Madeira)

Guimarães

Lisbon

Loulé

Óbidos

Oporto

Sagres

Santana (Madeira)

Setúbal

Silves

Sintra

Viana do Castelo

Vila do Conde

Churches and Monastaries

Basilica de Santa Luzia (Viana do Castelo)

Convento de São Gonçalo (Amarante)

Convento do Carmo (Lisbon)

Igreja de Sao Domingos (Guimarães)

Igreja do Carmo (Faro)

Mosteiro de Alcobaça (Alcobaça)

Mosteiro de Batalha (Batalha)

Mosteiro de Mafra (Mafra)

Mosteiro dos Jerónimos (Lisbon)

Sé (Lisbon)

Sé Velha (Coimbra)

Sinagoga de Tomar (Tomar)

Templo de Diana (Évora)

Museums

Museu Calouste Gulbenkian (Lisbon)

Museu de Arte Popular (Lisbon)

Museu de Grão Vasco (Viseu)

Museu de Machado de Castro (Coimbra)

Museu de Rafael Bordalo Pinheiro (Caldas da Rainha)

Museu do Convento de Jesus (Aveiro)

Museu Municipal de Viana (Viana do Castelo)

Ruinas de Conímbriga (Conímbriga)

Squares and Parks

Jardim de Monserrate (Setais)

Jardim do Antigo Paço Episcopal (Castelo Branco)

Parque Nacional de Peneda-Gerês (Braga)

Parque Nacional de Serra de Aire e Candeeiros (between Lisbon/Coimbra)

Praça da República (Viana do Castelo)

Praça de Comércio (Lisbon)

Praça de Dom Dûarte (Viseu)

Praça do Geraldo (Évora)

Serra d'Arrábida (near Setúbal)

Hotels

Buçaco Palace, Buçaco (*Very Expensive*)

Hotel Palácio, Estoril (*Very Expensive*)

Hotel Ritz, Lisbon (*Very Expensive*)

Hotel Dom Luís, Coimbra (*Expensive*)

Pousada da Ria, Aveiro (*Expensive*)

Pousada de Santa Marinha, Guimarães (*Expensive*)

Pousada de São Felipe, Setúbal (*Expensive*)

Pousada de São Pedro, Évora (*Expensive*)

Reids, Funchal (*Expensive*)

Albergaria Senhora do Monte, Lisbon (*Moderate*)

Arcada, Aveiro (*Moderate*)

Grande Hotel do Porto, Oporto (*Moderate*)

Hotel Grão Vasco, Viseu (*Moderate*)

Hotel Praia, Nazaré (*Moderate*)

Hotel Tivoli Sintra, Sintra (*Moderate*)

Casa de Lumena, Faro (*Inexpensive*)

Hotel Flamingo, Lisbon (*Inexpensive*)

Restaurants

Aviz, Lisbon (*Very Expensive*)

Tavares Rico, Lisbon (*Very Expensive*)

Buçaco Palace, Buçaco (*Expensive–Very Expensive*)

Cidade Velha, Faro (*Expensive*)

A Veranda da Sé, Viseu (*Moderate–Expensive*)

Golfinho, Funchal (*Moderate*)

Jardim d'Allah, Albufeira (*Moderate*)

O Alambique, Viana do Castelo (*Moderate*)

Pedro dos Letões, Curia (*Moderate*)

Rio Azul, Setúbal (*Moderate*)

Bom Jardim, Lisbon (*Inexpensive*)

O Peleiro, Figueira da Foz (*Inexpensive*)

Europe

World Time Zones

MONDAY
SUNDAY

International Date Line

+12 +13   -9   -4   -3

-10   -3

-11   -5   -4

-3:30

+11   +12   -11   -10   -9   -8   -7   -6   -5   -4   -3

Numbers below vertical bands relate each zone to Greenwich Mean Time (0 hrs.).
Local times frequently differ from these general indications,
as indicated by light-face numbers on map.

Algiers, **29**	Berlin, **34**	Delhi, **48**	Istanbul, **40**
Anchorage, **3**	Bogotá, **19**	Denver, **8**	Jerusalem, **42**
Athens, **41**	Budapest, **37**	Djakarta, **53**	Johannesburg, **44**
Auckland, **1**	Buenos Aires, **24**	Dublin, **26**	Lima, **20**
Baghdad, **46**	Caracas, **22**	Edmonton, **7**	Lisbon, **28**
Bangkok, **50**	Chicago, **9**	Hong Kong, **56**	London (Greenwich), **27**
Beijing, **54**	Copenhagen, **33**	Honolulu, **2**	Los Angeles, **6**
	Dallas, **10**		Madrid, **38**
			Manila, **57**

Prime Meridian

+5 +8 +10

+8 +9 +10 +11

+1 +2

+6 +7

+4 +5

+3

+4 +5 +8

+11

+12

+2

+9

+3 +3:30 +4:30

+5:45 +6

+8

+5 +5:30 +6:30

+8

0 +1 +2 +8

+3

+3

+9

+2

+8 +9:30 +10

Prime Meridian

-1 0 +1 +2 +3 +4 +5 +6 +7 +8 +9 +10

Greenwich
Mean Time

Mecca, **47**
Mexico City, **12**
Miami, **18**
Montréal, **15**
Moscow, **45**
Nairobi, **43**
New Orleans, **11**
New York City, **16**

Ottawa, **14**
Paris, **30**
Perth, **58**
Reykjavík, **25**
Rio de Janeiro, **23**
Rome, **39**
Saigon (Ho Chi Minh City), **51**

San Francisco, **5**
Santiago, **21**
Seoul, **59**
Shanghai, **55**
Singapore, **52**
Stockholm, **32**
Sydney, **61**
Tokyo, **60**

Toronto, **13**
Vancouver, **4**
Vienna, **35**
Warsaw, **36**
Washington, D.C., **17**
Yangon, **49**
Zürich, **31**

Introduction

By Jules Brown

Jules Brown is a travel-book editor and freelance writer who enjoys such destinations as Portugal, Sweden, and Hong Kong.

West across the Iberian peninsula, from Spain's arid plains and burning sun, Portugal's natural grandeur and color unfold to reveal a sweeping coastline and a mountainous, green interior. Those familiar with Spain and its treasures can expect the same gifts from Portugal, including fine food and wine, spectacularly situated castles, excellent beaches, and hilltop villages that date from the Middle Ages. These similarities, and the countries' close proximity to each another would suggest that Portugal and Spain are very much alike. For as much as they are, however, the two countries differ. First, Portugal sees far less tourism than Spain, so it's still possible to travel into the heart of the provinces and be among few, if any, visitors. Also, the languages spoken in the two countries are worlds apart, although Portuguese does have some Spanish influence, in addition to French and Arabic influences. Perhaps the most obvious difference, though, is that although it's firmly Atlantic-facing Portugal has a Mediterranean air, especially in its Moorish-influenced architecture.

High economic growth (in excess of that of most of its European partners) and heavy foreign investment have benefited large sectors of the population. Many people are employed in the tourism industry, which now accounts for about 10% of the country's gross national product. Accordingly, the resort areas and cities are now anything but undiscovered: The southern Algarve coast, for example, is one of Europe's most touristed regions. Lisbon, too, has rapidly acquired the trappings of a forward-looking commercial capital. Many of its turn-of-the-century buildings are being replaced by skyscrapers, and renovation and modernization have touched every part of the capital. Many of the architectural and cultural features that once made Portugal unique now stand side by side with contemporary styles, an all-too-familiar occurrence in late-20th-century Europe. However, away from Lisbon and the busy Algarve there are still country villages, isolated beaches, crumbling historic towns, and hidden valleys that have barely changed over the past 100 years or more.

Geography The major surprise for most visitors to Portugal is its topography: It's a far greener land than Spain, with a riot of flowers, trees, and shrubs that provide color and shade throughout the country. There's also an enormous variety of landscapes in what is a relatively small European nation. A long, rectangular area only slightly larger than the state of Indiana, mainland Portugal measures just 560 kilometers (350 miles) from north to south and 220 kilometers (138 miles) from east to west at its widest point. It's bordered on the north and east by Spain and on the south and west by the Atlantic Ocean, and is temperate year-round, especially along the coasts. Portugal rarely suffers the extreme heat of other Mediterranean countries.

This strip of land contains an extraordinary range of geographical variations unexpected in a country of Portugal's size. The mountainous northeast on the mainland provides the greatest contrast for travelers who have just left the central plains of Spain. Here is a seldom-visited region with the Shangri-la name of Trás-os-Montes (Beyond the Mountains), an unspoiled area of rugged beauty that offers tumbling rivers, expansive forests, hilltop castles, and sparsely populated villages that appear to have changed little through the centuries. Extremes of temperature dictate custom and the local economy: The long, often harsh, winters have earned the northern part of region the name Terra Fria (Cold Land); the months of June, July, and August are dry and hot, turning the land tawny. In the milder, more fertile, southern part of the region—the Terra Quente (Hot Land)—lie the vineyards of the Upper Douro valley. Grapes from this area contribute to the country's most famous export, port wine. The vineyards, like all the land of Trás-os-Montes, depend upon the Rio Douro (River Douro), whose tributaries (the Tamega, Corgo, and Tua) lace the region.

To the west, beyond the town of Vila Real, the region known as the Minho displays a gentler character. Touching the Atlantic and stretching from the northern Spanish border south to Oporto (the country's second largest city), the Minho contains the lush hinterland of Portugal's most renowned rivers, the Rio Minho itself, the Lima, and the Douro. In this mass of predominantly green landscape are the Costa Verde (Green Coast), the beautiful pine-tree-lined coast north of Oporto, and the inland hills and valleys where the slightly sparkling *vinho verde* (green wine) is produced. Winters are mild here, and the Minho is heavily cultivated with plenty of rain; summers are short and temperate—a climate akin to that of Galicia, in northwest Spain, which the Minho resembles at several points.

Moving southeast, the central Beira region contains Portugal's highest mountains, the Serra da Estrela (Estrela Mountains), which reach a height of 1,991 meters (6,530 feet) and offer the best hiking and skiing possibilities in the country. In the Beira Alta (Upper Beira)—between Viseu, Guarda, and Covilhã—the winter frost is fierce, and the wind whistles through a string of hilltowns which, while little known to foreigners, are the heart of Portugal's history. As in the very north of the country, there's a distinct geographical and climatic shift as you move west towards the coast, leaving the mountains behind for the fertile expanses of the Beira Litoral (Coastal Beira) plain. It's a temperate, low-lying country, threatened by flooding from the mountains, though at Aveiro in the north of the region the water has been tamed by an extensive network of canals and drainage channels. The coast itself, the pine-forested Costa da Prata, is one of the finest sandy stretches in the country, while inland from the main resort of Figuera da Foz is the famous university town of Coimbra, which lies on the banks of the Rio Mondego (Mondego River).

The mountains finally peter out on the southern edge of the Beira. The provinces of the Estremadura and the Ribatejo extend south and west to Lisbon, following a line drawn by the wide valley of the Rio Tejo (River Tagus). The Estremadura is highly populated, and contains some of the country's most famous towns and monuments scattered about its rolling hills and glorious coastline. Summers are long, hot, and bright, particularly in the seaside resorts, which stretch south as far as the Estoril Coast, west of Lisbon. In this region there's a unique microclimate, which ensures that the winters are milder than in the capital; in summer, the resorts of Estoril and Cascais enjoy a permanent breeze that offsets the high temperatures that plague Lisbon itself. Out of the capital, and across the Rio Tejo, you're soon in the Ribatejo (literally translated as the "banks-of-the-River Tagus"), famous as a bull-breeding district, and whose mainly flat lands fade into the vast plains of the southern Alentejo region.

Once known as the granary of Portugal, the Alentejo is a thinly populated, largely agricultural region of grain fields, cork, and olive trees, and is as remote in its way as Trás-os-Montes, though with none of the compensating grandeur. That said, there are some impressive Atlantic beaches (whipped year-round by a strong wind), and a pretty eastern section, where the Rio Guadiana (River Gaudiana) forms the frontier with Spain. In the Alentejo summer starts early (March), and there's little shade from the sun. There's also very little rainfall, except perhaps in early spring and autumn.

Dividing the Alentejo from Portugal's southernmost coastal province, the Algarve, is a continuous range of mountains—the Serra de Monchique (Monchique Mountains) and the Serra de Caldeirão (Caldeirão Mountains). The Algarve boasts some 3,000 hours of sunshine annually, and its low-lying plains, rocky coastline (in the west), sand-bar islands (in the east), and sweeping beaches comprise Portugal's busiest tourist region. In August, when the sun is hottest, this is probably the Portuguese province where the midday heat is most unbearable, though it's easy to cool off in a pool or in the sea. The Algarve is also the only real year-round destination in Portugal, despite the general clemency of the climate elsewhere. The region feels semi-tropical: Coastal winter days are warm and bright, the wildflowers strung across the low hills start to bloom early in February, and temperatures stay high until late-October.

Lying 1,220 kilometers (760 miles) due west of Lisbon are the volcanic islands of Madeira and the Azores. These islands, which are under Portuguese jurisdiction, have an equable subtropical climate tempered by the Gulf Stream, with warm summers and mild winters.

A result of Portugal's varied geography and climate has been that the country has become a fascinating target for nature lovers. Many regions have been turned into nature reserves, which are excellent places to see the country's flora and fauna. The oldest reserve is Peneda-Gerês, in the extreme north of the country, reaching up to the Spanish border, where wild boar and horses roam the mountains. Lesser northern reserves are those of Alvão, near Vila Real, and the Serra da Malcata on the Spanish frontier, east of the peaks of the Serra da Estrela. Interesting wildlife areas farther south include the mountainous regions around Sintra, near Lisbon, and the Serra da Arrábida (Arrábida Mountains), near Setúbal, while water-based reserves include the estuary of the Rio Sado, south of Lisbon, and the Algarve coast, from Faro east to Vila Real de Santo António. This last region is a stop-over for waders and sea-birds on their migration south.

History Blessed with this salubrious climate, abundant game, and fish from the rivers and long coastline, the part of the Iberian peninsula that is now Portugal supported a once-flourishing prehistoric population. Few traces of the culture remain, however, save the ancient sculpted stone boar fertility symbols found in Trás-os-Montes, and the huge Colussus of Pedralva, a mysterious seated figure in granite, on display in the Museu Martins Sarmento in Guimarães. The later arrival of the Celtic (700 BC–600 BC) peoples in northern Portugal is recorded in a series of *citanias* (fortified hill settlements), which appear throughout the Minho; the most impressive example is at Briteiros, between Braga and Guimarães. Phoenicians traded at the site of present-day Lisbon, and the Carthaginians and Greeks set up trading posts on Portugal's southern shore. However, it wasn't until the Roman annexation of the peninsula after the Second Punic War (218–202 BC) that the region came under any kind of unified control. There was resistance to the Roman advance, particularly in central Portugal, where the heroic chieftain Viriatus of the Lusitani tribe held the legions at bay for several decades, until his eventual defeat in 139 BC. Despite the subsequent colonization of much of the country, little of the Roman period survives in modern Portugal. Roads, acqueducts, and elegant bridges (like those at Chaves and Ponte de Lima) were built, and cities founded, though the only substantial remains are at Évora, where there's a fine temple from the 2nd century, and at the preserved Roman town of

Conimbriga, near Coimbra. A less obvious Roman relic is *latifundia*, the system of vast agricultural estates established in the Alentejo. Here the Romans introduced to Portugal new crops that have become mainstays of the domestic economy: wheat, barley, olives, and grapes.

The Moorish invasion of the Iberian peninsula in 711 has had a lasting effect on the country, particularly in the south where place names and peoples' features still echo from Moorish times. The Moors established a capital at Silves in the Algarve (derived from the Moorish, *al-Gharb*, meaning "west of the land beyond"); allowed freedom of worship; planted great orchards on irrigated land; and spread a Moorish-Arab culture of great significance. Arab rule stood firm until the 12th century, when Christian forces under Dom (King) Afonso Henriques moved south from their stronghold at Guimarães in the Minho to take successive Moorish towns and castles at Leiria, Santarém, and Sintra. The ramparts and battlements of these fortresses are all visible today, a reminder both of the Moorish genius for siting defences and of the Christian effort involved in overcoming them. The most significant victory was at Lisbon in 1147, with the storming of the Moorish fortress on the site of the present–day Castelo de São Jorge. A Burgundian by descent, Afonso Henriques was by now being called the first king of all Portugal, and he ordered the building of Lisbon's proud Sé (Cathedral) in celebration of the victory. Many other churches in Portugal mark the path of the reconquest (as the Moors were pushed south), particularly the numerous Romanesque chapels that cover the landscape between the Rio Minho and Rio Douro.

Southern Alentejo and the Algarve remained in Arab hands until Christian reconquest in the mid-13th century, by which time the fledgling kingdom of Portugal extended to its current borders. The country took final shape in 1260 when Afonso III—conqueror of Faro and the western Algarve from the Moors—moved the capital from its early site at Coimbra to Lisbon.

The early kings of Portugal, from the dynastic House of Burgundy, moved quickly to establish their independent country. Recognition was gained from the neighboring Castilian rulers, although fortresses were built to guard the Spanish frontier as a precaution. Those at Beja and Estremoz are evocative examples. A *Cortes* (parliament) was assembled, and a university founded, initially in Lisbon in 1290 but transfered to Coimbra in 1308. The grand university buildings that you see today in Coimbra date from the 16th century, when the scholastic foundation was declared permanent, but the evident sense of pride in the city goes back to the university's origins; it remained the only university in Portugal until this century. The transitional Gothic style of building became replaced by a more typically Portuguese style, and some handsome cloisters, in particular, survive from this period, at Guimarães, Coimbra, Lisbon, and Évora.

The House of Burgundy was succeeded by the House of Aviz, whose first king, Dom João I, roundly defeated the Castilian army at the Battle of Aljubarrota (1385) to end any lingering Castilian thoughts of domination over Portugal. It was a significant victory that secured the independence of Portugal for nearly two centuries, and allowed Portuguese kings to turn their attention to the maritime ventures that were to guarantee them fabulous colonial wealth. João I marked the victory by building the extraordinarily beautiful abbey of Nossa Senhora da Vitoria at Batalha in Estremadura, not far from the battlefield. It's one of the finest expressions of Portuguese nationalism. Triumphant in tone, the abbey celebrates not only the Portuguese release from Castilian interference, but also the important historical link with England. The Treaty of Windsor, signed a year after the battle, confirmed the Anglo-Portuguese alliance, and in 1387 João I married Philippa of Lancaster, daughter of John of Gaunt. Philippa and João are buried side by side in the abbey's chapel, as are their children, one of whom was Prince Henry the Navigator, the man who did the most to influence Portugal's rapid 15th-century expansion.

Based at Sagres, on the western tip of the Algarve, Prince Henry surrounded himself with seamen, map-makers, and astrologers. Under the protection of the mighty *fortaleza* (fortress), which still stands, these men were the first to establish the principles of navigation on the high seas. The caravelle, a ship capable of navigating in a cross wind, was developed and the famous maritime discoveries were soon under way: Madeira and the Azores were discovered in 1419 and 1427 respectively, and by 1460 (when Henry died) the west coast of Africa was known to Portuguese seamen. There were no limits to the inquisitiveness, or to the bravery of the Portuguese sailors. Bartolomeu Dias rounded the southern tip of Africa in 1487, naming it the Cape of Good Hope; 10 years later, Vasco da Gama reached Calcutta; and in 1500 Pedro Alvares Cabral sailed to Brazil. By the mid-16th century, the Portuguese empire had spread over four continents, with trading posts in the Far East and a Portuguese monopoly in force throughout the Indian Ocean.

The wealth gained from this aggressive expansionism knew no bounds. Portugal was at the height of her influence, with Lisbon the richest city in Europe, and under Dom Manuel I (1495–1521), the Crown intervened to take a fifth of the maritime trading profits. With the proceeds, Manuel began to adorn Portugal with buildings and monuments worthy of an Imperial power, and the late-Gothic architecture that evolved has since come to be recognized as Manueline style. If there's any doubt about the brimming confidence of that era, one look at the Manueline buildings of Portugal will dispel it immediately. The elaborate decoration that is the hallmark of Manueline architecture is at once inspiring and instructive: inspiring in its sheer novelty, instructive in that it could only have been the child of a great maritime power. Buildings and monuments are supported by twisted stone columns and covered with sculpted emblems of Portugal's conquests on the high seas and in distant lands: Representations of anchors, seaweed, and rigging mingle with exotic animals and strange, occasionally pagan, symbols, a fusion of diverse cultures and civilizations brought together under the umbrella of a Christian Portuguese empire. The interior decoration of the Igreja de Jesus (Church of Jesus), begun in 1494 in Setúbal, near Lisbon, is generally considered to be the earliest appearance of the Manueline style in Portugal. It was soon overshadowed by exuberant works in the capital itself, at Belém, where the Mosteiro dos Jerónimos (Jerónimos Monastery) and the Torre de Belém (Belém Tower) are two of the most visited surviving examples in the country. The abbey of Batalha was transformed by its Manueline renovations, in particular the portal of the Capelas Imperfeitas (Unfinished Chapels), which is among the most impressive of all Manueline works. A tour of any of these buildings is a requisite to understanding the untrammeled power and influence of 16th-century Portugal, but also perhaps to recognizing the strong national identity that the Portuguese retain today. The pride in these buildings goes beyond mere architectural prowess, and is most evident in Tomar's Convento de Cristo (Convent of Christ), whose supreme Manueline ornamentation in the windows of the Chapter House stands as the most eloquent reminder of the Portuguese age of discovery.

Although the buildings have survived, the glories of the Portuguese empire were relatively shortlived. The disastrous crusade in Morocco by the young Dom Sebastião in 1578, where the king perished alongside most of the country's nobility, allowed Phillip II of Spain to renew his claim to Portugal. Spanish rule lasted 60 years (1580–1640), during which time many of Portugal's overseas posessions were lost, but in 1640 the Portuguese took back their throne when a nobleman from the powerful Portuguese House of Bragança was installed as Dom João IV. The Bragança dynasty was to last until the first years of the 20th century, but for the most part there was a hollow ring to its pretensions as a power. Fueled by the gold and diamonds extracted from Brazil, there was extravagant spending on irrationally grand projects, like the massive monastery at Mafra (which employed 50,000 workmen), the university library at Coimbra, and the excessive decoration of the Capela de São João Baptista (Chapel of St. John the Baptist) in Lisbon. However, with the domestic economy still weak, and society strictly feudal, it took the appalling devastation of the 1755 earthquake, which destroyed Lisbon, before renewed life was breathed into commerce and industry. The king's chief minister at the time, the Marquês de Pombal, ordered that the capital's dead be buried and the living fed. He then immediately set about creating a new, planned Lisbon that took heed of the most advanced architectural and social ideas of the age, resulting in an elegant but restrained style of building later known as "Pombaline." To walk through downtown Lisbon today is to walk through shades of the 18th century, starting in the elegant colonnaded riverside square, the Praça do Comércio, and through the gridded Baixa (Lower) district, expressly designed by Pombal to house the trades and commercial concerns he was keen to promote. Lisbon's glory is its 18th-century buildings, and its sense of measured space, an early example of town planning that's repeated elsewhere in Portugal, most notably in the gridded streets of Vila Real de Santo António, the easternmost town of the Algarve.

These developments proved to be mere diversions from the economic, social, and moral poverty of the Portuguese crown. Napoleon's invasions during the Peninsular War left the country devastated, and the monarchy was finally overthrown in 1910. A republic was proclaimed, but the rot of instability had set in and during the next 16 years 44 different governments attempted to rescue Portugal from its malaise. A coup d'etat followed in 1926, and from 1928 onward the country was governed by the right-wing dictatorship of António Salazar, who—first as Minister of Finance, then as Prime Minister—was strongly influenced by the contemporary Italian and Spanish Fascist movements led by Mussolini and Franco, respectively. The dictatorship was to last until 1974.

Art and Architecture The four-and-a-half decades of introverted Portuguese dictatorship were a chastening experience for a people whose ancestors had joyfully announced their political independence and superiority in innovative architecture, daring decorative arts, and challenging painting and literature. The Manueline style (described above) is perhaps the most obvious architectural manifestation of the Portuguese national character, but other developments proved to be of similar significance. Following the discovery of gold in Brazil at the end of the 17th century, churches, particularly, began to be embellished in an extraordinary rococo style, which employed *talha dourada* (polychrome and gilded carved wood) to stupendous, pictorial effect. Sadly, the great golden interior of the Cistercian abbey at Alcobaça was removed at the beginning of this century, leaving its structure evocative but bare. Nevertheless, there are superb surviving examples at the churches of São Francisco (St. Francis) in Oporto and SantoAntónio (St. Anthony) in Lagos, and at the Convento de Jesus (Convent of Jesus) at Aveiro. As a contrast, for rococo at its most restrained, you must visit the lovely royal palace at Queluz, in the environs of Lisbon.

Aside from the baroque and rococo work in buildings and churches all over the country, one of the most notable images of Portugal which visitors take away with them is the abundance of *azulejos* (painted ceramic tiles). Throughout the country, in nearly every town and village—adorning churches, palaces, fountains, public buildings, and private homes—you can see a veritable open-air art display of the tiles, reflecting the Portuguese love of decoration and ostentation. Originally introduced by the Moors, the tiles featured geometrical designs and a wide variety of colors, the best example of which is still in place at the Paco Real (Royal Palace) in Sintra. By the 17th century the early styles were being replaced by whole panels that depicted religious or secular motifs, often based on engravings and colored blue and white. These are the most enduring of all Portugal's azulejos, with fine examples throughout the country, especially at the Fronteira palace on the outskirts of Lisbon. Anyone particularly interested in the development of the tilework should visit at least one of the museums that feature some of the best-preserved examples: Lisbon's Museu do Azulejo and Museu de Arte Antiga, and Coimbra's Museu Machado de Castro. Also, *quintas* (baroque country residences) often feature the most delightful combination of styles, and the most interesting examples are found in the Minho region, in the north, though there are also attractive homes on the Setúbal Peninsula, in Lisbon's environs.

Sculpture and painting styles in Portugal evolved in a similar way, inspired first by the excitement of the newly emerging Portuguese nation and subsequently by the baroque experimentation allowed by the wealth available from the colonies. The earlier, rarer works still speak volumes about the confidence of those caught up in the Imperial age. A Portuguese tradition in sculpture found its first outlet in grand royal and noble funerary monuments, as witnessed by the realism on display on the Gothic tombs in the cathedrals of Lisbon, Guarda, and Braga. These were precursory of the masterpiece of their kind, the 14th-century tombs of Pedro and Inês at Alcobaça, while similarly eloquent are the hand-clasped figures of Dom João and his queen, Philippa, in the chapel at Batalha. Portuguese painting came into its own in the 15th century, with the completion of Nuno Goncalves' Flemish-inspired polyptych of São Vicente (St. Vincent), which portrayed the princes and knights, monks and fishermen, court figures and ordinary people of Imperial Portugal in six remarkable painted panels. It's on display in Lisbon's Museu de Arte Antiga. The next great Portuguese painter, the 16th-century Vasco Fernandes (known as *Grão Vasco*, "The Great Vasco"), was also influenced by the Flemish tradition, but his work has an expressive, realistic vigor. Grão

Vasco's masterpieces are on show in Viseu, at the Museu Grāo Vasco.

By way of contrast, the later baroque styles in art and sculpture said less about the country, and more about the indiscriminate use of wealth. There were flamboyant creations, to be sure, including the unsurpassed granite-and-plaster staircases, pilgrimage shrines, and sculptures at Bom Jesus and Lamego, in the Minho, but these were built at a time when the monarchy had lost the vision and moral will that had sustained it during earlier, greater periods. Nevertheless, there were always sculptors and artists ready to work in styles that drew on the strengths of the Portuguese character and not the weaknesses. The 18th century saw the emergence of the sculptor Machado de Castro, who produced perhaps the greatest equestrian statue of his time, that of Dom José I in Lisbon's Praça do Comércio. Domingos António Sequeira (1768–1837) painted historical and religious subjects of international renown, while portrait and landscape painting became popular in the 19th century; the works of José Malhoā and Miguel Angelo Lupi can be seen in the Museu de Jose Malhoā in Caldas da Rainha. Other museums throughout the country display the works of talented contemporaries. The Museu Soares dos Reis in Oporto—named after the 19th-century sculptor, António Soares dos Reis (1847–1889)—was the first national museum in the country. His pupil was António Teixeira Lopes (1866–1942), who achieved great popular success, and who also has a museum named after him in Oporto, in the suburb of Vila Nova de Gaia.

Literature In literature, there had been a long, barren period since the time of the great poet Camões, that was only briefly illuminated in the 18th century by the lyric poet, Bocage. Revival came in the 19th century, with the Romantic Movement, whose most brilliant exponent was Almeida Garrett, a novelist, dramatist, and poet, who died in 1854. Garret influenced a whole generation of remarkable writers, including novelists Camilo Castelo Branco and Julio Dinis; the historians Alexandre Herculano and Oliveira Martins; and the poets Antero de Quental and António de Castilho. The latter half of the 19th century almost exactly covered the life of the great Portuguese novelist Eca de Queiroz, an early realist, while the first half of the 20th century only produced one outstanding figure, the poet Fernando Pessoā, who died in 1935.

Contemporary Politics, Culture, and Economy In the 20th century, industrialization passed Portugal by, the economy remained agricultural, the political system was unreformed, and the lot of the people did not improve. The country preserved its age-old traditions and customs within an almost feudal social structure, causing it to fall behind developing nations. Portugal was ready for change. In 1968 its government appointed Dr. Marcelo Caetano to replace then-dictator António de Oliveira Salazar, who had just suffered a severe stroke. Long-brewing discontent in the African colonies of Angola and Mozambique led to the revolution that occurred six years later, on April 25, 1974, in which Caetono was ousted in a virtually bloodless coup (fewer than 20 people were killed) led by General António de Spinola. It was the move that the Portuguese people had long awaited, and huge demonstrations in support of the left-wing, officer-led *Movimento das Forcas Armadas* (Armed Forces Movement) left no doubt that Portugal had entered a new era. The remaining colonies were granted independence: Initially it was a relatively peaceful operation in Mozambique and Guinea-Bissau, but in Angola and East Timor it was fraught with conflict. Land on the huge estates of the Alentejo was redistributed, and in the name of democracy, free elections produced a popular Socialist government.

Almost 20 years later, Portugal is a stable country, its people keen to share in the prosperity offered by the developments within the European Community, of which it held the presidency in 1992. The government has shifted steadily to the right since the heady days of revolution; the Social Democrats have been the largest party in government since 1985. Visitors may find the obvious stability surprising, given the relatively short time since the revolution, and indeed it speaks well for the inherent qualities of the Portuguese people. Moreover, since 1975 more than 700,000 refugees from the former Portuguese colonies in Africa and Timor have been absorbed into the country, and there has been remarkable integration in that short period, especially if one considers that the number of refugees represents more than 7% of the total population.

The refugees have bestowed a welcome new face on Portugal: in Lisbon, for example, African music and dance is extremely popular. Performed in bars and clubs is the country's most famous music, *fado*, or "fate," a mournful, soulful, singing tradition thought to have originated in African slave songs, and imported to Portugal by way of the slave trade from the colonies. There are two distinct strands of fado: in Lisbon, emotive feeling is the dominant force in the lyrics, while the fado of Coimbra has a more intellectual edge, and is said to date to the age of the troubadours, in the 14th century. Whichever type, and wherever you hear fado, this is an essence of Portugal and the Portuguese that is timeless: It's the lament of time past, the acceptance of the future.

There's a bouyancy in other cultural matters, too, with Lisbon, Oporto, Coimbra, and other major towns providing visitors with plenty of opportunity to see the best in contemporary Portuguese art, music, and dance. Excellent modern art museums in both Oporto and Lisbon are high on many itineraries: Maria-Helena Vieira da Silva is the most famous name Portugal has produced this century, though others have also been influential, including pioneer modernist Almada Negreiros, and Amadeu de Sousa Cardoso (who has a separate gallery for his works in Amarante). Contemporary writers whose works are translated into English include José Cardoso Pires and José Saramago, and architects strive to recreate that Imperial Portuguese sense of confidence in their buildings—Lisbon's vast, colorful Amoreiras shopping and residential complex is as bold as such projects come.

Political stability and artistic confidence couldn't have been maintained without improvements in the economy, and there have been great strides forward since 1974. Membership in the European Community has undoubtedly helped, with grants and subsidies paying for the modernization of agriculture; massive aid and loans from the United States have also played a part in reviving the economy. However, one effect of this regeneration that regular visitors will notice is that Portugal has become a more expensive place over the last few years. It's no longer the very cheap destination it once was, though you're unlikely to find costs prohibitive, as they are rapidly becoming in Spain's Barcelona and Seville. The government, of course, faces its own problems, not least a marked disparity in economic development between the north and south of the country. In addition, there are relatively high illiteracy and infant mortality rates; inflation causes concern; and agriculture is stubbornly inefficient, despite modernization.

The challenges to the government and people of Portugal during the remainder of the 1990s are clear, and there are few countries in Europe better equipped to deal with them, since a young democracy often has an uncommon will to succeed. But there's a challenge to the visitor, too. If you come with preconceived ideas, perhaps expecting the culture, nationalism, and symbols of Spain, its Iberian neighbor, Portugal will confuse with its strangeness. You'll find elements of its unique character in the tourist areas of the Algarve, and in the modern cities of Lisbon and Oporto, but the challenge is to delve further. Take time to get off the beaten track, and you'll be rewarded—more than anywhere else in western Europe—with glimpses of a traditional life and culture that has been shaped by the memories of empire and tempered by the experience of revolution.

1 Essential Information

Before You Go

Government Tourist Offices

By Mary Ellen Schultz

Contact the Portuguese government tourist offices for information on all aspects of travel to and in Portugal.

In the United States
590 5th Ave., New York, NY 10036–4704, tel. 212/354–4403, fax 212/764–6137.

In Canada
60 Bloor St. W, Suite 1005, Ontario M4W 3G8, tel. 416/921–7376, fax 416/921–1353; 500 Sherbrooke W, Suite 930, Montréal, Québec H3A 36C, tel. 514/843–4623, fax 514/843–9328.

In the United Kingdom
New Bond St., 1–5 New Bond St. House, London W1Y ONP, tel. 071/493–3873, fax 071/409–3307.

Tour Groups

When considering a tour group, read the fine print in the brochure and expect only what it specifies. Be sure to find out exactly what expenses are included (particularly tips, taxes and service charges, side trips, additional meals, and entertainment); and their ratings of all hotels; and, if you are traveling alone, the cost of a single supplement. Note whether any of the arrangements offered are subject to change, and check out the operator's policy regarding cancelations, complaints, and trip-interruption insurance. Most tour operators request that bookings be made through a travel agent; there is no additional charge for doing so. Below is a sampling of the operators and packages available. For additional resources, contact your travel agent or a Portuguese National Tourist Office (*see* Government Tourist Offices, *above*).

General-Interest United States
American Express Vacations (300 Pinnacle Way, Norcross, GA 30071, tel. 404/368–5100 or 800/241–1700) arranges escorted and free-lance tours to Lisbon and Madeira in addition to tours combining highlights of both Spain and Portugal. Tours last one to three weeks. **TWA Getaway Vacations** (100 S. Bedford Rd., Mt. Kisco, NY 10549, tel. 800/439–2929) offers similar packages. **TAP Air Portugal** (399 Market St., Newark, NJ 07105, tel. 800/336–6690; in NY, 800/324–3520) offers a variety of escorted and fly-and-drive itineraries. **TRAVCOA** (Box 2630, Newport Beach, CA 92658, tel. 714/476–2800 or 800/992–2003; in CA, 800/992–2004) offers an 18-day tour of "Unusual Spain and Portugal." The tour begins in Madrid and goes to Segovia, Toledo, Oviedo, Leon, Salamanca, and several other Spanish cities before heading to Oporto, Coimbra, Fátima, Nazaré, and Lisbon. Travcoa's tours are small, usually 25 or fewer participants. **Maupintour** (1515 St. Andrews Dr., Lawrence, KS 66047, tel. 919/843–1211 or 800/255–6162) offers "Pousadas and Paradors," a 16-day tour of the western Iberian peninsula, with stops in Lisbon, Buçaco, Vila Nova de Cerveira, Estremoz, and several other Portuguese cities, as well as Benavente, Segovia, Madrid, and Salamanca in Spain. If you wish to tour Portugal without visiting Spain, **Abreu Tours, Inc.** (317 E. 34th St., New York, NY 10016, tel. 212/661–0555 or 800/223–1580) has several tours, including "North of Portugal," which begins and ends in Lisbon and passes through Nazaré, Fátima, Coimbra, Oporto, Viana do Castelo, Braga, Portalegre, Evora, and several other cities. Accommodations and most meals are included. **Sun**

Pleasure Tours (383 Rockdale Ave., New Bedford, MA 02740, tel. 508/997–9361 or 800/431–8810) and **Portuguese Tours** (Box 729, Elizabeth, NJ 07207, tel. 201/352–6112 or 800/526–4047) offer similar packages. **Cultural Heritage Alliance** (107–115 S. 2nd St., Philadelphia, PA 19160, tel. 215/923–7288) takes student and adult groups to Lisbon and the north of Portugal.

For cruises from Lisbon to the beautiful island of Madeira, contact **Cunard Line Ltd.** (555 5th Ave., New York, NY 10017, tel. 212/880–7500) and **Princess Cruises** (2029 Century Park E, Los Angeles, CA 90067, tel. 213/553–7000). **Royal Cruise Line** (1 Maritime Plaza, San Francisco, CA 94111, tel. 415/956–7200) also offers a cruise up the Portuguese coast, stopping at Oporto before heading out to the Atlantic Ocean and Madeira.

United Kingdom   **Abreu Travel Agency Ltd.** (109 Westbourne Grove, London W2 4UL, tel. 071/229–9905), **Caravela Tours** (38–44 Gillingham St., London SW1V 1JW, tel. 071/630–9223), **Club Mediterranee** (106–108 Brompton Rd., London SW3 1JJ, tel. 071/581–1161), **Hartland Holidays** (Brunswick House, 91 Brunswick Crescent, London N11 1EE, tel. 071/368–4422), **Sovereign Holidays** (Groundstar House, London Rd., Crawley, W. Sussex RH10 2B, tel. 293/561–444), **Thomas Cook Ltd.** (Box 36, Thorpe Wood, Peterborough, Cambridgeshire PE3 6SB, tel. 733/330–300).

Special-Interest   **Prospect Art Tours** (10 Barley Mow Passage, London W4 4PH,
Art and   tel. 081/995–2163) has several tours of Portugal, all staffed with
Architecture   expert guides and focusing on Iberian culture. **Serenissima Travel** (21 Dorset Sq., London NW1 6QG, tel 071/730–9841) has similar tours, and **Swan-Hellenic** (77 New Oxford St., London WC1A 1PP, tel. 071/831–1616) has art tours of Lisbon and the northern part of the country.

The Texas Connection (217 Arden Grove, San Antonio, TX 78215, tel. 512/225–6294) recently began a "Handicraft Tour" of Portugal. The "Village Weavers Tour" in 1991 was the first of what promises to be a fascinating series of expeditions to Portugal's myriad folk-art and handicrafts centers.

Bicycling   **Cycling Through the Centuries** (Rotan Charter Inc., Box 877, San Antonio, FL 33576, tel. 904/588–4132 or 800/245–4226) offers eight- to 10-night bicycle tours through many quaint and out-of-the-way parts of the country—from the lush, green Minho to the wine regions to the strikingly different Algarve in the south, with the pace as relaxed or as strenuous as you prefer. Bring your own bike or rent one of theirs. **Tip Tours** (Av. Costa Pinto 91-A, 2750 Cascais, tel. 01/483–3821) rents bicycles and runs bicycle tours throughout the country, with accommodations. Cyclists are accompanied by a guide, a mechanic, and a luggage van. During summer a "Volta de Portugal" (similar to the Tour de France) tests bicycle racers' endurance. Check with the tourist office for dates and more details.

Gastronomy   Altamira Tours (860 Detroit St., Denver, CO 80206, tel. 303/
and Wines   399–3660 or 800/747–2869) offers a 15-day food-and-wine tour of Portugal and Madeira. Both the host and the lodgings are first class. **Thomson Holidays** (Greater London House, Hampstead Rd., London NW1 7SD, tel. 071/387–1900) has a "Wine Routes of Portugal" tour, which includes excursions to Lisbon and Oporto, the Sandeman Port cellars, the Mateus estate, and the Dão wine cellars; it can be combined with seven nights in Estoril.

Golf **Adventure Golf Holidays** (815 North Rd., Westfield, MA 01805, tel. 413/568–2855 or 800/628–9655), and **Perry Golf** (8302 Dunwoody Pl., Suite 305, Atlanta, GA 30350, tel. 404/641–9696 or 800/344–5257) offer land packages to the best courses in the Algarve and Madeira. Also, contact the Portuguese National Tourist Office for a list of courses throughout the mainland, Madeira, and the Azores.

History For the 500th anniversary of Columbus's voyage to the New World, **Marsans International** (2121 Ponce de Leon Blvd., Suite 715, Coral Gables, FL 33134, tel. 305/441–1555 or 800/777–9110) offers "Medieval Odyssey," a tour through the north of Portugal, and "Woods of Portugal," which explores some of the most spectacular areas of Southern Portugal and includes historical tours and visits to relaxing beaches. **Odysseys and Adventures** (535 Chestnut St., Box 305, Cedarhurst, NY 11516, tel. 516/569–2812 or 800/344–0013) will entertain and enlighten travelers interested in Portugal's rich Jewish history with 10-day tours combining general-interest sightseeing with stops at important Jewish sites throughout the country. There is no traveling on the Sabbath, but these tours are not kosher. **American Jewish Congress International Travel Department** (15 E. 84th St., New York, NY 10028, tel. 212/879–4500) has tours to the Iberian peninsula, flying to Lisbon and returning from Madrid.

Spas Portugal has 44 hot springs on the mainland and the islands; contact the Portuguese National Tourist Office nearest you for a complete list of spas, or get in touch with the **Associação Nacional dos Industriais de Aguas Minero-Medicinais e de Mesa** (Rua de S. Jose, 93,1–1100 Lisbon, tel. 01/347–5623). **Custom Spa Vacations** (1318 2nd St., Suite 5, Brookline, MA 02146, tel. 617/566–5144 or 800/443–7727), offers several tours of varying lengths in different parts of the country, combining American- and European-style treatments. They also have a deluxe cruise program to Seville, the Canary Islands, and Morocco, including round-trip airfare to Lisbon.

Package Deals for Independent Travelers

Extra Value Travel (683 S. Collier Blvd., Marco Island, FL 33937, tel. 813/394–3384 or 800/255–2847) arranges self-drive programs of a week or more that provide a rental car, unlimited mileage, accommodations, and a daily Continental breakfast.

TWA Getaway Tours (tel. 800/438-2929), **American Express** (tel. 800/637-6200), and **TAP Air Portugal** (tel. 800/221–7370) will send you brochures of many tour packages (golf, bicycling, gourmet, pousadas, manor houses, castles, etc.) offered in conjunction with leading tour operators in the United States; **Abreu Tours** (317 E. 34th St., New York, NY 10016, tel. 212/661–0555 or 800/223–1580) offers escorted motor-coach tours of varying lengths that allow plenty of time to do your own exploring.

When to Go

The tourist season begins in spring and lasts through the autumn. In midsummer it is never unbearably hot (except in parts of the Algarve and on the mainland plains), and it is especially pleasant along the coast, where a cool breeze springs up in the evening. Winter is mild and frequently rainy, except in Madeira, where the winter season has long been popular; off-season travelers have the advantage of reduced hotel rates. In the Algarve, springtime begins in February with a marvelous range of wildflowers. Late September and early October herald Indian summer, ensuring warm sunshine through November.

Climate The following are average daily maximum and minimum temperatures for major cities in Portugal.

Faro

Jan.	59F	15C	May	72F	22C	Sept.	79F	26C
	48	9		57	14		66	19
Feb.	61F	16C	June	77F	25C	Oct.	72F	22C
	50	10		64	18		61	16
Mar.	64F	18C	July	82F	28C	Nov.	66F	19C
	52	11		68	20		55	13
Apr.	68F	20C	Aug.	82F	28C	Dec.	61F	16C
	55	13		68	20		60	10

Lisbon

Jan.	57F	14C	May	71F	21C	Sept.	79F	26C
	46	8		55	13		62	17
Feb.	59F	15C	June	77F	25C	Oct.	72F	22C
	47	8		60	15		58	14
Mar.	63F	17C	July	81F	27C	Nov.	63F	17C
	50	10		63	17		52	11
Apr.	67F	20C	Aug.	82F	28C	Dec.	58F	15C
	53	12		63	17		47	9

Oporto

Jan.	55F	13C	May	68F	20C	Sept.	75F	24C
	41	5		52	11		57	14
Feb.	57F	14C	June	73F	23C	Oct.	70F	21C
	41	5		55	13		52	11
Mar.	61F	16C	July	77F	25C	Nov.	63F	17C
	46	8		59	15		46	8
Apr.	64F	18C	Aug.	77F	25C	Dec.	57F	14C
	48	9		59	15		41	5

Current weather information for foreign and domestic cities may be obtained by calling **The Weather Channel Connection** at 900/WEATHER from a touch-tone phone. In addition to the weather report, The Weather Channel Connection offers local time and travel tips as well as hurricane, foliage, and ski reports. The call costs 95¢ per minute.

National Holidays

January 1 (New Year's Day), February 23 (Mardi Gras—a holiday in Lisbon and other towns), April 9 (Good Friday), April 25 (Liberty Day), May 1 (Labor Day), June 10 (Portugal's and Camões Day; also Corpus Christi), June 13 (St. Anthony's Day—Lisbon), August 15 (Assumption Day), October 5 (Republic Day), November 1 (All Saints' Day), December 1 (Independence Day), December 8 (The Feast of the Immaculate Conception), December 24 (Christmas Eve), and December 25 (Christmas Day).

If a national holiday falls on a Tuesday or Thursday, many businesses also close on the Monday or Friday in between, for a long weekend called a *ponte* (bridge).

Festivals and Seasonal Events

It is said that there is a different market day or festival every day of the year in Portugal. Market days, whether in big cities or small towns, are an irresistible attraction. In **Lisbon:** the Thieves Market, Tuesday and Saturday behind the Church of São Vicente de Fora. Near Lisbon: every Wednesday and Saturday in **Cascais;** the second and fourth Sunday of the month in **São Pedro de Sintra** (known for the antiques and handicrafts); every Thursday at **Malveira,** near Mafra, and **Carcavelos** on the Cascais train line; every first Sunday at **Azeitão** south of the Rio Tejo (Tagus). In the north: every Thursday at **Barcelos.** In the Algarve: every third Sunday at **Albufeira;** every first Saturday at **Lagos;** every first Monday at **Portimão;** every third Monday at **Silves;** every third Monday at **Tavira;** and every Saturday at **Loulé** and at **São Braz de Alportel.**

Religious festivals called *romarias* are held throughout the year. Some of the leading annual festivals, fairs, and folk pilgrimages are listed below. Verify the dates with the Portuguese tourism office, which can also send you its complete listing of the numerous events, plus advice on when to book hotel reservations (well in advance).

Mid-January: St. Gonçalo and St. Cristovão Festivities in Vila Nova de Gaia, Oporto; St. Gonçalinho Festivities in Aveiro.

Mid-late January: St. Sebastião or Fogaceiras Festivities in Santa Maria da Feira in Aveiro.

Early February: Our Lady of Candeias Festivities, Mourão (in Évora).

Early March: Festivities of Carnival (Mardi Gras), the final festival before Lent, are held throughout the country, with processions of masked participants, parades of vehicles decked out with satirical motifs, and exuberant flowers.

Mid-April: Holy Week Festivities are held in Braga, Ovar, Póvoa de Varzim, and other major cities, with the most important events taking place on Monday, Thursday, and Good Friday, when the faithful march in parades.

Early May: Festival of the Crosses (Festas das Cruzes) in Barcelos includes a large fair with handicrafts, concerts, an affecting Procession of the Holy Cross, and a spectacular display of fireworks on the Rio Cavado.

Early-mid-May: First Annual Pilgrimage to Fátima. Hundreds of thousands from all over the world travel to Fátima for the commemoration of the first apparition of the Virgin to the little shepherd children, on May 13, 1917.

Late May: Three days of Festivities honoring "Senhor Santo Cristo" in Ponta Delgada, S. Miguel Island, Azores climax when the 16th-century image of Christ of the Miracles, accompanied by its legendary treasure, parades for hours through the town.

May-June: Algarve Music Festival in the larger towns of the Algarve features more than 40 concerts by leading Portuguese and foreign artists.

Early June: The National Fair of Agriculture in Santarém is the most important agricultural fair in Portugal, with a colorful program of bullfighting, folk songs and dancing, and typical fair amusements.

Late June: Festivities in honor of St. Anthony in Lisbon honor the city's patron saint with an impressive show of *marchas* (walking groups of singers and musicians) parading along the Avenida da Liberdade while the various city districts carry on their own music, dances, and bonfires. **Festivities in honor of St. John** are held in many towns, but the festivities in Oporto are the most colorful. Every corner has its own *cascatas* (arrangements of religious motifs), bonfires, and all-night groups of singing and dancing merrymakers.

Early July: The Red Waistcoat Festival (Coletes Encarnado) in Vila Franca de Xira honors the *campinos*, Portuguese cowboys who guard the brave bulls in the pasturelands of the Ribatejo.

July–August: Estoril Music Festival features leading Portuguese and foreign artists in Estoril, Cascais, and other towns of the Estoril coast.

Early August: St. Walter's Festival (Festas Gualterianas) in Guimarães is a fascinating show of music bands, folk-dance groups, and the spectacular Procession of St. Walter.

Mid-August: Festival in honor of Our Lady of the Monte is held on "Monte," near Funchal, Madeira Island, with an evening amusement fair, groups of celebrants dancing and singing to the sound of live brass bands, and a procession of Our Lady.

Mid–late August: Our Lady of Agony Festivities in Viana do Castelo are some of the most colorful in Portugal, with the Lady paraded throughout the town over lush carpets of flowers, and a spectacular display of fireworks.

Late August–late September: Saint Matthew's Fair in Viseu is an important agricultural and livestock fair with folk dancing and singing, held since the Middle Ages.

Early September: The **Wine Harvest Festival** in Palmela has a colorful parade of harvesters, wine tastings, the election of the "Queen of the Wine," and a spectacular fireworks display.

Early–mid-September: Our Lady of Nazaré Festivities, held in one of Portugal's oldest and most typical fishing villages, has bullfights, folk dancing and singing, and three festive processions of Nazaré fishermen carrying the Lady's image on their shoulders.

Mid-September: In the **Annual Folk Music and Dance Festival,** singing and dancing in all the Algarve's larger towns culminate at Praia da Rocha with performances by groups from all over the country. **Our Lady of Good Voyage Festivities** take place in the ancient town of Moita (near Setúbal), bathed by the waters of the Rio Tejo, and center on the blessing of the fishing boats.

Early October: October Fair in Vila Franca de Xira, a short distance from Lisbon, has farming and agricultural activities, handicraft displays, bullfights, and the traditional running of bulls in the streets.

October 12–13: Last Pilgrimage to Fátima brings thousands of pilgrims from all over the world to Fátima to honor the last apparition of the virgin, on October 12, 1917.

Late October–early November: The National Gastronomy Festival in Santarém presents traditional dishes from all regions of the country as well as cooking contests and lectures by leading gastronomes.

Early November: St. Martin's Fair and the **National Horse Show** in Golega combine parades of saddle horses, horses for bullfights, and riding competitions with handicrafts exhibitions, wine tasting, and other amusements.

December 31: St. Sylvester's Festival for New Year's Eve transforms Funchal, Madeira Island, into a vast fairground, with a
breathtaking fireworks display over the city's beautiful bay.

What to Pack

Clothing   The Portuguese, like the Spanish, tend to dress up more than
do Americans or the British. Summer can be brutally hot,
spring and fall mild to chilly, and winter cold and rainy. Sightseeing calls for casual, comfortable clothing. Well broken-in,
low-heel shoes will make it easier to stroll along cobblestone
streets, up hills, and along dusty roads or beach promenades.
In the cities dressier outfits are required at fine restaurants
and nightclubs. American tourists can be spotted easily in Portugal because they wear sneakers; if you want to blend in, wear
leather shoes instead. In some small towns people still frown on
wearing shorts in churches, but for the most part there is no
dress code. Wearing bathing suits along the streets or in restaurants and shops is not considered in good taste.

Miscellaneous   Take along an extra pair of prescription glasses, contact lenses,
or sunglasses, just in case. Sunscreen is a good idea any time of
the year, since the sunshine in Portugal is particularly bright.
Pack any prescription or allergy medicine you take regularly;
in the case of prescription medicine, it might also be wise to
carry an extra prescription.

The electric current in Portugal is 220 volts, and plugs have two
prongs, so you'll need an adapter for hair dryers, electric ra-
zors, and other small appliances.

Carry-On Luggage   Airlines generally allow each passenger one piece of carry-on
luggage on international flights from both the United States
and the United Kingdom. This bag cannot exceed 114.3 centimeters (45 inches)—length + width + height—and must fit
under the seat or in the overhead luggage compartment.

Checked Luggage   Passengers are generally allowed to check two pieces of luggage, neither of which can exceed 157.5 centimeters (62 inch-
es)—length + width + height—or weigh more than 31.5
kilograms (70 pounds). Baggage allowances vary slightly
among airlines, so be sure to check with the carrier or your
travel agent before departure.

Taking Money Abroad

Traveler's checks and major U.S. credit cards are widely accepted, but you will need cash for some of the smaller regional
restaurants and shops. Although you can't get as good an exchange rate at home as abroad, it's wise to change a small
amount of money ($20–$50) into escudos before leaving, to
avoid long lines at airport currency exchange booths (Portela,
the airport at Lisbon, has a bank currency exchange open 24
hours a day). Most U.S. banks will not convert dollars into escudos, however, you can exchange money through **Thomas
Cook Currency Service Inc.** (630 5th Ave., New York, NY
10111, tel. 212/757–6915).

For safety and convenience it's always best to take traveler's
checks. The most widely recognized are **American Express,
Barclays, Thomas Cook,** and those issued through major commercial banks such as **Citibank** and **Bank of America. American**

Express checks can, of course, be purchased at their own offices worldwide.

Buy some of the traveler's checks in small denominations to cash toward the end of your trip; this will prevent you from ending up with more foreign money than you need. Hold on to your receipts after exchanging traveler's checks in Portugal—it's easier to convert foreign currency back into dollars if you have them.

American Express now offers "AMEX Traveler's Cheques for Two," which allow two travelers to sign and use the same checks. Since 80% of travelers go with a companion, this could be the most convenient option overall. American Express is represented by the **Star Travel Agency,** with offices in Lisbon (Praça dos Restauradores 14, tel. 01/346–2501), Oporto (Av. dos Aliados 202, tel. 2/200–3637), Estoril (Av. Nice 4, tel. 01/468–2906), and Faro (Rua Conselheiro Bivar 86, tel. 89/25125).

Getting Money from Home

There are at least four ways to get money from home: (1) Have it sent through a large commercial bank that has a branch where you are staying. The only drawback is that you must have an account with the bank; if not, you'll have to go through your own bank, and the process will be slower and more costly. (2) Have it sent through American Express. If you are a cardholder, you can cash a personal check or a counter check at an American Express office for up to $1,000; $200 will be in escudos and $800 in traveler's checks. There is a 1% commission on the traveler's checks. You can also receive money through an **American Express MoneyGram,** which enables you to obtain up to $10,000 in cash. It works this way: You call home and ask someone to go to an American Express office—or an American Express MoneyGram agent located in a retail outlet—and fill out an American Express MoneyGram. It can be paid for with cash or with any major credit card. The person making the payment is given a reference number and telephones you with it. The American Express MoneyGram agent authorizes the transfer of funds, and in most cases, the money is available immediately. You pick it up by showing identification and giving the reference number. Fees vary with the amount of money sent. For $300 the fee is $35; for $5,000 it's $170. For the American Express MoneyGram location nearest your home and to find out the locations in Portugal, call 800/543–4080. You do not have to be a cardholder to use this service. (3) Have money sent through **Western Union,** whose U.S. number is 800/325–6000. If you have a MasterCard or Visa, you can have money sent for any amount up to your credit limit. If not, have someone back home take cash or a certified cashier's check to a Western Union office. The money will be delivered to a bank near where you are staying. Fees vary with the amount of money sent and the precise location of the recipient. (4) Britons holding a **Eurocheque Card** and checkbook can cash checks for up to £100 a day at participating banks and can write checks in hotels, restaurants, and shops, again for up to £100. Look for the distinctive blue-and-red symbol in the window. To obtain a card and checkbook, apply at your bank.

Cash Machines   Automatic teller machines are becoming common in Portugal, with many banks on a central network called **Multibanco.** Before leaving home, you can arrange with your bank for a Personal Identification Number (PIN) to get money from your Visa or Mastercard at one of the cash machines belonging to this system. (Note that CIRRUS and PLUS are *not* available in Portugal, although plans to make both systems compatible with Multibanco are under way.) If you have not made such arrangements, you can still get a cash advance at most banks by presenting your credit card and passport at the foreign exchange counter.

Many cash machines will convert foreign currency (bills) into escudos. Machines are located outside several of the bigger banks throughout the country (in Lisbon there is one in the Praça dos Restauradores) and are easy to use, since instructions are provided in English.

Portuguese Currency

Portugal's currency unit is the escudo, which is divided up into 100 centavos. The number of escudos is written to the left of the $ sign and the centavos to the right; thus, 2 escudos and 50 centavos is written 2$50. Coins are issued for 200$00, 100$00, 50$00, 20$00, 10$00, 5$00, 2$50, and 1$00. Bills in circulation are for 10,000$00, 5,000$00, 2,000$00, 1,000$00, and 500$00. Units of 1,000$00 are often referred to as "contos." At press time (summer 1992), the exchange rate was about 143$00 to the U.S. dollar, 130$00 per Canadian dollar, and 240$00 to the pound sterling.

What It Will Cost

As Portugal moves to catch up with the rest of Europe, prices keep climbing; annual inflation runs around 8%. The weakening U.S. dollar has lost about 15% of its value against the escudo in recent years. Lisbon is still not as expensive as other international capitals, but it is not the extraordinary bargain it used to be. The coastal resort areas from Cascais and Estoril down to the Algarve can also be expensive, but lower-price hotels and restaurants catering mainly to the package-tour trade are certainly popular. The traveler who decides to head off the beaten track will find substantially cheaper food and lodging.

Transportation is still cheap in Portugal when compared to the rest of Europe. Gas prices are controlled by the government, and train and bus travel are inexpensive. Highway tolls are steep but may be worth the cost if you want to bypass the small towns and villages that second-class highways pass through. Flights within the country on the state-owned TAP airlines are costly.

Taxes Value-added tax (or sales tax) is called IVA in Portugal. It is charged on services such as hotels and restaurants and on many categories of consumer products. Restaurant menus generally state at the bottom whether tax is included *(IVA incluido)* or not *(mas 8% IVA)*. Higher-end restaurants are required to charge 8% IVA. When in doubt about whether tax is included in a price, ask, *Está incluido o IVA* (ee-vah)*?*.

Sample Prices Coffee in a bar: 40$00 (standing), 60$00 (seated). Beer in a bar: 70$00 (standing), 90$00 (seated). Small glass of wine in a bar: 60$00; bottle of beer, 100$00. Glass of Port: 160$00–300$00, depending on brand. Bottle of ordinary table wine *(vinho da* *casa*): 350$00; half bottle, 200$00. Coca-Cola: 70$00. Ham-and-cheese sandwich: 125$00. One-mile taxi ride: 200$00 (but the meter keeps ticking in traffic jams). Local bus ride: 110$00 if purchased from driver. Subway ride: 50$00. Ferry ride in Lisbon: 100$00–400$00 round-trip. Opera or theater seat: about 2,500$00. Nightclub cover-charge 3,000$00–5,000$00. Movie-theater seat: 450$00. Foreign newspaper: 180$00.

Passports and Visas

Americans All U.S. citizens need a passport to enter Portugal. Applications for your first passport must be made in person; renewals can be obtained in person or by mail. First-time applicants should apply at least five weeks before their departure date to one of the 13 U.S. Passport Agency offices. In addition, local county courthouses, many state and probate courts, and some post offices have forms and accept passport applications. Necessary documents include (1) a completed passport application (Form DSP-11); (2) proof of citizenship (birth certificate with raised seal or naturalization papers); (3) proof of identity (unexpired driver's license, employee ID card, or any other document with your photograph and signature); (4) two recent, identical, two-inch square photographs (black and white or color), with a white or off-white background; (5) $42 application fee for a 10-year passport (those under 18 pay $27 for a five-year passport). If paying in cash, you must have exact change. Passports should be mailed to you in about 10 working days, but it can take longer in early summer.

To renew your passport by mail, you'll need to complete Form DSP-82 and submit two recent, identical passport photographs; a recent passport, fewer than 12 years old from the issue date; and a check or money order for $35.

A visa is not necessary to visit Portugal for up to 60 days. For longer stays apply to the police for an extension when the original 60 days are about to end.

Canadians All Canadians need a passport to enter Portugal. Send your completed application (available at any post office or passport office) to the **Bureau of Passports** (Suite 215, West Tower, Guy Favreau Complex, 200 René Lévesque Blvd. W, Montréal, Québec H2Z 1X4). Include $35, three photographs, a guarantor, and proof of Canadian citizenship. Application can be made in person at the regional passport offices in Calgary, Edmonton, Halifax, Montréal, St. John's (Newfoundland), Toronto, Vancouver, Victoria, or Winnipeg. Passports are valid for five years and are nonrenewable.

Britons All British citizens need a valid passport or a British Visitor's Passport to enter Portugal. Application forms are available from most travel agents and major post offices, or contact the **Passport Office** (Clive House, 70 Petty France, London SW1H 9HD, tel. 071/729–3434) or regional passport offices located in Liverpool, Peterborough, Glasgow, and Newport (Gwent). The cost is £15 for a standard 32-page passport, £30 for a 94-page passport. British Visitor's Passports are valid for one year only and are nonrenewable. They cost £7.50. All applications must be made in person at a main post office and must be countersigned by your bank manager or by a solicitor, a barrister, a doctor, a clergyman, or a justice of the peace, and must be accompanied by two photographs.

Visa requirements are the same as for U.S. citizens—no visa is required for visits to mainland Portugal, Madeira, or the Azores for stays of up to 60 days. For longer stays apply to the police for an extension, when the original 60 days are about to end.

Customs and Duties

On Arrival Visitors aged 15 and over are permitted to bring in 200 cigarettes, or 100 cigarillos, or 50 cigars, or 250 grams of loose tobacco. Those 17 years of age and older may bring in one liter of liquor over 22 proof and two liters of wine. Perfume is limited to 50 grams, eau de cologne to .25 liter.

It is a good idea to carry along sales receipts for expensive personal belongings to avoid paying export duties when you leave.

For all visitors to Madeira and the Azores who are over 1 year old, and traveling from an infected area, a certificate of vaccination against yellow fever is required.

Dogs and cats are admitted, providing they have up-to-date vaccination records from the home country.

On Departure If you are bringing any foreign-made equipment from home, such as cameras, it's wise to carry the original receipt with you or register it with U.S. Customs before you leave (Form 4457). Otherwise, you may end up paying duties on your return.

Americans You may bring home duty-free up to $400 worth of foreign goods, as long as you have been out of the country for at least 48 hours and haven't made an international trip in 30 days. Each member of the family is entitled to the same exemption, regardless of age, and exemptions may be pooled. For the next $1,000 worth of goods, a flat 10% rate is assessed; above $1,400, duties vary with the merchandise. Included for travelers 21 and older are 1 liter of alcohol, 100 cigars (non-Cuban), and 200 cigarettes. Only one bottle of perfume trademarked in the United States may be brought in. However, there is no duty on antiques or works of art more than 100 years old. Anything exceeding these limits will be taxed at the port of entry and may be taxed additionally in the traveler's home state. Gifts valued at under $50 may be mailed to friends or relatives at home duty-free, but no more than one package per day may be sent to any one addressee, and packages may not include tobacco, liquor, or perfumes costing more than $5.

Do not bring home foreign meats, fruits, plants, soil, or other agricultural items when you return to the United States. It is illegal to bring in foreign agricultural items without permission, because they can spread destructive plant or animal pests or diseases. For more information, request the brochures *Know Before You Go* and *Travelers' Tips* from the U.S. Customs Service (1301 Constitution Ave., Washington, DC 20229).

Canadians Exemptions for returning Canadians range from $20 to $300, depending on length of stay out of the country. For the $300 exemption, you must have been out of the country for at least one week. For any given year, you are allowed one $300 exemption. You may bring in duty-free up to 50 cigars, 200 cigarettes, 1 kilogram (2.2 pounds) of tobacco, and 1.2 liters (40 ounces) of liquor, provided these are declared in writing to customs on arrival and accompany the traveler in hand or checked-through baggage. These restrictions apply to one calendar year only and after a minimum of seven days' absence. If you are out of Canada for fewer than seven days and for a minimum of 48 hours, there is a $100 exemption, with the same restrictions on alcohol and tobacco products. Personal gifts should be mailed as "Unsolicited Gift—Value under $40." Get a copy of the Canadian Customs brochure *I Declare* for further details. Copies can be obtained at local customs offices.

Britons There are two levels of duty-free allowance for people entering the United Kingdom: one for goods bought outside the European Community (EC) or in a duty-free shop in an EC country; the other for goods bought in an EC country but not in a duty-free shop.

In the first category you may import duty-free: (1) 200 cigarettes or 100 cigarillos or 50 cigars or 250 grams of tobacco (if you live outside Europe, these allowances are doubled); (2) two liters of still table wine and (3) one liter of alcoholic drink over 22% volume/proof or two liters of alcoholic drink under 22% volume (fortified or sparkling wine) or two more liters of still table wine; (4) 60 milliliters of perfume and 250 milliliters of toilet water; and (5) other goods up to a value of 32 pounds, but not more than 50 liters of beer or 25 lighters.

In the second category you may import duty-free (1) 300 cigarettes or 150 cigarillos or 75 cigars or 400 grams of tobacco; (2) five liters of still table wine and (3) 1.5 liters of alcoholic drink over 22% volume or three liters of alcoholic drink under 22% volume (fortified or sparkling wine) or three more liters of still table wine; (4) 90 milliliters of perfume and 375 milliliters of toilet water; and (5) other goods up to a value of £265, but not more than 50 liters of beer and 25 lighters.

Note that, although it is not classified as an alcoholic drink by EC countries for customs purposes and is thus part of the "other goods" allowance, you may not import more than 50 liters of beer.

For further information, contact **HM Customs and Excise** (Dorset House, Stamford St., London SE1 9PS, tel. 071/620–1313).

Traveling with Film

If your camera is new, shoot and develop a few rolls of film before leaving home. Pack some lens tissue and an extra battery if you have a built-in light meter. Invest about $10 in a UV or skylight filter and screw it on to the front of your lens: It will protect the lens and reduce haze.

Film doesn't like hot weather. If you're driving in summer, don't store it in the glove compartment or on the shelf under the rear window. Put it behind the front seat on the floor, on the side opposite the exhaust pipe.

On a plane trip, never pack unprocessed film in check-in luggage; if your bags are X-rayed, say goodbye to your pictures. Always carry undeveloped film with you through security and ask to have it inspected by hand. (It helps to keep your film in a plastic bag, ready for quick inspection.)

The old airport scanning machines, still in use in some countries, use heavy doses of radiation that can turn a family portrait into an early morning fog. The newer models used in all

U.S. airports are reputed to be safe for anything from five to 500 scans, depending on the film speed. The effects are cumulative: You can put the same roll of film through several scans without worry; after five scans, though, you're asking for trouble.

If your film becomes fogged and you want an explanation, send it to the National Association of Photographic Manufacturers (50 Mamaroneck Ave., Harrison, NY 10528). They'll try to determine what went wrong, and the service is free.

Language

Despite its Slavic-sounding inflections and nasal intonations, Portuguese is essentially a romance language of Latin origin, and is now the seventh most widely spoken language in the world. Roughly half the people a tourist comes in contact with (at least in the larger cities) will speak some English. Any attempt by visitors to speak Portuguese will be warmly appreciated. Written Portuguese resembles Spanish, although pronunciation can be markedly different (*see* the Glossary at the end of this guide).

Staying Healthy

Sunburn and sunstroke are common problems in summer in mainland Portugal and virtually year-round in Madeira and the Azores. On a hot, sunny day, even people not normally bothered by a strong sun should cover up with a long-sleeve shirt, a hat, and slacks or a beach wrap. Carry sun block for nose, ears, and other sensitive areas; be sure to drink enough liquids, and above all, limit your sun exposure for the first few days until you become accustomed to the heat.

No special shots are required before visiting Portugal (except for yellow-fever shots for visitors to Madeira or the Azores from infected areas). If you may need to purchase prescription drugs in Portugal, have your doctor write a prescription using the drug's generic name; brand names can vary widely.

The **International Association for Medical Assistance to Travelers (IAMAT)** (417 Center St., Lewiston, NY 14902, tel. 716/754–4883; 40 Regal Rd., Guelph, Ontario N1K 1B5, tel. 519/836–0102; 57 Voirets, 1212 Grand-Lancy, Geneva, Switzerland) is a worldwide organization offering a list of approved English-speaking doctors whose training meets British and American standards. Contact IAMAT for a list of physicians and clinics in Portugal that belong to this network. Membership is free.

Medical Treatment In Portugal there is no free medical treatment for visitors unless their countries of origin have reciprocal health agreements, as with the United Kingdom. There is a **British Hospital** (Rua Saraiva de Carvalho 49, Lisbon, tel. 01/602–020 daytime, 01/603–785 nighttime) for both in- and outpatients, with English-speaking doctors and nurses. There are local hospitals with emergency services in all the larger towns.

Insurance

Travelers may seek insurance coverage in three areas: health and accident, lost luggage, and trip cancellation. Your first step is to review your existing health and home-owner policies; some health insurance plans cover health expenses incurred while traveling, some major medical plans cover emergency transportation, and some home-owner policies cover the theft of luggage.

Health and Accident
Several companies offer coverage designed to supplement existing health insurance for travelers:

Carefree Travel Insurance (Box 310, 120 Mineola Blvd., Mineola, NY 11501, tel. 516/294–0220 or 800/343–3419) provides coverage for emergency medical evacuation and accidental death or dismemberment. It also offers 24-hour phone medical advice.

International SOS Assistance (Box 11586, Philadelphia, PA 19116, tel. 215/244–2500 or 800/523–8930), a medical-assistance company, provides emergency medical evacuation services, worldwide medical referrals, and optional medical insurance.

Travel Assistance International (1133 15th St. NW, Suite 400, Washington, DC 20005, tel. 202/331–1609 or 800/821–2828) provides emergency evacuation services and 24-hour medical referrals.

Travel Guard International, underwritten by Transamerica Occidental Life Companies (1145 Clark St., Stevens Point, WI 54481, tel. 715/345–0505 or 800/782–5151), offers reimbursement for medical expenses with no deductibles or daily limits, and emergency evacuation services.

Wallach and Company, Inc. (243 Church St. NW, Suite 100D, Vienna, VA 22180, tel. 703/281–9500 or 800/237–6615) offers comprehensive medical coverage, including emergency evacuation services worldwide.

WorldCare Travel Assistance Association (1150 S. Olive St., Suite T–233, Los Angeles, CA 90015, tel. 213/749–0909 or 800/666–4993 provides unlimited emergency evacuation, 24-hour medical referral, and an emergency message center.

Lost Luggage
On international flights, airlines are responsible for lost or damaged property to a value of $9.07 per pound (or $20 per kilogram) for checked baggage, and up to $400 per passenger for unchecked baggage. If you're carrying valuables, either take them with you on the plane or purchase additional insurance for lost luggage. Some airlines will issue extra luggage insurance when you check in, but many do not. Insurance for lost, damaged, or stolen luggage is available through travel agents or directly through various insurance companies. Luggage-loss coverage is usually part of a comprehensive travel insurance package that includes personal accident, trip cancellation, and sometimes default and bankruptcy. Two companies that issue luggage insurance are **TeleTrip** (Box 31685, 3201 Farnam St., Omaha, NE 68131, tel. 800/228–9792), a subsidiary of Mutual of Omaha), and the **Travelers** (Ticket and Travel Dept., 1 Tower Sq., Hartford, CT 06183, tel. 203/277–0111 or 800/243–3174). TeleTrip operates sales booths at airports and issues insurance through travel agents. Rates vary according to the length of the trip. Other companies with comprehensive policies include **Access America, Inc.,** a subsidiary of Blue Cross-Blue Shield (Box 11188, Richmond, VA 23230, tel. 800/334–7525 or 800/284–8300), **Near Services** (450 Prairie Ave., Suite 101, Calumet City, IL, 60409, tel. 708/868–6700 or 800/654–6700), and **Travel**

Guard International and **Carefree Travel Insurance** (*see* Health and Accident Insurance, *above*).

Before you go, itemize the contents of each bag in case you need to file an insurance claim. Be certain to put your home or business address on each piece of luggage, including carry-on bags. If your luggage is lost or stolen and later recovered, the airline will deliver the luggage to your home free of charge.

Trip Cancellation Flight-cancellation insurance is often included in the price of a ticket when paid for by American Express, Visa, and other major credit cards. It is usually included in combination travel insurance packages available from most tour operators, travel agents, and insurance agents.

In the United Kingdom, for free general advice on all aspects of holiday insurance, contact the **Association of British Insurers** (Aldermary House, 10–15 Queen St., London EC4N 1TT, tel. 071/248–4477). A proven leader in the holiday insurance field is **Europ Assistance** (252 High St., Croydon, Surrey CR0 1NF, tel. 081/680–1234).

Renting and Leasing Cars

Driver's licenses issued in the United States and Canada are valid for driving in Portugal. However, it is wise to get an International Driving Permit before you leave, especially if you plan to drive to other countries; it is printed in several languages and could smooth out difficulties if you have an accident. Permits are available for a small fee through local offices of the **American Automobile Association** (AAA) and the **Canadian Automobile Association** (CAA) or from the main offices (AAA, 1000 AAA Dr., Heathrow, FL 32746–0001, tel. 800/336–4357; CAA, 2 Carlton St., Toronto, Ontario M5B 1K4, tel. 416/964–3170). Alternatively, you can obtain an official translation of your license from a Portuguese consulate.

Renting Be sure to make your arrangements for car rentals before you leave home; cars rented on arrival in Portugal can cost up to twice as much.

If you are planning to begin your visit with a city stay, save money by arranging to pick up your car the day you are ready to start traveling. If you are already in Portugal and decide to rent a car, it may be cheaper to call home and have a friend or relative make the reservation for you, although cars must be reserved seven days in advance. Fly-drive and train-drive packages are also available for travel within Portugal, as are special weekend deals. Cars with automatic transmissions should be reserved well in advance, because manual transmissions are much more common. A 12% IVA tax and insurance will be tacked on to your bill, regardless of the vehicle you rent.

U.S. insurance companies do not cover car rentals in foreign countries, and an optional Collision Damage Waiver (CDW) is sold for about $10 a day. American Express and other credit cards now provide the CDW free if you charge the car rental; check before leaving.

Auto Europe (Box 1097, Sharps Wharf, Camden, ME 04843, tel. 800/223–5555; in ME, 800/342–5202; in Canada, 800/237–2456) will help you hedge against a falling dollar by guaranteeing advertised rates if you pay in advance. Other budget rental companies serving Europe include **Europe by Car** (1 Rockefeller Plaza, New York, NY 10020, tel. 212/245–1713 or 800/223–1516) and **Kemwel** (106 Calvert St., Harrison, NY 10528, tel. 800/678–0678).

Leasing For trips of 21 days or longer, you may save money by leasing a car. With a leasing arrangement, you are technically buying a car and then selling it back to the manufacturer after you've used it. Although leasing is not common in Portugal, companies offering some leasing arrangements include **Auto Europe, Europe by Car,** and **Kemwel** (*see above*).

Rail Passes

The **EurailPass,** valid for unlimited first-class train travel through 17 countries, including Portugal, is an excellent value for travel around the Continent. The ticket is available for periods of 15 days ($430), 21 days ($550), one month ($680), two months ($920), and three months ($1,115). For two or more people traveling together, a 15-day rail pass costs $298 per person. You need a minimum of three in your group to get this discount between April 1 and September 30. There is a **Eurail Youthpass** for those 25 years old and younger, allowing one or two months' unlimited second-class train travel at $470 and $640 respectively.

For travelers who like to spread out their train journeys, there is the **Eurail Flexipass.** With the 15-day pass ($280), travelers get five days of unlimited first-class train travel but can spread that travel out over 15 days. A 21-day pass ($450) gives you nine days of travel; a one-month Flexipass ($610) gives you 14 days of travel.

The Eurailpass does not cover Great Britain, and it is available only if you live outside Europe or North Africa. The pass must be bought from an authorized agent before you leave for Europe. Apply through your travel agent or through **Rail Europe** (610 5th Ave., New York, NY 10020, tel. 800/345–1990).

Student and Youth Travel

The **International Student Identity Card** (ISIC) entitles full-time students to rail passes, special fares on local transportation, student charter flights, and discounts at museums, theaters, sports events, and many other attractions. If purchased in the United States, the $14 ISIC also provides $3,000 in emergency medical coverage and $100 a day for up to 60 days of hospital coverage, as well as a collect phone number to call in case of emergency. Apply to the **Council on International Educational Exchange** (CIEE, 205 E. 42nd St., New York, NY 10017, tel. 212/661–1414). In Canada the ISIC is available for CN$12 from **Travel Cuts** (187 College St., Toronto, Ontario M5T 1P7, tel. 416/979–2406). In the United Kingdom contact **USIT London Student Travel** (52 Grosvenor Gardens, London SW1 W0AG, tel. 071/730–3402 for information about Europe, or 071/730–8111 for information about the rest of the world, including the United States).

Travelers under 26 can apply for a **Youth International Educational Exchange Card** (YIEE) issued by the **Federations of International Youth Travel Organizations** (FIYTO, 81 Islands Brugge, DK–2300 Copenhagen S., Denmark). It provides services and benefits similar to those of the ISIC card. The YIEE card is available in the United States from CIEE (*see above*) and in Canada from the **Canadian Hostelling Association** (CHA, 1600 James Naismith Dr., Suite 608, Gloucester, Ontario K1B 5N4, tel. 613/748–5638).

An **International Youth Hostel Federation** membership card is the key to inexpensive, dormitory-style accommodations at thousands of youth hostels around the world. Hostels aren't only for young travelers on a budget, though; many have family accommodations. Hostels provide separate sleeping quarters for men and women at rates ranging from $7 to $20 a night per person and are situated in a variety of facilities, including converted farmhouses, villas, restored castles, and even lighthouses, as well as specially constructed modern buildings. There are more than 5,000 hostel locations in 68 countries around the world. IYHF memberships, which are valid for 12 months from the time of purchase, are available in the United States through **American Youth Hostels** (AYH, Box 37613, Washington, DC 20013, tel. 202/783–6161). The cost for a first-year membership is $25 for adults 18–54. Renewal thereafter is $15. For youths (17 and under), the rate is $10, and for senior citizens (55 and older) the rate is $15. Family membership is available for $35. All national hostel associations arrange special reductions for members visiting their country, such as discounted rail fare or free bus travel, so be sure to ask for an international concessions list when you buy your membership.

Council Travel, a CIEE subsidiary, is the foremost U.S. student-travel agency, specializing in low-cost charters and serving as the exclusive U.S. agent for many student airfare bargains and student tours. CIEE's 80-page Student Travel catalogue and "Council Charter" brochures are available from any Council Travel office in the United States (enclose $1 postage if ordering by mail). In addition to the CIEE headquarters (205 E. 42nd St.) and branch office (35 E. 8th St.) in New York City, there are Council Travel offices in Berkeley, La Jolla, Long Beach, Los Angeles, San Diego, San Francisco, and Sherman Oaks, California; New Haven, Connecticut; Washington, DC; Atlanta, Georgia; Chicago and Evanston, Illinois; New Orleans, Louisiana; Amherst, Boston, and Cambridge, Massachusetts; Minneapolis, Minnesota; Durham, North Carolina; Portland, Oregon; Providence, Rhode Island; Austin and Dallas, Texas; Seattle, Washington; and Milwaukee, Wisconsin.

The Educational Travel Center (438 N. Frances St., Madison, WI 53703, tel. 608/256–5551) is another student travel specialist worth contacting for information on student tours, bargain fares, and bookings.

Students who would like to work abroad should contact CIEE's **Work Abroad Department** (205 E. 42nd St., New York, NY 10017, tel. 212/661–1414, ext. 1130). The council arranges various types of paid and volunteer work experiences overseas for up to six months. CIEE also sponsors study programs in Europe and publishes many books of interest to the student traveler. These include *Work, Study, Travel Abroad: The Whole World Handbook* ($12.95 plus $1.50 book-rate postage or $3.00 first-class postage) and *Volunteer! The Comprehensive Guide to Voluntary Service in the U.S. and Abroad* ($8.95 plus $1.50 book-rate postage or $3 first-class postage).

The Information Center at the **Institute of International Education** (IIE) has reference books, foreign-university catalogues, study-abroad brochures, and other materials, which may be consulted by students and nonstudents alike, free of charge. The Information Center is located on First Avenue between 45th and 46th streets in New York City (809 U.N. Plaza, New York, NY 10017, tel. 212/984–5413). It's open weekdays 10–4; closed holidays.

Traveling with Children

The Portuguese are very family-oriented and love children, so bring them along on your trip. You'll see children of all ages accompanying their parents everywhere, including bars and restaurants. Shopkeepers will smile and offer your child a *bombom* (candy), and, like many places, even the coldest waiters tend to be friendlier when you have a child with you. Kitchens are usually willing to fix something special for children, but you won't find children's menus anywhere. On the road, even the smallest *tasca* (town restaurant/bar) will be able to make a *sanduiche de queijo* (cheese sandwich), and roast chicken (*frango assado*) is on most menus. Museum admissions, buses, and metro rides are generally free for children under five, and half-price for children under 12.

Publications *Family Travel Times* is a newsletter published 10 times a year by Travel With Your Children (TWYCH, 45 W. 18th St., 7th Floor Tower, New York, NY 10011, tel. 212/206–0688). A one-year subscription costs $35 and includes access to back issues and twice-weekly opportunities to call in for specific advice.

Traveling with Children—And Enjoying It (The Globe Pequot Press, Box Q, Chester, CT 06412, $11.95) offers tips on how to cut costs, keep kids busy, eat out, reduce jet lag, and pack properly when traveling in the United States and abroad.

Hotels Generally children under six years stay free in the same room with parents, and children under 12 sharing the parents' room get a 50% discount. A travel agent should be able to confirm this for you.

Home Exchange Exchanging homes is a surprisingly low-cost way to enjoy a vacation abroad, especially a long one. The largest home-exchange service, the **International Home Exchange Service** (Box 590504, San Francisco, CA 94159, tel. 415/435–3497 or 800/756–4663) publishes three directories a year. Membership, which costs $45, entitles you to one listing and all three directories. Photos of your property cost an additional $10, and listing a second home costs $10. **Loan-a-Home** (2 Park La., Apt. 6E, Mount Vernon, NY 10552, tel. 914/664–7640) is popular with the academic community on sabbatical and business people on temporary assignment. There's no annual membership fee or charge for listing your home; one directory and supplement cost $35.

Getting There On international flights, children under two not occupying a seat pay 10% of the adult fare. Various discounts apply to children from ages two to 12, so check with your airline when booking. Reserve a seat behind the bulkhead of the plane, because there's usually more legroom and enough space to fit a bassinet, which the airlines will supply. At the same time, ask about special children's meals or snacks; most airlines offer them. See

TWYCH's Airline Guide, published in the February 1990 issue (and again in February 1992) of *Family Travel Times*, for more information about the children's services offered by 46 airlines.

Ask the airline in advance if you can bring aboard your child's car seat. For the booklet *Child/Infant Safety Seats Acceptable for Use in Aircraft*, write to the Federal Aviation Administration (APA–200, 800 Independence Ave. SW, Washington, DC 20591, tel. 202/267–3479).

Baby-Sitting Services The front-desk personnel in most Portuguese hotels will be able to find a reliable baby-sitter.

Hints for Disabled Travelers

The **Information Center for Individuals with Disabilities** (Fort Point Pl., 1st floor, 27–43 Wormwood St., Boston, MA 02210, tel. 617/727–5540) offers useful problem-solving assistance, including lists of travel agents who specialize in tours for the disabled.

Moss Rehabilitation Hospital Travel Information Service (1200 W. Tabor Rd., Philadelphia, PA 19141–3009, tel. 215/456–9600, TDD 215/456–9603) provides information on tourist sights, transportation (for example, toll-free telephone numbers for airlines with special lines for the hearing impaired and, again, listings of selected tour operators), and accommodations in destinations around the world for a small fee.

Travel Industry and Disabled Exchange (TIDE, 5435 Dona Ave., Tarzana, CA 91356, tel. 818/368–5648), for a $15 per-person annual membership fee, provides a quarterly newsletter and a directory of travel agencies specializing in tours to Europe for the disabled.

The Society for the Advancement of Travel for the Handicapped (347 5th Ave., Suite 610, New York, NY 10016, tel. 212/447–7288, fax 212/725–8253) offers access information. Annual membership costs $45, $25 for senior citizens and students. Send $2 and a stamped, self-addressed envelope.

Hints for Older Travelers

The **American Association of Retired Persons** (AARP, 601 E St., NW, Washington, DC 20049, tel. 202/434–2277) has the Purchase Privilege Program for independent travelers, which offers discounts on hotels, airfare, car rentals, and sight-seeing. (The program includes the member and member's spouse or the member and another person who shares the household.) The AARP also arranges group tours, through **AARP Travel Experience from American Express** (Box 5850, Norcross, GA 30091, tel. 800/927–0111). AARP members must be 50 years or older, and annual dues are $5 per person or per couple.

When using an AARP or other discount identification cards, ask for reduced hotel rates at the time you make your reservation, not when you check out. At participating restaurants show your card to the maitre d' before you're seated, because discounts may be limited to certain set menus, days, or hours. For a free list of hotels and restaurants offering discounts, call or write the AARP and ask for the "Purchase Privilege" brochure or call the AARP travel service. When renting a car, be sure to ask about special promotional rates that might offer greater savings than are available with your discount ID card.

Elderhostel (75 Federal St., 3rd floor, Boston, MA 02210–1941, tel. 617/426–7788) is an innovative educational program for people 60 and older. Participants live in dorms on some 1,200 campuses around the world. Mornings are devoted to lectures and seminars, afternoons to sightseeing and field trips. Fees for two- and three-week trips, including room, board, tuition, and round-trip transportation, range from $1,800 to $4,500.

National Council of Senior Citizens (1331 F St. NW, Washington, DC 20004, tel. 202/347–8800) is a nonprofit advocacy group with some 5,000 local clubs across the country. Annual membership is $10 per person or $14 per couple. Members receive a monthly newspaper with travel information and an ID for reduced hotels and car rentals.

Mature Outlook (6001 N. Clark St., Chicago, IL 60660, tel. 800/336–6330), a subsidiary of Sears, Roebuck & Co., is a travel club for people over 50, with hotel and motel discounts and a bimonthly newsletter. Annual membership is $9.95, and there are currently 800,000 members. Instant membership is available at participating Choice Hotels (Ramada, Sheraton, Howard Johnson, Marriot). Ask about ITC–50 Club discounts.

Saga International Holidays (120 Boylston St., Boston, MA 02116, tel. 800/343–0273) specializes in group travel for people over 60. A selection of variously priced tours allows you to choose the package that meets your needs.

Further Reading

A good place to begin is your local library. Check the library index, perhaps for the travel section first, and then the history books.

The Discoverers—An Encyclopedia of Explorers and Exploration, edited by Helen Delpar (McGraw Hill, 1980) will inform you about the Portuguese discoverers (Prince Henry the Navigator, Vasco de Gama, and Ferdinand Magellan, among others).

Portugal—Social Life and Customs, edited by Richard Herr and John Polt, and *Iberian Identity: Essays on the Nature of Identity in Portugal and Spain* (University of California International Studies, 1989) gives insight about the people of the Iberian peninsula.

Time Off in Spain and Portugal by Teresa Tinsley (Horizon Books Ltd./Harper & Row, 1989) is for travelers contemplating more than just a few days or weeks in the country—it includes historical facts as well as local contacts and advice on how to experience the everyday life of the Portuguese and be more than just a tourist.

Other books include:

History *A New History of Portugal* (Cambridge University Press, 1976); *A History of Portugal (2 Volumes)*, (Columbia University Press, 1972) by A. H. Marques de Oliveira; *Portugal: Ancient Country, Young Democracy* (Wilson Center Publishers, 1990), edited by Kenneth Maxwell and Michael H. Haltzel; *The Discoverers* (Random House, Inc., 1983), by Daniel Boorstin;

The Portuguese Land and Its People (Penguin Viking, 1991), by Marion Kaplan; *Portugal of the Portuguese* (The Gordon Press, 1976), by A. F. Bell.

Literature *The Lusiads* (Viking Penguin, 1975), by Luis de Camões, translated by W. C. Atkinson, was written by a contemporary of Cervantes and Shakespeare who wrote the definitive classic of his people during the time of the Discoveries. *Portugal, A Book of Folkways* (Cambridge University Press, 1936) is a collection of Portuguese folklore.

Gastronomy *The Food of Portugal* (William Morrow & Co., 1986), by Jean Anderson; *Wines of Spain and Portugal* (Price Stern, 1990), by Charles Metcalfe and Kathryn McWhirter.

Arriving and Departing

From North America by Plane

All transatlantic flights from the United States and Canada to Portugal pass through Lisbon, where you change for connecting flights to other destinations in the country or to Madeira or the Azores. Schedule and fare changes occur with breathtaking frequency, so consult with your travel agent on which bargains are currently available, and read the newspaper for special promotions.

Be sure to distinguish among (1) nonstop flights—no plane changes, no stops; (2) direct flights—no plane changes, but one or more stops; and (3) connecting flights—two or more planes, one or more stops.

Airports and Airlines Three airlines fly from the United States to Portugal: **TAP Air Portugal** (tel. 800/221–7370); **TWA** (tel. 800/892–4141); and **Delta** (tel. 800/241–4141). TAP flies to Lisbon's **Portela Airport** (tel. 01/802060) six times a week in winter; daily from New York and Newark from April till September; and twice weekly from Boston and Los Angeles. TAP also flies to Madeira and the Azores through Boston three times a week. TWA flies daily from New York in the summer, four times a week during the rest of the year. Delta flies from New York three times a week.

Air Canada (tel. 800/776–3000) has three flights a week from Toronto and Montréal; **TAP Air Portugal** has frequent service from both Montréal and Toronto, including flights to Madeira (through Lisbon) and the Azores (through Boston).

Although price will probably be your prime consideration in selecting an airline, try to avoid the delays involved in changing planes at New York's Kennedy Airport.

Flying Time From New York to Lisbon: 6½ hours. From Atlanta to Lisbon (including one stop): 12 hours. From Los Angeles to Lisbon (including one stop): 15 hours. From Toronto or Montréal to Lisbon: eight hours.

Enjoying the Flight Because the air on a plane is dry, it helps, while flying, to drink a lot of nonalcoholic beverages; drinking alcohol contributes to jet lag, as does eating heavy meals on board. Feet swell at high altitudes, so it's a good idea to remove your shoes at the beginning of your flight. If you want to sleep, you may prefer a window seat to curl up against; if you like to move about the cabin, ask for an aisle seat. Bulkhead seats (located in the first row of each cabin) have more legroom, but seat trays are attached rather awkwardly to the arms of the seat rather than to the back of the seat ahead. Generally, bulkhead seats are reserved for the disabled, the elderly, or parents traveling with babies.

Discount Flights The price of an airline seat can vary up to 300%, depending on the day of purchase. First Class, Business, and Economy fares are usually sold without restrictions and can be bought, used, canceled or changed at any time—but they are also all quite expensive compared to most APEX (advance purchase) fares. As a rule, the farther in advance you buy a ticket, the less expensive it is and the greater the penalty (up to 100%) for canceling.

An APEX fare on a major airline is not necessarily the best buy because it carries certain restrictions: It must be bought in advance (usually 21 days); it restricts your travel, usually with a minimum stay of seven days and a maximum of 90; and it penalizes you for changes—voluntary or not—of your travel plans. Check with the airlines for details. But if you can work around these drawbacks (and most travelers can), they are among the lowest fares available.

For comparison, at press time round-trip New York–Lisbon fares were: first class, $2,614; business class (TAP calls it "Navigator Class"), $2,606, which includes a year-round special companion fare, whereby the second ticket is half price; economy, $918; APEX, $690. Note that TAP Air Portugal does not offer first-class service.

Read the newspapers; sometimes airlines advertise amazingly low fares. For example, at press time it was possible to book a round-trip New York–Lisbon flight on at least two major airlines for under $300 (with airport tax, the total cost was $328).

Charter flights usually offer the lowest fares but often depart only on certain days, and seldom on time. Though you may be able to arrive at one city and return from another, you may lose all or most of your money if you cancel your trip. Don't sign up for a charter flight unless you've checked with a travel agency about the reputation of the packager. It's particularly important to know the packager's policy concerning refunds should a flight be canceled; some agents recommend that travelers purchase trip-cancellation insurance if they plan to book charter flights. One of the most popular charter operators to Europe is **Council Charter** (205 E. 42nd St., New York, NY 10017, tel. 212/661–0311 or 800/223–7402), a division of the Council on International Education Exchange (CIEE). Other companies advertise in the travel sections of Sunday newspapers.

Other discounted fares—up to 50% below the cost of APEX tickets—can be found through consolidators, companies that buy blocks of tickets on scheduled airlines and sell them at wholesale prices. Tickets are subject to availability, so passengers must generally have flexible travel schedules. Here again, you may lose all or most of your money if you change plans, but at least you will be on a regularly scheduled flight with less risk of cancellation than on a charter. As an added precaution, you may want to purchase trip-cancellation insurance. Once you've made your reservation, call the airline to confirm it. Among the best-known consolidators are **UniTravel** (Box 12485, St. Louis, MO 63132, tel. 314/569–2501 or 800/325–2222) and **Access International** (101 W. 31st St., Suite 1104, New York, NY 10001, tel.

212/465–0707 or 800/825–3633). Others advertise in the travel sections of Sunday newspapers.

Another option is to join a travel club that offers special discounts to its members. Such organizations are **Discount Travel International** (114 Forrest Ave., Narberth, PA 19072, tel. 215/668–7184), **Moment's Notice** (425 Madison Ave., New York, NY 10017, tel. 212/486–0503), **Travelers Advantage** (CUC Travel Service, 49 Music Sq. W, Nashville, TN 37203, tel. 800/548–1116), and **Worldwide Discount Travel Club** (1674 Meridian Ave., Miami Beach, FL 33139, tel. 305/534–2082). These cut-rate tickets should be compared with APEX tickets on the major airlines. **Travel World Leisure Club** (225 W. 34th St., Suite 2203, New York, NY 10122, tel. 212/444–3562 or 800/444–8952) offers discounts on hotels, on some cruises, and on a limited amount of air travel.

If you are willing to put up with some restrictions and inconveniences in exchange for a substantially reduced airfare, you may be interested in flying as an air courier. A person who agrees to be a courier must accompany shipments between designated points. A few sources of information on courier deals are: a telephone directory listing courier companies by the cities to which they fly (send $5 and a self-addressed, stamped, business-size envelope to Pacific Data Sales Publishing, 2554 Lincoln Blvd., Suite 275–F, Marina del Rey, CA 92091); *A Simple Guide to Courier Travel* (send $15.95—includes postage and handling—to Guide, Courier Travel Carriage Group, Box 2394, Lake Oswego, OR 97035; for more information, call 800/344–9375); and *Airfare Secrets Uncovered* (send $16.95 to Universal Information Corp., 2812 Santa Monica Blvd., Santa Monica, CA 90404, tel. 310/828–4727) by Sharon Tyler and Matthew R. Wunder, which includes tips on courier travel, as well as other ways get discounted airfare.

Smoking   If cigarette smoke bothers you, ask for a seat far from the smoking section. It is best to request a nonsmoking seat at the time you book your ticket. If a U.S. airline representative tells you there are no seats in the nonsmoking section, insist on one: Department of Transportation regulations require U.S.–flag carriers to find seats for all nonsmokers on the day of the flight, provided they meet check-in time restrictions. These regulations apply to all international flights on domestic carriers; however, the Department of Transportation does not have jurisdiction over foreign carriers traveling out of, or into, the United States. Space for nonsmokers on these flights may be minimal; check ahead of time for seating arrangements, especially in business class.

Lost Luggage   If your luggage appears lost when you arrive in Portugal, go immediately to the airline's baggage-complaint desk and file a claim. It's possible your bag is arriving on a later flight, and the carrier will deliver it to your hotel free of charge. Also inquire about a cash advance for toiletries and other necessary items to tide you over until your luggage is found (*see* Insurance—Lost Luggage in Before You Go, *above*).

From the United States by Ship

There are no regular transatlantic crossings from the United States to Portugal, but **Royal Viking** (95 Merrick Way, Coral Gables, FL 33134, tel. 800/422–8000) and **Cunard Line, Ltd.**

(555 5th Ave., New York, NY 10017, tel. 800/221–4770) include stops in Madeira. Royal Viking has several transatlantic crossings from Ft. Lauderdale, Florida, that stop in Madeira on the way to Rome. Cunard sponsors two crossings a year (May and August) on the QEII that stop in Madeira, via Southampton in England and the Canary Islands in Spain.

For details regarding freighter travel to or from Portugal, consult **Pearl's Freighter Tips** (Box 188, 16307 Depot Rd., Flushing, NY 11358).

From the United Kingdom by Plane, Car, Train, Bus, and Fly/Drive

By Plane   It's important to distinguish between scheduled services to Portugal, operated chiefly by **TAP Air Portugal** and **British Airways,** and inexpensive charter flights operated by a whole range of companies that serve Lisbon, Oporto, Faro, Madeira, and the Azores (more frequently in summer months). If you're looking for bargains, don't mind traveling at inconvenient times, and are prepared for delays (up to 48 hours at peak periods), then consider a charter flight. But if you value reliability—and don't mind paying for it—you're better off with a scheduled flight.

During summer there is one flight daily from London Heathrow to Lisbon by British Airways and one daily from Heathrow to Lisbon by TAP Air Portugal (two flights daily on Thursday, Saturday, and Sunday). Flying time is between two and two-and-a-half hours. There is also a British Airways flight every day (except Saturday) from London Gatwick. Oporto receives daily direct flights by British Airways and TAP Air Portugal from London Heathrow. TAP has three flights a week from Heathrow to Madeira. All flights to the Azores connect through Lisbon.

Faro is served by a British Airways scheduled flight every day from London Gatwick, and by TAP on three days (Thursday, Saturday, and Sunday) from London Heathrow. The fantastic boom in the popularity of the Algarve as a vacation destination has also fostered a larger number of regular charter flights to Faro, and to a lesser extent Lisbon. This gives a wider choice, especially from regional airports in the United Kingdom Charter seats are often sold off at a big discount at the last minute.

As of mid-April 1992, approximate prices for a round-trip British Airways Club Class ticket were £396, £180–£250 for a Super-Pex return. Book and pay any time before departure. Turpoa, the same price as APEX, allows you to change your return flight for £30.

Charter flights offer substantial savings, though booking conditions can be strict. You'll need to buy your ticket some time in advance (between two and four weeks), and most charter flights allow stays of no more than four weeks. On the other hand, there are charter flights to almost every Portuguese airport from practically every British regional airport. Most flights, naturally, are in summer. Prices vary so much that it's hard to give guidelines, but you can usually expect to pay between 10% and 15% less than on the cheapest scheduled flight. Check what's available with a good travel agent, take your time, and shop around.

Further bargains are available if you buy at the last minute off-season or only want a one-way ticket. Check the advertisements in *Time Out* and the Sunday paper.

For reservations and information: **British Airways** (tel. 071/897–4000) and **TAP Air Portugal** (tel. 071/828–0262).

By Car The least expensive route to Portugal by car, though not necessarily the fastest, is by cross-channel ferry to France. The drawbacks are that the shortest and cheapest ferry crossing (Dover–Calais) leaves you with the greatest amount of driving; this can be tiring and also expensive if you take toll roads through France and spend many nights en route. It is some 2,121 kilometers (1,318 miles) from Calais to Lisbon. For a distance such as this, unless time is short, consider going as far as possible by ferry or using Motorail for part of the journey to reduce the tiring drive to a minimum. **Brittany Ferries** (Millbay Docks, Plymouth, PL1 3EW, tel. 0752/221–321) offers a range of vacation tours for motorists to Spain and northern Portugal that are based on the famous paradors and pousadas and are an excellent value for the money. **French National Railroads/French Travel Board** (610 5th Ave., New York, NY, tel. 212/757–1125) can provide rate information and schedules only in the United States.

By Train Train services to Portugal are not as frequent, fast, or inexpensive as plane travel. Getting to Lisbon by rail takes between two and two-and-a-half days; the fastest connection to Paris is the *Hoverspeed City Link* rail-hovercraft-rail service from London's Victoria Station, with up to four departures daily to choose from. From Paris the luxurious overnight Paris–Madrid **TALGO** or the **Puerta del Sol** leave the Gare d'Austerlitz, transfer in Madrid to the Lisboa Express, and reach Lisbon in about nine hours. Advance reservations are obligatory in both trains; book well in advance to guarantee a place.

Eurotrain (52 Grosvenor Gardens, London SW1W OAG, tel. 071/730–3402) and **Transalpino** (71–75 Buckingham Palace Rd., London SW1W ORE, tel. 071/834–9656) both offer excellent deals for those under 26. Otherwise book through **British Rail Travel Centers** (tel. 071/834–2345).

Rail Europe (230 Westchester Ave., White Plains, NY 10604, tel. 914/682–2999) has introduced a series of "Rail-and-Drive" programs in 17 European countries; the Portuguese program allows three rail trips and three **Hertz** rental-car days within one month for $129–$189 per person. Their EurailDrive Pass allows four rail trips and three rental-car days within a 21-day period for $269 per person (two people traveling together).

By Bus The **Eurolines/National Express** consortium runs regular bus service to Lisbon (twice weekly); Faro and Lagos in the Algarve on the southern coast (twice weekly); and once weekly to Coimbra. Buses leave London Victoria Coach Station and reach Coimbra, Lisbon, and Faro on the third day. For more information and reservations: **National Express/Eurolines** (Coach Travel Center, 13 Regent St., London SW1Y 4LR, tel. 071/730–0202), **Eurolines** (52 Grosvenor Gardens, London SW1W OAU, tel. 071/730–8235), or any **National Express** appointed agent.

Fly/Drive This has proved one of the more popular touring vacations in Portugal, as it combines swiftness in getting to the country (in practice you can be driving along the roads of Portugal within hours of leaving the United Kingdom) with total freedom of movement—plus the advantages of the "package" with none of its attendant restrictions. Prices are calculated per person as a rule, with two sharing both the car and accommodations (if pre-booked); if four go together, the costs are lower. Fly/drive can start at any of Portugal's three mainland airports—Lisbon, Oporto, and Faro, with Lisbon and Faro being the most popular. Fly/drive is also available in Madeira, but packages are based on staying in one hotel and exploring from there (and be advised that driving in Madeira is not for the fainthearted).

Prices include flight, fully-insured car rental with unlimited mileage, and a variety of itineraries, with first and last nights' accommodations (or a fully worked out itinerary, if you prefer).

British Airways teams up with **Avis** for this, but there are a number of other car rental companies in the market. In some cases (the Algarve in particular) a car is offered as part of the package deal when you rent a villa or apartment.

Full details are available from travel agents, car rental companies, and the airlines. You might also want to contact the following companies: **AVRO** (AVRO House, 262 Haydons Rd., London SW19 8TT, tel. 081/543–6511, fax 081/540–3574), **City Travel Service** (16 City Rd., London EC1V 2NE, tel. 071/253–4271, fax 071/251–3479), **Falcon Travel** (Astley House, 33 Nottinghill Gate, London W11 35Q, tel. 071/221–0088, fax 071/727–0497), **Flights Delight** (164–B Heath Rd., Twickenham, Middlesex TW1 4BN, tel. 081/744–2744, fax 081/892–2619), or **British Airways Holidays** (Atlantic House, Hazelwick Ave., Three Bridges, Crawley, West Sussex RH10 1NP, tel. 293/518060, fax 293/552319).

Staying in Portugal

Getting Around

By Plane   **TAP Air Portugal** and its sister carrier, **LAR,** are the main domestic airlines in Portugal, with flights from Lisbon to all major cities and many interregional flights, including to Madeira and the Azores. **Portugalia** flies between Lisbon and Oporto and offers charter service to Funchal in Madeira. **SATA** (Azorean Airways) offers regular connections between islands in the Azores. **Air Atlantis** (a subsidiary of TAP) has charter flights all over the world. Travel in Portugal can be time-consuming; trains are slow and roads can be bad, so flying is sometimes the best option.

Portugalia operates a *Ponte Areo* (Air Bridge) commuter service between Lisbon and Oporto/Faro. Flights leave every hour or so, depending on the time of day, and no advance booking is needed; just show up at the airport, buy a ticket, and take the next flight out. At press time (spring 1992) the cost of a one-way ticket was 12,000$00 (approximately $84).

By Train   The Portuguese railway system, **Caminhos de Ferro Portugueses (CP),** is surprisingly extensive. Trains are clean and leave on time, but many of those away from the Lisbon–Oporto main line are old-fashioned and infrequent. Many of the branch lines serving the agrarian interior, especially in the north, are meter-gauge.

Some express trains between Lisbon and Oporto run virtually nonstop and have either restaurant or buffet facilities. They are first-class, and require advance reservations and supplementary fares. The fastest trains travel the 350 kilometers (215 miles) in under three hours. Fares from Lisbon to Oporto are about $17–$30 first class and $9.25–$18 second class, depending on time of travel and number of stops made. Several of the Oporto–Lisbon trains take cars, as do some of the Algarve trains (only in the summer) and one train a day between Lisbon, Castelo Branco, Regua, and Guarda. Prices are reasonable, but remember that cars must be at the station an hour beforehand and tickets are best purchased in advance.

One of the newest tourist attractions in the Alto Minho region of the north is the "trains of yesteryear," historic steam engines and 19th-century rail cars that follow the route between Viana do Castelo and Caminha along a route similar to that inaugurated in 1878. The train's crew don period costume to enhance the vintage experience.

Be sure to buy tickets at the station as there is a huge surcharge on the train.

Fares A *cartão jovem* (youth pass) for those 26 and under costs about $25 and offers a 50% discount on train tickets, except on peak travel days. A family ticket is available to family groups of at least three people, and group tickets are available for groups of 10 or more traveling a minimum of 75 kilometers (47 miles) one-way. Discounts range between 20% and 30%. Tourist tickets can be purchased for trips of seven, 14, and 21 days.

If you are under 26, inquire about a *Billet International Jeune* (BIJ) discount travel plan. The special one-trip tariff is offered by **EuroTrain International**, with offices in London, Dublin, Paris, Madrid, Rome, Zurich, Athens, Brussels, Budapest, Hannover, Leiden, Vienna, and Tangier. You can purchase a EuroTrain ticket at one of these offices or through travel agents, youth travel specialists, and at mainline rail stations. **Tagus Turismo Juvenil** (20 Rua Camilo Castelo Branco, Lisbon, tel. 01/352–5509; 9 Praça de Londres, 1100 Lisbon, tel. 01/848–4957, fax 01/532715), a well-known youth and student-travel agency, is another source for information and reservations.

Portuguese railways are covered by the Eurailpass. Details and up-to-date prices can be obtained in the United States at **Rail Europe** (610 5th Ave., New York, NY 10020, tel. 800/345–1990). **Wasteels Expresso** (Av. Antonio Augusto de Aguiar 88, 1000 Lisbon, tel. 01/579180) is reliable for all local and international train tickets and reservations.

Contact your nearest **Portuguese National Tourist Office** for their *Railroads of Portugal* booklet, which contains information on schedules, fares, and discounts.

Smoking CP provides nonsmoking cars on all long-distance trips and most short runs; be sure to specify if you want a nonsmoking seat or bunk, because many Portuguese will contentedly smoke all night long.

By Bus You can be sure a bus will go to almost any town not served by train—and the fare will be lower. **Rodoviaria Nacional** (Ave.

Columbano Bordalo Pinheiro 86, 1000 Lisbon, tel. 01/726–7123; Ave. Casal Ribeiro 18, tel. 01/545–439), the national bus company, runs regular services throughout Portugal.

Bus tours can give you a quick overview of large cities and the surrounding sights before you set off on foot to explore. Most of the following private companies in Lisbon offer tours in English: **Mundial Turismo** (Av. Antonio Augusto de Aguiar 90–A, tel. 01/575–740), **Novo Mundo** (Rua Augusto dos Santos 9, tel. 01/352–7709), **Sol Expresso** (Rua Entrecampos 1, tel. 01/797–3748, for Algarve and Alantejo), **Abreu Tours** (Av. da Liberdade 160, tel. 01/347–6441), **Citirama** (Av. Praia da Vitoria 12, tel. 01/352–2594); and **Melia** (Rua Rosa Araujo 2, tel. 01/315–7247). You can make bookings at hotels or travel agencies.

By Car   Major work is being done on Portugal's highway system; a new superhighway runs between Lisbon and Oporto, and **autoestradas** (four-lane toll roads) circumvent many of the more congested areas of these cities. However, most highway driving is on two-lane roads with long backups behind heavy trucks. Even so, driving is the best way to see the rural areas and get off the beaten track.

Tolls seem steep in Portugal, but time saved by traveling the autoestradas usually makes them worthwhile.

Rules of the Road   Residents of EC countries can use their national driver's license in Portugal. Others should have an International Driver's Permit (*see* Renting or Leasing Cars in Before You Go, *above*), although your national license and passport usually suffice. Driving is on the right, and a red warning-triangle must be carried. Seat belts are obligatory, and children under 12 must ride in the back seat. Horns are banned in built-up areas (but that doesn't seem to stop the Portuguese). The city speed limit is 60 kilometers per hour (37 miles per hour); on the autoestrada the limit is 120 kph (74 mph); on the Nacional (national two-lane highway) the limit is 100 kph (62 mph), and on other roads it is 90 kph (56 mph) unless otherwise signposted. Portuguese drivers are notoriously rash, and the country has one of the highest traffic fatality rates in Europe, so driving defensively is strongly recommended.

Gas   Gas stations are plentiful throughout Portugal. Prices are controlled by the government and are the same everywhere. At press time gasoline cost 140$00 a liter (approximately ¼ gallon) for normal (92 octane) and 146$00 a liter for super (97 octane). Credit cards are frequently accepted, especially along main roads.

Breakdowns   The large car-rental companies, Hertz and Avis, have 24-hour breakdown service. If you are a member of an automobile club (AAA, CAA, or AA), you can get assistance from the Portuguese Automobile Club (ACP/Automovel Clube de Portugal, Rua Rosa Araujo 24, 1200 Lisbon, tel. 01/736–121; Rua Goncalo Cristovao 2–6, 4000 Oporto, tel. 02/316–732).

By Bicycle   Portugal is one of Europe's more mountainous countries. Although country roads can sometimes be crowded with speeding trucks, bicycle trips can take you along some unforgettably scenic routes. Ask the tourist office for a brochure, or contact the **Direcção Geral de Desportos** (Av. Infante Santo 74–4, 1300 Lisbon, tel. 01/607–095 or 01/674–181).

Telephones

Local Calls Public phones can be frustrating, and phone numbers in Portugal are being changed, so you might have trouble getting through. Ask either at your hotel or at a local phone office for help. The easiest way to make a local call is to go into a café or bar and ask the bartender if you may use the phone. Bar phones are metered, and the bartender will charge you after you've finished.

At a pay phone, insert coins and wait for a dial tone. The minimum cost for a local call is 10$00, and 50$00 to call another province, for which you must dial the area code. On the old pay phones, you line up the coins in a groove on top of the dial, and they drop down as needed. The new CrediFone or T-Sete phone booths take phone credit cards, which can be purchased at post offices for either 750$00 or 1,750$00. These phones have digital readouts, so you can see your time ticking away, and they are uncomplicated to use—the booths have instructions in several languages, including English.

To make calls to other areas within Portugal, precede the provincial code with 0 (most phone booths have a chart inside listing the various province codes). The 0 is unnecessary when dialing from outside Portugal.

International Calls Calling abroad is awkward from public pay phones and can be expensive from hotels, which often add a considerable surcharge. The best way to make an international call is to go to the local telephone office and have someone place it for you. Every town has an office, and big cities have several. When the call is connected, you will be sent to a quiet cubicle and charged according to the meter. If the price is 500$00 or more, you may pay with Visa or MasterCard, or use the CrediFone card (*see* Local Calls, *above*). In Lisbon the main telephone office is located in the Praça dos Restauradores, right off the Rossio.

To make an international call yourself, dial 00 and wait for a tone. Then dial the country code (1 for the United States; 44 for the United Kingdom), followed by the area code and number. You can call the United States easily with **AT&T USA Direct** or **MCI,** both of which add a reasonable surcharge. Dial 05017–1–288, and you'll be connected with an AT&T operator in the States. For an MCI operator dial 05017–1–234. You can then make a collect or calling card call.

Operators and Information The national number for emergencies is 115; for general information in Portugal, dial 118; the international information and assistance operator is at 098. These are good numbers to keep handy, since Portugal is in the process of changing numbers and adding digits.

Mail

Postal Rates Airmail letters to the United States and Canada cost 110$00 up to 15 grams, postcards 80$00. Letters to the United Kingdom and other countries in the European Community cost 60$00 up to 20 grams. Letters within Portugal are 35$00. Postcards are charged the same rate as letters. Stamps (*selos*) can be bought at post offices and government-run tobacco shops.

Receiving Mail Because mail delivery can often be slow and unreliable, it is best to have your mail sent to **American Express** (tel. 800/543–

4080); call for lists of offices in Portugal. An alternative is to have mail held at a Portuguese post office; have it addressed to **Lista de Correios** (general delivery) in a town you will be visiting. Postal addresses should include the name of the province and district, for example, Figueira da Foz (Coimbra).

Tipping

Service is included in café, restaurant, and hotel bills, but waiters and other service people are poorly paid, and you can be sure your contribution will be appreciated. However, if you received bad service, never feel obligated (or intimidated) to leave a tip. An acceptable tip is 10%–15% of the total bill, and if you have a sandwich or *petiscos* (appetizers) at a bar, leave less, just enough to round out the bill to the nearest 100. Cocktail waiters get 25$00–50$00 a drink, depending on the bar.

Taxi drivers get about 10% of the meter, but more for long rides or extra help with luggage, and there is an official surcharge for airport runs and baggage.

Hotel porters are tipped 100$00 a bag; 100$00 also goes for room service or a doorman who calls you a taxi. If you stay in a hotel for more than two nights, tip the maid about 100$00 per night. The concierge should be tipped for any additional help he or she gives you.

Tour guides should be tipped about 200$00, ushers in theaters or bullfights 100$00, barbers at least 100$00, hairdressers at least 200$00 for a wash and set. Washroom attendants are tipped 100$00.

Opening and Closing Times

Banks   Banks are generally open weekdays 8:30–3. Money exchanges at airports and train stations are usually open all day (24 hours at Portela airport in Lisbon), and some hotels will be able to accommodate you, although at a slightly lower rate than at a bank.

Museums   Most museums open at 10, close for lunch between 12:30 and 2 and close at 5 (a few big ones stay open at midday—check beforehand). They are closed on Monday and holidays; palaces close on Tuesday and holidays.

Shops   One of the most inconvenient things about shopping in Portugal is that most shops close at midday for approximately two hours. Store hours are Monday–Friday 9–1 and Saturday 3–7. In December Saturday hours are the same as weekdays. Shops are closed on Sunday, although some *hipermercados* (supermarkets) and shopping centers are open seven days a week, 10 AM–midnight.

Shopping

Superbly woven baskets found in markets and gift shops make lightweight and practical gifts. Beautifully hand-embroidered table linens don't weigh much, nor do the embroidered organdy blouses or initialled handkerchiefs that are the specialty of Madeira. Traditional embroidered silk bedspreads are still made in Castelo Branco, and exquisite, hand-made lace in Vila do Conde near Oporto.

The country's lovely glazed tiles—azulejos—can be found in either single patterns or pictorial panels that can be shipped home by freight.

Porcelain and pottery are also very attractive and sometimes irresistible; *Vista Alegre* is the oldest and most famous porcelain, with works near Aveiro. Pottery differs from place to place. The brightly colored roosters (symbol of Portugal) are made in Barcelos, black pottery in Vila Real, polychrome in Aveiro, blue and white in Coimbra and Alcobaça. Caldas da Rainha is famous for green glazed plates and dishes made in the form of leaves, vegetables, fruit, and animals. In the Alentejo, particularly in Estremoz, you will find early Etruscan and Roman shapes reproduced in unglazed red clay pots and jars. There is also a large range of glazed cooking pots in all shapes and sizes, and colored figurines. Marinha Grande is the center for glassware of every kind, and Atlantis crystal is particularly worth seeking out; its local factory is renowned.

The Alantejo is the home of natural cork; here you'll find picture frames, lidded buckets (*tarros*) in which food can be kept hot or cold, and other lightweight gifts. Carved wooden spoons and boxes and lambskin and goatskin slippers are also from this part of the country. Attractive lanterns, fire screens, and outdoor furniture are made from tin, brass, copper, and other metals in the Algarve and Trás-os-Montes. Primitive as well as sophisticated musical instruments (such as guitars, horns, flutes, and bells) are made in the Minho, Trás-os-Montes, and the Beiras. Coimbra is famous for guitars, and clay whistles are made in Estremoz.

Fine leather shoes, handbags, and belts can be bought all over the country, as can textiles such as cotton and wool blankets in cheerfully colored stripes. Embroidered carpets and rugs are the specialty of Arraiolos in the Alentejo, and Portalegre has the finest tapestry shops in Portugal.

Portuguese jewelry is also lovely: The gold is 19.25 carats here, and you can find modern brooches, and earrings, as well as many exquisite pieces based on ancient designs. Fine-leather bookbinding is another specialty, along with other leather products, such as clothing, wallets, luggage, belts, and gloves. For children's gifts stop in at any stationery shop, where you'll find a wide selection of unusual pen-and-pencil boxes, notebooks, erasers, and other items not seen in the United States.

Tax Refunds A number of shops, particularly large stores and shops in holiday resorts, offer a refund of the 12% IVA sales tax on large purchases (the purchase must be a single item worth more than $500). Be sure to ask for your tax-free check; you show your passport, fill out a form, and the store mails you the refund at home. Or simply present the signed form and the merchandise at the tax-free counter at the airport for a cash refund before you leave the country.

Sports and Outdoor Activities

Tennis is becoming ever more popular. If your hotel doesn't have courts, most of the resort areas have a **Clube de Tenis** where you can swing a racket (usually for a small fee). Most courts are clay. Tennis pros offer classes almost all year long in the resorts; contact the tourism office for a list of courts in the resort areas. For further information, contact the **Federação Portuguesa de Tenis** (Portuguese Tennis Federation, Estadio Nacional, Caxias, 2480 Oeiras, tel. 41/95244 or 41/98472).

Sailing, boating, windsurfing, and other water sports are popular all along the Atlantic and Mediterranean coasts and around Madeira and the Azores. Yachting and sailing facilities can be found at the Cascais Yacht Club, the marinas of Lisbon, and the expanding Vilamoura Marina in the Algarve, which currently offers 1,000 berths. The tourism office publishes listings of facilities available all over the country. For further information contact the **Federação Portuguesa de Vela** (Portuguese Sailing Federation, Doca de Belem, 1300 Lisbon, tel. 01/641–2152 or 01/647–324) or **Federação Portuguesa de Actividades Subaquáticas** (Portuguese Underwater Sports Federation, Rua Almeida Brandao 39, 1200 Lisbon, tel. 01/396–4322); **Federação Portuguesa de Canoagem** (Portuguese Canoeing Federation, Rua Antonio Pinto Machado 60, 4100 Porto, tel. 2/697–350).

Portugal's rivers, streams, and almost 1,300 kilometers (800 miles) of coastline make the country a paradise for **fishing,** with a great variety of catches. The best freshwater fishing is in the Rio Minho and Ria Lima (lamprey, trout, salmon) and in the Ria Vouga and the Serra da Estrela lakes and streams (trout). Off Madeira and the Azores, the Gulf Stream ensures some of the best deep-sea fishing in the world.

Portugal also has year-round **golf.** Courses in Lisbon, Estoril, and the Algarve are reputed to be the best on the Continent, and challenging courses in the north of the country and on Madeira and the Azores are set amidst breathtaking scenery. Contact the tourism office for detailed descriptions of the courses and a list of greens fees or the **Federação Portuguesa de Golf** (Portuguese Golf Federation, 9 Rua Almeida Brandão 39, 1200 Lisbon, tel. 01/674–658).

Hiking is a wonderful way to get in touch with nature in Portugal. The Iberian Peninsula is on a main route of migrating birds, where there is an astounding variety of species. The oldest nature reserve in the country is at *Peneda-Geres* in the far north, where wild boar, civet cats, wolves, and wild horses roam the mountains.

For the equestrian, Portugal offers **horseback riding** along sandy beaches, mountain trails, and in small villages throughout the country. Most Algarve resorts have stables, as does the Campo Dom Carlos in Cascais. Contact the **Federação Equestre Portuguesa** (Portuguese Equestrian Federation, Av. Duque d'Avila 9–4, 1000 Lisbon, tel. 01/674–658).

Beaches

Despite the tourist boom that has almost completely developed large stretches of the Algarve and the Costa de Prata, you can commune with the sea and the sky in relative solitude along the Costa Azul and the beaches of the Minho and Costa Verde. Decide whether you want the excitement and glamour of a world-class resort complete with casino and 24-hour nightlife; or whether your spirit would be more refreshed by amber cliffs and yellow sand leading into an indigo sea down south in the

Algarve; or lush green mountains and oyster sand meeting the blue-gray ocean, as in the north.

Dining

Although it is a small country, Portugal has a large, rich, and varied gastronomy. The Portuguese introduced coriander, pepper, ginger, curry, saffron, and paprika in to Europe as a result of their explorations and establishment of trade routes with the East. They brought back tea from the Orient, coffee and peanuts from Africa, and pineapples, tomatoes, and potatoes from the New World.

Portugal's rivers and its proximity to the sea give it a fish- and seafood-oriented gastronomy: Be sure to try the *caldeirada* (national seafood stew) and fresh *sardinhas assadas* (grilled sardines). Chicken and pork are good everywhere, and the mention of golden and crunchy *leitao assado* (roasted piglet) in the north is enough to give anyone an appetite. Sautéed or grilled *bife á Portuguesa* (steak), often cooked in a Port wine sauce, is served throughout the country. *Bacalhau* (codfish) can be served 365 different ways (or so legend has it). The famous pork and clam dish, called *porco a alentejana*, is made with diced marinated pork and clams and served with outstanding potatoes or rice.

The country has a wealth of good wines. Apart from the unique Port and Madeira, there are more than 100 different varieties, ranging from table wines to extra-special ones, all reflecting the individual character of their regions' soils.

Mealtimes are similar to those in the United Kingdom. Breakfast is lightest; and lunch, the main meal of the day, is served between 12 and 2:30. (In large cities office workers nowadays often grab a quick sandwich in a bar instead of stopping for a big lunch.) Dinner is eaten sometime around 7, preceded by an afternoon break at about 5 for coffee or tea and a pastry.

As in many European countries, Portuguese restaurants use an *ementa (or prato) do dia*, or set menu. This can be a real bargain, covering all of the above at 80% of the cost of a single course ordered separately.

Ratings The government rates restaurants from five forks (deluxe) down to one fork (basic). We use four categories (Very Expensive, Expensive, Moderate, Inexpensive) to indicate average prices in escudos for a three-course meal excluding wine.

Lodging

Portugal offers accommodations to suit every taste and budget, from palaces to pensions, from mansions to ultra-modern hotels. Many visitors design their itineraries around *pousadas*, a chain of state-run hotels converted from old castles and historic buildings. Luxurious resorts provide self-contained surroundings that can tempt guests not to leave and explore surrounding areas. There are new high-rise hotels in cities, residences, and aparto-hotel-style pensions (with suites or one-bedroom units and kitchenettes) in the smallest of towns. By law prices must be posted at the reception desk and should indicate whether tax is included (IVA is 8% for hotels).

Hotels   High season means not only the summer months, but also Easter week and anytime a town is holding a fiesta. However, in the off-season (November through March) many hotels' rates are as much as 20% lower. In Portugal, a Continental breakfast is usually included in the price of the room.

Pousadas   The term **pousada** is derived from the Portuguese verb *pousar*, meaning "to rest." Portugal has an easily accessible network of more than 32 of these state-run hotels, which are located in wonderfully restored castles, palaces, monasteries, convents, and other charming historic buildings. Each pousada is set in a particularly scenic and tranquil part of the country and is tastefully furnished with traditional regional crafts and antiques and artwork. All have restaurants that present regional specialties; you may stop for a meal or a drink at a pousada without spending the night. Rates are reasonable, considering that most pousadas are four- and five-star hotels and a stay in a pousada can be the highlight of your visit. However, they are extremely popular with foreigners and Portuguese alike, so make reservations in advance, especially during summer months, since some have 10 or fewer rooms. For more information, contact the tourist office or **ENATUR** (Av. Sta. Joana a Pricesa 10–A, 1700 Lisbon, tel. 01/848–1221); in the United States, **Marketing Ahead** (433 5th Ave., New York, NY 10016, tel. 212/686–9213); in the United Kingdom, **Keytel International** (402 Edgeware Rd., London W2 1ED, tel. 071/402–8182).

Country Houses   Manors, farm estates, and country homes have been modified to receive small numbers of guests in a fairly new venture called *Turismo de Habitacão* (Country House Tourism), mostly operating in the north of the country. These guest houses are located in bucolic settings that offer an alternative kind of comfort, removed from the cities, and quite often near parks, monuments, or historic villages. Breakfast is always included in the price. For more details contact your tourism office or **Promocões e Ideaias Turisticas** (PIT: Alto da Pampilheira, Torre D-2-8A, 2750 Cascais, tel. 01/486–7958 or 01/284–4464) for homes in the center and south; **Direcção-Geral do Turismo, Divisão do Turismo no Espaço Rural** (Av. Antonio Augusto de Aguiar 86, 1099 Lisbon, tel. 01/575–015 or 01/575–086), or **TURIHAB** (Praça da República, 4990 Ponte de Lima, tel. 58/942–239 or 58/942–335), for accommodations in more rural areas of the country.

Camping   More than 100 good campgrounds are available in Portugal, where camping has been on the upswing over the past few years. One of the largest is the *Monsanto Parque Florestal*, along the Estoril autostrada not far from the city center, with tennis, a swimming pool, a bank, a restaurant, cafés, a chapel, a library, a game room, and a mini-market. Another very pleasant site is five minutes from Guincho Beach, Cascais; it's operated by **Orbitur** (Avenida Almirante Gago Coutinho 25, Lisbon 1000, tel. 01/892–938), which also has several other well-equipped camps, some with four-person chalets to rent.

For a relatively complete list of campgrounds, contact the **Turismo** offices or the **Federação Portuguesa de Campismo e Caravanismo** (Portuguese Camping and Caravanning Federation, Av. 5 de Outubro 15–3, 1000 Lisbon, tel. 01/522–715 or 01/522–3308).

Hostels There are about 17 **Pousadas de Juventude** (Youth Hostels) around the country, providing clean, somewhat spartan, and reasonably priced lodgings. Young travelers with membership cards validated by any Youth Hostel Association belonging to the International Federation of Youth Hostels are welcome. Although it's best to purchase an AYHA membership card at home, you will be able to get one in an overseas hostel. Not all hostels require the ID, but some do, so it may be worth the investment. Hostels provide linens, breakfast, and sometimes dinner. The official limit is three consecutive days, but you may stay longer if space is available. To join the International Federation of Youth Hostels, apply in the United States to **American Youth Hostels, Inc.** (Box 37613, Washington, DC 20013, tel. 202/783–6161), in Canada to **Canadian Hosteling Association** (18 Dyward Market, Ottawa, Ontario, K1N 7A1, tel. 613/748–5638), and in the United Kingdom to **Youth Hostels Association** (14 Southampton St., London WC2E 7HY, tel. 071/836–8541). IFYH recently introduced the name **Hostelling International** as a new, more global logo—look for it on signs and in their advertising.

Spas Portugal has been favored with a profusion of thermal springs, whose waters reputedly can cure whatever ails you. In the smaller spas, hotels are rather simple; in the more famous ones, they are first-class. Most are open from May through October. For complete listings and reservations information, contact the Portuguese tourism office nearest you or the **Associação Nacional dos Industriais de Aguas Minero-Medicinais de Mesa** (Rua de S. Jose 93–1, 1100 Lisbon, tel. 01/324–523).

Villas Renting a **villa** in Portugal is a romantic idea and can save you money on a long trip, but beware that glossy brochures usually make a villa look much better than it really is. The best way to find a villa is to do it yourself on arrival or inspect properties this year for next year's vacation. Use only reputable agents. Three U.S. companies offering villa rentals in Portugal are **At Home Abroad Inc.** (405 E. 56th St., New York, NY 10022, tel. 212/421–9165), **Sun Holidays** (26 6th St., Suite 603, Stamford, CT 06905, tel. 203/323–1166 or 800/243–2057), and **Mediterranean Destinations** (Suite 230, 7300 City Ave., Philadelphia, PA 19151–2286, tel. 215/879–3777).

In Britain try **Jean Harper Holidays** (20 Walton Rd., Stockton Heath, Warrington WA4 6NL, tel. 925/64234) or **Bartle Holidays** (Wingfield, High Dr. Woldingham, Caterham, Surrey CR3 7ED, tel. 883/652257).

2 Portrait of Portugal

Family Affairs

By Marion
Kaplan

In modern Portugal, there are still a few dukes, marquises and counts. Nobility has not been recognized since the fall of the monarchy in 1910, but the old families are still there—and social snobbery. I can gawp at the partying, if I want to, in the weekly *Semanário*'s magazine, *Olá*, which concentrates on the rich at play, their plush homes and glossy life-styles. Old families do not welcome the new rich to their clubs; there are no grandees among the northern industrialists. Wealth and power have shifted drastically. Yet despite the shock of revolution, the sudden development of a new class of money-market technocrats and impresarios, divisions are not just between old and new, rich and poor, success and failure. The aristocracy and landowning classes, feudal by history and rich by inheritance, have adapted, too.

Sons and daughters of the old families take little for granted. They go to university, marry correctly, enter the professions, participate actively in the modernizing of Portugal—outside the cut and thrust of party politics. These families have experienced and survived the shattering effects of revolution; the challenges of 1992 could never be as fearful as the shocks of 1974.

Family names ring across history and continents, yet it is no longer simple in the gusts and eruptions of new times—despite an astonishingly large and informative press—even for knowledgeable and socially aware Portuguese to be sure who is who.

For one thing, many Portuguese come from truly gigantic families. At a family reunion held in Lisbon's Estufa Fria greenhouse-park, 1,200 d'Oreys showed up.

In the house which had been her family's for three generations Maria Eugenia Sa da Bandeira—another historic and distinguished name—spoke of her large family to *Olá* magazine. "Imagine what it's like," she said, "buying shoes for fifteen, or toothbrushes." Another matriarch, Maria Simoes de Almeida, has seventeen children, a family that, with husbands and wives and their children, adds up to close to a hundred. In north Portugal's *vinho verde* country I have met many people for whom, for reasons that are as much custom as religion, anything but a large family would be unusual.

In Geraz do Lima the Casa dos Cunhas has belonged for centuries to the Sottomayor Correia de Oliveira family. One of the family is a lawyer, Antonio Correia de Oliveira, one of six children and, in his thirties, a father of six. "Not a lot," he said; "my grandparents had fifteen." I met dashing young Miguel Reymao, an agronomist who works for a bank. He is one of ten brothers and sisters whose family owns the Quinta de Luou, a member of the Association of Bottlers and Producers of Vinho Verde which aspires to a high quality and more individual wine. No Reymao lives on the estate, a flourishing 21-hectare farm near Ponte de Lima which is run in the manner of many such properties by a *caseiro* (manager). The future of the family's pleasant country house? Tourism, perhaps.

Transforming old family concerns into EC-conscious companies capable of strong competition became a business priority as the 1980s ended. Jerónimo Martins, a family grocery founded in 1792 and in the same family until about 1920, created a new group in 1989, built on a supermarket empire and a Unilever association, and a new image which left family considerations behind. But no proud Portuguese company would ignore its history. Bold publicity reminded everyone that Jerónimo Martins had outlasted five political regimes, the French invasions, two world wars, four revolutions and the Chiado fire that, in August 1988, burned its most distinguished shop to cinders.

Of the Costa Salema family, Helena Roseta—one of eight brothers and sisters—is the most forthright and conspicuous. Born in 1947, she is a qualified architect, has been *Presidente da Câmara* (mayor) of Cascais, a Member of Parliament within the PSD party and an independent deputy on the Socialists' bench outside it. She is not the only achiever. Her husband, Pedro Roseta, a PSD deputy, has been ambassador to the Organization for Economic Cooperation and Development, OECD. Each of her brothers and sisters is a professional success, their husbands and wives often public figures—one sister is married to Antonio Capucho, a PSD minister, one of the d'Orey clan and elected to the European Parliament in 1989. Another sister, Margarida Salema, a lawyer, was selected by Cavaco Silva for the PSD list and also won a seat at Strasbourg. In a profile on the family the newspaper, *O Independente*, found not a dud among them—even the upcoming generation showed every sign of intellectual brilliance in fields as diverse as architecture and maritime biology. The family's modest explanation for its strong public presence: 'The family is big, the country small.'

With its deep roots and long blood lines, traditions and kinsfolk and, increasingly, professional success and the money that goes with it, the classic Portuguese family is a rock of ages. The family might appear to have sundered where sons and daughters have left villages and farms to study, to work or to emigrate. But the glue holds. Wealth, class and life-style affect only the degree of sophistication of joyous, loud reunions.

Children, whether from aristocratic families, the bourgeoisie, or smallholdings and farms, love and respect their par-

ents, visit them frequently when they are away from home,
very often marry into their own community—and occasionally never break away at all. In the rural setting in which I
live, a young man quite often stays at home until he is married. He is doted on and spoiled. If he is talented he may
start a small business, like many a local plumber or electri-
cian—Edelberto Estrelo in Areeiro turned a teenage
knack with wiring into a successful enterprise. His living-
room, packed with refrigerators, television sets, washing
machines and other *electrodomésticos*, grew to a spacious
showroom—an extension of the family home. He does in-
stallations and repairs; his mother runs the shop. When he
marries, his wife—if she has no profession or job of her
own—will help out.

Young couples frequently live with one or other set of
parents—separate housing is too often prohibitive-
ly costly. When babies arrive, grandmothers are in-
stant babysitters. And when there is no handy mother-in-
law, grandmother, older sister, cousin or other relative,
then babies fit in with daily activity—tucked into the corner of a minimercado (a modernized village store), or
among the laundry in a *lavandaria*. Family life can sometimes be too close: mother-in-law may be a useful baby
minder but she may be as interfering and troublesome as
the mother-in-law jokes suggest. Mental breakdowns are
not uncommon; family pressures are the prime cause.

From birth to death, in a traditional rural family, links bind
tightly even across oceans where sons, daughters, cousins
have settled and extended the family further. In marriages
abroad Portuguese will most likely marry Portuguese.
Beldora, the lissom and beautiful American-born grand-
daughter of my hardworking neighbours, married a young
American whose Portuguese parents come from the same
freguesia (parish). Love bloomed from a casual encounter
and a comfortable convention made for a good marriage—
and, a year later, a bonny baby daughter.

However the Portuguese family is undergoing new challenges and trials every day. There is no enemy to fight, no
cause to defend, no dastardly regime to overcome or escape;
their concerns are closer to home, in the hopes, successes
and failures of children, in relationships between wife and
husband. The post-revolution generation faces the acute
problems of a developing country—in education, in housing, in jobs, in acquiring a suitably supercharged EC men-
tality. Suddenly, small Portugal is like an erupting volcano.
Are families suffering? Many, yes. But there have been worse
upheavals—emigration, Salazar's policies and repressions,
the revolution itself. The family, close and united, the frame
on which this new society is taking shape, on the whole stays
strong.

3 Lisbon

By Jules Brown

With a total population of about 1 million, Lisbon is one of Europe's smallest capital cities, and, to many visitors, it immediately becomes one of the most likeable. Lying north of the Rio Tejo (River Tagus) estuary and spread over a string of seven hills, Lisbon offers a variety of faces to anyone with the energy to negotiate its switchback streets. In the oldest parts of the city, tiny, stepped alleys are lined with pastel-color houses, across which drying laundry is strung; here and there lies a *miradouro*, a natural vantage point lending spectacular views of the city and river. In the grand 18th-century center, wide boulevards are bordered by black-and-white mosaic cobblestone sidewalks. There's a legacy of fine Art Nouveau buildings, too, and everywhere—on church walls, around fountains, and in restaurants and bars—you'll come across striking blue-and-white *azulejos* (painted and glazed ceramic tiles), for which the country is famous.

Lisbon's earliest history is a little unclear, but historians believe the city was probably founded by the Phoenicians. However, it was not until 205 BC, when the Romans colonized the city and linked it by road to the great Spanish cities of the Iberian peninsula, that Lisbon prospered. The Visigoths followed in the 5th century and built the earliest fortifications on the site of the Castelo de São Jorge, but it was with the arrival of the Moors in the 8th century that Lisbon came into its own.

The city became a flourishing trading center during the 300 years of Moorish rule, and the Alfama—the oldest district of Lisbon—retains its intricate Arab-influenced layout, although no original buildings exist. In 1147 the Moorish period ended, when the Christian army, led by Dom Afonso Henriques, took the city. The siege lasted 17 weeks, and, after the Moors were driven from Lisbon, Henriques planned to erect the city's cathedral in thanks. The building was founded three years later, in 1150.

The next great period in the city's history—"the Discoveries"—came in the 16th century, following the discoveries in India, Africa, and later in Brazil, led by the great Portuguese navigators. The wealth released by these voyages was phenomenal: Gold, jewels, ivory, porcelain, and spices helped finance grand new buildings and impressive commercial activity. Late–Portuguese Gothic architecture—called Manueline (after the king Dom Manuel I)—assumed a rich, individualistic style, characterized by elaborate sculptural details, often with a maritime motif. Torre de Bélém and the Mosteiro dos Jerónimos (Belém's tower and monastery) are supreme examples of this period. With independence from Spain in 1640 and the assumption to the throne of successive dukes of the House of Bragança, the most powerful noble family in Portugal, Lisbon became ever more prosperous, only to suffer calamity on November 1, 1755, when the city was hit by the last of a series of late-medieval earthquakes. Two thirds of Lisbon was destroyed, and tremors were felt as far north as Scotland; 40,000 people in Lisbon died, and entire sections of the city were swept away by a tidal wave.

Under the direction of the prime minister, the Marquês de Pombal, Lisbon was rebuilt quickly and ruthlessly. The old medieval quarters were leveled and replaced with broad boulevards and distinctive mosaic sidewalks; the Baixa, laid out in a grid, was designed as the city's commercial center; and the great Praça do Comércio riverfront square was planned. Essentially this is how downtown Lisbon appears to visitors today. Its 18th-century character largely consists of an elegant layout, which remains as pleasing and efficient in modern times as it was intended to be nearly 250 years ago.

Of course, there are parts of Lisbon that lack charm, particularly the modern city that extends beyond the center in a series of often dreary suburbs. Even some of the elegant downtown sections are losing their appeal, as restorations and renovations replace turn-of-the-century buildings with shiny new office blocks. But even so, the self-evident beauty of much of the city should compensate for almost any complaint the visitor may have. In parts of Lisbon—especially in the Alfama and the Bairro Alto—the centuries seem to collide: Out of 17th-century buildings trip designer-clad youths; the fish market at Cais do Sodré resonates with traditional sights and smells; and just a few minutes' walk from Lisbon's 18th-century aqueduct sits Portugal's most modernistic building, the Amoreiras shopping center.

Quite apart from the architecture and the obvious historic attractions, such as the St. George's Castle, the Cathedral, the Belém Tower, and Jerónimos Monastery, Lisbon has much to recommend it for a leisurely stop. The finest museum in Portugal—the Gulbenkian—is here, as are a host of other museums. The city transportation system is novel and entertaining, consisting of trams and a series of funicular railways and lifts that take you up the city's hills, as well as a subway system and the more usual buses. And whatever your vantage point, the river is never far away: Chances are either you'll be looking over it or walking alongside it, close to the fishing boats, container ships, and passenger ferries that make up its traffic.

The steep inclines of many Lisbon streets present a tough challenge to the casual tourist, and visitors are often surprised to find that because of the hills, places appearing close to one another on a map are actually on different levels and quite far apart. It will be worth your while—and indeed, pleasurable—to use various means of transportation to complement your walking tours of the city. As for the weather, it's best not to visit at the height of summer, when the city positively steams and lodgings are at their most expensive—and most difficult to obtain. Winters are generally mild and usually accompanied by bright blue skies, but for Lisbon's optimum climate, visit on either side of summer, in May or late September through October.

Essential Information

Important Addresses and Numbers

Tourist Information
Lisbon's main tourist office is in the **Palácio Foz** (Praça dos Restauradores, tel. 01/346–3314), at the Baixa end of Avenida da Liberdade, open Monday–Saturday 9–8, Sunday 10–6. The staff speaks English, and there are plenty of free brochures and maps. You can also reserve a hotel room from here.

There are other tourist offices at the **airport** (tel. 01/893689; open daily 9 AM–midnight), **Avenida António Augusto Aguiar 86** (tel. 01/575086, open daily 9–6), and **Santa Apolonia train sta-**

tion (Largo dos Caminhos de Ferro, tel. 01/867848, open daily 9–6).

Embassies **United States** (Av. das Forças Armadas, tel. 01/726–6600), **Canada** (Av. da Liberdade 144–3, tel. 01/347–4892), **United Kingdom** (Rua S. Domingos â Lapa 37, tel. 01/396–1191).

Emergencies **Police** (tel. 01/346–6141), **ambulance** (tel. 01/617777), **fire** (tel. 01/606060), **SOS Emergencies** (tel. 115). For general problems, or in case of theft, the **Tourism Police** (Rua Capelo 13, tel. 01/366141) has an office open 24 hours. If you need to make a claim against your travel insurance, you must file a report here.

Doctors Ask the staff at your hotel or at the embassy to recommend a reliable local doctor: Many doctors who have trained abroad speak English. Also, you can contact the British Hospital (*see above*), whose switchboard staff speaks English and will assist you.

Hospitals **British Hospital** (Rua Saraiva de Carvalho 49, tel. 01/602020; 24-hour emergency room; tel. 01/603785) has English-speaking doctors and nurses. Other hospitals include the **Hospital São José** (Rua José A. Serrano, tel. 01/864531); **Hospital Dona Estefânia** (Rua Jacinta Mareto, tel. 01/561954); and **Hospital Santa Maria** (Av. Prof. Egas Moniz, tel. 01/775171; emergency 01/793–2762).

Where to Change Money Most major banks have offices in the **Baixa,** and there are currency-exchange facilities at the **airport** and at **Santa Apolónia train station.** Throughout the city you will find automatic currency-exchange machines (equivalent to ATMs in the United States), but they only take European money cards; Cirrus and Plus networks cannot be accessed in Lisbon or anywhere in Portugal.

Mail and Telephones The **main post office** (Praça do Comércio) receives Poste Restante mail (General Delivery) and is open weekdays 9–7. You'll need your passport to collect your mail.

The **post office** on the eastern side of Praça dos Restauradores, at No. 58, is open daily 8 AM–10 PM. The **telephone office** here is the best place to make long-distance calls, but expect to wait in line. There's a second **telephone office** on the northwestern corner of the Rossio, at No. 65, that's open daily 8 AM–10 PM. At both of these locations you can use your Visa card.

If you have an AT&T or MCI calling card, you can dial the appropriate access number from your hotel phone (and some public phones) to be connected with an English-speaking operator to make an international call. For AT&T dial 05017–1–288 for access; for MCI dial 05017–1234. Be aware that you cannot get this service from all phones in the city, and you may need to use one of the telephone offices or your hotel operator to make the international connection.

English-Language Bookstores Most bookstores downtown carry at least a few English-language novels and guidebooks. **Livraria Bertrand** (Rua Garrett 75), **Livraria Britanica** (Rua de São Marcal 168), and **Livraria Bucholz** (Rua Duque de Palmela 4) have a broader selection than most bookstores. For American and European newspapers, go to one of the several small newsstands at the bottom of Praça dos Restauradores and on the Rossio, but expect periodicals to be a day or two out of date.

Late-Night Pharmacies Hours of operation and listings of late-opening druggists are posted on most pharmacy doors. For information on the nearest drugstore open weekends or after hours, call 118. Local newspapers also carry a current list of pharmacies with extended hours.

Travel Agencies You can save yourself a lot of time by purchasing train or bus tickets from one of Lisbon's many travel agencies. Major agencies include: **American Express Star Travel Service** (Av. Sidónio Pais 4, tel. 01/539841), **Wagon-Lits** (Av. da Liberdade 103, tel. 01/360706), **Wasteels–Expresso** (Av. António Augusto de Aguiar 88, tel. 01/579180), and **Viagens Rawes** (Travessa do Corpo Santo 15, tel. 01/370231). All main branches generally have an employee who speaks English.

Arriving and Departing by Plane

Airport and Airlines International and domestic flights land at Lisbon's small but recently modernized **Portela Airport** (tel. 01/802060 for arrival/departure information), north of the city. There is a tourist office here and an exchange bureau for changing money on your arrival. The airport is only about 20 minutes from the city center by car or taxi.

TAP, the Portuguese national airline, flies from New York, Newark, Boston, Los Angeles, Montréal, and Toronto, with some direct flights to Lisbon. Also, **TAP, British Airways, TWA, Delta,** and **Air Canada** link the city with London and other European capitals (*see* Arriving and Departing in Chapter 1).

Between the Airport and Downtown There are no trains or subways between the airport and the city, but getting downtown by bus or taxi is a simple matter and is relatively inexpensive.

By Bus There is a special express-bus service into the city center called the **Linha Verde** (Green Line, No. 90), which departs every 15–30 minutes 7:30 AM–1:30 AM and takes 30 minutes to travel downtown. The bus leaves from immediately outside the terminal building, costs 250$00, and stops at several useful points, including Praça Marquês de Pombal, the Avenida da Liberdade, the Rossio, and Santa Apolónia train station.

City buses (Nos. 44 and 45) costing about 125$00 one-way are cheaper than Linha Verde. They depart from the main road in front of the terminal building and pass through Praça dos Restauradores on the way to the Cais do Sodré train station. (From there you can continue by rail to Estoril and Cascais.)

By Taxi Taxis in Lisbon are so cheap and the airport is so close to the city center that many visitors make a beeline straight for a cab (lines form at the terminal). Expect to pay less than 1,000$00 to most destinations in the city center and 4,000$00–5,000$00 if you're headed for Estoril or Sintra. Note that you will probably have to pay extra for each piece of luggage.

By Car Car-rental firms and the tourist-information office at the airport provide free maps of Lisbon and the Lisbon Environs. The drive to the city center takes 20–30 minutes, depending on traffic conditions. It's best to follow the Linha Verde bus route (*see* By Bus, *above*). However, signs to the city center are posted along Avenida Marechal Craveiro Lopes, through Campo Grande, down Avenida da República, and to Praça Marquês de Pombal, and the main Avenida da Liberdade.

Arriving and Departing by Car, Train, and Bus

By Car Lisbon sees some of the most wreckless driving in all of Portugal. Add to this the notoriously difficult parking situation in the city center and the unsuitability of Lisbon's cramped old-town quarters for sightseeing by auto, and there's much to be said for not using a car in the capital. Nevertheless, most of the country's highways originate in Lisbon, including the fast roads west to Estoril, south to Setúbal, and north to Oporto.

Car Rentals Major car-rental companies have offices at the airport. In central Lisbon you'll also find: **Avis** (Av. Praia da Vitória 12, tel. 01/561176), **Budget** (Av. Fontes Pereira de Melo 62, tel. 01/537717), **Europcar** (Av. António Agusto de Aguiar 24, tel. 01/524558), and **Hertz** (Rua Tomas Ribeiro 6, tel. 01/539816).

By Train International trains from France and Spain and long-distance domestic services from Oporto and the north arrive at and depart from the **Santa Apolónia station** (Av. Infante D. Henrique, tel. 01/876025), on the riverfront, to the east of Lisbon's center. One daily train runs to and from Paris; two daily trains to and from Madrid; and frequent daily trains to and from Oporto from 7 AM–midnight. To reach the Rossio or Avenida da Liberdade from the station, take a taxi or bus No. 9 or 46 from outside the station.

Local trains to Sintra and all destinations in Estremadura use the central **Rossio station** (tel. 01/346–5022), an unmistakable neo-Manueline building that stands between Praça dos Restauradores and the Rossio itself. Trains to Sintra run daily every 15 minutes from 6 AM to 2:40 AM; three trains daily run to towns in Estremadura. The train-information office is on street level, but for tickets and platforms take the escalators (through the shopping center, in the station building).

Trains traveling along the coast to Estoril and Cascais arrive at and depart from the waterfront **Cais do Sodre station** (tel. 01/347–0181), a 10-minute walk west of the Praça do Comércio. Departures both ways are very regular—every 15–30 minutes, from 5:30 AM–2:30 AM.

Traveling by train to the Algarve and the south of the country is somewhat more complicated than train travel to other destinations. The **Barreiro station** (no tel.) is on the opposite side of the Rio Tejo but is linked to Lisbon by a ferry that docks at the **Terminal Fluvial** (also known as Sul e Sueste) adjacent to Praça do Comércio. The fare is included in the train-ticket price. There are seven daily trains to the Algarve, the first of which leaves at 6:40 AM, and the last one—an overnight service—departs around midnight.

By Bus Several bus companies provide services to and from Lisbon, and each has its own terminal. The **main terminal** (Av. Casal Ribeiro 18, tel. 01/577715) serves buses arriving from the north and is located very near Praça Duque de Saldanha. The Saldanha and Picoas metro stations are just a few minutes' walk away. Terminals at **Praça de Espanha** and **Campo Pequeno** serve the rest of Portugal and Europe; again, nearby metro stations provide onward transportation.

For bus transportation schedules it's best to inquire in advance at the main tourist-information office, since routes and companies change frequently (particularly on the popular summer express runs to the Algarve). Most travel agents can sell you a bus ticket in advance; if you buy from the company ticket office, give yourself plenty of time to purchase before you depart. In summer it's wise to reserve a ticket at least a day in advance for destinations in the Algarve. There are four daily departures from Lisbon for the Algarve and Oporto; towns closer to the capital receive more frequent service.

Getting Around

The best way to see central Lisbon is on foot (in combination with various forms of public transport). It's a small city by any standard, and most of the points of interest are contained within the well-defined older quarters. A stroll through the Baixa—the gridded 18th-century downtown shopping area—can take less than a half hour; from there you can walk to the Bairro Alto to the west or the Alfama to the east. The latter two areas are the most interesting of the old-town quarters. A 30-minute walk north up the central Avenida da Liberdade takes you to the large Parque Eduardo VII; the Gulbenkian Foundation is about 15 minutes farther.

If you plan to walk the city, it's important to remember that Lisbon is hilly and has cobblestone sidewalks that can make walking tiring (especially in the hot summer) even when you wear comfortable shoes. At some point you'll probably want to use the public-transportation system, if only to sample the old trams and funicular railways and elevators that link sections of the city.

There are ways to reduce public-transportation costs, especially if you're staying in Lisbon for more than a few days. To save about 50% off individual ticket purchases, you can buy blocks of 20 tickets for under 500$00, to be used on trams and buses; tickets are available at kiosks near principal bus stops along the main routes. Similarly, blocks of 10 tickets are available for use on the metro system and cost 400$00. Another option is a tourist pass that gives unlimited rides on all city transportation. It costs 1,100$00 for four days or 1,550$00 for a week and is available at Cais do Sodré station (at the booth by the Elevador de Santa Justa) and other terminals; take your passport along to qualify for the pass.

A note of warning: Avoid traveling on public transportation during rush hours, especially on the metro, which gets jammed. Also, be aware that pickpockets ply their trade on crowded trains, buses, and trams. Keep an eye on your possessions, and carry bags and purses with the zipper side facing your body.

By Tram Taking an *eléctrico* (tram) is one of the most amusing and enjoyable ways to get around Lisbon. The system built by British engineers at the end of the last century is one of the best in Europe and is easy to use. Stops are indicated by *paragem* (signs) suspended from cables above the street, and every stop has a route map for each tram that passes that way. The system operates 6:30 AM–midnight, and tickets cost 105$00 per journey; insert your ticket in the ticket-punch machine by the driver. Useful routes and an inexpensive tour of the city include Nos. 13, 24, 28, 29, and 30; Nos. 15, 16, and 17 will take you to Belém; No. 12 goes to the Alfama.

By Bus *Carris* (buses) are generally quicker than trams, although bus tickets are more expensive: There's a flat fare of 125$00 for most city journeys. Again, each stop is posted with full details of routes, so it's simple to determine the correct bus to take. City buses operate 6 AM–1 AM, and useful lines include No. 90, which links the airport with the main downtown areas, and Nos. 52 and 53, which make the spectacular journey across the Ponte 25 de Abril over the Rio Tejo. When you board, insert your ticket in the ticket-punch machine located behind the driver and wait for the pinging noise.

By Metro The metro, called the *Metropolitano*, is modern and efficient but covers a limited route and is used mostly by local commuter traffic. However, you may find it convenient for transport to and from the Gulbenkian Foundation; there are stops en route along Avenida da Liberdade and at the Parque Eduardo VII. The metro operates 6:30 AM–1 AM, and tickets cost 50$00 per journey. Insert your ticket in the ticket-punch machine at the barrier.

By Funicular and Elevator Small funicular-railway systems and an ingenious vertical lift (both are called the *elevador*) link some of the high and low parts of Lisbon. The lift, the Elevador de Santa Justa, whisks passengers from Rua de Santa Justa in the Baixa grid up to Largo do Carmo in the Bairro Alto. Of the funicular railways, the most useful are the Elevador da Glória, which runs from just behind Praça dos Restauradores to Rua de São Pedro de Alcântara in the Bairro Alto, and the Elevador da Bica, which runs from Rua do Loreto down to Rua Boavista, northwest of Cais do Sodré. Hours of operation for all three coincide with those of the other public-transportation systems; tickets cost 30$00 per journey, and departures are every few minutes.

By Taxi Taxis are plentiful and cheap, and if two to four people are traveling together a cab is often the cheapest option. Drivers are generally reliable and use meters; small tips are appreciated. Rates start at 130$00, and most city journeys will run 300$00–400$00; supplementary charges are added for luggage and for journeys outside the city limits. You may hail cruising vehicles, but it's sometimes difficult to get drivers' attention, especially late at night; there are taxi stands at most main squares. When you hail a cab, remember that when the green light is on it means the cab is already occupied. To phone a cab, try **Radio Taxis** (tel. 01/825061) or **Rossio Taxis** (tel. 01/827536).

By Ferry Ferries crossing the Rio Tejo leave from jetties at Praça do Comércio, Cais do Sodré, and Belém, and cost 75$00–200$00 one-way. The journey is worth making at least once for the spectacular view it affords of Lisbon from the water. For details of Lisbon-area destinations accessible by ferry, *see* Essential Information in Chapter 4.

Guided Tours

Orientation Many companies organize half-day tours of Lisbon and its environs and full-day trips to more distant places of interest. Listed below are a handful of reliable sources, and reservations can be made through any travel agency or hotel; some tours will pick you up at your door. A half-day tour of Lisbon costs about 4,000$00; a full-day trip out of the city to places such as Obidos, Nazaré, and Fátima costs about 10,000$00.

Try **Capristanos** (Av. Duque de Loule 47, tel. 01/543580), **Citirama** (Av. Praia da Vitória 12, tel. 01/560668), **Marcus & Harting** (Praça Dom Pedro IV 50, tel. 01/346–9271), and **Portugal Tours** (Rua D. Estefania 124–2, tel. 01/352–2902).

Personal Guides For names of personal guides, contact Lisbon's main tourist office (*see* Important Addresses and Numbers, *above*). Beware of unauthorized guides who approach you at popular monuments and attractions: These people are usually more concerned with "guiding" you to a particular shop or restaurant. But this is not to suggest that persons offering you a tour of the interior of a church or museum should be ignored. Often knowledgeable people associated with the particular institution volunteer their services for a tip of 100$00 or 200$00.

Exploring Lisbon

Orientation

The center of Lisbon stretches north from the spacious Praça do Comércio—one of the largest riverside squares in Europe—to the Rossio, a smaller square lined with shops and sidewalk cafés. The district in between is known as the Baixa (Lower Town), an attractive grid of parallel streets that was built after the 1755 earthquake and tidal wave destroyed much of the city.

The Alfama, the old Moorish quarter that survived the earthquake, lies east of the Baixa. Located in this part of town are the Sé (the city's cathedral) and, on the hill above, the Castelo de São Jorge (St. George's Castle). West of the Baixa, sprawled across another of Lisbon's hills, is the Bairro Alto (Upper Town), a fascinating area of intricate 17th-century streets, peeling houses, and churches. Five kilometers (3 miles) farther west is Belém, site of the famous Jerónimos Monastery, as well as several royal palaces and museums.

The modern city begins at Praça dos Restauradores, adjacent to the Rossio. From here the main Avenida da Liberdade stretches northwest to the landmark Praça de Marquês de Pombal, headed by the green expanse of the Parque Eduardo VII beyond.

The account of Lisbon below is divided into a series of walking tours that take you through the old- and new-town areas. Each quarter is pleasingly self-contained and can easily occupy half a day or more. By using taxis and public transportation you can combine two or three tours in a single day, but beware of trying to see too much too quickly. Walking in the summer heat is tiring, and, besides, some of Lisbon's greatest attractions and pleasures are to be found in the "hidden" squares and streets and in some of the agreeable café-bars for which the city is known. In Lisbon, slower is always better.

Highlights for First-Time Visitors

Amoreiras Shopping Center (*see* Tour 4)
Castelo de São Jorge (*see* Tour 1)
Elevador de Santa Justa (*see* Tour 2)
Fundação Calouste Gulbenkian (*see* Tour 4)
Igreja de São Roque (*see* Tour 3)
Instituto do Vinho do Porto (*see* Tour 3)

Mosteiro dos Jerónimos (*see* Tour 5)
Museu de Arte Antiga (*see* Tour 5)
Rossio Square (*see* Tour 2)
Torre de Belém (*see* Tour 5)

Tour 1: The Alfama District

Numbers in the margin correspond to points of interest on the Lisbon map.

The Moors, who imposed their rule on most of the southern Iberian peninsula during the 8th century, left their mark on much of Lisbon but nowhere so evidently as in the Alfama district. Here narrow, twisting streets wind up to an imposing castle set on one of the city's highest hills. This is a grand place to get your bearings and take in supreme views over the whole of Lisbon. The Alfama's streets and alleys are very steep, and its levels are connected by flights of stone steps, which means it is easier to tour the area from the top down. Take a taxi up to the castle or approach it by tram (No. 28 from Rua Conceição in the Baixa or No. 12 from Largo Martim Moniz, just northeast of the Rossio) and stroll down toward the center of town.

① Although the **Castelo de São Jorge** (St. George's Castle) was constructed by the Moors, the site on which it stands dates to the 5th century, when the Visigoths first raised a fortification here. At the castle's entrance is a statue of Dom Afonso Henriques, who in 1147 besieged the castle and ultimately drove the Moors out of Lisbon. Within the preserved Moorish walls and the castle's ramparts and towers (restored to their former glory in 1938) are remnants of a palace that was the residence of the kings of Portugal until the 16th century. The well-kept grounds are home to swans, turkeys, ducks, ravens, and other birds, and the outer walls encompass the small medieval village of Santa Cruz and its surviving church, some homes, restaurants, and shops. *Largo do Chão da Feira. Admission free. Open Apr.–Sept., daily 9–9; Oct.–Mar., daily 9–7.*

After leaving the castle, give yourself time to wander the warren of streets that make up the **Alfama,** the most ancient part of Lisbon. Because its foundation is dense bedrock, the district—a jumble of whitewashed houses with flower-laden balconies and red-tile roofs—has managed to survive the wear and tear of the ages, including the great earthquake of 1755. Nevertheless, time has taken its toll, and what in the Moorish period was the most exclusive part of the city is now a somewhat run-down working-class neighborhood but is full of interest nonetheless. June is a particularly joyous time to visit, during the festivals of the *Santos Populares* (Popular Saints), when the entire quarter turns out to eat, drink, and be merry.

Although the Alfama has a notoriously confusing layout, it is relatively compact, and you'll keep circling back to the same main squares and streets. Follow the castle walls around, and
② you'll emerge close to the **Museu da Marioneta** (Puppet Museum), with its unique collection of Portuguese and foreign puppets. The intricate workmanship that went into the creation of these dolls is remarkable. Occasionally the museum staff performs a traditional puppet show, but schedules are not regular so you should inquire at the museum about upcoming events. *Largo Rodrigues de Freitas 19, tel. 01/878396. Admission:*

Lisbon

*200$00 adults, children under 10 free. Open Tues.–Sun. 11–1
and 3–6.*

From the puppet museum it's a 10-minute walk down Rua de
❸ Santa Marinha and Rua São Vicente to the twin-tower **Mosteiro
de São Vicente** (St. Vincent's Monastery). The bright, Italianate facade heralds an airy church with a barrel-vault ceiling.
Although there's nothing left of the original 12th-century monastery, the present church (completed in 1704) features a tiled
cloister, and the former monastery refectory is the pantheon of
the Bragança dynasty. In the pantheon, among the great, solid
tombs and weighty inscriptions, lies Catherine of Bragança,
who married Charles II of England in 1661. *Largo de São
Vicente. Admission to church free; cloister 150$00 plus tip for
guide. Open daily 10–1 and 2:30–5.*

Time Out Behind São Vicente is the **Feira da Ladra,** Lisbon's flea market,
which is open every Tuesday morning 8 AM–1 PM, and all day
Saturday. There is the occasional antique here waiting to be discovered, but the browser will find mainly junk, army clothing,
and bric-a-brac. Still, this can be a fun way to spend an hour or so.

From outside the São Vicente church, tired legs can catch the
No. 28 tram (or walk 10 minutes) to the Alfama's prettiest
square, **Largo das Portal do Sol.** The terrace offers glorious
views of the streets below, dotted with drying laundry draped
across the stepped alleys.

❹ In the square you'll find the **Museu Escola de Artes Decorativas**
(Museum and School of Decorative Arts), a beautifully restored 17th-century palace in which tour guides exhaustively
point out every furnishing, including the lovely *arraiolos* (traditional, hand-embroidered Portuguese carpets that are
brightly colored and based on imported Arabic designs). The
more than 20 workstations located next to the museum teach
rare handicrafts, such as bookbinding, carving, and cabinetma-
king. *Largo das Portal do Sol 2, tel. 01/862184. Admission:
500$00. Open Tues.–Sat. 10–1 and 2:30–5.*

❺ Continue down the hill about 110 yards to the **Igreja de Santa
Luzia** (Church of Santa Luzia), with its fine exterior azulejos
upon which the story of the siege of the castle and the conquest
of Lisbon from the Moors is told. The adjacent terrace, the
Miradouro Santa Luzia, offers another sweeping view of the
Alfama and the river.

Time Out At both Largo das Portas do Sol and the Miradouro Santa
Luzia, you'll find a number of small café-bars with outside seats
from which you can watch the ships' activities on the Rio Tejo.
Cerca Moura (Largo das Portas do Sol 4)—named after the
Moorish walls that surround the district—is one of the best,
with a full menu of drinks and snacks from which to choose.

Head southwest from the miradouro along Rua do Limoeiro,
which eventually becomes Rua Augusto Rosa. This route takes
❻ you past the **Sé**—Lisbon's cathedral—which was founded
three years after the defeat of the Moors to commemorate the
Christian army's victory; to rub salt in the wound, the conquer-
ors built the sanctuary upon the site where Moorish Lisbon's
main mosque once stood. Aside from the austere Romanesque
interior and a fine rose window, there's little to detain you,

save a splendid 13th-century cloister. The ticket for the cloister also allows you entry to the sacristy, which contains the relics of the martyr St. Vincent. According to legend, the relics were carried from the Algarve to Lisbon in a ship piloted by ravens. *Largo da Sé. Admission to cathedral free; cloister 150$00. Open daily 9–noon and 2–6.*

Opposite the cathedral is the small church of Santo António da Sé, which retains a room (now a chapel) in which Saint Anthony was born, in 1195. The **Museu Antoniano,** in the chapel, features a curious collection of icons, books, and relics relating to the life of the saint. *Largo de Santo António da Sé, tel. 01/ 860447. Admission: 100$00; free Sun. Open Tues.–Sun. 10–1 and 2–6.*

To complete your tour of this district, walk around and below the cathedral to the **Casa dos Bicos,** a mansion that survived the 1755 earthquake. Its main attraction is its striking facade of pointed white-stone diamonds. The building is at the end of Rua dos Bacalhoeiros, a street close to the dockside and lined with modest fish-and-seafood restaurants. From here it's an easy walk to the adjacent Baixa district, or retrace your steps to the cathedral, outside which tram No. 28 stops before heading to the Baixa.

Tour 2: The Baixa District and the Chiado

Tremors caused by the earthquake of 1755, a massive tidal wave, and subsequent fires killed thousands of people and reduced proud 18th-century Lisbon to rubble. But within 10 years, frantic rebuilding under the direction of the king's minister, the Marquês de Pombal, had given the city a new look: a neo-Classical, grid design.

This can be seen perfectly today in the impressive **Baixa** district (Lower Town), which stretches from the riverfront to the square known as the Rossio. Pombal intended the various streets to house certain trades and crafts and the street names to tell the story, as do Rua dos Sapateiros (Cobblers' Street), Rua da Prata (Silversmiths' Street), and Rua do Ouro (now the Rua Aurea: Goldsmiths' Street).

Begin your tour in the enormous **Praça do Comércio,** the riverfront square that completed Pombal's design. Known also as the Terreiro do Paço, after the royal palace (Paço) that once stood here, it is indeed a regal space, lined with serene 18th-century buildings. The equestrian statue is of Dom José, who was king at the time of the earthquake and during subsequent rebuilding. Steps—once used by occupants of the royal barges that docked here—lead up from the water onto the square. The square itself is a hub for public transportation (trams to Belém leave from here), and although at times it may look like nothing more than a parking lot, recently it has become a popular spot for outdoor cafés. The best views are from any of the ferries that regularly cross the Tejo at this point.

Time Out   One of the original buildings on the square houses the elegant **Café Martinho da Arcada** (Praça do Comércio 3; *see* Dining, *below*), situated, as its name suggests, in the 18th-century arcade. Literary haunts since 1782, the main rooms now contain an expensive restaurant full of old-style atmosphere; there's also a more modest adjacent café-bar.

From the square a riverside path runs to the train station at **Cais do Sodré** and offers pleasant views over the Tejo. If you want a rest, settle on a park bench and watch the fishermen throwing out their lines. It's a 10-minute walk to Cais do Sodré from the Praça do Comércio, where there's an open-air produce market on the waterfront (and a handy taxi stand and bus stop in case you don't want to continue on foot).

Back at the Praça do Comércio, the most practical tour to make is through the grid of streets that makes up Lisbon's main shopping and banking district. The central street—**Rua Augusta**—and some of the cross streets have been closed to cars, making window shopping easy. Most days there's a small crafts market close to the Praça do Comércio, and scattered throughout the shopping district you'll find some of the best shoe shops in Europe; glittering jewelry stores; and a host of cafés and delicatessens selling wines, cheeses, and pastries.

9 The western side of the grid, the streets leading uphill from there to the Bairro Alto, is known as the **Chiado,** Lisbon's most chic shopping district. In 1988 this area suffered great damage from a calamitous fire that destroyed many of the older shops in the vicinity of Rua Garrett. Today, though, an ambitious rebuilding program is under way, and there is much hope that the area can be restored to its former glory. Despite the damage, the Chiado remains a fashionable place to shop.

If you're interested in the macabre, take the route through the ruins. Follow the newly built covered walkway through parts of the Rua Garrett and Rua do Carmo (where the fire began) and look down into the gaping shells of the burned-out buildings. A small crowd of onlookers usually gathers here to check on the progress and watch the acrobatics of workers who are trying to restore the area.

Time Out Rua Garrett, the Chiado's principal street, is lined with old department stores and a series of comfortable, turn-of-the-century, wood-paneled coffee shops that attract locals and tourists. The most famous of these is the **A Brasíleira** (Rua Garrett 120), which features a life-size statue of Portugal's national poet, Fernando Pessoa, seated at a table. This is a fine place for coffee or a beer anytime but Sunday, when the café is closed.

At Rua Garrett you aren't far from the Bairro Alto (*see* Tour 3, *below*), but the steep walk can be arduous. It may be better to drop back down to the Baixa, where—at the junction of Rua Aurea and Rua de Santa Justa—you'll find the extraordinary **10** **Elevador de Santa Justa,** a lift engineered in 1902 inside its own Gothic-style tower. In less than a minute the lift whisks passengers up to Largo do Carmo in the Bairro Alto. *Cost: 30$00. Open daily 7 AM–11 PM.*

11 If you walk north beyond the elevador, you'll enter the **Rossio,** Lisbon's main square since the Middle Ages. On the northern side of the praça—known officially as Praça Dom Pedro IV (whom the central statue commemorates)—is the mid-19th-century **Teatro Nacional** (National Theater), built on the site of the earlier Palace of the Inquisition. Unless you come to the theater for a performance (productions are in Portuguese), you'll probably do what the locals do when they come to the Rossio: sit at one of the sidewalk cafés lining the east and west sides of the square. The **Café Nicola,** on the west side, is one of the more traditional spots.

The Rossio, filled with hawkers, newspaper stands, and shoppers taking a break, is a lively place to end your tour. It's also a good place to have your shoes shined, by one of the roaming shoe-shiners who solicit their trade in the cafés. Before you agree to take their services, though, make sure you establish the price.

Tour 3: The Bairro Alto

Lisbon's **Bairro Alto** (Upper Town) extends west of the Baixa and, like the latter, is laid out in a grid. Unlike the Baixa, however, the streets of the Bairro Alto are narrow and cobbled and follow the contours of the hills, which makes getting around the district both pleasurable and confusing. Although the district dates to the 17th century, most of the buildings are from the 18th and 19th centuries and house restaurants, nightclubs, bars, churches, and antiques shops. Historically the area has been slightly Bohemian, but, with the opening of smart boutiques and trendy eateries, some gentrification has come. Yet the back streets are still lively with the sounds of daily life: Children scuffle amid the drying laundry, women carry huge bundles from shop to shop, and old men clog the doorways of neighborhood barrooms.

⑫ You can approach the Bairro Alto using the Elevador de Santa Justa (*see* Tour 2, *above*), but this tour starts at the **Elevador da Glória,** a funicular railway located on the western side of Avenida da Liberdade, by Praça dos Restauradores. Glória runs up the steep Calçada da Glória and takes only about a minute to reach the São Pedro de Alcântara miradouro, a viewing point that looks out over the castle and the Alfama (*see* Tour 1, *above*). *Cost: 30$00. Open 6 AM–midnight.*

⑬ Immediately across the street from the miradouro is the wonderful **Instituto do Vinho do Porto** (Port Wine Institute), where, in the cozy, clublike lounge, visitors can sample from more than 100 brands of port, from extra-dry white varieties to red vintages. Service can be a bit slow, but eventually someone will bring you a wine list, and you may order by the glass or bottle. *Rua de São Pedro de Alcântara 45, tel. 01/342–3307. Prices of tastings start at 100$00 a glass. Open Mon.–Sat. 10–10.*

Time Out While in the Bairro Alto you may want to sample from an *ementa turística* (tourist menu) that's offered in many of the small restaurants and bars. Typically, menus in this district include a set lunch of three courses, wine, and coffee and cost less than 1,500$00. **O Tacão Pequeno** (Travessa da Cara 3A), located on a side street opposite the upper station of the funicular railway, is a cheerful dining room that's often packed with people enjoying the hearty local food.

⑭ From the institute, turn right and walk down Rua São Pedro de Alcântara. At Largo Trindade Coelho, on your left, is the **Igreja de São Roque** (Church of St. Roque), a Renaissance church built by Felipe Terzi, the architect who designed São

Vicente (*see* Tour 1, *above*) in the Alfama. Curb your impatience
with its plain facade and venture inside. Its side chapels are superbly decorated. The last chapel on the left before the altar,
the 18th-century **Capela de São João Baptista** (Chapel of St.
John the Baptist) is particularly extraordinary: Designed and
built in Rome, with rare stones and mosaics that resemble oil
paintings, the chapel was taken apart, shipped to Lisbon, and
installed in 1747. You may find a guide who will escort you
around the church and switch on the appropriate lights so the
beauty of the chapels is revealed. *Open daily 8:30–6.*

⑮ Continue to follow Rua Nova da Trindade south down the hill,
and turn left at Rua Trindade toward the pretty Largo do
Carmo, on which stands the partially ruined **Convento do
Carmo** (Carmo Convent). The convent—once Lisbon's largest—was severely damaged in the 1755 earthquake, but open-
air summer orchestral concerts are held beneath its majestic
archways. Its sacristy houses the **Museu Arqueológico do
Carmo** (Archaeological Museum), a small but worthy collection
of ceramic tiles, medieval tombs, ancient coins, and other city
finds. *Museu Arqueológico, Largo do Carmo, tel. 01/346–0473.
Admission: 250$00. Open May–Sept., Tues.–Sat. 10–6; Oct.–
Apr., Tues.–Sat. 10–1 and 2–5.*

Down a narrow alley behind the Carmo Convent is the upper
station of the Elevador de Santa Justa; if you wish, you can return directly to the Baixa from there.

⑯ To complete your tour of the Bairro Alto, take the tram across
the quarter to the **Jardim da Estrêla** (Estrêla Gardens), on the
western edge of the district; No. 28 runs from Rua do Loreto,
near Praça Luis de Camões, which is just west of Largo do
Carmo. Towering above the attractive gardens is the impressive 18th-century **Basilica da Estrêla** (Estrêla Basilica), a spacious Baroque church with views of the city from its *zimborio*
(dome). Across the gardens, on Rua de São Jorge, is the **English Cemetery,** established in the early 18th century to allow
Protestants to be buried with due reverence in a Catholic city.
The most famous resident buried here is British author Henry
Fielding, who died in Lisbon in 1754 and is known for his classic
novel *Tom Jones.* You must ring for entrance at the cemetery
gates.

⑰ Lisbon's botanical gardens, the **Jardim Botânico** (Botanical
Gardens), are about 1.6 kilometers (1 mile) east of the Estrêla
Gardens, in the **Rato** district just north of the Bairro Alto. An
alternative appoach (but of the same distance) is to head north
from the Port Wine Institute (*see above*), instead of south.
Whichever way you get there, the botanical gardens, set on a
hillside and inhabited by varieties of birdlife, make a pleasant
stop. The four hectares of garden—laid out in 1874—contain
nearly 15,000 species of subtropical plants and also house a
19th-century meteorological observatory. *Rua da Escola
Politécnica 58, tel. 01/396–1521. Open May–Oct., daily 9–7;
Nov.–Apr., weekdays 9–6; guided tours year-round Sat. at 11.
Reservations required for tours.*

Tour 4: The Modern City

⑱ **Praça dos Restauradores,** the square adjacent to the Rossio,
marks the beginning of the modern city. Here the broad, tree-
lined Avenida da Liberdade starts its northwesterly ascent.

There's little of interest in the square, save the 18th-century **Palácio Foz,** on the west side, which houses the main tourist office. On the eastern side, a block east from the square and running parallel to it, is **Rua das Portas de Santo Antão,** famous for its row of seafood restaurants, most of which display in their windows great tanks of lobsters and fish on iced slabs.

⑲ Also on this road is the **Museu Etnografico,** sponsored by the Lisbon Geographical Society. Bizarre items such as shrunken heads, shells, and African musical instruments that have been retrieved from Portugal's former colonies are displayed here. *Rua das Portas de Santo Antão 100, tel. 01/325401. Admission free. Open only for tours Mon., Wed., and Fri. at 11 and 3.*

The city's main avenue—**Avenida da Liberdade**—is 1½ kilometers (1 mile) long and about 325 feet wide in places. Sadly, the thoroughfare that was laid out in 1879 isn't as grand as it once was: Many of the turn-of-the-century mansions and Art Deco buildings that graced the route have been demolished; others are covered in scaffolding as "renovation" work—the practice of turning historic buildings into soulless office blocks—continues. Nevertheless, you should take a leisurely stroll up the avenue from Praça dos Restauradores. Among the many cafés serving coffee and cool drinks is the open-air esplanada (garden-café), in its central, tree-shaded location.

It takes about 30 minutes on foot (or two stops on the metro) to ⑳ reach the top of the avenue and the **Praça Marquês de Pombal,** a large roundabout also known as the Rotunda. Dominating the site is a central statue of the Marquês, designer of the new Lisbon, that emerged from the ruins of the 1755 earthquake. From here you can take the metro north to the Gulbenkian Foundation (*see below*) or back to the Rossio (*see Tour 2, above*).

Alternately, go uphill to the west along Rua Joaquim António Aguiar to Lisbon's most ambitious post-modern building, the gigantic, pink-and-blue, commercial-and-residential complex ㉑ called **Amoreiras.** It's a 1-kilometer (⅔-mile) walk, or try to catch one of the free buses that runs during the day from the Rotunda. Designed by Tomás Taveira and visable from just about everywhere in the city, Amoreiras is adored as well as disdained. Inside there's a huge shopping center, a 10-screen movie theater, a "food street" of restaurants and bars, and information boards at every turn to help you cope with the complex's enormity. On weekends it seems all of Lisbon turns out to parade the corridors. *Av. Eng. Duarte Pacheco, tel. 01/ 692558. Shops and restaurants open daily 9 AM–11 PM.*

Rua das Amoreiras runs south from the shopping center to the Largo do Rato. As you approach the quiet Largo das ㉒ Amoreiras, look up at the **Aqueducto das Aguas Livres,** an 18th-century aqueduct supported by 14 arches, which formerly provided clean drinking water for the city. Nineteenth-century lore tells of one character who had a penchant for hurling his victims the 200 feet to the ground below.

Back at the Rotunda is the entrance to Lisbon's main park, the ㉓ **Parque Eduardo VII,** which was established at the beginning of this century and named in honor of King Edward VII of England, who visited Lisbon in 1903. Bordering the common, particularly on the western side, are several of Lisbon's luxury hotels, including the Ritz and the Lisboa Meridien. (Many of the hotels have private terraces that guarantee you a room with a view.) The park is best known for its two **estufas,** the *estufa fria* (cold greenhouse) and *estufa quente* (hot greenhouse), which contain rare flowers, trees, and shrubs from tropical and subtropical climes. The estufa fria is also one of the city's most bizarre concert venues, used on occasion by orchestras and soloists. *Tel. 01/682278. Admission to estufas: 60$00. Open Apr.–Sept., daily 9–6; Oct.–Mar., daily 9–5.*

Exit the park on the east side, and head north along Avenida António Augusto Aguiar. A 15-minute walk will bring you to the Praça de Espanha, to the right of which, in the Parque de Palhava, is the celebrated **Fundação Calouste Gulbenkian,** set on its own lush grounds. The museum of this cultural-trust foundation houses treasures collected by Armenian oil magnate Calouste Gulbenkian (1869–1955) and donated to the people of Portugal in return for tax concessions. The **Museu Calouste Gulbenkian** is the main part of the foundation's buildings and is easily Portugal's finest museum. The collection it houses is split in two: One part is devoted to Egyptian, Greek, Roman, Islamic, and Oriental arts and the other to European acquisitions. Both holdings are relatively small, but the quality of the pieces on display is magnificent, and you should aim to spend at least two hours here, or even the better part of a day. English-language notes are available throughout the museum.

You might first visit the astounding Egyptian room, highlighted by a haunting gold mummy-mask. Greek and Roman coins and statuary, Chinese porcelain, Japanese prints, and a set of rich 16th- and 17th-century Persian tapestries follow. No less comprehensive is the European art section, with pieces representing all major schools from the 15th through the 20th centuries. A room of vivid 18th-century Venetian scenes by Francesco Guardi, and paintings by Rembrandt, Rubens, Monet, and Renoir stimulate the senses, as do the Italian and Spanish ceramics, gleaming French furniture, textiles, and Art Nouveau jewelry. In short, this collection rates as one of the most satisfying and complete holdings of artistic brilliance in the world.

If it's all too much to take in at one time, break up your visit with a stop in the pleasant café-restaurant in the basement. There's an exhibition room here, too, which features temporary displays of art. Later, on your way out of the museum, at the main desk, you can buy superb (and inexpensive) posters and postcards. The foundation also houses two concert halls, where music and ballet festivals are held in winter and spring. Thanks to the Gulbenkian Foundation, modestly priced tickets are available at the box office. *Av. de Berna 45, tel. 01/793–5131. Admission: 200$00, free Sun. Open June–Sept., Tues., Thurs., Fri., and Sun. 10–5, Wed. and Sat. 2–7:30; Oct.–May, Tues.–Sun. 10–5.*

In the gardens outside the museum, sculptures hide in every recess. You may want to spend a little time here before following signs through the garden to the foundation's **Centro de Arte Moderna,** where modern and contemporary Portuguese and foreign art are displayed on two floors. There's also a special section set aside for drawings and prints. Although the range of exhibits here is more limited than that of the Museu Calouste Gulbenkian, modern-art fans will appreciate this venue for the finest collection of its sort in Portugal. Naturally, Portuguese artists are best represented: Look for pieces by Amadeo de

Sousa Cardoso, whose painting style varied greatly in his short life; abstract works by Viera da Silva; and the childhood themes explored in the paintings of Paula Rego. *Rua Dr. N. Bettencourt, tel. 01/793–5131. Admission: 250$00, free Sun. Open June–Sept., Tues., Thurs., Fri., and Sun. 10–5, Wed. and Sat. 2–7:30; Oct.–May, Tues.–Sun. 10–5.*

From the Modern Art Museum, walk back through the grounds of the Gulbenkian Foundation and exit east on to Avenida de Berna. Where the street crosses Avenida da República you'll **26** find the area (and metro stop) known as **Campo Pequeno.** This site—impossible to overlook—is the city's circular, red-brick, Moorish-style bullring, which sports small cupolas atop its four main towers. The bullring holds about 9,000 people, who crowd in to watch the twice-weekly bullfights (*see* Sports, *below*).

North of the downtown area, the modern city stretches into suburbs, with little to tempt the tourist except perhaps the **27** **Museu da Cidade** (City Museum), in Campo Grande. From the bullring take the metro to Campo Grande (the museum is just a few minutes' walk away), or bus No. 47, which stops close to the 18th-century Palácio Pimenta. The museum houses a collection of prints and paintings of Lisbon before the earthquake and a famous portrait of poet Fernando Pessoa, painted by the modernist Almada Negreiro, whose works are also displayed in the Gulbenkian's Centro de Arte Moderna. *Campo Grande 245, tel. 01/759–1617. Admission: 250$00, free Sun. Open Tues.–Sun. 10–1 and 2–6.*

Tour 5: Belém and the Museu de Arte Antiga

To see the best examples of the uniquely Portuguese, late-Gothic architecture known as Manueline, you should head for **Belém,** at the far southwestern edge of Lisbon. If you are traveling in a group of three or four, taxis are the cheapest means of transportation. Otherwise, for a more scenic—if bumpier—20–30-minute journey, take tram No. 15, 16, or 17 from Praça do Comércio.

Numbers in the margin correspond to points of interest on the Belém map.

28 The enormous bulk of Belém's famous **Mosteiro dos Jerónimos** (Jerónimos Monastery), the construction of which began in 1502, is Lisbon's most impressive building. Conceived and commissioned by Dom Manuel I to honor the discoveries of Vasco de Gama, the edifice was financed largely by treasures brought back from the so-called *descobrimentos*—the "discoveries" of Africa, Asia, and South America made by the Portuguese. The Manueline design of the monastery was created by Diogo de Boitac and his successor João de Castilho, a Spaniard. The latter architect was responsible for the superb southern portal that forms the main entrance to the church: The figure on the central pillar is Henry the Navigator, and the canopy shows a hierarchy of statues contained within niches. The spacious Gothic interior contrasts with the riot of decorative Renaissance detail on the six nave columns, which disappear into a complex latticework ceiling.

Don't leave the monastery without visiting the Gothic- and Renaissance-style **double cloister,** the lower level of which was also designed to stunning effect by Castilho. The arches and

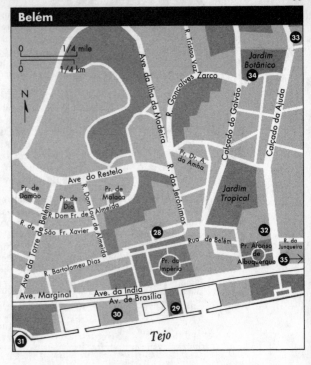

pillars are heavily sculpted with marine motifs typical of the Manueline style. *Praça do Império, tel. 01/362–0034. Admission to church free; cloister 400$00 June–Sept., 250$00 Oct.–May, free Sun. Church open June–Sept., Tues.–Sun. 10–noon and 2–6:30; Oct.–May, Tues.–Sun. 10–noon and 2–5. Cloister open June–Sept., daily 10–6:30.; Oct.–May, daily 10–5.*

There are two museums in the complex of buildings adjoining the monastery. For enthusiasts only, there's the **Museu Nacional de Arqueologia** (National Museum of Archaeology: admission 250$00, free Sun.; open Tues.–Sun. 10–noon and 2–5), a less-than-accomplished presentation of Portuguese archaeological relics from Paleolithic to medieval times. Far more inviting to the lay person is the **Museu da Marinha** (Maritime Museum: admission 200$00; open Tues.–Sun. 10–5), at the western edge of the building. The Maritime Museum is large, and there's something here for everyone, including early maps, navigational equipment, real and model ships, uniforms, and other items that reflect Portugal's seafaring tradition.

Time Out   For a real taste of Lisbon, stop at the impressive **Fabrica dos Pasteis de Belém** (Rua de Belém 86–88), a pastry shop and café that serves delicious hot-custard pastries sprinkled with cinnamon and powdered sugar. Although you can buy these treats throughout Lisbon, they're made best here.

Across from the monastery, at the water's edge (take the pedestrian underpass through the park), stands the **Monumento dos Descobrimentos** (Monument to the Discoveries). Built in

1960, this tall, white, angular slab was designed as a modern tribute to the country's seafaring explorers and built on what was the departure point for many voyages. Facing the water, at the prow, is Henry the Navigator; lined up behind him are the Portuguese explorers of Brazil and Asia, as well as other national heroes, including Camões the poet, who can be recognized by the book in his hand. Walk inside and take the elevator to the top for river views. *Admission: 225$00. Open Tues.– Sun. 10–5.*

③⓪ If you walk west for a few minutes along the waterfront you'll come to a squat modern building that houses the **Museu de Arte Popular** (Museum of Popular Art). Collected here are examples of the country's popular (or folk) art, as well as a collection of ceramics, costumes, furniture, domestic and farm implements, and other ethnographic pieces. Displays are organized according to the province from which the objects came. *Av. Brasilia, tel. 01/301–1282. Admission: 200$00, free Sun. Open Tues.– Sun. 10–12:30 and 2–5.*

③① Another kilometer (⅗ miles), or about a 15-minute walk, farther west along the waterfront will bring you to the fairytalelike **Torre de Belém** (Belém Tower). Its openwork balconies, and domed turrets make this perhaps the purest Manueline structure in the country. Although it was built in the early 16th century on an island in the middle of the Rio Tejo, today the chalk-white tower stands near what has become the north bank—evidence of the changing course of the river. Built to defend the entrance to the port, the tower served as a prison from the late 16th through the 19th century; its inmates were incarcerated in the dungeons. Cross the wood gangway and walk inside, not necessarily to see the rather plain interior but to clamber up the steep stone steps to the very top. From this vantage point you'll have a bird's-eye view of the Tejo and central Lisbon. *Av. da India, tel. 01/301–6892. Admission: 400$00 in summer, 250$00 in winter, free Sun. 10–2. Open June– Sept., Tues.–Sun. 10–6:30; Oct.–May, Tues.–Sun. 10–5.*

③② Make your way back to the center of Belém via the main Avenida da India. To the east of the monastery on Praça Afonso de Albuquerque is the **Museu Nacional de Coches** (National Coach Museum), with one of the largest collections of coaches in the world, in buildings that once accommodated a riding school. The oldest vehicle on display was made for Phillip II of Spain in the late 16th century, and among the most stunning exhibits are three gold coaches created in Rome for King John V in 1716. The collection of gloriously painted, gilded Baroque coaches is dazzling, but given the museum's limited subject, it may be hard to understand why this is among the most popular collections in Lisbon. *Praça Afonso de Albuquerque, tel. 01/ 363–8022. Admission: 400$00 June–Sept., 250$00 Oct.–May, free Sun. Open June–Sept., Tues.–Sun. 10–1 and 2:30–6:30; Oct.–May, Tues.–Sun. 10–1 and 2:30–5:30.*

③③ Calçada da Ajuda, on the east side of the coach museum, leads north up the hill to the overblown, fussily designed **Palácio da Ajuda** (Ajuda Palace). It's a 20-minute walk, or take bus No. 14, which stops here. In 1802 construction began on the palace, which was intended as a royal residence; its last royal occupant died here in 1911. Today the building is home to a museum of 18th- and 19th-century paintings, furniture, and tapestries, but unless you're especially interested in such works, this attraction is not an essential sight. *Largo da Ajuda, tel. 01/363–7095. Admission: 200$00, free Sun. 10–2. Open Thurs.–Tues. 10–5.*

㉞ Just southwest of the palace is the **Jardim Botânico da Ajuda** (Ajuda Botanical Gardens), the oldest botanical garden in Portugal (laid out in 1768) and an enjoyable place to spend a half-hour or so. The many species of flora, labeled in Latin, are contained in several greenhouses covering 10 acres. *Calçada da Ajuda. Admission: 50$00. Open June–Sept., Tues.–Sun. 10–7; Oct.–May, Tues.–Sun. 10–6.*

Having completed your tour of Belém, take a taxi or public transportation (*see above*) toward downtown Lisbon. About halfway you'll pass under the magnificent **Ponte 25 de Abril**, spanning the Rio Tejo. Standing 230 feet above the water and stretching almost 2.5 kilometers (1.6 miles), this is the longest suspension bridge in Europe. The bridge was completed in 1966 but later retitled; its name commemorates the 1974 revolution, in which the Portuguese army overthrew Prime Minister Marcelo Caetano, successor to the long-serving autocrat Dr. Salazar. Drive across the bridge on a clear day, if you can: The visibility extends for miles and the experience is unforgettable. Traveling to Setúbal (*see* Chapter 4), for example, will afford you the chance to enjoy the panoramic view.

Shortly after passing under the bridge, you approach the wealthy district of **Lapa,** with its many foreign embassies, as **㉟** well as the **Museu de Arte Antiga** (Ancient Art Museum), the only museum in Lisbon to approach the status of the Gulbenkian (*see* Tour 4, *above*). Bus No. 49 and tram Nos. 15, 16, and 17 run from Belém and stop near the museum on their way back to downtown Lisbon (tram No. 19 from Rua do Arsenal, near Praça do Comércio, stops outside the museum, if you are making a separate trip). Housed in a 17th-century palace, the museum features a beautifully displayed collection of Portuguese art dating mainly from the 15th through 19th centuries that superbly complements the Gulbenkian's general collection. Indeed, Gulbenkian himself donated several pieces to this museum, which opened in 1883.

Of all the holdings, the religious works of the Portuguese School (characterized by fine portraiture with a distinct Flemish influence) of artists stand out, especially the acknowledged masterpiece of Nuno Gonçalves, the *Saint Vincent Altarpiece.* Painted between 1467 and 1470 for the Saint Vincent chapel in Lisbon's cathedral; the altarpiece has six panels showing the patron saint of Lisbon receiving the homage of king, court, and citizens. Sixty different figures can be identified, including Henry the Navigator, the archbishop of Lisbon, and sundry dukes, monks, fishermen, knights, and religious figures. In the top left corner of the two central panels is a figure purported to be that of Gonçalves himself.

Besides the Portuguese works, there are pieces representing Flemish painters who influenced the Portuguese. There are also extensive collections of French silver, Portuguese furniture and tapestries, Oriental ceramics, and other works from former Portuguese colonies. *Rua das Janelas Verdes, tel. 01/672725. Admission: 200$00, free Sun. Open Tues.–Sun. 10–1 and 2:30–5.*

Lisbon for Free

There's a lot to do in Lisbon that's free. Indeed, on some walking tours around the city, it may be difficult to spend your money. The city's churches, for instance—including the Sé (Cathedral; *see* Tour 1)—charge no admission fee, although there often is a small charge to enter the cloisters.

Walking around the alleys, streets, and squares in the historic districts of the Alfama (*see* Tour 1), the Baixa (*see* Tour 2), and the Bairro Alto (*see* Tour 3) carries no charge, and for the price of a cup of coffee you can pull up a chair at a sidewalk café anywhere in downtown Lisbon and watch the fascinating world go by. For an equally marginal cost you can ride an *elevador* (lift or funicular railway) from the Baixa to the Bairro Alto (*see* Tours 2 and 3) or see the city from the windows of a rattling tram (*see* Getting Around in Essential Information, *above*).

Historic Sites　Some of Lisbon's most compelling historic sites are free, including the dramatic heights of the **Castelo de São Jorge** (*see* Tour 1), the **Capela de São João Baptista** (*see* Tour 3), and the Manueline **Mosteiro dos Jerónimos** (although not the cloisters; *see* Tour 5). The engaging **Torre de Belém** has free admission Sunday 10–2 (*see* Tour 5).

Museums　Many museums have free admission on Sunday, including the famous **Museu Calouste Gulbenkian** and the adjacent **Centro de Arte Moderna** (*see* Tour 4), the **Museu da Cidade** (*see* Tour 4), the **Museu Nacional de Arqueologia** (*see* Tour 5), the **Museu de Arte Popular** (*see* Tour 5), and the **Museu de Arte Antiga** (*see* Tour 5). At some of these museums free admission is limited to certain hours, so check with the tourist office or with the museum itself before you go.

Parks and Public Places　Enjoy Lisbon for free at the twice-weekly **Feira da Ladra** (flea market; *see* Tour 1), on the edge of the Alfama, or by dawdling in the main square, the **Rossio** (*see* Tour 2). The gardens and church at **Estrêla** (*see* Tour 3) are a pleasant spot, and a stroll up the main Avenida da Liberdade ends with a rest in the city's main park, **Parque Eduardo VII** (*see* Tour 4). Not far from here is an opportunity to window-shop until you drop at the **Amoreiras** shopping center (*see* Tour 4), open for business daily 9 AM–11 PM.

What to See and Do with Children

Keeping children amused in Lisbon should be no problem; kids love the rickety trams, funicular railways, ferries, and parks, and most bars and restaurants accommodate families with children. One attraction you can bet youngsters will enjoy is the summertime **Feira Popular**, a fair with rides, games, and a lot of food. *Entrecampos, opposite Entrecampos metro station. Admission: 100$00. Open May–Sept., weekdays 7 PM–1 AM, weekends and holidays 1–1.*

Museums　Not all of Lisbon's museums and galleries are appropriate for children, but plenty of them host special exhibits geared toward young visitors; also, most charge lower admission fees (or no fee at all) for kids under 10. The following museums may be of particular interest to families.

Museu da Marinha (*see* Tour 5)

Museu da Marioneta (*see* Tour 1)

Museu de Arte Popular (*see* Tour 5)

Museu Etnografico (*see* Tour 4)

Museu Miltar (Military Museum). The extensive collection of weapons, uniforms, and armor from the 15th century should intrigue any adventure-seeking child. Adults can study the historical text that accompanies the displays. *Largo dos Caminhos de Ferro (opposite Santa Apolónia station), tel. 01/867131. Admission: 150$00. Open Tues.–Sat. 10–4, Sun. 11–5.*

Museu Nacional de História Natural (Natural History Museum). Divided into three sections, this museum presents mineral and geological displays, zoological and anthropological exhibits, and a botanical garden (*see* Tour 3, *above*). *Rua da Escola Politécnica 58, tel. 01/396–1521. Admission free. Mineral/geological and zoological/anthropological sections open Mon. 2:30–4:30, Tues.–Sat. 9:30–11:30 and 2:30–4:30. Botanical gardens open May–Oct., daily 9–7; Nov.–Apr., Mon.–Fri. 9–5.*

Planetário (Planetarium). Located in Belém behind the Maritime Museum, the planetarium presents interesting astronomical shows and displays several times a week. A bulletin posted in the window announces the current program, or you can get updates from the Palácio da Foz tourist office. *Praça do Imperio, tel. 01/362–0002. Admission: 200$00. Showtimes: Wed. at 11, 3, and 4:15; Sat. and Sun. at 4 and 5. Schedules vary, so check in advance.*

Parks **Jardim da Estrêla** (*see* Tour 3, *above*)

Jardim do Campo Grande (metro: Entrecampos), in the north of the city, has a playground, tennis courts, a boating lake (rentals available), and two cafés.

Jardim Zoológico. With a menagerie of 2,000 animals, the city zoo is always a popular spot. In addition to the usual exhibits there is a children's zoo, with miniature houses and small animals, a dolphin show with twice-daily presentations at 11 and 3, and a cemetery for dogs. There are snack bars and restaurants on site, or you can pack a lunch for a picnic. *Estrada de Benfica 158, tel. 01/726–8041. Admission to zoo: 390$800 adults, 250$00 children. Admission to dolphin show: 800$00 adults, 600$00 children. Open daily 9–8.*

Parque Eduardo VII (*see* Tour 4, *above*)

Off the Beaten Track

To fully understand the craftsmanship that goes into making the ubiquitous azulejos visit the engaging **Museu do Azulejo** (Azulejo Museum), in the 16th-century Madre de Deus convent and cloister. Some of the ceramics on display date to the 1700s, with representative examples from each century to the present. A highlight of the display is the 118-foot, 18th-century *Panorama of Lisbon*, a beautifully detailed study of the city and waterfront and reputedly the country's longest azulejo work. While you're here you may want to take a look at the richly furnished convent-church, too, since it contains some noteworthy gilt Baroque decoration. To reach the museum, take tram No. 3 or 16 from Praça do Comércio to the eastern suburb of Xabegras (20 minutes away). *Rua Madre de Deus, tel. 01/ 814–7747. Admission: 200$00, free Sun. 10–2. Open Tues.– Sun. 10–5.*

Northwest of the city, in the suburb of São Domingo de Benfica (near the zoo), stands the **Palácio dos Marqueses da Fronteira,** one of the most beautiful private houses in the capital. Built in the late 17th century, the building contains splendid reception rooms with 17th- and 18th-century decorative tiles, contemporary furniture, and paintings. The grounds, which contain a terraced walk, a topiary garden, and statuary and fountains, are stunning. *Largo de São Domingo de Benfica 1, tel. 01/ 782023. Admission to gardens, 300$00; to palace and gardens, 1,000$00. Open Mon.–Sat. at 11 for 1-hour guided tour. All tours are guided; call ahead for details and restrictions.*

Shopping

Shopping in Lisbon can be a pleasant, even refreshing experience, not least because there are still many independent boutiques and few large stores. Handmade goods such as leather handbags, shoes, gloves, embroidery, ceramics, and basketwork are sold throughout the city at relatively reasonable prices. Most shops are open weekdays 9–1 and 3–7 and Saturday 9–1; shopping malls and supermarkets often remain open until at least 10, and some are open on Sunday, also.

Shopping Districts

In 1988 a fire destroyed much of the Baixa's **Chiado** district (*see* Tour 2, *above*), Lisbon's smartest shopping area, but there are still plenty of choice stores on and around the Chiado's Rua Garrett. The rest of the district, made up of the grid of streets from the Rossio to the Rio Tejo, remains a fine place to shop, with small stores given over mainly to fashion, jewelry, shoes, and delicatessen foods. Excellent shops continue to open in the new residential districts near the airport, at **Praça de Londres** and **Avenida de Roma.**

Of the shopping centers, easily the best is the **Amoreiras** (Av. Eng. Duarte Pacheco), west of Praça Marquês de Pombal, which contains a multitude of shops selling clothes, shoes, food, crystal, ceramics, and jewelry. It also has a hairdresser, restaurants, and 10 movie screens. For more information *see* Tour 4, *above*.

Markets

Lisbon has several markets and, although you are unlikely to find authentic antiques, you may find something traditional to take home. The best-known market is the **Feira da Ladra** (No metro; Campo de Santa Clara in the Alfama), a flea market held on Tuesday morning (8 AM–1 PM) and all day Saturday. Others worth considering are the daily clothes market at **Praça de Espanha** (metro; Palhava; open 9–5.); the covered, produce market at **Praça do Chile** (metro: Arroios; open Mon.–Sat. 9–5); the fish-and-flower market opposite **Cais do Sodré** (no metro; open daily dawn–dusk); and the food market opposite the Sheraton Hotel on **Avenida Fontes Pereira de Melo** (metro: Picoas; open Mon.–Sat. 9–5).

Specialty Stores

Antiques Most of Lisbon's antiques shops are concentrated in the district of Rato and in the Bairro Alto along one long street, which changes its name four times as it runs southward from Largo do Rato: Rua Escola Politécnica, Rua Dom Pedro V, Rua da Misericórdia, and Rua do Alecrim. Also look on the nearby Rua de São Bento for more stores. Two of the best-known shops are **Solar** (Rua Dom Pedro V 68–70), and **Abside** (Travessa dos Fieis de Deus 14–16), the latter in the Bairro Alto.

Ceramics **Viuva Lamego** (Largo do Intendente 25) offers the largest selection of tiles and pottery in Lisbon, at competitive prices. **Vista Alegre** (Largo do Chiado 18) founded its porcelain factory in 1824, and you can buy perfect reproductions of their original table services and ornaments. The **Fábrica Sant'Ana** (Rua do Alecrim 95), founded in the 1700s, sells wonderful hand-painted ceramics and tiles based on antique patterns; the pieces sold here may be the finest you'll find in the city. Also try **Aresta Viva** (Rua Antero de Quental 22), producers of hand-made and hand-painted tiles, some based on 16th-century designs seen at the Museu do Azulejo (*see* Off the Beaten Track, *above*).

Clothing Although Lisbon isn't on the cutting edge of fashion and design, there are young Portuguese clothing-designers whose products are featured alongside the more established fashion names in a variety of stores. **Praça de Londres** and **Avenida de Roma**—both in the modern city—comprise the newest fashionable shopping district. For big international names under one roof, **Amoreiras** shopping center (*see* Shopping Districts, *above*) can't be beaten.

Food and Wine There are some excellent delicatessens in the Baixa that sell fine foods, including delicious regional cheeses, and a wide selection of wines, especially varieties of port—one of Portugal's major exports. (The **Instituto do Vinho do Porto** [*see* Tour 3, *above*] offers more than 100 varieties to sample and bottles for sale.) Other places that sell local wines are delicatessens, supermarkets, and—oddly—any shop that sells *bacalhau* (dried cod), which you'll see stacked outside on the sidewalk or hanging in the window.

Other popular gourmet items are fresh chocolates, marzipan, dried and crystallized fruits, and pastries, on sale in most of the city's *pastelarias* (cafés specializing in cakes and pastries). Try the pastelaria **Suiça** (Rossio 96, eastern side), which has a particularly large selection of sweets.

Handicrafts **Rua da Conceição,** one of the crossroads in the Baixa, is known for buttons, wools, cottons, and all sewing materials. For embroidered goods and baskets from the Azores, try **Casa Regional da Ilha Verde** (Rua Paiva de Andrade 4). **Tito Cunha** (Rua Aurea 286) has a similar range of goods from Madeira, and near the Castelo de São Jorge, you'll find **A Bilha** (Rua do Milagre de Santo António 10), which sells embroidery, lace, copper, gold, and silver. Casa **Quintão** (Rua Ivens 30) has a large selection of *arraiolos*, the traditional hand-embroidered Portuguese carpets (here you can also buy a kit for making your own rug) and another showroom for traditional carpets is **Almoravida** (Rua da Senhora da Glória 130).

Jewelry The Baixa is a good place to look for jewelry: Rua Aurea (formerly Rua do Ouro: Gold Street) was named for the shops installed there under Pombal's 18th-century city plan. **Sarmento** (Rua Aurea 251) has a large display of characteristic Portuguese gold- and silver-filigree work. For antique silver and jewelry visit **António da Silva** (Praça Luis de Camoes 40) or **Barreto & Gonçalves** (Rua das Portas de Santo Antão 17).

Leather Goods Shoe shops can be found all over the city, but they may have limited selections of large sizes since the Portuguese tend to have small feet. However, all the better shops can make shoes to order.

Fine leather handbags and luggage are sold at **Galeão** (Rua Augusta 190) and **Casa Canada** (Rua Augusta 232) also has a large selection, although most of the products are not manufactured in Portugal. Gloves are sold or made to order in specialty shops in the **Rua do Carmo** and **Rua Aurea. Coelho** (Rua da Conceição 85) is excellent for leather belts and can also create leatherback fabric belts using your own material, if you wish.

Sports

Participant Sports

There are few sports facilities in Lisbon itself; for most outdoor activities—scuba diving, fishing, horseback riding, water sports—you'll have to journey to Lisbon's environs (*see* Sports and Fitness in Chapter 4).

Golf There are a half dozen golf courses in Lisbon's environs (*see* Sports and Fitness in Chapter 4), most of which are concentrated along the Estoril Coast. The nearest golf course to the city center is at **Lisboa Sport Club** (Casal da Carregueira, near Belas, tel. 01/960077), situated about 20 minutes by car from the city in a natural setting.

Swimming If your hotel doesn't have a pool you can visit **Piscina do Areeiro** (Av. de Roma, tel. 01/886794), **Piscina do Campo Grande** (Campo Grande, tel. 01/766303), or **Piscina dos Olivais** (Av. Dr. Francisco Luís Gomes, tel. 01/314630), 5 kilometers (3.1 miles) northeast of town. The **Lisboa Sport Club** (*see above*) also has a swimming pool.

Another option is the new **Aquaparque de Lisboa** (Av. das Descobertas, open daily 9:30–8), a complex of pools, slides, waterfalls, cafés, and restaurants in Restelo Park, near Belém.

Tennis There are public tennis courts at **Campo Grande** (Estádio 1 de Maio at Alvalade). To play, inquire at the main tourist office in Praça dos Restauradores (*see* Important Addresses and Numbers in Essential Information, *above*).

Spectator Sports

Bullfighting For those not disturbed by bullfights, the events are held Sunday and Thursday between Easter and September in the ornate Praça de Touros (bullring) at **Campo Pequeno**. Some people defend the Portuguese bullfight as entertainment because the bull is not killed in the ring but is wrestled to the ground by a group of *forçados* (a team of eight men who fight the bull) dressed in traditional red-and-green costumes. Nonetheless, any bull injured during the contest is later killed. The first-class riding skills displayed by the *cavaleiro* (horseback fighter) during the fight are undeniable. After the cavaleiro performs, the forçados goad the bull into charging them, and one man throws himself across the horns (which have been padded) while the other men pull the bull down by grabbing hold of whatever bits they can, including the tail. *Av. da República (metro: Campo Pequeno). Admission: 2,000$00–8,000$00, depending on seats. Exhibitions Easter–Sept., Thurs. and Sun.*

Soccer Soccer is Portugal's most popular sport, and Lisbon has three teams, which play at least weekly during the September–May season. The most famous team is **Benfica,** for whom the great Eusebio played in the 1960s, when he took his team to five European championship finals. Matches are held in the northwest part of the city, at the huge Estádio da Luz (tel. 01/726-6129), one of Europe's biggest stadiums. Great rivals of Benfica, the **Sporting Clube de Portugal,** play at the Estádio Alvalade near Campo Grande in the north of the city. Third best of the teams is Belém's **Belenenses,** which plays at Estadio do Rastelo. You can buy tickets on the day of a game at the stadiums, but for most big matches (certainly when Benfica and Sporting play each other, or when either play Oporto's main team, FC Porto), you should purchase tickets in advance from the booth in Praça dos Restauradores. Plan to arrive at the stadium in plenty of time, because there's usually a full program of entertainment first, including children's soccer, marching bands, and fireworks. (Note: Always be wary of pickpockets in the crowd.)

Dining

Although only a few of Lisbon's restaurants can compare with the best establishments in other European capitals, there's no doubt that dining here is taken seriously. Fresh ingredients—especially fish and shellfish—are used everywhere, and you can find excellent meals all over the city, often in seemingly modest places. On the other hand, the dining experience is boosted by the establishment's surroundings: Many restaurants are housed in ancient, converted buildings; some have city and river views; and others offer outdoor dining in summer.

With the exception of some very expensive restaurants, many of which feature French-influenced fare, a large number of properties serve Portuguese cuisine, characterized by grilled sardines, simple steaks and cutlets, fresh seafood (always ask the price before ordering), and salads. As long as you're happy with these standard foods you'll have few complaints. If you want variety, however, try restaurants specializing in colonial Portuguese food—principally Brazilian, but also Mozambican and Goan (Indian) cuisine. Wine is excellent and reasonably priced everywhere, especially the *vinho da casa* (house wine), which—in cheaper and more expensive restaurants, alike—is carefully selected for its quality.

Almost all restaurants offer an *ementa turistica* (tourist menu), usually at lunchtime. Meals vary in quality but generally include three courses, a drink, and coffee, all for about 1,500$00–2,000$00. The selections are nearly always good value but can be limited in scope. Lisbon's restaurants normally serve lunch from noon until 3 and dinner from 7:30 until 11; many establishments are closed Sunday.

Unless otherwise noted below, restaurants don't accept reservations; this is especially true of inexpensive places. In the traditional *cervejarias* (beer hall/restaurants), which frequently have huge dining rooms, it's likely you'll have to wait for a table, but usually not for more than 15 or 20 minutes. In the Bairro Alto, many of the reasonably priced *tascas* (taverns) are on the small side: If you can't reserve a table, either wait in line or move on to the next place. Throughout Lisbon, dress for meals is usually casual, but exceptions are noted below.

Highly recommended restaurants are indicated by a star ★.

Category	Cost*
Very Expensive	over 6,000$00
Expensive	3,500$00–6,000$00
Moderate	1,500$00–3,500$00
Inexpensive	under 1,500$00

*per person, excluding drinks and service.

Very Expensive **António Clara.** This classic French restaurant, named for its owner, is housed in an attractive Art Nouveau building in the north of Lisbon, in the modern part of the city. In addition to French fare, international dishes with a flourish are served in an elegant room that has a decorated ceiling, oil paintings, heavy draperies, and a huge chandelier. The menu is seasonal (fish is always well presented), the service extremely attentive, and there's a fine wine list. A private dining club for business people and the piano bar attract an up-market clientele. *Av. da República 38, tel. 01/766380. Reservations required. Jacket and tie required. AE, DC, MC, V. Closed Sun.*

★ **Aviz.** One of the best and classiest restaurants in Lisbon, Aviz has a rich but subtle Belle Epoque decor, which includes turn-of-the-century furnishings, fine wood paneling, leather chairs, and crisp linen tablecloths. This exclusive restaurant is hidden on a side street off the Baixa's Rua Garrett. The mainly French and international menu is enhanced by Portuguese elements such as *bacalhau* (dried cod). *Rua Serpa Pinto 12–13, tel. 01/342–8391. Reservations required. Jacket and tie required. AE, DC, MC, V. No Sat. dinner. Closed Sun.*

Casa da Comida. Imaginative French and Portuguese food is served in what was once a private residence. This grand house, with its flower-filled patio, offers a variety of options, from seafood to grilled steak with anchovy butter. You may have to look closely to find the entrance, situated just off the pretty Praça das Amoreiras. *Travessa das Amoreiras 1, tel. 01/659386. Reservations advised. AE, DC, MC, V. No Sat. lunch. Closed Sun.*

Gambrinus. One of Lisbon's older and smarter restaurants, Gambrinus is renowned for its fish and shellfish. Situated on a busy street that bulges with fish restaurants, this establishment is understated—a quality that only adds to its appeal: Once inside the front door you'll find many small dining rooms; your waiter will regale you with a list of the day's seafood specials, which vary enormously in price. (There are meat dishes, too.) For a less formal but satisfying meal, you can eat at the

Lisbon Dining

bar during lunchtime. *Rua Portas de S. Antão 23–25, tel. 01/ 346–8974. Reservations advised. AE, DC, MC, V.*

O Terraço. Set atop the central Tivoli Lisboa Hotel, The Terrace offers a panoramic view of downtown Lisbon. But the scenery is just one reason to dine here: Other reasons are the excellent international cuisine (especially the expertly cooked steaks and other meat dishes from the grill) and the quietly attentive service. *Av. da Liberdade 185, tel. 01/530181. Reservations advised. Jacket and tie advised. AE, DC, MC, V.*

Tagide. Delicious Portuguese food and wine are served in this fine old tiled house that looks out over the Baixa and Rio Tejo. Renovations have created an elegant dining room—a lovely backdrop for sampling the impressive list of Portuguese regional dishes, including the famous *presunto* (smoked ham) from Chaves. Also offered is a smaller but no less succulent selection of French-influenced international dishes. Try to sit at a table by the window. *Largo Academia das Belas Artes 18–20, tel. 01/346–0570. Reservations advised. AE, DC, MC, V. Closed weekends.*

★ **Tavares Rico.** Superb food, an excellent wine list, and a handsome Edwardian dining room have made this one of Lisbon's most famous and formal restaurants. Tavares Rico—founded as a café in the 18th century—is considerably older than the Aviz (*see above*) and includes the splendor in its furnishings, the quality of its service, and its French-inspired menu, which features seasonal ingredients. A wise choice for an entrée is the sole cooked in champagne sauce. *Rua Misericórdia 35–37, tel. 01/342–1112. Reservations required. Jacket and tie advised. AE, DC, MC, V. Closed Sat. dinner and Sun.*

Expensive   **A Gôndola.** This small country house opposite the Gulbenkian Foundation survives in the midst of otherwise modern development. In summer, enjoy atmospheric al fresco dining under a canopy of leaves, and for a pleasant winter experience eat in in the smartly decorated dining room. The Italian menu features cannelloni, but there are some good Portuguese dishes, too. *Av. Berna 64, tel. 01/770426. Reservations advised in summer. AE, DC, MC, V. No Sat. dinner. Closed Sun.*

Alcântara. Lisbon's newest "in" place, this large bar-restaurant has a glorious modernist design, which impressively and effectively combines wood, velvet, and steel. Old Portuguese specialties highlight the menu, and fish is always a good choice. There's a large wine list, too, and a splendid bar if you want to sip an aperitif before dinner. The restaurant is outside of the city center, near Ponte 25 de Abril, and the kitchen stays open until 2 AM. *Rua Maria Luísa Holstein 15, near Rua Coz. Económica, tel. 01/363–7176. Reservations advised. AE, DC, MC, V. No lunch. Closed Tues.*

Café Martinho da Arcada. This famous café-restaurant, founded in 1782 beneath the arcades of Praça do Comércio in Baixa, was once frequented by the Portuguese poet Fernando Pessoa and other literary stars. In the recently refurbished dining room you can choose from a Portuguese menu that offers dishes from various regions and some that reveal a French influence as well. Try a *cataplana* (clam stew) from the Algarve, especially if you won't be heading south on this trip. *Praça do Comércio 3, tel. 01/879259. Reservations advised. AE, DC, MC, V.*

Cais da Ribeira. Converted from an old fisherman's warehouse, this small restaurant perched on the waterfront behind Cais do

Sodré station specializes in fish grilled over charcoal and a filling *caldeirada* (fish stew). Whatever you order, the accompanying views over the river will complement your meal nicely. Remember that this is not the most desirable area for walking around late at night: You can get a taxi just around the corner, in front of the train station. *Cais do Sodré, tel. 01/323611. Reservations advised. MC, V. No lunch Sat. and Sun.*

Já Sei. Because of its prime location above the river at Belém, this is a fine lunchtime stop, especially in summer if you sit on the attractive outdoor terrace. Smooth service and impressive meals—*arroz de marisco* (seafood rice) for two, for example—make this a memorable choice. *Av. Brasília 202, Belém, tel. 01/615969. Reservations advised. AE, DC, MC, V. No Sun. dinner. Closed Mon.*

★ **Michel.** Innovative French cooking with Portuguese flourishes is served in this intimate and attractive, green-painted restaurant just outside the walls of St. George's Castle. Curtains—which add to the dignified ambience—shut out the sun beaming in from the dusty square outside. Choose from such dishes as bass fillet with champagne sauce, and *porco a alentejana* (pork fillet with clams), a Portuguese classic. *Largo S. Cruz do Castelo 5, tel. 01/864338. Reservations advised. AE, DC, MC, V. Closed Sun.*

São Jerónimo. Contemporary decor and classy presentation of Portuguese food attract Lisbon's elite to São Jerónimo. Favorites include grilled shrimp and other fresh seafood dishes, and there are daily-changing regional specials, too. This recently refurbished restaurant beside the monastery in Belém offers discreet and stylish dining. *Rua dos Jerónimos 12, Belém, tel. 01/648797. Reservations advised. Jacket and tie advised. AE, MC, V. Closed Sun.*

Solmar. Best known for its fish and shellfish (and the excellent seafood soup), Solmar's menu may surprise some with its occasional offering of boar or venison (when in season). Competent waiters move briskly about the two-floor dining area: A central fountain is the focus, and a huge mosaic of an underwater scene carries out Solmar's oceanic theme. *Rua Portas de S. Antạo 108, tel. 01/346–0010. AE, DC, MC, V.*

Moderate **Brasuca.** Eating in this comfortable Brazilian restaurant set in an old mansion on the edge of the Bairro Alto is almost like being invited into someone's home. The dining room still has domestic features that make it an intimate retreat, and the staff is genuinely welcoming. Before indulging in the Brazilian specialties and mainstream Portuguese fare—spicy meat stews and grilled meats are a good choice—try a traditional (but strong!) *caipirinha* (Brazilian rum cocktail). *Rua João Pereira da Rosa 7, tel. 01/342–8542. Reservations advised. AE, DC, MC, V. Closed Mon.*

★ **Cervejaria Trindade.** Relatively inexpensive and hearty Portuguese cuisine, including *açorda* (bread-and-shellfish stew) and grilled seafood, makes the relatively short wait for a table here worthwhile. The walls inside this 19th-century Bairro Alto beer hall/restaurant are adorned with colorful tiles, and high vaulted ceilings and frenetic service add to the restaurant's feeling of enormousness. The garden is an enjoyable spot for dining in summer. *Rua Nova da Trindade 20, tel. 01/342–3506. AE, DC, MC, V.*

Comida de Santo. Excellent Brazilian food served in an attractive, brightly painted dining room and lively Brazilian music ensure a steady clientele that keeps this place packed until closing time, at 1 AM. Come early and enjoy classic dishes, such as *fejoada* (meat-and-bean stew) or *vatapa* (a spicy shrimp dish). *Calçada Engenheiro Miguel Pais 39, tel. 01/396-3339. AE, DC, MC, V.*

O Alexandre. There are only a half dozen tables in this tiny restaurant, and you'll do better sitting outside on the sidewalk terrace, from which there are superb views of the Jerónimos Monastery. The Alexandre does a brisk lunchtime business, serving fish and seafood platters to a largely local clientele. Try the grilled *peixe espada* (scabbard fish) or one of the more unusual squid or octopus dishes. Note that the restaurant closes at 9:45. *Rua Vieira Portuense 84, Belém, tel. 01/363-4454. No reservations. MC, V. Closed Sat.*

O Madeirense. Even though it's set inside the Amoreiras shopping center, Lisbon's only Madeiran restaurant goes overboard making patrons feel they're on the island itself: The eatery features traditional food, wine, and handicrafts. Try the *espetada mista* (mixed meat on a skewer). *Loja 3027, Amoreiras Shopping Center, Av. Eng. Duarte Pacheco, tel. 01/690827. Reservations advised for Sun. lunch. AE, DC, MC, V.*

★ **Pap'Açorda.** Housed in an old converted bakery in the heart of the Bairro Alto, this popular restaurant, with its marble bar and pastel interior, is as fashionable as its fare is tasty. Among the offerings from the Portuguese menu is açorda, a bread stew cooked with shellfish and spices: The *açorda real* comes with lobster and shrimp. *Rua da Atalaia 57–59, tel. 01/346-4811. Reservations advised. AE, DC, MC, V. Closed Sun. and Mon.*

Ribadouro. Go to this bustling basement restaurant on the main avenue for the finely prepared seafood, including crabs and crayfish. The surroundings are functional, not fancy, but the layout allows you to watch crabs and crayfish being prepared at the counter. Try to arrive before 8, although even on the busiest nights you shouldn't have to wait too long to be seated. If you eat at the bar, prices are even more reasonable. *Av. da Liberdade 155, tel. 01/549411. AE, DC, MC, V.*

Inexpensive **A Quinta.** This homey, country-style restaurant at the top of the Elevador de Santa Justa commands fine views of the Baixa. The eclectic menu features Portuguese specialties, such as stuffed squid or sardines, and quirky international fare, from steak-and-kidney pie and goulash to spaghetti and Wiener schnitzel. *Passarela do Elevador de Santa Justa, next to Largo do Carmo, tel. 01/346-5588. AE, DC, MC, V. Closed Sun.*

★ **Bonjardim.** Known locally as Rei dos Frangos (the King of Chickens), Bonjardim—set in an alley between Praça dos Restauradores and Rua Portas de Santo Antão—specializes in superbly cooked spit-roast poultry, best eaten with fries and a salad. The restaurant is crowded at peak times (8–10 PM), but you shouldn't have to wait long for a table. Even if you do have a few minutes to wait, watching the frenzied waiters is entertainment in itself. *Travessa de S. Antão 11, tel. 01/324389. AE, DC, MC, V.*

Casa Faz Frio. Here is a traditional *adega típica* (traditional wine cellar) located on the edge of the Bairro Alto, complete with blue tile and bunches of garlic suspended from the ceiling. The list of Portuguese dishes changes daily, and all are a good value. *Rua de Dom Pedro V 96–98, no tel. No credit cards.*

Farah's Tandoori. A small, simple place, Farah's is known as one of the best and friendliest Indian restaurants in Lisbon. All the curries, served with Indian bread, are sure bets for a good meal. Two dining floors make finding a table a manageable task. *Rua de Sant'Ana à Lapa 73, tel. 01/609219. MC, V. Closed Tues.*

O Cantinho do Aziz. Hidden in the ring of tiny streets below the castle, this small, family-run Mozambican restaurant offers "Comida Indio-Africana"—plenty of rich curried meat and fish dishes accompanied by coconut-flavor rice. The surroundings are rudimentary and the TV occasionally deafening, but tasty food comes with a smile. Climb the flight of steps from Poco do Borratem, near Praça da Figueira to find the entrance. *Rua de S. Lourenço 3–5, tel. 01/876472. No credit cards. Closed Sun.*

Café-Bars and Pastelarias

Lisbon has some glorious old cafés, and you should make every effort to visit at least a few. Most are wonderfully decorated and have rich interiors of burnished and carved wood, mirrors, and traditional tiling. Also, many cafés have outdoor seating, so you can order a coffee, beer, or snack, and watch the city pass by. Pastelarias are perhaps the city's greatest contribution to the gastronomic arts: Make sure to sample some sweets at one of the places listed below, most of which are closed Sunday.

Café a Brasileira. Rather less exclusive than it once was, this coffeehouse in the heart of the shopping district is still the most famous of Lisbon's old haunts. For a feel of bygone days it's best to come before dark, because at night every table (and the long bar) is taken over by beer-drinking young people. *Rua Garrett 120.*

Café Nicola. With its grand interior and suitably aloof waiters, this "in" café is one of the prime and priciest spots for sitting down and taking in downtown Lisbon. *Rossio, western side.*

Leitaria a Camponeza. An old-fashioned Baixa Leitaria (specializing in milk products and pastries), whose blue-tiled walls display bucolic scenes. The coffee, cakes, and sandwiches are all good. *Rua dos Sapateiros 155–157. Closed Sun.*

Pastelaria Suiça. This huge café-pastelaria stretches all the way back to the adjacent Praça da Figueira. The renowned cakes draw such crowds that it may be easier to order pastries to go from the inside counter. Outdoor tables are at a premium, especially on nice days. *Rossio 96, eastern side.*

Versailles. Located in the modern part of the city, the Versailles (founded in 1929) has retained its grand furnishings. Homemade cakes and hot chocolate are house specialties. *Av. de República 15.*

Lodging

A spate of new hotels has gone up in Lisbon in recent years, and old favorites have been modernized, so guests of the city can now choose from a range of accommodations. However, hotels in Lisbon are not the bargain that, by and large, restaurants are, and staying in the top-rated hotels may cost as much here as in any European city.

Nevertheless, it's still possible to find reasonably priced rooms in the city's dozens of modest *pensões* (guest houses), many of which cost less than 6,000$00 a night. If you plan to stay in a pensõe, be aware that the toilet may be down the hall, and you may have to share a shower room with other guests. The quality varies greatly from one guest house to another, but the best are spotless and friendly, and many are concentrated downtown, around the Rossio, Praça dos Restauradores, and in the Bairro Alto. In summer it may be difficult to find a pensão with vacancies, so you may have to go door to door until you find a suitable place with rooms to let. The tourist office can make reservations for you, but they usually don't recommend the very cheap places, and you won't be able to see your room first.

There is no real tourist season in Lisbon because the capital hosts trade fairs and conventions year-round, so it's best to secure a room in advance of your trip. If you've arrived without accommodations, stop by the hotel-reservations desk at the airport or at the main downtown tourist-information office (Palácio Foz, Praça dos Restauradores, tel. 01/346-3643; open Mon.–Sat. 9–8, Sun. 10–6). The staff at both locations speaks English, and there's no fee for their services.

All lodgings listed below include private baths in rooms unless otherwise noted.

Highly recommended hotels are indicated by a star ★.

Category	Cost*
Very Expensive	over 40,000$00
Expensive	20,000$00–40,000$00
Moderate	14,000$00–20,000$00
Inexpensive	under 14,000$00

*All prices include tax and are for two people sharing a standard double room.

Very Expensive   **Lisboa Sheraton and Towers.** Typical of Sheraton properties, this hotel has a huge reception area but less-impressive guest quarters. A separate desk in the lobby and a private lounge accommodate visitors staying in the more deluxe Towers section; guest rooms in the Towers are about the same size as standards, but their appointments are luxurious. The range of facilities available to all guests is extensive, and the 30-floor hotel is centrally located, not far from Parque Eduardo VII and the Rotunda. *Rua Latino Coelho 1, 1000, tel. 01/575757, fax 01/547164. 386 rooms. Facilities: restaurant, bar, pool, gym, sauna, shops, garage. AE, DC, MC, V.*

Meridien Lisboa. The stepped facade and decorative metal canopy above the entrance are just two of the details that make this mid-'80s accommodation one of the most distinctive modern luxury hotels in Lisbon. Most rooms are small, but they're bright, soundproof, and attractively decorated; ask for one in front with a view of the Parque Eduardo VII. *Rua Castilho 149, 1200, tel. 01/690400, fax 01/693231. 318 rooms. Facilities: restaurant, bar, health club with sauna, shops, garage. AE, DC, MC, V.*

★ **Ritz Lisboa.** One of the finest hotels in Europe, this hotel, part of the Intercontinental Hotel chain, is renowned for its excellent service and comfortable surroundings. The large, handsomely decorated guest rooms have terraces and luxurious bathrooms, and the elegantly appointed public rooms feature

Lisbon Lodging

Albergaria Senhora do Monte, **21**
Altis, **10**
Avenida Palace, **17**
Casa de São Mamede, **13**
Duas Nações, **19**
Eduardo VII, **4**
Fénix, **7**
Flamingo, **8**
Flórida, **9**
Hotel Borges, **18**
Lisboa Penta, **1**
Lisboa Plaza, **15**
Lisboa Sheraton and Towers, **3**
Meridien Lisboa, **5**
Ninho das Aguias, **20**
Novotel Lisboa, **2**
Principe Real, **16**
Ritz Lisboa, **6**
Tivoli Jardim, **12**
Tivoli Lisboa, **11**
York House, **14**

tapestries, antique reproductions, and fine paintings. Rooms in the back looking over the park are the best choices. There's convenient dining at the restaurant and outstanding Ritz Grill Room, the latter considered to be among Lisbon's best. *Rua Rodrigo da Fonseca 88, 1000, tel. 01/692020, fax 01/691783. 304 rooms. Facilities: 2 restaurants, bar, shops, garage. AE, DC, MC, V.*

★ **Tivoli Lisboa.** Located on Lisbon's main avenue, this well-run property has a large public area furnished with inviting armchairs and sofas. Reasonable room rates, and pleasant, well-equipped—although modestly sized—guest quarters make the Tivoli a popular choice. Rooms in the rear are most quiet. In warmer months the outdoor pool and garden offer respite from the bustling city; the grill on the top floor presents wonderful views of the city and the Tejo. There's also a good restaurant off the lobby, where a filling morning buffet is presented. *Av. da Liberdade 185, 1200, tel. 01/530181, fax 01/579461. 344 rooms. Facilities: restaurant, grill, bar, pool, garden, tennis court, shops, garage. AE, DC, MC, V.*

Expensive **Altis.** A member of the Best Western group of hotels, this large modern lodging has a broad range of facilities, including an indoor pool and an art gallery. Rooms are welcoming, if unexceptional; those on higher floors have some fine views of Parque Eduardo VII, as does the grill restaurant, the Don Fernando Grill, on the top floor. *Rua Castilho 11, 1200, tel. 01/522496, fax 01/548696. 307 rooms. Facilities: 2 restaurants, 2 bars, pool, gym, sauna, art gallery, shops, garage. AE, DC, MC, V.*

Avenida Palace. Situated between the Rossio and Praça dos Restauradores, this is Lisbon's most-central big hotel. Rooms are comfortable, and furnishings and decor throughout reveal the turn-of-the-century style of Avenida Palace. Street noise can be a problem, but the hotel's proximity to the best downtown restaurants and bars may be compensation enough. *Rua 1 de Dezembro 123, 1200, tel. 01/346-0151, fax 01/322884. 92 rooms. Facilities: bar, parking. AE, DC, MC, V.*

Lisboa Penta. The city's largest hotel is located about midway between the airport and city center, next to the U.S. Embassy and near the Gulbenkian Foundation. The Penta provides shuttle-bus service downtown, but this is probably not the best choice for a tourist planning to do a lot of sightseeing in the center. Business travelers seem content here. The rooms are rather small, but each has a terrace that overlooks either the pool or garden. *Av. dos Combatentes, 1600, tel. 01/726-4554, fax 01/726-4281. 592 rooms. Facilities: restaurant, bar, outdoor pool, health club with sauna, squash courts, shops, garage. AE, DC, MC, V.*

Lisboa Plaza. A recent renovation of this family-owned hotel behind the main Avenida da Liberdade have made it a comfortable and welcoming lodging. Bathrooms have been refurbished to include marble baths, and rooms are air-conditioned; a complimentary American-style breakfast is served daily. The quiet bar is a particularly pleasant place to unwind after sightseeing. *Travessa do Salitre 7, 1200, tel. 01/346-3922, fax 01/371630. 93 rooms. Facilities: restaurant, bar, business services, parking. AE, DC, MC, V.*

Principe Real. Close to the botanical gardens, this small hotel has a large repeat clientele who enjoy the friendly atmosphere and comfortable rooms, each are decorated in a different style with harmonious color schemes. The lack of amenities is more than made up for by fine personal service. *Rua da Alegria 53, 1200, tel. 01/346–0116, fax 01/523492. 24 rooms. Facilities: bar. AE, DC, MC, V.*

Tivoli Jardim. A less-expensive annex to the Tivoli Lisboa, the Jardim sits behind its counterpart, and guests are welcome to use the Tivoli Lisboa's swimming pool and tennis courts. Guest rooms aren't as extravagantly decorated here, but still they are bright; public areas—clad in marble and Portuguese tiles—are dramatically designed. As at the pricier lodging, you get comfort and value for your money. *Rua Júlio Cesar Machado 7–9, 1200, tel. 01/539971, fax 01/556566. 119 rooms. Facilities: restaurant, snack bar, parking, access to pool and tennis court. AE, DC, MC, V.*

★ **York House.** A former 17th-century convent, this attractive *residencia* (inn) is near the Museum of Ancient Art and has its own shady courtyard garden. Despite its somewhat inconvenient location, west of the center, the York House has a loyal following (especially among English visitors), and you'll need to book well in advance. The best rooms look out over a courtyard in which breakfast is sometimes served. A small annex down the street takes the overflow of guests, but although the rooms are a little more spacious here, it's not as pleasing as the main house. *Rua das Janelas Verdes 32–1, 1200, tel. 01/396–2544, fax 01/672793. 46 rooms. Facilities: restaurant, bar, garden. AE, DC, MC, V.*

Moderate **Albergaria Senhora do Monte.** This small, unpretentious hotel
★ in the oldest part of town near St. George's Castle offers some of the best views of Lisbon, especially at night, when the castle is softly illuminated. When you book a room, specify that you want one with a terrace so you can take advantage of the scenery. The top-floor grill has a picture window, the neighborhood is quiet, and parking is available. Without a car, you'll face a steep walk every time you return to the Albergaria; tram No. 28 runs nearby. *Calçada do Monte 39, 1100, tel. 01/866002, fax 01/877783. 27 rooms. Facilities: bar, grill. AE, DC, MC, V.*

Eduardo VII. This elegant, reasonably priced old hotel is well situated in the center of the city, near the park of the same name. It's one of the best-value lodgings in the area, especially now that renovations have smartened the rooms: The most attractive ones face the front, although those in the rear are quieter. The top-floor restaurant captures a marvelous view of the city and the Tejo. *Av. Fontes Pereira de Melo 5, 1000, tel. 01/530141, fax 01/53879. 121 rooms. Facilities: restaurant, bar, shops. AE, DC, MC, V.*

Fénix. Located at the top of Avenida da Liberdade, on Praça Marquês de Pombal, this recently renovated hotel has marble trappings in its bright, air-conditioned public rooms, large guest rooms, and a pleasant first-floor bar. Many of the guest rooms benefit from the hotel's location, at the southern end of the Parque Eduardo VII. The restaurant, O Bodegon, serves good Spanish and Portuguese food in rustic surroundings. *Praça Marquês de Pombal 8, 1200, tel. 01/535121, fax 01/536131. 114 rooms. Facilities: restaurant, bar. AE, DC, MC, V.*

Flórida. Stylishly turned out, this hotel has a pleasant atmosphere and a decent location, near the Parque Eduardo VII. Guest rooms are comfortable, although not big, and have smart marble bathrooms. Breakfast is the only meal available, but

there is a bar that stays open late. *Rua Duque de Palmela 32, 1200, tel. 01/576145, fax 01/543584. 108 rooms. AE, DC, MC, V.*
Novotel Lisboa. The attentive staff and quiet, welcoming atmosphere contribute to the comfortable feel of this modern hotel near the U.S. Embassy. Although not centrally situated, the hotel benefits from the nearby Palharvã metro station and its range of facilities. Public rooms are spacious, and guest rooms are attractively furnished. *Av. Jóse Malhoa, Lote 1642, 1000, tel. 01/726–6022, fax 01/726–6496. 246 rooms. Facilities: restaurant, bar, terrace, pool, garage. AE, MC, V.*

Inexpensive **Casa de São Mamede.** Located behind the botanical gardens and halfway between the main avenue, Avenida da Liberdade, and the Amoreiras shopping center, this attractive, old-fashioned residencia (originally built as a private home) is a fine value, and recent renovations haven't destroyed its antique charm. The ambience of the old mansion in which the hotel is housed, combined with a friendly staff, make this a comfortable choice. *Rua da Escola Politécnica 159, 1200, tel. 01/396–3166. 25 rooms, 11 with bath. MC, V.*
Duas Nacões. What you're really paying for in this fairly basic, sometimes noisy pensão is its superb location, in the heart of the Baixa grid. Duas Nacões is comfortable enough but has few amenities. Quieter rooms face the back. *Rua da Vitória 41, 1000, tel. 01/346–0710. 66 rooms, 42 with bath. Facilities: bar. No credit cards.*
Flamingo. A good-value choice near the top of the Avenida da Liberdade, this small hotel has a friendly staff and cheerful guest rooms, which are a bit on the small side, but pleasant, nonetheless. Those in front tend to be noisy. Amenities include a Portuguese-Continental restaurant; a comfortable, relaxing bar; and a pay parking lot next door, a bonus in this busy area. *Rua Castilho 41, 1200, tel. 01/532191, fax 01/352–1216. 39 rooms. Facilities: restaurant, bar. AE, DC, MC, V.*
Hotel Borges. Set in the heart of the Chiado district, this dependable hotel, characterized by old-fashioned charm and good, modern service, is convenient for guests who plan to shop till they drop. The Borges offers decent-size rooms and an option for breakfast, but taking a meal at the famous Brasileira coffeehouse (located just steps away) is a better bet. *Rua Garrett 108–110, 1200, tel. 01/346–1951. 99 rooms with bath. Facilities: restaurant, bar. MC, V.*
Ninho das Aguias. Perched below the castle, within walking distance of the Alfama, this budget-price pensão is a good find, although it's a bit far from the center of Lisbon. Rooms are simply furnished, and the main attraction is the garden terrace, which has a superb view of the city center. *Costa do Castelo 74, 1100, tel. 01/867000, 16 rooms, 6 with bath. No credit cards.*

Pensoês

Inexpensive **Pensão Arco Bandeira.** The plain rooms in this friendly fourth-floor pensão are reasonably quiet, given its location, at the bottom of the Rossio (under the arch at the top of Rua dos Sapateiros). Guest areas, which include separate bathrooms, are spotless and cost about 4,000$00. *Rua dos Sapateiros 226, 1100, tel. 01/342–3478. 8 rooms. No credit cards.*
Pensão Beira-Minho. The best rooms in this second-floor pensão have sweeping views of one of Lisbon's busiest squares, and cost only about 4,000$00. The Beira-Minho's location

makes this a good base for city-center sightseeing, and it's just across from the Pastelaria Suiça, an excellent place for breakfast. *Praça da Figueira 6, 1100, tel. 01/346–1846. 19 rooms, 12 with bath. No credit cards.*

The Arts and Nightlife

Lisbon has an extensive arts-and-nightlife scene, and you'll find full details of films and events in the weekly *Sete* magazine, available at most newsstands. Although written in Portuguese, listings are fairly easy to decipher, or you can ask the tourist-information office or someone at your hotel reception desk to interpret. There's also a monthly booklet called *Lisboa Ao Vivo,* available for 300$00 from the tourist office and packed with useful cultural and tourist information, much of it in English.

Tickets to musical and theatrical performances are best purchased at the venues, but you can also get them at ticket booths, which are scattered around the city: There's one in Praça dos Restauradores, near the post office.

The Arts

The prime mover behind Lisbon's artistic and cultural scene is the **Fundação Calouste Gulbenkian** (*see* Tour 4, *above*), which not only presents exhibitions and concerts in its foundation buildings but also sponsors events throughout the city. The foundation publishes a frequently updated schedule of activities, which you can pick up at the reception desk. The tourist-information office can also assist with queries about upcoming events.

Art Galleries Lisbon's major art museums often put on temporary exhibitions alongside their permanent collections, and you'll find details in *Sete* and in the local press. Other galleries of interest include: **Galeria de Arte Cervejaria Trindade** (Rua Nova da Trindade 20, tel. 01/342–3506), **Galeria de Arte Hotel Altis** (Rua Castilho 11, tel. 01/527496), **Galeria de São Bento** (Rua do Machadinho 1, tel. 01/674325), and **Galeria Valentim de Carvalho** (Palácio Alcáçovas, Rua Cruz dos Poiais 111, tel. 01/608619).

Concerts Classical-music concerts are staged from about October through June by the **Fundação Calouste Gulbenkian** (*see* Tour 4, *above*), which has three concert halls. Of particular interest is the annual **Early Music and Baroque Festival,** held in churches and museums around Lisbon every spring. You may also be in town during a performance of the **Nova Filarmonica,** a recently established national orchestra, which performs concerts around the country throughout the year; consult local newspapers for details.

Other venues where regular concerts take place include the **Teatro Nacional de São Carlos** (*see* Theater, *below*), the **Sé** (see Tour 1, *above*), the **Igreja do Carmo** (Largo do Carmo, for summer outdoor concerts), and the **Basilica da Estrêla** (*see* Tour 3, *above*).

Film Surprisingly, all films shown in Lisbon appear in their original language accompanied by Portuguese subtitles, and you can usually find the latest Hollywood releases playing around town. Ticket prices are low and even cheaper on Monday; it's best to get to the movie theater early to be assured a seat. Some of the theaters are situated in preserved Art Deco buildings and are attractions in their own right. There are dozens of movie houses throughout the city, including a large selection on and around Praça dos Restauradores and Avenida da Liberdade. A more modern facility, in the **Amoreiras shopping center** (Av. Eng. Duarte Pacheco, tel. 01/692558), has 10 screens.

Theater Plays are performed in Portuguese at the **Teatro Nacional de Dona Maria II** (Praça Dom Pedro V, tel. 01/322210), Lisbon's principal theater. Performances are given August–June, and there's the occasional foreign-language production, too.

The **Teatro Nacional de São Carlos** (Rua Serpa Pinto 9, tel. 01/346–5914) hosts an opera season September–June.

If you're traveling with children it's worth inquiring about productions at the **Teatro Infantil de Lisboa** (Rua Leão de Oliveira 1, tel. 01/363–9974), a children's theater that stages productions in Portuguese but uses mime and other media that can be understood by children of all nationalities.

Nightlife

Lisbon has an extremely active nightlife, revolving mostly around the bars and discos of the Bairro Alto, where a 20- to 30-year-old crowd hangs out. Here, in a series of narrow streets and crowded buildings, you'll find dozens of places to eat, drink, and dance the night away. On weekends the mobs are shoulder to shoulder in the street, as each passing hour heralds a move to the next trendy spot. For a less boisterous evening out, visit one of the adegas tipicas (traditional wine cellars) in the Bairro Alto to hear *fado* (a Portuguese folk-music tradition, based on African slave songs). Still other venues host a variety of live events, from rock-and-roll to African-music performances.

Bars For late-night partying the Bairro Alto is the place to go. Not all bars have signs outside, so to discover the latest hot spots it may be necessary to follow the crowds or push open a half-open door. Most Bairro Alto bars stay open until 3 or so, which is true of those listed here unless otherwise noted. Don't expect to have a quiet drink: The company is generally young and excitable.

Without question the best place to start off your evening is the refined **Instituto do Vinho do Porto** (Rua de São Pedro de Alcântara 45, tel. 01/342–3307, open Mon.–Sat. 10–10), a formidable old building in which you can sink into an armchair and sample a menu of port. Farther up the street is **Harry's Bar** (Rua de São Pedro de Alcântara 57, tel. 01/346–0760), which attracts a mixed tourist and local clientele. Also in this area is the **Pavilhão Chinês** (Rua Dom Pedro V 89, tel. 01/342–4729), which is decorated with extraordinary bric-a-brac from around the world.

Back in the heart of the Bairro Alto, the well-heeled young crowd the loud and fashionable **Cena de Copos** (Rua da Barroca 103–105, tel. 01/347–3372). **Cerca Moura** (Largo da Portas do Sol 4, tel. 01/874859), in the Alfama, is a pleasant, quieter bar, with outdoor seating and views of the river.

Discos and Clubs The best concentration of discos and clubs is found in the Bairro Alto, but there is a smattering of cool, up-market places in the suburbs of Santos and Alcântara (note that new discos open and close frequently in Lisbon). Most charge about 1,000$00 (more on weekends), which usually includes one drink. Some clubs have strict door policies, and bouncers may scrutinize you and your clothes—it's best to ask around first about the likely age of the patrons. Clubs are open from about 11 until 4 or 5, although few get going until well after midnight. "In" spots in Bairro Alto are **Fragil** (Rua da Atalaia 126, tel. 01/369578), which attracts a partly gay crowd; **Nova** (Rua Rosa 261, tel. 01/346–2834), for the younger set; and **Sudoeste** (Rua Barroca 135, tel. 01/321672), a small place with rap and dance music.

The two top places in Alcântara are the exclusive **Banana Power** (Rua Cascais 51, tel. 01/631815), which also has a restaurant, and the ritzy **Alcântara Mar** (Rua da Cozinha Económica 11, tel. 01/649440), which is closed Monday and Tuesday. In Santos the current sensation is **Kremlin** (Escadinhas da Praia 5, tel. 01/665116).

Fado One of Lisbon's most famous nighttime diversions is going to an adega tipica (wine cellar) to hear fado (fate), a haunting, blues-style music rooted in African slave songs. During colonial times fado was exported to Portugal; later, Lisbon's Alfama was recognized as the birthplace of the style; and today most performances occur in the Bairro Alto. In the adegas tipicas food and wine are served, and fado plays late into the night: The singing starts at 10 or 11, and the adegas often stay open until 3. Unfortunately, it's becoming increasingly difficult to find an authentic adega tipica, since tourism has encouraged proprietors to charge admission fees and dilute real fado with other, more "accessible" forms of music. It's best to ask around for a personal recommendation of an adega tipica, but here are some suggestions: **Senhor Vinho** (Rua do Meio á Lapa 18, tel. 01/672681, closed Sun.); **Lisboa a Noite** (Rua das Gaveas 69, tel. 01/346–8557, closed Sun.), which is more expensive than most; the **Adega do Machado** (Rua do Norte 91, tel. 01/346–0095, closed Mon.), a typical, bustling tourist place; the intimate **Fado Menor** (Rua das Praças 18, tel. 01/671856); and **Timpanas** (Rua Gilberto Rola 24, tel. 01/672431, closed Mon.), which is farther out of the center but one of the most authentic.

Live Music For a change from fado, there are plenty of places offering live rock, pop, and jazz. Big-name American and British bands, as well as the superstar Brazilian singers so beloved in Portugal, often play in Lisbon's large concert halls and stadiums. *Sete* has details of upcoming performances, and keep an eye out for advertising posters around the city. Advance tickets may be bought at the venue or at the ticket booth in Praça dos Restauradores.

African music is immensely popular in Lisbon, with touring groups from Cabo Verde and Angola playing regularly alongside homegrown talent. The **Ritz** (Rua da Glória 55 is Lisbon's biggest African club. It's on the edge of the Bairro Alto in a rather seedy area but is renowned as a friendly place where you can dance to live music. In the Alfama **Pê Sujo** (Largo de São Martinho 6, tel. 01/865629, closed Mon.) is a similar club specializing in live Brazilian music washed down with superb *caipirinhas* (Brazilian rum cocktails).

4 Lisbon's Environs

By Jules Brown

The region that is considered Lisbon's environs stretches about 50 kilometers (31 miles) north and south of the Rio Tejo (River Tagus) from the capital, and encompasses a succession of coastal resorts and historic towns, each with unique traditions and characteristics. The environs' region is, properly speaking, the most southerly part of the province of Estremadura, which reaches as far north as Alcobaça (*see* Chapter 5) and borders on the province of Ribetejo to the east. This was the first land taken back from the Moors in the 12th century under the Christian Reconquest, which had originated farther to the north in the region of the River Douro: Estremadura means "farthest from the River Douro," an indication of the early extent of the Christian advance against the Moors.

Today this southern part of the Estremadura province is considered part of Lisbon's environs and indeed is best seen by using the capital as a base. The environs' scenery is highly varied and includes the glistening coastline, broad river estuaries, wooded valleys, and green mountains. Because of its proximity to Lisbon, the area tends to be heavily populated and geared toward the capital's needs: Beaches, restaurants, and hotels are filled with people escaping from the city, and coastal roads are often congested with slow-moving traffic.

All of the main towns and most of the sights in the environs are accessible by public transportation from the capital, and it's possible to visit each in separate day trips. Of course, staying overnight (or longer) in Estoril, Cascais, or Sintra is an attractive option and allows a deeper exploration of the region.

Lisbon and Lisbon's environs are complementary: It's necessary to visit both the city and its surrounding towns to get a real sense of how they have served each other through history. Even the country's earliest rulers appreciated the importance of one to the other. It was the Moors who first built a castle to the northwest of the capital at Sintra as a defense against Christian forces under Dom Afonso Henriques. The forces had moved steadily southward since the victory at Ourique in 1139. The castle at Sintra was lost to the Christians in 1147, a few days after the defeat of the Moors in Lisbon.

Once the Christian Reconquest had been consolidated in Estremadura, there was a less pressing need for defensive measures. The early Christian kings instead adopted the lush hills and valleys of Sintra as a summer retreat, and designed estates and glorious palaces that survive today. Like the Christians, Lisbon's 18th- and 19th-century nobility desired a more leisurely life outside the city and so developed small resorts along the Estoril coast; the amenities and ocean views are still greatly sought after. In this century, too, Lisboans search for local retreats: Across the Rio Tejo are the tourist beaches of the Costa da Caparica and the southern Setúbal Peninsula.

In whichever direction you travel and whatever your interests, you should be delighted with all the environs has to offer. The palaces, gardens, and luxury *quintas* (country manor houses) of Sintra are justly celebrated. At Cascais and Estoril life revolves around the sea, and visitors can take part in time-honored pastimes: a stroll along the shore, a seafood meal, a game of tennis, a flutter at the casino. To the north, around Guincho's rocky promontory and the Praia das Maças coast, the Atlantic Ocean is often windswept and rough but provides good surf-boarding, windsurfing, and scuba diving, as well as excellent views for coastal drives.

The best of the sand beaches lie to the south of the Rio Tejo, on the Setúbal Peninsula, a scenic area known for its rural traditions, festivals, and agriculture. Visitors can sample some of the county's best wines, explore the attractive dramatic mountain scenery of the Serra da Arrábida (Arrábida Mountains), and indulge themselves by lodging in one of two ancient castles, now converted into *pousadas* (luxury state-run hotels). At the large port of Setúbal, architectural history was made in the late-15th century with the building of the first church in the Manueline style—a design that was later to come into full bloom with the building of Lisbon's Jerónimos Monastery (*see* Tour 5 in Chapter 3) in the early 16th century.

Another reason for the region's ever-increasing popularity is its comprehensive sports facilities. Swimming and watersports are omnipresent, with the local climate encouraging a dip almost year-round. The superb golf courses lying between Lisbon and Estoril attract international players, and nearly everywhere you'll find good fishing, horseback riding, country walking, and tennis. Even grand prix racing is highly profiled at Estoril. The Lisbon environs can also be good for shopping and souvenir-hunting: The area hosts several traditional annual country fairs, where you'll be able to find a variety of local handicrafts and foods.

Essential Information

Important Addresses and Numbers

Tourist Information Lisbon's main tourist office in the Palácio Foz (Praça dos Restauradores, tel. 01/346–3314) can help with general inquiries concerning travel to the city's environs.

The local offices listed below are usually open June–September, daily 9–1 and 2–6, sometimes later in the tourist-resort areas. Hours are greatly reduced after peak season, and most offices are closed Sunday.

There are also tourist offices in **Cabo da Roca** (tel. 01/929–0981), **Cascais** (Av. Marginal, tel. 01/286–8204), **Colares** (tel. 01/929–2638), **Estoril** (Arcadas do Parque, tel. 01/286–0113), **Sesimbra** (Av. dos Naufragios, tel. 01/223–3304), **Setúbal** (Largo do Corpo Santo, tel. 065/24284), **Sintra** (Praça da Republica 3, tel. 01/923–3919 or 01/923–1157), and **Queluz** (tel. 01/436–3415).

Emergencies For all general emergencies dial **115;** for service numbers and contact addresses in the Lisbon area, *see* Important Addresses and Numbers in Chapter 3.

Mail There are main post offices in **Cascais** (Rua Manuel J. Avelar, tel. 01/483–3175) and **Sintra** (Av. Movimento F. Armadas 1, tel. 01/923–3699).

Arriving and Departing by Plane

The initial point of arrival for almost all the environs' destinations is Lisbon (*see* Essential Information in Chapter 3); from the city you may drive or take public transportation to the surrounding towns. If you are traveling north from the Algarve, tour Setúbal (*see* Tour 4, *below*) before moving on to Lisbon and the other environs.

Arriving and Departing by Train, Bus, Car, and Boat

By Train Electric commuter trains travel the entire Estoril coast, with departures from the waterfront Cais do Sodré station (tel. 01/347–0181), located in Lisbon, just 10 minutes west (by foot) of the Praça do Comércio. Trains depart every 15–30 minutes. The scenic trip to Estoril, with splendid sea views, takes about 30 minutes, and four more stops along the seashore bring you to Cascais, at the end the line. A one-way ticket to either costs 130$00; service operates daily 5:30 AM–2:30 AM.

Trains from Lisbon's Rossio station (tel. 01/346–5022), situated between Praça dos Restauradores and the Rossio, run every 15 minutes to Queluz (a 20-minute trip) and on to Sintra (40 minutes total). The service operates 6 AM–2:40 AM, and one-way tickets cost about 130$00.

Although you can reach Setúbal by train and ferry, it's much easier to take the bus (*see below*).

In summer an inexpensive narrow gauge railway runs for 8 kilometers (5 miles) along the Costa da Caparica from the town of Caparica, on the Setúbal Peninsula. It makes 20 stops to beaches along the way. You can reach Caparica by bus from Lisbon or from Cacilhas (*see below*).

By Bus Although the best way to reach Sintra and most of the towns on the Estoril coast is by car or by train from Lisbon, there are some useful bus connections between towns. At Cascais the bus terminal outside the train station operates regular summer services to Guincho (15 minutes) and Sintra (one hour). From outside the train station at Sintra, there are half-hourly departures in summer to the nearby coastal resorts of Praia das Maças and Azenhas do Mar (30 minutes) in the west, and north to Mafra in the Estremadura (one hour).

Buses to Caparica (45 minutes from Lisbon) depart from Praça de Espanha (metro: Palhavã) in Lisbon and travel over the Ponte 25 de Abril bridge, which provides superb panoramic views. Regular buses to Caparica also leave from the quayside at Cacilhas, the suburb immediately across the Tejo from Lisbon, which you can reach by ferry from the Terminal Fluvial, adjacent to Praça do Comércio. Both services can be very crowded in the summer months.

Buses to Setúbal (one hour), on the Setúbal Peninsula, leave regularly from Lisbon's Praça de Espanha (metro: Palhavã). At Setúbal you can connect with local services north to Palmela (20 minutes), and west to Sesimbra (30 minutes). Six buses daily run a 30-minute trip from Sesimbra to the southwestern cape of Cabo Espichel.

By Car Driving is certainly the most flexible way to see Lisbon's environs; without a car some Atlantic beaches and some of the manor houses near Sintra and Setúbal will be difficult to reach. Fast highways connect Lisbon with Estoril and Setúbal, and the quality of other roads in the region is generally good. Take special care on hilly and coastal roads, though, and if possible, avoid driving (or at least driving to Lisbon) at the end of a weekend or during public holidays. Bear in mind, too, that parking can be problematic, especially in the summer along the Estoril coast. When you do park, never leave anything visible in the car.

Car Rentals There are more choices for car rentals in Lisbon (*see* Arriving and Departing by Car, Train, and Bus in Chapter 3), though the tourist offices in Cascais, Estoril, Sintra, and Setúbal can advise you of the local possibilities. Two choices are **Avis** (Tamariz, Estoril, tel. 01/468–5728) and **Europcar** (Av. Marginal, Centro Comércial Cisne, Bloco B, Logas 4 and 5, Cascais, tel. 01/286–7295).

Taxis If you don't have your own car, it may pay in convenience to take a taxi to some environs towns that are close to Lisbon. Cabs can be reasonably inexpensive, and you can usually agree on a fixed price that will include the round-trip to a specific attraction (the driver will wait for you to complete your tour).

By Boat Ferries cross the Rio Tejo from Lisbon to the suburb of Cacilhas, every 10–15 minutes (7 AM–9 PM) from Fluvial terminal, adjacent to Praça do Comércio, or Cais do Sodré (24-hour service). One-way tickets cost 75$00, and the journey takes about 15 minutes.

From Setúbal there's an hourly ferry for cars and foot passengers across to the Tróia Peninsula; the journey takes about 20 minutes.

Getting Around

By Train and Bus *See* Arriving and Departing, *above.*

On Foot The Estoril coast and much of Sintra are ideal for walking. Most of the tours in this chapter are designed as walks, and the tourist offices will provide maps and brochures that detail local footpaths. If you visit Costa da Caparica in the summer, be prepared to walk a good distance before you find a relatively uncrowded beach.

By Bicycle **Tip Tours** (Av. Costa Pinto 91A, Cascais, tel. 01/286–5150) rents bicycles by the day or half-day, but be careful of the traffic.

Guided Tours

Catur (Largo da Academia Nacional de Belas Artes 12, Lisbon, tel. 01/346–7974) offers a seven-hour excursion (including lunch) to principal sites in Lisbon's environs, and costs 7,500$00. **Citirama** (Av. Praia da Vitória 12–B, Lisbon, tel. 01/560668) has various tours, including: half-day trips to Queluz, Sintra, and Estoril, or a tour of the area's royal palaces (both 5,500$00); nine-hour tours of Mafra, Sintra, and Cascais (9,000$00 including lunch); and even an evening visit to Estoril's famous casino (9,500$00, including dinner).

There are several other companies offering similar tours at comparable prices; for details *see* Guided Tours in Chapter 3, or ask local tourist offices for recommendations.

Exploring Lisbon's Environs

Orientation

Several of the destinations in this chapter make ideal day trips from Lisbon, particularly the seaside resorts of the Estoril coast, the palace at Queluz, and the beaches of the Costa da Caparica. Although other attractions and towns can be included on a day's outing from the capital, you may find you're trying to do too much in too short a time. The best solution is to plan ahead: See some of the sights on day trips from Lisbon, and include others in a regional tour that might last several days.

West of Lisbon consider Sintra and the Serra de Sintra for possible overnight stops; the beautiful surroundings can occupy two or three days' leisurely exploring. Estoril and Cascais—both easy day trips—have lively resorts and beaches that may tempt you to stop longer than planned. Setúbal—located across the Rio Tejo to the south—has a splendid pousada that makes a popular overnight stop for those driving on toward the Algarve.

With a car it's possible to cover the entire region in two days, visiting the areas north and south of the Rio Tejo separately. However, a week would not be too long to spend in Lisbon's environs, since there's much to be said for taking your time and savoring the scenery. Although driving gives you a lot of freedom, parking can be a real problem. Traveling by public transportation also allows you to get around with relative ease, especially between the major destinations; for example, even with only a day or so to spare, you can see a great deal of the Estoril coast and Sintra by train.

Highlights for First-Time Visitors

Cabo da Roca (*see* Tour 2)
Cascais (*see* Tour 1)
Costa da Caparica (*see* Tour 4)
Estoril Casino (*see* Tour 1)
Igreja de Jesus, Setúbal (*see* Tour 4)
Monserrate Gardens (*see* Tour 2)
Palácio Nacional de Pena (*see* Tour 2)
Palácio Nacional de Queluz (*see* Tour 3)
Palácio Nacional de Sintra (*see* Tour 2)
Sesimbra (*see* Tour 4)

Tour 1: The Estoril Coast

Numbers in the margin correspond to points of interest on the Estoril Coast, Sintra, and Queluz map.

The **Estoril coast** is a stretch of coastline extending for 32 kilometers (20 miles) to the west of Lisbon, taking in the major towns of Estoril and Cascais, as well as some smaller settlements that are part city suburb, part beach town. A favored residential area (thanks to its special microclimate), the coast has milder winters than nearby Lisbon. Partly for that reason, this entire stretch is also known as the Portuguese Riviera.

Over the years the casino at Estoril and the beaches there and in Cascais have been playgrounds for the wealthy, as well as homes for expatriates and exiled royalty of Europe. Today parts of the coastline and several of the hotels are still exclusive, but many of the easternmost towns (particularly those nearest Lisbon) are now firmly part of the city's commuter belt. Even in Estoril and Cascais—whose rich villas still imply wealth—you can count on sharing a visit in summer with great throngs of tourists.

Besides the crowds, the Estoril coast has had to face the problem of pollution due to an inadequate sewage system. Many of the beaches have been profoundly affected, but the quality and cleanliness of the water and sands differ greatly from beach to beach. The problem is a long-standing one, brought about by development, and although plans are underway to rectify the situation, you are strongly advised to avoid swimming in an area unless the water has been declared safe. The best way to determine this is to look for a blue Council of Europe flag, which signals a high standard of unpolluted water and beach. Consult local tourist offices if you are unsure.

None of this is to suggest that the Estoril coast should be avoided. Many of the beaches are still fine, the waterfront towns—especially Cascais—are attractive, and the train ride from Lisbon's Cais do Sodré station along the shore offers some of the most appealing views in the region. Unless you intend to tour the wider region over several days, taking the train can be better than joining the crowded roads. If you do choose to drive, leave Lisbon by car via the Estrada Marginal road (follow signs for Cascais/Estoril) and take the curving coastal route to Estoril (the N6); the parallel, faster Auto-Estrada da Oeste highway runs from the Praça Marquês de Pombal in Lisbon to Estoril.

① The first point of interest along the coastal route is at **Oeiras,** 17 kilometers (10½ miles) west of Lisbon. The suburb features the 18th-century Palácio do Marquês de Pombal, originally the country mansion of the man who redesigned Lisbon after the great earthquake of 1755. Unfortunately, only the grounds (including an interesting fishing pavilion and a water tank with the familiar blue-and-white tiling known as azulejo) are open to the public—sometimes.

② The town of **Carcavelos,** a couple of kilometers (just over a mile) farther west, has a small beach lined with café-bars and a busy Thursday market. After another 5 kilometers (3 miles) along the coastal road you'll enter the increasingly built-up environs of Estoril, at **São Pedro** and **São João do Estoril.** Both suburbs have their own beaches and train stations. From São João do Estoril, you can pick up the seafront promenade path that runs through Estoril to Cascais. This is a fine walk (about 5 kilometers/3 miles) with excellent seaside views and no shortage of places to stop for a cold drink or coffee.

③ The town of **Estoril,** 26 kilometers (16 miles) west of Lisbon, is filled with grand homes and gardens but otherwise has few specific attractions to interest visitors. Many of the mansions date from the last century, when the resort was preferred by the European aristocracy, and Estoril has managed to maintain a ritzy, jet-set veneer: The town still boasts numerous plush accommodations, restaurants, and sports facilities.

Perhaps the most distinctive attraction in Estoril is its **casino,** which opened in the center of town in 1968 and includes a restaurant, bar, concert venue, movie theater, and art gallery. If you fancy gaming, you won't want to miss a throw of the dice in the gambling salons, which have all the usual games, including banks of American and European slot machines. (To enter the casino, all foreign visitors must show their passports.) If you're making a night of it, there's dinner and an international floorshow, too. Every summer musical concerts and ballets are staged here, and a schedule is available at the tourist office. *Parque do Estoril, tel. 01/268-4521. Admission: 400$00. Casino and restaurant open 3 PM-3 AM, floor show nightly at 11. Reservations required for restaurant and show. Jacket and tie required. AE, DC, MC, V.*

The casino is set at the top of the formal gardens of the **Parque do Estoril,** a park that overlooks the sea and is lined on both sides by several pleasant cafés. People-watching is a famous pastime in this exclusive resort, and a prime spot is from one of the al fresco restaurants along the beachfront **Tamariz esplanade.** The best and longest local beach is at the adjacent **Monte Estoril,** which adjoins Estoril's beach: Here you'll find rest rooms and beach chairs for rent, as well as plenty of shops and snackbars.

Time Out   Facing the park is Estoril's luxurious **Hotel Palácio** (*see Dining and Lodging, below*), worth visiting, if for no reason other tha to take tea in one of its ample salons. During World War II the palace was an espionage center where—in neutral Portugal— the Germans and Allies kept watch on each other, and where exiled European courts awaited the end of the war.

④ Walk along the seafront promenade and across the bay to **Cascais,** just 3 kilometers (2 miles) to the west. Once a mere fishing village, this pretty town—with three small, sandy bays—is now a heavily developed tourist resort packed with shops, restaurants, and hotels. Regardless of the masses of people, Cascais is worth visiting because (unlike Estoril) it has retained some of its erstwhile small-town character and boasts a selection of sights both in and around the town. (However, what Cascais does have in common with Estoril is polluted water: The beaches are very attractive, but stay out of the sea.) Aside from the harbor, with its fishing boats and yachts, the nicest part of town is the area of old streets and squares off Largo 5 Outubro, behind the Hotel Baia, where you'll find lace shops, cafés, and restaurants galore. In the summer parking in Cascais is a real headache.

Walk south from the Hotel Baia, down Rua Marquês Porcada, to the Baroque **Igreja de Nossa Senhora da Assunção** (Church of Our Lady of the Assumption) with its plain white facade. Inside are fine paintings by Portuguese artist Josefa de Óbidos and an elegant golden altar. *Largo da Assunção. Admission free. Open 8–noon and 2–5.*

Opposite the church is one of the entrances to the municipal **Parque do Marechal Carmona** (open daily 9–6), in which there is a shallow lake, a café, a small zoo, and tables and chairs set out under the trees for picnickers. Walk through the park to its southern edge, and you'll find the **Museu Conde de Castro Guimarães,** a stately 19th-century home set on spacious grounds. The small, charming museum houses 18th- and 19th-century paintings, ceramics, furniture, and some archaeological artifacts that were excavated nearby. *Estrada da Boca do Inferno. Admission: 150$00. Open Tues.–Sun. 11–12:30 and 2–5.*

Time Out A short walk west from the museum along the coastal road will bring you to the café-terrace **Esplanada Santa Marta** (Estrada da Boca do Inferno), which overlooks the tiny Santa Marta beach and the adjacent lighthouse. This is a perfect spot for a cool drink on the way to or from the Boca do Inferno, a 20-minute walk beyond.

⑤ Continue on the coastal road for a little less than 2 kilometers (1¼ miles) to Cascais's most famous attraction, the **Boca do Inferno** (Mouth of Hell). Year-round the sea pounds this impressive natural grotto, one of several in the rugged local coastline. Walk along the fenced paths to the viewing platforms above the grotto, and peer down into the abyss: It's a lively spot anytime, though it's best when the incoming tide thrusts waves high onto the surrounding cliffs. A path leads down to secluded spots on the rocks below, from where fishermen cast their lines. Afterward, visit the daily roadside market of handicrafts, lace, and leather goods or one of the nearby cafés.

From the Boca do Inferno it's a scenic 9-kilometer (5½-mile) drive along the coastal road to the superb surfing beach at

❻ Guincho. Here rollers from the Atlantic pound onto the sand even on the calmest of days, providing perfect conditions for windsurfing (the annual world championships are often held here during the summer). But beware: The undertow at Guincho beach is notoriously dangerous, and even the best swimmers should take heed.

From Guincho you can return along the coastal road to Cascais and Estoril, or cut inland and drive northward on the N247 to Cabo da Roca and Sintra *(see* Tour 2, *below).*

Tour 2: Sintra and Environs

❼ Long considered one of the most beautiful places in Portugal, **Sintra,** 30 kilometers (18 miles) west of Lisbon, should not be missed. The district's lush, woods and valleys lying on the northern slopes of the **Serra de Sintra** (Sintra Mountains) have been inhabited since prehistoric times, though the Moors were the first to build a castle on its crags. Later Sintra became the summer residence of Portuguese kings and aristocrats, and its late medieval National Palace *(see below)* was the greatest expression of the royal wealth and power of the time. In the 18th and 19th centuries the area's charms were becoming widely known, as a succession of English travelers, poets, and writers—including an enthusiastic Lord Byron—were drawn to the region's beauty. The poet Robert Southey described Sintra as "the most blessed spot on the whole inhabitable globe." Today the town's palaces, gardens, wooded paths, and viewpoints are still scintillating, and horse-drawn carriages and elegant old hotels in the vicinity add to Sintra's 19th-century air.

The main drawback to visiting Sintra, especially in the summer, is the number of tour buses that sometimes clog the main square of the **Vila Velha** (Old Town). However, with a little effort you can escape the crowds by taking one of several lovely rural walks through the surrounding countryside. Ask the Sintra tourist office for their guidebook to local walks.

In the center of Sintra's old town stands the **Palácio Nacional de Sintra** (National Palace of Sintra), also called the Paço Real, whose conical twin chimneys are one of the region's most recognizable landmarks. There has probably been a palace here since Moorish times, although the present-day structure dates from the 14th century. The property was the summer residence of the House of Avis, Portugal's royal lineage, and displays a combination of Moorish, Gothic, and Manueline architectural styles. To see the interior you must join one of the guided tours, which is a pity since several of the rooms are exceptional and may demand more time than you're given. The kitchen, with the famous chimneys, is visited first, followed by a succession of rooms and a chapel decorated with some spectacular examples of mozarabic (Moorish influenced) azulejos from the 15th and 16th centuries. The Sala das Armas's ceiling is painted with the coats-of-arms of 72 noble families; another grand room has a ceiling of painted swans. Attached to one of the oldest rooms is a well-known tale about an encounter between Dom João I (1385–1433), for whom the palace was largely rebuilt, and a lady-in-waiting whom he kissed. The king had the room painted with as many magpies as there were chattering court ladies, in order to stop their gossiping by satirizing them as loose-tongued birds. *Largo Rainha D. Amelia, tel. 01/923–*

4118. Admission: 400$00 June–Sept., 200$00 Oct.–May, free Sun. 10–12:30. Open Thurs.-Tues. 10–12:30 and 2–4:30.

If you stand on the steps of the palace and look up toward the Sintra Mountains, you can spot the ruins of the 8th-century **Castelo dos Mouros** (Moorish Castle), which defied hundreds of invaders until it was finally conquered by Dom Afonso Henriques in 1147. For a closer look follow the steep, partially cobbled road that leads up to the ruins; or you may rent one of the horse-drawn carriages outside the palace for a more romantic trip. Vast, panoramic views from the castle's serrated walls help explain why Moorish architects chose the site. *Estrada da Pena. Admission free. Open daily 10–5.*

Several kilometers farther up the same road is the draw-bridged **Palácio Nacional da Pena** (Pena Palace), the most enjoyable of Sintra's palaces, with its turrets, ramparts, and domes. It's a long walk here from the center of Sintra (about 1½ hours), but buses run twice daily in summer, making this attraction easily accessible. For details contact the tourist office. Commissioned by the King Consort Ferdinand of Saxe-Coburg in 1840, to be built where a 16th-century convent once stood, the palace resembles a collection of clashing styles, from Arabian to Victorian. A splendid park filled with a lush variety of trees and flowers from every corner of the Portuguese empire in the mid-19th century surrounds the palace, and perched atop a nearby crag, overseeing the grounds, is an enormous statue of Baron Eschwege (the building's German architect) cast as a medieval knight. The final kings of Portugal lived here, the last of whom—Dom Manuel—went into exile in England in 1910 after a republican revolt. The pseudo-medieval structure, with its ramparts, towers, and great halls, is decorated in late Victorian and Edwardian furnishings—a rich, sometimes vulgar, and often bizarre collection of furniture, ornaments, and paintings that makes the guided tour surprisingly interesting. *Estrada da Pena, tel. 01/923–0227. Admission: 400$00 June–Sept., 200$00 Oct.–May, free Sun. 10–2. Open Tues.–Sun. 10–5.*

Above the palace beyond the statue, a path leads to **Cruz Alta, a** 16th-century stone cross that rests 540 meters above sea level, at the highest point of the Sintra Mountains. Naturally, the views from this altitude are stupendous, although you may find the climb arduous, especially in the summer sun. However, the walk from the Pena Palace back down to Sintra is delightful: You travel through shaded woods and have several opportunities to rest at viewpoints and take in the panoramic scenes.

If you want to speed up this tour take the high road (N247–3) west from Pena Palace for 4 kilometers (2½ miles) to the Convento de Santa Cruz dos Capuchos (*see below*). Otherwise, if you find you have extra time once you've returned to downtown Sintra, you might visit a museum. The **Museu Regional** (Regional Museum), housed in the old Hotel Costa, not only displays a permanent collection of local archaeological, ethnological, and historical collections but also hosts a variety of interesting temporary exhibitions. *Praça da República. Admission free. Open Tues.–Sun. 10–12:30 and 2:30–5.*

Just down the road, in the **Museu do Brinquedo** (Toy Museum), you'll find an enjoyable collection of locally made dolls and traditional Portuguese toys. *Largo Latino Coelho 9. Admission: 200$00. Open Tues.–Sun. 10–12:30 and 2:30–5.*

After you've explored the palaces and some of Sintra's other historic sights, you may want to browse around the souvenir and antique shops that line the town's central streets. Or, if, you visit on the second or fourth Sunday of the month, the near-

8 by village of **São Pedro de Sintra** (located just over a kilometer—under a mile—to the east) hosts the **Feira de Sintra** (country fair). Dating back to the time of the Christian Reconquest, the fair is one of the best in the country, with livestock and agricultural displays, and local crafts, antiques, bric-a-brac, and food for sale. While you're in town, you may want to sample *queijadas*, the sweet cheese tartlets that are a specialty in Sintra's cafés.

Aside from Sintra and its immediate attractions, most of the local points of interest lie to the west and can be reached via the road to Colares (*see below*). The gardens in Monserrate (*see below*) are about an hour's walk from Sintra, so to visit this and other attractions you'll probably want to drive or take a taxi.

Time Out On your way west follow signs to Seteais (a 20-minute walk from Sintra), where you can stop for a meal or afternoon tea at the 18th-century **Palácio de Seteais** (*see* Dining and Lodging, *below*). Built by the Dutch Consul in Portugal, the imposing building—once a palace—is now a luxury hotel, with an excellent (and very expensive) restaurant and beautiful formal gardens. The lunch menu offers a variety of specialties. *Rua Barbosa do Bocage 8, tel. 01/923–3200. Reservations advised. Jacket advised.*

Beyond the palace the road continues through a leafy neighborhood of private manor houses; some of the homes are part of the *Turismo de Habitação* system, an organization that lists lodgings for rent. About 3 kilometers (1.8 miles) from Seteais are

9 the world-renowned gardens of **Monserrate**, laid out by Scottish gardeners in the mid-1800s at the behest of a wealthy Englishman, Sir Francis Cook. The architecturally extravagant, Moorish-style domed pavilion—the ground's centerpiece—is closed to visitors, but the gardens with their streams, waterfalls, and imported Etruscan tombs, demand a stop. In addition to the dazzling array of tree and plant species is one of the largest collections of ferns in the world. *Admission: 50$00. Open daily 9–5.*

Past Monserrate the road leads west for 3 kilometers (2 miles)

10 to the small village of **Colares,** associated with the locally produced red wine. The town is also known for the local parish which is adorned with ceramic tiles, and the main square which is bordered by some 18th-century homes. The village's winding streets are alive with colorful flowers and trees. For terrific views of the sea and surrounding mountains, take the

11 winding road that climbs up to the nearby village of **Penedo** less than 2 kilometers (1½ miles) away.

Just out of Colares, the road from Sintra meets the N375, which runs east for 4 kilometers (2½ miles) to the tiny **Convento de Santa Cruz dos Capuchos** (Capuchos Convent), a friary built in 1560 by Franciscan monks. The 12 diminutive cells, the chapel and the refectory—all hacked out of solid rock—are insulated with cork, hence the nickname the "Cork Convent." *Admission free; tip expected. Open Tues.– Sun. 10–12:30 and 2:30–5.*

From the convent, follow the N375 back to where you turned beyond Colares; continue northwest and follow the hilly route to the Atlantic-facing resort village of **Praia das Maças,** with similar resorts of **Azenhas do Mar** to the north, and **Praia Grande** to the south. All three have good beaches (Praia Grande's is the longest) and a selection of small restaurants. If you're visiting Praia das Maças between July and September, a tram leaves from **Banzão** (just outside Colares) and offers particularly engaging views upon approach to the beach.

Time Out   At Praia Grande the **Angra** (tel. 01/929–0069) restaurant, with its beachfront views and rooftop terrace, is an ideal, moderately priced stop for lunch or dinner.

A novel stop when visiting Sintra's environs is the windswept **Cabo da Roca** and its lighthouse, continental Europe's westernmost point. Here, where the immense wild ocean stretches away from the rugged, barren land, you can purchase a certificate from the gift shop that verifies your visit. Also on site is a tourist desk. Many people visit just to say they've been to the western edge of the continent, but even without the certificate the memory of this desolate granite cape will linger. To reach the cape, retrace your steps to Colares and drive southwest on the N247; turn right after 3 kilometers (2 miles) for the minor road (N247–4), which leads, after another kilometer or so, to the cape.

Cabo da Roca marks the end of Tour 2, and from here you can drive back through Colares to Sintra. Another route is to take the main road that goes east (N247) and skirts the southern side of the Serra de Sintra; after about 9 kilometers (5½ miles) you'll reach the beach at Guincho, from where you're on course to link up with the towns of the Estoril coast (*see* Tour 1, *above*).

Alternatively, at the junction where the cape road (N247–4) and the main road (N247) meet, a minor road (sign-posted to Peninha) cuts inland and across the Serra de Sintra. This is the scenic route that runs 15 kilometers (9 miles) back to Sintra and passes the peak of Peninha, with a good overlook, and a turn-off for the Capuchos Convent, before the road climbs to Pena Palace and finally down to Sintra.

Tour 3: Queluz and Palácio Nacional de Queluz

Located halfway between Lisbon and Sintra (just off the N249) is the town of **Queluz,** with its magnificent **Palácio Nacional de Queluz** (Queluz Palace). The 15-kilometer (9-mile) drive from Portugal's capital takes about 20 minutes, making this a good half-day option or a fine stop on the way to or from Sintra (*see* Tour 2, *above*). If you take the train, get off at the Queluz-Belas station and walk about a kilometer (just over ½ mile) to the palace.

One of the most ttractive of the royal residences in Lisbon's environs, the Queluz Palace—with its salmon-pink rococo edifice that was ordered by Dom Pedro III in 1747 and took 40 years to complete!—was inspired in part, by the palace at Versailles. Intended as a royal summer residence, the building is surrounded by formal landscaping and waterways designed by

Frenchman Jean-Baptiste Robillon. The ponds, canal, statues, fountains, hedges—and the palace—all fit a carefully executed baroque plan that implies harmony and wholeness. In 1934 a disastrous fire caused much damage, but the palace has been restored and is used today for formal banquets, music festivals, and as accommodations for visiting heads of state. On the guest list have been dignitaries such as Queen Elizabeth II and President Eisenhower. In summer a month-long festival—the Noites de Queluz (Queluz Nights)—complete with costumed cast and orchestra, is staged in the gardens. This event mimics the concerts, fireworks displays, and other activities held in the gardens to amuse Queen Maria I (wife of Dom Pedro III), who lived in the palace throughout her long reign (1777–1816) and whose eccentric behavior earned her the name "Mad" Queen Maria.

Visitors may tour the richly furnished interior and walk through the elegant state rooms: the frescoed Music Salon, the Hall of Ambassadors, the mirrored Throne Room with its crystal chandeliers and gilt trimmings, and so on. The room appointments, gathered from all corners of the globe, including woods and precious metals from the old Portuguese colonies, are as ornate and spectacular as you might expect. *Tel. 01/ 950039. Admission: 400$00 June–Sept., 200$00 Oct.–May. Open Mon. and Wed.–Sun. 10–1 and 2–5.*

Time Out Reserve a table in advance to enjoy lunch in the old palace kitchens, now the **Restaurante de Cozinha Velha** (tel. 01/435– 0740). In addition to the excellent food, the fixtures and fittings that date to the 18th century make this an experience to savour. If you miss lunch, try to visit during afternoon tea. *See* Dining and Lodging, *below.*

Tour 4: The Setúbal Peninsula

Numbers in the margin correspond to points of interest on the Setúbal Peninsula map.

The extensive **Setúbal Peninsula,** situated south of the Rio Tejo, is visited mostly for its beaches on the northern Costa da Caparica, which provide the cleanest and closest ocean swimming to Lisbon. Other area attractions include the major port of Setúbal, and the scenic mountain range that separates the port from the peninsula's southernmost beaches and fishing villages.

If you're intent on spending the day at the beach or simply touring the town of Setúbal, then traveling by public transportation may be your easiest course of action. However, if you want to see most or all of the sites covered in this tour, renting a car will be your best move.

If you travel by bus or car, you'll approach the Setúbal Peninsula (and the sites covered below) by crossing the Ponte 25 de Abril suspension bridge from Lisbon. From this route you're guaranteed stupendous views of the capital.

Having crossed the bridge, you're now on the main highway (E4) to Setúbal. However, the first part of Tour 4 is contained within the northern coast of the peninsula. Therefore, as you leave the bridge, follow signs to the **Christo Rei.** The huge statue of Christ, built in 1959, was designed after the famous stat-ue of Christ the Redeemer that is in Rio de Janeiro. The figure, with outstretched arms that seem to embrace the city, is a wa-terfront landmark that can be seen easily from almost any-where in Lisbon. You can take the elevator to the top of the statue for remarkable panoramic views. *Open 10–noon and 2–6.*

17 The suburb above which the statue stands, **Cacilhas,** is noted for the numerous seafood restaurants lining the town's main street, Rua do Ginjal. Waiters armed with menus linger outside the establishments' doors, ready to pounce on passersby who can't decide where or what to eat. At night, and especially on weekends, this is a popular destination for city folk who have ferried their way from across the river. Ferries depart regu-larly from Lisbon's Cais do Sodré station and the quay at Praça do Comércio. (Buses from the ferry station on the Cacilhas's dockside can take you to the Christo Rei statue.)

18 Buses also connect Cacilhas with the **Costa da Caparica,** whose main town is **Caparica,** 14 kilometers (8½ miles) southwest of Lisbon. If you're driving, either return to the highway (E4) and follow the signs or take the minor N377 from Cacilhas—a slow-er, more scenic route—to reach the 20-kilometer (12-mile) stretch of beach on the northwestern coast of the Setúbal Pen-insula. Formerly a fishing village, Caparica is now a lively re-sort, bloated with Portuguese tourists who come to enjoy the relatively unpolluted waters.

Several new resorts near Caparica are on the verge of experi-encing a tourism boom, but you may be able to avoid the crowds if you keep heading south toward the less accessible, lonely dunes and coves at the end of the peninsula. During the sum-mer a small, narrow-gauge train departs from Caparica and travels along an 8-kilometer (5-mile) stretch of coast, making stops at different sandy beaches en route. Each town is unique: The areas nearest Caparica are family oriented, while the more southerly resorts tend to attract a younger crowd (among these beaches are some nudist spots as well).

19 From the Costa da Caparica, head back to the highway (E4) and drive southeast to **Palmela,** a small town located just 25 ki-lometers (15 miles) from Lisbon. Every September the commu-nity—situated in the center of a prosperous wine-growing area—takes part in festivities to celebrate the year's harvest. Palmela's cobbled streets are prettily laced with engaging, low whitewashed houses, and dominating the village are the re-mains of a 12th-century castle that was captured from the Moors and enlarged by successive kings. In the 15th century the monastery and church of Sant' Iago was built within the castle walls, although both the castle and monastic buildings were damaged in the 1755 earthquake. The structure lay aban-doned for many years, until, after extensive restoration, the pousada that now occupies the monastic buildings began opera-ting. The views from this height are extensive.

20 The main highway continues south to **Setúbal,** 40 kilometers (24½ miles) from Lisbon, at the mouth of the Rio Sado. This is the country's third-largest port, and, although it's one of Portugal's oldest cities, its character has become largely indus-trial. Nevertheless, you may be compelled to stop here, if for no other reason than to stay overnight before driving on to the

The Setúbal Peninsula

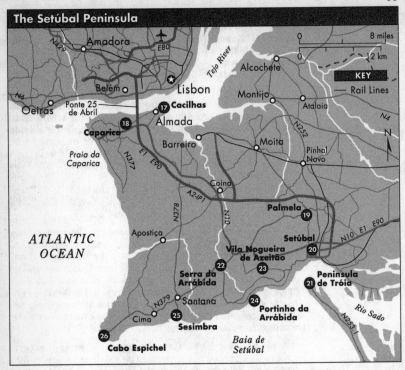

Algarve. If you do stay, consider lodging in the 16th-century Castelo de São Filipe (*see* Dining and Lodging, *below*), now one of Portugal's finest pousadas. Even if you decide to continue with your tour, you may want to dine here or just pause for a while to take in some commanding views that are provided from the castle's privileged position over the city.

There is more to Setúbal than just the castle, and many of the interesting elements can be found on the city's old central streets. The 15th-century **Igreja de Jesus** (Church of Jesus), for example, was built with local marble and is one of Portugal's earliest examples of Manueline-style architecture. Setúbal's sanctuary, which predates the Jerónimos Monastery at Belém, displays twisted, ropelike pillars that support the vault—the details of which would soon become the hallmark of Manueline style. The Church of Jesus's original monastic buildings and Gothic cloister now house a **municipal museum,** which contains a fascinating collection of 15th- and 16th-century Portuguese paintings, several by the so-called Master of Setúbal. Other museum attractions include some lovely azulejos, local archaeological finds, and a coin collection. *Praça Miguel Bombarda. Admission free. Open Tues.–Sun. 10–12:30 and 2–6.*

㉑ Across the river estuary from Setúbal is the **Península de Tróia,** a long spit of land running south and blessed with fine beaches and clean water. To answer the demands of tourists, the point has been much developed in recent years, evidenced by the large sports complex—**Tróia Tourist Complex**—which includes a golf course, tennis courts, and other amenities. The area has managed to retain a little of its history, though: The peninsula is the site of the Roman town of Cetobriga, which was destroyed by a tidal wave in the 5th century, and you can visit the scant ruins (opposite the marina). As with Caparica, the farther south you go, the thinner the crowds.

From Setúbal, drive west along the N10 and almost immediately you'll enter the **Serra de Arrábida,** a 5,000-foot-high mountain range whose wild crags fall steeply to the sea. There is profuse plant life at these heights, particularly in the spring, when the rocks are carpeted with wildflowers. The entire region is now a national park.

Ten kilometers (6 miles) from Setúbal is the **Quinta da Bacalhoa,** a late-16th-century L-shape mansion whose box-hedged gardens sport striking azulejo paths. You can't tour the villa (which is a private house), but the gardens are open to the public. The great water tank washes a pavilion with three pyramid-shape towers that houses the oldest azulejo panel in the country: It depicts the story of Susannah and the Elders and dates from 1565. *Admission free; tips expected. Gardens open Mon.–Sat. 1–5.*

Time Out Follow the road to the adjacent village of Vila Fresca de Azeitão, not far from the mansion, to find the 16th-century **Quinta das Torres** (tel. 065/208–0001), now an inn with a restaurant. The fine old building has been beautifully restored and features antique furniture and tapestries at every turn. Locally produced food served here is well prepared and moderately priced.

Two kilometers (1¼ miles) to the west of Vila Fresca de Azeitão is the town of **Vila Nogueira de Azeitão,** whose grandest building is the 16th-century **Tavora Palace,** once owned by the Duke of Aveiro. In the 18th-century the Marquês de Pombal accused the duke of collaborating in the assassination plot against the king, Dom José. Subsequently the duke was executed by the Marquês, and the Tavora coat of arms was erased from the Sala das Armas in Sintra's National Palace. Unfortunately, the palace is not open for visits.

On a more upbeat association, the village—home to the **José Maria da Fonseca Company,** one of the country's major wine exporters—is known for its winemaking. Visitors may tour the wine vaults of the Fonseca Company, and view all stages of the production process. There are two wineries: the New Winery, very near the Tavora Palace; and the Old Winery, right in the center of the village. Both are sign-posted. Among the vintages for sale is the dessert wine called Moscatel de Setúbal. *Open Mon.–Fri. 9–noon and 2–5. Admission free.*

Time Out On the first Sunday of every month, Vila Nogueira de Azeitão hosts an interesting **country market,** where you can buy the popular locally made *queijo fresco* (sheep's milk cheese). Enjoyed throughout Lisbon and its environs, this cheese is a good choice for a picnic lunch, and you can buy excellent fresh bread from one of the market's bakery stalls.

Continuing west from Azeitão, the N379 leads to Sesimbra *(see below)*. However, after about 2 kilometers (1¼ miles) the road forks, and you have the option to veer left toward the small fishing village of **Portinho da Arrábida.** The village is only about 8 kilometers (5 miles) farther and is sited at the foot of the **Serra de Arrábida** mountain range, a popular summer destination for Lisboans who appreciate the good local beaches. In summer, park above the port and walk down to the water, where you'll find several modest seafood restaurants that overlook the port. Although it's a steep walk, during peak season it's much better than trying to park closer to the water, when the number of visitors makes parking nearly impossible.

To return from Portinho da Arrábida you can take one of the two parallel roads leading west from the village toward Setúbal: The lower, coastal road hugs the shore nearly all the way; the upper road gives access to the ramshackle, white-walled **Convento de Arrábida,** an atmospheric 16th-century monastery built into the hills of the Serra de Arrábida. From here the views are glorious, but you'll have to contact the tourist office in Setúbal in advance to arrange for your visit to the monastery.

The N379 runs southeast to the junction at Santara, where you should turn left for the 3-kilometer (2-mile) drive south to **25 Sesimbra,** a lively fishing village to which many Lisboans retreat in the summer. The surrounding mountains and isolated bays and coves are only about 40 kilometers (24½ miles) south of the capital, a location that has contributed to the area's popularity. Despite high-rise apartments that now mar the town, Sesimbra has some central narrow streets that are still thoroughly agreeable. Perched on a hilltop, and northwest of town, an old castle with its five towers overlooks the port, which is guarded by a 17th-century fortress and littered with nets, coils of rope, and anchors. Packed with colorful fishing boats—which unload their catches at an entertaining daily fish auction—the port may be the best attraction in town.

26 Twelve kilometers (7 miles) to the west, the N379 ends at **Cabo Espichel,** a salt-encrusted headland on which 18th-century arcaded pilgrimage houses border a huge open space; at one end is a forsaken pilgrimage church. This is the southwestern point of the Setúbal Peninsula, a rugged and lonely place to end your tour. To the north unsullied beaches extend as far as Caparica, with only local roads and foot paths connecting them. Drivers heading north toward Lisbon should retrace their route to Santana and follow the N378, which joins the N10 after 18 kilometers (11 miles).

What to See and Do with Children

Take the narrow-gauge railway along Costa da Caparica (*see* Tour 4)
Pena Palace (*see* Tour 2)
Ferry ride to Cacilhas (*see* Tour 4)

Shopping

Throughout Lisbon's environs there are shopping opportunities galore, from ceramics sold in smart Cascais boutiques to weavings and leather goods featured at roadside stalls and weekly village markets. The quality and prices of the products vary greatly, so you may want to spend time "shopping around" before you actually purchase. Prices are fixed almost everywhere, although with a firm command of the Portuguese language you may be able to negotiate a small discount at some of the local markets and roadside stalls. However, bargaining is not practiced in stores or boutiques.

Cascais

Cascais, the best shopping area on the Estoril coast, has many pedestrianized streets lined with shops that are all within easy walking distance of each other. For smart fashions, gifts, and handmade jewelry, browse around **Rua Frederico Arouca.**

Markets are held north of town at Rua Mercado (off Avenida 25 de Abril) on Wednesday and Saturday and feature fruits, vegetables, cheeses, breads, and flowers. Also, on the first and third Sunday of each month, a market is held at the **Praça de Touros** (bullring) on Avenida Pedro Álvares, which is a larger affair with the same kind of goods.

For local crafts you may want to walk about 25 minutes from the center of town to the daily market at the entrance of **Boca do Inferno,** where specialty items such as lace and ceramics are sold.

Estoril

Each July and August Estoril hosts the **Feira do Artesanato,** an open-air handicrafts fair held close to the casino. Every evening, 5–midnight, stalls sell local arts and crafts and traditional Portuguese foods.

Setúbal Peninsula

There is limited shopping on the Setúbal Peninsula, but on the first Sunday of each month the **country market** in the center of Azeitão features fresh local produce.

Sintra

Sintra is a center for **antiques** and **curios,** with several of its streets dedicated to shops crowded with rare items, arts, and crafts. In nearby São Pedro de Sintra a **country fair** takes place on the second and fourth Sunday of every month and features produce, crafts, and antiques.

On the N9 road between Sintra and Mafra, the small town of Pero Pinheiro is known for its **marble,** evidenced by shops on both sides of the road that feature stacks of decorative objects.

Sports and Outdoor Activities

Participant Sports

Fishing **Sesimbra,** known as a deep-sea fishing center, is reknowned for the huge swordfish that are landed in the area. You may ask around for local people who rent boats, or more formally, both **Tip Tours** (Av. Costa Pinto 91A, Cascais, tel. 01/286–5150) and the **Clube Naval de Cascais** (Esp. Príncipe Luis Filipe, in front of Hotel Baia, tel. 01/280125), organize deep-sea fishing outings.

Golf The entire region boasts excellent golf courses, among them: **Clube de Golfe do Estoril** (Av. da República, Estoril, tel. 01/468–0176), which has an immaculate 18-hole championship course, with special rates and privileges for guests staying at the Hotel Palácio; **Quinta da Marinha** (4 kilometers/2½ miles west of Cascais, tel. 01/289881), with its new 18-hole course designed by Robert Trent Jones; and the **Tróia Golf Club** (Tróia, Setúbal, tel. 065/44151), presenting an 18-hole course in splendid countryside on the Rio Sado. On the Estoril-Sintra road the **Estoril Sol** (Logoa Azul, Linhó, tel. 01/293–2461) has a scenic nine-hole course.

Horseback Riding There's a particularly good equestrian center at the **Quinta da Marinha** (Cascais, tel. 01/289282), with year-round riding opportunities.

Swimming Most good hotels along the Estoril coast have indoor and outdoor swimming pools, and it's recommended that you use them rather than the sea, since the water on this stretch of the coast is polluted. The **Costa da Caparica** and the **southern side of the Setúbal Peninsula** have considerably cleaner waters and beaches.

Tennis Many of the hotels in the region have tennis courts. Some other options are: the **Clube de Tenis do Estoril** (Av. Amaral, Estoril, tel. 01/268–1675), **Oeiras Tennis Club** (Rua Miguel Bombarda, tel. 01/247–1010), the **Quinta da Marinha** (*see* Golf, *above*), and the sports complex on the **Tróia Peninsula,** which has 12 tennis courts.

Water Sports **Sailboarding** and **surfing** are popular sports along the Estoril coast. The beaches at Carcavelos and São Pedro do Estoril appeal to sailors and surfers, but the experts head for Guincho beach, one of the venues of the World Windsurfing Championships. Rental equipment is available from **Windsurfing Guincho** (Bairro da Assunção, Zona C, Lote 10, Loja P, 2750 Cascais, tel. 01/284–7180).

There are sailing clubs at Cascais, Sesimbra, and Setúbal, and local tourist offices can provide you with information on others. It's often possible to arrange a week-long sail with some of the clubs in the coastal towns. Check with your local sailing organization to see if it has reciprocity with any Portuguese marinas. The **Clube Naval de Cascais** (Esp. Príncipe Luís Filipe, tel. 01/280125) provides shelter for yachts in Cascais Bay.

Spectator Sports

Grand-Prix Racing The **Autódromo do Estoril** (Estoril Autodrome), on the Estoril–Sintra road, 5 kilometers (3 miles) north of Estoril, hosts Formula 1 car racing and can accommodate 40,000 spectators. The racetrack is also the start and finish point of the annual **Port Wine Rally,** an international car competition. Details about both events can be obtained from the Estoril tourist office.

Dining and Lodging

Dining   Interesting and sometimes unusual preparations of fresh fish and seafood are served in restaurants throughout Lisbon's environs. Although towns along the Estoril coast and the Setúbal Peninsula may receive the daily catch almost immediately after it's landed, most inland villages are close enough to the sea that you can be assured of quality and freshness in their restaurants, too. City dwellers make a point of crossing the Tejo to the suburb of Cacilhas to eat platefuls of *arroz de mariscos* (rice with seafood); *linguado* (sole) is especially popular, as are the mounds of shellfish displayed in restaurant windows.

As you travel through Portugal, you may find that different towns boast local specialties. In Sintra *queijadas* (sweet cheese tarts) are popular; in the Azeitão region of the Setúbal Peninsula, locals swear by the *quiejo fresco*, a delicious white sheep's-milk cheese. Lisbon's environs also produce good wines, many of which are offered as the house vintages in local restaurants. From Colares comes a light, smooth red wine, a fine accompaniment to a hearty lunch; Palmela, the demarcated wine-growing district of Setúbal, produces distinctive amber-colored wines of recognized quality; the Setúbal Peninsula is home to the famous José Maria da Fonseca winery and features a dessert vintage called Moscatel de Setúbal.

Dress in restaurants throughout the region is usually casual, especially in the coastal resorts, but any exceptions are noted below. Reservations are not necessary unless specified, although you should be prepared to wait in line at the more popular seafood restaurants.

Restaurant ratings correspond to Lisbon's dining chart, in Chapter 3. Highly recommended restaurants are indicated by a star ★.

Lodging   Many visitors are content to use Lisbon as a base from which to explore the city's environs. However, spending at least one night away from the capital, staying either at one of the popular resorts on the Estoril coast or Setúbal Peninsula, or at the rural retreat of Sintra may give you some perspective on the country. Regardless of where you stay, it's essential that in the summer you book a room in advance. If you do opt to spend a night or two in Lisbon's environs you'll have an opportunity to experience two types of accommodations not available in the capital itself: *pousadas* and members of the *Turismo de Habatição* scheme.

Pousadas, or state-run hotels, often are located in converted historic buildings, and they generally have superior facilities and restaurants. The two in this region are at Setúbal and Palmela: Both occupy ancient, hilltop castles and are well worth a stay. For more information contact **Enatur Pousadas de Portugal** (Av. Santa Joana Princesa 10, Lisbon, tel. 01/881221, fax 01/805846).

The second type of lodging in the region is the Turismo de Habitação system—old manor houses and country estates that offer rooms and sometimes meals. All lodgings listed with this association are located in rural areas and provide comfortable—if occasionally simple—accommodations. Some members of Turismo de Habitação are reviewed below, but since the homes typically have few rooms, availability is limited. For a full listing and more information, contact the **Promoções e Ideias Turísticas** (PIT: Alto da Pampilheira, Torre D2, 8A, 2750 Cascais, tel. 01/284–2901 or 01/284–4464). Tourist offices can also advise you about vacancies at local manor houses.

Hotel ratings correspond to Lisbon's lodging chart, in Chapter 3. Highly recommended hotels are indicated by a star ★.

Cascais
Dining

João Padeiro. Not only does this restaurant serve excellently prepared sole, but it's also reknowned for succulent lobsters accompanied by homemade mayonnaise. If you're a meat-eater, you'll find a few choices on the menu, too, with pork being the most reliable dish. The distinctive wood-and-leather-panel interior, although rather dim, is enlivened by cheery decorations. Service is brisk and assured, and the location—along the main road next to the tourist office—couldn't be more convenient for visitors who are unfamiliar with the town. *Rua Visconde da Luz 12, tel. 01/483–0232. Reservations recommended. AE, DC, MC, V. Closed Tues. Expensive.*

Beira Mar. One of several well-established and unpretentious restaurants situated behind the fish market, the Beira Mar has a comfortable interior decorated with blue-and-white azulejos. The menu includes a wide variety of fish and meat dishes, but seafood and shellfish are best picked from the usually impressive central display of the day's catch. *Rua das Flores 6, tel. 01/483–0152. AE, DC, MC, V. Closed Thurs. Moderate.*

O Pescador. Fish and shellfish, picked fresh from the market, are the reliable items served in this folksy restaurant, where a cluttered ceiling and maritime-related artifacts distract the eye. The sole is a house specialty, and this is also a good place to try bacalhau. *Rua das Flores 10, tel. 01/284–6037. AE, DC, MC. Moderate.*

Joshua's Shoarma Grill. This popular local spot specializes in tasty Middle Eastern food, including kebabs, pita bread, hummus dip, and the like. Joshua's is open daily until 2 AM, so it's a good place to know about when the late-night munchies strike. *Rua Visconde da Luz 19, tel. 01/284–3064. No credit cards. Inexpensive.*

Dining and Lodging

Hotel Albatroz. Situated on a rocky outcrop, this attractive old house—once an aristocrat's summer residence—is the most luxurious of Cascais's hotels. Though the Albatroz has been expanded and modernized, its genteel character has been retained, particularly in the charming bedrooms and the pleasant terrace bar. Most of the time this hotel is fully booked, so advance reservations are recommended, especially in summer. The hotel restaurant (also called the Albatroz), where fish dishes are the specialty, boasts superior views of the sea and the coast toward Lisbon. *Rua Frederico Arouca 100, 2750, tel. 01/282821, fax 01/284–4827. 40 rooms with bath. Facilities: restaurant, bar, pool, garage. AE, DC, MC, V. Very Expensive.*

★ **Estalgem do Farol.** Located just outside Cascais and adjacent to a lighthouse, this converted 19th-century Victorian mansion offers modern comforts and a peaceful secluded beach setting. The romantic Estalgem (meaning inn) is just a kilometer or so out of town on the coastal road to Guincho, so Cascais and its attractions are easily accessible. You may be tempted to spend some time at the lovely wood-panel piano bar before indulging in one of the freshly caught fish dinners served at the inn's excellent restaurant. *Av. Rei Humberto II Italia 7, 2750, tel. 01/*

483–0173 or 01/486–4732, fax 01/284–1447. 18 rooms with bath. Facilities: restaurant, bar, tearoom, saltwater pool, tennis court, parking. AE, DC, MC, V. Expensive.

Lodging **Hotel Baia.** This modern stone hotel fronted with white balconies overlooks fishing boats on the quayside and the glistening blue waters of Cascais Bay. Following renovations, the Baia presents an air of efficiency, and the comfortable rooms are well-appointed; try to secure one of the 66 that have sea views. There's a private esplanade along the ground floor, with a lounge, restaurant, grill, café, and bar. *Av. Marginal, 2750, tel. 01/483–1033 or 01/483–1034, fax 01/483–1095. 114 rooms with bath. Facilities: restaurant, grill, café, bar, roof terrace and pool. AE, DC, MC, V. Moderate.*

Estoril **A Choupana.** Situated just east of the town in adjacent São João
Dining do Estoril, this long-established restaurant with beach views offers quality fresh fish, seafood, and local dishes in comfortable, plant-filled surroundings. Live music accompanies dinner, and there's nightly dancing until 2. Parking is available. *Estrada Marginal, São João do Estoril, tel. 01/268–3099. Reservations advised. AE, DC, MC, V. Expensive.*

Furusato. This excellent new Japanese restaurant sits within a lovingly restored 19th-century house overlooking the central Praia do Tamariz and its promenade. Japanese cuisine is a rarity in Portugal, and Furusato serves a full range, including sushi, tempura, and teppanyaki dishes. *Praia do Tamariz, tel. 01/268–4430. AE, DC, MC, V. Expensive.*

The English Bar. Despite the British reference in the name and the mock-Tudor embellishments, this friendly establishment serves first-class Portuguese and international cuisine. Fish is always available, and the sole is a reliable choice; shellfish soup makes a fine starter. The hotel, situated near Monte Estoril's Hotel Atlantico, is only a few minutes' walk from the central beach and offers good views of Cascais. *Av. Sabola 9, off Av. Marginal, tel. 01/468–0413. Reservations advised. AE, DC, MC, V. Closed Sun. Moderate.*

Frolic. A bright, welcoming café-bar, set beside the Hotel Palácio, Frolic is worth considering for its delectable cakes and snacks. *Av. Clotilde, tel. 01/468–1219. AE, DC, MC, V. Closed Sun. Inexpensive.*

Dining and Lodging **Hotel Palácio.** During World War II exiled European courts
★ came to live in this luxurious 1930s hotel to await the end of the war. The hotel faces the town's central park and has pastel rooms decorated with Regency-style reproduction furniture and attractive and elegant public rooms. The Palácio boasts one of Portugal's most famous restaurants—the Four Seasons Grill—which serves buffets around the garden pool in summer and adjusts its menus seasonally, using the freshest ingredients in its quest for perfection. The hotel is a two-minute walk from the beach, and golfers can tee-up on the championship golf course. *Rua do Parque, Parque do Estoril, 2765, tel. 01/268–0400, fax 01/268–4867. 168 rooms with bath. Facilities: restaurant, bar, outdoor pool, tennis courts, golf, shops, parking. AE, DC, MC, V. Very Expensive.*

Lodging **Hotel Apartamento Estoril Eden.** The comfortable, tastefully decorated rooms in this modern apartment hotel are reasonably sized and come with kitchenettes, TVs, and VCRs, making the Eden a good bet for families. Superb views of the sweeping Estoril coast are an added attraction to the convenient Monte

Estoril beach location, a few minutes' walk to the ocean via an underpass. *Av. Sabóia 209, 2765, tel. 01/267–0573, fax 01/267–0848. 162 units with bath and kitchenette. Facilities: restaurant, bar, indoor and outdoor pools, sauna, gym, garden, parking. AE, DC, MC, V. Expensive.*

Estalgem Lennox Country Club. Set on a hillside a few minutes' walk from the casino, this small but attractive inn is a favorite with golfers: The rooms are named after famous golf courses, and there's free transportation to and from the greens. Accommodations are in either the original villa (which has a small pool) or in the new extension in the garden; complimentary tea and coffee are available to all guests. *Rua Eng. Alvaro Pinheiro de Sousa 5, 2765, tel. 01/268–0424, fax 01/267–0859. 32 rooms with bath. Facilities: terrace bar, pool, golf packages, parking. AE, DC, MC, V. Moderate.*

Hotel Lido. Set on a quiet street well away from the beach, the Lido is justly popular for its good-value rooms and amenities, which include a pool, garden, and decent restaurant. *Rua do Alentejo 12, 2765, tel. 01/268–4123, fax 01/268–3665. 62 rooms with bath. Facilities: restaurant, bar, pool, garage. AE, DC, MC, V. Moderate.*

Guincho
Dining and Lodging

Estalgem do Forte Muchaxo. The sound of the sea echoes through the dining room of this attractive, rustic restaurant nestled in the rocks over Guincho beach. Begun as a simple hut where fishermen could go for drinks and coffee, it's one of the area's oldest and best-known eating places. Today it features beautifully presented and consistently well-prepared fish specialties and Portuguese fare. The lovely location of this restaurant and inn may draw you here from Cascais (10 kilometers, 6 miles, away); there are rooms available for overnight guests and most have splendid ocean views, and there's also a pool and lounge room for relaxing. *Praia do Guincho, on the beach, 2750 Cascais, tel. 01/285–0221. 24 rooms with bath. Facilities: restaurant, pool. AE, DC, MC, V. Moderate.*

Monserrate
Lodging

Quinta da Capela. A member of *Turismo de Habitação*, this 16th-century manor home presents varied accommodations, from smart rooms with private bath in the main section to self-contained apartments with kitchenette. The latter sleep four and are suitable for families who can make use of kitchen facilities, since only breakfast is served here. There is also a lovely garden, an old chapel on the grounds, and a pool. The manor house is located just 3 kilometers (2 miles) west of Sintra, off the road to Colares. *Estrada de Monserrate, 2710 Sintra, tel. 01/929–0170. 6 rooms with bath, 2 apartments. Facilities: kitchen, garden, pool, gym, sauna, parking. MC. Closed Dec.–Feb. Moderate.*

Palmela
Dining and Lodging

Pousada de Palmela. Set 25 kilometers (about 15 miles) from Lisbon, on a hill at the end of the Arrábida range, this historic building was originally a fortress and later became a monastery. In 1979 the edifice was converted into a pousada, and the designers made use of the flagstone corridors and old cloister (now a lounge); most of the pleasant rooms provide superb views of the valley and the sea. The monks' former refectory is now a dependable restaurant, serving traditional Portuguese fare. *2950, tel. 01/235–1226, fax 01/235–0410. 27 rooms with bath. Facilities: restaurant, bar, garden, parking. AE, DC, MC, V. Expensive.*

Queluz
Dining

Restaurante de Cozinha Velha. Formerly the great kitchen of the adjoining Queluz Palace, this restaurant is magnificently dominated by an imposing open fireplace. Original cooking utensils hang from the walls, and guests dine at reproduction antique tables. There are some fine wines in the cellar that go well with the splendid, traditional Portuguese cooking; certain recipes have been inspired by popular 18th-century dishes. *Palácio Nacional de Queluz, tel. 01/435–0740. Reservations advised. AE, DC, MC, V. Expensive.*

Sesimbra
Lodging

Hotel do Mar. The fishing village of Sesimbra—west of Setúbal—is rapidly becoming a popular resort area, evidenced by new hotels such as this one. A low, stepped building tucked into the seaside cliffs, this property features reasonably sized modern rooms with balconies that overlook either the sea or the private garden and pool area. The plethora of public rooms and amenities enables guests to have a complete holiday within the confines of the hotel. *Rua General Humberto Delgado 10, 2970, tel. 01/223–3326, fax 01/223–3888. 120 rooms with bath. Facilities: restaurant, coffee shop, bar, garden, terrace, pool, tennis courts, children's playground, parking. AE, DC, MC, V. Moderate.*

Setúbal
Dining

Rio Azul. Locals frequent this popular seafood restaurant—hidden on a side street near the fishing harbor—for the fresh fish grilled to perfection and the *arroz de marisco* (seafood rice), a house specialty. *Rua Placido Stichini 1, tel. 065/522828. MC, V. Closed Wed. Moderate.*

Lodging

Pousada de São Filipe. Perched atop a hill where it overlooks the town and the Rio Sado, this 16th-century castle-turned-pousada makes an exciting overnight stop and is given excellent reviews by most visitors. Winter nights can be chilly, but the historic location, splendid views, and the hotel's unique features compensate considerably for any moments of discomfort. Rooms that are high up feel airy and open and provide expansive views; for a change from the usual hotel quarters, request one of the rooms in the old castle dungeons. Another relic is a lovely 18th-century chapel, decorated with azulejos depicting the life of São Filipe. *Castelo de São Filipe, 2900, tel. 065/523844. 14 rooms with bath. Facilities: restaurant, bar, parking. AE, DC, MC, V. Expensive.*

Quinta do Patricio. This manor house—a member of Turismo de Habitação—is situated close to the castle and provides a small-scale, pretty alternative to the grandness of the pousada. Furnishings throughout the property are homey, with bright-colored rugs and paintings, and from the garden you'll get some nice views of the town. Meals are available upon request; reservations made well in advance are essential. *Estrada de São Filipe, 2900, tel. 065/522088. 2 rooms and 1 self-contained apartment with bath. Facilities: bar, garden. No credit cards. Moderate.*

Sintra
Dining

Cantinho de São Pedro. Imaginative Portuguese cuisine with a French influence is presented at this busy restaurant in São Pedro de Sintra, an old village about a kilometer (about ½ mile) from Sintra. Locals consider the food well worth the wait for a table. *Prqca Dom Fernando II 18, São Pedro de Sintra, tel. 01/923–0267. AE, DC, MC. No dinner Thurs. Closed Mon. Expensive.*

Tacho Real. The high-quality international fare and helpful service make this restaurant a popular choice for locals. The changing menu features Portuguese specials. *Rua do Ferraria 4, tel. 01/923–5277. Reservations advised. AE, DC, MC, V. Closed Wed. Expensive.*

Café Paris. Well-placed in Sintra's central square for fine views of the National Palace, this café makes a pleasant stop for a drink, though outside seating can be difficult to score. If you're feeling hungry there's a full menu of Portuguese and international food, too. *Largo Rainha Dona Amelia, tel. 01/923–2375. MC, V. Moderate.*

Solar São Pedro. Highly recommended by habitués for its Portuguese and French-country cuisine, Solar also offers a good varied wine list, and fresh fish and grilled-steak specials. Avoid stopping here on the second and fourth Sunday of every month, since that's when the local country fair takes place and parking and tables are hard to come by. *Largo da Feira 12, São Pedro de Sintra, tel. 01/923–1860. Reservations advised. AE, DC, MC, V. Closed Wed. Moderate.*

Dining and Lodging **Hotel Palácio dos Seteais.** This luxurious 18th-century palace, ★ placed on pristine grounds, is just a kilometer or so (just over ½ mile) from the center of Sintra. The palace's name, Seteais—meaning "seven sighs"—supposedly tells of the relief felt by the Portuguese after the signing of the 1807 Treaty of Sintra with the French. Today the sighs are more likely to be of admiration for the conservation of such a beautiful building. You'll enter under a superb, classical arch that joins the palace's two wings: Its public rooms are gloriously decorated with period and reproduction furnishings, delicate frescoes, and Arraiolas carpets; the 18 guest rooms are individually styled, some with hand-painted wallpapers. (With so few rooms it's essential that you reserve in advance.) If you're not planning an overnight stay, at least have yourself pampered in the splendid restaurant, which serves a four-course set meal of impressively garnished Continental-style dishes. In summer, coffee or afternoon tea taken on the terrace is an added delight. *Rua Barbosa do Bocage 8, 2710, tel. 01/923–3200, fax 01/923–4277. 18 rooms with bath. Facilities: restaurant, bar, gardens, pool, parking. AE, DC, MC, V. Very Expensive.*

Lodging **Tivoli Sintra.** The ultramodern Tivoli (a member of the chain of hotels in Lisbon by the same name), positioned right in the middle of town, offers excellent views of the local valley and a welcoming restaurant, the Monserrate. Given the hotel's marvelous location, room rates are reasonable, especially in the winter, when they're reduced by at least 15%. Overall this is one of the region's best-value choices. *Praça da República 2710, tel. 01/923–3505, fax 01/923–1572. 75 rooms with bath Facilities: restaurant, bar, garage. AE, DC, MC, V. Moderate–Expensive.*

Hotel Central. Dating from the turn of the century and exuding a certain faded charm, the Central appeals despite its lack of facilities. Its location—in the same square as the Tivoli and opposite the National Palace—is prime (although rooms that face the square can be noisy), and the hotel's architecture allows the lodging to fit well with its surroundings. Amenities include a large terrace and a simple Portuguese restaurant. *Praça da República 35, 2710, tel. 01/923–0963. 14 rooms, 9 with bath. Facilities: restaurant, bar. Inexpensive.*

The Arts and Nightlife

With Lisbon so close by, many visitors choose to visit the capital's surroundings during the day and return to the city for its evening culture and entertainment. Nevertheless, the environs host several festivals worth experiencing, and Sintra, particularly, is known for events that compare favorably with similar ones held in Lisbon.

The Arts

Cascais The **Cascais music festival**, held every July and August, lures well-known orchestras and soloists to the town. Cascais also hosts an annual summer **jazz festival** in July.

There are **three cinemas** in Cascais that present first-release films in English: two in the Pão d'Açucar shopping center on Estrada Marginal near the train station and one on Rua 25 de Abril.

Estoril **Estoril Casino** (Parque do Estoril, tel. 01/268-4521) has regularly changing art exhibitions, a movie theater showing the latest films, and year-round theatrical and ballet performances. Call for details about performances and tickets, or ask at Estoril's tourist office (*see* Important Numbers and Addresses, *above*).

Queluz Every summer the **Noites de Queluz** (Queluz Nights) is held in the palace gardens. Characteristic of the 18th century, performances reflect the music and costumes popular when the palace was built. For more information, contact the Sintra Tourist Board (*see* Important Numbers and Address, *above*).

Setúbal Peninsula The **Feira de Santiago** takes place in Setúbal at the end of July and includes various folkloric events, a fair with rides and food stalls, and other entertainment.

In September Palmela sees the **Festa das Vindimas** (Grape Harvest Festival), with a symbolic treading of the grapes and a blessing of the harvest. Dancing, fireworks, wine tastings, and other celebrations accompany the festival.

Sintra The excellent **Sintra Festival** runs from June through September every year, and features piano recitals, operas, and ballet performances that take place in the town's palaces, churches, and parks. The **Sintra Tourist Board Cultural Department** (Praça da República, tel. 01/923–5079) can provide more details.

Besides its twice-monthly country fairs, the village of São Pedro de Sintra, hosts the large, annual **Festa de São Pedro** on June 29 (St. Peter's Day), with all of the riotous hulaballoo that the Portuguese inject into their religious festivities.

Nightlife

Not surprisingly, the resorts on the Estoril coast are responsible for most of the region's nightlife. Generally the towns have a plethora of bars, and most have at least one disco. (You may find, however, that the dance clubs are a bit tame compared to those in Lisbon's Bairro Alto.)

Cascais Cascais, a town that attracts a young crowd, is the best bet for a long night's entertainment, with plenty of bars and discos on and around the central, pedestrianized Rua Frederico Arouca that attract young people. For drinks, try the English-style pub, the **John Bull** (Largo Camões 4) and the trendy **Casa do Largo** (Largo da Assunção 6). For discos go to **Van Gogo** (Travessa de Alfarrobeia 9, tel. 01/283378), a converted fisherman's house that's open daily 11 PM–4 AM; or **Coconuts** (Estrada de Guincho, tel. 01/282861), with its outdoor bar, located just out of town near the Estalgem do Farol.

Estoril The **Casino** (Parque do Estoril, tel. 01/268–4521. Open 3 PM–3 AM) is the obvious place you'll find nightlife. Quite apart from the gaming tables and slot machines, there's a nightclub with floor shows, and a restaurant. Don't forget to take your passport if you intend to gamble. Tour companies organize evening excursions to the Casino, which include dinner and a show (*see* Guided Tours in Essential Information, *above*).

Nightlife elsewhere in Estoril is based around several well-known bars and clubs. Two to try are: **Frolic** (Parque do Estoril, tel. 01/268–1219), in front of the casino, which attracts an older, sophisticated clientele; and **Forte Velho** (Av. Marginal, in São João do Estoril, tel. 01/268–1337), an old fort on the edge of town that's been converted into a disco. Both are open 10 PM–3 AM.

5 Evora and Central Portugal

By Dennis Jaffe

As an American writer who has lived in Europe since 1975, Dennis Jaffe has become deeply involved in European travel. He and his wife, Tina, have written several books, including Biking Through Europe and the Camper's Companions to Northern and Southern Europe. He's also written extensively about Portugal, Turkey, Germany, and Switzerland.

The region we call central Portugal encompasses three provinces: the Alentejo, the Estremadura, and the Ribatejo, each with its own geography, traditions, and character.

The **Alentejo,** which means "the land beyond the Rio Tejo (River Tagus)," in Portuguese, is a vast, sparsely populated region of heath and rolling hills punctuated with stands of cork and olive trees. The undulating fields of wheat and barley surrounding Beja and Évora, the rice paddies of Alcácer do Sal, and the vineyards of Borba and Reguengos are representative of this rural province. Traditions here are strong. Herdsmen tending flocks of sheep and goats don the *pelico* (a traditional sheepskin vest), and women in the fields wear a broad-brim hat over a kerchief and a colorful, patterned dress over men's trousers. Dwellings are dazzling white; more elegant houses have wrought-iron balconies and grillwork. The windows and doors of modest cottages and hilltop country *montes* (farmhouses) are trimmed with blue or yellow, and colorful flowers abound.

The Alentejo is the country's largest province, stretching from the rugged west coast beaches all the way east to Spain and from the Tejo in the north to the low mountains separating the Alentejo from Portugal's southernmost province, the Algarve. Over the centuries this pastoral countryside has been the scene of innumerable battles: between Romans and Visigoths, Moors and Christians, Portuguese and Spaniards, Portuguese and French, and finally (in the 1830s) between rival Portuguese factions in a civil war. Few hilltops in the region are without at least a trace of a castle or fortress.

One of the Alentejo's major industries is cork, of which Portugal is the world's largest producer. This is not, however, an industry for people in a hurry. It takes two decades before the trees can be harvested, and they may be carefully stripped only once every nine years. The numbers painted on the trees indicate the year of the last harvest. Exhibits at several regional museums chronicle this delicate process and display associated tools and handicrafts.

The best time to visit the Alentejo is spring, when temperatures are pleasant and the fields are covered with a multicolored carpet of wildflowers. Summer can be brutal, with the mercury frequently topping 100°F. The Portuguese say, "In the Alentejo there is no shade but what comes from the sky."

The **Estremadura** occupies a narrow stretch of land along the coast, extending north from Lisbon to include the onetime royal residence of Leiria, 119 kilometers (73 miles) from the capital city. Closely tied to the sea, which at no point in the province is more than a few miles away, the region is known for its fine beaches, coastal pine forests, and picturesque fishing villages. Some of these—such as Nazeré—have evolved, for better or worse, into popular international resorts. Fruits and vegetables grow in fertile coastal valleys and livestock contentedly graze in rich pastures, but the Estremadura hasn't always been so peaceful. During the Wars of Reconquest, which raged from the 8th to the 13th centuries, it was the scene of a series of bloody encounters between Christians and Moors. In the aftermath of the wars Portuguese sovereignty was secured, with the rout of the Spanish at Aljubarrota, in 1385, and the turning back of Napoleon's forces in 1810, at Torres Vedras. The bloodshed left a positive legacy for today's traveler: Alcobaça and

Batalha, masterpieces of religious architecture, were built to commemorate Portuguese victories.

The **Ribatejo** developed along the Tejo, and it is this waterway, born in the distant mountains of Spain, that has shaped and sustained the province that carries its name. In the north the inhabitants tend small groves of olive and fig trees, and the peaceful, sparsely populated landscape has changed little since the Romans settled and cultivated the area.

Over the centuries Romans, Visigoths, Moors, and Christians built and rebuilt various castles and fortifications to protect the strategic Tejo. Some fine examples of these may be seen along the river at Belver, Abrantes, and Almourol. Tomar, spanning the banks of the Nabão (a tributary of the Tejo) is dominated by the hilltop Convent of Christ, an extraordinary example of medieval architecture, built in the 12th century by the Knights Templar. In the brush-covered hills at the western edge of the province lies Fátima, one of Christendom's most important pilgrimage sites. To the south, as it approaches Lisbon, the river expands, often overflowing its banks during the winter rains, and the landscape changes to one of rich meadows and pastures and broad, alluvial plains, where rice and other cereals grow in abundance.

The Ribatejans are said to be more reserved than their fellow Portuguese; that is, until they step into the arena to test their mettle against a ton or so of charging bull. The Ribatejo is bullfight country, the heartland of one of Portugal's richest and most colorful traditions. On the vast plains along the right bank of the Tejo, you'll encounter men on horseback carrying long wooden prods and often wearing the traditional waistcoats and stocking caps of their trade. These are *campinos*, the Portuguese "cowboys" who tend the herds of bulls and horses bred and trained for arenas throughout the country.

Essential Information

Important Addresses and Numbers

Tourist Information
The regional tourist office for Évora is the **Região de Turismo de Évora** (Praça do Sertario 8, tel. 066/28665.)

Estremadura
In the Estremadura the principal tourist offices are in **Alcobaça** (Praça 25 de Abril, tel. 062/42377), **Batalha** (Largo Paulo VI, tel. 044/96180), **Caldas da Rainha** (Praça da República, tel. 062/34511), **Ericeira** (Rua Eduardo Burnay 33, tel. 061/63122), **Leiria** (Jardim Lúis de Camões, tel. 044/32748), **Lourinhã** (Praia da Areia Branca, tel. 061/422167), **Mafra** (Av. 25 de Abril, tel. 061/812023), **Nazaré** (Av. Vieira Guimarães, tel. 062/561154), **Óbidos** (Praça de Santa Maria, tel. 062/959296), **Peniche** (Rua Alex. Herculano, tel. 062/79571), **Pombal** (Largo da Cardal, tel. 036/23230), **Torres Vedras** (Av. 5 de Outubro, tel. 061/23094), and **Vila Franca de Xira** (Rua Dr. Manuel de Arriagá 24, tel. 063/33219).

Lower Alentejo
In the Lower Alentejo there are tourist offices in **Beja** (Rua Capitão João de Sousa 25, tel. 084/23693), **Moura** (Largo Santa Clara, tel. 085/22301), **Odemira** (Trav. do Botequim 6, tel. 083/22247), **Serpa** (Largo D. Jorge de Melo 2–3, tel. 084/90335), and **Sines** (Largo do Mercado Municipal, tel. 069/634472).

Ribatejo
In the Ribatejo you will find tourist offices in **Abrantes** (Câmara Municipal, tel. 041/22555), **Constância** (Câmera Municipal, tel. 049/99205), **Fátima** (Av. D. Correia da Silva, tel. 049/531139), **Santerém** (Rua Capelo e Ivens 63, tel. 043/23140), **Tomar** (Rua Serpa Pinto 1, tel. 049/313013), and **Torres Novas** (Largo do Paço, tel. 049/24910).

Upper Alentejo
For the Upper Alentejo the regional office is the **Região de Turismo de São Mamede** (Estrada de Santana 25, 7300 Portalegre, tel. 045/21815). There are local offices in **Alcácer do Sal** (Solar dos Salemas, tel. 065/62603), **Alter do Chão** (Câmara Municipal, tel. 045/62454), **Arronches** (Câmera Municipal, tel. 045/52210), **Campo Maior** (Rua Mayor Talaya, tel. 068/686104), **Castelo de Vide** (Rua Bartolomeu A. da Santa 81/3, tel. 045/91316), **Elvas** (Praça da República, tel. 068/622236), **Évora** (Praça do Giraldo 73, tel. 066/22671), **Marvão** (Rua Dr. Matos Magalhães, tel. 045/93226), **Monforte** (Praça da República, tel. 045/53115), and **Portalegre** (Rua de Elvas, tel. 045/21815).

Emergencies
For emergencies in central Portugal, as well as throughout the country, dial 115.

Hospitals
The following cities have hospitals with emergency rooms, and their approaches are signed HOSPITAL; the emergency room is signed URGÊNCIAS. Beja (Hospital Distrital, Rua Dr. António F C Lima, tel. 084/22133), Caldas da Rainha (Hospital Distrital, Parque Rainha Dona Leonor, tel. 062/832133), Évora (Hospital Distrital, Largo Sr. Pobreza, tel. 066/22132), Leiria (Hospital Distrital, Largo D. Mel. Aguiar, tel. 044/32133), Tomar (Hospital Distrital, Av. Dr. Candido Madueira, tel. 049/313074).

Late-Night Pharmacies
All sizable towns have at least one pharmacy open weekends, holidays, and after normal store hours. Local newspapers usually keep a schedule, and notices are posted on the door of every pharmacy.

Travel Agencies
Many of the travel agencies in the region are small and offer limited services, and often the personnel does not speak English. The following agencies have English-speaking staff and provide a full range of services. In Évora, **RN Tours** (Rua República 131, tel. 066/24254); in Leiria, **Viajes Melia** (Av. Cidade Maringá 25, tel. 044/32286).

Arriving and Departing by Plane

The Estremadura and Ribatejo are best served by Lisbon's international airport. Évora and the Alentejo can be conveniently reached either from Lisbon or Faro. Évora is 160 kilometers (100 miles) from Lisbon and 245 kilometers (147 miles) from Faro.

Airports and Airlines
For flight information concerning Lisbon, *see* Chapter 3. **TAP Air Portugal** offers several flights daily between Lisbon and Faro, in the Algarve (*see* Chapter 6), from which the Alentejo can be reached.

Arriving and Departing by Car, Train, and Bus

By Car
The Estremadura and the Ribatejo can be reached easily from Lisbon, since both provinces begin as extensions of the city's northern suburbs. From Oporto there is easy access via the A1 tollway.

Three main roads connect the Alentejo with Spain: The N521 runs 105 kilometers (64 miles) from Caceres, Spain, to the Portuguese border near Portalegre; the N4 covers the 15 kilometers (9 miles) between Elvas and the Spanish city of Badajoz; and to the south the N433 runs from Seville, Spain, to Beja, 225 kilometers (136 miles) away. The Alentejo can also be easily reached from the Algarve, its southern neighbor. The smoothest of the main routes is the IP-1, which extends north from Albufeira.

By Train The train station for Marvão is located in the town of Beira 10 kilometers (6 miles) away and is served by the *Lusitania Express* and the *Lúis de Camões* which run daily between Lisbon (Santa Apolonia Station) and Madrid. The *Lúis de Camões* leaves Lisbon's Santa Apolonia Station at 12:15 PM and arrives at Madrid's Atocha Station at 9:12 PM; it arrives at Chamartin Station at 9:22 PM. The *Lusitania Express* departs Lisbon at 9:25 PM and arrives in Madrid's Chamartin Station at 8:55 the following morning. First-class seats cost 8,875$00. Second-class seats cost 5,140$00. Youth (under 26) seats cost 5,140$00. The *Sud Express*, linking Paris with Lisbon (Santa Apolonia Station)—via the Spanish cities of Burgos and Salamanca—stops at Pombal and Fátima. It leaves Lisbon's Santa Apolonia Station daily 2:45 PM and arrives at Paris's Austerlitz Station at 7 PM the following day. First-class costs 26,900$00; second-class costs 17,800$00. Youth 26 and younger pay 16,410$00. Sleepers (couchette) are 2,075$00 extra. Although the schedule reads "Fátima," the actual station is some 25 kilometers (15 miles) away, but a bus—on a coordinated schedule—runs between the town and the station.

Within the country the Alentejo towns of Alcácer do Sal, Évora, and Beja are connected with Lisbon (Terreiro do Paço) by several trains daily.

There is frequent service on the Lisbon– (Santa Apolonia Station) Oporto line to Santerém and Pombal. Torres Vedras, Caldas da Rainha, and Leiria, in the western part of the region, are served from Lisbon's Rossio Station.

By Bus There is regular bus service on **Euroline** that runs between Lisbon and Spain's Costa del Sol, Seville, Madrid, and Barcelona. Euroline coaches also stop in the Alentejo towns of Elvas and Estremoz. Euroline buses from France and northern Europe stop in Pombal, Leiria, Abrantes, and Santerém. For information and reservations in Lisbon contact: **Intercentro Eurolines** (Rua Actor Taborda 55, tel. 01/547300).

Getting Around

By Car A car is by far the most efficient way to tour this region, especially in the Alentejo, where distances between points are long and bus or train service is infrequent. Driving will give you access to many out-of-the-way beaches and villages. The roads are generally good and traffic, with the exception of weekend congestion along the coast, is light. There are no confusing big cities in which to get lost, although parking can be a major problem in some of the towns. The best map for motorists, both in scale and ease of reading, is the Michelin map #437, Portugal–Madeira, available at bookshops throughout Portugal; in the United States go to any major bookshop or contact **Michelin**

Travel Publications (1 Parkway S, Greenville, SC 29615, tel. 803/458–6330).

Car Rental Major car-rental agencies are located in Évora, Beja, Leiria and Nazaré.

By Train Travel by train within central Portugal, and particularly in the vast Alentejo, is not for people in a great hurry. Service to many of the more remote destinations is infrequent—and in some cases nonexistent. Even major tourist attractions such as Fátima, Nazaré, and Mafra have no direct rail links.

By Bus There are few, if any, places in this region that are not served by at least one bus daily. Express coaches run by the national bus line, RN (Rodoviária Nacional) travel regularly between Lisbon and the larger towns such as Évora, Santerém, Leiria, and Abrantes. If you have the time and patience, bus travel, which offers an opportunity to come in close contact with locals, can be a rewarding and inexpensive way of getting around. The main bus terminal in Lisbon is located on Avenida Casal Ribeira 18. For schedules call tel. 01/545439.

Guided Tours

General-Interest Walking tours of Évora and bus tours of the Alentejo are available from **Mendes and Murteira** (Rua Corredoura 8, 7000 Évora, tel. 066/23616).

Few regularly scheduled sightseeing tours originate within the region; however, Évora, Nazaré, Óbidos, Tomar, Mafra, and the other major attractions are covered by a wide selection of one-day tours from Lisbon. For information contact **RN Tours** (Av. Fontes Pereira de Melo 12–14, tel. 01/577523) or **Cityrama** (Av. Praia da Vitoria 12–B, tel. 01/530425).

Special-Interest Boat trips on the São Cristovão, along the Rio Zêzere, depart daily in summer from the dam at Castelo de Bode and include lunch. The 4½-hour cruise costs 4,000$00. For reservations and information in Tomar, contact Hotel dos Templários (Largo Candido dos Reis 1, 2300 Tomar, tel. 049/312121) or the Estalagem Lago Azul (Estrada Nacional 378, Castanheira, 2240 Ferreira do Zêzere).

Frescuras (Estrada da Luz 197, 1600 Lisbon, tel. 01/726–2183) offers four-wheel drive tours of the backroads and remote villages of the Alentejo, the west coast beaches and the marshlands, and the bull-breeding areas of the Ribatejo. Hot-air balloon flights and four-wheel drives through the Alentejo are offered by **Turibalão Lda.** (Rua Miguel Bombarda 44 r/c, 7000 Évora, tel. 066/26323). **Cavalgada** (Apartado 68, 7050 Montemar O Novo, tel. 066/82230) sponsors half-, full-, and two-day horseback riding trips. **Promocões e Ideaias Turisticas** (PIT: Alto da Pampilheira, Torre D–2, 2750 Cascais, tel. 01/486–9958, fax 01/284–2901) will arrange custom tours with overnight accommodations in historic manor houses.

Exploring Evora and Central Portugal

Orientation

For convenience the following tours are designed so that each falls easily within the confines of one of the three provinces, the Alentejo, the Estremadura, or the Ribatejo. However, these itineraries are not carved in stone: At times you may be tempted to cross from one tour to another or to link up with tours in another chapter. By all means do so!

Our first tour explores the rich architectural treasures of Évora, the capital of the Alentejo. We then head north across the rolling hills and past the fortresses of Estremoz and Elvas to the Alentejo's only mountain range, the Serra de São Mamede, which lies along the Spanish border.

The lower Alentejo—which includes the rice paddies and salt marshes around Alcácer do Sal and the rugged west coast beaches—is the subject of our third tour. The last two circuits, through the Estremadura and Ribatejo, suggest visits to some of Portugal's most outstanding monuments and architectural treasures including Mafra, Alcobaça, Óbidos, Tomar, and Batalha. Featured in the latter tour are such diverse places as the bull-fighting centers of Vila Franca de Xira and Santerém, the shrine at Fátima, and the fishing port of Nazeré.

Highlights for First-Time Visitors

Castle of Almourol (*see* Tour 6)
Cathedral of Évora (*see* Tour 1)
Convent of Christ in Tomar (*see* Tour 6)
Convent of the Conception in Beja (*see* Tour 4)
Fortified town of Marvão (*see* Tour 3)
Fortified town of Monsaraz (*see* Tour 3)
Monastery at Alcobaça (*see* Tour 5)
Monastery at Batalha (*see* Tour 5)
Monastery at Mafra (*see* Tour 5)

Tour 1: Évora

Numbers in the margin correspond to points of interest on the Central Portugal and Évora maps.

Shepherds and farmers in traditional garb, with wizened faces bearing markings of a lifetime in the baking Alentejo sun, stand about Giraldo square; a group of pretty young college girls dressed in jeans and T-shirts chat animatedly at a sidewalk café; a local businessman in coat and tie purposefully hurries by; and clusters of tourists, the ubiquitous cameras in hand, capture the historic monuments on film. This is all part of **①** a typical summer's day in downtown **Évora**, the flourishing capital of the rich agricultural Alentejo province, a university center, and one of the world's great architectural treasures, which was officially classified as such in 1986 by UNESCO.

Located atop a small hill in the heart of Portugal's foremost cork-, olive-, and grain-producing region, Évora—with its as-

tonishing variety of inspiring architecture—stands out from practically any other provincial farm town of its size in the world. The entire inner city is itself a monument.

Although the region was inhabited some 4,000 years ago—as attested to by the dolmens and phallic menhirs in the countryside surrounding Évora—it was during the Roman epoch that the town once known as "Liberalitas Julia" first achieved importance as one of the major settlements in the Roman province of Lusitania. A large part of present-day Évora is built upon Roman foundations. The Temple of Diana with its graceful Corinthian columns, is the most conspicuous reminder of the town's Roman heritage.

The Moors were another group that made a great historical impact on the area. They arrived in 715 and remained more than 450 years before they were driven out in 1166, thanks in part to a clever ruse perpetrated by the Portuguese counterpart to El Cid, Geraldo Sem Pavor (Gerald the Fearless). Geraldo was able to trick Évora's Moorish ruler into leaving unguarded a strategic watchtower that protected one of the entrances to the town. With the small force, Geraldo took control of the tower, which prompted the main body of Moorish troops to leave its post at the principal entrance to the city, in an attempt to regain control of the watchtower. With the main entrance now undefended, the bulk of Geraldo's forces was able to storm the city unopposed.

Toward the end of the 12th century, Évora's fortunes increased, as the town became the favored locale for the courts of the Burgundy and Avis dynasties; situated less than 164 kilometers (100 miles) from Lisbon, it attracted many of the great minds and creative talents of Renaissance Portugal. Gil Vicente, the founder of Portuguese theater; the sculptor Nicolas Chanterene; and Gregorio Lopes, the painter known for his renderings of court life, were some of the more prominent residents of the time. This concentration of royal wealth and Renaissance creativity superimposed upon the existing Moorish town was instrumental in the development of the delicate Manueline-Mudejar style. You can see fine examples of this in the graceful lines of the Palace of Dom Manuel and the multiturreted São Bras Hermitage.

Évora is, above all, a town for walking. Wherever you glance as you stroll the maze of narrow streets and alleys of the old town, amidst arches and whitewashed houses, you'll come face to face with reminders of the town's rich architectural and cultural heritage.

❷ Begin your walking tour in the **Praça do Giraldo,** the bustling, arcade-lined square in the center of the old town named after the city's liberator, Gerald the Fearless. During Caesar's time the square, marked by a large arch, was the Roman forum; in 1571 the arch was destroyed to make room for the fountain across from the entrance to the church. The graceful, flattened sphere made of white Estremoz marble was designed and executed by the Renaissance architect Afonso Alvares.

❸ Note the striking white Renaissance facade of the **Igreja de St. Antão,** which stands at the top of the square. A medieval hermitage of the Templar Knights was razed in 1553 to make way for the present church, which, with its massive round pil

Évora

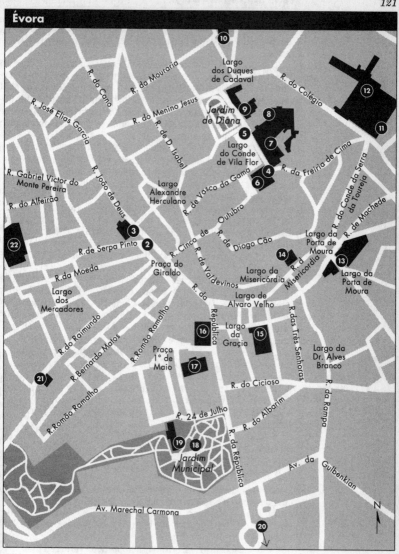

Largo dos Duques de Cadaval

R. do Colégio

R. da Mouraria

R. do Cano

R. José Elias Garcia

R. do Menino Jesus

Jardim de Diana

R. de D. Isabel

R. da Freiria de Cima

R. Gabriel Victor do Monte Pereira

R. João de Deus

Largo do Conde de Vila Flor

R. de Vasco da Gama

R. do Alfeirão

Largo Alexandre Herculano

R. Cinco de Outubro

R. do Conde da Serra da Tourela

R. de Machede

R. de Diogo Cão

Largo da Porta de Moura

R. de Serpa Pinto

R. de Valdevinos

R. d Misericórdia

Praça do Giraldo

Largo da Misericórdia

Largo da Porta de Moura

R. da Moeda

Largo de Alvaro Velho

Largo dos Mercadores

R. do Raimundo

R. da República

R. das Três Senhoras

Largo da Graça

Largo da Dr. Alves Branco

R. Romão Ramalho

R. Bernardo Matos

Praça 1° de Maio

R. do Cicioso

R. da Rampa

R. Romão Ramalho

R. 24 de Julho

R. do Albarim

R. da República

Jardim Municipal

Av. da Gulbenkian

Av. Marechal Carmona

N

lars and soaring vaulted ceilings, is the finest example of the German style *Hallenkirche* to be found in the Alentejo. The marble altar in bas-relief is a holdover from the primitive hermitage.

Time Out   The **Café Arcadia,** opposite the fountain on the Praça do Giraldo, is an Évora institution. The large hall, divided into snack bar and restaurant sections, is decorated with photos of the big bands that played here in the 40s. Outside tables set on the square are just the place from which to watch Évora on parade.

From the square head up the narrow, cobblestoned Rua 5 de Outubro. This pedestrianized thoroughfare lined with shops, hanging lanterns, and whitewashed houses with wrought-iron balconies is one of the town's most attractive streets. The massive twin towers and the battlement ringed walls give the **Sé** (cathedral) a fortresslike appearance, a type of construction also seen in the Lisbon and Coimbra cathedrals. The cathedral, one of Portugal's most striking architectural achievements, is a transitional Gothic-style building constructed in 1186 from huge granite blocks. It has been enhanced over the centuries with an octagonal, turreted dome above the transept, a blue tiled spire atop the north tower, a number of fine Manueline windows, and several Gothic rose windows. At the entrance the Gothic arches are supported by marble columns bearing delicately sculpted 14th-century statues of the Apostles. With the exception of a fine baroque chapel, the granite interior is somber. The cloisters, a 14th-century Gothic addition with Mudejar vestiges, is one of the finest of its genre in the country. Statues of the Evangelists decorate the four corners. Housed in the towers and chapter room are the Treasury and Museum of Sacred Art. Of particular interest is a 13th-century triptych, a set of three panels or compartments set side by side that bear scenes carved in ivory. What is unique about this piece, however, is that it displays a wood head that was added in the 16th century and is strangely out of proportion. *Admission to museum: 150$00. Open Tues.–Sun. 9–noon and 2–5. Closed Mon. and holidays.*

Leave the cathedral, and turn right. After a few steps the view opens onto a large plaza dominated by the well-preserved ruins of the **Templo Romano,** or Roman temple. The edifice, considered one of the finest of its kind on the Iberian peninsula, makes use of the Corinthian style, and was built during the second and third centuries. Although it has been referred to as the Temple of Diana, historians are uncertain as to which of the many Roman deities it was actually dedicated. The temple, largely destroyed during the invasions of the barbarian tribes in the early 5th century, has been used at various times as a fortification and, in the 14th century as a municipal slaughter house for animals. It was uncovered and restored to its present state just over 100 years ago.

The stately late-17th-century baroque building across from the temple was once a palace that accommodated bishops but is now home to the **Museu Regional de Évora** (Museum of Évora). It contains a rich collection of sculpture and paintings as well as a number of interesting archaeological and architectural artifacts. The first-floor galleries arranged around a pleasant garden include several excellent carved pillars and a fine

Manueline doorway. Among the early Portuguese paintings on display in the upstairs gallery are works attributed to the 16th-century Mestre of Sardoal. *Largo do Conde de Vila Flor, no tel. Admission: 150$00. Open Tues.–Sun. 10–12:30 and 2–5. Closed Mon. and holidays.*

To the right of the museum, in the former town hall, is the ❼ **Biblioteca Pública** (Municipal Library), with an outstanding collection of rare books and manuscripts. *Open Mon.–Sat. 9–1 and 2–6.*

Around the corner from the library and adjacent to the Pousada ❽ dos Lóios (*see* Dining and Lodging, *below*) is the **Igreja e Convento dos Lóios** (Church and Convent of Lóios). To enter the church go down several steps and through a portal framed by a series of fan-shaped arches in the flamboyant Gothic style. The sanctuary, dedicated to St. John the Evangelist, was founded in the 15th century by the Venetian-based Lóios Order. Its interior walls are covered with 18th-century heroic *azulejo* (traditional Portuguese tiles of Arabic origin) panels created by Oliveira Bernardes, the foremost master of this unique Portuguese art form. The blue-and-white tiles depict scenes from the life of the church's founder, Rodrigo de Melo, who, along with members of his family, is buried here. The bas-relief marble tombstones at the foot of the high altar are the only ones of their kind in Portugal. Note the two metal hatches on either side of the main aisle: One covers an ancient cistern, which belonged to the Moorish castle that predated the church (an undeground spring still supplies the cistern with potable water), and beneath the other hatch lie the neatly stacked bones of hundreds of monks that have been collected over the centuries. This bizarre ossuary was uncovered in 1958 during restoration work. Enhanced by the 16th-century Renaissance gallery, the cloister is now an integral part of the Pousada dos Lóios. *Largo Conde de Vila Flor. Admission: 250$00. Open Tues.–Sun. 10–12:30 and 2–5. Closed Mon. and holidays.*

As you leave the church, just to your right will be two stone towers with pointed battlements. A part of a medieval castle that once protected the town, these towers were incorporated ❾ into the **Palacío dos Duques do Cadaval** (Palace of the Dukes of Cadaval), a former residence of Kings João I and João IV. A small ground-floor gallery contains historical documents, paintings, and the unusual Flemish-style bronze tomb of Rui de Sousa, a signatory of the Treaty of Tordesilhas. In 1494 the treaty divided the world into two spheres of influence: Spanish and Portuguese. Today the palace is being used by the city road department. *Admission, opening times, and ticket for the gallery are the same as those for the Lóios Church.*

Opposite the Roman temple a restful, tree-lined park looks out over an aqueduct and the plains. From this park—in one sweeping glance that takes in the temple, the spires of the Gothic cathedral, the Church of Lóios, and the 20th-century pousada housed in the convent—you can span nearly two thousand years of Portuguese history.

Time Out | A snack bar at the corner of the park that overlooks the temple is a great spot to sit and reflect upon the architectural marvels spread out before you.

Once you're refreshed and suitably inspired, go down the hill past the palace, turn right, at the bottom, and continue along the Rua Dukes de Cadaval. The small church to your left is the **Igreja de São Mamede** (Church of St. Mamede), which contains a vaulted ceiling decorated with baroque frescoes. Note the fine azulejos that cover the wall of the nave. On the east wall is a marble bust of the Renaissance humanist Andre de Resendeby, created by João Cuteliero, a well-known contemporary Portuguese sculptor.

From the church follow the Rua de Colégio until it converges on the square called the Largo de Colégio. Along the way, to your right, you'll have a good view of the ancient town walls, and in some places, vestiges of the Roman foundations are visible. At the square is the 16th-century **Igreja de Espirito Santo** (Espirito Santo Church), a squat structure with five arches in front that was originally a part of the ancient Évora University. The interior contains some fine azulejos and paintings, including artist Gregorio Lopes's rendition of *The Last Supper*.

Take a left turn after you leave the church to get to one of several campuses of **Universidad de Évora.** From 1555 until its closure by the Marquis of Pombal in 1759, this was a Jesuit college; in 1979, after a lapse of more than 200 years, Évora University resumed classes. Athough the enrollment is small, the college's presence has given new life and vigor to this ancient city. The large courtyard is flanked on all sides by a series of graceful buildings with double-tier, white-limestone arched galleries in Italian Renaissance style. From the main entrance you'll see the imposing Baroque facade of the gallery, known as the **Sala dos Actos** (Hall of Acts), which is crowned with allegorical figures and coats of arms carved in white marble quarried in the region. Lining the gallery's interior are azulejos that represent historical, mythological, and biblical themes.

From the university return to the Largo do Colégio, then take a downhill stroll on Rua Conde de Serra da Torrega. This is a lovely part of town with whitewashed houses and wrought-iron grillwork. At the **Largo de Portos de Moura**—perhaps Évora's most beautiful square—paired stone towers guard one of the principal entrances to the walled old town. Spires of the cathedral rise above the towers, and in the center of the square is an unusual Renaissance fountain. The large white marble sphere supported by a single column bears a Latin inscription dated 1556; overlooking the fountain is the **Cordovil Mansion** (closed to public), on whose terrace are several particularly attractive arches decorated in the Manueline-Mudejar style.

Return to the post office near the square, via Rua da Misericórdia. The small church at the end of the road, along Largo da Porta de Moura, is the 16th-century **Igreja de Misericordia** (Misericordia Church). Go inside to see the large azulejo panels depicting scenes from the life of Christ; the unsigned 18th-century tiles are thought to be the work of António de Oliveira de Bernardes, one of Portugal's foremost tile-makers.

Follow the Rua da Misericórdia into the Largo de Alvaro Velho, an inviting square lined with metalsmith shops. Just past the Hotel Planice turn down the Travessa Manuelinho. The **Igreja a Nossa Senhora da Graça** (Church of Our Lady of Grace) is a splendid piece of classical Italian-style architecture. Note the impish figures perched above the portal: According to local legend, these four figures represent the first victims burned to death in the Inquisition in Évora in 1543.

16 Cross the Largo da Graça, and continue to the Rua da República. On your left is the **Museu do Artesanato** (Crafts Museum), whose exhibits include a comprehensive collection of handicrafts from the Alentejo. *Rua da República. Admission: 200$00. Open Tues.–Sun. 10–12:30 and 2–5. Closed Mon. and holidays.*

17 The imposing building across from the museum is the **Igreja de São Francisco** (Church of St. Francis). After the cathedral this is the grandest of Évora's religious structures. Its construction in the early 16th century, on the site of a former Gothic chapel, involved the greatest talents of the day; these included Nicolas Chanterene, Oliver of Gehnt, and the Arruda brothers, Francisco and Diogo. The magnificent religious architecture notwithstanding, the bizarre **Casa dos Ossos** (House of the Bones) is the main attraction. The translation of the chilling inscription over the entrance reads: "We bones who are here are waiting for yours." The bones of some 5,000 skeletons dug up from cemeteries in the area line the ceilings and supporting columns. With a decorative flair that would do Charles Adams justice, a 16th-century Franciscan monk placed skulls jaw-to-cranium, so they formed arches across the ceiling; and arm and leg bones are neatly stacked to shape the supporting columns. *Admission to the Bones Chapel: 25$00. Open Mon.–Sat. 8:30–1 and 2:30–6; Sun. 10–11:30 and 2:30–6.*

As you walk out of the church across the tiered portico and onto the Praça 1 de Maio, you'll see a large sprawling building, the **municipal market,** across the square. Wander around the stalls crammed with fresh fruits and vegetables and fish and meat to get a good idea of what the Alentejo produces and consumes. Mornings, except for Sunday, the pavement in front of the market overflows with displays of colorful pottery.

18 The **Jardim Municipal** (Municipal Gardens), across from the church, offer a pleasant respite from the rigors of sightseeing. The extensive gardens are planted with a variety of exotic plants and trees from all over the world. At the entrance is the **19** **Palácio de Dom Manuel** (Dom Manuel Palace). Only a part of the former royal palace—restored after a fire in 1916—remains. The existing wing displays a row of paired, gracefully curved Manueline windows. On the south side of the building note the arcade of red brick Mudejar sawtooth arches. Currently used as an art gallery, the palace has witnessed a number of historical events since its construction in the late 15th century. It was here, for instance , in 1497, that Vasco da Gama received his commission to command the fleet that discovered the sea route to India.

Time Out In the Municipal Gardens is a snack bar where you can get sandwiches and drinks. From a park bench or the Victorian gazebo, you'll have a lovely view of the Church of St. Francis.

From the palace you may head south on the Avenida Dr. Barahona to the **St. Blaise Chapel** (a 15-minute walk), or go on to the Museum of Decorative Arts.

20 The **Ermida de São Bras** (St. Blaise Chapel), a curious structure built in the late 15th century, was the first important building in the Alentejo to join Gothic and Moorish elements to form the Gothic-Mudejar style. The fortified church is characterized by massive battlement-topped walls and a series of round towers crowned with steep spires.

To continue the tour walk through the Municipal Gardens following the line of the ancient fortifications. At the Rua do Raimundo turn right, and continue for several minutes until you see a small church sandwiched between a garage and a car dealership. The church, the **Igreja das Mercês**, is now the **Museu de Artes Decorativas** (Museum of Decorative Arts). Inside the late 17th-century building are several good examples of azulejos with scenes from the life of St. Augustine, the patron saint of the founding order of this church. There are also two unusual confessionals concealed behind tile panels. *Rua do Raimundo. Admission: 50$00. Open Tues.–Sun. 10–12:30 and 2–5. Closed Mon. and holidays.*

From the museum cross the street, turn left, and then right onto the Travessa da Palmeira, a narrow alleyway bordering the old Quinta da Palmeira. Stay on this until it runs into the Rua de Serpa Pinto, then turn right on this busy thoroughfare and you'll come to the baroque facade of the **Igreja de Santa Clara** (Santa Clara Church). The interior is adorned with paintings, including a fine rendition on wood of the Procession of Santa Clara by the 16th-century Évora painter Francisco João. Now return to the Praça do Giraldo, along the Rua de Serpa Pinto, or wander along one of the narrow passageways that leads through the old town.

Tour 2: Évora Environs

From within Évora you may view the aqueduct by walking along the Rua do Cano. This can be picked up by taking the Rua do Muro for about 200 yards from the entrance of the Arraiolos road (N114–4) into the town. Best seen in the northwest corner of Évora and along the road to Arraiolos is **Aqueduto da Agua da Prata** (Aqueduct of the Silver Water), a graceful, arched structure that once carried water to Évora from the springs at Graça do Divor, some 18 kilometers (11 miles) away. Constructed in 1532 under the patronage of Dom João III, the aqueduct was designed by the famous architect Francisco de Arruda. Extensive parts of the system remain intact and can be seen.

A trip through the countryside surrounding Évora will take you to some of the earliest inhabited sites in Portugal, including the **Cromlech** and the **Menhir of Almendres.** Follow N114 toward Montemar-O-Novo, and after 14 kilometers (8½ miles) turn off to Guadalupe, the site of a 17th-century chapel. In Guadalupe, near the grain-storage bins of the Agricultural Cooperative, is the Menhir of Almendres, a massive eight-foot-tall neolithic stone obelisk. Several hundred yards in the same direction is the Cromlech, some 95 granite monoliths arranged in an oval configuration in the middle of a large field. From the N380—the road to Alcaçovas—take the turnoff to Valverde and the 20-foot-high **Dolmen of Zambujeiro,** the largest of its kind ever discovered on the Iberian peninsula. This prehistoric monument is typical of those found throughout Neolithic Europe: Several great stone slabs stand upright, supporting a flat stone that serves as a roof. These structures were designed as burial chambers.

㉖ **Arraiolos,** 22 kilometers (13 miles) northwest of Évora and dominated by the ruins of a once-mighty fortress, is a typical hilltop Alentejo village of whitewashed houses and narrow streets. What distinguishes Arraiolos from so many similar villages is its worldwide reputation as a carpet-producing center. In the 16th century, as Portuguese trade with the East grew, an interest developed in the intricate designs of the carpets from India and Persia, and these patterns served as models for the earliest hand-embroidered Arraiolos carpets. The colorful rugs are not mass-produced in factories but are handmade by locals in their homes and cottages. An authentic Arraiolos rug, made of locally produced wool, has some 44,000 ties per square meter. To discourage imitations, in 1992 the town council designed a special blue seal of authenticity to be affixed to each carpet. There is a permanent exhibition of carpets in the **town hall.** *Admission free. Open weekdays 9–12:30 and 2–5; weekend hours vary, so call the tourist office (Praça Lima Brito, tel. 066/42105) for information.*

Tour 3: The Upper Alentejo

From Évora take N18 for 35 kilometers (21 miles) southwest to ㉗ **Reguengos de Monsaraz,** a sleepy little Alentejo town arranged around a large square. Note the unusual pentagonal bell tower on the 19th-century Victorian church. Reguengos, in the center of a large wine-producing region, is also known for its hand-woven rugs.

Five kilometers (3 miles) out of Reguengos on the road to ㉘ Monsaraz is the tiny hamlet of **São Pedro do Corval,** one of Portugal's major centers for inexpensive hand-painted pottery.

Continue on the same route toward the fortified hilltop town of ㉙ **Monsaraz.** Just before the road begins to climb, you'll see an intriguing Moorish-style domed fountain across from the public laundry area. The Roman numerals inscribed on the structure read "1723." The road now snakes up the hill to a parking area outside the village walls; no cars except those of residents are permitted inside. The entire village is a living museum of narrow, stone-surfaced streets lined with ancient white houses. The town's 150 or so permanent residents (mostly older people) live mainly from tourism, and because they do so graciously and unobtrusively, Monsaraz has managed to retain its essential character.

Old women clad in black still sit in the doorways of their tiny cottages and chat with neighbors, their ever-present knitting in hand (as in villages all over the country for generations). At the south end of the walls stand the well-preserved towers of a formidable castle. The view from atop the pentagonal tower sweeps across the Alentejo plain to the west and to the east over the Ria Guadiana to Spain. Within the castle perimeter is an unusual arena with makeshift slate benches at either end of an oval field. Several times a year and in the second week of September (during the festival of Senhora Jesus dos Passos, which commemorates the village's patron saint), bullfights are held here.

The small **museum** next to the parish church displays religious artifacts and the original town charter signed by Dom Manuel in 1512. The former tribunal contains an interesting 15th-century fresco, which depicts Christ presiding over figures representing truth and deception. *Admission: 100$00. Open Wed.–Mon. 10–12 and 2–5; closed Tues.*

The area around Monsaraz is dotted with megalithic monuments. The **Menhir of Outeiro,** 3 kilometers (2 miles) north, on the road to Monsaraz, is the one of the tallest ever discovered.

To continue the tour, return to Reguengos, pick up N255, and head north 28 kilometers (17 miles) across the cork- and olive-tree-covered hills to **Terena.** This little jewel of a town, with a charter dating to 1262 and a castle on a hill, is a place where tourists are still a pleasant curiosity. Drive—or better yet, stroll—along the narrow Rua Direita past the white houses, some with Gothic doorways, others with baroque or Renaissance ones. The small, well-preserved castle was one of several built in this area to defend the border with Spain, which lies across the Ria Guadiana just 11 kilometers (7 miles) to the east.

Vila Viçosa, a quiet town with a moated castle, occupies a gentle elevation in the heart of the fertile Borba plain and has been closely linked with Portuguese royalty since the 15th century. But this royal association was not always favorable: In 1483 King João II, seeking to strengthen his grip on the throne, moved to eliminate the 2nd Duke of Bragança, his brother-in-law and most formidable rival, who, from Vila Viçosa, controlled more than 50 cities, castles, and towns. After much intrigue and counter intrigue, the unfortunate Duke was beheaded in the main square of Évora.

Court life in Vila Viçosa flourished in the late 16th and early 17th centuries, when the huge palace constructed by the 4th Duke of Bragança (Jaime) was the scene of great royal feasts, theater performances, and bullfights. This all came to an abrupt end in 1640, when King João IV, the 8th Duke of Bragança and the first Portuguese to occupy the throne after 60 years of Spanish domination, elected to move his court to Lisbon. Thereafter, Vila Viçosa slipped into relative oblivion. In more recent times Portugal's last king, Carlos I, and the young Prince Luis Filipe spent their last night in the palace. The following day, February 1, 1908, they were assassinated by members of a secret political society in response to a royal decree that mandated exile for "political" crimes. The murders occurred while they were crossing Lisbon's Terreiro do Paço in an open carriage.

The **Paço Ducal** (Ducal Palace), still in the hands of the Braganças, draws people from all over. Built of locally quarried marble, the main wing extends for some 360 feet and overlooks the expansive Palace Square and the bronze equestrian statue of Dom João IV. The interior of the palace was extensively restored in the 1950s and contains all that you'd expect to find: Azulejos, Arraiolos rugs, frescoed ceilings, priceless collections of silver and gold objects, Chinese vases, Gobelin tapestries, a long dining hall adorned with antlers and other hunting trophies. The enormous kitchen is equipped with spits large enough to accommodate several oxen and enough gleaming copperware to keep a small army of servants busy polishing. The apartments where the unfortunate Dom Carlos spent his last night have been maintained as they were. Carlos was quite an accomplished painter—some say a better painter than he was king—and many of his works (along with private photos of Portugal's last royal family) line the walls of the apartments.

Following the tour of the palace you may visit the adjacent **Museu dos Coches** (Coach Museum), which features a collection of horse-drawn coaches and antique automobiles and is a pleasant postscript to your visit of the palace. However, if you've already seen the coach museum in Lisbon, you should skip this one. Vila Viçosa's is interesting but isn't in the same league. *Admission to palace: 400$00; to museum, 100$00. Open Oct.–May, Tues.–Sun. 9:30–1 and 2–5; June–Sept., Tues.–Sun. 9:30–1 and 2–6; closed Mon. and holidays.*

Located at the north end of the palace square is the **Knot Gate** with its massive stone ropes—an intriguing example of the Manueline style.

㉜ Between Vila Viçosa and the town of **Borba** (4 kilometers [2½ miles] northwest of Vila Viçosa on N255) are mountainous dirt-and-rock piles strewn about the countryside. These tailings are the result of centuries of extracting high-quality marble from the many local quarries. As you travel throughout the region, notice the generous use of marble even in the most modest of buildings.

Borba is also one of the Alentejo's major wine producers, and the town's vintners have won many national prizes. The village boasts a pleasant conglomeration of modest whitewashed houses, noble mansions, and small churches—all beautifully decorated with marble. Borba's most notable monument is the 18th-century **Fonte das Bicas,** a neoclassical, white-marble fountain built to honor Queen Maria I, known as Maria the Pious, who reigned from 1777 to 1816.

㉝ What was **Estremoz** lies on the ancient road that connected Lisbon with Mérida, Spain, and has been a site of strategic importance since Roman times. The castle, which overlooks the town, was one of the most important of the Alentejo's many fortresses. To many Portuguese, Estremoz is most closely associated with the Queen Saint Isabel, though she spent only a short time here. Married to Dom Dinis—a Portuguese king—in 1282, she arrived in 1336 and after a brief stay became ill and died. The luxurious Pousada da Rainha Santa Isabel (*see* Dining and Lodging, *below*) occupying the castle was named for her. It was also in Estremoz, in 1367, that the Queen's grandson Pedro, the lover and secret husband of Inês de Castro, died. The Portuguese people loved Queen Saint Isabel, and many tales and legends of her humility and charity have been handed down over the ages, and a statue in the castle square commemorates her. From atop the castle tower you'll have a magnificent view over the Alentejo plains.

Across from the castle, housed in a 16th-century alms house, is the **Municipal Museum.** Its displays chronicle the development of the region and range from Roman artifacts to contemporary pottery. *Admission: 120$00. Open Tues.–Sun. 10–11:45 and 2–6; closed Mon. and holidays.*

The lower town, a maze of narrow streets and white houses, radiates out from the Rossio, a huge, unpaved square. Stands lining it sell the colorful pottery for which Estremoz is so well known. In addition to the multicolored, hand-painted plates, pitchers, and dolls, note the earthenware jugs decorated with bits of locally quarried white marble.

Time Out There are several refreshment stands and snack bars along the
Rossio. For more substantial fare try the **Café Alentejo,** on the
Rossio. From this popular 50-year-old café and restaurant, you
can watch the goings-on in the square.

The tiny **Rural Museum,** on the opposite side of the Rossio from
the Café Alentejo, is chock full of handmade miniatures depict
ing various aspects of Alentejo country life. The museum wa
once a *Casa do Povo* (a sort of Portuguese senior citizen's cer
ter), where all the exhibits were originally made. Note that the
finely carved bulls' horns are crafted in a fashion similar to the
scrimshaw carvings of New England whalers. *Rossio. Admis
sion: 100$00. Open Oct.–May, Tues.–Sun. 10–1 and 3–5
June–Sept., Tues–Sun. 10–1 and 2–6; closed Mon. and holi
days.*

34 **Évoramonte,** on N18, 17 kilometers (10 miles) southwest o
Estremoz, is a medieval town that sits along the western flan
of the **Serra da Ossa,** and has an altitude of 1,550 feet. Drive u
to the castle for a spectacular panoramic view that extends a
far as the **Serra da Estrela.** The Évoramonte castle, built in Ital
ian-Renaissance style, is distinguished by a massive, roun
tower at each of its four corners. Also note the heavy Manuelin
ropes that run, like ribbons on a Christmas package, aroun
the outside of the castle; they're joined together at the entranc
with two tidy cement knots. (An interesting gastronomic aside
It was in Évoramonte that the famous *sopa Alentejana* is sai
to have originated. The convention held here in 1834 to end the
civil war between the Liberals and Miguelists took so long t
conclude that at the end only stale bread was left to eat—an
thus was born the popular Alentejo soup, made with stal
bread, garlic, olive oil, coriander, and water.)

Return to Estremoz, and follow N4 38 kilometers (23 miles) to
35 **Elvas,** another of the white, fortified Alentejo towns. Locate
about 6 kilometers (less than 4 miles) from the Spanish tow
of Badajoz, Elvas, since its founding, has been an importan
bastion in warding off attacks from the east. The extensiv
fortifications, 17th-century Portugal's most formidable, ar
characterized by a series of walls, moats, and reinforced tow
ers. The enormousness of the complex can be best appreciate
by driving around the periphery of the town. Another di
tinguishing landmark, the 8-kilometer-long (5-mile-lon
Amoreira Aqueduct—which took more than a century to co
struct—is still in use today. Started in 1498 under the directic
of one of the era's great architects, Francisco de Arruda—wl
also designed the Aqueduto da Agua da Prata (*see above*)—
was not until 1622 that the first drops of water flowed into th
town fountain.

The former **Gothic Cathedral,** situated within the town walls,
worth a visit, if for no other reason than to see the 16th-centu
Manueline–style refurbishment, as designed by Francisco c
Arruda. The blue and yellow azulejos lining the interior wal
were added in the 17th century. From the Cathedral, which si
at the head of the Praça da República, walk up the hill past
pillory and two stone towers (spanned by a graceful Moori
loggia) to the castle. At the battlements you'll have a sweepi
view of the town and its fortifications. *Praça da República. A
mission: Open Fri.–Wed. 9:30–12:30 and 2:30–5:30; clos
Thurs.*

From Elvas head north 19 kilometers (11½ miles) on N373 to ③⑥ **Campo Maior,** and you'll traverse rows of gentle hills covered with the Alentejo's ubiquitous cork and olive trees. This is a quiet, sparsely populated corner of the country where little has changed over the years. You may notice the smell of roasting coffee lingering in the air: It isn't coming from a nearby café but from the several coffee-roasting plants in the area. Campo Maior is the center of Portugal's coffee industry.

Try to make it to this town during the first week of September, when nearly 100 streets and squares are covered with a rainbow-colored mantle of paper flowers and decorations. The decorations for each neighborhood are a closely held secret for months as the women nimbly assemble the paper flowers and the men construct the wooden framing. When the festival opens, all is revealed in a blaze of color and festivity. Check with the local or regional tourist office for exact dates.

At the top of the hill is a castle that was reconstructed after a disastrous explosion in 1732 destroyed it and much of the town. As you walk around the fortifications, you'll notice some tiny whitewashed dwellings with laundry fluttering about like flags in the breeze. The little buildings are the old army barracks, the only part of the military complex that is still occupied. Before leaving Campo Maior, take time to stroll through the lower part of town, where the narrow streets are lined with many fine examples of wrought-iron grills and balconies, giving the town a Spanish appearance.

③⑦ Continue on N371 toward **Portalegre,** the gateway to the Alentejo's most mountainous region, where the parched, expansive plains of the south give way to a greener, more inviting landscape. The town of Portalegre, which sits at the foot of the Serra de São Mamede, lacks the charm of the whitewashed hamlets in the south of the province but has long been noted for the quality of its tapestries. (It gained added prominence in the 17th century with the establishment of silk mills, however, these are now gone.) Near the town center, on the second floor of an unmarked, dilapidated Jesuit monastery (Rua Guilherme Gomes Fernandes 26) is a tapestry factory you may tour. Go up the stairs, turn left, and ring the bell. The workshop, Dickensian in appearance, is an ancient, wooden-floor hall with two long rows of looms. World-famous tapestries are made here by hand, either copies of classical patterns or originals made to order. Note that this is not a place for bargain hunters: It takes approximately two years before a piece is completed, and the current price is about $5,000 per square meter. *Rua Guilherme Gomes Fernandes 26, tel. 045/23283. Admission free. Open weekdays 9:30–11 and 2:30–4:30.*

Time Out   Located in the municipal park in the town center, the **O Tarro** restaurant and snack bar has a pleasant terrace, which overlooks a pond and the sprawling park.

To explore Portalegre, start at the park in the center of the lower town and walk uphill past a maze of shops and old houses to the twin-towered **cathedral.** The 18th-century facade of this, the town's most prominent landmark, is highlighted with marble columns and wrought-iron balconies. *Open Mon.–Sat. 8:30–11:30 and 2–6; Sun. 8;30–11:30.*

The **Municipal Museum,** located in a former seminary next to the cathedral, contains a wealth of religious art including a gilded, 16th-century Spanish pietà. *Admission: 100$00. Open Tues.–Sun. 9:30–12:30 and 2–6; closed Mon. and holidays.*

From the cathedral square, head east about 400 yards to the ruins of a once-formidable castle, whose tower walls afford a splendid view of the cathedral and its surroundings.

The **José Regio Museum,** located just off the Avenida Poeta José Regio, is roughly midway between the cathedral and the castle. It was named for the local poet who died in 1969 and bequeathed his varied collection of religious and folk art to the museum. The collection is located in the poet's former residence. *Praça Municipal, tel. 045/23625. Admission: 100$00. Open Tues.–Sun. 9:30–12:30 and 2–6; closed Mon. and holidays.*

Portalegre is also the gateway to a recently established national-al park called the **Parque Natural da Serra de São Mamede,** which encompasses some 80,000 acres and extends north to include the fortified town of Marvao and the spa of Castelo de Vide.

Hugging the Spanish border, the park reaches south from Portalegre to the little hamlet of Esperança. Rural in character, the sparsely inhabited park is made up of small family plots, and sheepherding is the major livelihood. The region is rich in wildlife and includes many rare species of birds, along with wild boar, deer, and wildcat. This is not a spectacularly scenic park like Yellowstone or Yosemite but is a quiet place for hiking, riding, or simply communing with nature. For information about activities contact the **park office** (Praceta Herois da India 8, 7301 Portalegre, tel. 045/23631, fax 045/27501).

If you're interested in horses, a visit to the **Coudelaria Real** (National Stud Farm) is a must. The former Royal Stud Farm, founded by Dom João V in 1748, was established to furnish royalty with high-quality mounts. The Coudelaria—the most important stud farm in Portugal—is located on a dusty track 3 kilometers (2 miles) northwest of the town of **Alter do Chão.** From Portalegre take N119 west for 21 kilometers (13 miles), and head south toward Alter do Chão (which has an interesting castle opposite its main square). The road to the farm is marked COUDELARIA. If, at the farm, you try to speak Portuguese or you seem interested in horses, the sympathetic employees may show you around. Otherwise, you can roam the farm yourself and look at the horses or maybe catch a training session. Of special interest is the annual horse auction held in late April. *Follow signs to Coudelaria. Open daily 9:30–12 and 2–4:30.*

For the most scenic approach to the Serra de São Mamede, backtrack to Portalegre on N119, then take N359 toward Marvão. Another route is to take N245 north to the intersection at N246 to Castelo de Vide and Marvão. The narrow but well-surfaced serpentine N359 rises to an elevation of 2,800 feet, past stands of birch and chestnut trees and small vegetable gardens bordered by ancient stone walls. At **Portagem** take note of the well-preserved Roman bridge.

The views of the mountains as you approach the fortress-town of **Marvão,** 18 kilometers (11 miles) away, are spectacular. Perched atop the face of a sheer rock cliff, the town's castle commands a sweeping, 360-degree panorama. Although it's possible to drive through the constricted streets of this medieval mountaintop village, Marvão is best appreciated on foot. First head for the castle, and climb to the tower. From there you can trace the course of the massive stone walls, adorned at intervals with Vauban-style (a 17th-century style characterized by concentric lines of trenches and walls) bartizans, to enjoy breathtaking vistas from different angles. Given its strategic position, it's no surprise that Marvão has been a fortified settlement since Roman times or earlier. The present castle was built under Dom Dinis in the late 13th century and modified some four centuries later, during the reign of Dom João IV.

At the foot of the path leading to the castle is the **Municipal Museum,** housed in the recently renovated 13th-century Church of Saint Mary. The small gallery contains a diverse collection of religious artifacts, azulejos, costumes, ancient maps, and weapons. *Admission: 150$00. Open daily 9–12:30 and 2–5:30.*

The village, with some 300, mostly older inhabitants, is laid out in several long rows of tidy, white stone dwellings terraced into the hill. The newly remodeled Pousada de Santa Maria (*see* Dining and Lodging, *below*) and the few guest houses and restaurants are well integrated into the village and do not detract from Marvão's pleasing traditional architecture. Head north on the small country road and follow signs to **Santo António das Areias,** where some two dozen prehistoric dolmens are scattered among the chestnut groves.

An intriguing backcountry lane connects Marvão with Castelo de Vide. About halfway down the hill from Marvão, turn to the right toward Escusa, and continue through the chestnut- and acacia-covered hills to **Castelo de Vide.** This hilltop spa town is graced with flowers, which sprout from nearly every nook and cranny. When you encounter the local people it will be clear that the beauty of Castelo de Vide has reached the hearts of its residents, who have kind and gentle natures. Start out in the Praça Dom Pedro V, the large, baroque square bordered by the Church of Santa Maria and the town hall. From here wander down the alleyway to the right of the church; this route will take you to the village fountain, which taps one of the many springs in the area. (The waters are alleged to cure a wide variety of disorders ranging from diabetes to dermatitis.) The canopied, clam-shaped marble fountain is the town symbol.

Follow the cobblestone alley leading from the fountain up to the *Juderia* (Jewish Quarter). On the Rua da Juderia you'll come to a **medieval synagogue,** a modest, one-story building that was once the center of a thriving Jewish community. In medieval times, as the town prospered, many Jews and Marranos (Jews forced to convert to Christianity) settled here. As you walk along, notice the many houses with Gothic doorways and their various designs. (The tourist brochures proclaim that Castelo de Vide has the largest number of Gothic doorways of any town in Portugal.) From the Juderia it's a short climb to the ruins of the castle. Climb up into the tower and inside the well-preserved keep to the large Gothic hall with a picture window looking down on the town square and the church. *Admission free. Open Oct.–May, daily 10–5:30; June–Sept., daily 10–8.*

Tour 4: The Lower Alentejo

Extending across a small knoll midway between Spain and the
sea, **Beja** is the Lower Alentejo's principal agricultural center.
Along the town's streets and squares, shepherds wearing
broad-brimmed hats and the traditional sheepskin vests mingle easily with the townspeople. In the fields at the edge of
town, gypsies often set up camp, with makeshift tents, horse
carts, and open campfires. These scenes from a rapidly disap-
pearing way of life contrast sharply with the modern jets taking off and landing at the nearby German Air Force base.
However, much of the old part of Beja still retains a significantly Arabic flavor, the legacy of more than 400 years of Moorish
occupation. Students of the Portuguese language even claim
that the local dialect has Arabic characteristics.

In the first century Beja, founded by Julius Caesar and known
as Pax Julia, was an important town in the Roman province of
Lusitania. The name Pax Julia was chosen because it was here,
after a long struggle, that peace was finally established between the Lusitanian chiefs and Julius Caesar. Artifacts from
the Roman era can be viewed at the Museu Regional on the second floor of the Convento da Conceição and at the excavations in
nearby Pizões.

The convent, located on a broad plaza in the center of the old
town, was founded in 1459 by the parents of King Manuel I. Favored by the royal family, the Franciscan convent that was
once a Moorish *mesquita* (mosque) thrived and became one of
the richest of the period. The **Church of Santa Maria,** located
across the square, can be easily recognized by its massive
round pillars, Mudejar arches, and its bell tower similar in design to that of the famed Giralda Tower in Seville. The church
and cloisters display some fine azulejos from the 16th and 17th
centuries, including panels depicting scenes from the life of St.
John the Baptist, and a section of multicolor Moorish tiles. Upstairs, at the far end of the second-floor gallery, is one of the
most famous windows in the country, the so-called "Mariana
Window," named after a young Beja nun, Mariana Alcoforado.
As the story goes, in the mid-17th century Mariana fell in love
with a French count by the name of Chamilly, who was in the
Alentejo fighting against the Spaniards. When he went back to
France, the nun waited longingly and in vain, at the window,
for him to return. The publication in France in 1669 of five pas-
sionate love letters known as *The Portuguese Letters*, written
by Mariana to the count and documenting the scandalous affair,
brought a measure of lasting international literary fame to this
provincial Alentejo town. The recently established **Visigoth
Museum** next door houses an impressive collection of artifacts,
such as tombstones, weapons, and pottery, that help document
the Visigoth presence in the region. The museum is situated in
the 6th-century Visigoth Church of Santo Amaro. *Largo da
Conceição. Admission to convent and museum: 100$00. Open
Tues.–Sun. 9:45–1:30 and 2–5:15.*

Time Out The **Café Pastelaria Santa Maria,** opposite the church, has outside tables looking out on the convent square and is a pleasant
spot for cake and coffee or a light lunch.

Beja Castle is an extensive system of fortifications whose crenellated walls and towers chronicle the history of the town from

its Roman occupation through its 19th-century battles with the French. The castle keep houses a military museum where weapons from the 16th century through modern times are displayed. *Admission free. Open Oct.–May, daily 9–12 and 1–4; June–Sept., daily 10-1 and 2-6.*

44 **Serpa,** 29 kilometers (18 miles) east of Beja on N260, is a sleepy agricultural town, which seems to have missed the train of progress and development that's changed much of Portugal. Here men pass the time of day by gathering together in the compact Praça da República, under the shadow of the ancient, stone clock tower. Unemployment is high, and there is little else for many of the men to do. In tiny cubbyholes along narrow, cobbled streets, carpenters, shoemakers, basket weavers, and other craftsmen work in much the same manner as their forefathers did generations earlier.

From the 13th-century castle walls, you can get a bird's-eye view of the town. Note how an aqueduct forms an integral part of the walls. As for the huge sections of the walls tottering precariously above the entrance, they're the result of explosions ordered by the Duke of Ossuna during the 18th-century War of the Spanish Succession. Within the castle walls there's a small municipal museum with a particularly unusual exhibit—a life-size bronze-colored papier-mâché artwork replica of *The Last Supper. Admission: 100$00. Open Tues.–Sun. 9–12:30 and 2–5:30; closed Mon. and holidays.*

Now head north on N265, a narrow road that parallels the Rio Guadiana as it runs through an isolated stretch of rolling hills and cork trees. At the intersection with N258, follow signs to **45** **Vidigueira,** a quiet farm town in the middle of the Alentejo plain, best known as the one-time home of Vasco da Gama, the Portuguese explorer whose voyage in 1497 opened the sea route to India. A statue of the heroic explorer stands in the main square.

At the edge of town, in a setting of gardens and ponds, is the Carmelite chapel where the explorer's body once laid, from the time it was returned from India in 1539 until it was moved in 1898 to its current resting place, Lisbon's Jeronimos Monastery.

Five kilometers (3 miles) west of Vidigueira on N258, standing in an olive tree orchard, are the 2,000-year-old ruins of a Roman villa. The two-story structure known as the **Ruins of São Cucufate** was part of an extensive Roman settlement. (Coins and other artifacts that have turned up indicate a first-century Roman presence here.) It's believed that the ground floor was used as a barn, with the living quarters above it. Remnants of the original heating and drainage systems are visible. The building was later adapted and used in the 13th century as a convent; the frescoes were done in the late 15th and early 16th centuries, and have not been restored. *N258. Admission free; donations accepted. Open Tues.–Fri. 10–12 and 2–5; closed Sat., Sun., and Mon.*

47 Continue on N258 to **Alvito,** a typical, sleepy Alentejo town that occupies a low hill above the Rio Odivelas. Noted for its fortress-like 13th-century parish church, the town also boasts a rectangular, early 16th-century castle with round towers at three of its corners and a number of fine Mudejar windows. (The castle will soon be converted into a pousada.) In the village a surprising number of modest houses bear graceful Manueline doorways and windows.

48 The castle at **Viana do Alentejo,** 10 kilometers (6 miles) north of Alvito on N258, with its rough stone walls, brick battlements, and round turrets, is one of the most attractive in the Alentejo. It was constructed in 1313 to the very specific orders of Dom Dinis, who decreed that the pentagonal walls that formed a pentagon be tall enough that a horseman with a lance measuring nine covados (an ancient unit of measure that equals 66 centimeters, or 26 inches) wouldn't injure anyone between the battlements. The fortified parish church—designed by the famous architect Diogo de Arruda—located within the walls of the castle, has an eye-pleasing combination of battlements, spires, and ornate Manueline elements. Below the castle a delightful Renaissance fountain enhances the town square. Viana do Alentejo is also noted for its primitive-style pottery, sold in several of the small shops in town.

Take N383 south and then west to Torrão, then follow N5, which runs along the Rio Sado through a sparsely populated re-
49 gion of pine and olive trees, to **Alcácer do Sal,** whose hilltop castle is the most prominent attraction. The town's buildings form long, horizontal rows reaching down the hill to the riverbank. Because of its favored location, Alcácer was one of the first inhabited sites in Portugal; parts of the castle foundations are some 5,000 years old. The Greeks were here, and, of course, so were the Romans, who established the town of Salatia Urbs Imperatoria—a key intersection in their system of Lusitanian roads. During the Moorish occupation, under the name of Alcácer de Salaria, this became one of the most important Moslem strongholds in all of Iberia. In the 16th century Alcácer prospered as a major producer of salt, and a brisk trade was conducted with the northern European countries, which used the product to preserve herring.

Drive west on N253 through the **Reserva Natural do Sado** (Sado River Nature Reserve). The riverbanks are lined with extensive salt pans and rice paddies, and the reserve gives shelter to wildlife such as dolphin, otter, white stork, and egret. From the beach town of Comporta, head south along the coast on N261 to Santiago do Cacém. This mostly deserted stretch of dunes and pine trees has some wonderful, undeveloped sandy beaches.

50 **Santiago do Cacém,** located about 16 kilometers (10 miles) from the sea at the junction of N120 and N261, is a quiet regional market town. The castle built by the Knights of the Order of Santiago (St. James), on the site of Moorish ruins, dominates the town and affords sweeping views that reach to the sea; the vista is marred only by the oil refineries at Sines. Inside the parish church, which is surrounded by the fortifications, you can see a sculpture of Saint James battling the Moors. The old town, which occupies a maze of narrow streets just below the castle, has a number of well-preserved 17th- and 18th-century manor houses. The **regional museum,** housed in a former prison in the center of town, offers several well-organized exhibits portraying various aspects of Alentejo life, including a display showing the stages of and implements used in cork production. *Admission: 100$00. Open Sun.–Thurs. 10–12:30 and 2–5:30; closed Fri., Sat., and holidays.*

At the edge of town, just off of the road to Lisbon, you can explore the excavations of the Roman city of **Mirobriga.** Originally this site was settled by the Celts in the 4th century BC; later, in the 1st century, it became a Roman town. The ruins, although not nearly as extensive or as well preserved as those at Conimbriga near Coimbra, contain several interesting features, including the sanctuaries of Venus and Aesculapius (god of medicine). The excavations—some of which were done in the 1980s by a team from the University of Missouri—are not currently being worked. *Rd. to Lisbon. Admission: 100$00. Open Oct.–May, Tues.–Sun. 9–noon and 1–5:30; June–Sept., Tues.–Sun. 9–1 and 2:45–6:45.*

From Santiago do Cacém head south either along the motorway, which passes the refineries and power plant at

🟡 Sines, or along the inland N120 to **Vila Nova de Milfontes.** Although the town itself is just another small beach resort without any special architectural merit, its location at the broad mouth of the Rio Mira is delightful, and it has soft sandy beaches on both sides of the river. Overlooking the sea is an ivy-covered fortress built on Moorish foundations in the late 16th century to protect Milfontes from the Algerian pirates who regularly terrorized the Portuguese coast. With the subsidance of the pirate threat, the fortress was abandoned and the ruins were sold at auction in 1906; in 1939 it was taken over by the present owner, who has converted it into a delightful inn called the Castelo de Milfontes (*see* Dining and Lodging, *below*).

Tour 5: The Estremadura

In 1711, after nearly three years of a childless union with his Hapsburg queen, Mariana, a despairing João V vowed that should the queen bear him an heir, he would build a Franciscan monastery dedicated to St. Anthony. In December of that same year, a girl—later to become queen of Spain—was born; João's eventual heir, José I, was born three years later. True to his word, the King had built the enormous **Palácio Nacional de Mafra** (Monastery and Royal Palace) that loom above the small

🟡 farming community of **Mafra,** some 25 kilometers (15 miles) northwest of Lisbon. The original project—entrusted to the Italian-trained German architect Fredrich Ludwig—was to be a modest-size facility that could house 13 friars. What finally emerged after 18 years of construction was an immense, rectangular complex that contained a monastery large enough for 300 monks, an imposing basilica, and a grandiose royal palace, which has been compared to Spain's El Escorial outside Madrid. The numbers involved in the construction are mind-boggling: At times 50,000 workers were used; there are 4,500 doors and windows, 300 cells, 880 halls and rooms, and 154 stairways; and perimeter walls that total some 19 kilometers (12 miles) surround the park. The story of the monastery is the subject of a bizarre but fascinating novel titled *Baltasar and Blimunda* by the Portuguese author José Saramago.

There are a number of details to note as you take the two-hour guided tour, but the highlight is the magnificent baroque library: The barrel-vaulted, two-tiered hall contains some 40,000 volumes of mostly 16th-, 17th-, and 18th-century works, and a number of ancient maps are displayed. The Basilica, constructed entirely of limestone and containing 11 chapels, was patterned after St. Peter's Basilica in the Vatican. The balcony of the connecting corridor overlooks the high altar and was a favorite meeting place for Dom João and Mariana. This midway point between the "his" and "hers" royal bedrooms was considered "neutral territory." When you're in the gilded **throne room,** you may want to spend some time observing the life-size renditions of the seven virtues, as well as the impressive figure of Hercules, by Domingos Sequeira. On display in the game room is an early version of a pinball machine. Note the hardplanked beds in the monastery infirmary; the monks used no mattresses.

You'll be fortunate if you arrive on a Sunday morning, when the sonorous tones of the 92-bell carillon—played by Francisco Gato, a TAP Air Portugal pilot—ring out across the countryside. *Admission: 200$00. Open: Wed.–Mon. 10-1 and 2-5; closed Tues.*

Time Out | The **Pasteleria Dom João V,** situated directly across the street from the monastery, offers a welcome respite from the rigors of sight-seeing. Homemade pastries and ice cream are specialties.

53 **Ericeira,** an old fishing village located on the rocky coast 11 kilometers (7 miles) northwest of Mafra, on N247, is a popular seaside resort. The core of the village fans out from the sheer cliff beneath which the fishing boats are hauled up onto a small, sheltered beach. Either end of the village has good sand for sunbathing, but the south end is preferred by surfers.

54 Take N247 for 20 kilometers (12 miles) along the rugged coast to the turnoff for **Torres Vedras.** Today a bustling commercial center crowned with the ruins of a medieval castle, the town is best known for the extensive system of trenches and fortresses, for which the Torres Vedras is named. It was here, at the Lines of Torres Vedras—a system of fortifications that were erected by Wellington in 1810 as part of a secret plan for the defense of Lisbon—that the surprised French Army, under Napoleon's Marshal Masséna, was routed. Remnants of the fortifications can be seen throughout the region.

55 Continue north along N247 for 40 kilometers (24 miles) to **Peniche.** The rocky coast is interrupted with fine beaches at Santa Cruz, Ribamar, and Areia Branca. Peniche, situated in the lee of the rocky Cape Carvoeiro Peninsula, is a major fishing and canning port with a bustling harbor watched-over by a sprawling, 16th-century fortress. The town, a popular summer resort, is also known for its lace. The most interesting of the area's several churches is the 13th-century Church of São Leonardo in nearby **Atouguia da Baleia.**

For a good view of the fortress and the harbor, drive out to **Cape Carvoeiro.** The narrow road winds around the peninsula, along the rugged shore, and past the lighthouse and bizarre rock formations. Within the fortress walls there's a small museum. *Admission free. Open Tues.–Sun. 10–12 and 2–5; closed Mon.*

56 The harbor at Peniche is the jumping-off point for excursions to the offshore **Berlenga Islands.** The six small islands are a nature reserve and a favorite place for fishermen and divers. Berlenga, the largest of the group, is the site of the **Forte de São João Baptista,** a 17th-century fortress built to defend the area from pirates. There's also a hostel on the island. For more information about accommodations, contact the Peniche tourist office (Rua Alex Herculano, tel. 062/79571). *Boats depart Peniche for Berlenga between June and Sept. at 9 and noon and return at 11:30 AM and 6 PM. The trip takes approximately 1 hour and costs 1,200$00.*

57 **Óbidos,** once a strategic seaport but now 10 kilometers (6 miles) from the ocean (due to siltation), is surrounded by fertile farmland. Cottages and cultivated fields abut the town walls, where fishing boats and trading vessels once docked. As you approach Óbidos from the distance, you can see the bastions and crenellated walls standing as a hilltop sentinel guarding the now-peaceful valley of the Ria Arnoia. Enter the town through the massive, arched gates, and it may seem that you've been transported into medieval Portugal. The narrow Rua Direita, lined with boutiques and flower-bedecked white houses, runs the length of the town from the main gates to the foot of the castle: You may want to do a bit of shopping for ceramics and clothing on this street. The rest of the town is crisscrossed by a labyrinth of stone footpaths, tiny squares, and decaying stairways. Explore any route or all of them, for the town is small and you can't really get lost. Each nook and cranny will offer its own reward. Just be sure to include the castle in your explorations: Extensively restored after having been severely damaged in the 1755 earthquake, the multitowered complex—one of the finest medieval castles in Portugal—displays both Arabic and Manueline elements. Parts of the castle have been occupied as a pousada since 1952.

Óbidos has a long association with women who have been prominent figures in Portuguese history. In the 14th century Inês de Castro sought refuge in this castle. So enchanted was the young Queen Isabel with Óbidos—which she visited with her husband, Dom Dinis, shortly after their marriage in 1282—that the king gave it to her as a gift along with Abrantes and Porto de Móso; the town stayed the property of the queens of Portugal until 1834. Another queen associated with Óbidos was Leonor (the wife of João II), who came here to recuperate after the death of her young son; the town pillory bears Leonor's coat of arms. The 17th-century artist Josefa de Óbidos is yet another famous woman linked with the town. Evidently, she was born in Seville but came to Óbidos as a small child and lived here until her death in 1684. Some of her work may be seen in the azulejos-lined **St. Mary's Church,** which dates back to the 8th century.

58 Five kilometers (3 miles) north of Óbidos on N8 lies the spa of **Caldas da Rainha** (The Queen's Baths). The hub of a large farming area, Caldas da Rainha is best known for its sulfur baths. In 1484 Queen Leonor, en route to partake in a memorial service in Batalha for her father-in-law, Afonso V, noticed some people bathing in a malodorous pool. Having heard of the wondrous healing properties of the water, the queen interrupted her journey to soak in the pool. Convinced of the benefits of the sulfurous waters, the Queen decided to build a hospital on the site. She was so enthusiastic about the project that, according to the story, she sold her jewels to help finance it, and Caldas has been a spa ever since. There is a large bronze statue of Leonor in front of the hospital. The expansive, wooded park surrounding the spa contains two interesting museums: The **Malhoa Muse-**

um, which is primarily dedicated to the works of the local 19th-
and 20th-century painter José Malhoa, and the **Rafael Bordalo
Pinheiro Ceramics Museum,** which is located in the house of the
19th-century ceramist for whom the museum was named. *Admission: 250$00. Open Tues.–Sun. 10–noon and 2–5.*

From Caldas head west along the lagoon to the beach town of
Foz do Arelho. Then follow the coast road 26 kilometers (16
⑤⑨ miles) to **Nazaré.** Not so long ago tourists could mingle on the
beach with the black-stocking-capped fishermen and even help
as the oxen hauled the fishing boats in from the crashing surf.
One of the first quaint Portuguese fishing villages to feel the
impact of tourism, Nazaré is no longer a village and has long
ceased to be quaint. The boats now motor comfortably into a
safe, modern harbor, and the oxen have been put to pasture.
But tourists still flock here, and in summer the broad, sandy
beach is covered with a multicolored quilt of tents and awnings
and the beachfront boulevard is lined with the usual assortment of restaurants, bars, and souvenir shops. To find what's
left of the Nazaré once hailed by many as "the most picturesque
fishing village in Portugal," come in the winter, and either
climb the precipitous trail or take the funicular to the **Sitio,** the
361-foot cliff overlooking the beach. Clustered at the cliff's
edge is a small community of fishermen who live in tiny cottages
and seem unaffected by all that's happening below.

⑥⓪ From Nazaré head east on N8-5 to **Alcobaça,** site of one of
Portugal's most impressive religious monuments. Like the
monastery at Mafra, the Monastery of Saint Mary of Alcobaça
was built as the result of a kingly vow, this time not to give
thanks for a royal heir but in gratitude for a battle won. In 1147,
faced with stiff Moslem resistance during the battle for
Santerém, Portugal's first king, Afonso Henriques, vowed that
if he were victorious, he would build a monastery dedicated to
St. Bernard and the Cistercian Order. The Portuguese were
victorious, Santerém was captured from the Moors, and shortly thereafter a site was selected. Construction on the monastery was begun in 1153 and concluded in 1178. The church, the
largest in Portual, is awe-inspiring: The unadorned, 350-foot-
long structure of massive granite blocks and cross-ribbed
vaulting is a masterpiece of understatement: There's good use
of clean, flowing lines, with none of the clutter found in the later rococco and Manueline architecture. At opposite ends of the
transept, placed foot-to-foot some 30 paces apart, are the delicately carved tombs of King Pedro I and Inês de Castro, their
serene faces looking upwards. The story of Pedro and Inês, one
of the most bizarre love stories in Portuguese history, was immortalized by Camões in the *Lusiads,* one of the most
reknowned pieces of Portuguese literature. Because of the
work, their legend has been kept alive.

Pedro, son of King Afonso IV and heir to the throne, fell in love
with the beautiful young Galician Inês de Castro, a lady-in-
waiting to Pedro's Castilian wife, Constanza. Fearful of any
Spanish influence on his heir, the king banished Inês from the
court. Upon the death of Constanza, Pedro and Inês secretly
married, and she lived in a home in Coimbra, which later came
to be known as the *Quinta das Lagrimas* (The House of Tears);
two sons were born of this union. King Afonso, ever wary of
foreign influence on Pedro, had Inês murdered. Subsequently,
Pedro took the throne and had Inês's murderers pursued: Two

of the three were captured and executed, their hearts wrenched from their bodies. Pedro publicly proclaimed that he had been married to Inês and arranged an elaborate and macabre funeral for his wife. Before the procession, Inês's fleshless body, garbed in royal robes, was placed on the throne beside him, and the courtiers were forced to kiss her lifeless hand. She was then placed in the tomb in Alcobaça that Pedro had designed and which lay, according to his wishes, opposite his own tomb—so that on Judgment Day the lovers would ascend to heaven facing one another.

The graceful twin-tiered **cloister** was added in the 14th and 16th centuries. The Kings Hall, just to the left of the main entrance, is lined with a series of 18th-century azulejos illustrating the building of the monastery. *Admission: 300$00. Open daily 9–5.*

While you're in Alcobaça, you may want to make time for the interesting **Wine Museum,** with wine making implements and presses, that's located in an old winery at the edge of town on N8 in the direction of Leiria. *N8. Admission: 100$00. Open Mon.–Sat. 9–12:30 and 2–5:30; closed Sun.*

Stay on N8 for the next 18 kilometers (11 miles) to the town of ⑥⑴ **Batalha.** The monastery church of **Santa Maria da Vitoria** (Saint Mary of Victory) was built to commemorate a decisive Portuguese victory over the Spanish on August 14, 1385, in the battle of Aljubarrota. In this battle the Portuguese king, John of Avis, who had been crowned only seven days earlier, took on and routed a superior Spanish force. In so doing he maintained independence for Portugal, which was to last until 1580, when the crown finally passed into Spanish hands. At the battle of Aljubarrota, John of Avis, realizing the onerous consequences of defeat, made a vow to the Virgin Mary to build a monastery in her honor should he emerge victorious. The monastery church of Saint Mary of Victory, commonly referred to as Batalha, was the fulfillment of that vow.

The monastery is a masterful combination of Gothic and Manueline styles and was built from 1388 to 1533. Some 15 architects were involved in the project, but the principal architect was Alfonso Domingues, whose portrait, carved in stone, graces the wall in the chapter house. In the great hall lie the remains of two Portuguese unknown soldiers who died in World War I, one in France, the other in Africa.

The tomb in the center of the Founder's Chapel, beneath the star-shaped, vaulted ceiling, is that of John of Avis, lying hand-in-hand with his English queen, Philippa of Lancaster. The tombs along the south and west walls are those of the couple's children, including that of Henry the Navigator.

The graceful lines and proportions of the Royal Cloister manifest a pleasing blending of the Gothic and Manueline styles. Perhaps the finest parts of the entire project lie in the Unfinished Chapels, seven chapels radiating off of an octagonal rotunda, started by Dom Duarte in 1435, and left roofless due to lack of funds. Note the incredible filigree-like detail of the main doorway. *Admission to the cloisters: 250$00. Open daily 9–5.*

The statue of the heroic mounted figure in the forecourt is that of Nuno Álvares Pereira, who, along with John of Avis, led the Portuguese army at Aljubarrota. There is a small battlefield museum 5 kilometers (3 miles) to the south on N8. *Admission: 100$00. Open Tues.–Fri. 10–12, Sat.–Sun. 10–12 and 2–5; closed Mon. and Tues.–Fri. afternoons.*

㉒ Leiria, 11 kilometers (7 miles) north of Batalha on N1, is a pleasant, modern, industrial town situated at the confluence of the Rios Liz and Lena. The region is known for its handicrafts, particularly the fine hand-blown glassware from Marinha Grande. Among the most interesting features of Leiria are the hilltop castle and, beneath it, the old town quarter and the cathedral. The castle, built in 1135 by Prince Afonso Henriques (later Portugal's first king), was an important link in the chain of defenses along the southern border of what was at the time the Kingdom of Portugal. When the Moors were driven from the region, the castle lost its strategic significance and lay dormant until the early 14th century, at which time it was restored and modified and became the favorite residence of King Dinis and his queen, Isabel of Aragon. With these modifications the castle became more of a palace than a fortress and remains one of the loveliest structures of its kind in Portugal. Within the perimeter walls you'll encounter the ruins of a Gothic church, the castle keep, and—built into the section of the fortifications overlooking the town—the Royal Palace. Lined by eight arches, the balcony of the palace affords a lovely view of the town. *Admission: 40$00. Open daily 9–6:30.*

Tour 6: The Ribatejo

㉓ If you want to see a bullfight in Portugal, **Vila Franca de Xira** is the place to do it. The town is 30 kilometers (18 miles) north of Lisbon via the A1 motorway. The Portuguese version of this ancient spectacle—known as the *courada*—is quite different from any bullfight you might have seen in Mexico or Spain. In Portugal the bull's principal opponent is not a sword-carrying matador but a *cavaleiro*—a horseman elegantly attired as an 18th-century nobleman with plumed hat and embroidered coat. Displaying finely tuned equestrian skills he provokes the bull and, just inches away from the animal's padded horns, manages to deftly place a colorfully festooned *bandarilha* (dart) in a designated part of the bull's back. With each pass of an ever shorter bandarilha, the danger to horse and rider increases—in spite of the bull's blunted horns. At the proper moment, when the bull is sufficiently fatigued, the final dart is placed, and with a flourish the cavaleiro exits the arena. (Following a decree by the Marquis of Pombal in the 18th century, bulls are not killed in Portuguese rings.) The stage is now set for the *pega*, an audacious display of bravery with burlesque overtones. A file of eight men—the *forcados*—dressed in bright-crimson vests and green stocking caps parades into the arena and, hands on hips, confronts the tired but still-enraged bull. When the bull charges, the leader meets him head-on with a running leap and literally seizes the bull by the horns. The other men rush in and by grabbing the bull's tail, try to force the animal to the ground. At times this can be quite an amusing sight, though there is the ever-present element of danger, and forcados have been killed during the pega. At the end of the spectacle, a few cows are led in to lure the bull from the ring. If he has shown exceptional bravery, the bull will be spared for stud purposes; otherwise, he will be slaughtered. Bullfights are held from

Easter to October. Call the tourist office (tel. 063/33219) for more information.

The best time to visit Vila Franca de Xira is during the first week in July for the *Festa do Colete Encarnado* (Festival of the Red Waistcoat). Had Hemingway and his buddies taken a wrong train and wound up in Vila Franca de Xira some 60 years ago, perhaps Pamplona would have remained an unsung, grimy industrial town, and the world would have flocked instead to the Ribatejo each July for one of Portugal's greatest parties. The downtown streets are cordoned off, and the bulls are let loose as would-be bullfighters try their luck at dodging the charging beasts. At night the streets are alive with *fado* (traditional folk) music and flamenco dancing. The running of the bulls also takes place during the Autumn Fair held in early October. The bullring, one of Portugal's finest, contains a small museum with a collection of bullfighting memorabilia. For more information call the tourist office (tel. 063/33219). *Admission: 150$00. Open Tues.–Sun. 10–12:30 and 2–6; closed Mon. and holidays.*

There are two routes to Santerém. The more interesting follows the right bank of the Rio Tejo and takes you through the **64 Leziria,** the marshy plain along the river, and across rich pasturelands with stud farms. From Vila Franca de Xira cross the bridge, and follow N118 north. As you drive through the town of **Benavente** and surrounding countryside, look for *campinos* (farmhands) in the fields working the bulls and **65** horses. The road runs through **Almeirim,** where you may visit a working stud farm and a winery at the **Quinta da Alorna.** From Almeirim head back across the river to Santerém.

66 Present-day **Santerém,** perched high above the Tejo, is an important farming and livestock center. Some historians believe that its beginnings date to as early as 1200 BC and the age of Ulysses. Lured by its strategic location, several kings chose Santerém as their residence, and the *Cortes* (Parliament) frequently met here.

To get the feel of the town, walk up to the **Portas do Sol,** a lovely park within the ancient walls. From this vantage point you can look down on a sweeping bend in the Rio Tejo and beyond to the rich farmlands stretching into the neighboring Alentejo. Thanks to its royal connections, Santerém is more richly endowed with treasures and monuments than other towns of its size. The Portuguese refer to it as their "Gothic Capital." Of particular interest are the 17th-century **Seminary Church,** built on the ruins of a royal palace, and the azulejo-bedecked **Marvila Church.**

Inside the **Archaeological Museum** you'll find the finely sculpted tomb of Duarte de Meneses, which, according to legend, contains a single tooth, all that remained of the nobleman after his brutal murder by the Moors in Africa. The museum is on Rua Figueiredo Leal, directly across from the bell tower known as the Torre das Cabaças. *Admission free. Open Tues.–Sun. 9:30–1 and 2–3; closed Mon. and holidays.*

Time Out   **Xantarin** (Travessa da Misericordia 6), one of the region's most popular bars, was once a Roman cistern. Today you may snack and sip your drinks under the original ceiling with Roman arches.

Also in Santarém, on the Largo Pedro Alvares Cabral, is the **Graça Church,** which contains the gravestone of Pedro Cabral, the discoverer of Brazil. There is a tomb of the explorer in Belmonte, the town of his birth, too, but no one is really sure just what is in which tomb! Of note in this 14th-century Gothic church is the delicate rose window carved from a single stone. *Largo Pedro Alvares Cabral.*

(67) When you cross the Rio Tejo on N368 in nearby **Alpiarça,** you'll have the chance to see how a wealthy country gentleman lived at the beginning of this century. The **Casa dos Patudos,** now a museum, was the estate of Jose Relvas, a diplomat and gentleman farmer. The unusual three-story manorhouse with its zebra-striped spire is surrounded by gardens and vineyards. An impressive assemblage of furnishings, including Portugal's foremost collection of Arraiolos carpets, is contained in the museum. *Admission: 200$00. Open Wed.–Sun. and holidays 10–12 and 2–5; contact Alpiarça town hall for other opening hours.*

(68) From Alpiarça continue north on N243 through the horse-breeding center of **Golegã.** During the first two weeks of November, this is the site of the colorful **National Horse Fair,** the most important event of its kind in the country. Another 10 kilometers (6 miles) north on N243 will bring you to the fortified
(69) town of **Torres Novas.** The crenellated, 14th-century hilltop castle encloses a delightful garden. At the foot of the castle stands a caricature-like statue of Dom Sancho I created by João Cutiliero, one of Portugal's most prominent contemporary sculptors.

Some 20 kilometers (12 miles) to the northwest on N357, across the scrub-covered limestone hills of the Serra de Aire, lies
(70) **Fátima,** site of one of the world's most important religious pilgrimages. (Ironically, this great Christian pilgrimage takes place in a village named after the daughter of Mohammed, the prophet of Islam!) If you visit this sleepy little Portuguese town in between pilgrimages, it will be difficult to imagine the roads, squares, parks, and virtually every square foot of space crammed with thousands of the faithful who come from all corners of the world to make this religious affirmation. Many of the pilgrims crawl the last miles on their knees.

During Pope John Paul II's visit in 1991, it was estimated that more than one million people flocked to Fátima. Where there are so many people, there are bound to be opportunists. That Fátima is no exception is attested to by the presence of such places as the "Virgin Mary Souvenir Shop" and the "Pope John Paul II Snack Bar."

The origin of all of this attention goes back to May 13, 1917, a sunny spring Sunday, when three young shepherds—Lúcia dos Santos and her cousins Francisco and Jacinta—reported having seen the Virgin Mary in a field at Cova de Iria, near the village of Fátima. Apparently, the Blessed Mother told them she had descended from heaven and promised to return on the 13th of each month for the next six months. Amid much controversy and skepticism, and each time accompanied by increasingly larger crowds, the three children reported successive apparitions. On October 13 the sixth and final appearance of the Virgin was reported by the three young shepherds, who by this time were under great pressure to admit that their story was a hoax. This was during a period of great anticlerical sentiment in Portugal, and the children were even arrested and interrogated. But they insisted that the Virgin did speak to them and had told them three secrets. Two of these, revealed by Lúcia in 1941, were interpreted to foretell the coming of World War II and the spread of communism and atheism. The third secret is still held by the Vatican. Francisco died in 1919 just short of his 11th birthday, and Jacinta died of tuberculosis in 1920 at the age of 10. Lúcia entered a convent in Coimbra. She was present in Fátima during the Pope's visit in May 1991. In 1930, in a Pastoral Letter, the Bishop of Leiria declared the apparitions worthy of belief, thus approving the "Cult of Fátima." On the 13th of each month, and especially in May and October, the faithful flock here. They stand in the great square of the Sanctuary (a larger plot than St. Peter's Square in Rome) to witness the passing of the statue of the Virgin through the throngs, to participate in candlelight processions, and to take part in solemn masses.

At the head of the huge esplanade is a large, neoclassical basilica (built in the late 1920s) flanked on either side by a semicircular peristyle. The basilica contains the tombs of Francisco and Jacinta. Other pilgrimage sites include the cottages in the nearby hamlet of Aljustrel, where the children were born, and the **Chapel of Apparitions,** built on the spot where the appearances of the Virgin Mary are said to have taken place. There is a **Wax Museum** in the center of town with tableaux representing the story. *Admission: 450$00. Open daily 9–5.*

The hills to the south and west of Fátima are honeycombed with limestone caves, the largest such caverns in Portugal. Within about a 25-kilometer (15-mile) radius of Fátima, there are four sets of these chambers that are equipped with artificial lighting and elevators; here visitors can see the subterranean world of limestone formations, underground rivers and lakes, and multicolored stalagmites and stalactites. They are: **São Mamede Caves, Mira de Aire Caves, Alvados Caves,** and **Santo António Caves.** The tourist office can assist you with further details. *Admission: 300$00. Open Oct.–Mar., daily 9–6; Apr.–June and Sept., daily 9–8; July–Aug., daily 9–9.*

71 From Fátima take N113 east to **Tomar,** a town laid out on both sides of the Rio Nabão, with the new and old parts linked by a graceful, arched stone bridge. The river flows through a lovely park with weeping willows and an old wooden waterwheel.

Atop a hill rising from the old town is **The Convent of Christ,** one of Portugal's most remarkable architectural achievements. You can drive to the top of the hill or hike for about 20 minutes along a path through the trees; at the top you'll be treated to a sweeping panoramic view from the castle walls. The entrance is through a formal garden lined with azulejo-covered benches. From 1160 until the order was forced to disband in 1314 due to pressure from Philip the Fair of France, this was the headquarters of the order of the Knights Templar. Identified by their white tunics emblazoned with a crimson cross, the Templars were at the forefront of the Christian armies in the Crusades and during the years of struggle to regain the lands in Spain and Portugal that had been lost to the Moslem invaders. King Dinis in 1334 resurrected the order in Portugal under the banner of the Knights of Christ and re-established Tomar as its headquarters. In the early 15th century, under the leadership of Prince Henry the Navigator (who for a time resided in the castle), the order flourished. The caravels, which opened up vast parts of the distant world to Portugal, sailed under the order's blazing crimson cross.

When they constructed the original fortifications in 1160, the Templars drew heavily upon their experiences with the Moslems during the Crusades. The buildings within the battlements are made up of a series of cloisters formed around the **Templar's Rotunda**—the complex's showpiece. This two-story, octagonal church, constructed in the Byzantine style, is patterned after the Church of the Holy Sepulchre in Jerusalem and is part of the original 12th-century construction. The paintings and wooden statues are 16th-century Portuguese. To see what the Manueline style is all about, stroll through the nave with its many examples of the twisted ropes, seaweed, and nautical themes, which typify the style. Be sure to look at the **Chapter House Window,** probably Europe's most photographed and described window. This lichen-encrusted sculpture manifests the Manueline style and evokes the feeling and spirit of the great age of discovery.

Back in the old town walk along the narrow, flower-lined streets, particularly Rua Dr. Joaquim Jacinto, where in the heart of the old Jewish quarter you'll find the **Sinogoga de Tomar** (Synagogue of Tomar), a much more modest religious building. Built in the mid-15th century, this is the oldest Jewish house of worship in Portugal. Inside is a small museum with exhibits chronicling the Jewish presence in the country. The once-sizable Jewish population was considerably reduced when in 1496 Dom Manuel issued an edict that ordered the Jews either to leave the country or convert to Christianity. Many, who became known as *Marranos,* converted but secretly practiced their original religion. *Rua Dr. Joaquim Jacinto. Admission free; donations accepted.*

To leave Tomar head south on N210 for 7 kilometers (4 miles) to N358–2, the turnoff for **Castelo de Bode.** Follow this road across the dam. The huge lake—which fans out north from the dam—formed by the damming of the Rio Zêzere, is a popular watersports area. For information regarding boat excursions on the lake, inquire at the Hotel dos Templários in Tomar or at the dock by the Pousada de São Pedro (*see* Dining and Lodging, *below*). The road N358–2 follows the Zêzere to join the Tejo. The storybook castle sitting on a craggy island in the middle of the river is **Almourol Castle.** For a closer look take the mile-long dirt road leading down to the river; the riverbank in this area is practically deserted, making it a wonderful picnic spot. (In summer you can take a boat to the island.) The setting could hardly be more romantic: an ancient castle with crenellated walls and a lofty tower, all sitting on a greenery-covered rock in the middle of a gently flowing river. This is the stuff of poetry and legends: Francisco de Morais used Almourol as the setting for his epic *Palmeirim of England.*

Time Out   **Restaurante Almourol,** on N3 just west of the castle, is in a lovely old house with gardens, orange trees, and a terrace overlooking the castle that makes a good luch stop.

Back on N3 head east to **Constância,** a peaceful hamlet where the Zêzere joins the Rio Tejo. The town is best known as the place where Camôes was exiled in 1548, the unfortunate result of his romantic involvement with Catarina de Ataide, the "Natercia" of his poems and a lady-in-waiting to Queen Catarina. There is a bronze statue of the bard in a reflective pose at the riverbank.

Farther along the Rio Tejo on a hill is the strategically situated
(75) town of **Abrantes.** During the 16th century, when the Rio Tejo was navigable all the way to the sea, Abrantes flourished and became one of the country's most populous and prosperous towns. With the coming of the railroad and the development of better roads, the town's commercial importance waned. The main attraction here is the castle (built in the 16th century). Walk up through the maze of narrow, flower-lined streets to the ruins of the ancient fortress. Much of the castle is in disrepair, but with a bit of imagination, you can conjure visions of what an impressive structure this must have been. The attractive garden that's been planted between the twin fortifications makes a wonderful place to watch the sunset: The play of light upon the river and the lengthening shadows along the olive groves provide an inspiring setting for an evening picnic.

Situated some 12 kilometers (7 miles) north of Abrantes on N2
(76) is **Sardoal,** an island of white- and red-tile roofed houses in a sea of wooded hills. It's an enchanting place of narrow streets paved with pebbles from nearby streams, modest, yellow-trimmed white houses, and flowers everywhere—hanging from windows and from balconies and lining the winding streets and alleys. In such a spot you might expect art to flourish, and in fact the 17th-century **Parish Church** contains a collection of fine 16th-century paintings by the "Master of Sardoal," an unknown painter whose works have been found in other parts of the country and whose influence on other artists has been noted.

Leave Sardoal on N244–3 and follow it through the pine-covered hills to Chão de Codes, then take N244 south toward Gavião. As you come down from the hills toward the Rio Tejo, you'll see a cone-shaped hill (looking as if its top has been sliced off) and a fairy-tale castle planted on top. This is the fortress of
(77) **Belver,** built in the last years of the 12th century by the Knights of the Hospitallers under the command of King Sancho I. In 1194, when the order to build the castle was given, this region was threatened by the Moorish forces who had control of the lands south of the Rio Tejo, with the exception of Évora. As it turned out, the expected attack never took place, and the present structure is little changed from its original design. The walls of the keep, which stands in the center of the courtyard, are some 12 feet thick, and on the ground floor is a great cistern of unknown depth. According to local lore, if an orange is dropped into the well, later it will appear bobbing down the Rio Tejo.

What to See and Do with Children

Lucena Karting, a go-cart track in Évora, provides an outlet for pent-up youthful energy. *N114 to Montemor, tel. 066/734990. Admission: 400$00–6,000$00, depending on vehicle and length of rental time. Open Tues.–Sun. 10–8; closed Mon.*

Young aviation enthusiasts will enjoy seeing old planes at the **Museu do Ar** (Aviation Museum), in Alverca, at the airport. *Tel. 01/958–2782. Admission: 100$00. Open Tues.–Sun. 10–8.*

Beja Aquatica, a waterslide park in Beja, will occupy young water rats for a good part of the day. *On N260, toward Sapa, tel. 084/329755. Admission: 1,400$00 (full day), 1,100$00 (half day) adult; 900$00 (full day), 700$00 (half day) children under 12. Open daily 10–8.*

Peniche Sportaga, a large water-park complex with a separate slide area and adults' and children's swimming pools, also has a restaurant, cafeteria, and disco. *Av. Monsehnor M. Basto, R. Sonsa, tel. 062/789125. Admission: 1,500$00 (full day), 1,000$00 (half day) adult; 1,000$00 (full day), 900$00 (half day) children under 12.*

The **boat trip** from Peniche to the Berlenga Islands is great fun for kids as well as adults. *See* Tour 5.

Children will love exploring the **caves** near Fátima. *See* Tour 6.

Of the many castles in the region, **Marvão** (*see* Tour 3), **Óbidos** (*see* Tour 5), and **Monsaraz** (*see* Tour 3) are the most fun for kids to scamper about.

Off the Beaten Track

The **Parque Natural das Serras de Aire e Candeeiros** is a sparsely populated rural region that straddles the boundary between the Estremadura and the Ribatejo and is roughly midway between Lisbon and Coimbra. Within its 75,000 acres of scrublands and moors, you'll find small settlements, little changed in hundreds of years, where farmers barely eke out a living. In this rocky landscape stones are the main building material for homes, windmills, and the miles of walls used to mark boundary lines. In the village of Minde, you can see women weaving the rough patchwork rugs for which this region is well known.

Shopping

Crystal and Glass

Marinha Grande, just west of Leiria, is the center for the production of Stephens Lead Crystal. The Stephens Brothers Factory School (Bairro Benta, tel. 044/568680), where much of the glass is still produced by hand, may be visited. The school is open weekdays 9–12 and 2–5. **Alcobaça** is another center for quality crystal and hand-blown glass.

Pottery and Ceramics

The brightly colored hand-painted plates, bowls, and figurines from the upper Alentejo are popular throughout Portugal. You'll find the best selection of this distinctive type of folk art in and around **Estremoz,** where the terra-cotta jugs and bowls are adorned with chips of marble from local quarries. Saturday morning the Rossio is chock-full of venders displaying their wares. **Redondo** and the village of **San Pedro do Corval,** near Reguengos, are also good sources of this type of pottery.

An entirely different type of ceramics is produced in **Caldas da Rainha,** a large ceramics-manufacturing center. Its characteristic cabbage-leaf and vegetable-shaped pieces are famous throughout the country. To visit a ceramics factory and showroom contact: **SECLA** (Rua S. João de Deus, tel. 062/842151) and **Armando Baiana** (Rua Casais da Ribeira 37, tel. 062/24355). South of Batalha (on N8) there are a number of roadside shops with good selections of hand-painted ceramics in classical patterns. In **Alcobaça** try the **Casa Lisboa,** across from the monastery.

Rugs

The village of **Arraiolos,** near Évora, is famous for its hand-embroidered wool rugs, and the main street is lined with showrooms and workshops. Some of the best selections can be found at **Calantica** (Rua Alexandre Herculano 20, tel. 066/42356) and **Condestavel** (Rua Bombeiros voluntarios 7, tel. 066/42219), a large shop with branches in Évora and Lisbon.

Sweaters

The beachfront promenade in **Nazaré** is lined with shops selling the traditional cable-stitch Portuguese fishermen's sweaters. The best are made of pure wool rather than acrylic blends. You'll also find a wide selection of wool plaid shirts and caps. It pays to shop around, as prices vary widely and bargaining is the order of the day.

Sports and Outdoor Activities

Participant Sports

Golf The one golf course in the region is located at the beach at **Praia de Porto Nova** (Hotel Praia do Porto Nova, 2560 Torres Vedras, tel. 061/984157) and is part of the Hotel Golf Mar. The par 67, nine-hole course designed by Frank Pennink is 5,259 yards long. Reserve greens in advance, even if you're a hotel guest.

Horseback Riding **Sela Real** (Caldas da Rainha, tel. 062/842096) offers a riding school as well as excursions in Vale da Couto. Contact **Centro Hipico de Caldas da Rainha** (tel. 062/35851) for information.

In Évora contact **Centro Hipico de Évora** (tel. 066/21376). In Montemor-o-Novo contact **Cavalgada** (tel. 066/82230) for Alentejo trail rides. For riding along the beach near Sines, contact **Centro Equestre de Santo Andre** (Monte V. Cima, Santo Andre, tel. 069/71235). Half-day escorted trail rides in small groups for all levels of riders through the Alentejo farmlands are available from **Cavalgada,** (Apt. 68, 7050 Montemor-o-Novo, tel. 066/8223). Half-day rides are 3,500$00 and full-day rides cost 6,500$00; two-day weekend rides are also offered. The price of 9,500$00 includes one night's accommodation in a B&B along the way. Reservations are advised. Because most tourists are not familiar with the terrain it is difficult to arrange unescorted rides. Hourly rates for groups of as many as five persons are about 2,000$00 per person. Riding lessons cost 1,200$00 per half-hour.

Water Sports Most of the larger towns and many smaller ones have modern municipal swimming pools, so even in the middle of the dry Alentejo, you'll never be very far from a refreshing dip.

The Óbidos Lagoon at Foz do Arelho is popular with **sailboarders,** and Windsurfers can be rented at the beach. The cost for just the rig is about 1,200$00 per hour; rental and lessons cost about 2,500$00 per hour.

Surfers, on the other hand, prefer beaches at Penniche, Ericeira, and along the rugged Alentejo coast.

The clear waters and bizarre rock formations off the Berlenga Islands are frequented by **scuba divers**; spearfishing with scuba gear is prohibited. Boats may be rented at the harbor in Penniche.

Fishermen like these waters, too. The most commonly caught fish in this area are sea bass, bream, and red mullet. A fishing license is not necessary.

Beaches

From Odeceixe in the south, where the Alentejo and Algarve join, to the northern end of the Estremadura just south of Figuiera da Foz, there's an almost-continuous, 241-kilometer (150-mile) stretch of sandy beach. There are beaches to meet just about every need. If you like quiet, uncrowded areas with fine, soft sand and clear waters, your best bet is on the Alentejo coast. Even in July and August, when most of Europe's beaches are packed elbow to elbow, you can find solitude by heading west on almost any of the unmarked tracks along the coast. The following signposted beaches, all south of Lisbon, are seldom crowded: **Carvalhal, Zambujeira, Almograve,** and **Fontainhas.**

Some of the more popular beaches (but not necessarily approved of by the European Common Market) where you will find the customary range of facilities, hotels, restaurants, and equipment are at: **Nazaré, Peniche, Foz do Arelho, Ericeira,** and **Milfontes.**

Beaches in the region that fly a blue banner, indicating they've met European Common Market standards for safety and hygiene are at: **Pedrogão, São Pedro de Moel Foz do Arelho, Baleal, Consolação, Porto Dinheiro, Santa Cruz,** and **Porto Covo.**

Dining and Lodging

Dining In the Alentejo, a region known as the country's granary, bread is a major ingredient in the cuisine. It's the basis of a popular dish known as *açorda,* a thick, stick-to-the-ribs bread porridge to which various ingredients such as fish, meat, eggs, or shellfish are added. *Açorda de marisco,* a tasty combination of bread, eggs, seasonings, and a hearty portion of assorted shellfish, is one of the more popular varieties. Another version, *açorda da Alentejana,* is a clear broth with olive oil, slices of bread, garlic, and a poached egg floating on the surface. Pork from the Alentejo is the best in the country and often is combined with clams, onions, and tomatoes in the classic dish *carne de porco Alentejana.* Cheese, particularly the tangy sheep's cheese from the Serpa region, is quite good, Elvas, near the Spanish border, is known for its tasty sugar plums. Alentejo wines—especially those from the Borba and Reguengos regions—are regular prize winners at national tasting contests.

In the Ribatejo and the Estremadura restaurants, the culinary emphasis is on fish, including the ubiquitous *bacalhau* (dried salt cod) and *caldeirada* (a hearty fish stew). The seaside resorts of Ericeira, Nazaré, and Peniche are famous for fresh lobster and other *mariscos* (shellfish). In Santerém and other spots along the Rio Tejo, a bread soup made with *savel*, a shadlike fish from the river, is popular, as are *enguias* (eels) prepared in a variety of ways. Roast lamb and kid are also widely enjoyed. Portuguese nuns have the reputation of making wonderful sweets, and the abundance of convents in the region has added many tasty and colorful sounding dishes—such as *queijinhos do ceu* (little cheeses from heaven)—to local dessert menus. The straw-color white wines from the Ribatejo district of Bucelas rank with the country's finest.

Between mid-June and mid-September reservations are advised at upscale restaurants. However, most of the establishments we list are moderate or inexpensive and do not accept reservations and have informal dining rooms where it's quite acceptable to share a table with other diners. Dress at all but the most luxurious restaurants is casual; any exceptions to the dress code or reservation policy are noted within the individual review.

Highly recommended restaurants are indicated by a star ★.

Category	Cost*
Very Expensive	over 5,000$00
Expensive	3,500$00–5,000$00
Moderate	2,500$00–3,500$00
Inexpensive	under 2,500$00

per person for 3-course meal, including service and tax and excluding drinks

Lodging The vast, primarily agricultural Alentejo and the Ribatejo are lacking in first-class hotels; the best accommodations in this region are the government-run inns called *pousadas*. Two of the finest in the country are in the Alentejo, one located in the ancient convent in Évora and the other in the castle at Estremoz. The pousadas are small, some with as few as six rooms, so reserving well in advance is essential. There are also a number of quality, government-approved private guest houses in the region. Look for signs reading *Turismo Rural* or *Turismo de Habitacão*. Several of these are included in our listings. For information about additional guest houses, contact: **Promocões e Ideaias Turisticas** (PIT: Alto da Pampilheira, Torre D–2, 2750 Cascais, tel. 01/486–7958, fax 01/284–2901). The more densely populated Estremadura is better equipped with quality lodgings, especially along the coast. In all areas during the summer months, reservations are recommended. Most establishments offer substantial off-season discounts.

Highly recommended hotels are indicated by a star ★.

Category	Cost*
Very Expensive	over 15,000$00
Expensive	12,00$00–15,000$00
Moderate	8,000$00–12,000$00
Inexpensive	under 8,000$00

*Unless noted otherwise, all prices are for standard double room with bath in high season, including tax and breakfast.

Abrantes
Dining

Cristina. In a town where good restaurants are scarce, this attractively decorated, rustic, family-run place on N3, 5 kilometers (3 miles) west of Abrantes, is worth the drive. Ask the restaurant's namesake, Cristina Mota, to tell you the daily special and hope it's *bacalhau com natas* (dried cod baked in a casserole with cream and potatoes), one of her most popular creations. *Rio de Moinhos, tel. 041/98177. MC, V. Closed Mon. Inexpensive.*

Dining and Lodging

Hotel Turismo. This hotel is perched in such a spectacular location, on a hill high above the Rio Tejo, that it's a shame the architect didn't create a more pleasing exterior design than this nondescript, pink-stucco eyesore. But inside is a different story, with an inviting, clubby lounge featuring a fireplace and comfy leather chairs. Guest rooms are on the small side but are comfortably furnished, and many of the newer rooms have terraces with wonderful vistas. The dining room—surrounded with picture windows—affords inspiring views, and is an excellent place to sample the delicious *palha de Abrantes* (straw of Abrantes), a tasty local dessert specialty that consists of thick egg and almond paste topped with yellow threadlike wisps made of eggs and sugar. *Largo de Santo António, 2200, tel. 041/21261, fax 041/25218. 41 rooms. Facilities: restaurant, bar, pool, tennis, parking. AE, DC, MC, V. Expensive.*

Alcácer do Sal
Dining

O Brazão. Don't be put off by the run-down exterior of this no-frills restaurant: It's the favorite eating place of local businesspeople. The open kitchen allows you to peek in and see for yourself what looks good. Sample *ensopa da garoupa* (fish stew), a typical dish from this part of the country. *Largo Prof. Francisco Gentil, tel. 065/62576. No credit cards. Closed Sun. Inexpensive–Moderate.*

Dining and Lodging

Pousada do Vale do Gaio. Located 27 kilometers (16 miles) east of Alcácer do Sal and 8 kilometers (5 miles) from Torrão in a secluded wooded area overlooking a man-made lake, this small, rustic lodge was built to house the engineers who constructed the nearby dam. In 1977 it was converted into a pousada and has become a favorite spot for hunters and fishermen. The rooms are utilitarian but comfortable and look out over the lake, and a surprising variety of excellent local dishes come out of the tiny restaurant. This is a good place to get away from it all. *Pousada do Vale do Gaio, 7595 Torrão, tel. 065/66610. 7 rooms. Facilities: restaurant, bar, water sports and fishing in lake, parking. AE, DC, MC, V. Moderate.*

Alcobaça
Dining

Trindade. An unpretentious, popular restaurant, Trindade is considered one of the town's best. The intimate dining room, lined with old photos of local scenes, reveals some of Alcobaça's history. Try the house specialty, *açorda de marisco*, and for dessert the homemade pastry. *Praça D. Afonso Henriques 22, tel. 062/42397. MC, V. Inexpensive.*

Lodging
★
Casa da Paderia. In this family establishment mom cooks and keeps house while son Luis manages the place. Guests mingle freely with the hosts of this delightful country inn, 5 kilometers (3 miles) outside of Alcobaça on N8, where comfortable living and sitting rooms are shared with the proprietors as well as other visitors. The bedrooms are large, and each is furnished with period reproductions and covered with dainty flowered wallpaper. Breakfast features hot, fresh, out-of-the-oven homemade bread, and Senhora Ventura will cook you a wonderful dinner upon request. *Aljubarrota, 2460, tel. 062/48272, fax 062/48242. 8 rooms, 2 apartments. Facilities: bar, pool, billiards, minigolf, parking. MC, V. Expensive.*

Batalha
Dining and Lodging
★
Pousada do Mestre Afonso Domingues. This pousada named for the architect who designed the famous Batalha Monastery offers 20th-century comfort in a modern, two-story, white-stucco building and is just steps away from the historic monument. The good-size upstairs rooms with patterned wallpaper are furnished in 17th- and 18th-century style, and several look out on the monastery. The first-floor restaurant, with its polished calçada floor and wood ceiling, faces the monastery. The menu includes several types of bacalhau and features an extensive wine list. *Pousada do Mestre Afonso Domingues, 2440, tel. 044/92260. 20 rooms, 1 suite. Facilities: restaurant, bar, parking. AE, DC, MC, V. Very Expensive.*

Lodging
Quinta do Fidalgo. This historic, two-story manor house adjacent to the monastery features a homey ambience: Guests gather and chat in the spacious living room or outside on the large terrace and in the pleasant garden. The rooms are comfortably and traditionally furnished. Reservations in summer are advised. *Quinta do Fidalgo, 2440, tel. 044/96114, fax 044/96114. 5 rooms. Facilities: bar, parking. No credit cards. Moderate.*

Beja
Dining
Gatus. Located in a quiet alley, close to the convent, the Gatus is a small, intimate establishment with a marble floor and wood paneling and is one of the best choices in this restaurant-poor town. The *ensopado de borrego* (lamb stew) or *bife Gatus* (braised beef with mushrooms and cream) are recommended. *Rua João Conforte 16–18, tel. 084/25418. MC, V. Closed Mon. Inexpensive.*

Lodging
Cristina. Until the new hotel on the edge of town is completed, this is the best accommodation in Beja. The property is a clean, modern, five-story building, conveniently located on one of the main shopping streets. Light and airy rooms have been newly decorated but are a bit sterile. *Rua de Mértola 71, 7800, tel. 084/42035, fax 084/29874. 28 rooms, 3 suites. Facilities: bar. AE, DC, MC, V. Inexpensive.*

Caldas da Rainha
Dining
★
Adega do Borlão. Tucked away on a quiet back street near the courthouse and decorated as an old winery with wine barrels and farm implements, the Adega has become popular with the young professionals in the area who come here to relax and enjoy a good meal. The open kitchen enables you to watch your food being prepared. A house special to try from the strictly Portuguese menu is the *javali* (wild boar), if it's in season. Also, the bread is baked fresh each day in a brick oven. *Rua Eng. Cancela de Abreu 11, tel. 062/842690. Reservations advised. MC, V. Closed Sun. Moderate.*

Dining and Lodging **Hotel Malhoa.** Most business travelers to the area choose this modern, eight-story hotel conveniently placed near the town center. The rooms are comfortable, but there aren't many details to indicate you're in Portugal. *Rua António Sergio 31, 2500, tel. 062/842180, fax 062/842680. 111 rooms, 2 suites. Facilities: restaurant, bar, pool, sauna, disco, bingo, garage. AE, DC, MC, V. Moderate.*

Lodging **Quinta da Foz.** This large, two-story manor house dating from
★ the 16th century is beautifully situated amidst lawns and trees at the edge of the Óbidos Lagoon, some 15-minutes' walk to the beach. This can be a quiet base from which to explore Caldas da Rainha, only 9 kilometers (5½ miles) away, or other towns in the region. The bedrooms are large and comfortably furnished with lots of flowers about. *Largo do Arraial, 2500, tel. 062/979369. 5 rooms. Facilities: tennis, horseback riding, parking. No credit cards. Expensive.*

Castelo de Vide **O Cantinho Particular.** This tiny place on a side street near the
Dining town square engages the help of all the family members—Mom cooks while Dad and Junior take care of the customers. The dining room is old but clean, and the basic Portuguese fare is simple and tasty. Your best bet is to ask Senhor Bernardo what he recommends. *Rua Miguel Bombarda 9, tel. 045/91151. No credit cards. Inexpensive.*

Dining and Lodging **Sol e Serra.** This modern, three-story, Mediterranean-style hotel sitting at the edge of town is just a five-minute walk to the castle and Juderia. Large rooms have balconies looking over the park, and the bar and spacious lounge that overlooks the pool is the town's most popular gathering place. The tastefully decorated restaurant with wooden beams is considered Castelo de Vide's best eatery and is one of the few places in Portugal where you can get a kosher menu. *Estrada de São Vincente, 7320, tel. 045/91301. 51 rooms. Facilities: restaurant, bar, parking. AE, DC, MC, V. Expensive.*

Constância **Quinta de Santa Barbara.** If you're looking for a place to im-
Dining and Lodging merse yourself for a while in the peace and quiet of the Portu-
★ guese countryside, look no farther. The Quinta, located about 3 kilometers (2 miles) east of Constância, has several sprawling buildings (a few of which date back to the 16th century) and occupies some 45 acres of farmland and cork and olive groves overlooking the Rio Tejo. Tired of the hectic life in Germany, Jan and Angelika Hild decided to open a country inn in 1988. They have achieved a wonderful blend of old-world charm and modern convenience. Each of the eight spacious rooms in the main house is individually furnished with 18th-century Portuguese reproductions and has a modern tiled bathroom. The small restaurant with a barrel-vault ceiling and stone walls specializes in local dishes prepared from old recipes (many of the ingredients are from the Quinta's own organic gardens). *Quinta de Santa Barbara, 2250, tel. 049/99150. 8 rooms. Facilities: restaurant, bar, tennis, pool, horseback riding, parking. No credit cards. Moderate.*

Elvas **Pousada de Santa Luzia.** Opened in 1942, this was Portugal's
Dining and Lodging first pousada, and its convenient location—just 12 kilometers
★ (7 miles) from one of the major border crossings between Spain and Portugal—was no accident. The two-story, Moorish-style building has been remodeled several times: All bedrooms on the second floor are good-sized and cheerfully decorated with

hand-painted Alentejo furniture and bright floral fabrics. The modern tiled bathrooms are small but adequate. The large restaurant has arched windows overlooking an attractive garden and is a favorite with Elvas residents. One of the most popular dishes is *bacalhau dourado* (cod fish sautéed with eggs, potatoes, and onions). Reserve a room in advance of your visit. *Pousada de Santa Luzia, 7350, tel. 068/622194, fax 068/622127. 15 rooms, 1 suite. Facilities: restaurant, bar, parking. AE, DC, MC, V. Very Expensive.*

Ericeira
Dining and Lodging
★
Hotel de Turismo. Strangely reminiscent of a New York state Catskills Mountain resort hotel transplanted to the seashore, the Turismo is a sprawling, self-contained, low-rise—a classic old Portuguese beach hotel. The dramatic location at the edge of the breakers adds to the distinctive feel of the place. Public rooms are decorated with a delightful variety of colored tiles, and flowers and plants seem to be everywhere. Most of the spacious guest rooms have balconies with sea views. When you dine, choose your setting: The large restaurant is lined with picture windows looking out on the water, or you can be served on the seaside terrace. The international menu emphasizes seafood, and the quality is good. *Hotel de Turismo da Ericeira, 2655, tel. 061/864045, fax 061/63146. 250 rooms. Facilities: restaurant, bar, tennis, 3 pools, beach, disco, parking. AE, DC, MC, V. Expensive.*

Pedro O Pescador. If you prefer your hotels on a small scale, then you'll like this intimate, pastel blue-colored, family-run hotel located within walking distance of the beach. Cheerful rooms have planked floors and are decorated with flowered Alentejo furniture. The small, modern restaurant is frequented mostly by hotel guests. *Rua Dr. Eduardo Burnay 22, 2655, tel. 061/62504, fax 061/62321. 25 rooms. Facilities: restaurant, bar. AE, DC, MC, V. Moderate.*

Estremoz
Dining
★
Adega do Isaias. Hidden away on a narrow side street a few minutes' walk from the town square, this is the best place in town for hearty, no-nonsense roasts and grilled meats. The front part of the former wine cellar is a rough-looking bar; walk through to the dining area—a sloping, cement-floored cave that's lined with huge terra-cotta wine jugs. During your meal you sit on benches at planked tables; expect the service to be casual, at best, but the food is great and the place, popular with the locals, is always jammed. *Rua do Almeida, 21, tel. 068/ 22318. No credit cards. Inexpensive.*

Dining and Lodging
★
Pousada da Rainha Santa Isabel. Occupying a hilltop castle steeped in history, this pousada is the most luxurious in the country. The sumptuous lobby and other public rooms display literally tons of gleaming Estremoz marble and are decorated with 15th-century tapestries, Arraiolos rugs, and original paintings. The generous-size bedrooms are furnished with 17th- and 18th-century reproductions, and some of the rooms have elaborate four-poster beds. Just to sit in the baronial dining hall is a treat, and the food and service—in tune with the decor—are fit for a queen. Reservations are advised. *Pousada da Rainha Santa Isabel, 7100, tel. 068/00618, fax 068/23982. 20 rooms, 3 suites. Facilities: restaurant, bar, parking. AE, DC, MC, V. Very Expensive.*

Lodging
★
Monte Dos Pensamentos. This comfortable old country manor house surrounded by olive and orange trees is just 2 kilometers (1¼ miles) from Estremoz. The living room and large bedrooms

are cluttered with enough painted plates, dolls, and antiques to stock a good-size museum. The mood is casual and relaxed, and guests typically sit around the fire and share the cozy sitting room. *Estrada, Estacão Ameixial, 7100, tel. 068/22375, fax 068/284290. 4 rooms. Facilities: bar, pool, parking. No credit cards. Moderate.*

Évora
Dining
★

Fialho. Amor and Gabriel Fialho are the third generation of Fialhos to operate this popular, traditional restaurant, one of Évora's best. The beamed ceiling and painted plates on the walls lend a rustic ambience to what is quite a sophisticated kitchen. You might start with a selection of appetizers that includes an excellent *salada de polvo* (marinated octopus salad), and as a main course try *coehlo de convent a cartuxa* (breasted rabbit with potatoes and carrots, according to a recipe from a nearby monastery). A wide selection of Alentejo wines is offered. *Travessa das Mascarenhas 16, tel. 066/23079. Reservations advised. AE, DC, MC, V. Closed Mon. Expensive.*

★ **A Choupana.** Popular with the locals, this is a pleasant restaurant just off the main square. In one of its two rooms, there are a few tables and a counter with stools, and in the other there's a small, paneled dining area. Service is friendly, and the food is good. Try *açorda de mariscos* (bread porridge with shellfish). *Rua dos Mercadores 20, tel. 066/24427. MC, V. Closed Sun. Moderate.*

Dining and Lodging
★

Pousada dos Lóios. Located in an historic 15th-century monastery opposite the Roman Temple of Diana, this rates among the most luxurious pousadas in the chain. With the exception of the small size of the rooms and the need for anyone under 5' 2" to duck when entering the former monks' cells, there's nothing to remind one of the austerity of a monastery. The opulent period furnishings compensate for the slightly cramped quarters, while the elegant lounges and public rooms deserve a visit even if you don't plan to spend the night. In the former cloister, on the lower level, is the restaurant—a marvel of Manueline ceilings and columns and where superbly prepared Alentejo specialties are served. *Largo Conde de Vila Flor, 7000, tel. 066/24051, fax 066/27248. 31 rooms, 1 suite. Facilities: restaurant, bar, pool. AE, DC, MC, V. Very Expensive.*

Lodging

O Eborense. Located in an historic building with a delightful arch-lined gallery in the heart of the old town, this comfortable, family-run guesthouse offers quiet, old-fashioned hospitality. The rooms, while small, are comfortably furnished, as is the TV lounge. *Largo da Misericórdia 1, 7000, tel. 066/22031. 24 rooms, 1 suite. Facilities: bar. No credit cards. Moderate.*

Riviera. This cozy, three-story old manor house is well situated between Giraldo Square and the Roman Temple. The small, cheerful entry is decorated with colorful azulejos, and the rooms are covered with flowered wallpaper. Furnishings are in the traditional, painted Alentejo style. *Rua 5 de Outubro 49, 7000, tel. 066/23304, fax 066/20467. 22 rooms. Facilities: lounge. AE, DC, MC, V. Moderate.*

Fátima
Dining
★

Tia Alice. Considered the best restaurant in the area, Tia Alice, which means "Aunt Alice," is concealed in an inconspicuous old house with French windows and sits across from the parish church in the village of Fátima, near the Sanctuary at Cova de Iria. Inside, the flight of wooden stairs leads to the small, intimate dining area with a wood-beam ceiling and stone walls. Try the *borrego assado* (roast lamb). *Rua do Adro, tel. 049/531737.*

Reservations advised. MC, V. No dinner Sun., closed Mon. Moderate.

Retiro dos Caçadores. A big brick fireplace, wood paneling, and stone walls set the mood in this cozy hunter's lodge, where the food is simple, but portions are hearty and the quality good. This is the best place in town for fresh game, especially *coelho con arroz* (rabbit with rice) and *perdiz* (partridge). *Lombo Egua, tel. 049/531323. MC, V. Closed Thurs. Inexpensive.*

Lodging **Hotel de Fátima.** Sporting a four-star rating by DGT, the government tourist agency, this modern, four-story building—part of the Best Western chain—is in close proximity to the Sanctuary. Although it's generally considered to be Fátima's top hotel, with its spacious lobby with green-marble floors and wood-paneled walls, Hotel de Fátima seems otherwise institutional and undistinguished. The dining area and simply furnished but functional rooms are nondescript. *Rua João Paulo II, 2496, tel. 049/532351, fax 049/532691. 126 rooms, 7 suites. Facilities: restaurant, bar, garage, parking. AE, DC, MC, V. Moderate.*

Casa Beato Nuno. This large, pink-stucco inn, located in a quiet setting just a few minutes' walk from the Sanctuary, is run by the Carmelite Fathers but is open to visitors of all denominations. The austere rooms are clean and comfortable. *Casa Beato Nuno, Apt. 4, 2496, tel. 049/532199, fax 049/532757. 132 rooms. Facilities: restaurant, parking. No credit cards. Inexpensive.*

Leiria **O Casarão.** Located 5 kilometers (3 miles) south of Leiria in
Dining Azoia, at the Nazaré turnoff, O Casarão occupies a large rustic
★ house surrounded by gardens. This is a family enterprise in which Chef José Rodrigues supervises the outstanding kitchen staff while his wife, Clarissa, presides over the dining room. The service and presentation are flawless without being pretentious, and the extensive menu includes several ancient recipes from nearby monasteries. One of the best dishes is *bacalhau Tibarna* (thick cod filets baked in a casserole with olive oil, corn bread, and potatoes). Be sure to leave room for the *bolo pinão* (pinenut cake). The comprehensive wine list presents labels and lists 120 different wines. *Cruzamento de Azoia, tel. 044/871080. AE, DC, MC, V. Closed Mon. Moderate.*

Lodging **Eurosol.** A pair of modern, "medium-rise" hotels, the Eurosol and Eurosol Jardim occupy a hilltop location that's about a 15-minute walk from the town center. These hotels are popular stops for businessmen working in the area. The recently remodeled lobbies and bedrooms are spacious and smartly furnished, and the eighth-floor restaurant is ringed with picture windows affording bird's-eye views of the town. *Rua Dom José Alves Correia da Silva, 2400, tel. 044/812201, fax 044/811205. 128 rooms, 7 suites. Facilities: restaurant, bar, pool, fitness room, garage. AE, DC, MC, V. Moderate.*

Liz. Conveniently situated in the town center across from the park, the Liz is a cozy old hotel with creaking floors and a lived-in feel. The large lounge with its fireplace can be particularly homey. Clean and comfortable bedrooms offer plain furnishings. *Largo Alex, Herculano 10, 2400, tel. 044/31017, fax 044/25099. 41 rooms. Facilities: bar. AE, DC, MC, V. Inexpensive.*

Lourinhã **Golf Mar.** This hotel's idyllic location—on a rise overlooking a
Lodging broad, sandy beach—is the main reason you'd choose to stay

here: The high rise's huge, concrete-block facade is hardly alluring, and the uninspiring interior suffers here and there from peeling paint and frayed carpets. However, if you're a golfer looking for a course, this is your only option in the region. *Praia do Porto Novo, 2560 Torres Vedras, tel. 061/984157, fax 061/984261. 267 rooms, 9 suites. Facilities: restaurant, bar, 9-hole golf course, tennis, horseback riding, indoor and outdoor pools, disco, billiards, parking, AE, DC, MC, V. Very Expensive.*

Estalagem Areia Branca. This is a small, modern hotel with a favored cliff-top location, about 10 minutes by foot from a lovely sandy beach. The furnishings are serviceable and not much more, and the place could use an injection of charm (save for the fantastic views from some of the rooms). The restaurant looks out over the ocean and serves mostly seafood, including fresh shellfish taken from a large tank. *Praia da Areia Branca, 2530, tel. 061/412491, fax 061/413143. 34 rooms. Facilities: restaurant, bar, pool, parking. AE, DC, MC, V. Moderate.*

Areia Branca Youth Hostel. This large, full-facility hostel situated on the beach has 116 beds (56 for women, 56 for men, 2 for couples), a lounge, bike rentals, and three meals a day. *Areia Branca beach, 2530, tel. 061/422127. Inexpensive.*

Marvão
Dining and Lodging
★

Pousada de Santa Maria. In 1976 several old houses within the city walls were joined together to create the Pousada de Santa Maria and in 1992 the inn was enlarged and remodeled. The rooms have spectacular views and are decorated with traditional Alentejo furnishings and the restaurant serves some of the best food in the village, especially local favorites such as *migas a Alentejana com carne de porco* (marinated pork with a bread and sausage stuffing). *Pousada de Santa Maria, 7330, tel. 045/93201, fax 045/93202. 27 rooms. Facilities: restaurant (reservations advised in summer), bar. AE, DC, MC, V. Very Expensive.*

Dom Dinis. This comfortable country inn at the foot of the castle occupies a restored 200-year-old house with massive stone window and door frames. Bedrooms, which have fantastic cliffside views, are furnished with light pine furniture. In the adjacent building is the restaurant, where you sit at planked-wood tables while enjoying good hearty regional fare. *Rua Dr. Matos Magalhaes, 7330, tel. 045/92236. 15 rooms, 8 with bath. Facilities: restaurant, bar. AE, DC, MC, V. Inexpensive.*

Monsaraz
Dining
★

Casa do Forno. The labor of love of two ambitious women (Gloria and Mariana), Casa do Forno is an upscale restaurant in a picturesque fortified village. At the entrance is a huge, rounded oven with an iron door, hence the name O Forno—Portuguese for "oven." Picture windows line the dining room and offer a spectacular view over the rolling plains. The Alentejan menu appropriately features roasts, and one special dish worth trying is the *borrego Convento Orado* (roast lamb from an ancient recipe obtained at the nearby monastery). *Travessa de Sanabrosa, tel. 066/55190. Reservations advised in summer. MC, V. Closed Tues. Moderate.*

Lodging

Horta da Moura. This self-contained mini-resort 15 kilometers (9 miles) east of Reguengos de Monsaraz, on a well-signed dirt road, is set on a working farm between the walled city and the Ria Guadiana. The main house, whose white-stucco facade is highlighted with blue trim and an arched portico, is typical of Alentejo-style architecture. Inside, vaulted brick ceilings with wood beams and traditional furnishings make the atmosphere comfortable. The outlying buildings include stables, a riding school, a crafts room, a winery, and a recreation center with a large fireplace. The helpful staff eagerly arranges walking, horseback-riding, and cycling trips along the nearby Ria Guadiana, as well as four-wheel-drive and canoe excursions. Hunting and fishing trips can also be arranged. *Horta da Moura, Apt. 64, 7200 Reguengos de Monsaraz, tel. 066/55206, fax 066/55241. 4 rooms, 7 suites, 1 apartment. Facilities: pool, tennis, horseback riding, bicycling, snooker, fishing, hunting. AE, DC, MC, V. Very Expensive.*

Casa Nuno. This small, rustic guest house occupies a restored old white house on the main street of the walled town. Clean rooms with modern furnishings offer fantastic views over the valley, and the sunsets, alone, are worth the price of a room. Casa Nuno is a perfect little romantic hideaway in an ancient village. *Rua José Caeiro 6, 7200, tel. 066/55146. 8 rooms. Facilities: parking. MC, V. Inexpensive.*

Nazaré **Arte Xavega.** Set on a hill overlooking the town, this is by far
Dining Nazaré's classiest restaurant. Gardens and plants help to establish the comfortable blend of elegance and intimacy that owner Antonio Figueira has achieved for Arte Xavega. The international menu emphasizes local seafood specialties, including *arroz de marisco* (shellfish with rice). *Ladeira Sitio-Meia Laranja, tel. 062/552136. AE, DC, MC, V. Expensive.*

Dining and Lodging **Ribamar.** Situated on the main drag across from the beach, this family-run restaurant and boardinghouse couldn't hope for a more convenient location, though sometimes in summer it's noisy. Bedrooms are small, but all are clean and well-kept; ask for one that faces the sea. The restaurant, decorated like a country tavern, has large windows overlooking the beach; seafood is the main attraction, particularly the *caldeirada* (a hearty fish stew favored by the local fishermen). *Rua Gomes Freire 9, 2450, tel. 062/551158. 23 rooms. Facilities: restaurant (reservations advised in summer), bar. AE, DC, MC, V. Moderate.*

Lodging **Hotel Praia.** In spite of its popularity, Nazaré lacks a really first-rate hotel, but the 25-year-old, six-story Praia comes closest to filling the bill. The hotel is comfortable and clean, but still, it's uninspiring. *Av. Vieira Guimaraes 39, 2450, tel. 062/561423, fax 062/561436. 40 rooms. Facilities: garage. AE, DC, MC, V. Moderate.*

Óbidos **Alcaide.** From the upstairs dining room of this rustic tavern on
Dining the main street, patrons can enjoy a lovely view of the old town. The Alcaide is often jammed with hungry sightseers, especially from May through October; this is not the place for those seeking a quiet, romantic hideaway. The food, however, is always carefully prepared, and the service is attentive. Try the *coelho a Alcaide* (grilled rabbit with potatoes). *Rua Direita between main gate and castle, tel. 062/959220. AE, DC, MC, V. Closed Mon. Moderate.*

Dining and Lodging **Pousada do Castelo.** If you've ever fantasized about living in
★ luxury within a medieval castle, this is a wonderful place to fulfill that wish. Pousada do Castelo occupies parts of the historic castle that King Dinis presented in 1282 to his young bride, Isabel, as a wedding gift. Except for the electric lights and the relatively modern plumbing in the bathrooms, the style of the

Middle Ages prevails throughout the inn, from the guest rooms to the beautifully tiled lounge and dining room—where the food and service are worthy of a royal castle. Room #2—situated within one of the massive stone towers—is especially evocative of ancient times; other rooms are uniquely furnished with 16th- or 17th-century reproductions. The restaurant boasts a curtained alcove where you can dine in privacy but still enjoy a splendid view of the castle walls and valley below. Try the *cabrito assado* (roast kid). *Pousada do Castelo, 2510, tel. 062/959105, fax 062/959148. 6 rooms, 3 suites. Facilities: restaurant, bar, parking. AE, DC, MC, V. Very Expensive.*

Albergaría Josefa d'Óbidos. Built into the hillside at the main gate, this attractive, flower-bedecked country inn is the next best thing to Pousada do Castelo. The rooms are outfitted with comfortable 18th-century reproductions, including massive wood furnishings that enhance the old-country-inn feeling, even though this accommodation is only 10 years old. The Albergería features several reproductions of Josefa d'Obidos's works in the bar; and a large, rustic restaurant with an open brick grill features a variety of regional specialties. Try the *arroz de tamboril* (monkfish with rice) or one of the many preparations of *bacalhau* (codfish). The ambience of the otherwise-charming dining room is sometimes disturbed by the presence of large tour groups. *Rua D. João de Ornelas, 2510, tel. 062/959228. 40 rooms, 2 suites. Facilities: restaurant, bar, disco. AE, DC, MC, V. Moderate.*

Peniche **O Canhoto.** Unlike many of the expensive touristy restaurants
Dining along the harbor, O Canhoto puts less emphasis on the trappings and more on the simple but tasty food. This is a typical, no-frills Portuguese fish restaurant—set on a narrow side street—where you're almost always assured a good meal, especially if you ask for the *peixe do dia* (fish of the day). *Rua 13 de Infantaria 22, tel. 062/74512. No credit cards. Inexpensive.*

Lodging **Praia Norte.** Praia Norte, a modern three-story hotel, sits on the outskirts of town and offers reasonable rates. Most rooms are generous in size and overlook the hotel's large pool. Guest quarters are light and simply furnished but lack charm. The large water park adjacent to the hotel is a nice feature for families with children. *Av. Monsenhor Basto, 2520, tel. 062/781166, fax 062/781165. 97 rooms, 3 suites. Facilities: restaurant, bar, pool, parking. AE, DC, MC, V. Moderate.*

Portalegre **O Abrigo.** This is a small, very "local" restaurant, set on a quiet
Dining street around the corner from the cathedral. The small, cork-lined dining room, presided over by owners Adriano and Pedro, is entered through a snack bar—indication that this is a modestly run establishment. One of the best dishes on the menu is *açorda de marisco* (bread porridge with eggs and shellfish, served steaming hot in a terra-cotta bowl). *Rua de Elvas 74, tel. 045/22778. No credit cards. Closed Tues. Inexpensive.*

Dining and Lodging **Dom João III.** This is a modern multistoried hotel situated across from the city park. Although the lobby and hallways are somewhat institutional, rooms are more pleasant: Many have balconies overlooking the park. The large, top-floor restaurant, a favorite with local businessmen, is ringed with picture windows looking over the town. An international menu offers regional specialties. *Av. da Liberdade, 7300, tel. 045/21192, fax 045/24444. 58 rooms, 2 suites. Facilities: restaurant, bar, pool. AE, DC, MC, V. Expensive.*

Portalegre Youth Hostel. This hostel is located in the center of town in a 13th-century monastery. It offers 44 beds (22 for women, 22 for men), a lounge, a kitchen, and serves breakfast. *Praça da República, 7300, tel. 045/23568. Inexpensive.*

Santa Clara
Dining and Lodging
★
Pousada de Santa Clara. Its remote hidden setting, overlooking the Santa Clara dam and a huge lake, and its proximity to the Algarve (an hour's drive from the crowded beaches) make this pousada a great retreat. At press time, however, the hotel was closed for extensive remodeling and to add a new 26-room annex. By early 1994 the pousada should be open. *Enatur, Pousadas de Portugal, Av. Santa Joana a Princesa 10, 1700 Lisbon, tel. 01/8481221, fax 01/805846. 32 rooms. AE, DC, MC, V. Very Expensive.*

Santerém
Dining
Portas do Sol. A small restaurant in the town's most scenic location, the Portas do Sol is surrounded by flowers and trees in the gardens of the same name. This is a good place to combine a pleasant lunch on the brick-walled terrace with a walk around the gardens. Good regional dishes are offered here: Try the *bacalhau a bras* (cod slivers with scrambled eggs and onions). *Jardim das Portas do Sol, tel. 043/29520. AE, DC, MC, V. Moderate.*

Lodging
Quinta de Vale de Lobos. This is a delightful two-story, 19th-century farmhouse situated on N3, 6 kilometers (4 miles) from Santerém, among trees, ponds, and gardens. Guests enjoy lounging in the large comfortable living rooms and strolling in the adjacent woods. The four generously sized bedrooms are comfortably furnished. *Azoia de Baixo, 2000, tel. 043/429264, fax 043/429313. 4 rooms, 2 apartments. Facilities: pool, access to 600-acre hunting estate, parking. Expensive.*

Victoria. Situated on a quiet street, in a residential apartment building, Victoria provides a relaxed stopover. The owner of this eponymous family-run lodging, Senhora Victoria will make you feel right at home. The old section is a bit drab, so try for a room in the new wing. *Rua Visconde 2, 2000, tel. 043/22573. 25 rooms. Facilities: limited parking. MC, V. No credit cards. Moderate.*

Santiago do Cacém
Dining
★
O Retiro. The joint efforts of an Austrian and his Portuguese wife have turned this Alentejo cottage in the heart of town into a cozy international restaurant. Farm implements adorning the walls help set a "down-home" tone in this friendly but professional restaurant, which serves good solid Portuguese fare. *Rua Machado dos Santos 8, tel. 069/22659. Reservations advised in summer. MC, V. Closed Sun. Moderate.*

Dining and Lodging
★
Pousada de Santiago. Sitting atop a small rise at the end of town is this rose-colored, ivy-clad manor house surrounded by mature trees and gardens. One of the first pousadas created, the Santiago has had time to cultivate comfort: Over the years its guest and public rooms have been extensively remodeled so that visitors feel almost as if they're staying in a private home. Some rooms view the castle; all units are furnished with decorative Alentejan pieces. As for the restaurant, the intimate dining room has a wood-beamed ceiling and a tiled fireplace, and you'll be served quality local favorites such as *carne de porco Alentejana* (pork and clams). In summer the terrace opens up for meals under the stars. *Pousada de Santiago, 7540, tel. 069/22459. 8 rooms. Facilities: restaurant, bar, pool, parking, AE, DC, MC, V. Moderate.*

★ **Quinta da Ortiga.** This lovely old country estate, located just 5 kilometers (3 miles) from Santiago do Cacém, sits amidst some 10 acres of trees and farmland and features interior decor—wood-panel ceilings and Arraiplos carpets—that can best be described as "luxury rustic." The ambience is reminiscent of a comfortable rural villa, and the intimate restaurant, which features gastronomy of the region, is more like an old-style family dining room than a commercial establishment. Try this inn—managed by ENATUR—the same government owned and operated organization that handles the pousadas, for a quiet, comfortable base from which to enjoy the Alentejo's beaches. *Apartado 67, 7540, tel. 069/22871, fax 069/22073. 7 rooms. Facilities: restaurant, bar, chapel, pool, horseback riding, parking. AE, DC, MC, V. Minimum 7-night stay with ½-board required July–Sept. Moderate.*

Serpa
Dining and Lodging
★
Pousada de São Gens. Perched on a hill next to the Chapel of Guadalupe and overlooking the white houses and fortifications of Serpa, this modern, white-domed, Moorish-style pousada offers a relaxed and informal lodging option. The Arabic influence accompanies you as you walk through the green-tiled entrance to the lobby with its ubiquitous arches and vaulted ceilings. Each of the rooms has a small terrace, and bright, cheery fabrics nicely offset the white walls and ceilings. The restaurant has a small, brick-floored dining room with an open fireplace, and in summer guests may dine on the terrace looking over the pool and the plains. Tasty local specialties include *poejada de bacalhau* (dried cod fried with bread and seasoned with pennyroyal). *Pousada de São Gens, 7830, tel. 084/90327, fax 084/53337. 16 rooms, 2 suites. Facilities: restaurant, bar, pool, parking. AE, DC, MC, V. Very Expensive.*

Terena
Dining and Lodging
★
Casa de Terena. A few years ago Susanna Bianchi and her partner, Arnaldo Aboim, gave up successful careers in Lisbon to buy and restore a dilapidated 18th-century townhouse in this out-of-the-way village. Now a charming inn, Casa de Terena offers six comfortably furnished bedrooms featuring period reproductions. In the morning guests dine in what was once the stable, but is now a delightful breakfast room. Across the street the rustic Migas Restaurant—named after the family dog—serves simple but tasty traditional fare. *Rua Direita 45 7250 Alandroal, tel. 068/45132, fax 068/45155. 5 rooms, 1 suite. Facilities: restaurant, bar, parking. Moderate.*

Tomar
Dining
★
A Bela Vista. The date on the polished *calçada* (stone pavement with small black stones on a white background) floor reads 1922—when the Sousa family opened this attractive little restaurant located next to the old arched bridge. For summer dining there's a small, rustic terrace with views of the river and the Convent of Christ. Carrying on the family tradition, son Eugenio Sousa presides over the kitchen, which turns out great quantities of hearty regional fare. Try one of the house specialties such as *cabrito assado* (roast kid) or *dobrada com feijao* (tripe with beans), and wash it down with a robust local red wine. *Marquês de Pombal 68, tel. 049/312870. No credit cards. Closed Tues. Moderate.*

Dining and Lodging
★
Hotel dos Templários. A large, modern hotel set in a tranquil park along the Rio Nabão, the Templários offers a number of rooms in a completely new wing and many units with views of the Convent of Christ. The big, airy dining room has picture

windows facing the park and good, though uninspiring, food. With its spacious grounds and several swimming pools, the hotel makes a good base from which to visit the area's many attractions. *Largo Candido dos Reis 1, 2300, tel. 049/321730, fax 049/322191. 172 rooms. Facilities: restaurant, bar, indoor and outdoor pools, tennis, barbershop, beauty parlor, parking. AE, DC, MC, V. Expensive.*

★ **Pousada de São Pedro.** Originally built in 1946 to house engineers working on the construction of the dam on the Rio Zezere, this pousada, which sits on a wooded hill and overlooks the Albufeira do Castelo do Bode, the largest man-made lake in Portugal, is undergoing extensive remodeling. The project, scheduled for completion by early 1993, promises to produce 10 additional rooms among other improvements. Pousada de São Pedro's location 18 kilometers (11 miles) from Tomar, in Castelo de Bode, makes a good place from which to explore nearby villages. The restaurant was not open at press time, but the menu is expected to feature regional fare, The setting is lovely. *Pousada São Pedro, Castelo de Bode, 2300, tel. 049/381175, fax 049/381176. 25 rooms. Facilities: restaurant, water sports, parking. AE, DC, MC, V. Expensive.*

Torres Novas
Dining
★

A Tavolá. This simple, friendly, family-run neighborhood restaurant, presided over by Francisco and Isabel Vieira, emphasizes regional dishes, and their *cabrito assado no forno* (roast kid filled with bacon, sausage, and olives) garnered first prize at a regional gastronomic fair. Since it's only about a 10-minute walk from the castle, A Tavolá makes a good dining spot after seeing the sights. *Av. Dr. Manuel de Figueiredo 12, tel. 049/23983. MC, V. Closed Sat. Moderate.*

Dining and Lodging

Hotel dos Cavaleiros. Conveniently located facing the main square, this modern three-story hotel blends in well with the surrounding 18th-century buildings. Rooms are moderately sized and have plain, light-wood furnishings; ask for one with a terrace on the third-floor. In spite of its sterile, coffee-shop appearance, the restaurant serves generous portions of well-prepared traditional dishes. Try the *espetada mista* (grilled pork, squid, and shrimp on a spit). *Praça 5 de Outubro, 2350, tel. 049/811951, fax 049/812052. 57 rooms, 3 suites. Facilities: restaurant (closed Sun.), bar. AE, DC, MC, V. Moderate.*

Vila Franca de Xira
Dining
★

Redondel. Located inside the walls of the famous bullring, this restaurant sees a lot of action and is considered Vila Franca's top eatery. There are high-vaulted brick ceilings and, in keeping with the theme, the dining room is adorned with bullfighting posters and memorabilia. On the menu are regional dishes including *açorda de saval* (bread porridge with fish from the Rio Tejo). *Arcadas da Praça de Touros, tel. 063/22973. Reservations required on bullfight and festival days. AE, DC, MC, V. Closed Mon. Moderate.*

Marisqueira Fartazana. In this spotlessly clean local fish restaurant, the accent is on good, simple food rather than decor, and the specialty is shellfish of all kinds. Try the *arroz de mariscos* (an assortment of shellfish served in a bowl with rice), a good filling dish. *Rua Almirante Cândido Reis 131, tel. 063/32943. No credit cards. Closed Mon. Inexpensive.*

Dining and Lodging

Flora. For simple but well-maintained budget accommodations, try this modern, four-story hotel conveniently located in the center of town. The small, homey restaurant provides good food at reasonable prices. *Rua Noel Perdigão 12, 2600, tel. 063/*

23127. 14 rooms, 7 with bath. Facilities: restaurant, bar, limited parking. MC, V. Inexpensive.

Lodging ★ **Lezíria Parque Hotel.** This four-story, modern hotel-and-apartment complex offers the first new accommodations to be built in Vila Franca de Xira in many years. Conveniently situated off the main Lisbon–Porto road, the hotel provides a comfortable base from which to explore the bull- and cattle-breeding region across the Rio Tejo. The rooms are small and plainly furnished; there's a pleasant coffee shop on the ground floor. *Estrada Nacional 1, Povos, 2600, tel. 063/33813, fax 063/26364. 71 rooms. Facilities: indoor pool, parking. AE, DC, MC, V. Moderate.*

Quinta do Alto. Once you drive through the massive iron gates of this hotel, you may have a hard time leaving. Situated on 50 choice acres of orchards, gardens, and vineyards in the hills high above the Rio Tejo and just 30 minutes from the Lisbon airport, the Quinta do Alto—once the exclusive summer residence of a prominent Portuguese family—has been recently opened for paying guests to have the run of the spacious house and grounds. The feeling here is more that of visiting a wealthy friend or relative than of being a lodger. Each of the 10 large bedrooms is comfortably furnished and has a luxurious bathroom; half the units provide terraces and views of the countryside overlooking the Rio Tejo. Red brick adorns the vaulted ceilings, and the tile floors are enhanced with Arraiolos carpets. The price includes use of the extensive facilities and transportation to and from the airport. Breakfast and snacks are available for guests. *Quinta do Alta, 2600, tel. 063/26850, fax 063/26027. 10 rooms. Facilities: bar, disco, snacks, pool, tennis, squash, fitness room, sauna, kennels, parking. AE, DC, MC, V. Very Expensive.*

Vila Nova de Milfontes
Dining **O Quebra Mar.** If you're looking for fresh grilled fish and a fantastic view of the estuary and sand dunes, there's no better place in town than this simple beach bar-restaurant. *End of beach rd., tel. 083/99263. No credit cards. Inexpensive.*

Dining and Lodging ★ **Castelo de Milfontes.** This 16th-century castle was built on ancient foundations, for it was believed that the spirits there would ward off marauding Algerian pirates. In recent times owner and hostess Dona Margarida de Castro e Almeida has lovingly transformed this ivy-covered edifice into a comfortable guest house. Nearly everything you would expect a castle to have is still intact: battlements, a drawbridge, moat, and a suit of armor. The rooms are comfortably furnished and offer inspiring views over the dunes and estuary. There is no public restaurant, but the hotel provides meals for guests, and there's a lovely intimate family-style dining area that's lined with tiles. Full board is required. *Castelo de Milfontes, 7645, tel. 083/96108. 7 rooms. Facilities: restaurant (hotel guests only), bar. Moderate.*

6 The Algarve

By Jules Brown

The Algarve, Portugal's southernmost coastal region, is the most favored destination of foreign visitors to the country. It's a well-known holiday center with clean, sandy beaches and excellent sports facilities, coupled with an equable climate and a highly reasonable economy. Many Europeans fly here directly and rarely stray more than a few kilometers from their resorts. Even for those visitors based in Lisbon, the Algarve is an easy 300-kilometer (183-mile) drive south, and it provides an interesting contrast to the rest of the country.

Along with the region's popularity has come progress, and during the past two decades, the Algarve has been heavily developed, with parts of the once pristine, 240-kilometer (146-mile) coastline now seriously overbuilt. In certain areas apartment complexes, hotels, discos, and bars sprout from every bay and clifftop.

However, just 60 years ago the Algarve was rarely visited by tourists, and for centuries before that it remained isolated from the rest of Europe. Phoenicians, Romans, and Visigoths established fishing and trading communities here, but it wasn't until the arrival of the Moors in the 8th century that the region became an important strategic settlement. The Moorish capital of El Gharb (the land beyond), established at the inland town of Silves (in those days called Chelb), had direct access to the sea and at its peak was a grand city with a population of more than 30,000. Silves fell to the Christians in 1189, but the Moors weren't completely pushed out of the region until the middle of the 13th century, a 500-year rule that left many tangible reminders, extant even in today's Algarve: the Arabic place names; the white, cube-like houses in the coastal fishing villages; the popular fruits and sweets of the region; and the physical features of much of the population.

In the 15th century Prince Henry the Navigator established a town and a pioneering navigational school at Sagres, where the principles were learned that would enable Portuguese mariners of the 16th century to explore much of the world. However, after this flurry of attention, the Algarve once again settled into obscurity until modern times.

The Algarve, a mere 40 kilometers (25 miles) long, is bordered in the north by the Serra de Monchique (Monchique Mountains) and the Serra de Caldeirão (Caldeirão Mountains) and in the east by the Ria Guadiana, a river that isolated the Algarve from contact with neighboring Spain. Over the centuries it's been easy for the region's inhabitants to keep to themselves, as the area has many natural advantages: That the Algarve is in the southern part of Portugal and is protected by hills makes it much warmer here than any other place in the country; the vegetation is far more luxuriant; the land, originally irrigated by the Moors, supports a profusion of fruits, nuts, and vegetables; and the fishing industry has always flourished.

Despite the development the region still makes a fine coastal vacation: There are small fishing villages and secluded beaches (particularly in the west) that so far have escaped attention; an abundance of extraordinary rock formations and idyllic grottoes, also in the west; and (to the east) a series of isolated sandbar islands and sweeping beaches that balance the crowded excesses of the middle. Even where tourist development is at its heaviest, new construction means landscaped villa and apartment complexes that use local materials that not only fit in well with the surroundings, but keep money circulating within the community. But the Algarve is often seen at its best by visitors who are prepared to abandon the popular beaches for a drive inland. Here, rural Portugal still survives in hill villages, market towns, and agricultural landscapes which, though only a few kilometers from the coast, seem a world away in attitude.

Year-round the Algarve's weather is welcoming: Winters are mild, and spring is positively delightful, with blossoms covering the hillsides. Summer is, of course, high season, when lodgings are at a premium, prices at their highest, and crowds at their thickest. But you'll also find warm seas, piercing blue skies, and golden sands at the foot of glowing, ocher-red cliffs.

Warning The Algarve is one of Europe's most popular sites for holiday or retirement homes. If you didn't know that before you arrived, you'll soon get the picture in towns such as Albufeira and Praia da Rocha, where an entire industry exists to persuade visitors to tour apartment developments and proposed sites, with hope that they'll sign on the dotted line. You may be approached by agents offering all sorts of inducements (such as free gifts and meals and drinks) to encourage you to visit time-share properties and villa complexes. Even if you do agree to go on a tour— *never* sign anything, regardless of the promises made.

Essential Information

Important Addresses and Numbers

Tourist Information Albufeira (Rua 5 de Outubro, tel. 089/512144), **Armação de Pêra** (Av. Marginal, tel. 082/312145), **Faro** (Airport, tel. 089/822582; Rua da Misericórdia 8–12, tel. 089/803604), **Lagos** (Largo Marquês de Pombal, tel. 082/763031), **Loulé** (Edifício do Castelo, tel. 089/414336), **Monte Gordo** (Av. Marginal, tel. 081/44495), **Olhão** (Largo da Lagoa, tel. 089/713936), **Portimão** (Largo 1 de Dezembro, tel. 082/23695), **Praia da Rocha** (Av. Marginal, tel. 082/22290), **Quarteira** (Av. Infante de Sagres, tel. 082/312217), **Sagres** (Promontório de Sagres, tel. 082/64125), **Silves** (Rua 25 de Abril, tel. 082/442255), **Tavira** (Praça da República, tel. 081/22511), **Vila Real de Santo António** (Praça Marquês de Pombal, tel. 081/44495; Frontier Tourist Post, tel. 081/43272).

Consulates American and Canadian citizens must contact their consulates in Lisbon (*see* Important Addresses and Numbers in Chapter 3). However, there are two British consulate offices in the Algarve: at Portimão (Rua de Santa Isabel 21, tel. 082/23071) and Vila Real de Santo António (Rua General Humberto Delgado 4).

Emergencies For emergencies dial 115, the national emergency number.

Hospitals **Lagos** (Rua do Castelo dos Governadores, tel. 082/63034); **Faro** (Rua Leão Pinedo, tel. 089/22011); **Portimão** (tel. 082/22132).

Police **Lagos** (Rua General Alberto Silveira, tel. 082/62930); **Faro** (Rua Serpa Pinto, tel. 089/22022), **Portimão** (tel. 082/22510).

Late-Night Pharmacies Each town in the Algarve has at least one late-opening pharmacy; check with the local tourist office for current schedules.

Travel Agencies   There are travel agencies on practically every corner in every town in the Algarve, and most of them will assist you with purchasing tickets and choosing tours. Reliable agencies include: **Star** (agents for American Express: Rua Conselheiro Bivar 36, Faro, tel. 089/25125); **Marcus & Harting** (Rua Conselheiro Bivar 69, Faro, tel. 089/24034; Rua Caetano Feu 2, Praia da Rocha, tel. 082/22175); **Viagens Rawes** (Rua Conselheiro Bivar 72–78, Faro, tel. 089/803195; Rua da Hortinha 34C, Portimão, tel. 082/23092); **Wagon-Lits** (Rua do Pé da Cruz 14, Faro, tel. 089/28403).

Arriving and Departing by Plane

Airport and Airlines   International and domestic air services use **Faro airport** (tel. 089/23081), which is 6 kilometers (3½ miles) west of the town. Considerably expanded in 1989, the airport now accommodates frequent direct international flights from various European cities, and TAP—the Portuguese national airline—has regular daily services from Lisbon and Oporto, in the North. Flying time from Lisbon is 45 minutes; from Oporto it takes 90 minutes. At the airport you'll find car rental agencies and a tourist office. (The staff can assist you in finding a hotel room in town if you don't already have reservations.)

Between the Airport and Faro   The easiest way to reach the center of Faro is to take a taxi from outside the terminal building. The cost should be about 1,000$00, but ask the price before departing. Buses nos. 16 and 18 make the same journey and stop at Faro harbor in the center of town.

Arriving and Departing by Car, Train, Bus, and Ferry

By Car   To reach the Algarve from Lisbon, cross the Rio Tejo bridge and take the toll road to Setúbal, then follow signs for Alcácer-do-Sol, and Grândola/Ourique. Seventy kilometers (43 miles) south of Ourique is the intersection with the N125, the Algarve's main east-west thoroughfare. To reach Portimão, Lagos, and the western Algarve, turn right; go straight to reach Albufeira; and turn left for Faro and the eastern Algarve. The drive from Lisbon to Faro, Lagos, or Albufeira takes about four hours, longer in the summer weekend and holiday traffic.

Visitors heading to the Algarve from Spain by car can now drive from Ayamonte (the Spanish frontier town) across a new suspension bridge over the Ria Guadiana to Vila Real de Santo António, the easternmost town of the Algarve. The border is open year-round 7AM–11PM; from July through September and at Easter and Christmas, it's open 24 hours.

By Train   There are regular daily departures to the Algarve from Barreiro station, which is 10 kilometers (6 miles) south of Lisbon, across the Rio Tejo (*see* Essential Information in Chapter 3). The route runs through Setúbal to the rail junction of Tunes (3 hours from Barreiro): Trains continue from Tunes on to Albufeira (another 10 minutes), Faro (another 40 minutes), and all stations east to the border town of Vila Real de Santo António (another 2 hours). For the western route to Silves (20 minutes) and Lagos (1 hour), you must change trains at Tunes.

By Bus   There are daily express-bus services between Lisbon and several towns in the Algarve, including Portimão (4 hours 30 minutes), Lagos (5 hours 30 minutes), Faro (5 hours 30 minutes), Tavira (5 hours), and Vila Real de Santo António (5 hours 30 minutes). Generally this is a more comfortable experience than traveling by train, and some of the luxury coaches have a toilet, TV, and food service. Various companies operate the services, and any travel agency in Lisbon can reserve you a seat. In summer book your seat at least 24 hours in advance. For details of travel agencies in Lisbon, *see* Essential Information in Chapter 3.

A new bus route is planned that will cross the suspension bridge from the Spanish town of Ayamonte to Vila Real de Santo António, but at press time the service was not in operation. The tourist office will have up-to-date information.

By Ferry The car-passenger ferry that runs between Ayamonte in Spain and Vila Real de Santo António operates and is an alternative to driving over the new suspension bridge. In season ferries run April through October, daily 7AM–11PM with departures every 30 minutes; November–March, daily 9AM–9PM, with hourly departures. The journey takes 15 minutes and costs 100$00 per person, 600$00 per car.

Getting Around

Public transportation in the Algarve is fairly good due to the demands of the tourist industry, although sometimes service can be infrequent. Regardless, this region is one of the few in Portugal where having a car isn't essential (but, of course, you'll have more flexibility with a car).

By Car The main east-west highway in the Algarve is N125, which extends 165 kilometers (100 miles) from Vila Real de Santo António on the Spanish border to Vila do Bispo, north of Cabo São Vicente in the far west of the Algarve. It's an inland road running parallel to the coast but has clearly signed turnoffs to beachside destinations along the route. New, faster stretches of highway are under construction throughout the Algarve, but at present drivers should expect congestion in the summer near the busy resorts. In inland areas of the Algarve, minor country roads that are not always well maintained are typical, so as in the rest of the country, drive with care.

Car Rentals Almost all major international firms have offices at Faro airport, and many have branches elsewhere in the Algarve, too. Tourist offices can advise about local firms. Try **Auto Jardim** (Albufeira: Av. da Liberdade, tel. 089/859715; Faro: airport, tel. 089/818433); **Avis** (Albufeira: Rua da Igreja Nova 13, tel. 089/52678; Faro: airport, tel. 089/818538; Lagos: Largo das Portas de Portugal 11, tel. 082/63691; Praia da Rocha: Hotel Algarve, Av. Tomás Cabreira, tel. 082/415029; Quarteira: Centro Comercial Abertura Mar, tel. 089/314519; Vilamoura: Hotel Dom Pedro, 8125 Quarteira, tel. 089/314519); **Budget Rent-a-Car** (Faro: airport, tel. 089/24888, and Hotel Eva, Av. da República 1, tel. 089/803493; Albufeira: Cerro Grande, tel. 089/54997; Praia da Rocha: Av. Tomás Cabreira, tel. 082/415370); **Europcar** (Faro: airport, tel. 089/818777 or 089/818316; Monte Gordo: Praça Luis de Camões, Loja D, tel. 081/41747; Praia da Rocha: Av. Tomás Cabreira, tel. 082/415465); **Hertz** (Faro: Rua 1 de Maio, tel. 089/24877).

By Train The Algarve's railroad connects Lagos in the west with Vila Real de Santo António in the east—a route that's similar to the main highway. Several trains run daily along the entire route, which takes between three and four hours to complete; tickets are very reasonably priced. Traveling by train can be enjoyable in the scenic Algarve, but note that some of the stations may be several kilometers from the towns they serve, though there is usually a connecting bus service into the center. Good examples are the stations for Albufeira (6 kilometers/3½ miles from town) and Silves (2 kilometers/1¼ miles from the center). Also note that some of the faster trains don't stop at every station.

For train information contact the main stations: Faro (Largo da Estação, at the end of Av. da República, tel. 089/22653) and Lagos (across the river from town, tel. 082/62987).

By Bus The main form of public transportation in the Algarve is bus, and every town and village has its own terminal. Services are operated by many different companies, with major terminals at Lagos and Faro. Local tourist offices are the best place for information, although some routes are mentioned in the tour details below. Note that some local services are infrequent or don't run on Sundays. Distances between towns are usually short, so ticket prices tend to be relatively inexpensive, though a bus ride always costs more than the comparable train journey.

In Faro the bus station is on Avenida República behind the Hotel Eva. In Lagos most buses arrive at and depart from the station at the eastern end of town, opposite the bridge to the train station (buses to Portimão, however, depart from stops along the riverfront Avenida dos Descobrimentos).

Guided Tours

Orientation Organized guided bus tours of some of the Algarve's most noteworthy villages and towns depart regularly in summer from Faro, Quarteira, Vilamoura, Albufeira, Portimão, and Lagos. As there are various companies offering similar tours and prices, it's best to ask for recommendations from your hotel reception staff or the local tourist office representatives. **Abreu** (Av. da República 124, Faro, tel. 089/805335; Rua Infante Dom Henrique 83, Portimão, tel. 082/27151) is one of the largest and oldest travel agencies in the country.

Special-Interest A unique tour for the Algarve is a jeep "safari," which involves traveling to fascinating inland villages on minor, rural roads; lunch is usually included in the price. One company that operates such a tour is **Miltours** (Rua Veríssimo de Almeida 14, Faro, tel. 089/802030).

Coastal Excursions Many companies and individual fishermen along the Algarve coast hire out boats for excursions. These range from one-hour tours of local grottos and rock formations to full-day excursions that usually involve a stop at a beach for a barbecue lunch. Main centers for coastal excursions are Albufeira, Vilamoura, Portimão, Tavira, Lagos, Sagres, Vila Real, and Armação de Pêra. Consult the tourist offices in these towns for details, or simply wander down to the local harbor, where the prices and times of the next cruise will be posted on boards close to the boats.

Exploring the Algarve

Orientation

The Algarve may be the easiest region in Portugal to explore, since there is one main road—the N125—and a train line that connects towns and villages along almost the entire length of the coast. Journeys between towns are never very long, and it's possible to see all of the Algarve in a week's time, going at a fairly relaxed pace. Of course, you may want to spend several days at just one of the splendid beaches and resorts along the way; but do make an effort to see both the eastern and western ends of the Algarve and an inland town or two, for each has a very distinct character.

Most of the tours in the Exploring section begin in Faro—the Algarve's capital—from where various beaches and inland towns are accessible. The second tour moves east along the coast to the border town of Vila Real de Santo António, a point from which, you may cross into Spain. The third suggested route covers the area of the central Algarve, from Faro west to Portimão, the most built-up part of the coast, which bursts with enjoyable attractions. The final tour begins in Lagos, the main town of the western Algarve, and continues as far as Cabo São Vicente, the most southwesterly point of the European continent.

Highlights for First-Time Visitors

Albufeira (*see* Tour 3)
Cabo São Vicente (*see* Tour 4)
Cidade Velha, Faro (*see* Tour 1)
Fortaleza de Sagres (*see* Tour 4)
Igreja de Santo António, Lagos (*see* Tour 4)
Olhão's beaches (*see* Tour 1)
Portimão's harbor (*see* Tour 3)
Serra de Monchique (*see* Tour 3)
Silves (*see* Tour 3)
Tavira (*see* Tour 2)

Tour 1: Faro and Environs

Numbers in the margin correspond to points of interest on the Algarve and Faro maps.

❶ **Faro,** the provincial capital of the Algarve, is a prosperous city with around 30,000 residents. Many visitors fly into the nearby airport and pass straight through on their way to beaches east and west, but Faro has an attractive harbor and old town that is worthy of at least one night's stay. Moreover, if you intend to tour the region rather than simply laze at a beach resort, Faro makes a fine base for trips into the eastern and central Algarve.

Founded by the Moors, the city was taken by Afonso III in 1249, which marked the end of the Arab domination of Portugal. But despite its long history, much of Faro's architectural value was lost when the city, now in Spanish hands, was sacked by English forces under the command of the Earl of Essex in the late 16th century. Faro was further damaged by two 18th-century earthquakes, the last being the great one of 1755,

The Algarve

which also destroyed Lisbon. Nevertheless, remnants of the city's surrounding medieval walls and a series of historic buildings can still be seen in the delightful Cidade Velha (Old Town), the district across the harbor.

2 The main gate to the old town, the 18th-century **Arco da Vila** (Vila Arch), which stands in front of the central **Jardim Manuel Bivar** (Manuel Bivar Gardens), has a white marble statue of Saint Thomas Aquinas in a niche at the top.

The narrow, cobbled Rua do Municipio leads up to the Largo da Sé, a grand square bordered by orange trees and whitewashed **3** palace buildings. The squat mostly Renaissance-style **Sé** (Cathedral), at the top of the road, retains a Gothic tower, but the cathedral is mostly of interest for its stunning interior of decorated 17th- and 18th-century azulejos. Another highlight is the red Chinoiserie organ, which dates from 1751 and rests to one side of the nave. *Largo da Sé. Admission free. Open weekdays 10–noon, Sat. at 5PM for services, Sun. 8AM–1 for services.*

To the south of the cathedral, in Praça Afonso III, the 16th-century Convent of Nossa Senhora da Assunção has been con-**4** verted to house the **Museu Municipal** (Municipal Museum). The conversion makes fine use of the convent's beautiful two-story cloister. The best displays are the archaeological collections: These include fascinating Roman remains from local settlements predating Moorish Faro as well as Roman statues from the excavations at Milreu (*see below*). *Praça Afonso III 14, no tel. Admission: 120$00. Open Mon.–Sat. 9–noon and 2–5.*

The quiet streets and squares of the old town, with balconies and tilework that decorate even the most unappealing facade, are perfect for strolling through. Other than this there's nothing to do in Old Town unless you can gain entry to one of the churches. Many of them are locked, but you may want to ask **5** the tourist office about seeing the **Igreja de São Francisco** (Church of Saint Francis), east of the Municipal Museum, whose plain facade gives no hint of the richness of its baroque, interior. Inside are glorious 18th-century blue-and-white azulejos and a chapel adorned with giltwork. *Largo de São Francisco. Admission free.*

Walk back past the Cathedral and down through the town gate **6** to the water. The **porto** (harbor), flanked by Faro's main square and the Manuel Bivar Gardens, is one of the prettiest places in town. Here, at one of the many outdoor cafés, you can sit and watch the yachts ply the water.

Continue around the harbor in either direction, and on the **7** dockside past the Hotel Eva you'll find the **Museu Maritimo** (Maritime Museum), mainly of interest to boat enthusiasts. Models of local fishing craft are displayed alongside the real, sturdier boats of war and exploration, from the time when Portugal was a great seafaring nation. *Faro harbor, no tel. Admission: 100$00. Open Mon.–Sat. 10–noon and 2:30–4:30.*

Time Out The **Café Alianca** (Rua Francisco Gomes 7–11) is an old-style coffeehouse situated halfway around the harbor between Rua Francisco Gomes and Rua Marinha. Inside you'll find a time-worn ambience, and outside is a sidewalk café facing the water.

Behind the harbor, in the pedestrianized shopping streets
around Rua de Santo António, is everything that makes Faro
tick as a tourist town: There are dozens of bars and restaurants, shops, and sidewalk hawkers who sell souvenirs and
snacks. Spare some time for for a few cultural pursuits, too, in-
8 cluding a visit to the nearby **Museu Etnografico Regional** (Ethnographical Museum), which lies just off Rua de Santo António,
on Rua do Pé da Cruz. This gallery sheds light on the local fishing industry by way of various models and diagrams and also
features local crafts and reconstructions of typical house interiors. *Rua do Pé da Cruz, no tel. Admission: 50$00. Open week-
days 9:30–12:30 and 2–5:30.*

Ten minutes' walk in the other direction, across the city center,
9 stands the Baroque **Igreja do Carmo** (Carmo Church), which is
flanked by twin bell towers and looks very out of place amidst
the modern buildings surrounding it. The real interest is inside, where a door to the right of the altar leads to the **Capela
dos Ossos** (Chapel of the Bones): The chapel walls are covered in
skulls and bones taken from nearby monks' graves—an eerie
sight, to say the least! *Largo do Carmo. Admission free. Open
weekdays 10–1 and 3–5.*

After touring the city, most visitors are keen to head for the
10 local beaches, and the nearest one to Faro is on the **Ilha de Faro**
(Faro Island), a sand-bar island 5 kilometers (3 miles) to the
southwest of town. You can reach the long, sandy beach—the
Praia de Faro—by car, but in the summer it's far more enjoyable to make the 20-minute crossing by the hourly ferry that
departs from the jetty below Faro's old town. (Because of its

proximity to the city, the Praia de Faro has been heavily developed and in the summer is thick with crowds.)

It's better to head east from Faro on the N125 for the less-crowded sand-bar beaches that are accessible from the small **⑪** 18th-century port town of **Olhão,** 8 kilometers (5 miles) away on the Ria Formosa (River Formosa). Regular trains and buses from Faro also run here. During the Napoleonic Wars, Olhão's inhabitants defied the French blockade on trade with Britain and profited greatly from smuggling. With the proceeds residents built a town of North African-styled, cube-shaped whitewashed buildings. From Olhão local fishermen reputedly sailed to Brazil in 1808 to inform the exiled Dom João VI that the French had departed Portugal—for which service, undertaken without navigational aids, Olhão was granted a town charter.

Though modern construction has destroyed a great deal of its former charm, Olhão's fishing port is still colorful, and its intricate old town quarter has retained some of its earlier attraction. For a view over Olhão, visit the 17th-century **parish church,** from whose bell tower you can look down upon the narrow streets and cube houses. The church is located at the southern end of the main Avenida da República.

Also in town is one of the best food **markets** (open Monday through Saturday, 7–2) in the Algarve, housed in the buildings on the riverfront in the town gardens. Feast your eyes upon the shellfish for which Olhão is renowned: Mussels, in particular, are a local specialty.

To get to the local beaches, take a ferry from the jetty east of the town gardens. (You must buy tickets from the kiosk before boarding.) The sandy islands of **Armona** and **Culatra** lie to the east and are reached in 15 to 40 minutes, respectively. Armona is the best, with some fine, isolated stretches of sand, holiday villas, and café–bars; Culatra supports several ramshackle fishing communities, although at the southern village of **Farol** (meaning lighthouse), you'll find agreeable beaches. This entire section of coastline, including the islands and river inlets, has been declared a nature reserve, since a great number of migratory birds flock to the area on their way south for the winter. *Ferries run June through Sept., hourly, and cost 100$00–200$00; Oct.–May service is reduced.*

Other destinations close to Faro are inland. About 9 kilometers (6 miles) north of Faro, a road branches east from the N2 to the **⑫** village of **Estói,** which receives buses from Faro. Here the 18th-century **Palácio do Visconte de Estói** (Palace of the Counts of Estói) is closed to the public, but the caretaker allows visitors to stroll around the formal gardens (a tip of 200$00 or more is always welcome).

Close by, to the west of the village, are the extensive Roman **⑬** ruins at **Milreu,** first excavated in 1876. The settlement was once known as Roman *Ossonoba*, and the remains date from the second to the sixth centuries; they include a temple (later converted into a Christian basilica) and some mosaic fragments that adorn some of the third-century baths. You will have seen some of the more portable remains in the gardens of the nearby palace; others are in Faro's Municipal Museum. *Admission free. Open Tues.–Sun. 9–noon and 2–5.*

Seven kilometers (4 miles) farther north on the N2 is the village of **São Brás de Alportel,** which boasts one of the Algarve's two *pousadas*, or government-run inns (*see* Dining and Lodging, *below*). On the N2 turn to the west, and it's a 13-kilometer (8-mile) drive along the N270 to **Loulé,** a little market town in the hills. Once a Moorish stronghold, the town has preserved the ruins of its medieval **Castelo** (Castle), which houses the Loulé's historical museum and archives, as well as its tourist office. Nearby is the restored 13th-century **Igreja Matriz** (Parish Church): It's decorated with handsome tiles and wood carvings and features an unusual wrought-iron pulpit. *Castle and museum: Largo Dom Pedro I, no tel. Admission free. Open daily 9–12:30 and 2:30–5; Igreja Matriz: Largo da Matriz. Open Mon.–Sat. 9– noon and 2–5:30.*

Loulé is best known for its crafts, and the tiny, cobbled streets and their whitewashed homes that run between the castle and the church are lined with workshops where lace, leather, and copper goods are manufactured. It's fascinating to wander this area, watch the craftspeople at work, and explore the nooks and crannies of the old town. Note the many houses with sculpted plasterwork on the white chimneys, a typical Algarve sight. The rest of Loulé is more developed and is overwhelmed by the main boulevard and modern buildings, but there's a pleasant municipal park at the top of town.

Loulé is connected directly with Faro by bus, and the 17-kilometer (10-mile) journey makes visiting the town an easy half-day trip. To return to Faro by car, take the N125-4 southeast, which, after 8 kilometers (5 miles), joins the main N125.

Tour 2: The Eastern Algarve

Travel northeast from Faro along the N125 for 30 kilometers (18 miles) to reach **Tavira,** which is often described as the prettiest town in the Algarve. Situated at the mouth of the Rio Gilão (River Gilão), the town is one of the most immediately endearing, its old streets and pastel-colored houses straddling both sides of the quiet river, which is spanned by two low bridges. The bridge adjacent to the main, arcaded Praça da República is of Roman origin, though it was rebuilt in the 17th century. Throughout town many of Tavira's white, 18th-century houses retain their original doorways and coats-of-arms; others have peculiar, four-sided roofs. The best views of the town are from the battlemented walls of the central **Castelo** (Castle. Admission free. Open weekdays 8–5:30, weekends 9–5:30), reached by a stepped street leading from the main Rua da Liberdade, from where you can look down over the spires of Tavira's many churches and across the river delta to the sea.

If it's open, take a look inside the adjacent church of **Santa Maria do Castelo,** which was built upon the site of a Moorish mosque in the 13th century. Although almost all of it was destroyed by the 1755 earthquake, the church retains its original Gothic doorway. Tavira's other major church, located just west of the main square, is the nearby **Igreja da Misericórdia** (Church of the Misericórdia. Open daily 10–noon and 2–5), and is a beautiful Renaissance building with a portal dating from 1541.

Tavira is best known in the region as a tuna-fishing port, and it's an enjoyable town to walk through, especially along the riverfront gardens, past the vibrant covered market, to the harbor. The market always boasts an impressive array of fresh fish, while farther up the quayside is an entertaining tangle of fishing boats and nets, which makes a good snapshot.

Time Out You should be sure to sample the local catch, *atum* (tuna), while you're in Tavira. Fresh tuna steaks, often grilled and served with onions, are on sale in restaurants throughout the town at remarkably inexpensive prices. For a touch of real local color—no-frills dining at its best, with the local fishermen—walk past the market to the line of small, basic café-restaurants that face the fishing boats.

⓰ There are good beaches on the nearby **Ilha de Tavira** (Tavira Island), a long, offshore sand bar much like those near Olhão to the southwest. You can reach the beaches by ferries that leave several times daily from a jetty located 2 kilometers (1¼ miles) from Tavira. In summer there's a bus (marked Quatro Águas) that shuttles from the center of town to the jetty. *Ferries run June through Sept., daily 8–8; Mar.–May and Oct., 4 times daily.*

East of Tavira are more good beaches: A particularly nice one is located at the tiny, undeveloped village of **Cacela Velha,** 10 kilometers (6 miles) away, which also has its own offshore sand ⓱ bar. A few kilometers farther is the excellent **Monta Rota** beach, although the protective sand bars that stretch from Faro finally merge here with the shore. Unfortunately, the resulting long, unbroken beaches make terrain for heavy touristic development.

Six kilometers (4 miles) east of Monta Rota on N125, pine woods and orchards break up the flat landscape around the ⓲ large resort of **Praia de Monte Gordo,** which lies just 4 kilometers (2½ miles) from the Spanish border. A town of brightly colored houses and extensive tourist facilities, Monte Gordo features plenty of hotels and restaurants, as well as a casino, nightclubs, and discos. The long, flat stretch of beach is very popular, and visitors enjoy the highest average seawater temperature in the country. Be careful, though: The beach is steeply sloped, and swimmers quickly find themselves in deep water.

⓳ **Vila Real de Santo António,** the Portuguese border town, is the last stop before Spain, the country that lies across the Ria Guadiana. The original town was destroyed by a tidal wave in the 17th century and was not rebuilt until the late 18th century, when the Marquês de Pombal constructed a new, gridded town following the same pattern as the Baixa section of Lisbon. Consequently, Vila Real, which took only five months to complete, is a showpiece of 18th-century town planning. Like most border towns, it's a lively place, with plenty of bars and restaurants and some traffic-free central streets that encourage evening strolling. For all that, however, there's very little to see.

You might want to take an hour or so to visit the **Museu de Manuel Cabanas,** which contains some paintings, engravings, and local ethnographical items and is situated on Praça Marquês de Pombal, the attractive main square. *Praça Marquês de Pombal, no tel. Admission free. Open Tues.–Sun. 11–1 and 2–7.*

If you are driving on to Spain, the new suspension bridge is open for traffic; otherwise, ferries still cross the river to the

Spanish town of Ayamonte (Seville is another 160 kilometers/ 98 miles to the east on the N431).

If you're staying in Portugal, you can make an excursion north of Vila Real by following the minor N122, which runs through low hills and parallels the course of the Ria Guadiana. **Castro Marim,** 5 kilometers (3 miles) to the north, was the first head-quarters of the monastic Order of Christ, founded in the 14th century after the dissolution of the Knights Templar. The town has the remains of what was once a massive castle, which was built by Afonso III and was unfortunately laid to waste by the 1755 earthquake. However, the views from here are grand, and the surroundings have been turned into a nature reserve; there are paths through the nearby river marshes.

Tour 3: The Central Algarve

The central Algarve lies between Faro and Portimão and sees the heaviest concentration of tourist development: Some of the resorts are household names in Europe. Nevertheless, in be-tween the built-up areas, you can still discover quiet bays, amazing rock formations, and a series of exclusive, secluded ho-tels and villas that offer high standards and levels of comfort. With a car it's easy to travel the few kilometers inland that make all the difference: Minor roads lead into the hills, to towns that have resisted much of the changes wrought upon the devel-oped coast.

After about 10 kilometers (6 miles) along the northwest drive from Faro on the main N125, you'll see signposted minor roads that branch off south to the adjacent luxury resort villages of **Quinta do Lago** and **Vale do Lobo,** the latter being one of the Algarve's earliest resort developments. Both have superb facil-ities—from golf to sailboarding—and the tennis center at Vale do Lobo is among the best of its kind in Europe.

Drive on the N125 for 13 kilometers (8 miles) from Faro to reach the town of **Almansil** with its 18th-century chapel of **São Lou-renço** (St. Lawrence), situated just off the highway. What's most interesting about this chapel, built in 1730, is its blue-and-white azulejo panels and its intricate gilt work. The cottages next to the church have been transformed into an art gallery that exhibits contemporary Portuguese works and hosts occa-sional classical music concerts.

Just off the N125 is the N396 which, after about 6 kilometers (4 miles) to the southwest, will bring you to **Quarteira,** a bustling high-rise resort that was once a quiet fishing village but now offers golf courses, tennis courts, and an excellent beach. The remains of a Roman villa have been unearthed in the area. The adjacent town of **Vilamoura,** 4 kilometers (2½ miles) to the west, has no historical pedigree and is one of the most highly developed resort centers in the Algarve: There are an impressively large yacht marina, several golf courses, a major tennis center, and other sports facilities, as well as mod-ern luxury hotels and a casino.

Beaches to the west of Vilamoura—Falesia, Olhos d'Agua, and Praia da Oura—fall within the ambit of **Albufeira,** which lies 4 kilometers (2½ miles) south of the main road. Once an attract-ive fishing village, Albufeira has since mushroomed into the Algarve's largest and busiest resort area: It's considered too brash for many tastes but is a favorite with British holidaymakers. The town beach (reached by tunnel from the main street, Rua 5 de Outubro), with its interesting rock formations, caves, and grottos, attracts thousands of visitors daily; the noisy center, around Praça da República, is dominated by cafés, bars, restaurants, discos, and souvenir shops.

Despite the crowds, Albufeira has much to commend it, and a lunchtime stop at one of the cafés in the old town may be worth your while. One of the last Algarve towns to hold out against the Christian army in the 13th century, Albufeira still has a distinctly Moorish flavor that's apparent in the steep, narrow streets and hundreds of whitewashed houses snuggled on the slopes of nearby hills. There are the remains of a Moorish castle on the heights above town—under the Arabs the town was called *Al-Buhera* (castle on the sea)—and the bustling fish market and old harbor retain some interest, too.

On most summer days the town beach at Albufeira is so crowded that it may be difficult to enjoy: Those who require more space will have to move farther afield. Possibilities are just 4 kilometers (2½ miles) to the west and can be reached by minor local roads. They include the beautiful beaches of São Rafael and Praia da Galé, though there's been much recent development here, too. The coves and rocks are very attractive, but don't expect them to be deserted.

Fourteen kilometers (8½ miles) west of Albufeira, the bustling resort of **Armação de Pêra** has the largest beach in the Algarve, a wide, sandy stretch with a pretty promenade. Local boats take sightseers on cruises to the caves and grottos along the shore, past the Praia Senhora da Rocha (the Beach of Our Lady of the Rocks) to the west, named after the Romanesque chapel sited above the beach.

Return to the main road—N125—and at **Porches,** 16 kilometers (10 miles) to the west, you'll have an opportunity to stop at a variety of roadside shops that sell handmade pottery. Five kilometers (3 miles) farther west is **Lagoa,** a market town known for its wine, *vinho Lagoa;* the red is particularly good. It's possible to tour the winery here, but you must ask the tourist office in Portimão to help you arrange for the visit.

The local beach is 5 kilometers (3 miles) to the south, at **Carvoeiro,** whose picturesque harbor will merit the diversion. Sadly, and like many small-scale fishing villages in the region, Carvoeiro is beginning to buckle under the strain of recent development.

Return to Lagoa and turn north for the 7-kilometer (4-mile) drive up the N124-1 to **Silves,** on the Rio Arade (River Arade). A visit to this town will give you an opportunity to see the rural side of the Algarve: It's not unusual to be stuck for miles behind tractors or donkey carts, and you may have to be bold and take initiative when you pass. But don't neglect to absorb the surrounding fields planted with orange groves and nut trees (almonds, in particular).

Once the Moorish capital of the Algarve, Silves is one of the region's most intriguing inland towns. Rich and prosperous in medieval times, Silves remained in Arab hands until 1249, though not without earlier attempts by Christian forces to take the city: In 1189, following a siege led by Sancho I, the city was sacked by Crusaders, who subsequently put thousands of Moors to the sword. Silves finally lost its importance after it was almost completely destroyed by the 1755 earthquake. Today it makes an enjoyable day trip from the coast, as it's just 20 kilometers (12 miles) north of Portimão (train and bus connections are available).

The Moors built an early fortress in Silves, which survived untouched until the Christian sieges. The remains that you see today from the 12th-century sandstone **fortress,** with its impressive parapets, was restored in 1835 and still dominates the upper part of the town. You can walk around the walls for expansive views over Silves and the surrounding hills. The rest of the castle is mere shell, its interior with a modern garden, watched over by a statue of Sancho I. *Admission free. Open daily 9–1 and 2:30–5:30.*

Immediately below the fortress stands the 12th- to 13th-century **Santa Maria da Sé** (Cathedral of Saint Mary), which was built upon the site of a Moorish mosque and which saw service as the Cathedral of the Algarve until the 16th century. The effects of the earthquake in 1755 and indifferent restoration have left it rather plain inside, but its exterior gargoyles and tower still are interesting to see. *Admission free; donations accepted. Open June–Sept., daily 8:30–1 and 2:30–6; Oct.–May, until 5:30.*

Silves's excellent new **Museu Arqueologia** (Archaeological Museum) is located a few minutes' walk below the cathedral, off Rua da Sé. Although the artifacts' explanations are in Portuguese, the items on display still give some interesting insight into the history of the area from prehistoric times until the 16th century. One of the best attractions of the museum, is that the building preserves, in situ, an Arab water cistern—with a 10-meter- (30-foot-) deep well—which is among the most impressive Arab remains in town. *Rua das Portas de Loulé. Admission: 250$00. Open Mon.–Sat. 10–1 and 2–5.*

Time Out From the archaeological museum, walk back to the main Praça do Municipio. From here, you can walk straight downhill to the foot of town where, close to the medieval bridge that spans the river, is the local **produce market.** It's at its liveliest during the morning, but if you arrive at lunchtime, you'll find a number of simple restaurants that face the river and have outdoor barbecues, from which you can choose a delicious meal of spicy grilled chicken or fish. The market is open Monday through Saturday.

Drive northeast for 12 kilometers (7 miles) along the N124, to the scenic **Barragem de Arade,** a manmade dam set in the hills. Facilities here include a restaurant, picnic area, and boat rentals. Another 8 kilometers (5 miles) farther the road passes **29** through the attractive countryside village, **São Bartolomeu de Messines,** whose parish church dates from the late 14th century and has interior columns of spiraling, rope-like stonework. You can take a coffee break in the village before you return to the N124, back through Silves, and finally regaining the main N125.

Once back on the main road, continue for another 9 kilometers **30** (5½ miles) to **Portimão,** the most important fishing port in the Algarve. Even before the Romans arrived, there was a settlement here, at the mouth of the Rio Arade. Unfortunately, the town lost most architectural evidence of its heritage in the 1755 earthquake. Revived by the fish-canning industry in the 19th century, modern Portimão sprawls with concrete high-rise buildings but remains a cheerful, busy place: Tourists from nearby resorts come here especially to shop. The colorful fishing boats now unload their catch at a modern terminal across the river, but you can still sample charcoal-grilled sardines—a local specialty—at most of the open-air restaurants along the harbor.

Time Out Lunch at an open-air restaurant in Portimão's **harborside** is a must, the air thick with barbecue smoke and the tang of the sea. There are many inexpensive eateries that offer excellent grilled sardines, chewy fresh bread, a simple salad, and local red wine.

Across the bridge, in the former fishing hamlet of **Ferragudo,** are the ruins of the 16th-century castle of São João, which was built to defend Portimão from attack by marauding English, Dutch, and Spanish forces. Although it has not yet gone the tourist route of nearby Praia da Rocha (*see below*), Ferragudo is becoming developed for those who are attracted to the beach to the south, where sailboard rentals are available, and there are restaurants and bars.

31 **Praia da Rocha,** just 3 kilometers (2 miles) south of Portimão on the N125, was one of the first resorts in the Algarve to undergo a transformation for the mass market and is now dominated by high-rise apartments and hotels. Despite its development, the town boasts an excellent beach, made all the more interesting by a series of huge colored rocks worn into strange shapes by the wind and sea. Praia da Rocha also retains the 16th-century **Santa Catarina,** a defensive castle that has been partially restored and contains an open-air café. Regular buses run throughout the day and depart from Portimão to Praia da Rocha, and vice versa. Other beaches near Portimão are to the **32** west, around the handsome old port of **Alvor,** whose central narrow streets and whitewashed houses are increasingly being encroached upon by villa and hotel development in the vicinity. The crowds are attracted to Alvor's huge beach which, while not one of the region's best, does usually have space to spare.

To wind down your tour of the central Algarve, drive (there are buses, too) north from Portimão on route N124 (which changes after 7 kilometers/4 miles to become the N266), into the green hills of the **Serra de Monchique,** which form the northern boundary of the region. After 18 kilometers (11 miles) you'll **33** reach the beautifully sited spa town of **Caldas de Monchique,** whose natural therapeutic waters have been in use since Roman times. (The cool breezes here will provide a welcome respite from the coastal heat in the height of summer). A revival in popularity in the 19th century left the town with an attractive set of period houses and municipal buildings, including a casino, which is now in use as a handicrafts market. Unfortunately, the modern spa buildings themselves are less than attractive. If you want to sample the health-inducing waters between June and October, call 082/92205 for an appointment.

The N266 climbs another 6 kilometers (4 miles) to the market **34** town of **Monchique,** also known for its handicrafts: Many locals are skilled in carving and carpentry. From here it's 8 kilometers (5 miles) west along the minor road N266-3 to the highest point of the mountain range, at the town of **Foia** (902 meters), where there's a café and superb views over the western Algarve.

Having taken in the views, you can return the way you came, to Portimão, from where the N125 will either take you east back to Faro, or west and on to Lagos (*see* Tour 4, *below*).

Tour 4: Lagos and the Western Algarve

From the bustling holiday town of Lagos, the rest of the western Algarve is easily accessible. This is the most unspoiled part of the region, with some genuinely isolated beaches and bays along a wind-buffeted route that reaches to the southwesterly Cape of Saint Vincent.

Numbers in the margin correspond to points of interest on the Algarve and Lagos maps.

㉟ **Lagos**—an attractive, busy fishing port with some beautiful and startling cove beaches in the vicinity—draws a mixed international crowd. Unlike many Algarve towns, Lagos has a venerable history, with sights to prove it: Here, you feel, is a town whose inhabitants follow a way of life that goes beyond simply catering to tourists. However, there is no shortage of attractions for visitors, and the main pedestrianized streets
㊱ leading off the central **Praça Gil Eanes** are lined with shops, restaurants, cafés, and bars—all of which do a roaring business in the summer months.

Lagos's deep-water harbor and wide bay have made it a natural choice for various groups of settlers, starting with the Carthaginians, who founded the town around 400 BC. Under the Moors Lagos was a center for trade between Portugal and Africa, and even after the town fell to the Christians in 1241, trade continued and was greatly expanded under the rule of Prince Henry the Navigator, who used Lagos as his base. Lagos later became capital of the Algarve, a role it lost in 1756 after the great earthquake had reduced much of the city to rubble. Nonetheless, some interesting buildings remain, as does the circuit of defensive walls, built between the 14th and 16th centuries over older, Moorish defenses. Some of the best-preserved parts of the walls can be seen from near the Praça da República, at the seaward end of Avenida dos Descobrimentos.

㊲ The old **Casa Da Alfandega** (Customs House), at the back of the Praça da República, was the site of an African slave market held under the arches of the building in the 15th century.

㊳ Across the square stands the **Igreja da Santa Maria** (Church of Saint Mary), from whose Manueline-styled windows the king Dom Sebastião purportedly addressed his troops before setting off on his crusade of 1578. The crusade was a failure, and the king and his men died in Morocco at Alcácer-Quibir; Dom Sebastião is remembered by a much-maligned modernistic statue that stands in Praça Gil Eanes. *Praça da República. Admission free. Open daily 10–1 and 2–5.*

A short walk away, up Rua Henriques Correira Silva, is Lagos's most extraordinary building, the early 18th-century
㊴ Baroque **Igreja de Santo António** (Church of Saint Anthony), off

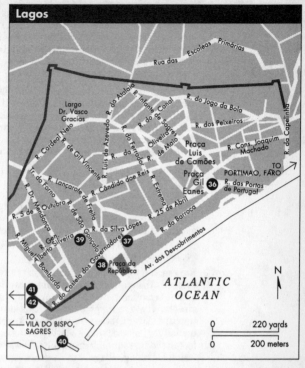

Lagos

Rua das Escoleas Primárias

Rua das

Largo Dr. Vasco Gracias

R. da Atalaia

R. Infante de

R. do Jogo de Bola

R. do Canal

R. do Ferrado

R. dos Peixeiros

R. Cardeal Neto

R. de Gil Vincente

R. Luís de Azevedo

R. do Sagres

Oliveira de Maio

R. de Maio

R. Cons. Joaquim Machado

R. da Capelinha

Praça Luís de Camões

TO PORTIMÃO, FARO

Tr. do Forno

R. Dr. Mendonça

R. Lancarote de Freita

R. Cândido doe Reis

R. Extrema

Praça Gil Eanes **36**

R. das Portas de Portugal

R. 5 de Outubro

R. de São Gonçalo

R. 25 de Abril

R. da Silva Lopes

R. da Barroca

R. Miguel Alberto Bombarda

R. Gen. R. Silveira **39**

R. Gonçalo dos Governadores **37**

Av. dos Descobrimentos

R. do Castelo dos Governadores

38 Praça da República

41
42

TO VILA DO BISPO, SAGRES

40

ATLANTIC OCEAN

N

0   220 yards

0   200 meters

Rua General Alberto Silveira. The decoration inside is a magnificent riot of gilt extravagance made possible by the import of gold from Brazil. Dozens of male and female cherubs and angels clamber over the walls, while in between lie fancifully carved woodwork and azulejos. Alongside the church is the **Museu Municipal** (Municipal Museum), housing an amusing jumble of exhibits, including mosaics, archaeological finds, and ethnographical items—all arranged haphazardly. Also displayed is an early town charter dating back to 1504. *Rua Henriques Correira Silva. Admission to church and museum: 200$00. Open Tues.–Sat. 9:30–12:30 and 2–1.*

The largest beach near town and one of the best centers for water sports is the 4-kilometer (2½-mile) stretch of Meia Praia to the northeast. Buses run here from the riverfront Avenida dos Descobrimentos, or there's a summer ferry service from close to the 17th-century fort at **Ponta da Bandeira,** from where the entrance to the harbor was defended in bygone days. From the inside you can look out onto decent ocean views. *Av. dos Descobrimentos. Admission: 200$00. Open Tues.–Sat. 10–1 and 2–6, Sun 10–1.*

All the other good beaches are south of town and can be reached on the main road (an extension of Avenida dos Descobrimentos) running past the fort. You could drive to the prettiest one—**Praia de Dona Ana**—by following the signs for the Hotel Golfinho (*see* Dining and Lodging, *below*), but the 30-minute walk along the clifftop is also very enjoyable. If you choose to hoof it, pass the fort, turn left at the fire station, and follow the footpaths, which go all the way to the most southerly point,

42 **Ponta da Piedade,** and its lighthouse. Along the way are several delightful cove beaches with fascinating rock formations and some beach-cafés. An interesting perspective is a view of the rocks and caves from the water: Fishing boats near the Ponta da Bandeira advertise cruises; check for departure times at the boards on the quayside.

Lagos is the western terminus of the railway that runs from Vila Real de Santo António; to head farther west, it's convenient to have a car. However, if you are not driving, there are good bus services from Lagos to all the destinations on this tour, but you may have to walk from the stops on the main N125 highway to the more isolated beaches.

43 Six kilometers (4 miles) to the west along the N125 is the resort town of **Luz** with its beautiful beach, which is 3 kilometers (2 miles) south of the highway, down a signposted minor road. Most visitors stay in fairly new villa or apartment complexes that have excellent watersport facilities. Despite the modern nature of the development, Luz is an attractive place, and if you would like to stay, the tourist office in Lagos can advise about accommodations.

44 **Burgau,** a few kilometers farther on the N125, is similarly developed, though this town retains something of its erstwhile village character, with its surviving square and narrow streets. It's a very popular vacation destination for British tourists. After another 5 kilometers (3 miles) you'll come to the **45** turnoff for **Salema,** with its lovely, 600-meter-long beach at the foot of the surrounding green hills. The town was until recently a simple fishing village, but new development is fast changing the face of this pretty place. Still, Salema is one of the most relaxed of local towns.

46 The N125 highway ends its run 8 kilometers (5 miles) farther west, at the small inland town of **Vila do Bispo,** a quiet place whose church—sited right in the center—has an interior covered in 18th-century azulejos. Once you've seen this, and stopped for a coffee at one of the cafés on the central square, you'll probably be ready to move on.

47 From Vila do Bispo the minor road, N268, leads south to reveal rugged terrain as you approach the windy headland at **Sagres,** 10 kilometers (6 miles) away. In the 15th century, on this harsh, barren moorland, Prince Henry the Navigator established his famous school of navigation, where he trained his captains before they set out on their voyages of discovery.

In the 19th century the village of Sagres was rebuilt over earthquake ruins and today contains little of note apart from a series of fine, sweeping beaches in the vicinity. Mainly a young crowd vacations here, and apartments and villas are growing steadily in number, with the expansion threatening to overwhelm the little square and fishing harbor.

You'll see the road that leads from the village to the tunnel-like entrance of the **Fortaleza de Sagres** (Sagres Fortress), an enormous run of defensive walls that sit high above the crashing ocean. On foot from the village, it's about a 15-minute walk, and the views are spectacular. The fortress was rebuilt in the 17th century and contains buildings often claimed to be Prince Henry's house and navigational school (it's now used as the tourist office and a youth hostel). More likely, is that Henry built his residence and school at Cabo São Vicente (*see below*), but this doesn't detract from the powerful atmosphere at the fortress. Certainly the **Venta da Rosa** (Wind Compass) dates from Prince Henry's period: It's a large circular construction made of stone and packed earth, and set in the courtyard just inside the fortress. It was only uncovered this century, though it is of the same age as the fortress's other relic, the partially ruined and forlorn Graça chapel, which stands near the tourist office.

Even more breathtaking than the views from the fortress are the sights from **Cabo São Vicente** (Cape of Saint Vincent), 6 kilometers (4 miles) to the west, at the end of the flat coastal road. At this point—the most southwesterly tip of the European continent—the landmass juts into the rough waters of the Atlantic and justly has been called *"O Fim do Mundo"*—"the end of the world." Legends attach themselves easily to this desolate place that the Romans once considered sacred. It takes its modern name from the martyr Saint Vincent, whose relics were brought here in the 8th century; it is said that they were transported to Lisbon 400 years later in a boat piloted by ravens.

Most historians agree that it was here where Henry built his house and school, and where Vasco da Gama, Ferdinand Magellan, and other great explorers learned their craft 500 years ago. The ancient buildings are long gone—having been destroyed by pirates and earthquakes—and the only structure that remains is a working **lighthouse,** the grounds of which are open to the public. Splendidly isolated, the beacon is said to have the strongest reflectors in Europe—as they cast a beam 96 kilometers (59 miles) out to sea. And the views from the surrounding walls of the Fortaleza de Sangres are remarkable: Turquoise water whips across the base of the rust-color cliff base below; the fortress is visible to the east; and beyond, lies the immense Atlantic.

On your return from the cape to Sagres you can stop halfway at **Belixe,** which has a couple of café-bars that you may wish to visit for a drink or a bite. Sagres is only a few kilometers farther east, and if you're not staying overnight at the Pousada do Infante (*see* Dining and Lodging, *below*), you can retrace your route along the N125 to Lagos.

What to See and Do with Children

The Algarve has several aquatic theme parks, where you'll find huge water slides, rapids, surf pools, other water-based amusements, and restaurants and snack bars. **Slide & Splash,** located near Portimão, is one of the largest, and it offers half-day trips with pickups from the region's hotels. *Estrada Nacional 125, Vale de Deus, Estômbar, tel. 082/341685. Admission: 2,000$00 adults, 1,300$00 children 5–10. Open mid-May–Sept., daily 10–6.*

Other attractions that would be of interest to children include: the splendid castle at **Silves** (*see* Tour 3); a **boat trip** around local caves and grottoes at Lagos (*see* Tour 4) or Armação de Pêra (*see* Tour 3); the dramatic fort at **Sagres** (*see* Tour 4); and **Cabo São Vicente** (*see* Tour 4).

Off the Beaten Track

Almost any deviation north from the main N125 highway will soon put you in open countryside, which, while not exactly uncharted territory, will show you a rural side of the Algarve that many visitors never see. Besides the inland destinations covered in the tours above, you may wish to try the following route:

Take the N122 north from just outside the border town of Vila Real de Santo António. This road climbs into low hills and parallels the course of the Ria Guadiana as it passes through **Castro Marim** (*see* Tour 2). After 37 kilometers (22½ miles) a branch road, the N122-1, leads northeast to the Spanish border town of Alcoutim, a quiet little village with a ruined castle. Return to the main road junction of the N122 and the N122-1, and drive west along the N124, a 65-kilometer (40-mile) route that offers fine views. The road will join the main N2 south to Faro, 14 kilometers (8½ miles) north of São Brás de Alportel.

Shopping

In every Algarve town you'll be able to find a selection of local crafts and souvenirs, in centrally located shops or at the markets and country fairs. In summer all the main tourist resorts have a lot of casual sidewalk stalls, where you can buy items such as jewelry, handicrafts, art, and clothes.

Probably the best place to shop in the Algarve is in Portimão, where many visitors enjoy spending at least half a day. The main shopping street is **Rua do Comércio,** while **Rua de Santa Isabel** specializes in crafts, leather goods, ceramics, crystal, and fashion. For shopping under one roof in Portimão, visit the enormous **Prisunic Shopping Center** (open daily 10 AM–10 PM), with 150 shops and restaurants. It's on the N124 (toward Praia da Rocha) at the junction with Avenida Miguel Bombarda.

Albufeira also boasts a new **Prisunic Shopping Center** (open daily 10 AM–10 PM), a complex with more than 60 shops on the bypass road above town. In Faro the best shopping area is the pedestrianized **Rua do Santo António** and the surrounding streets, where you'll find local handicrafts, ceramics, and leather goods.

Markets and Country Fairs

All the main towns and villages have regular **food markets,** usually held daily from 8–2. Among the best are those in Olhão, Tavira, Lagos, and Silves. Larger weekly and monthly markets where a wider variety of produce and goods are sold are organized in Loulé every Saturday; Lagos on the first Saturday of every month; Portimão on the first Monday of every month; Quarteira on the second Wednesday of every month; and Silves on the third Monday of every month. Ask the local tourist office for up-to-the-minute details and directions on how to get there.

Every town of any consequence in the Algarve also hosts an annual **country fair,** where alongside the market stalls you'll find crafts and entertainment. The dates vary from year to year, so check with local tourist offices.

Specialty Stores

Ceramics The **Olaria Pottery** (on the main N125), directly opposite the turn-off for Porches, produces fine traditional and originally designed tiles and tableware. In Portimão there's a branch of the well-known **Vista Alegre** (Rua de Santa Isabel 21), a showroom displaying high-quality, hand-painted porcelain. The same town also hosts **O Aquario III** (Rua Direita, Loja 10), which sells ceramics, porcelain, and crystal. Albufeira has **Infante Dom Henrique House** (Rua Cândid o dos Reis 30), whose stock includes porcelain dishes and baskets, as well as handmade Portuguese earthenware designed with 17th-century motifs.

Clothing The center for reasonably priced, hand-knitted sweaters is **Sagres,** where you'll see stalls outside the fortress.

Crafts For handmade copper items and other metal crafts, visit Portimão's **O Aquario II** (Rua Vasco da Gama 41).

Small woven sisal baskets make good souvenirs and are available nearly everywhere in the Algarve. You'll sometimes see women sitting in the doorways of their houses as they weave.

Loulé supports several craft workshops (closed Sundays) in the streets of its old town, particularly along **Rua 9 de Abril.** Also visit the spa town of Caldas de Monchique in the Serra de Monchique, where the 19th-century casino is now a **handicrafts market** (closed Sundays).

Leather Goods There are branches of the Parisian shoe store **Charles Jourdan** in Portimão (Rua de Santa Isabel 26) and in Albufeira (Edificio Tural, Av. de 25 Abril), where prices are considerably lower than in France.

For other leather goods, including bags and purses, visit Potimão's **Gaby's** (Rua Direita 5 and Praça Visconde Bívar 15), which sells high-quality items.

Sports and Outdoor Activities

Fishing

Individuals and charter companies offer organized fishing trips from various ports along the Algarve coast. Check the boards on quaysides for prices and departure times, or consult local tourist offices. The best fishing grounds are considered to be the waters off Sagres and Carrapateira, to the north, and local fishermen recommend October through January as the most fruitful fishing months. Fish you're likely to catch include gray mullet, sea bass, moray eels, scabbard fish, and bluefish.

Golf

The Algarve has some of Europe's best golf courses: They've been designed to very high standards by world-class professionals including Henry Cotton, Frank Pennink, and William Cotton. The game can be played in the region year-round, and almost all the courses have full facilities that usually include a clubhouse with bar and restaurant, practice grounds, and equipment rentals. Contact the **Quinta do Lago Golf Club** (Almansil, tel. 089/396002), a 36-hole course on the superb Quinta do Lago estate; the **Vale do Lobo Golf Club** (Vale do Lobo, tel. 089/394444), with three 9-hole courses; the **Vilamoura Golf Club** (Vilamoura I, tel. 089/313652; Vilamoura II, tel. 089/315582; Vilamoura III, tel. 089/380722), which has three different courses: two with 18 holes and one with 27; the 18-hole **Parque da Floresta** (Budens, 16 km/9.7 mi west of Lagos, near Salema, tel. 082/65333); or the **Palmares Golf Club** (Monte Palmares, Meia Praia, Lagos, tel. 082/62953 or 082/62961), whose 18 holes overlook Lagos Bay. Local tourist offices can give you details on the many other courses that were under construction at press time.

Guests at the many hotels with golf facilities can of course take advantage of them, and the privilege is included in the room rate. Those staying at the Hotel Dona Filipe in Vale do Lobo have free use of the new **San Lorenzo Golf Club** (Almansil, tel. 089/396522) and a 20% discount at the Vale do Lobo Golf Club. Guests at Alvor's Golfe da Penina may use the hotel's own course, the **Penina Golf Club** (Montes de Alvor, tel. 082/415415).

The Quinta do Lago Golf Club hosts the Portuguese Open Golf Championship in October.

Horseback Riding

Equestrian centers in the region include: **Quinta dos Amigos** (Almansil, tel. 089/39436); **Centro Hipico de Vilamoura** (Vilamoura, tel. 089/313033); and **Paradise Inn** (Almansil, Quinta do Lago road, tel. 089/396864).

Sailing

Vilamoura Marina (8125 Quarteira, tel. 089/312023 or 089/302925), 10 kilometers (6 miles) from Albufeira, is a self-contained marina complex of enormous proportions: It includes apartments, shops, hotels, and sporting and leisure facilities—and has 1,000 berths with power and water supplies.

Elsewhere there are anchorage and harbor facilities at the following ports: Faro, Lagos, Olhão, Portimão, Sagres, and Vila Real. The tourist office will provide details.

Sailboats are available for rental at the marinas at Vilamoura (tel. 089/313933), Vale do Lobo (tel. 089/394444), and Torralta, Alvor (tel. 082/20462).

Tennis

Tennis can be played in every resort, and many hotels and villa complexes have their own courts for guests' use. Vale do Lobo boasts the famous **Roger Taylor Tennis Center** (tel. 089/394311), one of Europe's best, with 12 all-weather courts, a clubhouse, sauna, pool, and restaurant. Other centers include the **Carvoeiro Tennis Club** (tel. 082/357847), with 10 courts; the **Vilamoura Tennis Center** (tel. 089/380088), with four courts; and the **Luz Bay Ocean Club** (tel. 082/789472), with three courts.

Water Sports

Snorkeling and scuba diving are possible at several places along the coast, and can be excellent in the western Algarve, where certified, experienced divers can take advantage of the many caves and rock formations. The **Sea Sports Center** (Av. dos Pescadores 4, tel. 082/789538) at Praia da Luz rents all the neccessary equipment and organizes dives.

Windsurfing equipment is available throughout the Algarve, and you can also rent from stands on the beaches at Meia Praia (Lagos), Quarteira, Vale do Lobo, Albufeira, Armação de Pêra, Ferragudo, Burgau, and the Luz Bay Club.

Waterskiing is less widely practiced, although it's possible to arrange a skiing excursion at the **Sea Sports Center** (*see above*) as well as at several of the beaches where windsurfing is popular.

Beaches

The Algarve's glory is its beaches, which are generally clear and impressive. Most (especially those in the main resorts) feature beachside snack bars and showers, and many offer watersports equipment rentals.

The Algarve's beaches are among the finest in the country. There are hundreds from which to choose along the long stretch of coast, many of which are described in the tours above. You may find that children, particularly, prefer the small, cove beaches to the crowded expanses of sand at resorts. Remember that although it's possible to wade out for a swim from most Algarve beaches, it's always wise to heed local warnings about currents and steeply sloping seabeds.

The best cove beaches are at **Lagos** (*see* Tour 4). Other interesting beaches are those with enormous rock formations such as the ones at **Albufeira** and **Praia da Rocha** (*see* Tour 3). If you require more breathing space, particularly if traveling with young children, try the strands near **Olhão** (*see* Tour 1) and **Tavira** (*see* Tour 2); these and the beaches near Sagres (*see* Tour 4) are less populated than those at major resorts.

Dining and Lodging

Dining Algarvian cooking is of very high quality and usually features the best of the day's catch from the sea. Nowhere is this seen better than with that most unusual of regional appetizers, *espedate fumada* (smoked swordfish), served in thin slices with a salad and appreciated all the more if accompanied by a dry white wine. Most restaurants serve their own version of *sopa de peixe* (fish soup) and a variety of succulent shellfish: *perceves* (barnacles), *santola* (crab), and *gambas* (shrimp). Main courses often depend on what's been landed that day, but there's generally a choice of *roballo* (sea bass), *pargo* (bream), *atum* (fresh tuna), and *espabarte* (swordfish). Perhaps the most famous Algarvian dish is the *cataplana*, a stew of clams, pork, onions, tomatoes, and wine, which takes its name from the lidded utensil used to steam the dish. You will generally have to wait for the dish to be specially prepared, but once you've tasted it, you won't mind waiting again and again.

Inland, in rural areas, game highlights most menus, with many meat dishes served *o forno* (oven-roasted). Specialties include *cabrito* (kid), *leitão* (suckling pig), and *codorniz* (quail), as well as *ensopado de borrego* (lamb stew).

You don't need to dine in a proper restaurant to taste the best that the Algarve has to offer. At simple beach cafés and harbor stalls the unmistakable smell of *sardinhas assadas* (charcoal-grilled sardines) wafts through the air: It's prepared anywhere for a tempting lunch to be served with fresh bread and smooth red wine. The splendid climate means that *alfresco* dining is possible throughout the year—and also that during any season you're assured a wonderful array of fresh fruit: The Algarve is particularly known for its oranges and figs.

For dessert the Algarve is famous for the rich egg, sugar, and almond custards that reflect the Moorish influence still found here. These include: *doces de amendoa* (marzipan cakes shaped into animals, birds, and flowers); *bolos de Dom Rodrigo* (almond sweets with egg-and-sugar filling); *bolo Algarvio* (cakes made of sugar, almonds, eggs, and cinnamon); and *morgado de figos do Algarve* (fig and almond paste).

Unless otherwise noted the dress code in restaurants is casual, and reservations are not needed off-season. During the busy summer, you'll need reservations at many of the best restaurants, but in the larger resorts you'll have little difficulty finding a seat at one of dozens of places that serve good food of comparable price and quality.

Restaurant ratings correspond to Lisbon's dining chart, in Chapter 3. Highly recommended restaurants are indicated by a star ★.

Lodging The Algarve has some of Portugal's best, and most relaxing, hotels, whose leisure and sports facilities are second to none. Visitors may choose from busy beachside hotels in the center of large resort areas or secluded retreats in luxuriant country estates. In summer advance reservations at most places are essential and can be arranged either through a travel agent or the Portuguese National Tourist Office.

The climate allows year-round sporting activities, and visitors may want to book a hotel that has special facilities included in the room rate—golf, tennis, and water sports, for example. The selection of hotels below details several places with superior offerings.

Apartment and villa complexes with luxurious amenities are popular in the Algarve. Some properties—built on the most beautiful parts of the coast—are fancy indeed. These accommodations, may be a good distance from major towns, but as most have bars, restaurants, and shops, and other facilities vacationers are usually content to stay on site.

In addition to accommodations listed below, budget lodging are available. In most of the region's main towns and resorts travelers will be approached by people offering very reasonably priced *quartos* (rooms) in private houses. The rooms are almost always clean and cheerful, if small, with a shared bathroom, and you can expect to pay from 3,000$00 to 4,000$00 for a double. Don't ever agree to an accommodation without seeing it first since the room may be farther from the town center than you have been led to believe.

Traveling off-peak (October–April) can be enjoyable in the Algarve, since the weather is still good and most hotels reduce their rates by up to 50%. It's worthwhile to check in every instance whether a discount applies to your chosen accommodation.

Hotel ratings correspond to Lisbon's lodging chart, in Chapter 3. Highly recommended hotels are indicated by a star ★.

Albufeira
Dining

La Cigale. This restaurant, located just 7 kilometers (4½ miles) east of Albufeira, is one of the best-known in the Algarve for its excellently prepared French and Portuguese cuisine. The establishment sits right on the beach and the terrace is the most popular place to dine, though you'll have to reserve in advance since La Cigale is so well known among the locals and repeat visitors. It's closed December–February and serves only dinner March–May. *Olhas d'Agua, tel. 089/501637. Reservations recommended. AE, D. Closed Dec.–Feb. Expensive.*

A Ruina. This big, multilevel rustic restaurant on the beach is the place to go for charcoal-grilled seafood, especially the fresh sardines or tuna steak (the day's catch comes from the nearby fish market). You may elect your dining preference: alfresco, on the beach, or inside in one of two attractively furnished dining rooms. There's a top-floor bar, too. *Cais Herculano, Praia dos Pescadores, tel. 089/512094. DC, MC. Moderate.*

Cabaz da Praia. You'll have spectacular views of the beach from the cliffside terrace of this long-established restaurant, named "beach basket" in Portuguese, and converted from an old fisherman's cottage. The kitchen prepares entrées from an international menu, including fish and chicken served in various styles, and desserts feature traditional Algarvian sweets. Try the souffle, perhaps the restaurant's most popular dish. *Praça Miguel Bombarda 7, tel. 089/512137. Reservations recommended. No credit cards. Closed Sat. lunch and Sun. Moderate.*

★ **Jardim d'Allah.** Sited in the old quarter of Albufeira, this family-run restaurant, decorated in attractive Moorish style, offers romantic courtyard dining. Specialties include excellent fresh fish dishes such as tuna; meat choices are available as well. *Beco Joséc Bernardino de Sousa, tel. 089/52296. MC, V. Moderate.*

Dining and Lodging
★

Estalgem Vila Joya. This is one of the most luxurious inns and restaurants in the Algarve, situated above the Praia da Gale, just 4 kilometers (2½ miles) west of town. The 13 spacious, Moorish-style rooms and three opulent suites are superbly appointed. The inn has direct access to the beach, a heated pool, and excellent à la carte lunches. At night you'll choose from the mostly French menu and dine in a candlelit setting. *Praia da Galê, tel. 089/591795, 13 rooms and 3 suites all with bath. Facilities: restaurant (very expensive; reservations and jacket and tie required), bar, pool. AE, DC, MC. Very Expensive.*

★ **Hotel Montechoro.** One of the most modern developments in Albufeira, the Montechoro—situated 3½ kilometers (2 miles) north of town—is ideal for those who wish to relax in the privacy of their own resort complex. Among the health facilities are two pools, tennis and squash courts, and a sauna. Guest rooms are furnished in up-to-the-minute style and look out over the surrounding coastal countryside. If you wish to never go off the property, you'll be fulfilled here: there are four separate bars, the Montechoro Restaurant, and the rooftop Amendoeiras

Grill, from which you can get stupendous views. *Av. Dr. Francisco Sá Carneiro, tel. 089/859423, fax 089/859947. 362 rooms
with bath. Facilities: restaurant (expensive), grill, 4 bars, 2
pools, sauna, gym, tennis and squash courts, billiards, shops,
garden, parking. AE, DC, MC, V. Expensive.*

Lodging **Hotel da Aldeia.** Adjacent to the Praia da Oura, 2 kilometers
(1¼ miles) east of Albufeira, this pleasant hotel within a large
tourist village complex is built from local materials, in traditional Algarvian style. Most rooms in the well-planned, low-
rise building have terraces overlooking the pool and gardens.
Room rates are very reasonable, especially given the hotel's excellent leisure facilities. *Av. Dr. Francisco Sá Carneiro,
Areias de São Joáo, tel. 089/858861, fax 089/858864. 133 rooms
with bath. Facilities: restaurant, bar, 2 pools (one for children), tennis courts, mini golf, billiards, health club and spa,
shops, parking. AE, MC, V. Expensive.*

Hotel-Apartamente Auramar. This pleasant beachside complex, situated on a low cliff just east of town, offers well-appointed self-service apartments with terraces and a full range
of facilities. This is a great place for families since units include
kitchenettes, and there are a children's playground and kiddie
pool on the premises. *Praia dos Aveiros, Areias de São João,
tel. 089/513337, fax 089/513327. 282 units with kitchenette. Facilities: restaurant, bar, pool, tennis courts, garden, shops,
parking. AE, DC, MC, V. Moderate.*

Alvor **Golfe da Penina.** This impressive golf hotel situated on 360 well-
Dining and Lodging maintained, secluded acres off the main road between Portimão
★ and Lagos has elegant public rooms and offers attentive ser-
vice. It was one of the first luxury hotels in the Algarve and is
now a member of the Trusthouse Forte chain. Most of the
smartly furnished guest rooms have balconies; those in the
back face the Monchique Mountains and have the best views.
The superlative golf course was designed by Henry Cotton, and
hotel guests enjoy free greens fees. There's a shuttle bus that
services the hotel beach (5 minutes away), which has a restaurant and water sports facilities. Back at the hotel there's a
large outdoor pool and a "Fun Village" for children. The village
has its own pool, zoo, and restaurant. You can eat either in the
hotel's Grill Room, which serves excellent Portuguese-style
dishes, or in the Harlequin, which specializes in Italian fare.
*Montes de Alvor, Penina, 8500 Portimão, tel. 082/415415, fax
082/415000. 202 rooms with bath. Facilities: restaurant (very
expensive; reservations required), grill, bar, 18-hole golf
course plus two 9-hole courses, tennis courts, horseback riding, Olympic-size pool, children's pool, sauna, private beach,
shops, small private airport, parking. AE, DC, MC, V. Expensive.*

Lodging **Hotel Alvor Praia.** This very comfortable, luxury split-level hotel is set on low cliffs overlooking the beach and bay that separates Portimão from Lagos and backed by the Monchique
Mountains. Naturally the views are excellent, and the rooms
facing the sea have spacious balconies. Among the amenities
are a dining room with picture windows overlooking the coast,
a large pool, and a deck where you can enjoy alfresco lunches.
An elevator (or an easy walk) will take you down to the pleasant
sand beach below the hotel. Guests of this hotel can benefit
from a 30% discount offered at nearby golf courses. *Praia dos
Tres Irmãos, 8500 Portimão, tel. 082/458900, fax 082/458999.*

241 rooms and suites with bath. Facilities: restaurant, bar, pool, sauna, gardens, mini-golf, tennis courts, boating, shops, garage. AE, DC, MC, V. Very Expensive.

Aparthotel Torralta. Offering good-size rooms, fully equipped kitchens, and daily maid service, this large apartment complex near the beach is a very good value all around. (If you come during winter, be sure to ask about the low, off-peak rates.) Some of the leisure facilities are appealing to children, making this an excellent choice for families. *Praia de Alvor, 8500 Portimão, tel. 082/459211, fax 082/459171. 644 units. Facilities: restaurant, disco, bar, 2 pools, horseback riding, boating, golf, tennis courts, billiard room, supermarket, parking. AE, DC, MC, V. Moderate.*

Armação de Pêra
Dining

A Santola. Just west of Albufeira, this delightful restaurant, with windows that look out to the beach, is considered the best in town for everything it offers, but the seafood is especially good—the restaurant's name means "crab." Try the excellent cataplana, a real Algarve specialty. *Largo 25 de Abril, tel. 082/312332. Reservations recommended. AE, DC, MC, V. Closed Sun. Moderate.*

Lodging

Hotel Garbe. The bar, lounge, and restaurant—all with terraces that provide unhindered views of the sea—maximize the superb location of this British-owned hotel. It sits on top of a cliff and is built on several levels: Rooms are modern and smartly furnished, and there's direct access from the hotel by steps to the beach below. The public rooms are bright and attractive, and the main lounge has an open fireplace as its best feature. *Av. Marginal, tel. 082/312194, fax 082/312201. 109 rooms with bath. Facilities: restaurant, coffee shop, bar, pool, garage. AE, DC, MC, V. Expensive.*

Hotel Viking. The prime location of this hotel, set not far from a good sandy beach and within a kilometer of town, makes this amenity-packed accommodation a fine place to stay. The Viking itself sits near the coast, but its swimming pools (one for children), tennis courts, and bars are situated between the main building and the clifftop. You may bargain with the town's fishermen for a sail around the impressive local grottos. *Praia Nossa Senhora da Rocha, tel. 082/312336 or 082/312339, fax 082/312826. 184 rooms with bath. Facilities: restaurant, bar, disco, 2 pools, tennis courts, boating, shops, garage. AE DC, MC, V. Expensive.*

Faro
Dining
★

Cidade Velha. Located in an 18th-century house beside the cathedral and within the walls of the Old Town, this small, intimate restaurant is easy to reach and serves excellent international cuisine. Many of the imaginative dishes utilize classic Portuguese ingredients: Try the pie made with *bacalhau* (dried codfish) or the rich house specialty—filet of pork stuffed with dates and walnuts and cooked in port. *Rua Domingos Guieiro 19, tel. 089/27145. Reservations recommended. MC, V. Closed Sat. lunch and Sun. Expensive.*

Restaurante Adega Nova. This atmospheric *adega* (wine cellar) offers excellently prepared traditional Portuguese dishes and down-to-earth surroundings that foster the lively atmosphere. Drinks are served at the tile-covered bar, and you sit at long wooden tables and benches for dining service. The restaurant is close to the train station, in an otherwise dreary area. *Rua Francisco Barreto 24, tel. 089/813433. No credit cards. Moderate.*

Restaurante Dos Irmãos. In business since 1925, this pretty and centrally located restaurant (one of several on the square) specializes in cataplana, as evidenced by the utensils hanging from the wood-beamed ceiling. Almost any of the other fresh fish and shellfish dishes are worth trying, too, but save room for the homemade *pudim caseiro* (crème caramel). Choose your wine from one of the hundreds of bottles of vintages that line the upper part of the wall of this large restaurant. *Largo do Terreiro do Bispo 14–15, tel. 089/823337. MC, V. Moderate.*

Lodging
★ **Hotel Eva.** Boasting the best location in town, this well-appointed hotel provides guests with unique views of the yacht-filled harbor, the sea, and the old town; moreover, its main-square location and novel rooftop pool and top-floor restaurant add all the ambience to be hoped for in a hotel. Public rooms are comfortably furnished and include a bar with evening entertainment. The guest rooms are modern and adequately furnished, though the best are enhanced by spacious balconies with vast views. There's also a courtesy bus to the town beach on nearby Faro Island. *Av. da República 1, tel. 089/803354, fax 089/802304. 146 rooms with bath. Facilities: restaurant, bar, disco, pool. AE, DC, MC, V. Expensive.*

★ **Casa de Lumena.** This graceful 150-year-old mansion has been tastefully converted into a small hotel and has some rooms overlooking the pretty square on which it's set. Each guest quarter, with unique furnishings, reveals its own character and reflects the care that the English owners have taken in restoring Casa de Lumena. The courtyard bar is an especially pleasant place for a drink. The hotel is near the central Rua de Santo António and is just a five-minute walk from the harbor. *Praća Alexandre Herculano 27, tel. 089/801990, fax 089/804019. 12 rooms with bath. Facilities: restaurant, bar. AE, DC, MC, V. Inexpensive.*

Hotel Faro. The only other harbor-front hotel in town, the functional but friendly Faro, is decidedly second-best to the Eva but is still a remarkably good value, considering its location. The rooms are of reasonable size, and the ones in the front offer water views (but you must ask for them). Other amenities include a rooftop terrace and a darkly lit bar with picture windows. *Praça D. Francisco Gomes 2, tel. 089/803276, fax 089/803546. 52 rooms with bath. Facilities: restaurant, bar, rooftop terrace. AE, DC, MC, V. Inexpensive.*

Lagos **Alpendre.** One of the oldest and best restaurants in the
Dining Algarve, Alpendre is renowned for its French-style meat dishes and local fish and shellfish specials. On a side street just off the Praça Luis de Camões, the comfortable restaurant has a relaxed interior that includes a wood-beam ceiling and walls adorned with porcelain plates. The service is leisurely and the food excellent. *Rua António Barbosa Viana 17, tel. 082/62705 Reservations recommended. AE, MC, V. Expensive.*

★ **Dom Sebastião.** Portuguese cooking, charcoal-grilled fish specials, and unobtrusive service are the attractions at this cheerful restaurant on Lagos's main pedestrianized street. You can dine inside at elegant, candle-lit tables that sit upon a cobblestone floor, or outside on the sidewalk terrace. While you ponder the menu, you'll be served an impressive array of appetizers (included in the cover charge). You may wish to start your meal with smoked swordfish and follow it with grilled tuna or the cataplana—all extremely good. *Rua 25 de Abril 20*

You've Let Your Imagination Go, Now Get Up And Follow Your Dreams.

For The Vacation You're Dreaming Of, Call American Express® Travel Agency At 1-800-YES-AMEX.*

American Express will send more than your imagination soaring. We'll fly you, sail you, drive you to any Fodor's destination and beyond. Because American Express believes the best vacations happen from Europe to the Orient, Walt Disney® World to Hawaii and everywhere in between.

For dependable service, expert advice, and value wherever your dreams take you, call on American Express. After all, the best traveling companion is a trustworthy friend.

AMERICAN EXPRESS Travel Agency

It's easy to recognize a good place when you see one.

American Express Cardmembers have been doing it for years.

The secret? Instead of just relying on what they see in the window, they look at the door. If there's an American Express Blue Box on it, they know they've found an establishment that cares about high standards.

Whether it's a place to eat, to sleep, to shop, or simply meet, they know they will be warmly welcomed.

So much so, they're rarely taken in by anything else.

Always a good sign.

tel. 082/62795. Reservations recommended. AE, DC, MC, V. Closed Sun. Oct.–May. Expensive.

Mirante. Perched on the cliff above the beautiful Praia de Dona Ana and just to the south of the town center, this restaurant shouts its fishermen's credentials loudly: A cork ceiling, ropes, and nets decorate the narrow interior. Mirante makes an excellent lunch stop, or come for an early dinner in summer when the views over the sea are lovely. Try the splendid tuna steak stewed with onions and, for dessert, the filling homemade cream tart. The staff is very friendly and efficient. *Praia de Dona Ana, tel. 082/62713. Reservations recommended for dinner. MC, V. Moderate.*

Piri-Piri. This small, low-key restaurant, decorated with understated pastel furnishings, is situated on one of the main tourist streets and offers an inexpensive but extensive menu. The long list of Portuguese dishes includes a variety of market-fresh fish, but the house specialty is the tasty *piri–piri* (spicy) pork and chicken that give the restaurant its name. *Rua Afonso d'Almeida 10, tel. 082/63803. MC, V. Inexpensive.*

Lodging **Hotel de Lagos.** This state-of-the-art hotel is attractively laid out at the eastern edge of the Old Town but is still within easy walking distance of the center. The rooms are strung across several levels, and the uniquely designed building includes gardens, tasteful lounges, and patios. Guest rooms are large and elegantly appointed. A regularly scheduled courtesy bus shuttles guests to the Meia Praia beach, where the hotel has some outstanding club facilities. Guests are also entitled to reduced greens fees at nearby golf courses. *Rua Nova da Aldeia, tel. 082/769967, fax 082/769920. 304 rooms with bath. Facilities: restaurant, bar, 2 pools, children's pool, shops, beach club, tennis courts, golf, parking. AE, DC, MC, V. Expensive.*

Hotel Golfinho. Set on the cliffs overlooking one of the prettiest cove beaches in Lagos, this hotel maximizes its location with balconies providing optimal views of the lovely sea and inland stretches. The Golfinho is a large, modern hotel, but its guest rooms are decorated in traditional Portuguese style and furnished with attractive wood and leather furniture. Geared toward tour-group vacationers, the amenities tend to be practical and include the ground-floor coffee shop and terrace, where many guests congregate. The hotel is just 1½ kilometers (almost a mile) from the town center, and a courtesy bus is available to shuttle patrons back and forth throughout the day. Clifftop paths lead from the Golfinho to beautiful cove beaches nearby. *Praia de Dona Ana, tel. 082/769900, fax 082/769999. 262 rooms with bath. Facilities: restaurant, bar, coffee shop, pool, disco, bowling alley, shops, garage. AE, DC, MC, V. Expensive.*

Pensão Mar Azul. Its choice central location makes this simple, budget-priced *pensão* (pension) a terrific value, although rooms that face the street (above the pedestrianized thoroughfare) can be noisy in high season. Nonetheless, the sparsely furnished quarters—some with a terrace—are more than adequate (four share a bath and toilet), and there's a comfortable community lounge. *Rua 25 de Abril 13–1. tel, 082/769749. 17 rooms, 13 with bath. No credit cards. Inexpensive.*

Monchique **Tereshina.** The interior decor of this modest restaurant is sim-
Dining ple, but real atmosphere can be found on the outdoor terrace,
★ which overlooks a lovely valley and the coastline. Located just west of Monchique, Tereshina offers good country cooking and

a particularly tasty local ham as well as chicken specials. *Estrada da Foia, tel. 082/92392. MC, V. Closed Mon. Inexpensive.*

Dining and Lodging
Estalgem Abrigo da Montanha. This pleasant, rustic inn—sited in the heart of the Serra de Monchique—is noted for its magnolia trees and camelia-filled garden and panoramic views. A leisurely lunch in the restaurant, where dependable regional dishes are prepared, always makes for an enjoyable afternoon. Stay longer to take in the scenery, and be sure to reserve one of the six welcoming rooms (all with views). It's best to reserve in advance. *Corto Pereiro, Estrada da Foia, tel. 082/92131. 6 rooms with bath. Facilities: restaurant (moderate), bar, garden, parking. AE, DC, MC, V. Inexpensive.*

Monte Gordo
Dining
Mota. A large, lively, unpretentious restaurant, the Mota is located on the sands of the Praia de Monte Gordo, 5 kilometers (3 miles) west of Vila Real de Santo António. Seafood, grills, and regional cuisine highlight the menu, and in the evening, live music accompanies the meal. *Praia de Monte Gordo, tel. 081/42650. No credit cards. Inexpensive.*

Lodging
Alcazar. Flaunting an unusual exterior and interior design, this hotel is easily one of the most striking in Monte Gordo. The white-colored balconies contrast with the red-brick facade, while inside a set of arches recalls the Arabic influence. All guest rooms have their own terrace. Alcazar also boasts a pleasant atmosphere and a convenient location, just 2 blocks off the beach. The staff is very accommodating. *Rua de Ceuta, tel. 081/42184. 95 rooms with bath. Facilities: restaurant, snack bar, bar, pool, disco, shops. AE, DC, MC, V. Moderate.*

Vasco da Gama. Occupying one of the prime beach sites in town, this long, low-lying hotel is well-equipped with water sports facilities and many other amenities. Families, especially, enjoy the extensive stretch of sandy beach, the children's pool, and the capable and friendly staff. *Av. Infante Dom Henrique, tel. 081/44321, fax 081/42322. 165 rooms with bath. Facilities: restaurant, bar, pool, children's pool, tennis courts, mini-golf, billiards, bowling, water sports, disco, parking. AE, DC, MC, V. Moderate.*

Portimão
Dining
A Lanterna. This well-run restaurant, situated on the main road just over the bridge at Parchal (on the Ferragudo side), features rich, exceptional fish soup and smoked swordfish, both of which are genuine Algarvian treats. Other seafood specialties are available, too. *Parchal, tel. 082/23948. Reservations recommended. MC, V. Closed Sun. Moderate.*

A Vela. A pleasant restaurant set on one of Portimão's back streets, A Vela provides guests with a serene, welcoming ambience. The cool, shaded dining area is decorated in Moorish fashion with a white-and-blue tiled interior and a spacious open kitchen that produces a varied selection of tasty Portuguese and international specialties. The accommodating staff adds to the enjoyable experience of dining here. *Rua Dr. Manuel de Almeida 97, tel. 082/414016. Reservations recommended in summer. AE, DC, MC, V. Closed Sun. Moderate.*

Flor da Sardinha. This is one of several open-air eateries situated next to the bridge and by the fishing harbor. Fresh sardines, superbly grilled on ranges at the quayside, are served to the crowds sitting at rows of informal plastic tables and chairs. A plateful of the delicious fish, with fries and a bottle of the local red wine, provides one of Portimão's finest dining experiences—at giveaway prices. *Cais da Lota, tel. 082/24862. No credit cards. Inexpensive.*

Lodging Portimão has a selection of hotels and pensões of reasonable quality and the local tourist office can assist you with finding accommodations. However, most visitors to the region choose to stay at one of the excellent local beach resorts instead, rather than to stay in the town itself. If you would prefer the latter option, which will allow you to visit Portimão as a day trip, *see* Alvor, *above*, and Praia da Rocha, *below*.

Praia da Luz **Luz Bay Club.** You may rent these well-appointed self-service
Lodging villas (with daily maid service) for either short or long stays. One of the best (and earliest) complexes in the Algarve, the Luz Bay Club blends well with the old village surroundings yet still provides a high level of comfort in its carefully decorated units, all of which are near the beach. Local water sports facilities are excellent, and there are several restaurants and bars nearby. The club is located off the main road on the way from Lagos to Sagres. *Rua Direita, tel. 082/789640, fax 082/789641. 131 villas with bath and kitchen. Facilities: 2 restaurants, 3 pools, tennis courts, water sports, gardens. AE, DC, MC, V. Expensive.*

Praia da Rocha **Fortaleza de Santa Catarina.** The 16th-century fortress of San-
Dining ta Catarina, on the esplanade, has been converted into a bar, restaurant, and *salão de cha* (tearoom) complex. Come for a moderately priced full meal (the food is good, and there are picture windows that look out to the beach) or simply afternoon tea (inexpensive) or a snack. Either way, the fort makes an atmospheric stop. *Av. Tomás Cabreira, tel. 082/22066. No credit cards. Moderate.*

Safari. Set on a cliff above the beach, this lively Portuguese restaurant has a distinctly African flavor. Seafood and delicious Angolan recipes are the best choices: Try the chicken curry or one of the charcoal grills, and enjoy your meal on the terrace. *Rua António Feu, tel. 082/415540. Reservations recommended. AE, DC, MC, V. Moderate.*

Lodging **Algarve.** Perched atop a cliff, this modern luxury hotel—the best in Praia da Rocha—provides marvelous sea views and even has an evening disco set into the rocks! Many of the public rooms are brightly decorated in Moorish style, and spacious guest rooms have tile floors and feature balconies facing the water. Among the numerous facilities are two salt water pools and a beach bar. The staff at all levels is most helpful. *Av. Tomás Cabreira, tel. 082/41500, fax 082/415999. 220 rooms with bath. Facilities: restaurant, bar, disco, 2 pools, tennis courts, health center, mini-golf, boating, water sports, garden, shops, parking. AE, DC, MC, V. Very Expensive.*

Bela Vista. A small, tastefully decorated beachfront hotel, the Bela Vista was originally built as a private residence at the turn of the century in Moorish style. Its remarkable furnishings—including magnificent azulejos and a large open fireplace—make this one of the most delightful accommodations in the Algarve. The guest rooms that face the sea are more expensive than the others but are worth the extra escudos. Early reservations are essential. *Av. Marginal, tel. 082/24055, fax 082/415369. 14 rooms with bath. Facilities: restaurant, bar. AE, DC, MC, V. Expensive.*

Sagres
Dining and Lodging
★

Pousada do Infante. Beautifully sited on the cliffs across the bay from the fortress, this modern pousada (built in 1960) is housed in a delightful two-story country house. There are relatively few facilities here, but the inn boasts the one attraction that really matters—the glorious view. The public rooms are tastefully decorated with Moorish embellishments and are comfortable, particularly the bar/terrace, a perfect place to watch the sun set. Guest rooms feel homey, and little touches around the property—such as the minarets and arches alongside the pool—make this place unique. The restaurant serves locally caught fish and is well respected. *Sagres, 8650 Vila do Bispo, tel. 082/64222. 23 rooms with bath. Facilities: restaurant (expensive), bar, pool, tennis court, parking. AE, DC, MC, V. Expensive.*

★ **Fortaleza do Belixe.** Resting 2 kilometers (1¼ miles) from Sagres on the coastal road to Cabo São Vicente, the remnants of an isolated cliff-top fortress have been converted into the Fortaleza do Belixe. The restaurant and very small hotel, with four rooms, is an annex of the Pousada do Infante (*see above*). Although it has similar features—the furnishings are smart and the rooms comfortable—room rates are a considerably better value. This is also an excellent spot for a meal, with good food served in the strikingly decorated dining room. *Sagres, 8650 Vila do Bispo, tel. 082/64124. 4 rooms with bath. Facilities: restaurant (expensive), bar, parking. AE, DC, MC, V. Moderate.*

Santa Bárbara de Nexe
Dining and Lodging

Hotel Apartamento La Reserve. Tucked in the hills and set within a six-acre park located 10 kilometers (6 miles) inland from Faro, this intimate luxury hotel promises seclusion, privacy, and comfort. High-class amenities including tennis courts and a pool and air-conditioned suites (all with terrace and kitchenette) provide guests with an atmosphere condusive to total relaxation. Patrons may enjoy a variety of outdoor activities in the rural surroundings and after working up an appetite may satisfy it in the formal gourmet restaurant. Elegant cuisine with a French accent (dinner only) is the fare, with seasonal game dishes as specialties. Advance reservations are required for both the hotel and restaurant. *Santa Bárbara de Nexe, 8000 Faro, tel. 089/91234, fax 089/56790. 20 suites. Facilities: restaurant (very expensive; closed Tues.), bar, garden, tennis courts, pool, garage. Closed Nov. Expensive.*

São Brás de Alportel
Dining and Lodging

Pousada de São Brás. This inland town 18 kilometers (11 miles) north of Faro has one of the region's only pousadas, a delightful 1940s-built hotel set in low hills. Rooms are comfortably furnished, and there's a rustic restaurant serving good regional dishes and other Portuguese specialties. The major attractions are the peaceful surroundings and the splendid views of the hills that can be seen from the terrace. *Estrada de Lisboa, 8150 São Brás de Alportel, tel. 082/842305. 29 rooms with bath. Facilities: restaurant (expensive), bar, pool, parking. AE, DC, MC, V. Moderate.*

Silves
Dining

Rui Marisqueira. The food is the main event here, as the functional decor doesn't offer much by way of ambience. The fish and shellfish are a remarkably good value, which explains why the crowds from the coast come up into the hills in the summer to dine. Grilled sea bream and bass are usually offered, and there's locally caught game—wild boar, rabbit, and partridge—in season. *Rua Comendador Vilarinho 23–27, tel. 082/*

443106. Reservations recommended in summer. MC, V. Closed Tues. Moderate.

Churrasqueira Valdemar. At this inexpensive grillroom on the riverfront behind the market, whole chickens are barbecued outside over charcoal. Eat under the stone arches, and enjoy your piri-piri (spicy) chicken with salad, fries, and local wine. *Facing the river, behind the market. No tel. No credit cards. Inexpensive.*

Tavira
Dining

Restaurante Imperial. The best restaurant on the riverfront, the Imperial—located behind the riverside gardens—is well-known for its fish and shellfish dishes, including tuna (the local catch) and a tasty mixed fried fishplate. Unfortunately, the staff is less than accommodating, and service can be brusque. *Rua José Pires Padinha 22–24, tel. 081/22234. Closed Wed. in winter. Moderate.*

Lodging

Residencial Princesa do Gilão. Across the river from the main square, this gleaming white *residencia* (small hotel) stands on the quayside, offering fine views of the fishing harbor and castle walls. All rooms are modern and compact and have tile floors, but you should try to secure one that faces the front and has a balcony. The landings and reception areas sparkle with cool marble and Portuguese tiles. *Rua Borda de Água de Aguiar 10–12, tel. 081/325171. 20 rooms, some with bath. No facilities. No credit cards. Inexpensive.*

Vale do Lobo
Dining and Lodging
★

Dona Filipa. This is one of the best-serviced and most luxurious hotels in the Algarve, with its lavish and striking interior and pleasant, air-conditioned rooms with balconies (most of which overlook the sea). Set on extensive, beautifully landscaped grounds near the beach and west of Faro, the Dona Filipa features a number of facilities including a chic restaurant offering an excellent international menu and an impressive wine list. Sports fans will be happy to find that greens fees for the fine nearby 18-hole golf course are included in room rates; and in addition to its own tennis courts, the hotel is very close to the famous Roger Taylor Tennis School. *Vale do Lobo, 8136 Almansil, tel. 089/394141, fax 089/394288. 136 rooms with bath. Facilities: restaurant, grill, bar, disco, gardens, pool, tennis courts, golf, shops, parking. AE, DC, MC, V. Very Expensive.*

Vilamoura
Dining and Lodging

Vilamoura Marinotel. One of the Algarve's newest accommodations, the luxurious Marinotel overlooks Vilamoura's stupendous marina and is perfectly positioned for anyone who favors everything nautical. The guest rooms come equipped with the most up-to-the-minute hardware including VCRs, and the lodging's facilities are wide-ranging. Many guests insist that the Marinotel is the best place to eat in Vilamoura. The extra-smart grill overlooks the boats and offers fresh fish and live music, while the restaurant specializes in Spanish and Portuguese dishes and looks into the hotel gardens. *Vilamoura 8125, Quarteira, tel. 089/889988, fax 089/889869. 399 rooms with bath. Facilities: restaurant (expensive), grill, bar, gardens, pool, children's pool, tennis, boating, terrace, shops, parking. AE, DC, MC, V. Expensive.*

Lodging

Hotel Dom Pedro Golf. Situated in the heart of this highly successful vacation complex, the Dom Pedro is the best of the three hotels here operated by the Dom Pedro Hotel Group. It's close to the casino and not far from the beach. Each bright room is

attractively furnished and has its own balcony facing the sea.
Guests may take full advantage of the excellent sports facilities
provided by the complex. *Vilamoura, 8125 Quarteira, tel. 089/
889650, fax 089/35482. 261 rooms with bath. Facilities: restaurant, bar, 2 pools, children's pool, shops, tennis courts, golf,
parking. AE, DC, MC, V. Expensive.*

Vila Real de **Caves do Guadiana.** Located in a large, old-fashioned building
Santo António facing the fishing docks and the river estuary, this accommoda-
Dining ting restaurant is popular for its well-prepared seafood and
Portuguese specialties. Stop for lunch on the way to or from the
Spanish border crossing. *Av. da República 90, tel. 081/44498.
DC, MC. Closed Thurs. Inexpensive.*

The Arts and Nightlife

The Arts

Most of the towns in the Algarve have annual festivals lasting
several days, and locals and tourists alike join in on the parades
and celebrations. Nearly every town and village also features
religious celebrations during Easter week and on Saint John's
Eve (June 23–24).

The **Algarve Regional Tourist Board** (Rua Ataide de Oliveira
100, Faro, tel. 089/803667) produces a monthly calendar of
events, which you may pick up at local tourist offices and hotels
throughout the Algarve. The Tourist Board also provides information on venues and ticket prices for the annual **Algarve Music
Festival,** a series of concerts and recitals sponsored by the
Gulbenkian Foundation, throughout May and June.

Faro Mid-July sees the **Festa e Feira da Senhora do Carmo** (Festival
and Fair of Our Lady of Carmen), a religious procession followed by an agricultural fair. In October the **Feira de Santa Iria**
(Fair of Santa Iria) is another happpy excuse for traditional celebrations held over several days.

Loulé An annual **street carnival**—or Mardi Gras—is held every February and is an enjoyable local affair with a procession of floats,
mask competitions, dancing, and more. On the second Sunday
after Easter, Loulé hosts the **Romaria da Senhora da Piedade,** a
pilgrimage and procession to the local shrine of Monte da
Piedade. There are also flower-decked celebrations here on
May 1, enlivened further by performances of traditional song
and dance.

Monchique The **Feira de Outubro** (October Fair), held at the end of the
month, gathers together crafts, goods, and produce from villages throughout the Serra de Monchique. It's one of the best of
the Algarve's annual fairs.

Praia da Rocha In previous years the first week in September has seen a **folklore festival** held at various venues around the resort of Praia da
Rocha. During each evening of the festival, there is traditional
song and dance performed by special folkloric groups.

Silves In July, Silves hosts a thoroughly enjoyable **Beer Festival** on the
castle grounds, where apart from being able to sample all the
different kinds of Portuguese beer, visitors may watch folk
dances and listen to traditional and orchestral music.

Nightlife

It won't be difficult to find an exciting venue where you can be entertained: There are more bars, discos, and clubs in the Algarve than anywhere else in Portugal. In the major resorts new places open and close with alarming speed or suddenly attract a different clientele, so it's not guaranteed that spots listed here will still be the trendiest when you visit; but they are representative of the range of nightlife available. If you prefer a quieter evening, the Algarve's open-air cafés are perfect for a drink and people-watching, and sometimes a traveling musician will stroll by. Many hotels also put on *fado* (traditional folk music) performances and other traditional music.

To gamble head for one of the Algarve's three casinos: at **Alvor** (tel. 082/23141), **Vilamoura** (tel. 089/65319), and **Monte Gordo** (tel. 081/42224). (Remember to take your passport for entry.)

Albufeira Albufeira tries hard to maintain its reputation as the Algarve's number-one nightspot. Enormously popular with the young, many bars and discos here have promotional nights, with free or reduced-price drinks and entry. Of the discos **Kiss** (Montechoro) and **Boite 7** (Rua São Gonçalo de Lagos) are still very lively and stay open nightly until 4 AM. Rua São Gonçalo de Lagos also boasts similar discos that guarantee a lively crowd. For a less energetic evening, **Sir Harry's Bar,** off the main square, is an English-style pub with an interesting clientele of different nationalities. It's open daily 10 AM–2 AM.

Faro Faro's central pedestrianized streets are filled at night with throngs of café-goers, while Rua do Prior, in particular, is known for its wide selection of stylish bars. The town's best disco is **Sheherazade** (at the Hotel Eva, Av. da República 1), and the Eva puts on traditional music and fado at least once a week in summer as well.

Lagos A good bar in Lagos is **Mullens** (Rua Cândido dos Reis 86), whose enthusiastic staff makes things swing until 2 AM; full meals are served here, too. For late-night dancing, **Phoenix** (Rua 5 de Outubro 11) plays disco and pop until 4 AM.

Sagres Sagres is a well-known haunt of young travelers, who stay the summer for the laid-back beach scene. Consequently, there are several music-bars near the village square. **A Rosa dos Ventos,** in the square, and **The Last Chance Saloon,** on the road down to Praia da Mareta, are both loud, lively, and open late.

7 Coimbra and the Beiras

By Dennis Jaffe

It's not far from one point in the Beiras to any other. In fact, you can drive from the Atlantic shore to the Spanish border in the time it takes many residents of Los Angeles or London to commute to work. However, within this small area you will encounter tremendous diversity.

To the east Portugal's highest mountains, the Serra da Estrela, rise to a height of nearly 6,600 feet and provide a playground of alpine meadows, wooded hills, and clear, rushing streams. High in the granite reaches of the Serra, a tiny trickle of an icy stream begins its tortuous journey to the sea. This is the Mondego, praised in song and poetry as the most Portuguese of all rivers. The longest river entirely within Portugal and the lifeblood of the Beiras, it provides vital irrigation to fruit orchards and farms as it flows through the heart of the province. Coimbra, the country's first capital and home to one of Europe's earliest universities, rises above its banks. Closer to the sea, under the imposing walls of Montemor Castle, the river widens to nurture rice fields, before finally merging with the Atlantic at the popular beach resort of Figueira da Foz.

In the mountains and along the border with Spain, life is difficult. The winters are cold and harsh and the summers broiling hot. Crops do not flourish here, and many of the villages have lost their ablest workers to the factories of France and Germany. In this part of the country, where the climate is most severe and tourists are still somewhat of a curiosity, you will find perhaps the warmest welcome.

The coastal region presents a much gentler face. The long, sandy beaches and sun-baked dunes are some of the most inviting you will find in all of Europe. The great lagoon at Aveiro, with its colorful kelp boats, is unique. A bit farther inland are the lush forests of Buçaco and the sedate spa resorts of Curia and Luso.

Historically, this region has played an important role in Portugal's development. The Romans built roads, established settlements, and, in 27 BC, incorporated into their vast empire, the remote province known as Lusitania, which emcompassed most of what is now central Portugal, including the Beiras. They left many traces of their presence in the region, including the well-known and well-preserved ruins at Conimbriga, near Coimbra.

Next came the Moors, who swept through the territory in the early 8th century and played a leading role for several hundred years. Many of the region's elaborate castles and extensive fortifications show a strong Moorish influence. The fortified towns stretching along the Spanish frontier have been the scene of many fierce battles, from the see-saw struggle against the Moors known as the wars of Christian reconquest to battles with the Spanish, as the fledgling Portuguese nation fought the invaders from neighboring Castile.

The Beiras also played a part in Portugal's golden age of discovery. In 1500 Pedro Álvares Cabral, a nobleman from the town of Belmonte, on the eastern flank of the Serra da Estrela, led the first expedition to come upon what is now Brazil. Much of the wealth garnered during this period, when tiny Portugal controlled so much of the world's trade, financed the great architectural and artistic achievements of the Portuguese Renaissance. Throughout the region there are fine examples of the

Manueline style, the uniquely Portuguese art form that reflects the nation's nautical heritage. The cathedrals at Guarda and Viseu, the Monastery of Santa Cruz at Coimbra, and the Convent of Jesus in Aveiro are especially noteworthy.

During the Peninsular War, fought between Napoleon's armies and Wellington's British and Portuguese forces in the early 19th century, a decisive battle was fought in the tranquil forest of Buçaco. Later in the same century, this area witnessed a much more peaceful invasion, as people from all corners of Europe came to take the waters at such well-known spas as Luso, Curia, and Caramulo. Around the turn of the century, when the now tourist-packed Algarve was merely a remote backwater, Figueira da Foz was coming into its own as an international beach resort.

Essential Information

Important Addresses and Numbers

Tourist Information The regional tourist offices for **Coimbra** and the surrounding area, including **Figueira da Foz**, are the **Região de Turismo do Centro** (Largo da Portagem, 3000 Coimbra, tel. 039/23886; Edificio Marisol, Av. 25 de Abril, 3080 Figueira da Foz, tel. 033/28895). Within this region there are local tourist offices in: **Arganil** (Praça Simões Dias, tel. 035/22859), **Buarcos** (Largo Tomas de Aquino, tel. 033/25019), **Condeixa** (Edificio da Câmara, tel. 039/941114), **Curia** (Largo da Rotunda, tel. 031/52248), **Figueiro dos Vinhos** (Av. Padre Diogo Vasconcelos, tel. 036/52178), **Lousa** (Edificio da Câmara, tel. 039/991502), **Luso/Buçaco** (Rua Emidio Navarro, Luso, tel. 031/93133), **Mira** (Edificio da Câmara, tel. 031/451506), **Montemor-O-Velho** (Praça da República, tel. 039/68187), and **Penacova** (Miradouro do Terreiro, tel. 039/477115).

For information about **Aveiro** and the **Rota da Luz** region, consult the **Região de Turismo da Rota da Luz** (Rua João Mendonça 8, 3800 Aveiro, tel. 034/23680). The principal local tourist offices in this region are in: **Águeda** (Estrada Nacional 1, tel. 034/601412), **Costa Nova** (Praia da Costa Nova, at the beach, tel. 034/369560, open June–Sept.), **Ilhavo** (Av. Mario Sacramento), **Ovar** (Edificio da Câmara, Praça da República, tel. 056/572215), and **Torreira** (Av. Hintze Ribeiro, tel. 034/48250).

The regional tourist office for the **Dão-Lafões** area is the **Região de Turismo de Dão-Lafões** (Av. Gulbenkian, 3500 Viseu, tel. 032/422014). Local tourist offices are in: **Caramulo** (Estrada Principal do Caramulo, tel. 032/861437), **Nelas** (Largo Prof. Veiga Simão, tel. 032/944384), and **São Pedro do Sul** (Largo dos Correios, tel. 032/711320).

The **Serra da Estrela** district is represented by the **Região de Turismo da Serra da Estrela** (Praça do Município 1, 6200 Covilhã, tel. 075/322170). There are local tourist offices in: **Belmonte** (Praça Pedro Álvares Cabral, tel. 075/911488), **Castelo Branco** (Alameda da Liberdade, tel. 072/21002), **Fundão** (Av da Liberdade, tel. 075/52770), **Gouveia** (Av. dos Bombeiros Voluntarios, tel. 038/42185), **Guarda** (Praça Luis Camões, tel 071/212251), **Manteigas** (Rua Dr. Gaspar de Carvalho, tel. 075/981129), **Oliveira do Hospital** (Praça do Município, tel. 038

52522), **Penamacor** (Praça 25 de Abril, tel. 090/314316), and **Seia** (Praça do Mercado, tel. 038/922272).

Emergencies The national emergency number is tel. 115. **Hospitals** with emergency rooms (urgências) are located in Castelo Branco (Hospital Distrital de Castelo Branco, Av. Pedro A. Cabral, tel. 072/322133), Coimbra (Hospital da Universidade Coimbra, Praça Prof. Mota Pinto, tel. 039/722115), Figueira da Foz (Hospital Distrital da Figueira da Foz, Gala, tel. 033/31033), and Guarda (Rua Dr. Francisco Prazeres, tel. 071/222133).

Mail The central post office in Coimbra, **CTT Estação Central** (Av. Fernão de Magalhães 223), is adjacent to the train station and is the center for poste restante (general delivery). Most other towns have just one central post office, where poste restante is received.

Late-Night Pharmacies Pharmacies in all sizable towns operate a rotating system for staying open after normal closing hours, including weekends and holidays. Consult a local newspaper or the notice posted on the door of every pharmacy.

Travel Agency In Coimbra, a useful agency is **Abreu** (Rua da Sota 2, tel. 039/27011).

Arriving and Departing by Plane

Although there are some international flights into Oporto (to the north), Lisbon is the preferred choice for the international air traveler. It's 160 kilometers (99 miles) northeast from the Lisbon airport to Coimbra via the newly completed A 1 highway.

Arriving and Departing by Car, Train, and Bus

By Car Although you can zip from Lisbon to Coimbra on the A 1 *autoestrada* (tollway) in less than two hours or drive from Oporto to Coimbra in under an hour, smaller roads provide a much richer and more varied travel experience. The eastern part of the Beiras is readily accessible from Spain. It's 90 kilometers (56 miles) on N620 from Salamanca and 320 kilometers (199 miles) from Madrid to the border crossing at Vilar Formoso.

By Train Coimbra, Guarda, Mangualde, Ovar, and Aveiro are on the main Lisbon/Oporto–Paris line. Two trains arrive from Paris and two depart daily. There is also regular train service linking the principal cities in the Beiras with Madrid, Lisbon, and Oporto. In summer a daily car-train operates between Paris and Lisbon. There are two train stations in Coimbra: **Coimbra A** (Estação Nova), located along the Rio Mondego, a five-minute walk from the center of town (for domestic routes), and **Coimbra B** (Estação Velha), 5 kilometers (3 miles) west (for international trains). There are frequent bus and rail links between stations. For information call 039/27263. Schedules for all trains are posted at both stations.

By Bus The **Rodoviária Nacional** (RN) provides comfortable motorcoach service between Lisbon, Oporto, and Coimbra. RN stations in Coimbra (Av. Fernão de Magalhães, tel. 039/27081), Castelo Branco (Rodrigo Rebelo 3, tel. 072/323301), and Covilhã (Largo das Forcas Armadas, tel. 075/24914) all have international as well as domestic service. International **Euroline** motor coaches link Coimbra with London, Paris, Amsterdam, and Frankfurt. For information call Euroline in Lisbon (tel. 01/547300), or contact a travel agent.

Getting Around

By Car   The Beiras, with their many remote villages, are particularly well suited to exploration by car. Distances between major points are short. (For example, it's only 160 kilometers (99 miles) from Aveiro, on the coast, to the line of fortress towns guarding the approaches from Spain.) There are no intimidating major cities to negotiate, and, except for the coastal strip in July and August, traffic is light. Roads in general are quite good and destinations well marked; however, parking is a problem in most towns.

Although it is possible to whiz through the region in a few hours, utilizing the Lisbon–Oporto highway or the newly completed IP5, which links Aveiro (on the coast) with Vilar Formosa (at the Spanish frontier), resist the temptation. The heart and soul of the Beiras are to be found along the many kilometers of those squiggly yellow and white lines lacing the road map of Portugal. The best map for motorists, both for scale and ease of reading, is Michelin map number 437 (Portugal-Madeira), available at bookstores throughout Portugal and in the United States from Michelin Travel Publications (1 Parkway S, Greenville, SC 29615, tel. 803/458–6330).

In addition to the numerous car-rental agencies in Lisbon, there are Hertz and Avis offices in Coimbra (Hertz, Av. Fernão de Magalhães 133, tel. 039/37491; Avis, Coimbra A, Làrgo das Ameias, tel. 039/34786) and Viseu (Hertz, Rua da Paz 21, tel. 032/421846; Avis, Hotel Grão Vasco, Rua Gaspar Barreiros, tel. 032/25750). If you plan to drive to Spain, be sure your *carta verde* (green insurance card) is valid there.

By Train   Although the major destinations in this chapter are linked by rail, service to most towns, with the exception of Coimbra, is infrequent. The equipment on the Beira line, which connects Lisbon with Guarda and the Serra da Estrela, has recently been upgraded.

Using Coimbra as a hub, there are three main rail lines serving the Beiras. Line 110 extends west to include Luso, Viseu, Mangualde, Celorico da Beira, and Guarda. Line 100 extends south through the Ribatejo to intersect with line 130, which runs from Lisbon's Santa Apolonia station to Covilhã, the gateway to the Serra da Estrela. After running along the Tejo through the towns of Santerém, Abrantes, and Belver, line 130 sweeps north to service the Beira Baixa towns of Castelo Branco, Fundão, and Covilhã. Going north from Coimbra, line 100 services Curia, Aveiro, and Ovar and continues north to Oporto and Braga. Schedules are posted at all train stations.

By Bus   If you choose not to drive, an extensive bus network provides the next best way of getting around. Vehicles of various vintages can take you to almost any destination, and unlike train stations, which are often located some distance from the town center, bus depots are centrally located. Rural buses, often packed with people going to and from regional markets, provide a wonderful microcosm of Portuguese life. Regional and local bus schedules are posted at the terminals. Information may also be obtained at local tourist offices.

Guided Tours

There are very few regularly scheduled guided tours originating in the Beiras. **RN Tours** (Rua da Sofia 102, 3000 Coimbra, tel. 039/22944) offers a half-day tour of Coimbra on Wednesday and Sunday during summer. **Mivitur** (Av. do Ramalhâo, 3220 Miranda do Corvo, tel. 039/52304) has an all-day tour of the Rio Mondego region on Tuesday and Thursday, mid-June–mid-September. There are also one- to seven-day tours that leave from Lisbon and Oporto and cover the Beiras. For further information contact a travel agency or, in Lisbon, **RN Tours** (Av. Fontes Pereira de Melo 14–12, tel. 01/577523) or **Tip Tours** (Av. Costa Pinto 91–A, tel. 01/286–5159).

From mid-June to mid-September, excursion boats cruise the Ria de Aveiro, the vast, 45-kilometer (28-mile) hydralike estuary formed by the Ria Vouga. Boats leave daily at 10 AM from the main canal just in front of the tourist office and return at 5 PM. Tickets are 1,750$00. There's a small bar on board, and a stop is made along the way for lunch.

With advance notice, horseback tours of the countryside around Aveiro can be arranged with the **Escola Equestre de Aveiro** (Equestrian School of Aveiro, Quinta Chão Agra, Vilarinho, tel. 034/912108). The school is about 6 kilometers (3½ miles) north of Aveiro on N109.

Exploring Coimbra and the Beiras

Orientation

The Beiras region encompasses the provinces of the Beira Litoral (Coastal Beira), the Beira Baixa (Lower Beira), and the Beira Alta (Upper Beira), which together make up roughly one quarter of continental Portugal's landmass. Extending from the rolling Atlantic breakers on the west coast to the lonely, fortified towns along the Spanish frontier some 160 kilometers (100 miles) east, this part of Portugal is on the verge of being discovered. Many discriminating travelers, who've traditionally limited their Portuguese vacation itineraries to Lisbon and the Algarve, are finding within the Beiras some of the last remaining areas in Europe unscathed by the mass tourism that's left its permanent and not always positive mark on so much of the Old World.

To provide a bit of historical perspective, the tours begin with Portugal's first capital, the ancient university town of Coimbra. The rest of the region is divided into two parts. The western tour takes in the seaside resort of Figueira da Foz and the canals and lagoons in and around Aveiro; moves inland to Viseu, with its wonderful parks and historic old quarter; follows the spa trail, visiting the mountain resort of Caramulo and the *Belle Epoque* spas of Luso and Curia; and passes through the dense forest of Buçaco before heading back toward Coimbra along the Mondego. The last tour travels into Portugal's highest mountains, the Serra da Estrela, and to the chain of ancient fortified towns along the Spanish border.

Highlights for First-Time Visitors

Centum Cellas (*see* Tour 3)
Palace Hotel Buçaco (*see* Tour 2)
Palácio des Condes de Anadia, Mangualde (*see* Tour 2)
Ria, Aveiro (*see* Tour 2)
Roman ruins, Conimbriga (*see* Tour 2)
Sé and Largo da Sé, Viseu (*see* Tour 2)
Sé Velha, Coimbra (*see* Tour 1)
University, Coimbra (*see* Tour 1)
Walled city, Sortelha (*see* Tour 3)

Tour 1: Coimbra

Numbers in the margin correspond to points of interest on The Beiras and Coimbra maps.

❶ The exact origins of **Coimbra** lie deeply buried in prehistoric times. However, from its emergence as the Roman settlement of Aeminium to the present, this city on the banks of the Rio Mondego has played an influential and often crucial role in the country's development. In Roman times, it was an important way station, the midway point on the road connecting Lisbon with Braga to the north. Several of today's main thoroughfares are built on top of this ancient road. The open-air café on the Praça do Comércio is actually on the site of a Roman circus.

The year 711 marked the beginning of a centuries-long period of Moorish domination, which, except for one hiatus, lasted until the final reconquest by Christian forces in 1064. At that time, Coimbra became the capital of a vast territory extending north to the Rio Douro and encompassing much of what are now the Beiras. By the 12th and 13th centuries, it had become the capital of the young Portuguese nation.

Coimbra is best known for its university, even though the country's first university, established by King Dinis I in 1290, was actually located in Lisbon. Transferred back and forth between Coimbra and Lisbon, it was finally installed on its present site high above the Mondego in 1537. Since then the university has been one of Europe's major learning centers and is important in the life of both the city and the nation. Dr. António Salazar, the dictator who ruled Portugal from 1932 until 1968, was a student and later a professor at Coimbra. During the 1960s the university was a focal point for much of the unrest preceding the 1974 revolution. Many of the current political leaders were educated there.

Essentially a college town, Coimbra is best visited when school is in session. The students, even in today's era of jeans and T-shirts, proudly wear the traditional black capes and adorn their briefcases with colored ribbons denoting which faculty they attend (for example, red for law, yellow for medicine). Their presence adds much color and life to the streets, bars, and restaurants of the city. In May, after final exams, students, with great exuberance, burn their colored ribbons in a ceremony called *Queima das Fitas* (Burning of the Ribbons). It's quite a party.

To devotees of that uniquely Portuguese art of musical expression, the *fado* (traditional folk music), Coimbra has a very special significance. It is here on the banks of the Mondego that the fado of Coimbra was born. With the exception of a few bars where it is performed mostly for tourists, you won't find fado "shows" in Coimbra. The authentic fado of Coimbra is more a form of personal expression than an entertainment medium. Wandering through the narrow, steep passageways of the old university quarter, you are likely to hear plaintive sounds drifting through the night air, perhaps from a student serenading his love. In contrast to the brasher Lisbon version, the Coimbra fado is performed only by men. Musical accompaniment is played on the traditional heart-shape, 12-string guitar, and tradition dictates that one does not applaud. During the *Queima das Fitas*, the square in front of the old cathedral is full of people who listen in silence to fado. During the student demonstrations of the '60s, this music was used as a form of protest in much the same manner as the folk song was in America.

Coimbra's romantic side is reserved for those willing to devote a bit more time than that required for quick hit-and-run visits to the obligatory sights. Sit in the cafés and student restaurants, watch young lovers walking hand in hand through parks, and stroll through the gardens of the *Quinta das Lágrimas* (House of Tears), where more than six centuries ago the ill-fated Inês de Castro was murdered. The tragic love story of Dom Pedro and the young Inês—part legend, part history—has been immortalized in the epic *Os Lusíadas* (The Lusiads), by Luis de Camões, Portugal's national poet. Evidence of the lovers' story can be found throughout the Beiras and in other parts of Portugal as well.

② The tour of Coimbra begins at the **Largo da Portagem,** the triangular plaza at the foot of the Ponte Santa Clara. The statue of Joaquim António de Aguiar with pen in hand represents the signing, in 1833, of a decree banning religious orders throughout Portugal.

A few hundred yards up the busy Rua Ferreira Borges, one of the city's principal shopping streets, you will see a tall, graceful, arched opening in a massive stone wall: the **Arco de Almedina** (Almedina Gate). The 12th-century arch is one of the last vestiges of the medieval city walls. Above the arch is a Renaissance carving of the virgin and child and an early Portuguese coat of arms. The adjacent tower houses the city's historical archives and the **Sino de Correr** (Warning Bell) used from medieval times until 1870 to signal the populace to return to the safety of the city walls. The tower is also used as an art gallery.

④ Go through the gate into the old city and head up the hill along one of Coimbra's most famous streets, **Rua Quebra Costas** (Street of the Broken Backs). Try carrying a heavy load of groceries up this steep street, and you will see where the name came from! Quebra Costas is the main pedestrian link between **⑤** the Baixa (Lower Town) and the **Sé Velha** (Old Cathedral). The cathedral was designed and constructed in the 12th century by the French master builders Robert and Bernard. Made of massive granite blocks and crowned by a ring of battlements, the cathedral looks more like a fortress than a house of worship. (Engaged in an ongoing struggle with the Moors, the Portuguese, who were building and reconstructing castles for defensive purposes throughout the country, often incorporated fortifications in their churches.) The harsh exterior is softened

The Beiras

Coimbra

somewhat by graceful 16th-century Renaissance doorways. The somber interior has several interesting features, including a gilded wood altarpiece, a late-15th-century example of the Flamboyant Gothic style by the Flemish masters Olivier of Ghent and Jean d'Ypres. The walls of the Chapel of the Holy Sacrament are lined with the touching, lifelike sculptures of Jean de Rouen, whose life-size Christ figure is flanked by finely detailed representations of the apostles and evangelists. The **cloisters**, built in the 13th century, are distinguished by a well-executed series of transitional Gothic arches. *Larga da Sé Velha, tel. 039/25273. Admission: cathedral free; cloisters: 40$00. Open daily 9:30–12:30 and 2–5:30.*

Time Out   The cathedral square is ringed with cafés and restaurants. **Café Sé Velha** (Rua da Joaquim António Aguiar 136), decorated with *azulejo* (traditional Portuguese tile) panels depicting local scenes, is one of the most inviting. Drop in for a meal or just drinks and snacks; you can sit outside in summer.

Continue uphill from the Largo da Sé Velha along Rua Borges Carneiro, the narrow street to the left of the cathedral, and you'll come to the **Museu Machado de Castro** (Machado de Castro Museum). The building, itself a work of art, was constructed in the 12th century to house the prelates of Coimbra; it was extensively modified 400 years later and was converted to a museum in 1912. It contains one of Portugal's finest collections of sculpture, including work by Jean de Rouen and Master Pero and an intriguing little statue of a mounted medieval knight. The Bishop's Chapel, adorned with 18th-century azulejos and silks, is a highlight of the upstairs galleries, which also contain a diverse selection of Portuguese paintings and furniture. Be sure to take in the view from the terrace of the Renaissance loggia. As you exit the museum, note the large 18th-century azulejo panel depicting Jeronimo translating the bible. *Largo Dr. José Rodrigues, tel. 039/23727. Admission: 200$00, Sun. morning free. Open Tues.–Sun. 10–5.*

As you leave the building, you'll see two churches. The first, on your left, with the Romanesque facade, is the 12th-century São Salvador Church, currently closed to the public. Across the street and to the right is the **Sé Nova** (New Cathedral). This 17th-century Jesuit church was, as were many such churches of the day, patterned after the church of Jesus in Rome. *Admission free. Open daily 9:30–12:30 and 2–5:30.*

Leaving the cathedral, follow the Rua São Pedro through the university to the Praça Porta Férrea, at the end of which is the **Porta Férrea** itself. Built in 1634 as a triumphal arch, it is adorned with the figures of the kings Dinis and João III. *Open daily 9:30–12:30 and 2–5.*

Walk through the gate, and you're in the principal courtyard of the **Velha Universidade** (Old University). Steeped in centuries-old tradition, Coimbra's university, with an enrollment of 20,000, is Portugal's most prestigious institution of higher learning. Although there are modern dormitories and apartments available, many students, some because of tradition and some for economic reasons, choose to live in one of the approximately 30 old, ramshackle *repúblicas* (student republics) scattered around the university quarter. Occupying old houses with the bare minimum in creature comforts, groups of students live together (coed since the revolution), sharing costs and chores; the one indulgence they allow themselves is a cook. Traditionally to the left on the political spectrum, the repúblicas were a hotbed of anti-Salazar activity during the years of the dictatorship. The República Bota-Abaixo (Rua São Salvador 6), near the Machado de Castro Museum, is a typical example of this Portuguese-style cooperative. The repúblicas are not really tourist attractions, nor are they open to the public, but if you're able to secure an invitation, don't pass up this opportunity for a glimpse of Portuguese student life.

The statue in the center of the courtyard is of Dom João III; it was during his reign that the university moved permanently to Coimbra. Walk to the far end of the courtyard for a view of the Mondego and across it to the Convento de Santa Clara-a-Nova. The double stairway rising from the courtyard leads to the graceful colonnade framing the **Via Latina** (Latin Way) the scene of colorful student processions at graduation time. Amid much pomp and ceremony, doctoral degrees are presented in the **Sala dos Capelos** (Ceremonial Hall) which is capped with a fine paneled ceiling and lined with a series of portraits of the kings of Portugal. *Admission: 250$00. Open daily 9:30–12:30 and 2–5.*

The 18th-century clock-and-bell tower rising above the courtyard is one of Coimbra's most famous landmarks. The bell, used to summon students to class and, in centuries past, to signal a dusk-to-dawn curfew, is derisively called the *cabra* (goat). In the southwest corner of the courtyard is a building with four huge columns framing a set of massive wooden doors. It contains one of the world's most beautiful libraries, the **Biblioteca Joanina.** Constructed in the early 18th century, the library contains three dazzling book-lined halls and has one of the loveliest Baroque interiors in the country. The large painting in the center is of Dom João V, the monarch responsible for the library's construction. *Admission: 250$00. Open Mon.–Sat. 9:30–12:30 and 2–5.*

Leave the courtyard, and return to the lower town via the Rua do Norte. Along the way you will pass the **Casa dos Melos,** an elegant, 16th-century building now housing the School of Pharmacy.

Return to the old cathedral, and follow the Rua Coutinhos to ⑨ the **Palácio de Sobre Ribas** (Palace above the Riverbanks). A tower in the ancient walls, it was converted into a private residence in the 16th century. The exterior of the building is graced by several Manueline doorways and windows. A short distance along the same street is another converted tower, the ⑩ **Torre de Anto** (Tower of Anto), now a regional handicrafts center. Anto is the nickname of the Portuguese poet Antònio Nobre, who lived in the tower during the 19th century. *Rua Sobre Ribas. Handicrafts center: Open weekdays 9–12:30 and 2–5:30.*

Continue down the hill and through the Almedina Gate to the Rua Ferreira Borges. Across the street and down a short flight of steps is the **Praça do Comércio,** one of the lower town's most attractive and active plazas. A variety of fashionable shops occupy the 17th- and 18th-century town houses lining the square. In the corners of the Comércio, street vendors sell everything from combs to carpets. In Roman times this was the site of the circus. Currently closed to the public, the Church of Sant'Iago, in the northeast corner, is a small, late 13th-century stone structure with finely carved Romanesque columns. At the opposite corner is the Church of São Bartolomeu. Dating back to 957, this is one of the oldest churches in the city. Destroyed several times, it was rebuilt in its present form in 1756. The interior is of no special interest.

Leave the Comércio along the Rua Eduardo Coelho. Lined on both sides with shoe shops, this was once known as the Street of the Shoemakers. At the Rua do Corvo turn right, and continue until you emerge onto a bustling elongated plaza, Praça 8 de ⑪ Maio. Your eyes will be drawn to the magnificent **Igreja e Mosteiro de Santa Cruz** (Church and Monastery of Santa Cruz), one of the country's richest in history and culture. The stark, 12th-century, stone facade is greatly enhanced by the Renaissance entrance, added as part of an extensive renovation in 1507. Unfortunately, much of the fine detail has been damaged by corrosion. Inside you will see the delicate features of the Renaissance altar carved in 1521 by Nicolas Chanterene. The high altar is flanked on either side by the intricately detailed tombs of the first two kings of Portugal, Dom Alfonso Henriques and his son, Dom Sancho I. In the sacristy there are several notable examples of 16th-century Portuguese painting The lower portions of the interior walls are lined with azulejos depicting various religious motifs. From the sacristy a door opens to the **Casa do Capitulo** (Silent Cloister); this double-tier Manueline cloister contains scenes from *The Passion of Christ* attributed to Nicolas Chanterene. *Praça 8 de Maio, tel. 039*

22941. Admission: church free; cloister: 150$00. Open daily 9–noon and 2–6.

Time Out Even if you are not hungry or thirsty, take the time to stop at the **Café Santa Cruz,** one of the most popular and unusual watering holes north of Lisbon. Until its conversion to more pedestrian uses in 1927, this was an auxiliary chapel for the Santa Cruz Monastery. Now its high-vaulted Manueline ceiling, stained-glass windows, and wood paneling provide a wonderful setting in which to indulge a favorite Portuguese pastime: sitting in a café with a strong, murky *bica* (Portugal's answer to espresso) and a brandy, reading the day's newspaper. In summer there are tables outside. *Praça 8 de Maio. Closed Sun.*

Turn right at the northeast corner of the Praça 8 de Maio onto the broad Rua Olímpio Fernandes. Continue past the public library to a small park with an odd assortment of domed, rose-color turrets grouped around a fountain. This is part of the **⑫ Jardim de Manga** (Manga Garden). Once belonging to the cloisters of the Santa Cruz Monastery, the garden was designed by Jean de Rouen in the 16th century. The fountain symbolizes the fountain of life and the eight pools radiating from it, the rivers of paradise. The impressive fountain on the other side of the **⑬** Rua Olímpio Fernandes is known as the **Fonte dos Judeus** (Jewish Fountain), which dates to 1725 and marks one of the boundaries of the old Jewish quarter. A few steps past the fountain, back toward the Praça 8 de Maio, is a small alley, Rua Pedro da **⑭** Rocha, which leads into the notorious **Patio da Inquisição** (Patio of the Inquisition). This once-feared site is now home to the local Red Cross.

Stay to your right after leaving the Patio, and you'll reach a broad, one-way street branching off from the Praça 8 de Maio. **⑮** This is the renowned **Rua da Sofia.** Developed in the 16th century, the rua is famous for its many fine religious monuments, including the Carmo, Graça, São Pedro, and Santa Justa churches. To preserve the architectural integrity of the neighborhood, the entire street has been classified as a national monument.

⑯ The **Palácio da Justiça** (Hall of Justice), on the Rua da Sofia, just around the corner from the new Tivoli Coimbra Hotel, occupies a stately, 16th-century building that was once the College of St. Thomas. To the left of the main entrance is a large azulejo panel showing the goddess of justice watched over by a Knight Templar. The three panels in front read "Work, Justice, and Order." Gracing the interior is a two-tier cloister, decorated with azulejo panels depicting historical themes associated with Coimbra. *Rua da Sofia. Admission free. Open weekdays 9–12:30 and 2–5:30.*

To return to the starting point at the Portagem, follow the Praça 8 de Maio to the shop-lined Rua Visconde da Luz and the Rua Ferreira Borges.

Time Out Why not succumb to the temptation of the pastry-filled windows of the inviting cafés along the Rua Ferreira Borges? The **Café Nicola** (Rua Ferreira Borges 35) is a good choice for sampling *arrufada,* Coimbra's most notable contribution to the great pastries of the world. This curved confection is said to represent the tortuous course of the Rio Mondego.

From the Portagem, cross the bridge over the Mondego, turn left on the Rua António Augusto Gonçalves, and left again down the Rua de Baixo. There you will see a stark Gothic structure with a single pointed tower—the **Convento de Santa Clara-a-Velha** (Old Santa Clara Convent). Although the convent is steeped in history, there isn't much left to see of the original 13th-century building, since the periodic flooding of the Mondego has taken its toll. At one time both Inês de Castro and Queen Isabel, the patron saint of Coimbra, were interred here.

Continue along the Rua António Augusto Gonçalves for about 15 minutes to reach the **Quinta das Lágrimas** (House of Tears), where Dom Pedro and Inês de Castro lived with their three children. It was here, as the legend goes, on a black, January night in 1355, that Inês was killed by agents of Dom Pedro's father, Alfonso IV. (For more on the story, *see* Alcobaça in Chapter 5.) The 19th-century manor house on the grounds is closed to the public, but you can wander around the gardens and pause at the celebrated **Fonte dos Amores** (Fountain of the Lovers). *Admission free. Open daily 9–7.*

The **Convento de Santa Clara-a-Nova** (New Santa Clara Convent) is located on a hill overlooking the city. On foot it's about a 20-minute climb after crossing the river. The term "new" is relative; it was built nearly 300 years ago to escape the periodic flooding that beset the old convent, which was abandoned in 1677. The new building was consecrated in 1696, and the body of Queen Isabel was relocated. The original painted stone tomb may be seen at the end of the lower chancel, and the 17th-century tomb, a fine example of the silver craftsmanship of the time, is in the main chancel. The church also contains an impressive statue of Isabel in nun's garb, carved from a single 10-foot-high block of limestone. During the Peninsular War, the French general Massena used the convent as a hospital for 300 troops wounded during the battle of Buçaco. The carefully hidden convent treasures escaped the desecration inflicted on so many Portuguese monuments during this period. Don't leave Santa Clara without a relaxing stroll through the enormous cloisters. *Admission free. Open daily 9–12:30 and 2–5:30.*

Tour 2: The Western Beiras

Conimbriga, in a bucolic setting 16 kilometers (10 miles) southwest of Coimbra, is one of the Iberian Peninsula's most important archaeological sites. It began as a small settlement in Celtic or possibly pre-Celtic times. In 27 BC, during his second Iberian visit, the emperor Augustus established the Roman province called Lusitania. It was in this period that, as the Portuguese historian Jorge Alarção described, "Conimbriga was transformed by the Romans from a village where people just existed into a city worth visiting." You enter via a brick reception pavilion with pools and gardens surrounding a museum. Exhibits chronicle the development of the site from its Iron Age origins, through its heyday as a prosperous Roman town to its decline following the 5th-century barbarian conquests. The museum is best appreciated after visiting the excavations.

At the site's entrance is a portion of the original Roman road that connected Olissipo (as Lisbon was then known) and the northern town of Braga. If you look closely, you can make out ridges worn into the stone by cart wheels. The uncovered area represents just a small portion of the Roman city, but within this area are some wonderful mosaic floors. The 3rd-century House of the Fountains has a large, macabre mosaic depicting Perseus offering the head of Medusa to a monster from the deep, an example of the amazing Roman craftsmanship of the period.

Across the way is the **Casa do Cantaber** (House of Cantaber), named for a nobleman whose family was captured by invading barbarians in 465. A tour of the house reveals the comfortable lifestyle of Roman nobility at the time. Private baths included a *tepidarium* (hot pool) and *frigidarium* (cold pool). Remnants of the under-floor central heating system are also visible. Fresh water was carried 3 kilometers (2 miles) by aqueduct from Alcabideque; parts of the original aqueduct can still be seen. There is daily bus service between Conimbriga and Coimbra. *Condeixa-a-Velha, tel. 039/941177. Admission: ruins and museum: June–Sept. 300$00, Oct.–May 200$00; ruins only: Mon., 100$00. Open: ruins: daily 9–1 and 2–6, until 8 during summer; museum: Tues.–Sun. 10–12:30 and 2–5, until 6 during summer; closed holidays.*

For the most scenic route, return to Coimbra, and from there take N341, which runs along the south bank of the Mondego to **㉑ Montemor-o-Velho.** Occupying a strategic hilltop position overlooking the fertile Mondego basin between Coimbra and Figueira da Foz, Montemor figures prominently in the history and legends of the region. One popular story tells how the castle's besieged defenders cut the throats of their own families to spare them a cruel death at the hands of the Moorish invaders; many died before the attackers were repulsed. The following day the escaping Moors were pursued and thoroughly defeated. Legend has it that all those slaughtered at Montemor were resurrected but forever carried a red mark on their necks as a reminder of the battle.

The castle walls and tower, which command the hill and fertile plains below, are largely intact, although little remains inside the impressive ramparts to suggest that this noble family's home once garrisoned 5,000 troops. Archaeological evidence indicates that the hill has been fortified for more than 2,000 years. Although Montemor Castle played an important role in the long-standing conflict between the Christians and Moors, changing hands many times, the structure seen today is primarily of 14th-century origin. The two churches on the hill are also part of the castle complex. The Church of Santa Maria de Alcaçova dates back to the 11th century and contains some well-preserved Manueline additions.

Here again are threads of the story of Inês de Castro, for in January of 1355, Dom Alfonso IV, meeting in the castle with his advisers, made the decision to murder her. In 1811, during the Napoleonic invasions, the castle was badly damaged. *Admission free. Open Tues.–Sun. 10–12:30 and 2–5.*

㉒ There are various theories as to the origin of the name **Figueira da Foz.** The consensus around the fishing harbor at this popular seaside resort favors the literal translation: the fig tree at the mouth of the river. The belief is that when this was just a small settlement, oceangoing fishermen and traders from up the river would arrange to meet at the big fig tree to conduct their business. Although today there are no fig trees to be seen at this busy fishing port, the name has stuck.

Shortly before the turn of the century, with the improvement of road and rail access, Figueira developed into a popular seaside resort with a long, sandy beach and a mild climate. Today, although the beach is little changed, a broad, four-lane, divided boulevard runs along its length. The town side is lined with the usual beach resort melange of apartments, hotels, and restaurants, but, fortunately, the beachfront has been spared from development.

One of the more curious sights in the town is the 18th-century **Casa do Paço,** the interior of which is decorated with about 7,000 Delft tiles. These traditional Dutch tiles were salvaged from a shipwreck at the mouth of the harbor. *Largo Prof. Vitor Guerra 4, around corner from main post office. Admission free. Open weekdays 9:30–12:30 and 2–5.*

The triangular, 17th-century **Fortaleza da Santa Catarina** (Santa Catarina Fortress), adjacent to the beachfront tennis courts, was occupied by the French during the early days of the Peninsular War.

Time Out   There are a number of brightly painted, wooden-shack restaurants sitting directly on the beach. These are wonderful places for fresh grilled fish or just a cold drink. **A Platforma** is one of the best.

Palácio Sotto Mayor (Sotto Mayor Palace), a luxurious, elegantly furnished, French-style manor house, was constructed as part of the wave of development in the late 19th and early 20th centuries that made Figueira da Foz a world-class resort. Long in the hands of one of Portugal's leading families, the palace now belongs to the owners of the casino (*see* The Arts and Nightlife, *below*). Local gossip has it that it was "donated" as payment for gambling debts. Its collection includes paintings and fine furnishings. *Rua Joaquím Sotto Mayor, tel. 033/ 22121. Admission: 100$00. Open weekends 2–6.*

One of the things to do here or in any Portuguese fishing town is to go down to the docks early in the morning to watch the *lota* (the auctioning of the day's catch). Although this colorful spectacle is closed to the public, if you are lucky, perhaps the customs police will look the other way.

❷❸   Just north of Figueira, **Buarcos,** with a fine sandy beach, has managed to retain some of the character of a Portuguese fishing village in spite of a heavy influx of tourists. Here colorfully painted boats are still pulled up onto the beach, and fishermen sit around mending nets. From Buarcos take a trip to the Cape Mondego lighthouse for a wonderful, uncluttered view of the coastline. Then continue climbing through a wooded area to the little village of Boa Viagem (Good Journey); from here you can trace the course of the Rio Mondego as it flows into the sea. Now head north, following the narrow road running along the dunes to Aveiro.

❷❹   To refer to **Aveiro** as the Venice of Portugal, as is sometimes done, does not really do justice to this pleasant coastal town. Yes, there are a few canals running through its center, and the swan-necked *moliceiros* (kelp boats) do remotely resemble Venetian gondolas, but that's the extent of the similarity.

Aveiro's mood is not the drama and splendor of Venice but rather a quiet confidence and dignity.

Aveiro is first and foremost a water city. Its traditions are closely tied to the sea and to the **Ria de Aveiro,** the vast, shallow lagoon that formed in 1575 when a violent storm caused shifting sand to block the flow of the Ria Vouga into the ocean. This unique combination of fresh and salt water, narrow waterways, and tiny islands is bordered by salt marshes and lush pine forests, and the ocean side is lined with lovely sandy beaches. The tranquil Ria is the realm of the moliceiros, the graceful, colorfully painted swan-necked craft that glide along the shallow waterways harvesting seaweed. A boat tour through the Ria is a must (*see* Guided Tours in Essential Information, *above*), or, if you have a car, a drive through the Ria's backroads is also recommended.

With the loss of its seaport, Aveiro, once a major center for boats working the Newfoundland codfish banks, suffered a prolonged decline. It was only in 1808, when a breakwater was built of stones from the old city fortifications, that a passage to the sea was reestablished and the town once again flourished. Deep-sea fishing was reinstituted, new industries were established, and the city took on the prosperous air it maintains today.

Aveiro is great for walking, since most of the industry and the new university are situated on the periphery and places of interest in the old town are easily accessible on foot. In many parts of town, the sidewalks and squares are paved with *calçada* (a traditional Portuguese style of hand-laid pavement) in intricate nautical patterns.

The most attractive buildings date back to the latter half of the 15th century. In 1472 the princess Joana, daughter of King Alfonso V, retired, against her father's wishes, to the **Mosteiro de Jesus** (Convent of Jesus), where she spent the last 18 years of her life. This royal presence gave impetus to the city's economic and cultural development. The convent, which now houses the **Museu de Aveiro** (Aveiro Museum), was established by papal bull in 1461. The late-18th-century facade is not particularly interesting, but the interior of the church, completed in the early 18th century, is a masterpiece of Baroque art. The elaborately gilded wood carvings and ornate ceiling, done by António Gomes and José Correia from Oporto, are among the finest in Portugal. Scenes depicting the life of Joana, who was canonized in 1693, can be seen on azulejo panels, and Joana's tomb is in the lower choir. The multicolor, inlaid marble sarcophagus is supported at each corner by delicately carved angels. The museum contains an assortment of sculpture, coaches and carriages, artifacts, and paintings, including a particularly fine 15th-century portrait of the Princess Joana by Nuno Gonçalves. *Rua Santa Joana Princesa. Admission: museum: 200$00. Open Tues.–Sun. 10–12:30 and 2–5.*

The austere stone structure across from the convent is the Aveiro Cathedral, more commonly known as the Church of São Domingos. The interior of the church has no definitive architectural style but does contain some fine azulejos.

Time Out   The **Sonatura,** overlooking the central canal, offers a rare opportunity to have a vegetarian snack or meal. Service is cafeteria-style inside a health-food store. To your right, as you leave the restaurant, note the modern tile relief showing kelp gatherers at work. *Praça Humberto Delgada, Rua Clube dos Galitos 6. Closed Sun.*

The Praça da República has two interesting buildings: the graceful, three-story Town Hall, with a pointed bell tower, and the 18th-century Misericórdia Church, whose imposing Baroque portal is set against a background of blue-and-white azulejos.

Also of interest in Aveiro is the headquarters of the port captain, an attractive, two-story building perched on arches in the middle of the central canal. The best place for viewing the brightly decorated fishing boats is along the Canal de São Roque. To the west are huge, glistening mounds of white salt, recovered by evaporation from the lagoon. At the northeast edge of the city, the train station displays some lovely azulejo panels depicting traditions and customs of the region.

26 **Ilhavo,** 4 kilometers (2½ miles) south of Aveiro, is a small town of attractive, tiled manor houses. The **Museu do Mar** (Museum of the Sea), situated in a drab, concrete building next to a fish-processing plant, documents the region's close relationship with the sea and has a collection of local pottery and Vista Alegre china. *Rua Vasco da Gama, tel. 034/321797. Admission: 100$00. Open Wed.–Sat. 9–12:30 and 2–5:30, Sun. and Tues. 2–5:30.*

27 Continue south from Ilhavo for 2 kilometers (1¼ miles) to **Vista Alegre,** where Portugal's finest china is produced. The business was started in 1824 as a sort of commune, with housing furnished for workers from all parts of the country. Training was provided by French master craftsmen, and the clay came from the nearby town of Ovar. The large, tree-filled square is bordered by the factory, a china museum, a gift shop, and a small 17th-century chapel with the delicately carved tomb of the chapel's founder. *Fabrica Vista Alegre, tel. 034/322365. Admission free. Museum and gift shop open weekdays 9–12:30 and 2–5:30.*

Back in Aveiro head north on N109 to Estarreja; then turn off and follow N109-5 through quiet farmlands. After crossing the
28 bridge over the Ria, continue north on N327 to **Ovar.** Situated at the northern end of the Ria, Ovar provides a convenient jumping-off point for visiting the string of beaches along the narrow northern peninsula. This small town with its many tiled houses is a veritable showcase of azulejos. The courthouse, built in the 1960s, is adorned with some unusually beautiful multicolor tile panels, and the exterior of the late-17th-century Parish Church is completely covered with blue-and-white azulejos. The small **Museu Regional de Ovar** (Regional Museum), located in an old house in the town center, also exhibits many tiles and local handicrafts. *Rua Heliodoro Slagado, tel. 056/52822. Admission: 100$00. Open Sat.–Thurs. 10–noon and 2–4 except holidays.*

29 Drive 10 kilometers (6 miles) on N223 from Ovar to **Santa Maria de Feira,** and you will be rewarded with the lovely fairy-tale Castle of Vila da Feira. The four square towers are crowned with a series of cone-shaped turrets in a display of Gothic architecture more common in Germany or Austria than in Portugal.

Although the original walls date back to the 11th century, the present structure is the result of modifications made 400 years later. From atop the tower you can make out the sprawling outlines of the Aveiro Ria. *Admission: 200$00. Open Tues.–Sun. 9–12:30 and 2–6.*

After visiting the castle, it's a scenic but twisting, bone-jarring 70-kilometer (43½-mile) drive on N227 across the Serra da Gralheira mountains to **Viseu.** (The new IP 1 and IP 5 highways offer a smoother, faster, but much less interesting alternative.) A thriving provincial capital situated in one of Portugal's prime wine-growing districts, the Dão region, Viseu has managed to preserve the ambience of a country town in spite of its obvious prosperity. The newer part of town is comfortably laid out. Parks and wide boulevards radiate from a central traffic circle, but, unlike many Portuguese towns, through-traffic does not have to go through its center.

A good place to start a visit is the tree-lined **Praça da República,** also known as the Rossio. This pleasant square is framed at one end by a massive azulejo mural depicting scenes of country life. The heroic figure in bronze, standing sword in hand, is Prince Henry the Navigator, the first duke of Viseu. The stately building across from the tile mural is the **Câmara Municipal** (Town Hall). Walk inside to admire the colorful Aveiro tiles and fine woodwork, and be sure to see the courtyard. Just to the south of the square, a graceful stairway leads to the 18th-century, baroque **A Igreja dos Terceiros de São Francisco** (Church of the Terceiros de São Francisco). Behind the church is a large, wooded park with walking paths and ponds, offering an ideal respite from the summer heat.

From the Rossio walk up the hill past a garden with a bronze figure of a mother and child to the Moorish-style mansion on the hill. This is the **A Casa-Museu de Almeida Moreira** (Almeida Moreira Museum). Almeida Moreira, the first director of the Grão Vasco Museum, bequeathed his house and a diverse collection of paintings, furniture, and ceramics to the city. The house alone is worth the admission price. *Rua Soar Cima, tel. 032/ 23769. Admission: 100$00. Open Tues.–Sun. 10–12:30 and 2–5 except holidays.*

Continue along the Largo Pintor Gata into the old town, and you will emerge onto the **Largo da Sé.** Bounded by three imposing edifices—the cathedral, the palace housing the Grão Vasco Museum, and the Misericórdia Church—this is one of the most impressive squares in Portugal.

The **Sé Catedral** (Cathedral), a massive stone structure with twin bell towers, lends a solemn air to the large plaza. Construction was started in the 13th century and continued on and off until the 18th century. The interior is marked by a mixture of Gothic and Manueline elements. Massive Gothic pillars support a network of twisted, knotted forms that reach across the high, vaulted roof. The dazzling gilded Baroque high altar contrasts with the otherwise somber stone interior. To the right of the Mannerist main portal is a double-tiered cloister. The lower level was constructed in the 16th century in the style of the Italian Renaissance. The harsh lines of the upper level (added 200 years later) appear awkward in contrast to the graceful Italianate arches below. The walls of the lower level are adorned with a series of excellent azulejo panels depicting various religious motifs. A well-preserved, transitional, Gothic-style doorway connects the cloister with the cathedral. *Admission free. Open daily 9:30–12:30 and 2–5:30.*

Directly adjacent to the cathedral is the former 16th-century Bishop's Palace, which now houses the **Museu de Grão Vasco** (Grão Vasco Museum). The second-floor galleries are devoted to the display of the works of the great 16th-century Portuguese painter Vasco Fernandes (Grão Vasco) and his Viseu school. *Adro de Sé, tel. 032/26249. Admission: 200$00, free weekends. Open Tues.–Sun. 10–12:30 and 2–5 except holidays.*

The other principal attraction in the Largo da Sé is the 18th-century **Misericórdia Church.** Directly opposite the cathedral, the white, rococo Misericórdia has soft, graceful lines, in sharp contrast to the harsh, gray lines of the cathedral. *Admission free. Open daily 9:30–12:30 and 2–5:30.*

Return to the lower town by way of the **Praça de Dom Duarte,** one of those rare places where just the right combination of rough stone pavement, splendid old houses, wrought-iron balconies, and views of an ancient cathedral come together to produce a magical effect. Try to be here at night, when the romance of the setting is further enhanced by the soft glow of the streetlights.

At the edge of town on the road toward Aveiro is a statue of a warrior standing on a rock. This is a monument to Viriáto, the leader of the Lusitanian resistance to the Roman invasion in the 2nd century BC. Some historians believe that this was the site of his encampment.

③① The market town of **Mangualde** is 13 kilometers (8 miles) southeast of Viseu on N16. The principal attraction is the **Palácio des Condes de Anadia** (Palace of the Counts of Anadia). The two-story, 17th-century, rococo manor house is one of the best from this era in the region. The walls are decorated with 18th-century Coimbra azulejos, and the interior contains period furniture and paintings from the 17th–19th centuries. *Admission: 300$00. Open Oct.–Aug., Tues.–Sun. 9–noon and 2–6.*

Driving through the heart of the Dão region from Mangualde to Caramulo, you will see many vineyards, some carefully terraced. The wines pressed from these grapes are some of Portugal's finest.

③② In the early part of this century, when tuberculosis was rife, people came to **Caramulo** for the beneficial effects of the fresh mountain air. Tuberculosis is no longer a problem, but Caramulo has not lost its appeal. People still come to enjoy the heather-clad, wooded slopes and to walk through the lovely parks and gardens. Mineral water bottled at the nearby spring is popular throughout the country.

The town has an unusual museum, the **Museu de Arte do Caramulo** (Caramulo Art Museum), founded and supported by Abel Lacerda, a local doctor. The varied collection, consisting solely of donations, includes jewels, ceramics, and a fine assortment of paintings, representing such diverse artists as Salvador Dali, Picasso, and Grão Vasco. Next door is the **Museu do Automóvel,** whose collection of perfectly restored antique cars includes such rare items as a 1902 Darracq. Also on exhibit are vintage bicycles and motorcycles. *Tel. 032/86270. Admission: both museums 300$00. Open Tues.–Sun. 10–12:30 and 2–6.*

Caramulinho and **Cabeço da Neve,** two nearby observation points, offer spectacular vistas. Take Avenida Abel de Lacerda west from town until it runs into N230-3. After 3 kilometers (2 miles) on N230-3, you come to a trail leading to Caramulinho. It's about a 30-minute climb to the top. Here at the tip of the Serra do Caramulo mountains, at an elevation of 3,500 feet, you can look out across a vast panorama taking in the coastal plain to the west and the Serra da Estrela to the southeast. On the drive back, take the turnoff marked Cabeço da Neve. From there you have a bird's-eye view of the Mondego basin.

㉝ As you continue west on N230, the road snakes down the mountain following the course of the Ria Águeda as it flows into the great Aveiro lagoon. The industrial town of **Águeda** is a center for the production of paper products. With the exception of the parish church, the town has little of interest.

㉞ Head south on N1 to **Curia,** a small but popular spa in the heart of the Bairrada region, an area noted for its fine wines and roast suckling pig. The waters of the spa, with their high calcium and magnesium sulphate contents, are said to help in the treatment of kidney disorders. Curia offers a quiet retreat of shaded parks, a small lake, and grand, *Belle Epoque* hotels just a half-hour's drive from the clamor of the summer beach scene. In fact, any of the three resorts in this area, Curia, Luso, or Buçaco, make good, quiet bases for visiting the beaches and other attractions of the region. Coimbra, Aveiro, Figueira da Foz, the Serra do Caramulo, and Viseu are all within an hour's drive.

㉟ **Luso,** another charming town built around "the taking of the waters," is located on the main Lisbon–Paris train line. It sits in a little valley at the foot of the Buçaco forest and attracts visitors from all over the world. Like Curia, it has an attractive park with a lake, elegant hotels, and medicinal waters. The Luso water emerges at a warm 27°C (81°F) from the *Fonte de São João,* a fountain in the center of town. Slightly radioactive and with a low sodium and high silicate content, the water is said to be effective in the treatment of a wide range of kidney and rheumatic disorders.

In the early 17th century, the head of the Order of Barefoot Carmelites, searching for a suitable location on which to found a monastery, came upon an area of dense virgin forest. Having rejected an offer to settle in Sintra because there were too many distractions, he chose instead the tranquil forest of **㊱** **Buçaco.** A site for the monastery was selected halfway up the hill on the greenest slope, and by 1630 the simple stone structure was occupied. To preserve their world of isolation and silence, the monks built a wall enclosing the forest. Their only link with the outside world was through one door facing toward Coimbra, which one of them watched over. The Coimbra Gate, still in use today, is the most decorative of the eight gates constructed since that time.

So concerned were the Carmelites for the well-being of their forest that they obtained a papal bull in 1643 calling for the excommunication of anyone caught cutting down even a single tree. They planted many trees, including a number of exotic varieties, and the forest flourished. Attracted by the calm and tranquility of the forest, individual monks would leave the monastery to be alone with God and nature. They built simple hermitages, where they would stay, without human companionship, for several months at a time. You can still see vestiges of these hermitages as you walk through the forest.

In 1810 this serenity was shattered by a fierce battle in which the Napoleonic armies under Massena were repulsed by Wellington's British and Portuguese troops. An obelisk marks the site of the Battle of Buçaco, a turning point in the French invasion of the Iberian peninsula. Nearby is the small **Museu da Guerra Peninsular** (Peninsular War Museum), with uniforms, weapons, and various memorabilia from the battle. *Admission: 75$00. Open June 15–Sept. 15, Tues.–Sun. 9–5:30; Sept. 16– June 14, Tues.–Sun. 10–4.*

A decree in 1834 banned religious orders throughout Portugal, and the monks were forced to leave the monastery. In the early years of this century, much of the original structure was torn down to construct what was to be a royal hunting lodge. The commission was given to the Italian architect Luigi Manini, and the project grew and grew. The opulent, multiturreted, pseudo-Manueline extravaganza that is now the **Palace Hotel Buçaco** was the result (*see* Dining and Lodging, *below*). With the exception of one brief vacation and a dubious romantic fling involving the 20-year-old Manuel II, Portugal's last king, this "simple hunting lodge" was never used by the royal family. The hotel prospered, and in the years between the two world wars it became one of Europe's most fashionable vacation addresses. Tales told in the local villages have it that during World War II, when neutral Portugal was a hotbed of espionage activity, Nazi agents ensconced in the hotel's tower rooms beamed radio signals to submarines off the coast. Today the hotel is still going strong, somewhat of a dinosaur among the sleek new breed of glass-and-steel hostelries. Many come to Buçaco just to view this unusual structure, to stroll the shaded paths that wind through the forest, and to climb the hill past the Stations of the Cross to the **Alta Cruz** (High Cross), their efforts rewarded by the spectacular view extending all the way to the sea.

③⑦ From Buçaco take N235 through the wooded countryside along the foot of the Serra do Buçaco to **Penacova,** a delightful little town perched on a hill at the confluence of three low mountain ranges. There are panoramic views wherever you look and wonderful opportunities for hiking. Several paths lead over the hills to the Monastery of Lorvão or through the vineyards and fields down to the Mondego. The attractive parish church in the town square was built in 1620.

Another 2 kilometers (1¼ miles) along N235 toward Coimbra takes you to the turnoff for the monastery in Lorvão. In a delightful setting among the hills above the Mondego, it is patterned after the massive, Baroque edifice at Mafra. Archaeological evidence places the existence of a monastery here as far back as the 6th century, but the present church is principally an 18th-century construction. It has a fine carved choir and the intricate silver tombs of Teresa and Sancha, daughters of Dom Sancho I. A large part of the original monastery has been taken over by a psychiatric hospital, but it is possible to visit the church, choir, and sacristy. There is also a small museum next to the church. *Admission free. Open daily 10–5.*

From Lorvão it's a pleasant 22-kilometer (14-mile) drive along the Mondego back to Coimbra.

Tour 3: The Serra da Estrela and Fortified Towns

The third tour covers a part of Portugal seldom visited by foreign tourists. The rugged mountains of the Serra da Estrela and sparse vegetation of the stone-strewn high plateau along the border with Spain present a sharp contrast to the sandy beaches, lush valleys, and densely forested mountains along the coast. As you drive east, the red tile roofs and brightly trimmed, white stucco houses are replaced by stone and slate construction, reflecting the harsher, more somber environment.

38 The start of the tour is **Castelo Branco,** a modern town of wide boulevards, parks, and gardens and the provincial capital of Beira Baixa. Lying at the confluence of three major roads, the N112 from Coimbra; the N118, which runs along the Tejo; and the N18, which connects Guarda in the North with the Alentejo (Portugal's largest province), it is easily accessible from all parts of the country.

Start with a stroll through the **Jardim do Antigo Paço Episcopal** (Gardens of the former Episcopal Palace). These 18th-century gardens are planted with rows of hedges cut in all sorts of bizarre shapes and contain a most unusual assemblage of sculpture. Bordering one of the park's five small lakes are a path and stairway lined on both sides with granite statues of the Apostles, the Evangelists, and the kings of Portugal. The long-standing Portuguese disdain for the Spanish is graphically demonstrated here; the kings who ruled when Portugal was under Spanish domination are carved to a noticeably smaller scale then the "true" Portuguese rulers. Unfortunately, many statues were damaged by Napoleon's troops when the city was ransacked in 1807. *Admission: 100$00. Open daily 9–6.*

Adjacent to the gardens is the old Episcopal Palace, which houses a small regional museum, the **Tavares Proença National Museum.** In addition to the usual Roman artifacts and odd pieces of furniture, the collection contains some fine examples of *bordado*, the embroidery for which Castelo Branco is so well known. Adjacent to the museum is a workshop where embroidered bedspreads in the traditional patterns are made and sold. *Rua Bartolomeu da Costa, tel. 072/24277. Admission: 150$00, Sun. free. Open daily 10–12:30 and 2–5:30 except holidays.*

Leave the park, and wander through the old town past the curious clock tower to the Praça Luis de Camões, the town's best-preserved medieval square. The building with the arched stone stairway is the 16th-century town hall. At the top of the hill are the ruins of the 12th-century Templar's Castle. Not much remains of the series of walls and towers that once surrounded the town. Adjoining the castle is the flower-covered **Miradouro de São Gens** (Terrace of São Gens), which provides a fine view of the town and surrounding countryside.

Time Out   For a refreshing pause, drop into the **Cervejeria Bohemia** (Av. 1 de Maio, near tourist office), an inviting snack bar–restaurant with a long, marble-top bar.

Travel north from Castelo Branco on N18. As you cross the broad plains dotted with olive trees, you can see the Serra da Estrela mountains in the distance. **Alpedrinha,** a village known for its fine fountains, also has well-preserved remnants of the Roman road that connected this fertile agricultural region with the Spanish town of Merida. From here N18 climbs to **Fundão,** the principal market town for the area's many orchards. The pears and cherries grown here are the best in Portugal. The 18th-century parish church is noted for its azulejos and decorative ceiling. Fundão is also a convenient gateway to the fortified towns along the Spanish border.

Head east on N345 to the intersection with N346. Then take N346 to **Penamacor.** Dominated by the ruins of an ancient castle that guarded the northern approaches to the Rio Tejo, Penamacor was a key link in the chain of strategically placed fortified towns. Many of the newer stucco houses that you see on the outskirts of the towns in this region were built by Portuguese emigrants with money earned working in France and Germany. Head up the hill to the **castle.** In the wake of the 11th- and 12th-century campaigns to reconquer this region from the Moors, Penamacor lay in ruins; it was Dom Sancho I who, in 1180, ordered the reconstruction of the fortifications. Although you can still find traces from that period, much of what you now see, including the solitary watchtower, dates from the early 16th century. The tower, which has no entrance, was used as an observation post and has a direct line of sight with the fortifications at Monsanto to the south and Sortelha to the north. *If castle is closed, ask for key at tourist office.*

Also of interest are the 16th-century Misericórdia Church, distinguished by a fine Manueline entrance, and a rare octagonal pillory in front of the old town hall. The town has a small but interesting **Regional Museum,** housed in a building that was a political prison until the 1974 revolution. One of the original cells has been kept intact, and among the other exhibits is the only complete Roman crematorium on the Iberian Peninsula. *Admission free. Open daily 9–12:30 and 2–5:30.*

Follow N233 north for 35 kilometers (22 miles) across the high plateau to **Sabugal.** This harsh, rocky country is a tough place to make a living. Traditionally, many inhabitants of these towns supplemented their meager farming incomes by smuggling contraband across the nearby border with Spain. The region was greatly affected by the wave of emigration to northern Europe between 1950 and 1970; a half million Portuguese went to France alone. As a consequence many villages are populated primarily by old people.

The main attraction in Sabugal is the 13th-century **Sabugal Castle,** which sits majestically atop a grassy knoll and is noted for its unusual pentagonal tower. Some historians maintain that the five sides represent the five shields of the Portuguese national coat of arms. Climb the stone stairs in the courtyard and walk around the battlements. The castle overlooks the Ria Côa, an important tributary of the Douro. *Admission free Open Mon.–Sat. 10–5. If castle is closed, ask for key at touris office.*

If you only have time to visit one fortified town, then **Sortelha** should be it. From the moment you walk through its massive ancient, stone walls, you feel like you are experiencing a time

519 M.P.H.

190 M.P.H.

75 M.P.H.

0 M.P.H.

WE LET YOU SEE EUROPE AT YOUR OWN PACE.

gardless of your personal speed limits, Rail Europe offers
thing to get you over, around and through anywhere you
in Europe. For more information, call
travel agent or **1-800-4-EURAIL**.

Rail Europe

MCI brings Europe and America closer together.

Call the U.S. for less with MCI CALL USA®.

It's easy and affordable to call home when you use MCI CALL USA!

- Less expensive than calling through hotel operators
- Available from over 65 countries and locations worldwide
- You're connected to English-speaking MCI® Operators
- Even call 800 numbers in the U.S.

Call the U.S. for less from these European locations.

Dial the toll-free access number for the country you're calling from. Give the U.S. MCI Operator the number you're calling and the method of payment: MCI Card, U.S. local phone company card, Telecom Canada Card or collect. Your call will be completed!

Austria	022-903-012	Hungary	00*800-01411	Poland	0*-01-04-800-222
Belgium	078-11-00-12	Ireland	1800-551-001	Portugal	05-017-1234
Czechoslovakia	00-42-000112	Italy	172-1022	San Marino	172-1022
Denmark	8001-0022	Liechtenstein	155-0222	Spain	900-99-0014
Finland	9800-102-80	Luxembourg	0800-0112	Sweden	020-795-922
France	19*-00-19	Monaco	19*-00-19	Switzerland	155-0222
Germany	0130-0012	Netherlands	06*-022-91-22	United Kingdom	0800-89-0222
Greece	00-800-1211	Norway	050-12912	Vatican City	172-1022

* Wait for 2nd dial tone. Collect calls not accepted on MCI CALL USA calls to 800 numbers

Call 1-800-444-4444 in the U.S. to apply for your MCI Card® now!

warp. Except for a few TV antennas, there is little else to evoke the 20th century. The streets are not littered with souvenir stands, nor is there a fast-food outlet in sight. Stone houses are built into the rocky terrain and arranged within the walls roughly in the shape of an amphitheater.

Time Out The **Bar Dom Sancho I,** in the main square, occupies the lower level of a carefully restored stone house. A "hobby project" of a local mining engineer, it is a pleasant place to pause for drinks and snacks. Upstairs you can purchase locally made handicrafts.

Perched above the village are the ruins of a small but imposing **castle.** The present configuration dates back mainly to a late-12th-century reconstruction, done on Moorish foundations; additional alterations were made in the 16th century. Note the Manueline coat of arms at the entrance. Wear sturdy shoes so that you can walk along the walls (it's possible to circle the entire village this way). As you walk along, there are views of Spain to the east and to the west of the Serra da Estrela. The three holes in the balcony projecting over the main entrance were used to pour boiling oil on intruders. Just to the right of the north gate are two linear indentations in the stone wall. One is exactly a meter in length, and the shorter of the two is a *covada* (66 centimeters). Traveling merchants used these in medieval times to ensure an honest measure.

❹ From Sortelha take N18–3 west and N345 north to **Belmonte.** As you approach the town, three distinct objects, which say a lot about Belmonte, catch your eye. The first two, the ancient castle and the church, represent the town's historic past, while the third structure, an ugly water tower, symbolizes the new industry of the town, now a major clothing manufacturing center. Historically Belmonte's importance can be traced back to Roman times, when it was an important outpost on the road between Merida, the Lusitanian capital, and Guarda. Elements of this road may still be seen.

Ask a Portuguese, or better yet any Brazilian, what Belmonte is best known for, and the answer will undoubtedly be Pedro Álvares Cabral. In 1500 this native son "discovered" Brazil and in doing so contributed to making Portugal one of the richest and most powerful nations of that era. The monument to Cabral in the town center is an important stop for Brazilians visiting Portugal.

Head up through the old town to the **castle.** Only the tower and battlements remain intact from what once was a mighty complex of fortifications and dwellings. As you enter the castle, note the scale-model replica of the caravel that carried Cabral to Brazil. On one of the side walls is a coat of arms with two goats, the emblem of the Cabral family. (*Cabra* means goat in Portuguese.) The graceful Manueline window incorporated into the heavy fortifications seems misplaced. *Admission: 100$00. Open Mon.–Sat. 10–12:30 and 2–5:30.*

As you leave the castle, you will see a cluster of old houses to your right. This was the *judería* (the old Jewish quarter). Belmonte had (and, in fact, still has) one of the largest Jewish communities in Portugal. Many present-day residents are descendants of the *Morranos,* the Jews who were forced to convert to Christianity during the Inquisition.

Adjacent to the castle is the 12th-century, stone **Igreja de São Tiago** (Church of Saint James), which contains fragments of original 12th-century frescoes and a fine pietà carved from a single block of granite. The tomb of Pedro Cabral is also in this church. Actually there are two Pedro Cabral tombs in Portugal, the result of a bizarre dispute with Santerem, where Cabral died. Both towns claim ownership of the explorer's mortal remains, and no one seems to know just who or what is in either tomb. *Admission free. Open daily 10–6. If closed, ask at tourist office.*

45 Just outside Belmonte, on a dirt track leading off the N18 toward Guarda, is a strange archaeological find, **Centum Cellas.** This massive, solitary tower constructed of granite blocks is thought to be of Roman origin, and some archaeologists believe it's part of a much larger complex. Excavations of the surrounding area are planned.

46 Although its origins go back to Roman times, there is little in present-day **Covilhã** of historical significance. Built into the foothills of the Serra da Estrela, the mostly modern town is closely linked to sheep raising. Its tangy *queijo da Serra,* a ewe's-milk cheese, is popular throughout the country, and the town is Portugal's most important wool-producing center. However, most visitors come to Covilhã because it is a convenient gateway to the Serra da Estrela (*see* National Parks in Sports and Outdoor Activities, *below*).

47 Nestled into the western side of the Mondego valley, **Gouveia,** a quiet town of parks and gardens, is another popular base from which to explore the Serra da Estrela. The exterior of the Baroque parish church is covered with blue and white tiles. Across the street a series of well-executed azulejos depicting the Stations of the Cross line the inside walls of the small, dimly lit chapel. The **Museu Abel Manta** (Abel Manta Museum), in an 18th-century manor house, displays the paintings of this local, 20th-century artist. *Admission free. Open Tues.–Sun. 10–noon and 2–5.*

Gouveia is the principal center for the famous Serra da Estrela dogs, beautiful sheepdogs known for their loyalty and courage. In earlier days, when marauding wolf packs were an ever-present menace, the dogs wore metal collars with long spikes to protect their throats. You can visit **Montes Herminios Kennels,** one of the major breeding kennels in the Vale do Rossim on N232 between Gouveia and Manteigas. *Solar do Cão da Serra, Estrada da Serra, tel. 038/42426.*

48 Follow N232 as it winds its way to **Manteigas,** a pleasant spa town at the foot of the Zêzere valley and another popular base for visiting the park. From Manteigas take N232 and N18–**▶** north, passing a lovely 12th-century church in **Valhelas.** The **49** road then climbs to **Guarda,** which, at an altitude of just over 3,300 feet, is Portugal's highest city. Guarda is aptly referred to by the four Fs: *forte, feia, fria, e farta* (strong, ugly, cold and wealthy). A somber conglomeration of austere granite buildings set in a harsh, uncompromising environment, it is no charming mountain hamlet. The winters are cold and gloomy, often cutting into the short springtime.

From pre-Roman times, Guarda has been a strategic bastion on the northeastern flank of the Serra da Estrela, protecting the approaches from Castile. The town is thought to have been military base for Julius Caesar. Following the fall of the Roman Empire, the Visigoths and later the Moors gained control. Guarda was liberated in the late 12th century by Christian forces and, along with a number of towns in the region, enlarged and fortified by Dom Sancho I.

The castle tower, perched on a small knoll above the cathedral, and a few segments of wall are all that remain of these extensive fortifications. From atop the ruins there is an impressive view across the rock-strewn countryside toward the Castilian plains. Walk down the hill to the fortresslike Sé (Cathedral). Although construction started in 1390, it was not completed until 1540. As a consequence, the imposing Gothic building also shows Renaissance and Manueline influences. Although built on a smaller and less majestic scale, the cathedral shows similarities to the great monastery at Batalha. Inside, a magnificent, four-tier relief contains more than 100 carved figures. The work is attributed to the 16th-century sculptor Jean de Rouen.

Leave the cathedral by the side door, and you are in the Praça Luis de Camões, a square lined with some fine 16th- and 18th-century houses. The statue is of Dom Sancho I. The **Regional Museum,** in a stately, early 17th-century palace adjacent to the 18th-century Misericórdia Church, is worth a visit. *Rua Alves Rocadas, tel. 071/23460. Admission: 200$00, Sun. free. Open Tues.–Sun. 10–12:30 and 2–5:30.*

From Guarda take either N16 or IP 5 east to N324 north. Enclosed within a star-shaped perimeter of massive stone walls, moats, and earthen bulwarks lies the quiet little town of ㊿ **Almeida.** Less than 10 kilometers (6 miles) from the Spanish border, the town has been the scene of much fighting over the centuries. This is a place for walking, for clambering along the walls and bulwarks, and for giving your imagination free reign, perhaps to conjure up ghosts of battles past.

Travel north on N332 to **Castelo Rodrigo,** an old, fortified town that is now mostly deserted; here turn south on N221, crossing ㉛ the Serra da Marofa and a desolate, rocky moonscape to **Pinhel.** The town, which sits atop a hill in the Marofa range, was a key bastion during the 17th-century wars of restoration. The most striking remnants from that period are the two solitary towers rising above the town. On one of the towers, below the balcony facing the town, you can make out the graceful form of a Manueline window.

㉜ **Trancoso,** to the west of Pinhel, is best approached along the scenic but tortuous N226. Portions of the well-preserved castle walls and towers date to the 9th century. The town reached its pinnacle in 1282, when King Dinis chose this as the site for his marriage to Isabel of Aragon. Above one of the gates, the **Porta do Carvalho,** you can make out the figure of a knight. This was a local lad who during one of the many battles with the Spanish left the safety of the castle walls to capture the Spanish flag. He was caught, but before being spirited away, he was able to defiantly hurl the flag over the wall.

㉝ **Celorico da Beira,** 18 kilometers (11 miles) south, is a major producer of Serra cheese and the site of one of Europe's largest cheese markets, held every other Friday. The cheese is made from the best-quality ewe's milk, using traditional methods. Cheese production takes place between December and March.

Celorico also has the requisite **fortress,** and a large portion of the castle walls and an impressive tower have remained intact. *Key to castle can be obtained at town hall (open Mon.–Sat. 10–12:30 and 2–5).*

54 Continue south on N17 from Celorico for 12 kilometers (7 miles), and take the turnoff to the left to **Linhares.** The road climbs to a rocky outcrop on the northeastern shoulder of the Serra da Estrela. At an elevation of 2,625 feet, a good place for a lookout, stand the fortifications of Linhares. Much of the outer walls and two square, crenellated towers from the time of King Dinis remain intact. Encircled by the walls is a small, quiet village of stone houses, a church, and a few shops. There's a 16th-century pillory in front of the church.

What to See and Do with Children

At Coimbra's **Portugal dos Pequenitos** (Portugal of the Little Ones), children will have great fun poking around the models of Portugal's most important buildings, built to the scale of a five-year-old child. Then they can compare them with what they have seen firsthand. *Admission: 200$00, 50$00 children under 11. Open daily 9–5:30, until 7 in summer. Closed Easter, Christmas, and November 1.*

A day at the beach is a treat for children of all ages. The beaches at Figueira da Foz, Tocha, Mira, and Furadouro (Ovar) are particularly well suited for children; they all have lifeguards and have met the European Common Market standards for safety and hygiene. (*See* Beaches in Sports and Outdoor Activities, *below.*)

Places of interest to children in the Western Beiras (*see* Tour 2, *above*) include the city parks in Aveiro and Viseu, which have playgrounds; the antique car museum in Caramulo; and the Museum of the Sea in Ilhavo. Watching the unloading of the big ships in Aveiro and Figueira da Foz can be fun for the whole family, as is the morning fish auction (officially off limits) at any of the harbors. The Curia Palace hotel, with its old, water-powered mill, antique cars, and animals of all kinds, is a wonderful place to stay with children (*see* Dining and Lodging, *below*).

The many castles along the third tour provide wonderful opportunities for children to let their fantasies run wild. The ruins at Almeida, Sortelha, and Belmonte are particularly suitable for scrambling and scampering about. In addition, the miles of hiking trails in the Serra da Estrela are enough to absorb the energy of even the most restless of children (*see* National Parks in Sports and Outdoor Activities, *below*).

Off the Beaten Track

Relief from Coimbra's oppresive summer heat can be found in the shade and greenery of the **Jardim Botânico** (Botanical Gardens), adjacent to the university, and in the city's fine parks. **O Choupal,** near the railroad bridge, is a lovely wooded area along the river at the west end of the city. **Parque de Santa Cruz** (Santa Cruz Park), at the Praça da República, offers a pleasant mixture of luxuriant vegetation, ornate fountains, and meandering walking paths.

Shopping

The Beiras are rich in artisans' traditions. Surprisingly, even today much of what is made is only available within a limited geographic area. For example, the intricate, hand-carved **willow toothpicks** of Penacova are rarely found outside this little town on the Mondego.

The **ceramics** produced in and around Coimbra, mostly blue-and-white reproductions of delicate 17th- and 18th-century patterns, are among the loveliest in the country. A good selection may be found at **Bazar de Louças** (Rua das Padeiras 44, Coimbra, across from the Hotel Oslo).

The region around Aveiro produces Portugal's finest **china,** including the well-known Vista Alegre brand. There is a retail outlet with a good selection of this fine-quality bone china at the factory just outside of Ilhavo (*see* Tour 2, *above*). In Aveiro the **Armazéms de Aveiro** (Rua Conselheoro Luis de Magalhaes 1) sell the leading Portuguese brands, including Vista Alegre, Quinta Nova, and Artebus, and they will ship your purchases.

In Viseu, a walk along the Rua Direita in the old town can be rewarding. The narrow street is lined with shops displaying locally made **wood carvings, pottery,** and **wrought iron.**

Tradition in Castelo Branco dictates that a new bride makes an **embroidered bedspread** for her wedding night. This custom is still followed, and these delicately patterned, hand-embroidered linen and silk spreads are among the finest examples of Portuguese handicrafts. There is a display-and-sales room next to the regional museum (*see* Tour 3, *above*).

In the Serra da Estrela the famous **Serra cheese** and **presunto** (cured ham) are available in most towns in the region, along with hand-carved, wood kitchen implements and wicker baskets.

Sports and Outdoor Activities

Participant Sports

Biking You can rent bikes and mopeds in Figueira da Foz at **AFGA Travel Agency** (Av. Miguel Bombarda 79). In Aveiro bicycles can be rented in summer in front of the tourist office.

Fishing There is excellent trout fishing in the rivers and lakes of the Serra da Estrela and in the Ria Vouga. The coastal strip known as the Beira Litoral is full of beaches and rocky outcroppings where you can try your luck with a variety of fish, including bass, bream, and sole. Check with the local tourist offices for information about obtaining permits. No permit is required for ocean fishing.

Hiking The Serra da Estrela National Park has a number of well-marked hiking trails. For a detailed booklet and maps, contact the regional tourist office in Covilhã (*see* Tourist Information in Essential Information, *above*).

Horseback Riding There is a well-equipped riding center near Aveiro: **Escola Equestre de Aveiro** (Quinta Chãs Agra, Vilarinho, tel. 034/ 912108).

Water Sports The Quiaios Lakes near Figueira da Foz are well suited for windsurfing and sailing. The bay at Buarcos is also a popular windsurfing location. Windsurfers can be rented at most of the popular beach resorts. Board surfers often find 10- to 12-foot waves at Quiaios Beach (just north of Cape Mondego) and good surf at Furadouro and Torreira beaches (near Aveiro). In summer there are kayak trips down the Mondego from Penacova to Coimbra. Information can be obtained from the Penacova tourist office (*see* Tourist Information in Essential Information, *above*).

Beaches

If you haven't already discovered that Portugal's beaches are some of the best in Europe, then you should during the course of Tour 2. There is a virtually continuous stretch of good sandy beach along the entire Beira Litoral from Praia de Leirosa in the south to Praia de Espinho in the north. One word of caution: If your only exposure to Portuguese beaches has been the Algarve's south coast, be careful at west coast beaches, which tend to have heavier surf and stronger undertows. If you see a red or yellow flag, do not go swimming. The water temperature on the west coast is usually a few degrees cooler than the south coast.

You can take your choice of beach types. There are fully equipped resorts, such as Figueira da Foz and Buarcos, or, if you prefer sand dunes and solitude, you can lay your mat down at any one of the beaches to the north. Just point your car down one of the unmarked roads between Praia de Mira and Costa Nova and head west.

National Parks

The **Serra da Estrela** is Portugal's largest national park. Until the end of the 19th century, this mountainous region was little known except by shepherds and local hunters. The first scientific expedition to the Serra was in 1881. Since that time it has developed into one of the country's most popular recreation areas. In summer the high, craggy peaks, alpine meadows, and rushing streams become the domain of hikers, climbers, and trout fishermen. The lower and middle elevations are heavily wooded with large stands of deciduous oak, sweet chestnut, and pine. Above the tree line, at about 4,900 feet, is a rocky, subalpine world of scrub vegetation and boggy meadows, which in late spring are transformed into a vivid, multicolored carpet of wildflowers. The Serra da Estrela is home to many species of animals, the largest of which include wild boar, badger, and, in the more remote areas, the occasional wolf.

This is a hiker's paradise, amply supplied with well-marked trails. A comprehensive trail guide is available at tourist offices in the region, and, although it's in Portuguese, the maps, elevation charts, and pictures are useful. There are several official campsites within the park, but if you are discreet about it, you can pitch a small tent just about anywhere without being bothered. The Zêzere, which cuts through one of Europe's deepest glacial valleys, is excellent for trout fishing. There is also good fishing in the Comprida and Loriga lakes. If you prefer to take in the scenery from the comfort of your car, the roads through the Serra da Estrela, although hair-raising at times, are well maintained and offer many inspiring vistas. The drive between Covilhã and Seia on N339, the highest road in the country, affords a breathtaking view of the Zêzere valley. Along the way you will pass a small fountain marking the source of the Rio Mondego.

With the coming of winter and the first snows, the area becomes a winter playground, offering many Portuguese their only exposure to winter sports. Although there are two ski lifts at **Torre,** the highest point in continental Portugal with an elevation of 6,539 feet, the conditions and facilities are not on a par with ski resorts in the rest of Europe.

One of Portugal's newest national parks, the **Serra da Malcata,** is virtually unknown to foreign tourists. The 50,000-acre area along the Spanish border between Penamacor and Sabugal was created primarily to protect the natural habitat of the Iberian lynx, which was threatened with extinction. This is not a place of rugged beauty and spectacular vistas like you would find in Yosemite or even in the Serra da Estrela; it is a quiet region of heavily wooded, low mountains with few traces of human habitation. In addition to the lynxes, the park shelters wildcats, wild boars, wolves, and foxes.

Dining and Lodging

Dining The cuisine found in this region reflects the geographical diversity of the Beiras. Along the coast, as would be expected, the accent is on fresh fish. At almost any of the ubiquitous beach-bar/restaurants, you can't go wrong by ordering the grilled *peixe do dia* (fish of the day). In most cases it will have been caught hours before and will be prepared outside on a charcoal grill. You will usually be served the whole fish along with boiled potatoes and a simple salad. Wash it down with a chilled white Dão wine, and you have a tasty, healthy, and relatively inexpensive meal. In Figueira da Foz and also in the Aveiro region, *enguia* (eels), *lampreia* (lamprey), and *caldeirada*, a fish stew that is a distant cousin of the French bouillabaisse, are popular.

Moving inland, although fish is readily available, the emphasis shifts to meat dishes. The Bairrada region and, in particular, the town of Mealhada are well known for *leitão assado* (roast suckling pig). In Coimbra the dish to try is *chanfana;* this is traditionally made with tender young kid braised in red wine and roasted in an earthenware casserole. In the mountains, *truta* (fresh trout), pan fried with bacon and onions, is often served, as is *javali* (wild boar). *Bacalhau* (salt cod) is found in one form or another on just about every menu in the region. *Bacalhau a brás* (slivers of cod fried in olive oil with eggs, onions, and sometimes potatoes) is one of many popular salt-cod dishes.

The Beiras contain two of Portugal's most notable wine districts: Bairrada and Dão. Particularly good years for these wines are 1983 and 1985; if you see a 1983 Porta dos Cavaleiros

Reserva *tinto* (red) on a wine list, grab it. The full-bodied Dão will go wonderfully with your chanfana or leitâo assado.

This region is also justly famous for its contribution to the country's dessert menus, although many of these pastry delights, such as the arrufada of Coimbra, are rarely found far from home. The tangy sheep's cheese of the Serra da Estrela is popular throughout the country.

With the exception of some luxury hotel dining rooms, restaurants are casual in dress and atmosphere. The emphasis is generally more on the food than on the trappings. Good restaurants are found throughout the region, and in many towns hotel dining rooms are popular places to eat. With the exception of pizza, ethnic food is virtually nonexistent outside of Lisbon and the Algarve. Reservations are not necessary unless noted otherwise.

Restaurant ratings correspond to Évora and Central Portugal's dining chart, in Chapter 5. Highly recommended restaurants are indicated by a star ★.

Lodging Until recently, the visitor to the Beiras in search of high-quality accommodations was almost solely dependent upon the government-run chain of *pousadas* and a few venerable old luxury hotels, such as the Palace Hotel Buçaco. During the past few years, especially near the coast, a number of new hotels and inns have been built, and, to keep up with the competition, many existing facilities have been refurbished. However, accommodations in the eastern portions of the Beiras are still limited. If you plan on traveling during the busy summer months, study the maps and lodging recommendations, and make advance reservations to avoid disappointment. There are six pousadas within the Beiras, which can be used as bases to explore the entire region. (These pousadas are small; the one at Caramulo has just six rooms.) In addition, there are several government-approved private manor houses that take guests. Most establishments offer substantial off-season discounts. (High season varies by hotel but generally runs July 1–September 15.)

Hotel ratings correspond to Évora and Central Portugal's dining chart, in Chapter 5. Highly recommended hotels are indicated by a star ★.

Águeda **Palácio.** There are few good reasons to come to the industrial
Dining and Lodging town of Águeda. This converted early 17th-century manor
★ house, just off the N1 toward Coimbra, is one of them. Completely rebuilt to the highest standards and first opened as a hotel in 1990, the Palácio has that rare blend of old-world charm and elegance with modern convenience. The generous-size bedrooms are furnished with excellent 15th- and 16th-century French reproductions. The reception area, lounges, and reading room tastefully combine elements ranging from Baroque to Italian Romantic. The 5 acres of ponds and gardens are a delight for strolling. There is even a private chapel. The intimate restaurant overlooking the gardens puts a strong emphasis on such regional dishes as leitão assado. The house specialty is *bacalhau a palácio* (cod filets baked with cheese, onions, mayonnaise, and potatoes). The Palácio has become a favorite with the Lisbon film-and-TV set. *Quinta da Borralha, 3750, tel. 034/601977, fax 034/601976. 41 rooms, 7 suites. Facilities: res-*

taurant, bar, pool, tennis court, parking. AE, DC, MC, V. Very Expensive.

Pousada de Santo António. Conveniently located outside Águeda in Serem, near the junction of the new IP1 and IP5 highways, this comfortable, three-story, pink-stucco country house is based on a concept of Raul Lino, one of the country's foremost architects. A tranquil retreat with good access to the region's attractions, it is 48 kilometers (30 miles) to Coimbra and 19 kilometers (12 miles) to Aveiro. The pousada sits atop a knoll surrounded by trees and looks over the Ria Vouga valley. Although it was built in 1942 and was one of the first in the pousada chain, it has been recently remodeled, and the 12 wood-floor bedrooms are comfortably furnished in traditional style. The circular dining room has large windows facing the valley, and the walls are trimmed with azulejos. There is a small terrace for outside dining and a bar with a brick fireplace. The restaurant does well with regional dishes. One tasty specialty that you probably won't find at your favorite restaurant back home is *ensopada da enguias* (a delicate stew made with eels from the Aveiro Ria). *Serem, 3750 Águeda, tel. 034/ 523230, fax 034/523192. 12 rooms. Facilities: restaurant, bar, pool, tennis court, parking. AE, DC, MC, V. Very Expensive.*

Almeida
Dining and Lodging
★

Pousada Senhora das Neves. Portuguese architect Cristiano Moreira has mastered the difficult task of integrating this modern hotel into historic fortress walls. The bedrooms as well as the public rooms are spacious and light, and there are large terraces that look out across the high tablelands into Spain. You can sip your afternoon glass of chilled white port and imagine Wellington's troops facing Napoleon's armies on this very spot. The restaurant, divided into two inviting plank-floor dining rooms, serves a wide variety of regional dishes, including *sopa de peixe do rio Côa* (a rich, tomato-based soup made with fish from the nearby Ria Coa). The extensive wine list offers more than 60 selections. *6350, tel. 071/54283, fax 071/54320. 20 rooms, 1 suite. Facilities: restaurant, bar, parking. AE, DC, MC, V. Very Expensive.*

A Muralha. This modern *residencial*, located just outside the fortifications, is the creation of two ex-schoolteachers, Manuel and Eliza Dias. He has traded teaching English for running the 24-room residencial, and Eliza gave up her geography courses to oversee the small restaurant. The rooms are clean and simply furnished. Cork floors in the bedrooms and cork paneling in the hallways contribute to a homey atmosphere. The restaurant's specialties include roast suckling pig and curried shrimp. *Bairro de São Pedro, 6350, tel. 071/54357. 24 rooms. Facilities: restaurant, bar, parking. MC, V. Inexpensive.*

Aveiro
Dining
★

A Nossa Casa. Located on a quiet street a few blocks from the town center, this small, unassuming, family-operated restaurant produces some of the best meals in town. The dining room is lined with wine bottles, and the tables are separated by wooden dividers. The favorite dish of proprietor Manuel Facteira is *parrilhada de peixes e mariscos no churrasco* (a generous assortment of grilled fish and shellfish served on a large platter around a special sauce made from ground shellfish). *Rua do Gravito 10, tel. 034/29236. MC, V. Closed weekends. Moderate.*

O Mercantel. This restaurant is the brainchild of Sr. Costa da Lota, who, after 13 years of working at the nearby fish market, decided to try his hand at the other side of the business. He's done quite well. In 1990 O Mercantel took first prize in the national gastronomic fair in Santerem. Specialties include fresh fish, fish stew, and *arroz de marisco* (shellfish with rice). *Rua António dos Santos Le 16, tel. 034/28057. MC, V. Closed Sun. Moderate.*

Dining and Lodging ★

Pousada da Ria. Built on the edge of the lagoon, this light and airy, two-story inn is filled with and surrounded by plants and flowers. The entry is a tasteful blend of wood and tile with a loft sitting area. Ten of the 16 cheerfully furnished rooms have large picture windows and look out over the water; you can stand on your balcony and watch the colorfully painted moliceiros glide by. Midway down the narrow, pine-covered peninsula separating the lagoon from the sea, the pousada is in a great location for exploring the lagoon and neighboring beaches. It's about 30 minutes by car to Aveiro. The restaurant has an open, spacious feeling and a view of the lagoon. There is also a terrace for outside dining during the summer. The tasty *ensopada de cabrito* (kid stew) is recommended. *3870 Murtosa, tel. 034/48332, fax 034/48333. 16 rooms, 3 suites. Facilities: restaurant, bar, pool, tennis court. AE, DC, MC, V. Very Expensive.*

Imperial. If you like an efficient, business-oriented, modern hotel in the heart of a city, then the Imperial is for you. The rooms are comfortable but lack charm. Some rooms on the upper floors have views and small balconies. The restaurant is luxurious without being ostentatious and is popular with the business community. Specials include *enguias fritas* (fried eels) and *bacalhau com natas* (cod with cream). The breakfast buffet is the best in town. *Rua Dr. Nascimento Leitão, 3800, tel. 034/22141, fax 034/24148. 100 rooms, 8 suites. Facilities: restaurant, 2 bars, solarium. AE, DC, MC, V. Expensive.*

Lodging ★

Arcada. The location, at the foot of the bridge over the central canal, couldn't be more convenient. This is a comfortable, family-owned Portuguese classic. The 50-year-old, arched, red-tile-roofed, four-story building is well kept up. Room size is adequate, and the furnishings vary from blonde 1950s to traditional Portuguese. The lounge and bar are reminiscent of a gentleman's club slightly past its prime. *Rua Viana do Castelo 4, 3800, tel. 034/23001, fax 034/21886. 49 rooms, 1 suite. Facilities: bar, breakfast room. AE, DC, MC, V. Moderate.*

Belmonte Dining and Lodging

Belsol. Pleasant and modest, the hotel is conveniently situated in a quiet spot off N18 between Castelo Branco and Guarda. Rooms are large, and a number have balconies with views of the Zêzere. Owner João Pinheiro is representative of a new breed of enterprising young Portuguese businesspeople looking to provide quality and service. The downstairs restaurant, although simple in decor, offers excellent food and is a favorit with local businesspeople. Try the fresh trout from the local rivers. *Quinta do Rio, 6250, tel. 075/911322, fax 075/912315. 50 rooms. Facilities: restaurant, bar, solarium, playground parking. MC, V. Inexpensive.*

Buçaco Dining and Lodging ★

Palace Hotel Buçaco. They just don't make them like this any more. This is one of the few remaining great old hotels in the world. Staying at the Palace, even if just for one night, is an experience to be remembered. Yes, there is an elevator, but who can resist the temptation to walk up the grand, red-carpeted stairway, its walls lined with heroic azulejo panels, and pas the suit of armor with the electric lights for eyes—a refreshin bit of kitsch in the midst of so much splendor? A former royal hunting lodge set in an historic, 250-acre forest, the hotel is a hodgepodge of architectural styles, ranging from Gothic to neo-Manueline to early Walt Disney. It's worth ordering a meal in the dining room just to sit at the finely laid table and take in the ornate, carved-wood ceiling, inlaid hardwood floors, and massive, arched Manueline windows. In keeping with the decor, Chef Manuel Lorenço turns out some masterpieces of his own. The hotel also has its own winery: The fine Buçaco wines laid down in the cellars, which contain some 200,000 bottles, are only available here. *3050 Mealhada, tel. 031/930101, fax 031/930509. 53 rooms, 6 suites. Facilities: restaurant, bar, parking. AE, DC, MC, V. Very Expensive.*

Caramulo
Dining and
Lodging
★

Pousada de São Jeronimo. One of the smallest pousadas, with just six rooms, this one is located in the Serra do Caramulo between Viseu and Coimbra, and, reminiscent of an alpine chalet, sits alone on a hill 1 kilometer (⅔ mile) from the spa resort of Caramulo. The reception area has lovely Arraiolos carpets hung on a knotty pine wall. Rooms are small but adequate, each with a modern marble bathroom and small balcony with a table and chairs. Views are spectacular. The lounge, restaurant, and bar are divided by a see-through wood partition, and there is an inviting open fireplace. The cozy dining room's picture windows frame a mountain panorama extending to the Serra da Estrela. The fare is country style, with *chanfana de borrego* (roast lamb with red wine) one of the favorites. The pool, cabana bar, and a badminton court are in a private wooded park across from the main building. *3475, tel. 032/861291. 6 rooms. Facilities: restaurant, bar, pool, badminton, parking. AE, DC, MC, V. Moderate.*

Castelo Branco
Dining
★

Praça Velha. Set in an historic stone building on a lovely square (the plaque outside reads 1685), this is by far the best restaurant in town. Of the two dining rooms, the older section with the beamed ceiling and stone floors is preferred. One intriguing specialty is *bife na pedra* (grilled beefsteak served on a hot slab of marble). *Largo Luis Camões 17, tel. 072/286330. Reservations advised. AE, DC, MC, V. Moderate.*

Lodging

Arraina. At present Castelo Branco lacks a first-rate hotel, although a new facility is planned by the owners of the Hotel Turismo in Guarda. This modern residencial is conveniently located and offers small but clean rooms; it is strictly a one-nighter. *Av. 1 de Maio 16, tel. 072/21634, fax 072/31884. 31 rooms. Facilities: bar. MC, V. Inexpensive.*

Celorico da Beira
Dining and
Lodging

Mira Serra. This modern, four-story hotel is conveniently located just off IP5. Owner Fernando Batista was formerly the manager of a five-star luxury hotel in the Algarve before striking out on his own. The rooms are comfortable and furnished in traditional style; some have a small balcony. The restaurant serves the best food in the area. Try the *bacalhau a brás* (slivers of dried cod fried with eggs and onions). *6360, tel. 071/72604, fax 071/73382. 42 rooms. Facilities: restaurant, bar, garage. AE, DC, MC, V. Moderate.*

Coimbra
Dining
★

Dom Pedro. The entrance, next to a car dealer, is hardly impressive, but once inside it's a different story. The tasteful blend of arches, tile, and wood creates just the right atmosphere in which to enjoy some of Coimbra's best food. The service is efficient without being stuffy. The chanfana is excellent, as is the *açorda de mariscos* (a sort of bread porridge mixed with eggs and mounds of fresh shellfish). There is an extensive list of Portuguese wines. The restaurant is just a few steps along the riverfront from the tourist office. *Av. Emidio Navarro 58, tel. 039/29108. DC, MC, V. Moderate.*

Democratia. The best that can be said about the decor is that it is functional. The students and locals who frequent this popular old establishment are here for the food and not the atmosphere. The fare is simple and inexpensive. A tasty *caldo verde* (potato soup with shredded cabbage and sausage) and some fresh, grilled fish make a typical meal. *Travess da Rua Nova 7, tel. 039/23784. No credit cards. Closed Sun. Inexpensive.*

Kanimambo. A pleasant, small, no-frills restaurant on a side street off of the Praça Comércio, it offers pleasant service and occasional live music. Try their special desert: *doce da casa* (a layered vanilla and chocolate pudding with cream). *Rua das Azeiteiras 65–69, tel. 039/33348. No credit cards. Inexpensive.*

★ **Zé Manel.** It's just a hole-in-the-wall in a back alley. The open kitchen is a jumble of pots and pans, and the walls are plastered with an odd assortment of yellowing paper announcements. Simple wooden tables and chairs constitute the decor, but the food is great and cheap. If you can get in, don't pass this one up. It's a favorite with students and hasn't yet succumbed to the tourist trade. There is an amazing choice of dishes for such a small place. They make a wonderful *sopa da pedra* (a rich vegetable soup served with hot stones in the pot to keep it warm). *Beco do Forno 10/2, tel. 039/23790. No reservations. No credit cards. Inexpensive.*

Dining and Lodging

★ **Astoria.** Occupying a prominent downtown location facing the Mondego, the domed, triangular Astoria has been a Coimbra landmark since its construction in 1927. The ownership is the same as that of the Buçaco Palace. In spite of a recent facelift, the 1920s ambience has been largely maintained, although the aluminum windows around the balconies seem out of step. If you like your hotels with old-world charm and tradition and almost state-of-the-art comforts, then you will like this veteran. When Portuguese president Mario Soares was in Coimbra recently, this was where he stayed. Ask for a room facing the river. The wood-paneled L'Amphitryon Restaurant is one of city's finest in both ambience and quality. Buçaco wines are served here. *Av. Emidio Navarro 21, 3000, tel. 039/22055, fax 039/22057. 64 rooms. Facilities: restaurant, bar. AE, DC, MC, V. Expensive.*

★ **Tivoli.** This four-star addition to the Coimbra hotel scene, opened in 1990, is currently the best address in town. It's sleek, efficient, well located, and outfitted with all of the latest gadgets. The only thing lacking is that certain sense of place that the other great hotels in the Tivoli chain have achieved: Once in your comfortable room, you could be anywhere. The Porta Férrea restaurant serves excellent food, both international and regional, in a subdued setting. *Rua João Machado 4–5, 3000, tel. 039/33340. 90 rooms, 10 suites. Facilities: restaurant, bar, health club, pool, garage. AE, DC, MC, V. Expensive.*

Lodging **Coimbra Youth Hostel.** The hostel occupies a large house near the Santa Cruz Park. Breakfast is available. *Rua Henrique Seco 12–14, 3000, tel. 039/22955. 80 beds in multibed rooms, family rooms. Facilities: members' kitchen. Inexpensive.*

Larbelo. A quiet, family-run residencial in an old, green-tiled building, it has a good central location facing the Largo d

Portagem, adjacent to the tourist office. The 17 upstairs rooms have high, ornate ceilings, and some have views to the river. Room 209 has the best view. Only breakfast is served. *Largo da Portagem 33, 3000, tel. 039/29092. 17 rooms (9 with bath and toilet, 8 with shower). Facilities: No credit cards. Inexpensive.*

Covilhã
Dining and Lodging

Hotel Serra da Estrela. Originally built in the early part of this century as a tuberculosis sanitorium, the hotel was completely renovated and reopened in 1989. Rooms are large, and those in the front have good views looking down into the valley. At an elevation of 3,936 feet and 12 kilometers (7½ miles) from Covilhã, the hotel provides an excellent base for a few days in the mountains. The restaurant is light and spacious, with lots of glass and wood. *Penhas da Saude, 6203 Covilhã, tel. 075/313809, fax 075/323789. 38 rooms. Facilities: restaurant, snack bar, bar, tennis courts, parking. AE, DC, MC, V. Moderate.*

Solneve. In the town center, Solneve has been the prime hotel in Covilhã since its opening some 50 years ago. It's now starting to fray a bit around the edges, but until the new Ibis Hotel at the edge of town is completed in 1993, it remains the best of a limited selection. The restaurant, in spite of a decor reminiscent of a high school cafeteria, offers a nice variety of tasty regional dishes, including *truta a solneve* (fresh trout grilled with cured ham and onions). *Rua Visconde da Coriscada 126, 6200, tel. 075/323001, fax 075/323001. 32 rooms, 6 suites. Facilities: restaurant, bar. MC, V. Inexpensive.*

Lodging

Penas da Saude Youth Hostel. The hostel is in a large, rustic mountaintop building. Meals are available. *Penas da Saude, 6200 Covilhã, tel. 075/25375. 163 beds in multibed rooms. Facilities: bar, members' kitchen, library, recreation room. Inexpensive.*

Curia
Dining
★

Pedro dos Leitões. Of the several restaurants clustered together on the EN1 from Coimbra to Oporto that specialize in roast suckling pig, "Pete of the Suckling Pigs," as the name of this restaurant translates, is the most popular. A meal here is one of those traditional things that you do when you visit Portugal. You eat sardines by the old bridge in Portimão, and you have suckling pig at Pedro's in Mealhada. The size of the parking lot is a dead giveaway that this is no intimate little bistro. In the busy summer season, Pete's spitted pigs pop out of the huge ovens at an amazing rate. In spite of the volume, quality is maintained. *EN 1, Sernadelo, tel. 031/22062. MC, V. Closed Mon. Moderate.*

Dining and Lodging
★

Curia Palace. The approach down a long, tree-lined drive past formal gardens is like the beginning of an old movie. In fact, parts of *The Buster Keaton Story* were filmed here. Enter the spacious, polished, marble-floored reception area, and you will be transported back to the Europe of the 1920s. The four-story hotel is the centerpiece of 15 acres of gardens, vineyards, a deer park, an aviary, orchards, and a duck pond, all of which support the hotel kitchen. A meticulously restored, 18th-century, water-power mill grinds wheat and corn for the bakery. There are also a winery, a distillery, and a chapel on the premises. The swimming pool is 60 feet by 107 feet, one of the largest in Portugal. For car buffs there is a small collection of antique autos. Bedrooms are large, with high ceilings and modern bathrooms, and the spacious corridors all have names (the Avenue of the Roses, for example). Room 255 is one of the larger rooms and has a fine view of the gardens. The dining room is light and airy, the enormous height of the ceiling broken somewhat by an encircling mezzanine. The cuisine, prepared from garden-fresh ingredients, is excellent. *3780 Anadia, tel. 031/512131, fax 031/ 515531. 114 rooms. Facilities: restaurant, bar, pool, miniature golf, 2 tennis courts, billiards, playground, boarding kennels, horseback riding, parking. AE, DC, MC, V. Closed Nov.– Mar. Very Expensive.*

★ **Grande Hotel de Curia.** The task of taking a grand old 1890s spa hotel and bringing it up to 1990s standards is not an easy one, but the Belver Hotel Group did just that. And it was not merely a cosmetic face-lift. New polished-marble floors, dark mahogany furniture and paneling, elegant bathroom fixtures, and fine carpets and drapes are some of the more visible changes. The hotel also has its own fully equipped, state-of-the-art health center with a full-time medical staff. Various exercise and diet programs are available. The restaurant, with wood-plank floors and soft draperies, exudes a subdued elegance. The menu is primarily international with a few regional specialties. *3780 Anadia, tel. 031/515720, fax 031/515317. 78 rooms, 6 suites. Facilities: restaurant, bar, library, indoor and outdoor pools, tennis, gym, whirlpool, sauna, Turkish bath, massage, parking. AE, DC, MC, V. Very Expensive.*

Lodging **Quinta de São Lourenço.** A delightful 18th-century country manor house surrounded by vineyards and pine groves, this is located in the tiny village of São Lourenço do Bairro, 3 kilometers (2 miles) from Curia. The house has five comfortable-size bedrooms with wood floors, period furniture, and modern bathrooms. There is also a small apartment. Meals can be arranged upon request. *São Lourenço do Bairro, 3780 Anadia, tel. 031/528168. 5 rooms, 1 apartment. Facilities: bar, library, card room, billiards. MC, V. Moderate.*

Figueira da Foz **Covil do Caçador.** An open kitchen and a dining room with a
Dining vaulted, beamed ceiling cluttered with hanging strings of corn, garlic, and other herbs and vegetables give this restaurant a comfortable country feeling. It's located across the river from downtown at the foot of the bridge and looks out over the bay. Chef José Olivio does a fine job with a varied menu. Try the *arroz de tamboril* (cubes of monkfish mixed with rice and seasonings). *Morraceira, tel. 033/31507. AE, DC, MC, V. Moderate.*

Teimoso. Located in Buarcos, about 2 kilometers (1¼ miles) from Figueira da Foz, this seaside restaurant with large picture windows has become a local institution. Although the menu choices are varied, seafood is what put this place on the map. Shellfish comes fresh from the restaurant's own huge saltwater tanks. *Estrada do Cabo Mondego, Buarcos, tel. 033/ 22785. MC, V. Closed Wed. Moderate.*

★ **O Peleiro.** Located in the quiet village of Paio, 10 kilometers (6 miles) from Figueira, this popular restaurant was once a tannery, and that's what the name means. Owner Henrique has achieved a tranquil ambience through the use of wood and tile. The menu is heavy on regional specialties. The *sopa da pedra* (stone soup), a thick vegetable soup with sausage, beans, and potatoes served in a tureen with hot stones, is a must. Grilled pork or veal on a spit is excellent, and there's a good wine selection. *Paio, tel. 033/940159. Closed May 1–15, Sept. 1–15, and Sun. MC, V. Inexpensive.*

Dining and Lodging **Grande.** This five-story, '50s-vintage hotel enjoys a favored location overlooking the broad, sandy beach. Public and guest rooms are spacious and airy, and sea-front rooms have a small balcony. A large swimming pool has a view of the beach. The hotel is popular with tour groups. The restaurant is a large, rather sterile room with picture windows. The menu is international with regional specialties. This dowager of a hotel is beginning to show her age, but a comprehensive face-lift is planned, with completion promised by early 1993 (check before you book). With surgery complete, this should be a winner. *Av. 25 de Abril, 3080, tel. 033/22539, fax 033/22420. 91 rooms. Facilities: restaurant, piano bar, pool. AE, DC, MC, V. Very Expensive.*

Clube Vale de Leão. This is a self-contained cluster of Mediterranean-style, semidetached villas unobtrusively nestled in the hills high above Buarcos. Rooms and apartments are small but comfortable, and the views over the bay are magnificent. The restaurant, a bit garish in decor, does a good job with both international and regional dishes. *Vais-Buarcos, 3080, tel. 033/33057. 6 rooms, 17 studios, 1 apartment. Facilities: restaurant, piano bar, tearoom, movies, pool, tennis, squash, gym, sauna, massage, parking. AE, DC, MC, V. Expensive.*

Lodging **Aparthotel Atlantico.** This is a high-rise tower at the beach containing apartments with kitchenettes. The rooms are small but adequate, with plain, functional furnishings. Some apartments have a wonderful sea view. *Av. 25 de Abril, 3080, tel. 033/24045, fax 033/22420. 70 apartments. Facilities: bar, pool. AE, DC, MC, V. Moderate.*

★ **International.** A comfortable, small hotel on a quiet street just a five-minute walk from the beach; the classic stone building was built in 1914 and completely remodeled in 1989, retaining the original ambience. *Rua da Liberdade 32, 3080, tel. 033/22051, fax 033/22420. 50 rooms. Facilities: bar, breakfast room, pool. AE, DC, MC, V. Moderate.*

Pensão Esplanada. This turn-of-the-century corner house is across from the beach. The floors creak and the rooms have seen better days, but it's clean and well maintained. Ask for a room with a sea view. *Rua Engenheiro Silva 86, 3080, tel. 033/22115. 19 rooms, 10 with bath. No credit cards. Inexpensive.*

Fundão **O Casarão.** This quiet neighborhood restaurant's three small
Dining dining areas have beamed ceilings and are divided by brick pillars. Owner José Pereira proudly proclaims that he serves the best food in Fundão, and in this restaurant-poor town he is probably right. Try the Oporto-style tripe. *Rua José Germano da Cunha 2/4, tel. 075/52844. No credit cards. Inexpensive.*

Dining and **Estalagém da Neve.** A small, cozy, Victorian-style inn on the
Lodging road from Castelo Branco, it has small but comfortably furnished rooms. The restaurant, with its beamed ceiling and tiled walls, provides an inviting setting in which to enjoy a fine Portuguese meal. Try the trout or roast kid. *Calçada de São Sebastião, 6230, tel. 075/52215, fax 075/53816. 22 rooms, 6 with bath. Facilities: restaurant, bar, pool, parking. MC, V. Inexpensive.*

Gouveia **O Foral.** Located on the ground floor of the Hotel Gouvia, this
Dining comfortable restaurant is the eatery of choice among the town's civic and business community. Service is attentive, and the kitchen is noted for its roast kid. *Av. 1 de Maio, tel. 038/42890. AE, DC, MC, V. Inexpensive.*

★ **O Julio.** This simple, unassuming restaurant, thanks to the talents of chef and owner Julio, was chosen to represent the Serra da Estrela region at the 1992 national tourist fair in Lisbon. Julio recommends the *vitela estufada na maneira antiga* (veal stew). *Travessa do Loureiro 1, tel. 038/42142. No credit cards. Closed Tues. Inexpensive.*

Lodging **Hotel Gouvia.** A small, modern hotel on one of the main approaches to the Serra da Estrela, it offers comfortable rooms furnished in traditional style. Several have small balconies. *Av. 1 de Maio, tel. 038/42890. 27 rooms, 4 suites. Facilities: restaurant, bar, pool, tennis, parking. AE, DC, MC, V. Inexpensive.*

Guarda **Belo Horizonte.** Outside of the Hotel Turismo dining room,
Dining Guarda is not noted for its good restaurants. Belo Horizonte, a modest establishment in the old quarter, is one of the few exceptions. It features hardy regional fare and a different type of bacalhau daily. *Largo de São Vicente 2, tel. 071/21454. MC, V. Closed Sat. Inexpensive.*

Dining and **Hotel Turismo.** Since it opened in 1940 in a stately, country-
Lodging style manor house, the Turismo has been Guarda's leading ho-
★ tel. Extensively remodeled in 1988, the hotel has maintained its position, albeit in a town with little competition. The extensive use of wood and leather in the bar and lounges lends a comfortable, clubby atmosphere to the place. Bedrooms are adequate in size and furnished in traditional style. The restaurant serves the best food in town in a quiet, refined atmosphere. *Av. Cor. Orlindo de Calvalho, 6300, tel. 071/212206, fax 071/212204. 100 rooms, 2 suites. Facilities: restaurant, bar, pool, garage. AE, DC, MC, V. Expensive.*

Filipe. Across the street from the Misericórdia Church, this newly redecorated, family-run residencial offers plain but comfortable rooms and a personal touch not found at the more-formal Hotel Turismo. Owner Americo Alexis has traveled the world and will be happy to pass the time of day in just about any language. The upstairs restaurant, the domain of Senhora Alexis, is a good place to enjoy *camaroes piri-piri* (giant prawns with hot-pepper sauce). *Rua Vasco da Gama 9, 6300, tel. 071/212658, fax 071/221402. 41 rooms. Facilities: restaurant, bar. AE, DC, MC, V. Restaurant closed Nov.–Jan. Moderate.*

Luso **O Cesteiro.** Situated at the western edge of town just past the
Dining Luso bottling plant, this is a plain but popular local restaurant. The fare is simple and includes several types of cod, roast kid, and fresh fish. *Rua Dr. Lucio Abranches, tel. 031/939360. MC, V. Closed Wed. Inexpensive.*

Dining and **Grande Hotel das Termas.** The hotel is a large, yellow-stucco
Lodging complex in a park at the center of town. The buildings, constructed in 1945, are an architectural zero, but the recently remodeled interior is attractive. Rooms are large and airy, with modern tiled bathrooms; some bedrooms have terraces overlooking the Olympic-size pool. The hotel is adjacent to the renowned Luso Spa, which offers a wide range of therapeutic programs. If you are looking for a hotel where you can settle in and really make use of the facilities, either this or the Palace in nearby Curia are ideal. The restaurant offers a good selection of international and regional foods in a pleasant environment overlooking the pool. *Luso-3050 Mealhada, tel. 031/940450, fax 031/930350. 173 rooms. Facilities: restaurant, bar, disco, so*

larium, indoor and outdoor pools, tennis, miniature golf, sauna, parking. AE, DC, MC, V. Very Expensive.

Lodging **Vila Duparchy.** As you pass through the old gate and go up the
★ long, curved, tree-lined driveway, you'll soon realize that this
is no ordinary hotel. The two-story stucco house was built in
the late 19th century. In 1988 Maria and Oscar Santos, the current resident owners, opened it as a guest house. Upstairs
there are just six rooms; each has a fireplace, modern bath, and
individually selected period furnishings. On the ground floor
are three comfortable sitting rooms, which guests share with
the Santos. The spacious grounds are full of trees and flowers,
and there is a small swimming pool. Breakfast is included, and
other meals, which are far superior to the local restaurant fare,
are prepared on request. *Luso-3050 Mealhada, tel. 031/939120.
6 rooms. Facilities: pool. No credit cards. Expensive.*

★ **Pensão Alegre.** On a hill overlooking the park, this 19th-century
manor house has been receiving guests since 1931. The present
owner, Manuel Alegre, took over the pension from his father.
Filled with colorful tiles and rich woods, it exudes charm. If
you're after Old-World ambience and hospitality at bargain
prices, look no farther. There are 20 rooms, all with high ceilings and plank floors. Ask for number 103; it has a large terrace. Home-cooked meals are available on request. *3050, tel.
031/939251. 20 rooms. Facilities: parking. No credit cards. Inexpensive.*

Mangualde **Quinta Magarenha.** Opened in 1991, this large, attractive,
Dining French-style manor house has been a great success for owner
Jose Oliviera. There is a comfortable lounge with plush sofas
and tiled walls. The single large dining room has an attractive
wooden ceiling and tile floors. The atmosphere is gregarious,
with rows of long tables, and the food is Portuguese, with an
emphasis on fish. The *lombino de pescada* (filets of whiting
with a sauce made from ground shellfish) is recommended.
Exit Viseu-leste from IP5. V. Moderate.

Dining and **Senhora do Castelo.** A large, four-story complex that shares a
Lodging hilltop park with the church of the same name, the 10-year-old
hotel is conveniently located adjacent to the new IP5 highway
but far enough away to avoid the noise. The buildings are pseudo-Mediterranean. Many of the rooms have small balconies;
those facing south have the best view. The restaurant and public rooms, while spacious and cheerful, lack character. However, the views, especially from the terrace restaurant, are
spectacular. Of the two indoor restaurants, the Grill Restaurant has a warmer atmosphere. Try the *bacalhau espiritual*
(the translation is "spiritual codfish"), what you get on your
plate is a tasty combination of dried, salted cod baked with potatoes, onions, and tomatoes. *3531, tel. 032/611608, fax 032/
623877. 85 rooms, 3 suites. Facilities: restaurants, bar with
live music, indoor and outdoor pools, sauna, 2 tennis courts.
AE, DC, MC, V. Expensive.*

Manteigas **Pousada de São Lourenço.** The pousada is located 13 kilometers
Dining and (8 miles) from Manteigas in the heart of the Serra da Estrela at
Lodging an elevation of 4,231 feet. This granite mountain lodge is a fa-
★ vorite stopover for Portuguese as well as foreign visitors. The
ample use of wood and brick in the rooms and a cozy fireplace
in the lounge contribute to the high-country ambience. Ask for
room 207; it has a loft for sleeping and one of the best views. If
you are just driving through, stop for lunch at the restaurant,

and try the unusual but delicious *bacalhau a lagareiro* (baked cod with corn bread, olive oil, and potatoes). *6260, tel. 075/ 981321, fax 075/981664. 21 rooms, 1 suite. Facilities: restaurant, bar, parking. AE, DC, MC, V. Very Expensive.*

Oliveira do Hospital
Dining and Lodging
★

Pousada de Santa Barbara. Located in the pines high on the western flank of the Serra da Estrela, this mountainside pousada offers a restful and cool respite from the summer heat. Many of the rooms have balconies supported by massive stone columns. The restaurant features a variety of tasty local dishes. *Povoa das Quartas, 3400, tel. 038/52252, fax 038/50545. 16 rooms. Facilities: restaurant, bar, pool, tennis court, parking. AE, DC, MC, V. Very Expensive.*

Penacova
Dining

O Panorâmico. This small, family-run restaurant is an ideal spot to have lunch while driving through this lovely countryside. It's easy to see where the name came from: There is a wonderful panoramic view looking down on the Rio Mondego as it snakes its way along to Coimbra. Maria da Graça, the proprietress, suggests the house specialty, *lampreia a mode de Penacova* (lampreys cooked with rice). *Tel. 039/477333. AE, DC, MC, V. Inexpensive.*

Penamacor
Dining and Lodging
★

Vila Rica. If you like to "collect" quaint country inns, this is a place to add to your collection. The 19th-century converted farmhouse is surrounded by trees and gardens and is adjacent to a popular hunting area. Not just by coincidence, the excellent restaurant serves many game dishes, including rabbit, quail, and wild boar. The 10 large bedrooms are simply but comfortably furnished. *6090, tel. 077/94311. 10 rooms. Facilities: restaurant, bar, private chapel, parking. Inexpensive.*

Seia
Dining
★

Cabana do Pastor. A cozy mountain restaurant with a fireplace and panoramic views, this is a good place to partake of the locally made cheese, quiejo da Serra, and presunto (cured ham). *Behind souvenir shop on N339 between Seia and Torre, tel. 038/ 22073. AE, DC, MC, V. Inexpensive.*

Lodging
★

Albergaria Senhora do Espinheiro. This newly built mountain inn is next to the Cabana do Pastor restaurant. Both are the labors of love of Antonio Mora, a big, gentle, bear of a man who will enhance your stay or meal. The use of wood and tile throughout gives the inn a warm feeling. The rooms are small and furnished in pine. Ask for a room at the back, where the views are best. *N339, 6270, 24 rooms. Facilities: bar, parking. AE, DC, MC, V. Inexpensive.*

Sortelha
Dining
★

Albaroque. This is the sort of place that interior designers are always trying to create with imitation wood beams and plastic rocks. The Albaroque, the town's only real restaurant, occupies an ancient stone building. You walk up some rickety wood stairs to a cozy, stone-wall dining area with massive wood beams overhead. Owner Raul Clara has done more than create an atmosphere; he also manages to turn out some wonderful food in this inviting restaurant. Specialties include wild boar and venison in season as well as a first rate *caldeirada de borrego* (lamb stew). *Tel. 071/68129. No credit cards. Inexpensive.*

Lodging

Although this medieval town has no hotels or pensions, several ancient stone houses have been converted into tourist accommodations. These are comfortable but not luxurious. They do have running water and bathrooms and offer an unusual opportunity to actually live in a medieval Portuguese village.

Casa Arabe. *Sortelha, 6320 Sabugal, tel. 071/68276 or 01/269–0149. 1 apartment, sleeps 4. Facilities: parking. No credit cards. Inexpensive.*

Casa do Vento que Soa. *Sortelha, 6320 Sabugal, tel. 071/68182. 2 rooms. Facilities: parking. No credit cards. Inexpensive.*

Viseu
Dining
★
A Veranda da Sé. After 37 years of running a restaurant in Rio de Janiero, João Correira became homesick for his native Portugal. Now back in the town of his birth, he is doing what he does best: running a restaurant. In an ancient stone building that was once a warehouse, he has created a cozy Portuguese bistro. There is a small loft for dining, and the original stone walls and floor remain. The menu is Portuguese with an accent on grilled meats. On Sunday, João, saluting his days in Brazil, serves *feiojoada da Brasil* (a tasty stewlike dish of beans, sausage, and meat). *Rua Augusto Hilario 55, tel. 032/421135. AE, DC, MC, V. Closed Tues. Moderate.*

O Fontelo. This is a storefront grill restaurant specializing in grilled chicken, which tastes as good as it looks in the window. *Av. Alfonso da Melo 45, tel. 032/424221. No credit cards. Closed Sat. Inexpensive.*

Dining and Lodging
★
Grão Vasco. For many years the Grão Vasco has been Viseu's leading hotel, and, recently remodeled, it still retains that distinction. Its location in a wooded park just a few steps from the main square is ideal, offering the convenience of the city and the quiet of the countryside. Many of the rooms have balconies looking out on the oval pool. The restaurant, which serves a wide variety of principally Portuguese dishes, is one of the best in town. If it's in season, try the *javali* (wild boar). *Rua Gaspar Barreiros, 3500, tel. 032/423432, fax 032/427047. 88 rooms. Facilities: restaurant, bar, pool, parking. AE, DC, MC, V. Expensive.*

★
Hotel Maná. Owner and manager Nelson Campos has done a fine job of putting together just the right combination of tasteful decor and modern comfort to make this small hotel on the outskirts of Viseu one of the best of its kind in the region. Ask for a room on the third floor with a balcony facing the Serra da Estrela. The restaurant produces a surprisingly high quality of service and cuisine. If you've acquired a taste for bacalhau, try their version of the tasty *bacalhau a Zé do Pipo* (a wonderful combination of baked, breaded cod with mayonnaise, pimentos, onions, and potatoes). *N16, Via Caçador, 3500, tel. 032/ 479243, fax 032/478744. 60 rooms. Facilities: restaurant, bar, pool, parking. AE, DC, MC, V. Moderate.*

Lodging
Bela Vista. This comfortable residencial on a quiet street about a mile from the center of town has rooms that are small but comfortable. *Rua Alexandre Herculano 510, 3500, tel. 032/426026. 44 rooms. Facilities: parking. No credit cards. Inexpensive.*

Campgrounds
As might be expected, the greatest concentration of campgrounds is along the coast. There are also well-equipped campgrounds in Coimbra, Viseu, Guarda, Castelo Branco, and the Serra da Estrela. Camping fees in Portugal are considerably less than in most of the rest of Europe. Two people with a camper can plan on paying 1,000$00–1,500$00 per night, electrical hookup included. Many campgrounds also rent inexpensive cabins. Here are a few recommendations.

Aveiro **Camping Costa Nova.** It's right at the beach, less than 10 kilometers (6 miles) from Aveiro. There's a bus to town, and stores and restaurants are nearby.

Castelo Branco **Camping Castelo Branco.** This is a level, partly shaded municipal site on N18, 1½ kilometers (1 mile) north of the town center. There is a bus to town.

Coimbra **Camping Municipal Coimbra.** This is a city-run facility adjacent to the sports stadium and the municipal swimming pool. There is a bus to town.

Covilhã/ Serra da Estrela **Camping Pião.** On a wooded hillside on EN339, 5 kilometers (3 miles) from Covilhã, this is a good base for visiting the Serra da Estrela. *Closed Nov.–Apr.*

Figueira da Foz **Camping Municipal Figueira da Foz.** This large site is in a pine grove 1½ kilometers (1 mile) from town and beach. A bus, playground, and tennis are available.

Guarda **Camping Orbitur.** The campground is in a pleasant, parklike setting at the northwest edge of town. There is a bus to Guarda center and a swimming pool.

Ovar **Parque de Campismo Furadouro.** In a wooded site at the beach, this is a good base for exploring the Aveiro lagoon. Tennis and outdoor movies are available.

Viseu **Parque do Fontelo.** In a wooded park just north of N16 at the east end of town, the campground makes for difficult maneuvering for large campers. There is a bus to town.

The Arts and Nightlife

The Arts

The Beiras are not merely an area rich in tradition and folklore but a region where these traditions are strongly respected. Just about every town and village celebrates some sort of festival or fair. In many cases dates vary from year to year. Check with local tourist offices for details.

Aveiro The *Feira do Marco* (March Fair), has been celebrated for more than 500 years. This large, regional fair is held in March, with folk music and dancing on weekends.

Coimbra In addition to the *Quiema das Fitas* (*see* Tour 1, *above*), the *Festas da Rainha Santa* (Festival of the Queen Saint) is held during even years in early July. It's marked by colorful processions and fireworks along the Mondego.

Figueira da Foz Every year during the last week in June, the *Festas de São João* (Festival of Saint John) features dancing around huge bonfires until dawn. The exhausted dancers then plunge into the sea for the ancient ritual of the "holy bath."

Gouvia The *Festa do Senhor do Calvario* (Festival of Our Lord of Calvary), during the first week in August, starts on a Sunday with a colorful procession. Other events include a handicrafts fair, games, and contests, including a sheepdog competition.

Viseu Held from mid-August through mid-September, the *Feira de São Mateus* (Fair of Saint Matthew) is like a giant county fair where agricultural products and handicrafts are exhibited. There is also folk music and dancing.

Nightlife

With the exception of the casino at Figueira da Foz, this region is not known for its nightlife. In most of the larger towns, you can find theaters showing recent English-language films.

Figueira da Foz   The casino is part of an entertainment complex that, although small by Las Vegas standards, is pretty big stuff for this part of the world. Built in 1886, the gambling room, with its frescoed ceilings and chandeliers, provides a subdued atmosphere in which to try your luck at a variety of games, including blackjack, American and Continental roulette, and an old European game played with three dice, known simply as the French table. Within the same building, there is also a large *Belle Epoque* show room featuring a Vegas-type revue. *Av. Bernado Lopes, tel. 033/22041. Gambling room: admission: 1,300$00; minimum age 18; open daily 3PM–3AM. Show room: minimum admission: Fri.–Sat. 2,500$00, Sun.–Thurs. 1,750$00; shows 10 PM and 1 AM. Reservations advised July–Sept. No jeans or T-shirts.*

8 Oporto and the North

By Jules Brown

The city of Oporto (Porto in Portuguese) is famous the world over for the wine that bears its name—port. However, the rest of the North is still undiscovered country for most visitors to Portugal. Intrepid travelers may visit the valley of the Rio Douro (River of Gold) or cross the bare uplands of the far north-eastern Trás-os-Montes (Beyond the Mountains). Some towns, like Chaves (Keys), bear curious names and complicated histories. Festivals such as the Holy Week parade at Braga (complete with a torch-lit procession through dark, old-town streets) evoke an earlier time. The North can be beautiful, as it is in the deep, rural heartland of the Minho, the coastal province to the north of Oporto. It can also be hostile, as typified by the Terra Fria (Cold Land), the name given to the remote, rugged parts of the northern Trás-os-Montes. From here come the mysterious, prehistoric *porcas* (stone pigs), reminders of early tribes who scratched a living from the cold earth.

The remote corners of northern Portugal seem far away in Oporto, a trading center since pre-Roman times and still a vibrant, cosmopolitan city. Oporto makes a fine contrast to Lisbon. The Moors never had the same strong foothold here that they did farther south, and the city remained largely unaffected by the great earthquake of 1755; as a result, Oporto shows off a Baroque finery lacking in the capital. Its grandiose granite buildings were financed by the trade that made the city wealthy: Wine from the upper valley of the Rio Douro was transported to Oporto and from there exported. Visitors may still follow that trail today, by boat or by the beautiful Douro Line train route along the river.

Though it's not immediately apparent, northern Portugal *is* a popular holiday destination—with the Portuguese. The Minho, which takes its name from the river forming Portugal's northern border with Spain, is bounded by the Atlantic in the west and cut by the long, peaceful Lima and Cávado rivers. The Minho coast is advertised as the Costa Verde (Green Coast), a sweeping stretch of beaches and fishing villages. Some locations have been appropriated as resorts by the Portuguese, but there are still plenty of places where you can find solitary dunes or splash in the brisk Atlantic away from crowds. Inland you can lose yourself in ancient villages with country markets and fairs that have changed little for hundreds of years. You'll also see that little of the green countryside is wasted. Vines are trailed on poles and trees high above cultivated fields, forming a natural canopy, for this is *vinho verde* (green wine) country. (The Costa Verde is named for its lush, green landscape, and vinho verde is so called because it is drunk young; it also has a slightly greenish cast.) This refreshing wine, which comes only from the Minho region, is a true taste of the North, one to which you'll quickly become accustomed as you sit, glass in hand, by a river or the coast and reflect upon the day's events.

To the northeast there's adventure at hand, in the winding mountain roads and remote towns and villages of the Trás-os-Montes region. After centuries of isolation, the area is being accessed by new roads, but there's still great excitement in the rattling trans-mountain train ride from Oporto to Bragança, in the far northeastern corner of the country. The imposing, medieval castle towers and fortress walls of this frontier region are a great attraction, but—unusual in such a small country—it's often the journey itself that's the greatest prize: traveling past voluminous man-made lakes, through forested valleys rich in wildlife, across bare crags and moorlands, and finally down to coarse, stone villages where TV aerials sit oddly in almost medieval surroundings.

It's best to visit the North in summer, when Oporto and the Costa Verde have a generally warm climate, though be prepared for drizzling rain at any time. Temperatures in the North are a good few degrees cooler than in the south. Inland, and especially in the northeastern mountains, traveling in winter can be cold, hard going.

Essential Information

Important Addresses and Numbers

Tourist Information
There are two tourist offices in **Oporto:** one just east of Avenida dos Aliados (Praça Dom João I 43, tel. 02/317514) and one to the west of the town hall, at the top of Avenida dos Aliados (Rua Clube dos Fenianos 25, tel. 02/312740). Both will provide maps of the city, information about tours, and help in finding accommodations.

There are local tourist offices providing similar services in the following towns: **Amarante** (Rua Cândido dos Reis, 4600, tel. 055/422980), **Arcos de Valdevez** (Av. da Marginal, 4970, tel. 058/66100), **Barcelos** (Torre de Menagem, Largo da Porta Nova, 4750, tel. 053/811882), **Braga** (Av. da Liberdade 1, 4700, tel. 053/22550), **Bragança** (Av. Cidade de Zamora, 5300, tel. 073/22273), **Caminha** (Rua Ricardo Joaquim Sousa, 4910, tel. 058/921952), **Chaves** (Rua de Santo António 213, 5400, tel. 076/21029), **Espinho** (Angulo das Ruas 6 e 23, tel. 02/720911), **Esposende** (Rua 1 de Dezembro, 4740, tel. 053/961354), **Gerês** (Av. da Liberdade 1, 4700, tel. 053/22550), **Guimarães** (Av. Resistentes ao Fascismo 83, 4800, tel. 053/412450), **Lamego** (Av. Visconde Guedes Teixeira, 5100, tel. 054/62005), **Monção** (Largo do Loreto, 4950, tel. 051/652757), **Ponte da Barca** (Largo da Misericórdia, 4980, tel. 058/42899), **Ponte de Lima** (Praça da República, 4990, tel. 058/942335), **Póvoa de Varzim** (Av. Mouzinho de Albuquerque 166, tel. 052/624609), **Valença do Minho** (Av. de Espanha, 4930, tel. 051/23374), **Viana do Castelo** (Rua do Hospital Velho, 4900, tel. 058/822620), **Vila do Conde** (Rua 25 de Abril, 4480, tel. 052/631472), **Vila Nova de Cerveira** (Rua Dr. A. Duro, 4920, tel. 051/95899), **Vila Nova de Gaia** Câmara Municipal, Rua Álvares Cabral, 4400, tel. 02/370 2559, **Vila Praia de Âncora** (Av. Ramos Pereira, 4915, tel. 058/911384), **Vila Real** (Av. Carvalho Araújo 94, 5000, tel. 059/22819).

Consulates
In Oporto: **United States** (Rua Júlio Dinis 826–3, tel. 02/690008), **United Kingdom** (Av. da Boavista 3072, tel. 02/684789). There isn't a Canadian consulate in the North.

Emergencies
The general emergency number is tel. 115. In Oporto specific services include: **The Red Cross** (tel. 02/60720), **Hospitals** (Hospital de Santa Maria, Rua de Camões, tel. 02/410–4844; Hospital Geral de Santo António, Largo Professor Abel Salazar, tel. 02/200–5241; Hospital de São João, Alameda Professor Hernâni Monteiro, tel. 02/487151), **Police** (Rua Augusto Rosa, tel. 02/200–6821), **Fire** (tel. 02/484121).

Late-night Pharmacies Pharmacies take turns staying open late. Schedules and addresses are posted on the door of each pharmacy, and listings of late-night services are carried in the local press.

Travel Agencies Travel agencies are the best places to obtain tickets and travel information without difficulty. In Oporto, many are found around the central Avenida dos Aliados. Reliable ones include: **Star,** agents for American Express (Av. dos Aliados 202, Oporto, tel. 02/200–3637; Av. Dom Afonso Henriques 638, Guimarães, tel. 053/515750); **Viagens Rawes** (Largo Ferreira Lapa 34, Oporto, tel. 02/666148); **Wasteels–Expresso** (Rua Pinto Bessa 29, Oporto, tel. 02/570589).

Mail and Telephones The main post office in Oporto is in Praça General Humberto Delgado (tel. 02/208–0251). It is open weekdays 8 AM–10 PM, Saturday 8–8. General delivery mail is received here, and telephones are available for international calls.

Arriving and Departing by Plane

Airports and Airlines Oporto's **Pedras Rubras Airport** (tel. 02/948–2141) is 13 kilometers (8 miles) north of the city and is the gateway to all of northern Portugal. There is direct service from European and South American cities but not from the United States. TAP, Portugal's national airline, runs regular flights from Lisbon. The airport has car-rental agencies and money-exchange facilities. In addition, there are regional airports handling domestic flights in Bragança (tel. 073/22075) and Chaves (tel. 076/21995). For regional service, contact the airline LAR Transregional at the Oporto airport.

Between the Airport and Downtown Bus Nos. 56 and 87 run from the airport to downtown Oporto and cost 130$00. It takes up to an hour, depending on the traffic, to reach the stop at Cordoaria, the area behind the Clérigos Tower. Taxis are available, too, outside the terminal.

Arriving and Departing by Car, Train, and Bus

By Car Oporto is a key destination for travelers driving to the North, since all of the region's major roads fan out from the city. It takes about 3½ hours from Lisbon on the fast highway. From Spain, the closest border crossing is at Tuy/Valença do Minho; from there it's 125 kilometers (77½ miles) south to Oporto on the N13. Other border crossings are to the east, at various points in the Trás-os-Montes region. Chaves, Bragança, or Miranda do Douro are your first stops; from each you face a long and winding drive across the country to Oporto. Visitors arriving in this remote northeastern part of the region would be advised to undertake Tour 5 (*see* Exploring Oporto and the North, *below*) before moving on to Oporto and the rest of the North.

By Train Most trains into Oporto (including those from Lisbon) arrive at **Estação de Campanhã** (Campanhã, tel. 02/565645), just east of the city center. From here, you take a five-minute connecting ride to the central **Estação de São Bento** (Praça Almeida Garrett, tel. 02/200–2722); connecting trains run regularly. When leaving Oporto, be sure to double-check your departure time and leave plenty of time for the connection from São Bento Station so that you make your train in Campanhã. For the express service to and from Lisbon, it's necessary to reserve your seat at least a day in advance.

A few trains, those from Guimarães and from the coast immediately north of the city, use the **Estação da Trindade** (Rua Alferes Malheiro, tel. 02/200–5224), which is a few minutes' walk from downtown Oporto, behind the town hall at the top of Avenida dos Aliados.

From Spain, the Vigo–Oporto through-train uses the Tuy/Valença border crossing and runs south down the Costa Verde to Oporto via Viana do Castelo. These trains usually stop at the Campanhã and São Bento stations, but on some runs the train will stop at Campanhã, and you'll have to connect to the more central São Bento station.

By Bus There are several bus terminals in Oporto. The main areas where buses arrive and depart from are at Praça Filipa de Lencastre (close to Av. dos Aliados) and in the streets behind São Bento Station (particularly Rua de Alexandre Herculano and Av. de Rodrigues de Freitas). For information on buses to Lisbon, contact **Caima,** (Rua das Carmelitas 32, tel. 02/318668). The journey to or from Lisbon takes about five hours, and you should reserve seats at least a day in advance in summer.

Getting Around

You'll be able to walk around most of central Oporto, although be prepared for the hills, which can prove tiring in the summer heat. Only a few sights are far enough away to require transportation, and taxis are readily available. Away from Oporto you'd do well to have a car, or try one of the beautiful train lines throughout the North.

By Car Oporto is very congested, so, though you'll want to have a car to see the surroundings and the rest of the North, leave it at your hotel while sightseeing in the city. Central parking is difficult to find, and much of the downtown area (in particular, the riverside and the winding streets of the old town below the cathedral) is not accessible to cars.

Outside Oporto a car is the most convenient way to get around, but be prepared for lengthy journeys, particularly in the northeast, where roads can be tortuous. Many roads have been improved in recent years—the fast N15 highway between Oporto and Bragança is nearing completion, and there are quick routes from Oporto to towns both north and south, as well as to Braga to the northeast—but, given the nature of some Portuguese terrain, some journeys will never be anything but slow. Examples are the routes Bragança–Chaves–Braga (N103), Vila Real–Chaves (N2), and Bragança–Mirando do Douro (N218). It's best simply to accept the roads' limitations, slow down, and appreciate the scenery.

Off the beaten track, particularly in the northeast, always check with local tourist offices to make sure that the routes you wish to follow are still navigable. Road work and winter land slides can cause detours and delays. In isolated regions, take special care at night, since many roads are unlit and unpaved.

Car Rentals All the major companies are represented at Oporto's airport and some have offices at the larger hotels. Other addresses include: **Avis** (Rua Guedes de Azevedo 125, Oporto, tel. 02/315947; Braga train station, Rua Gabriel P. Castro 28, tel. 053/72520; Rua do Gontim 35, Viana do Castelo, tel. 058/823994); **Europcar** (Rua de Santa Catarina 1158, Oporto, tel. 02/318398;

Campanhã Station, Oporto, tel. 02/580723), **Hertz** (Rua de Santa Catarina 899, Oporto, tel. 02/312387; Av. da Liberdade 20, Braga, tel. 053/79650; Av. Conde da Carreira, Viana do Castelo, tel. 058/822250). In other towns consult the tourist office for the best deals with local companies.

By Taxi In Oporto there is a taxi stand in Praça da Liberdade, or you may phone for a cab (tel. 02/488061, 02/482691, or 02/676093). Make sure that the driver switches on the meter. Note that taxis add a surcharge for crossing the Ponte Dom Luis I to Vila Nova de Gaia, the suburb known for its port wine.

By Bus and Tram Oporto has a decent public transportation system, consisting of *carris* (buses) and *eléctricos* (trams). The tourist office provides a city map with all the main routes and numbers. Main stops are at Praça da Liberdade, Praça de Dom João I, and Cordoaria, behind the Clérigos Tower. A useful bus route is No. 78, which runs from Praça da Liberdade, past the Soares dos Reis museum and the Palácio de Cristal gardens, along the main Avenida da Boavista, to the Museum of Modern Art. The tram system is of less use to visitors, though Nos. 1 and 18 make a pleasant run along the river to the beach at Foz.

Ticket prices vary according to the distance traveled, but most trips through the downtown area cost 130$00. The driver will tell you how much to pay when you get on. If you're going to make considerable use of public transportation, purchase a block of 20 tickets (1,210$00) or a four-day (1,210$00) or seven-day (1,680$00) *Passe Turístico* (Tourist Pass), all of which provide large discounts. All are available at kiosks at the main bus stops.

Outside the city system there's a confusion of bus companies in the North, with several providing service between the same destinations. Generally, however, companies use one central station in each town. Major terminals are found at Oporto, Braga, Guimarães, Vila Real, and Chaves. The best source of information about departures is the local tourist office, since bus station staff invariably speak no English. However, most bus stations do offer timetables for main routes, which you should be able to decipher with the aid of a dictionary. Always arrive at the station with enough time to buy your ticket.

The main company operating in Trás-os-Montes is **Cabanelas,** whose terminal in Oporto is at Rua da Alegria (tel. 02/200–2870). Bus trips in this region are slow and, on some of the minor routes, uncomfortable.

One useful tip is to take the bus rather than the train between the neighboring towns of Guimarães and Braga (*see* Tour 3 in Exploring Oporto and the North, *below*). It's only 22 kilometers (14 miles) on the road, but the circuitous train ride involves two changes, since both towns are at the end of branch lines.

By Train All of the region's train routes originate in Oporto; from here some of the finest lines in the country stretch out into the river valleys and mountain ranges of the northeast. Even if you've rented a car, try to take a day trip on at least one of the minor train lines, since the countryside is often best seen from a rattling train window. The **Douro Line** runs from Oporto's São Bento Station east to Pocinho via Livração, Peso da Régua, and Tua (a four-hour journey). Three narrow-gauge lines branch off of it: the **Tâmega Line,** linking Livração with beautiful

Amarante (25 minutes); the **Corgo Line,** from Peso da Régua to Vila Real (one hour); and the **Tua Line,** from Tua to Mirandela/ Bragança (two hours/four hours). The trains on these lines generally have just one class of car and stop at every station. Journeys are slow but rewarding. (Tickets are reasonably priced.) Recently there have been service cuts on the minor lines, and some route sections have been closed altogether. The lines mentioned above should still be operational, but for reservations and current schedules contact São Bento Station (tel. 02/ 311616) or the tourist office in Oporto.

The region's main train route runs north from Oporto (with approximately hourly departures from both São Bento and Campanhã stations) along the Costa Verde, through Barcelos and Viana do Castelo, as far as Valença do Minho. Branch lines connect with Braga and Guimarães.

By Boat   Cruises on the Rio Douro are offered by various companies based in Oporto. These range from short trips taking in Oporto's bridges and the local fishing villages to one- and two-day cruises that include meals and accommodations. Expect to pay around 1,500$00 for one- to two-hour cruises, most of which depart several times daily from the Cais da Ribeira quay, at the foot of Oporto's old town (*see* Tour 1, *below*). The longer cruises usually depart weekly and often involve taking a train from São Bento Station that connects with a boat farther down the Douro. The cost for these is 11,000$00–24,000$00 per person. Service is limited in the winter months.

One of the main cruise companies, with the best reputation, is **Endouro** (Rua da Reboleira 49, Oporto, tel. 02/324236, fax 02/ 317260). More information can be obtained from the tourist office in Oporto.

Guided Tours

Orientation   In Oporto, consult a tourist office or travel agency (*see* Important Addresses and Numbers, *above*) for the latest information on bus tours of the city. Usually these last half a day and take in all the principal sights, including a visit to the port-wine lodges (where the vintage is stored) at Vila Nova de Gaia. Short river cruises from Oporto are also a pleasant way to orient yourself (*see* By Boat in Getting Around, *above*).

For tours farther afield, **RN Tours** (Rua Sá da Bandeira 629, Oporto, tel. 02/382303) operates half- and full-day coach tours throughout the region, to destinations as diverse as the Douro valley, the Costa Verde, and Peneda-Gerês National Park. Consider, too, the longer cruises operated by Endouro (*see* By Boat in Getting Around, *above*), which cover the towns of the Douro valley.

Special-Interest   All of the port-wine lodges at Vila Nova de Gaia offer free tours of the production process as well as wine tastings. (*See* Tour 1 in Exploring Oporto and the North, *below*.)

Exploring Oporto and the North

Orientation

Oporto is just 3½ hours north of Lisbon by highway or express train, so even a short trip to Portugal can include a night or two in the country's second-largest city. Tour 1 takes in the most interesting sights and monuments in Oporto and allows time for a visit to the famous port-wine lodges. Tour 2 shows how a second or third day in the city could be used to explore Oporto's environs, including the local beaches and the lovely scenery of the Rio Douro valley. The third tour encompasses the two most intriguing historical towns of the Minho region, Guimarães and Braga, and also includes a visit to the country's biggest weekly market at Barcelos. Tour 4 continues from here, covering the beautiful Costa Verde coastline and the peaceful inland towns and villages along the region's main rivers, the Lima and the Minho. The final tour strikes off into the remote northeastern region of Portugal, Trás-os-Montes, where a long circuit takes in the fascinating towns of Bragança and Chaves before cutting back to the area covered in Tour 3.

Following all the tours in this chapter would be a major undertaking, requiring at least two weeks on top of your time in Oporto, perhaps longer if you have to rely on public transportation. However, in a week you could see the best parts of the coast and Minho province or travel widely in Trás-os-Montes. With just a few days for exploration, you could follow Tours 2 and 3, which cover varied towns and landscapes easily accessible from Oporto.

Highlights for First-Time Visitors

Amarante (*see* Tour 2)
Baroque staircase and shrine of Bom Jesus, Braga (*see* Tour 3)
Cais da Ribeira district, Oporto (*see* Tour 1)
Chaves (*see* Tour 5)
Citadel, Bragança (*see* Tour 5)
Guimarães (*see* Tour 3)
Ponte de Lima (*see* Tour 4)
Port-wine tasting at Vila Nova de Gaia, Oporto (*see* Tour 1)
Solar de Mateus, Vila Real (*see* Tour 5)
Thursday market, Barcelos (*see* Tour 3)
Viana do Castelo (*see* Tour 4)
View from the Torre dos Clérigos, Oporto (*see* Tour 1)

Tour 1: Oporto

Numbers in the margin correspond to points of interest on the North and Oporto maps.

❶ Industrious **Oporto**—Portugal's second city, with a population of half a million—considers itself the capital of the North and, more contentiously, the economic center of the country. Locals support this claim by quoting a typically down-to-earth maxim: "Coimbra sings, Braga prays, Lisbon shows off, and Oporto works." Certainly wherever you look there's evidence of a city

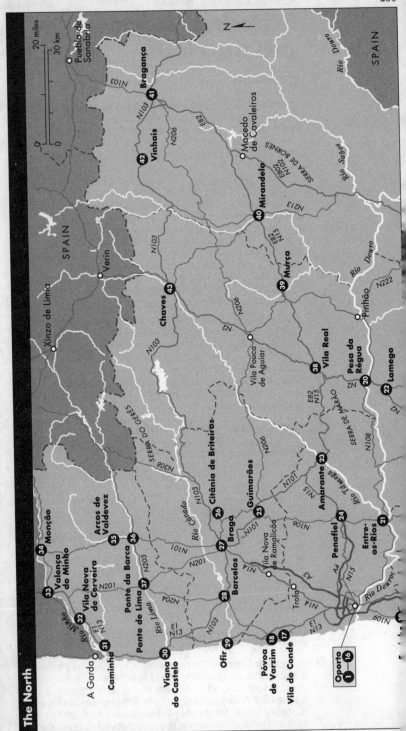

The North

256

in rude financial health. Massive new business developments on the outskirts give way to a fashionable commercial area in the heart of town; shops and restaurants bustle with high-spending locals; and the city's buildings, churches, and monuments—both old and new—impress with their solid construction. There's poverty here, of course, in the ragged old-town areas near the river; parts are positively medieval. But in the shopping centers, the stately Stock Exchange building, and the affluent port-wine industry, Oporto oozes confidence. Hard work, one feels, is the city's biggest asset.

This emphasis on worth rather than beauty means that Oporto is not a graceful city. Significant sights are few, and aesthetically pleasing monuments are rare. Visitors may find their first impression disappointing, although the city's glorious location—on a steep hillside above the Rio Douro—does much to compensate. The river has influenced the city's development since pre-Roman times, when the town of Cale on the left bank prospered sufficiently to support a trading port, called Portus, on the site of today's city. Under the Romans this twin town of Portus-Cale became a thriving commercial center, and it continued to be successful despite the later ravages of Moorish occupation and Christian reconquest. Significantly, given the outward-looking nature of its inhabitants, Henry the Navigator—the great explorer king—was born here at the end of the 14th century.

The importance of the river trade to the city is reflected in its current name, whose use began in early medieval times. Oporto, from the Portuguese *O Porto*, means simply "the port," and over the centuries the city has traded widely in fish, salt, and wine. As the result of an agreement with England in 1703, the region's most notable product—wine, made from the grapes of the Douro's vineyards—found a new market and was shipped out of the city in ever-increasing quantities. The port-wine trade is still big business, based just over the river from the city in the suburb of Vila Nova de Gaia (site of the Roman town of Cale).

❷ Having reached the city center (often a slow business because of the traffic), you'll do best to tour Oporto on foot, taking buses or taxis to the few outlying attractions. Start at the **Avenida dos Aliados,** an imposing, sloping boulevard that lies at the commercial heart of the city and points toward the river. Providing some welcome open space in Oporto's busy center, it is planted with bright flower beds and lined with grand buildings, including the broad **Câmara Municipal** (Town Hall), which stands at the top of the avenue. The roof of this early 20th-century palace-like building sprouts a tall bell tower, and inside is displayed an impressive Portuguese wall tapestry. At the other end of the avenue, **Praça da Liberdade** is the hub from which downtown Oporto radiates. Two statues adorn the square: a cast of Dom Pedro IV sitting on a horse and an unusual, modern statue of the great 19th-century Portuguese poet and novelist Almeida Garrett. *Town hall: Praça General Humberto Delgado, tel. 02/200–9871. Admission free. Open weekdays 9:30–noon and 2–5.*

Time Out The city has several fine old-style coffee houses, which, like those in Lisbon, feature turn-of-the-century decor. The large **Café Imperial,** on the eastern side of Praça da Liberdade, is a

Oporto

N

0 ———— 500 yards
0 ———— 500 meters

Avenida dos Aliados, **2**
Bolsa, **12**
Cais da Ribeira, **7**
Casa do Infante, **10**
Casa Museu de Guerra
Junqueiro, **6**
Estação de São
Bento, **4**

Igreja da
Misericórdia, **13**
Igreja de São
Francisco, **11**
Jardim do Palácio de
Cristal, **16**
Museu de Etnografia e
Historia, **14**

Museu Nacional
Soares dos Reis, **15**
Ponte Dom Luis I, **8**
Sé, **5**
Torre dos Clérigos, **3**
Vila Nova de Gaia, **9**

good place to watch the busy traffic and shoppers; there are tables inside and out. Around the corner, the similarly decorated **A Brasileira** (Rua Sá da Bandeira 61. Closed Sun.) has brisker service. For just a drink or snack, pay first at the cash desk and present your receipt at the busy bar. Both are inexpensive.

Rua dos Clérigos leads smartly uphill to the west from Praça da Liberdade, culminating in an odd oval-shaped church, whose tower is an immediately recognizable finger on the Oporto skyline. The **Torre dos Clérigos** (Clérigos Tower), designed by Italian architect Nicolau Nasoni and begun in 1754, consists of six stories that leap to a height of 249 feet, making it one of the tallest towers in the country. There are 225 steep stone steps to the belfry at the top, and the very considerable effort required to climb them is rewarded by stunning views of the old town, the river, and beyond to the mouth of the Douro. The **Igreja dos Clérigos,** a church that was also built by Nasoni, predates the tower and is an elaborate example of Italianate Baroque architecture. *Rua dos Clérigos, tel. 02/200–1729. Tower: Admission: 50$00. Open Thurs.–Tues. 10–noon and 2–5, Sun. to 5:30. Church: Admission free. Open Mon.–Sat. 7:30–9, 10–noon, 2–5, and 6–7:30; Sun. 10–1.*

Back at Praça da Liberdade, use the pedestrian underpass to cross to the **Estação de São Bento** (São Bento Station), Oporto's most central railroad station, whose main hall is decorated with enormous *azulejos* (ceramic tiles) depicting the history of Portuguese transportation. From the steps of the station you can look across to the granite **Sé** (Cathedral), situated on a sweeping terrace and perched over the old town, which is a few minutes' walk to the south. Originally constructed in the 12th century by the parents of Afonso Henriques (the first king of Portugal), the cathedral has been rebuilt twice: first in the late 13th century and again in the 18th century, when the architect of the Clérigos Tower, Nasoni, was among those commissioned to work on its expansion. Despite these renovations, it remains a severe, fortress-like structure, and, as such, is an uncompromising statement of the city's medieval wealth and power. Sheer size apart, the cathedral's interior is unusually disappointing, and only when you enter the two-story, 14th-century cloister does the building come to life. Decorated with gleaming azulejos, a staircase added by Nasoni leads to the second level and into a magnificent, richly furnished chapter house, from which there are fine views of the old town through narrow windows. *Terreiro da Sé, tel. 02/314837. Admission: cathedral free; cloister: 100$00. Open daily 9–12:30 and 3–6.*

Nasoni also designed the **Archbishop's Palace,** behind the cathedral, although since its conversion to public offices, visitors can see no farther than the impressive 60-meter-long facade. However, you may visit the elegant interior of another 18th-century building attributed to Nasoni, the **Casa Museu de Guerra Junqueiro** (Guerra Junqueiro House and Museum). It lies on Rua de Dom Hugo, a narrow street that curves around the eastern side of the cathedral. This white mansion was home to the poet Guerra Junqueiro (1850–1923) and is a quiet retreat. However, the short tour of his enviable collection of furniture, sculpture, paintings, and silver is less than enlightening if you don't speak Portuguese. *Rua de Dom Hugo 32, tel. 02/313644. Admission: 96$00. Open Tues.–Sat. 11–12:30 and 2:30–6.*

Continue along Rua de Dom Hugo and then head down, by way of the steep steps that cut through surviving sections of the medieval city walls, into a web of tangled alleys, leaning housing, and down-at-the-heel street markets. This decaying neighborhood has missed out on the city's economic progress, and there's much poverty here, however colorful the timeworn buildings with their long rows of balconies may appear. Whichever route you follow, the stepped alleys all eventually emerge ⑦ at the riverfront **Cais da Ribeira,** the quayside of the fascinating Ribeira district. Here there's a small daily market and a string of excellent fish restaurants and *tascas* (taverns) built into the street-level arcade of the old buildings above (*see* Dining and Lodging, *below*). In the Praça da Ribeira, people sit and chat around the odd, modern, cube-like sculpture, while farther on, steps lead up to a raised walkway, backed by tall houses, that runs above the river. There are good views from here of the port-wine lodges at Vila Nova de Gaia.

From the quayside there's access to the lower level of the two-tier **Ponte Dom Luis I** (Dom Luis I Bridge), the middle of three ⑧ bridges that span the Douro in Oporto. This bridge was built in ⑨ 1886 and leads directly to the suburb of **Vila Nova de Gaia,** which has been the headquarters of the port-wine trade since the late 17th century. Import bans on French wine had led British merchants to look for alternate sources, and by the 18th century the British had established companies and a regulatory association at Oporto to control the quality of the wine they were importing from Portugal. The wine was transported from vineyards on the upper reaches of the Rio Douro, 160 kilometers (100 miles) away, to port-wine "lodges" (warehouses) at Vila Nova de Gaia, where it was allowed to mature before being shipped out of the country. Very little has changed in the relationship between Oporto and the Douro since those days, as wine is still transported to the city, matured in the warehouses, and bottled. However, instead of traveling down the river on traditional *barcos rabelos* (flat-bottomed boats), the wine is now carried by truck. A couple of the boats are moored at the quayside on the Vila Nova de Gaia side, as a reminder of bygone days.

There are over 25 companies with **port-wine lodges** in Vila Nova de Gaia (many still foreign-owned), from such well-known names as Sandeman, Croft, and Cockburn to less-well-known Portuguese firms, such as Ramos Pinto and Borges. All are signposted within a few minutes' walk of each other, and their names are displayed in huge white letters across their roofs. Each company offers guided tours of the premises and the fascinating port-wine making and bottling process—tours that always end with a tasting of one or two wines and an opportunity to buy bottles from the company store. Tours begin regularly, usually when enough visitors are assembled. Even without taking a tour, you'll find the back streets of this suburb entertaining; they are filled with trucks loading and unloading in narrow alleys and offer glimpses of huge vats and technical equipment inside warehouses. The tourist office at Vila Nova de Gaia (*see* Important Addresses and Numbers in Essential Information, *above*) offers a small map of the main port-wine lodges, though note that not all lodges have the same opening hours. Opening hours for the larger lodges are given below, but the tourist office can advise about smaller operations. *Admis-*

*sion free. Open June–Sept., weekdays 9–12:30 and 2–7, Sat. 9–
12:30; Oct.–May, weekdays 9–12:30 and 2–5.*

Vila Nova de Gaia isn't solely devoted to the port-wine trade.
Combine a tour of the wine lodges with a visit to the **Casa
Museu de Teixeira Lopes,** the home of the sculptor António
Teixeira Lopes (1866–1942), who was born in town. It contains
some excellent sculpture as well as a varied collection of paintings by Teixeira Lopes's contemporaries. A selection of books,
coins, and ceramics is also interesting. *Rua Teixeira Lopes 32,
tel. 02/301224. Admission free. Open Oct.–May, Tues.–Sat.
9:30–12:30 and 2–5:30; June–Sept., Tues.–Sat. 9:30–12:30
and 2–5:30, Sun. 1–7.*

You may cross back to the city using the narrow footway on the
upper level of the Ponte Dom Luis I, which puts you on Avenida
de Vimara Peres, close to the cathedral. But at 200 feet above
the river and with traffic thundering past, this is no crossing
for faint hearts or for those who have tasted not too wisely but
too well of the port.

To continue the city tour, retrace your path to the Cais da
Ribeira. Away from the water, Rua do Infante Dom Henrique,
which used to be known as Rua dos Ingleses (English Street),
contains shipping offices and warehouses. Where it meets Rua
de São João stands the granite **Feitoria Inglesa** (Factory House
of the British Association), built at the end of the 18th century
as the headquarters of the Port Wine Shippers' Association. It
retains an impressive interior, but the general public is not ad-
❿ mitted. Farther west is the **Casa do Infante** (House of the
Prince), a foursquare, restored mansion said to be the birthplace of Oporto's most famous son, Prince Henry the Navigator
(born in 1394). The building now holds part of the city archives
and is open to the public for temporary exhibitions. *Rua do Infante, tel. 02/316025.*

Follow Rua do Infante Dom Henrique to the square of the same
name, which is marked by a statue of Prince Henry. Here the
⓫ late 14th-century **Igreja de São Francisco** (Church of Saint
Francis) appears to be an unremarkable Gothic building on the
outside but reveals its astounding interior to inquisitive visitors. The profusion of gilt-surfaced carving was added in the
mid-18th century and swarms over every inch of the building—
up the pillars, over the altar, and across the ceiling. (An adjacent museum, housing valuable pieces once belonging to the
Franciscan monastery that first stood here, is closed for restoration.) *Rua do Infante Dom Henrique, tel. 02/200–6493. Admission: 100$00. Open Tues.–Sat. 10–1 and 2–5.*

Behind the church, facing the square, Oporto's 19th-century,
⓬ neoclassical **Bolsa** (Stock Exchange) takes up much of the site
of the old Franciscan monastery. Guided tours (the only way to
see the interior) stroll around the huge, showy edifice, and
much of it is in questionable taste. The Arab-style ballroom, in
particular, has critics as numerous as the glowing adjectives
with which the guides describe it. *Rua Ferreira Borges, tel. 02/
200–4497. Guided tours: 300$00; May–Sept., Mon.–Sat. 9–
noon and 2–5:30, every 15–20 min.; Oct.–Apr., weekdays 9–
noon and 2–5:30, every 30 min.*

North of the stock exchange, at Largo de São Domingos, Rua
das Flores—a street known for its silversmiths and striking
wrought-iron balconies—leads back toward São Bento Station.

⑬ On the left is the **Igreja da Misericórdia** (Church of the Misericórdia), which dates from the 16th century but was largely remodeled two centuries later by Nicolau Nasoni. Call at the adjacent offices, and you will be shown the *Fons Vitae* (Fountain of Life), considered one of the country's finest paintings. It is an anonymous Renaissance work of brilliant colors, showing the founder of the church, Dom Manuel I, his queen, and their eight children kneeling before a crucified Christ. *Tel. 02/200–0941. Admission free. Open weekdays 10–noon and 2–5.*

⑭ Retrace your steps to Largo de São Domingos, and follow Rua de Belomonte west to Largo de São João Novo. The **Museu de Etnografia e Historia** (Ethnographic and History Museum) is contained within an early 18th-century mansion facing the square. It's one of the city's most rewarding museums, displaying a feast of cultural exhibits in every nook and cranny, from ink pots and quills to a sedan chair and spinning wheel. Some of the most amusing pieces are children's toys and games, including a doll's house of extraordinary intricacy. There are also local historical pieces, archaeological finds, demonstrations of local manufacturing, and a reconstruction of a 19th-century kitchen interior. The entrance is completely unmarked: Look for the mansion opposite the Igreja de São João Novo (church). Push the door for entry. *Largo de São João Novo, tel. 02/200–2010. Admission free. Open Tues.–Sat. 10–noon and 2–5.*

Having seen the graceful, balconied houses of Rua de Belomonte, walk north, following Rua das Taipas, until you reach the **Jardim João Chagas** (João Chagas Gardens), where the **Palácio da Justiça** (Palace of Justice) towers on your left. Facing the corner of the gardens is the large, 18th-century **Hospital de Santo Antonio,** ⑮ and a little farther west is the **Museu Nacional Soares dos Reis** (Soares dos Reis Museum), located in a former royal palace. The building was the headquarters of Marshal Soult in the Peninsular War, which pitted Napolean's French army against British and Portuguese forces. (In 1809, Soult was forced to flee before the rapid advance of the British expeditionary force.) Regarded as the city's most important museum, it is named after the 19th-century Portuguese sculptor whose works are contained within. Of wider interest, however, is the large art collection, which includes several Portuguese primitive works of the 16th century as well as superb collections of silver, ceramics, glassware, and costumes. *Rua de Dom Manuel II, tel. 02/200–7110. Admission: 200$00, free on Sun. Open Tues.–Sun. 10–noon and 2–5.*

⑯ Continue west on Rua de Dom Manuel II to the **Jardim do Palacio de Cristal** (Crystal Palace Gardens), named for a 19th-century palace that once stood here but that was replaced in the 1950s by an enormous domed pavilion used for sports and exhibitions. Follow Rua de Entre Quintas on the far side of the gardens to reach the **Quinta da Macierinha**. This is a charming 19th-century country house containing the so-called **Museu Romântico** (Romantic Museum), featuring period furniture and decoration. The ground floor of the Quinta is of special interest, for here the **Solar do Vinho do Porto** (Port Wine Institute) offers relaxed tastings of port wine, in much the same fashion as its counterpart in Lisbon; however, Oporto's Solar has a much friendlier reputation, and, in addition, the wine has only had to travel across the river before being served! Tasting prices vary but start at 100$00 per glass. This is a fine place to end your tour of the city, and, when it's time to return downtown, either catch Bus No. 78 (which runs along Rua de Dom Manuel II, past the Soares dos Reis Museum, to Praça da Liberdade) or jump into a taxi. *Rua de Entre Quintas 220. Museum: Tel. 02/691131; open Tues.–Sat. 10–noon and 2–5, Sun. 2–5:30. Solar: Tel. 02/697793; open weekdays 11 AM–11 PM, Sat. 5–11:30.*

Tour 2: Environs of Oporto— The Coast and the Rio Douro

Both north and south of Oporto are beach resorts much favored by locals. To the north there are beaches in **Foz do Douro,** 4 kilometers (2½ miles) from Oporto, and Matosinhos, 8 kilometers (5 miles) away, but they are unattractive places, much influenced by the industrial port of Leixoes. It's better to drive as far as **Vila do Conde,** 27 kilometers (17 miles) north, which has a long sweep of fine sand and retains an interesting fishing port, ship-building industry, and medieval quarter. The town is further distinguished by the huge **Convento de Santa Clara** (Convent of St. Clara), overwhelming the north bank of the Rio Ave, on which the town is situated. The convent was founded in the 14th century by Dom Afonso Sanches and his wife, Dona Teresa Martins, and it retains its original cloister and the beautiful tombs of its founders. The **Igreja Matriz** (Parish Church), in the center of town near the market, is also worth seeing. Completed in the 16th century, it features a superb Gothic portal. If you're looking for souvenirs, Vila do Conde is the center of a flourishing lace industry, and the tourist office will direct you to a lacemaking school in the town center that welcomes visitors. *Convent open Mon.–Sat. 9–noon and 2–5.*

Póvoa de Varzim, four kilometers (2½ miles) north, also has a long beach, but the town has little of Vila do Conde's charm. It is, instead, a major resort, with high-rise hotels used mostly by Portuguese on vacation. The recently refurbished casino (open daily 3 PM–3 AM) on the waterfront attracts much attention. Entertainment includes nightly floor shows; to gamble, take along your passport.

South of Oporto, frequent trains and route N109 run past a string of quiet family beaches to **Espinho,** 18 kilometers (11 miles) from the city. Built on a grid pattern, it has become an increasingly fashionable resort over the years, with a casino of its own, a full range of other leisure facilities, and good shopping. The long, sandy beach is very popular in summer, but you can find some space by walking through the pinewoods to less developed areas to the south. The Oporto Golf Club, founded in 1890 by members of the Port Wine Shippers' Association, is just 2 kilometers (1¼ miles) south of Espinho (*see* Sports and Outdoor Activities, *below*).

The beaches are pleasant, but a more interesting attraction is the **Rio Douro,** which makes its presence felt throughout Oporto and its surroundings. Visitors can see the beauty of the river and the local countryside by train, car, or boat (*see* Getting Around in Essential Information, *above*).

Even if you are traveling by car, it's worth considering at least a day trip using the Douro Line train. The main route cuts 60 kilometers (37 miles) inland from Oporto to join the Douro and follows the north bank of the river as far as **Peso da Régua,** a

2½-hour journey. This small river port is in the heart of port-wine country, and through it passes all the wine from the vineyards of the Upper Douro valley on its way to Oporto. Local wine lodges offer tours of their cellars, which make a nice contrast to the large-scale operations in Vila Nova de Gaia. From Peso da Régua the train continues east to the end of the line at Pocinho, providing a glorious 70-kilometer (43½-mile) ride that hugs the Rio Douro all the way. Unfortunately, service to the Spanish border has been discontinued. The Tâmega Line branches off the main line and runs north up the Rio Tâmega tributary to Amarante (*see below*). Service on both routes is currently under review, since they're used less and less by locals, who prefer the fast inland roads gradually extending from Oporto.

Drivers can get some of the same sense of rural splendor by following the minor N108 east from Oporto along the north bank of the river to Peso da Régua. It makes for a grand, if slow, journey that you can continue all the way to the Spanish border. One of the most striking sights in the valley is the point at which the Douro and the Tâmega join, at **Entre-os-Rios**, 40 kilometers (25 miles) southeast of Oporto.

At Peso da Régua you have a choice of routes. It's 25 kilometers (15½ miles) north along the N2 to Vila Real, the town marking the start of the tour of Trás-os-Montes (*see* Tour 5, *below*). Alternatively, cross the Rio Douro and follow the N2 south for 13 kilometers (8 miles) to **Lamego.** A prosperous wine-producing town, Lamego is rich in Baroque churches and mansions, though none so impressive as the town's most famous monument—the 18th-century pilgrimage church and shrine of **Nossa Senhora dos Remedios.** It stands on a hill to the west of the town center, and a marvelous granite staircase leads up the hillside to the church. The steps and terraces are decorated with azulejos, small chapels, and statues. During the annual pilgrimage on September 8, many penitents climb the steps on their knees, just as they do at the shrine of Bom Jesus near Braga (*see* Tour 3, *below*). Rest at the top under the chestnut trees, and enjoy the view over the town to the distant mountains.

Return to the Douro and Peso da Régua, and take the N108 west to Mesão Frio. Then take the N101, which climbs north out of the Douro valley and across the Serra do Marão (Marão Hills) before descending to join the N15. Forty kilometers (25 miles) from Peso da Régua is the small, agreeable town of **Amarante,** situated on both sides of the Ria Tâmega, a tributary of the Douro. It's also possible to reach Amarante on the Tâmega Line, with a change at Livração. The 70-kilometer (43½-mile) route runs through beautiful countryside distinguished by meadows and woods, and the last 13 kilometers (8 miles) are particularly impressive, for the train runs close to the river.

Amarante itself is charming, if ever a town deserved the adjective, and it's the one place in Oporto's environs that really demands an overnight stop. Its two halves are joined by a narrow 18th-century bridge, sitting above the river's tree-shaded banks. Although the river itself is polluted (which precludes swimming), it's beautiful to look at. Rowboats and pedal boats are for hire at several points along the riverside paths.

Time Out Along Rua 31 de Janeiro, the narrow main road leading to the bridge, several small cafés and restaurants have terraces overlooking the river. Enjoy a drink, snack, or a meal as you soak up the views.

On the north side of the river, across the bridge from the main part of town, is the imposing, 16th-century **Convento de São Gonçalo** (Convent of Saint Gonçalo). The effigy of the saint, on the left of the altar, is reputed to guarantee marriage to anyone who touches it. Not surprisingly, his features have almost been worn away over the years, as desperate suitors try one last time for success. *Praça da República. Admission free. Open daily 9–noon and 2–5.*

Adjacent to the church are the cloisters and associated buildings of the convent, now housing the tourist office and the **Museu Municipal Amadeo de Souza-Cardoso,** a small but intelligent collection of modern art revolving around the largely abstract paintings of Cardoso, who was born in the area. In 1906 Cardoso moved to Paris and shared a studio with Modigliani, but he returned to Portugal in 1914 and died four years later at the young age of 31. The museum also hosts exhibitions of other artists' work, and there's some intriguing modern sculpture displayed in the attractive courtyard. *Alameda Teixeira de Pascoais, tel. 055/432663. Admission free. Open Tues.–Sun. 10–12:30 and 2–5:30.*

Beyond the museum is the riverside site of the local **market,** held every Wednesday, which is perhaps the best day to be in Amarante. Until lunchtime this entire area is alive with activity, and the usually peaceful town is disturbed by manic traffic racing along the main street and over the bridge.

From Amarante the fast, new N15 highway runs 36 kilometers (22 miles) east to Vila Real, which marks the start of Tour 5 (*see below*). But to complete this tour, follow the road west, back toward Oporto. About halfway the highway passes just north of the town of **Penafiel,** which is also accessible from the Douro Line train. The surrounding valleys are terraced with vineyards, not of the heavy port variety but of the slightly sparkling vinho verde (green wine). Other than some fading granite mansions, there's little in the town itself see, but do stop for a glass of this always-refreshing local wine.

Many of the small villages between Penafiel and the Tâmega and Douro rivers, to the south, have lovely Romanesque churches. The closest is a little way off the main road, at **Paço de Sousa,** just to the southwest of Penafiel and 2 kilometers (1¼ miles) south of the train station at Cete. Here the 12th-century church is part of the Convento de São Salvador and contains the tomb of Egas Moniz, who was adviser to Afonso Henriques, the first king of all Portugal. Back on the highway you're just 40 kilometers (25 miles) from Oporto.

Tour 3: Guimarães, Braga, and Barcelos

Guimarães and Braga are of sufficient historical interest to warrant at least a day spent in each. Both make easy day trips from Oporto by road or rail, although they can be seen in a more relaxed fashion on a driving tour of the southern part of Minho province, which also takes in the market town of Barcelos. The tour below begins in Guimarães, but remember that you should visit Barcelos on market day, Thursday; you may have to revise your tour accordingly.

㉕ Guimarães, 51 kilometers (32 miles) northeast of Oporto, is the birthplace of Afonso Henriques. Born in 1110, within 20 years he was being referred to as king of *Portucale* (the united Portuguese lands between the Minho and Douro rivers) and had made Guimarães his capital. From this first "Portuguese" capital, Afonso Henriques drove south, taking Lisbon back from the Moors in 1147. Today Guimarães is a provincial town proud of its past, which is evident in a series of delightful medieval buildings and streets. In the narrow, cobbled thoroughfares of the old town, small bars open onto the sidewalk; balconied, pastel-colored houses overhang little squares; and flowers brighten every windowsill.

It's best to start at the **Castelo** (Castle) at the top of the town, which is, after all, where the story began. It was built (or at least reconstructed from earlier remains) by Henry of Burgundy; his son, Afonso Henriques, was born within its great battlements and flanking towers. Standing high on a solid rock base above the town, the castle has been superbly preserved. A path leads down from the walls to the tiny Romanesque **Igreja de São Miguel de Castelo,** the plain chapel where it's believed that Afonso Henriques was baptized. *Rua D. Teresa de Noronha. Admission free. Castle: Open Tues.–Sun. 9:30–12:30 and 2–5; Church: Open irregular hours.*

Below the chapel is the **Paço dos Duques** (Palace of the Dukes), a much-maligned, renovated 15th-century palace belonging to the dukes of Bragança. Critics claim that the restoration during the Salazar regime, which turned the building into an official state residence, damaged it irrevocably. Certainly the palace's brick chimneys and turrets bear little relation to the original structure, which was an atmospheric ruin for many years, but you can judge for yourself on a guided tour of the interior. The collections inside contain much of interest, from tapestries and furniture to porcelain and paintings. Guided tours are available at the main desk. *Tel. 053/412273. Admission: 300$00, June–Sept.; 200$00 Oct.–May. Open daily 10–12:30 and 2–5.*

Walk down Rua de Santa Maria into the peaceful old town, and the centuries roll away with every step: You'll see granite archways, wooden balconies, iron grilles, and paving stones underfoot. In Largo da Oliveira, a delightful square enclosed by buildings, stands the **Colegiada de Nossa Senhora da Oliveira** (Church of Our Lady of the Olive Branch). It was founded in the 10th century to commemorate one of Guimarães's most enduring legends. Wamba, elected king of the Visigoths in the 7th century, refused the honor and thrust his olive-branch stick into the earth, declaring that only if his stick were to blossom would he accept the crown—whereupon the stick promptly sprouted foliage. In the square in front of the church, an odd 14th-century Gothic canopy sheltering a cross marks the alleged spot.

The adjacent convent buildings, surrounding the Romanesque cloister, house the **Museu Alberto Sampaio,** a beautifully displayed collection of religious art. The cloister itself holds medieval statuary, sarcophagi, and various coats-of-arms, but the interior rooms provide the highlight: a 14th-century silver triptych of the Nativity, full of animation and power. This is said to have been captured from the King of Castile at the crucial Battle of Aljubarrota and presented to the victorious Dom João I, whose tunic, worn at the battle, is preserved in a glass case nearby. *Largo da Oliveira, tel. 053/412465. Admission: 200$00. Open Tues.–Sun. 10–12:30 and 2–5.*

Time Out An inexpensive café in Largo da Oliveira, **A Medieval** has seats outside in the square. Relax over coffee and a cake. *Closed Sun.*

The old-town streets peter out at the Almeida da Liberdade, a swath of gardens at the southern end of Guimarães, whose benches and cafés are often full. Here the **Igreja de São Francisco** (Church of Saint Francis) is worth seeing. Its chancel is decorated with 18th-century azulejos depicting the life of the saint. The church also boasts a fine Renaissance cloister. *Largo de São Francisco, tel. 053/412228. Open daily 9–noon and 3–6.*

Around to the west, at the top of the adjacent Largo do Toural, is Guimarães's other museum, the excellent **Museu Martins Sarmento.** It, too, is contained within the cloister and buildings of a church, the **Igreja de São Domingos.** The museum contains rich finds from the Celtic settlement of Citânia de Briteiros (*see below*), as well as Lusitanian and Roman stone sarcophagi, a strange miniature bronze chariot, various weapons, and elaborate ornaments. Two finds stand out: the decorative, carved stone slabs known as the *Pedras Formosas* (beautiful stones), one of which was found in situ at a funerary monument at Briteiros, and the huge, prehistoric, granite *Colossus of Pedralva,* a figure of brutal power, thought to be related to an ancient fertility cult. *Rua de Paio Galvão, tel. 053/415969. Admission: 250$00. Open Tues.–Sun. 10–noon and 2–5.*

Go north from Guimarães toward Braga on the N101, and after 8 kilometers (5 miles) turn right at Caldas das Taipas (Caldelas on some maps). This leads to **Citânia de Briteiros,** the fascinating remains of a Celtic *citânia* (hill settlement). It dates back to around 300 BC and was probably not abandoned until AD 300, making it one of the last Celtic strongholds against the Romans in Portugal. The walls and foundations of 150 huts and a meeting house have been excavated (two of the huts have been reconstructed to show their original size), and paths are clearly marked between them. Parts of a channeled water system also survive. The site was excavated in the late 19th century by Dr. Martins Sarmento, who gave his name to the museum in Guimarães (*see above*), where most of the finds from Briteiros were transferred. If you intend to visit the site, don't miss the museum. *Site open daily 9–6.*

Braga, fifteen kilometers (9 miles) north, is one of the outstanding surprises of northern Portugal. Its attractive city center is a delight to negotiate, featuring many fine buildings whose Baroque facades front on small squares and pedestrianized streets. A city of ancient origin, Braga prospered under the 6th-century Visigoths, when it became an important bishopric, marking the start of the religious authority it maintains today. Braga's later archbishops often wielded greater power than the Portuguese kings themselves. During the city's golden age, in the 16th century, Braga was beautified with churches, palaces, and fountains, many of which were subsequently altered (some say ruined) in the 18th century.

The city feels like the country's religious capital. Shops selling religious artifacts line the streets around the cathedral, and Braga hosts the most impressive of Portugal's Easter celebrations. It also has a conservative reputation, since it was at Braga that the military coup began that brought Salazar to power. However, Braga seems increasingly dynamic, both in its local economy and artistic life, and the city of 65,000 is growing fast. The preserved city center is now surrounded by noisy streets and apartment blocks, and traffic congestion is assuming legendary proportions.

The center of the old town is marked by the huge **Sé** (Cathedral), originally Romanesque in character but now an impressive blend of styles. The delicate Renaissance stone tracery on the roof is particularly eye-catching. Enter from the main Rua do Souto through the 18th-century cloister; the cathedral interior is on your left, and there are various interesting chapels. Steps by the entrance to the cathedral lead to the Museu de Arte Sacra, which has a fascinating collection of religious art and artifacts, including a 14th-century crystal cross set in bronze. From the magnificent *coro alto* (upper choir), which you cross as part of the treasury tour, there are views of the great Baroque double organ. Across the cloister, you'll see the *Capela dos Reis* (Kings' Chapel), a 14th-century chapel containing the tombs of Afonso Henriques's parents, Henry of Burgundy and his wife, Teresa. *Tel. 053/23317. Admission: cathedral free; treasury: 200$00. Open daily 8:30–12:30 and 2:30–6:30.*

Across narrow Rua do Souto from the cathedral is Largo do Paço. It is flanked by the impressive, well-proportioned **Paço dos Arcebispos** (Archbishop's Palace), which overlooks an attractive, castellated fountain. Parts of the building date from the 14th century. Today it's occupied by faculties from the city's university and functions as the public library, which is among the most impressive in the country, containing over 300,000 volumes.

The pedestrianized Rua Diogo de Sousa leads down from the cathedral and Archbishop's Palace to one of the city's former gateways, the 18th-century **Arco do Porta Nova.** Pass through here and turn right for the **Palácio dos Biscainhos** (Biscainhos Palace), a Baroque mansion typical of many in the city. The elegant rooms are furnished in 18th-century style and display silver and porcelain collections. Interestingly, the ground floor of the palace is stone flagged, which allowed carriages to run through the interior to the stables beyond. At the back of the palace is a formal garden with decorative tiles. *Rua dos Biscainhos, tel. 053/27645. Admission: 200$00. Open Tues.–Sun. 10–noon and 2–5:30.*

Walk back past the gateway to the area beyond the Igreja de São Sebastião (Church of Saint Sebastian). Here you'll find the **Zona Arqueologica** (Archaeological Zone), which contains the excavations of an old Roman city known as *Bracara Augusta* (The site isn't usually open to the public.) To the east, the Roman city stretched as far as the large Largo de São Tiago, where an imposing building contains the **Museu Pio XII e Medina** (Pio XII Museum). It contains two collections, one of religious works and the other of paintings and sculpture, though perhaps the most interesting elements of the museum are the few architectural and archaeological fragments gathered from local sites and churches. *Largo de São Tiago, tel. 053/23370. Admission: 150$00. Open Tues.–Sun. 10–12:30 and 3–6.*

From Largo de São Tiago, Rua do Anjo leads back toward the city center, eventually emerging at **Praça da República,** the square at the head of Braga's elongated central gardens. The west side of the square is arcaded, while behind it stands the dominating 14th-century tower, the **Torre de Menagem,** currently being restored.

Time Out There are two inexpensive cafés in the arcade at Praça da República, either of which makes a pleasant stop. **Café Astoria** is the most elegant, with mahogany-paneled walls, mirrors, marble tables, and a molded ceiling. **Café Vianna** has been in business since 1871 and serves a wider variety of snacks. It's also a good place for breakfast and offers views of the fountain and gardens. *Both cafés open 8 AM–11 PM.*

Many people visit Braga specifically to see the pilgrimage center of **Bom Jesus do Monte,** a 400-meter-high, densely wooded hill, 5 kilometers (3 miles) east of the city. Here, a stone staircase, started in 1723, climbs up to an 18th-century sanctuary-church, whose terrace commands wonderful views. But it's the stairway itself—a marvel of Baroque art—that is the most extraordinary attraction. Many pilgrims climb up on their knees. Fountains placed at various resting places represent the five senses and the virtues, and small chapels display a series of tableaux, with life-size figures illustrating the Stations of the Cross. If you don't want to climb up the staircase (which would be a pity!), you can take the funicular or drive up the winding road. There are restaurants, refreshment stands, and even a couple of hotels beside the sanctuary at the top. On weekends the area is popular with local families, who come here to picnic. Buses run every half hour from the center of Braga. *Funicular: 50$00.*

From Braga you can follow the N103 due west to the small market town of **Barcelos,** 20 kilometers (12 miles) away. Attractively situated on the banks of the Rio Cávado, Barcelos is the center of a flourishing handicrafts industry, particularly ceramics and wooden toys and models. It pays to come here if you plan to carry home a host of souvenirs. Unquestionably, the best time to visit is during the famous weekly **Feira de Barcelos** (Barcelos Market), a vast affair—the largest in the country—held every Thursday in the central Campo da República starting very early in the morning. Stalls appear overnight, and on market day the square resembles a small city, with rows of covered stalls selling mounds of vegetables, fruits, fresh bread and cakes, clothes, shoes, ceramics, leather, kitchen equipment, and almost anything else you can think of. At times, when the early mist rises off the ground and the cries of the vendors echo across the square, it seems almost medieval. This is the place to buy traditional Barcelos ceramics (brown pottery with yellow and white decoration) as well as more workaday earthenware, baskets, rugs, and figurines. From the Campo da República, Rua Dom António Barroso leads down through the old town toward the river. On the left, the former medieval town tower now houses the tourist office and the excellent **Centro Artesanato** (Artesan's Center), which brings together some of the best local handicrafts at very reasonable prices. Ceramic dishes and bowls, often signed with the artist's name, are a good buy. Figurines, too, are popular, though none approach the individuality of those made by the late Rosa Ramalho, a local potter whose work first made famous the ceramics of Barcelos. *Largo de Porta Nova, tel. 053/811882. Open Mon.–Sat. 9–5:30.*

The river, crossed by a medieval bridge, is the most attractive part of town, shaded by overhanging trees and bordered by municipal gardens. High above the river stands the ruin of the medieval Paço dos Condes (Palace of the Counts), whose grounds constitute the **Museu Arqueologico** (Archaeological Museum). Among the empty sarcophagi and stone crosses is the 14th-century crucifix known as the *Cruzeiro do Senhor do Galo* (Cross of the Gentleman of the Cock). According to a local legend, after sentencing an innocent man to death, a judge prepared to dine on a roast fowl. When the condemned man said, "I'll be hanged if that cock doesn't crow," it flew from the table. The Barcelos cock is on sale in pottery form throughout the town; indeed, it's become almost a national symbol. *Admission free. Open daily 10–noon and 2–6.*

Barcelos is just 54 kilometers (33½ miles) north of Oporto, to which it's connected by train. The quickest way back to Oporto by car is to follow the minor N205 south until you reach the N13, just north of Póvoa da Varzim. However, it's also enjoyable to stop overnight in Barcelos and, after the market, to move on to Viana do Castelo, which is covered in the next tour.

Tour 4: Costa Verde and the Minho and Lima Rivers

The coastline of Minho province, north of Oporto, is known as the **Costa Verde** (Green Coast), a largely unspoiled stretch of small towns and sandy beaches that runs all the way to the border with Spain. The weather in this northwestern region of Portugal is more inclement than elsewhere, a fact hinted at in its very name: The Costa Verde is green because it sees a disproportionate amount of rain. Summers can be cool, and swimming in the Atlantic is bracing at best. But visitors will find much of interest in a tour of the little-known region. Days spent at the coast can be alternated with trips inland, to medieval towns along the lush Ria Lima or through the historic border settlements along the Rio Minho. Most coastal towns are easily accessible by train from Oporto, and regular buses connect with the most interesting inland destinations. By car, a leisurely tour of the major points of interest could occupy three or four days.

Driving north on the N13, the first beach worth noting is at **Ofir,** on the south bank of the Rio Cávado estuary, 46 kilometers (29 miles) from Oporto. The sweeping white sands, dunes, pinewoods, and water sports have made this a popular resort in recent years. On the opposite bank of the river, **Esposende,** which also has a beach, retains elements of the small fishing village it once was. If you travel by train, you won't get to see either place, since the line runs inland at this point, passing through Barcelos (*see* Tour 3, *above*).

The train rejoins the coast at **Viana do Castelo,** 25 kilometers (15½ miles) farther north. An enjoyable resort at the mouth of the Ria Lima, it has been a prosperous trading center since it received its town charter in 1258. While you shouldn't miss the excellent local beach, Praia do Cabedelo (reached by ferry from the riverside at the end of the main street), there's plenty in town to occupy an inveterate stroller. Ask at the tourist office for their English-language brochure, which includes a walking tour of the town.

Many of Viana's finest buildings date from the 16th and 17th centuries, the period of its greatest prosperity, and the town's best face is presented in the old streets and squares that radiate from the charming Praça da República. The most striking building here is the **Misericórdia,** a 16th-century almshouse whose two upper stories are supported, unusually, by tall caryatids (carved, draped female figures). The stone fountain, also Renaissance in style, harmonizes perfectly with the surrounding buildings, which include the restored town hall and its lofty arcades.

Cross the main avenue, and take a 10-minute walk west to the **Museu Municipal** (Municipal Museum), housed in one of Viana's most impressive mansions. The early 18th-century interior has been carefully preserved, and the collection of 17th-century ceramics and ornate period furniture shows how wealthy many of Viana's merchants were. A little way beyond the museum are the great ramparts of the **Castelo de São Tiago da Barra,** the 16th-century fortification that added the words "do Castelo" to the town's name and protected Viana against attack from pirates eager to share in the town's wealth. Outside the walls Viana holds a large market every Friday. *Museum: Largo de São Domingos, tel. 058/24223. Admission: 100$00. Open Tues.–Sun. 10–noon and 2–5.*

An *elevador* (funicular railway) behind the train station climbs to the modern basilica of **Santa Luzia,** a white, domed building overlooking the town from its wooded heights. The views from the steps of the basilica are magnificent, and a staircase to the side (marked *Zimbório*) allows access to the very top of the dome for some extraordinary coastal views. Be warned that this steep climb, up a very narrow staircase to a little viewing platform, is for the agile only. *Estrada de Santa Luzia. Funicular: Cost: 60$00; operates 10–7, every 30 min. Basilica: Open 10–noon and 2–6. Admission to dome: 25$00.*

Leaving Viana, both the train and the road (N13) continue north, following the coast, and pass a succession of small villages with delightful beaches. There are good stretches of sand at the local resorts of **Vila Praia de Âncora** and **Moledo,** but if you keep your eyes open, you'll find some side roads that lead to fairly isolated beaches.

31 At **Caminha** you reach the Rio Minho, which forms the border with Spain. The fortified town hall on the main square once formed part of Caminha's defenses. There's a 16th-century clock tower in the square, too, while the nearby **Igreja Matriz** (Parish Church) dates from a century earlier, when Caminha was an important trading port. The rich interior of the church and the surviving mansions in the surrounding streets are reminders of the town's former wealth, but by the 17th century Caminha had lost much of its business to flourishing Viana do Castelo.

32 **Vila Nova de Cerveira,** twelve kilometers (7½ miles) farther up the river, has a medieval castle that has been converted into a luxurious pousada (government-run inn): the Pousada de Dom

Dinis (*see* Dining and Lodging, *below*). A minor ferry crossing
㉝ connects to the Spanish town of Goian, but it's **Valença do
Minho,** another 15 kilometers (9 miles) northeast, that is the
major crossing point, with road-and-rail service to Spain. The
old town of Valença is enclosed by perfectly preserved walls,
which face the similarly defended Spanish town of Tuy. Strolling along the river and ramparts is very pleasant—even more
so in the evening, when the day-trippers from Spain have re-
treated to their own side of the river. As at Vila Nova de
Cerveira, Valença's fortifications contain a pousada, from
which there are fine river views.

Beyond Valença, the N101 leads east 16 kilometers (10 miles) to
㉞ the riverside town of **Monção.** Once again, this is a fortified border settlement with a long history of skirmishes with the Spanish. In town there are the remains of a 14th-century castle,
which withstood a desperate siege in 1368, when a local woman
baked some small cakes with the last of the flour and sent them
to the Spaniards with the message that there was plenty more
where that came from. The bluff worked, the Spanish re-
treated, and the little cakes are still on sale in town in honor of
the event. There is a spa to the east of Monção, which attracts
some tourists, but the town is generally peaceful. If you stop,
try a glass of the local vinho verde, a noteworthy wine available
in several bars.

South of Monção the N101 traverses glorious rural countryside
before descending to the valley of the Rio Vez, a tributary of the
㉟ Lima. **Arcos de Valdevez,** 35 kilometers (22 miles) south of
Monção, makes a nice stop. It is a typically serene little river
town, where you can rent rowboats for a closer look at the surroundings.

Five kilometers (3 miles) farther south you arrive at the **Rio
Lima** itself, one of the most beautiful rivers in the country. It
was known to the Romans as the River of Oblivion, because its
blissful beauty was said to make travelers forget their home.
You may not fall into the same reverie as the Romans, but two
towns along the river do make very enjoyable stops. You'll pass
both if you continue south to the N203 and travel west back toward Viana do Castelo.

㊱ At the old town of **Ponte da Barca,** the *ponte* in question is a
beautiful, 10-arched bridge, built in the 15th century. At the
junction of four main roads, the small town has been an important market center for centuries, and the Tuesday market here
is well worth catching. On other days you can spend time quite
happily walking along the riverbank.

㊲ **Ponte de Lima,** eighteen kilometers (11 miles) down the road, is
as delightful a town as you're likely to come across in the region. The graceful bridge here is of Roman origin, long and
low, and open only to foot traffic; drivers cross a new concrete
bridge at the edge of town. The square tower near the old
bridge still stands guard over the town, while beyond, in the
narrow streets, there are several fine 16th-century mansions
and a busy market. Walking around town, you'll return again
and again to the river, which is the real highlight of a visit. A
wide beach usually displays lines of drying laundry, and a riverside avenue lined with plane trees leads down to the Renaissance church of São Antonio. The twice-monthly Monday
market, held on the riverbank, is the oldest in Portugal, dating

back to 1125. On market days and during the New Fairs festival in mid-September, also held since the 12th century, you'll see the town at its effervescent best.

Time Out   The main square by the old bridge in Ponte de Lima has a central fountain and benches and is ringed by little cafés. It's a perfect place to stop for a leisurely drink.

From Ponte de Lima you have your choice of routes. To the west lies Viana do Castelo (23 kilometers [14 miles]), Valença do Minho is to the north (38 kilometers [24 miles]), and Braga is to the south (33 kilometers [20½ miles]). Buses run to all these places from the town's bus station, by the market. To the east is Ponte da Barca, and 30 kilometers (19 miles) beyond that is the village of Lindoso, a point of entry for the Peneda-Gerês National Park (*see* National Park, *below*).

Tour 5: Trás-os-Montes

The remote and beautiful region of Trás-os-Montes, in Portugal's extreme northeast, attracts very few foreign visitors. The name means "Beyond the Mountains," and though new roads have made it easier to reach in recent years, exploring the region still requires a certain sense of adventure. Great distances separate the fascinating towns, and twisting roads can drive you to the point of distraction. Medieval villages exist in a landscape that alternates between splendor and harshness, and the population, thinned by emigration, retains rural customs that have all but disappeared elsewhere. Having a car is obviously the easiest way to tour the region, but driving exclusively would mean missing out on some of the finest train journeys in the country. The trip from Oporto to Bragança provides an excellent opportunity to see the changing landscape, but it is slow going. Trains stop at every village, and the entire journey, a distance of 280 kilometers (174 miles), takes eight to nine hours.

38 **Vila Real** is the first sizeable town in the province you'll come to if traveling inland from Oporto. By train you'll need to change at Peso da Régua (*see* Tour 2, *above*) to the Corgo branch line, which ends at Vila Real. The capital of Trás-os-Montes, it is superbly situated between two mountain ranges and boasts the only significant industry in the northeast—along with which have come modern suburbs and a traffic-choked center. Still, Vila Real retains a pleasant, small-town air. Although there's no great wealth of sights, it's worth stopping in town to stroll down the attractive central avenue, which ends at a rocky promontory poking out over the gushing Rio Corgo below. A path around the church at the head of the promontory provides views of stepped terraces and green slopes. At the southern end of the avenue, a few narrow streets are filled with 17th- and 18th-century houses, their entrances decorated with coats of arms. The finest Baroque work in town is the **Capel dos Clérigos**, also called the Capela Nova (New Chapel). This is a curious fan-shape building set between two heavy columns. *Between Rua 31 de Janeiro and Rua Direita. Admission free. Open daily 10–noon and 2–6.*

An exceptional Baroque mansion built in the mid-18th century, the **Solar de Mateus** is 4 kilometers (2½ miles) east of town. Its U-shape facade with high, decorated finials at each corner (which adorns the Mateus Rosé wine label) is recognized world-wide. The building is believed to have been designed by Nasoni (architect of Oporto's Clérigos Tower), and, typically, the huge portal is approached by a double staircase. Set back to one side is the chapel, with an even more extravagant facade. The elegant interior is open to the public, as are the formal gardens, which are enhanced by a cypress tunnel, with trees trained to shade the path. *N322, Sabrosa road, Mateus, tel. 059/323121. Admission: 350$00. Open for guided tours daily 9–1 and 2–6.*

The **Sogrape** winery, just before the mansion, offers tours of its premises. At the end of the tour, you'll have an opportunity to taste the wine and perhaps purchase a bottle. *Circuito Internacional, tel. 059/323074. Admission free. Open weekdays 10–noon and 2–5.*

The main road northeast of Vila Real (the N15) has recently been straightened for much of its length. You'll drive through exceptionally fine, high countryside; rolling, arable land continues as far as **Murça,** 40 kilometers (25 miles) away. Here you'll see the largest of the Iron Age porcas (stone pigs), which are found all over the region. This particular granite boar stands on a plinth in the town's central square and is presumed to be a fertility symbol.

Thirty-one kilometers (19 miles) farther northeast, is **Mirandela,** midway between Vila Real and Bragança and the point at which the train route meets the road. Train travelers from Vila Real will have to return to the main line at Peso da Régua and then change at Tua, to the east, to reach Mirandela. The train runs through superb country, following the course of the Rio Tua, a tributary of the Douro. Mirandela, an attractive town, has a medieval bridge with 17 arches, but its grandest monument is the 17th-century **Palacio dos Tavoras** (Tavora Palace), right in the center of town. Its great facade has elaborate pediments and Baroque ornaments. Once the residence of the famous Tavora family, it's now used as the town hall.

Beyond Mirandela the road passes through groves of poplars and willows before climbing into the Serra de Nogueira (Nogueira Mountains). Eventually the great castle at **Bragança** appears in the distance. An ancient town in the very northeastern corner of Portugal, Bragança has been inhabited since Celtic times (from about 600 BC). The town lent its name to the noble family of Bragança (or Braganza), whose most famous member, Catherine, married Charles II of England. Descendants of the family ruled Portugal until 1910; their tombs are contained within the church of São Vicente de Fora in Lisbon (*see* Chapter 3). Unfortunately, the approaches to Bragança have been spoiled by many ugly new buildings, since improved roads have encouraged development.

Above the modern town rises the magnificent, 12th-century **Castelo** (Castle) and a ring of battlemented walls that surrounds a perfectly preserved medieval village—one of the most thrilling sights in Trás-os-Montes. This citadel developed as the medieval community drew close to its castle for protection, and within the walls you'll find the **Domus Municipalis** (City Hall), a rare Romanesque civic building dating from the 12th century. If it's closed, the key can be obtained from one of the local cottages, as can the key to the 18th-century **Igreja de Santa Maria** (Church of Saint Mary), which has a superb painted ceiling. Another prehistoric granite boar stands below the castle tower, this one with a medieval stone pillory sprouting from its back. The tower itself, the **Torre de Menagem,** now contains a military museum, well worth visiting for the opportunity to imagine yourself fighting off a besieging army from the castle walls. *Castle and walls always open. Tower and museum: tel. 073/22378; open daily 10–noon and 2–5.*

On your way back down to town, along this route, you'll pass the Renaissance **Igreja de São Bento,** with a fine Mudejar (Moorish-style) vaulted ceiling and a recently regilded retable. The church may or may not be open. Farther along, however, you can be assured of entry to the excellent **Museu do Abade de Baçal,** housed in Bragança's former bishop's palace. The exhibits were collected by a local priest, the Abade de Baçal, who died in 1947, and include more prehistoric pigs, ancient tombstones, some nice furniture, local costumes, fine silver, coins, and paintings—anything that caught the priest's eye. *Museum: Rua do Consilheiro Abílio Beca 27, tel. 073/23242. Admission: 100$00. Open Tues.–Sun. 10–12:30 and 2–5.*

Once you've seen the castle and nearby buildings, you've seen almost everything Bragança has to offer. The central cathedral is unusually small and disappointing, but the modern town center is attractive in its way, with a wide central avenue and several cafés that open onto the sidewalk in summer. You'll easily exhaust all the local sights in under a day, but it's worth staying overnight for the views of the castle from the pousada on the outskirts of town (*see* Dining and Lodging, *below*).

The N103 runs west from Bragança toward Chaves. One of the most spectacular roads in the country, it winds through bleak uplands, with the mountains of Spain to the north and the distant mass of the Serra da Estrela (Estrela Mountains) to the south. After 31 kilometers (19 miles), you'll arrive at **Vinhais,** which provides a welcome break. Its most notable sight is the great Baroque facade of the former **Convento de São Francisco** (Convent of St. Francis). Shortly before reaching Chaves, you'll see the ruins of the 13th-century **Castelo do Monforte** (Monforte Castle), built upon the site of an earlier Roman fort, a remote outpost of the great empire.

43 **Chaves,** 96 kilometers (59½ miles) west of Bragança, was known to the Romans as Aquae Flaviae (Flavian's Waters), in honor of the emperor Flavian. They established a military base here and popularized the town's thermal springs, which are still in use today. The impressive, 16-arch Roman bridge across the Rio Tâmega, at the southern end of town, dates from the first century AD and displays two original Roman milestones. Today Chaves is characterized most by a series of fortifications built during late-medieval times, when the city was prone to attack from all quarters. The town lies only 12 kilometers (7½ miles) from the Spanish border. Its name means "keys"; whoever controlled Chaves held the keys to the north of the country.

Of the three surviving defensive structures, the most obvious landmark is the great, blunt fortress overlooking the river, the 14th-century **Torre de Menagem.** As at Bragança, this now houses a military museum, and its grounds offer views of the town. The tower is surrounded by narrow, winding streets filled with elegant houses, most of which have lovely ironwork balconies on their top floors. In Praça de Camões, the main square below the tower, the late 17th-century **Igreja da Misericórdia** (Misericórdia Church) is lined with huge panels of blue-and-white azulejos that depict scenes from the New Testament. Adjacent to this, the **Museu da Regiao Flaviense** (Regional Museum) is thoroughly recommended; it contains an indiscriminate hodgepodge of local archaeological finds and relics that tell the town's history. *Tower: Largo da Câmara Municipal de Chaves, tel. 076/21965; open daily 9-noon and 2-5. Museum: open Tues.-Fri. 9:30-12:30 and 2-5, weekends 2-4:30.*

The spa buildings are contained within the **Parque Termal** (Thermal Park), below the tower and close to the river. Local legend has it that the hot water here was cast up from the entrails of the underworld, which is exactly what a mouthful tastes like, so be warned. *Largo das Termas, tel. 076/21446. Open Apr.-Oct., daily 9-5.*

At Chaves you have a choice of routes to the south and west. The N2, south to Vila Real, is a glorious road down the Corgo valley. It used to be accessible by train, but that part of the Corgo branch line has been closed, leaving only the short section to the south of Vila Real (*see above*). Alternatively, you may continue west along the N103; after 35 kilometers (22 miles) begins an enormous system of lakes and hydroelectric dams along the Rio Cávado. At this point it's possible to make a short side trip to see the ruined castle at **Montalegre**, which is visible from miles around. Take a right turn onto the N308, and drive for 12 kilometers (7½ miles). The views are worth the detour.

Back on the N103, you'll follow along the edge of the great lake system, skirting drowned valleys in an endless series of long loops. Allow plenty of time, because you're sure to want to stop often to take in the incredible views. To the north is the Peneda-Gerês National Park; there are occasional access points along the road (*see* National Park, *below*). Finally, after passing the village of Cerdeirinhas, the road runs for 30 kilometers (19 miles) through rocky heights and down tree-clad slopes to reach Braga, where you are firmly in Minho province and back in civilization.

What to See and Do with Children

The north of Portugal is not the most obvious choice for a place to travel with children. Away from Oporto and the Costa Verde, facilities of all kinds—not just for children—are often limited. Hotels are comfortable enough, but they generally don't offer the range of distractions, such as pools and game rooms, that children enjoy. Traveling distances, especially in Trás-os-Montes, require long hours spent in a car or on a train. However, on balance, it's worth the occasional trying journey in order to introduce children to the unspoiled delights of the north.

In Oporto (*see* Tour 1, *above*), children will enjoy the climb to and view from the **Torre dos Clérigos** and the toys and other artifacts at the **Museu de Etnografia e Historia.** Have lunch in the **Cais da Ribeira district,** where you can watch the river as you eat, and then walk across the exciting **Ponte Dom Luis I bridge** (watch the traffic). Children are usually welcome on the tours of **Vila Nova de Gaia's** port-wine lodges, which show off their huge warehouses and all sorts of interesting machinery. (Double-check with the tourist office first.)

The **beaches** of the Atlantic and the many northern rivers provide some great entertainment (*see* Beaches, *below*, and Tours 2 and 4, *above*). In addition to swimming, children can enjoy boating at several river towns. During the summer Amarante (*see* Tour 2, *above*) has rowboats and pedal boats for rent along a particularly beautiful stretch of river.

In a border region dotted with ancient defenses, there are plenty of **castles** to visit, some of them so complete as to provide a virtual medieval playground. The best include those at Guimarães (*see* Tour 3, *above*), Monção (*see* Tour 4, *above*), and Bragança and Chaves (*see* Tour 5, *above*). Don't miss the region's two vast ornamental staircases, good for clambering up, at the pilgrimage sights of Lamego (*see* Tour 2, *above*) and Bom Jesus do Monte (*see* Tour 3, *above*).

The busy **markets** of the Minho are fascinating, and children will love the noises and smells of a genuine local affair. All sell food, toys, and games, in addition to handicrafts and clothes. The best is the weekly market at Barcelos, but there are smaller ones at Viana do Castelo, Ponte de Lima, and Ponte da Barca (*see* Shopping, *below*).

Off the Beaten Track

In the west of Oporto, beyond the range of the walking tour, is the **Museu Nacional de Arte Moderna** (Museum of Modern Art), run by the Gulbenkian Foundation, which administers a similar collection in Lisbon. The museum occupies the Serralves mansion, set on impressive grounds, and displays the work of a representative selection of modern Portuguese painters, sculptors, and designers. Exhibitions change constantly, and the museum closes for two weeks at a time for rehanging. Check with the tourist office for the latest information. You can take either a taxi or bus No. 78, which takes 30 minutes from the town center and passes the Palácio de Cristal. *Rua de Serralves 977, tel. 02/680057. Admission: 250$00. Open Tues.–Sun. 2–8.*

Also take time to visit the **Igreja de São Martinho da Cedofeita** (Church of Saint Martin), north of the city center, near the main Av. da Boavista. It was rebuilt in the 12th century from the remains of a mid-6th-century church erected by the Suevi king Theodomir. Suevi was an early tribe, originally from Germany, that settled in northern Portugal. Some claim this is one of the oldest Christian buildings in Europe, but because of the rebuilding, points of architectural interest are few. *Cedofeita* means "built quickly," and it's assumed that the church was erected in a hurry to house the relics of Saint Martin. *Rua de Anibal Cunha, tel. 02/200–0635. Admission free. Open daily 10–noon and 2–5.*

Trás-os-Montes (*see* Tour 5, *above*) is remote to begin with, but the minor roads running south of Bragança to the Spanish border are even more isolated. The N218 leads through high, cultivated country to **Miranda do Douro;** it's a winding, 84-kilometer (52-mile) journey that takes the better part of two hours. Miranda do Douro is a small town with a Renaissance cathedral and cobbled streets. It has an excellent pousada, where you can stop before crossing into Spain: Zamora is due east. Back in

Portugal the N221 shadows the frontier for the 50-kilometer (31-mile) drive southwest to **Mogadouro,** formerly a border stronghold and now a market town with a 13th-century tower. Continue south for 46 kilometers (29 miles), and you'll reach the oddly named town **Freixo de Espada à Cinta** (Ash Tree of the Girded Sword), which retains a tall defensive tower and a fine parish church. Or turn off the N221 14 kilometers (9 miles) before Freixo, and take the N220 to **Torre de Moncorvo,** which surrounds an enormous church with a high, solid tower. Just to the north you can pick up the main N102, which eventually joins the N15, running between Vila Real and Bragança. Alternatively, you could wander westward through the network of minor roads that flank the Rio Douro until you reach Peso da Régua.

Shopping

The North is an excellent region in which to shop for souvenirs, with a wide range of crafts available in many towns and villages. Oporto, of course, has the best selection of shops, but don't miss the smaller towns of the Minho, which often specialize in particular handicrafts. The region's weekly and monthly markets are also famous throughout Portugal, for here you can buy some of the best local crafts at very reasonable prices. The main post office in Oporto can help you send gifts overseas.

Barcelos

The great Thursday **market** at Barcelos is the place to purchase ceramics, glazed figurines (including the famous Barcelos cock), basketry, and wooden toys. There's also a handicrafts center in the old town tower, which houses the tourist office. (*See* Tour 3, *above.*)

Braga and Guimarães

In Braga, many shops in the pedestrianized streets around the cathedral sell **religious artifacts,** from candles to statues. The town's weekly market is on Tuesday. Guimarães, nearby, is a center for the local **linen** industry. The linen is hand spun and handwoven, then embroidered, all to impressive effect; it is available in local shops. Here the weekly market is on Friday.

Oporto

New **shopping centers** are a feature of Oporto's burgeoning commercial life. One of the best, with lots of shops on several floors, is the **Centro Comercial de Brasileira** (Av. da Boavista), in the city's northwest, or try **Centro Comercial Dallas** (Av. da Boavista 1588).

Excellent shopping can also be found in the downtown streets off the central Praça da Liberdade—particularly on Rua 31 de Janeiro, Rua dos Clérigos, Rua de Santa Catarina, Rua Sá da Bandeira, and Rua das Flores. Traditionally, Rua das Flores has been the street for **silversmiths. Pedro A. Baptista** (Rua das Flores 235) deals in antique and modern silver. **Gold-plated filigree** is also a regional specialty, and examples are numerous along the same street and along Rua de Santa Catarina. Rua 31 de Janeiro and nearby streets are the center of the **shoe** trade and many shops make made-to-measure shoes upon request. For a general **handicrafts** emporium, try **Artesanato dos Clérigos** (Rua da Assunção 33, next to the Clérigos Tower). The **Artesanato Centro Regional de Artes Tradicionais** (Center for Traditional Arts), at Rua da Reboleira 37, in the Cais da Ribeira district, sells an excellent selection of regional arts and crafts. For a good general **market,** visit the **Bolhão** market, off Rua Sá da Bandeira (closed Sun.). There's a daily **flea market** in the streets below the cathedral, particularly lively on Calçada Vandoma.

You'll see **port** on sale throughout the city. First taste the wine at either the Solar do Vinho do Porto or the lodges at Vila Nova de Gaia (*see* Tour 1, *above*). You may want to buy a bottle of the more unusual white port, drunk chilled as an aperitif, as it's not commonly sold in the United States or Britain.

Trás-os-Montes

Both Chaves and Bragança have locally made **ceramics.** Also in Bragança, there's a good **crafts** shop within the walls of the citadel. In Vila Real you can purchase some of the world-famous, slightly sparkling **wine** from the winery close to the Solar de Mateus (*see* Tour 5, *above*).

Viana do Castelo

Viana is regarded as the folk capital of the region and specializes in producing traditional **embroidered costumes,** which are worn at its most important festivals. These make colorful souvenirs, though the town also sells less elaborate **crafts,** including ceramics, lace, and jewelry. The large Friday market is a good place to shop, and the tourist office also displays a nice selection.

Vila do Conde and Póvoa de Varzim

Vila do Conde is known for its **lace** and has supported a lace-making school since the beginning of the century. The town also produces excellent hand-knit and embroidered **sweaters,** which are on sale here and in neighboring Póvoa de Varzim. An international handicrafts exhibition takes place in Vila do Conde every year, usually at the end of July.

Sports and Outdoor Activities

Participant Sports

Canoeing There's canoeing on the Rio Cávado near Braga. Contact the **Clube Nautico de Prado** (Prado, tel. 053/921101).

Fishing Inland, especially in the northeast, fishing is a traditional leisure activity. The best freshwater fishing is in the Lima and Minho rivers, where trout can be caught. Local tourist offices can assist with fishing licenses, or contact Direcção Geral dos Desportos (tel. 02/666227) in Oporto.

Golf There are two golf clubs at resorts south of Oporto. The 18-hole **Oporto Golf Club** (Pedreira-Silvalde, tel. 02/722008) is 2 kilometers (1¼ miles) south of Espinho; the **Miramar Golf Club** (Praia de Miramar, tel. 02/762–2067) has nine holes and is a few kilometers farther north.

Swimming Swimming pools are not standard in northern hotels, other than along the Costa Verde and in the largest of the region's other hotels. If you want to stay at a hotel with a pool, check the facilities in Dining and Lodging, *below*, and book accordingly. There are public pools in Barcelos, Braga, Bragança, Chaves, Oporto, Viana do Castelo, and Vila Real.

Spectator Sport

Soccer As in Lisbon, the main sporting obsession in Oporto is soccer, and the city has one of the country's best teams, **FC Oporto**, which rivals Lisbon's Benfica for domestic fame and fortune. Matches are played September through May at the Antas Stadium (Av. de Fernão de Magalhães, tel. 02/410–5844) in the east of the city; Bus Nos. 6, 78, and 88 run past it. The other team in the region to watch is **Guimarães,** a small soccer club that has enjoyed unexpected success in recent years.

Beaches

Swimming in the Atlantic can be very cold, even at the height of summer, and beaches along the Costa Verde are notoriously windswept. More pleasant is river swimming in the small towns along the Lima and Minho rivers, though take local advice about currents and pollution before plunging in. Ponte de Lima has a particularly nice wide, sandy beach.

Espinho, south of Oporto, and the main Costa Verde resorts to the north (Póvoa de Varzim and Ofir) are the best places for water-sports enthusiasts. Equipment rental is usually available at the beaches, or inquire at local tourist offices. (For details on particular ocean beaches, *see* Tours 2 and 4, *above;* for river beaches, *see* Tour 4, *above.*)

National Park

Northeast of Braga, the 172,900-acre **Parque Nacional da Peneda-Gerês** (Peneda-Gerês National Park) was created in 1970 to preserve the diverse flora and fauna that exist in the region. Even just a short trip to the main towns and villages contained within the park shows you wild stretches of land framed by mountains, great woods and lakes, and the peaceful beauty of a region allowed to live a traditional, unmolested life.

Bordered to the north by the frontier with Spain, the park is divided into two sections: a northern area encompassing the **Serra da Peneda** (Peneda Mountains), and a southern area around the **Serra do Gerês** (Gerês Mountains). Access is free, and accommodations are concentrated mostly in the attractive spa town of **Caldas do Gerês,** in the southern section. It's a two-hour drive from Braga; turn off the N103 just after Cerdeirinhas, along the N304. (There are buses, too.) To see the northern part of the park, it's best to come from Melgaço, a small town on the Rio Minho, 25 kilometers (15½ miles) east of Monção. From Melgaço, it's 27 kilometers (17 miles) on the

N202 to the village of Castro Laboreiro, at the northernmost point of the park. There's just one small hotel—and lots of fine, long-distance hiking. The central region of the park is accessible from Ponte da Barca, from which the N203 leads to Lindoso, or from Arcos de Valdevez, from which the minor N202 leads to the little village of Soajo. Both offer basic accommodations and superb hiking.

General information about the park is available at tourist offices in Oporto, Braga, and Caldas do Gerês. There's also a park information center at Caldas do Gerês, which can provide a walking map and more specific hints and help.

Dining and Lodging

Dining This chapter covers various regions, each with its own cuisine. The cooking in Oporto is rich and heavy. It is typified by the city's favorite dish, *tripas á moda do Porto* (Oporto tripe), which is made with beans, chicken, sausage, vegetables, and spices to make a heavy concoction suitable for winter. So fond are the locals of tripe that elsewhere in Portugal they're known as *tripeiros* (tripe-eaters)—a nickname earned when the city was under siege during the Napoleonic Wars and tripe was the only meat available. However, tripe doesn't dominate the menu in Oporto, and dishes tend to resemble those served in the Minho region. *Caldo verde* (literally "green soup") is ubiquitous; it's made of potato and shredded kale (cabbage) in a broth and is usually served with a slice or two of *chouriço* sausage. Fresh fish is found all the way up the coast, and every town has a local recipe for *bacalhau* (dried cod); in the Minho it's often cooked with potatoes, onions, and eggs. *Lampreias* (lampreys), oily, eel-like fish, are found in Minho rivers from February to April and are a particular specialty of Monção. Pork is the meat most often seen on menus, appearing in inventive stews and sausages, though *cabrito* (kid) is popular, too, served roasted.

In the mountains there is little fish and shellfish to offer, except for the wonderful *truta* (trout), available at any town or village close to a river. Trás-os-Montes menus are enlivened by hearty meat stews, which usually include various parts of the pig you may wish had been left out (turning up an ear or a trotter is common!). Sausages are a better bet, particularly *alheira* or chouriço, the spicy, smoked variety. The other smoked specialty of the region is *presunto de Chaves*, a delicious smoked ham from Chaves.

The wine available throughout the North is of very high quality. The Minho region is home to vinho verde, a light, slightly sparkling red or white wine that is drunk young. The taste is refreshing, both fruity and acid. Both reds and whites are served chilled (most people prefer the white), and vinho verde goes exceptionally well with fish and shellfish. Port is, of course, the most famous of the local wines (ask for *vinho do Porto*). Try a chilled white port as an aperitif. Other good regions for wine include the area around Chaves, particularly at Valpaços, which produces some excellent reds.

On the whole, restaurants in Oporto and the North offer extremely good value. Aside from a very few restaurants (noted below) dress throughout the region is informal, and reservations are usually unnecessary; often, they do not accept credit cards.

Restaurant ratings correspond to Lisbon's dining chart, in Chapter 3. Highly recommended restaurants are indicated by a star ★.

Lodging Most of the lodgings in the Minho and Trás-os-Montes are very reasonably priced compared to their counterparts elsewhere in the country—perhaps a reflection of the previous lack of attention paid by tourists to these regions. In Oporto, however, matters are much the same as in Lisbon, and, if at all possible, you should reserve a room well in advance to avoid disappointment. The North also hosts some of the country's most famous festivals and markets, at which times the sources of available lodging quickly dry up. For these dates (*see* Arts and Nightlife, *below*), book rooms well in advance.

The **Turismo de Habitação** (Manor House Tourism) system allows visitors to spend time at a variety of private, historic manor houses and country farms scattered throughout the Minho. Most of these converted 17th- and 18th-century buildings are found in the lovely rural areas around Ponte de Lima. The nearby Ria Lima provides guests with opportunities to walk, fish, and swim. You will also find manor house accommodations near Barcelos, Caminha, Guimarães, Monção, and Viana do Castelo. Reservations have to be made in advance through *Turihab* (Praça da República, 4990 Ponte de Lima, tel. 058/942335 or 058/942729, fax 058/941864), and bookings are for a minimum stay of three nights at each house. The cost includes bed and breakfast, although some manor houses will also arrange other meals on request. Full addresses and descriptions of the houses in the system are available from Turihab, and there is some information in the Ponte de Lima entry (*see below*).

Hotel ratings correspond to Lisbon's lodging chart, in Chapter 3. Highly recommended lodgings are indicated by a star ★.

Amarante **Zé da Calçada.** Situated on the town's narrow main street, this
Dining restaurant specializes in regional food, including a traditional baked bacalhau (dried salt cod) dish that takes the restaurant's name. Sweets and wines are local, too. A very elegant reception area leads into a comfortable dining room decorated in homey fashion; there's a fireplace, too, and a terrace that provides admirable riverside views. If you're taken with the decor, there are a few similarly turned-out, inexpensive rooms available. *Rua 31 de Janeiro, tel. 055/422023. Reservations advised. MC, V. Expensive.*

Restaurante Estoril. This simple, family-run restaurant makes a good lunch stop. It features river views from its windows and summer terrace and serves up plenty of good-value, standard Portuguese dishes. There's a short local wine list, and service is cheerful and friendly. The English-speaking owner also has some inexpensive rooms available on the other side of the river. *Rua 31 de Janeiro 49, tel. 055/422291. No credit cards. Inexpensive.*

Dining and Lodging **Pousada de São Gonçalo.** The small, modern São Gonçalo pousada lies 16 kilometers (10 miles) east of Amarante on the road to Vila Real. Located in the Serra do Marão at an altitude of nearly 3,000 feet, it offers wonderful views. The rugged terrain outside is matched by rustic decor within, and the pousada has lovely wood furniture, a large fireplace, and tile floors.

Having worked up an appetite in the hills, you can count on the restaurant to satisfy you with good, hearty, regional cooking. *Curva do Lancete, Ansiães, 4600 Amarante, tel. 055/461113. 15 rooms with bath. Facilities: restaurant, bar, parking. AE, DC, MC, V. Inexpensive.*

Lodging **Hotel Navarras.** A new three-star hotel (according to the Portuguese rating system), the Navarras is part of a modern shopping complex in the center of Amarante, a five-minute walk from the river. Decor throughout is smart and up-to-date, though unexceptional, and service is competent. Given the local river pollution, which prevents swimming, perhaps the greatest attraction is the hotel's covered pool. *Rua Antonio Carneiro, 4600, tel. 055/424036, fax 055/425891. 58 rooms with bath. Facilities: restaurant, bar, pool, shops, garage. AE. Inexpensive.*

Hotel Silva. This modest, friendly hotel lies on the road past the convent. Rooms in the back have French windows opening on a long balcony with splendid views of the river and adjacent gardens; there's also a pretty terrace for calm contemplation of the river. The interior has seen better days, though the simply furnished rooms remain comfortable, and bathrooms are functional. Breakfast is the only meal served, taken outside on the terrace in summer. *Rua Cândido dos Reis 53, 4600, tel. 055/423110. 21 rooms, 7 with bath. Facilities: riverside terrace. No credit cards. Inexpensive.*

Barcelos
Dining and Lodging
★

Pensão Bagoeira. The Bagoeira is a genuine and friendly old inn on the edge of the main square, perfect for a night's rest before an early visit to the Thursday market. The few large, bright rooms are individually furnished, with some nice old pieces, and there's a spotless bathroom down the hall. Downstairs, the excellent country restaurant does a fast and furious business on market day, as the vendors call in for a bowl of warming soup. Dishes are prepared in full view on a huge range, with all the spluttering flames and hisses that entails. Decor is rustic to the point of parody, with a wood ceiling, great metal chandeliers, and fresh flowers at every turn. Specialties include homemade corn bread, good vegetable soup, and any number of meat and fish grills, including tasty cod steaks. *Av. Dr. Sidonio Pais 495, 4750, tel. 053/811236. 6 rooms share bath. Facilities: restaurant, bar. Restaurant reservations advised for Thurs. lunch; room reservations advised, especially for Wed. night. No credit cards. Inexpensive.*

Braga
Dining
★

A Ceia. One of the city's best finds, A Ceia is a truly local haunt, with crowds of regulars digging into vast helpings of authentic Portuguese food. As the restaurant fills up, service becomes frenetic, but it's always friendly and lively. Try the spit-roasted chicken platter, and save room for one of the homemade desserts; the almond cake is good. There's a short list of reasonably priced local wines. If you haven't reserved a table and don't want to wait in line, it's possible to eat diner-style at the long bar. *Rua do Raio, tel. 053/23932. Reservations advised after 8 PM Fri. and Sat. No credit cards. Closed Mon. Moderate.*

Restaurante Inácio. Just outside the 18th-century town gate, the Arco da Porta Nova, this appealing restaurant emphasizes locally inspired dishes. Bacalhau is a favorite, and there's usually roasted *cabrito* (kid), too. The house wine is just fine, or try one of the other local wines that appear on the decent wine list. Service in the stone-clad interior is brisk and efficient.

Campo das Hortas 4, tel. 053/22355. Reservations advised. AE, DC, MC, V. Closed Mon. Moderate.

Lodging **Hotel de Turismo.** Braga is not well endowed with hotels, and the Turismo is among the best of a rather poor selection. It's a smart high rise located on a main road, just a few minutes away from the old town. Everything is uncompromisingly modern, from the soaring lobby to the spacious rooms, whose balconies provide views of the downtown traffic. There's a comfortable bar, a good restaurant, and the bonus of a rooftop pool. *Praceta João XXI, Av. da Liberdade, 4700, tel. 053/612200, fax 053/612211. 132 rooms with bath. Facilities: restaurant, bar, pool, parking. AE, DC, MC, V. Moderate.*

Residencial Inácio Filho. This central, old-town *residencial* (guest house)—a two-minute walk from the cathedral—is a wonderful bargain. A friendly private home, the well-cared-for building is decorated with antiques and bric-a-brac: Bellows, old typewriters, and porcelain lie side by side on the polished wooden floors and staircase. The few, simple rooms are spotless, if rather bare. There are no facilities, but many cafés and restaurants are within easy walking distance. Be sure to reserve in advance for a summer visit. *Rua Francisco Sanches 42–2, 4700, tel. 053/23849. 8 rooms, 6 with bath. No credit cards. Inexpensive.*

Bragança **La Em Casa.** This low-key but attractive, rustic town-center
Dining restaurant lies between the castle and the cathedral. It serves regional Portuguese food with—unusual this far inland—a decent menu of fish and shellfish. These are expensive, though. A more moderately priced meal can be had by picking from the extensive selection of meat dishes, and there's a particularly reasonable tourist menu available, too. *Rua Marquês de Pombal, tel. 073/22111. Reservations advised. AE, DC, MC, V. Closed Mon. Moderate–Expensive.*

Dining and Lodging **Pousada de São Bartolomeu.** Bragança's pousada is located on a
★ hill just to the west of the town center and offers terrific views of the citadel. It's a modern building, though very comfortable; its bar and lounge feature an open fireplace and wooden furnishings. Guest rooms are rustically decorated and have scenic balconies. The pousada is a few kilometers from the town and its restaurants, but it doesn't matter, since the formal dining room is the best in Bragança. It serves fine regional mountain cooking, including good stews and game. This would make an excellent first-night's stop if you have just crossed from the Spanish border, to the east. *Estrada do Turismo, 5300, tel. 073/22493, fax 073/22494. 16 rooms with bath. Facilities: restaurant, bar, tennis court, parking. AE, DC, MC, V. Inexpensive.*

Chaves **O Pote.** A little way out of town on the Bragança road, this fami-
Dining ly-run restaurant has no pretensions. It serves tasty Portuguese food to an enthusiastic local clientele. Ask about the daily specials, or follow what everybody else is eating. To reach the restaurant, cross the bridge from the town center and drive for 1 kilometer (⅗ mile). The restaurant is on the right, and parking is available. *Estrada da Fronteira, tel. 076/21226. No credit cards. Closed Mon. Inexpensive.*

Dining and Lodging **Trajano.** The basement restaurant of the Hotel Trajano is a good place to try the *presunto* (smoked ham) for which the town is famous. *Truta a Transmontana* (river trout) is another good choice, served with boiled potatoes and salad. There's a reasonably priced selection of local wines to accompany your meal, served promptly on monogrammed plates. Such touches, and the very attentive service, more than make up for the rather subdued basement surroundings. The good service continues upstairs, where the hotel's pleasant guest rooms are decorated in Portuguese country style. *Travessa Cândido dos Reis, 5400, tel. 076/22415. 39 rooms with bath. Facilities: restaurant, bar. MC, V. Inexpensive.*

Lodging **Hotel Aquae Flaviae.** Although it bears the ancient Roman name for Chaves, this is a brand-new, gleaming hotel, adjacent to the Parque Termal (thermal waters) and a cannon shot away from the town's fortified tower. It's well equipped, and rooms are spacious and attractively decorated. The facade has an art deco touch—it looks more like an enormous movie house than a hotel—and the interior impresses with its smooth lines and polished surfaces. *Praça do Brasil, 5400, tel. 076/26711, fax 076/26497. 86 rooms with bath. Facilities: restaurant, bar, piano bar, garden, pool, shops, garage. AE, DC, MC, V. Expensive.*

Guimarães **Pousada de Santa Marinha.** Guimarães has two pousadas: one in
Dining and Lodging the town center (*see below*) and this one, overlooking the town,
★ in the Penha National Park to the northwest. The Santa Marinha is one of the finest in the country, occupying a beautifully converted 12th-century monastery, which was originally founded by the wife of Dom Afonso Henriques to honor Santa Marinha (patron saint of pregnant women). The history contained within the building is almost tangible: Some of the attractive guest rooms used to be monks' cells; antiques from Lisbon's Ajuda Palace brighten the public rooms; and the great stone dining room (serving regional and Continental dishes) was once the monastery kitchen. *Estrada de Penha, 4800, tel. 053/514453, fax 053/514459. 51 rooms with bath. Facilities: restaurant, bar, garden, parking. AE, DC, MC, V. Expensive.*
Pousada da Nossa Senhora da Oliveira. An elegant mansion, this pousada was fashioned when various adjacent 16th- and 17th-century town houses in the center of Guimarães were remodeled. Antique reproductions throughout provide old-style atmosphere, and service, too, is straight from the old school—courteous and efficient. Guest rooms are not particularly large, but there's compensation at hand in the superb restaurant, whose windows overlook the lovely Largo da Oliveira. A large fireplace catches the eye, and the menu features a wide range of regional Minho dishes. Even if you don't stay here, this would make a fine place for lunch while sightseeing. *Rua de Santa Maria, 4800, tel. 053/514157, fax 053/514204. 16 rooms with bath. Facilities: restaurant, bar, parking. Restaurant reservations advised. AE, DC, MC, V. Moderate.*

Oporto **O Escondidinho.** The Escondidinho is situated on a central
Dining shopping street and serves high-quality food from the Douro region, as well as a range of French-influenced dishes. Steak is served no less than six different ways, and the sole is always good. The surroundings are engaging; a tiled entrance announces the restaurant's country-house decor. *Rua dos Passos Manuel 144, tel. 02/21079. Reservations advised. AE, DC, MC, V. Closed Sun. Expensive.*
★ **Portucale.** On the top of the modern building that houses the hotel Albergaria Miradouro, the Portucale is known equally for

the excellence of its food and the city-wide views from its windows. Dishes are rich, making imaginative use of local ingredients, such as tripe and game, and mountain-style cabrito is sometimes served. There's a pleasing attention to detail, typified by expert service. *Rua da Alegria 598, tel. 02/570717. Reservations required. Jacket and tie advised. AE, DC, MC, V. Expensive.*

★ **Casa Filha da Mãe Preta.** One of the best choices at the riverside Cais da Ribeira, this restaurant is part of the parade of tall buildings facing the river. The lovely first-floor dining room is decorated with azulejos. Reserve ahead, or arrive early enough, and you can eat by the arched windows and look across to the port-wine suburb of Vila Nova de Gaia. There's a reasonable tourist menu, and—as at every restaurant down here—any of the fish specialties is worth trying. Many dishes, including grilled sardines, come with an ample serving of rice and beans. *Cais da Ribeira 39–40, tel. 02/315515. Reservations advised for window tables. AE, DC, MC, V. Closed Sun. Moderate.*

Taverna do Bebobos. A stone tavern in business since 1876, the gloomily authentic Bebobos has survived the century's floods (water levels are marked on the wall outside) to offer modern-day diners the atmosphere of a crumbling, rustic interior. There's a very pleasant upstairs dining room with views of the river. Specialties are mostly fish, though there are some meat dishes on the menu, too. Choose local wine; it comes from a cask balanced on the bar. *Cais da Ribeira 24–25, tel. 02/313565. Reservations advised. No credit cards. Closed Sun. Moderate.*

Tripeiro. This is just the place to try tripe, which is nearly always on the menu in one form or another. In case you don't appreciate Oporto's favorite food, the spacious restaurant is also good for most meat dishes, and there are several bacalhau specialties, too. Along with the typically Portuguese food comes typically Portuguese decor: wooden ceiling beams, whitewashed walls, and potted plants throughout. *Rua de Passos Manuel 195, tel. 02/200–5886. AE, DC, MC, V. Closed Sun. Moderate.*

Majestic Café. One of Oporto's grand old coffeehouses, the art deco Majestic doubles as a reasonably priced grill-restaurant. Sit amid the sculpted wood, carved nymphs, and mirrors, and choose from a fair list of steaks, burgers, and omelets, or just take coffee and cake. Service is brisk (and occasionally brusque), but you'll have plenty of opportunity to observe the bustling local crowd, both inside and outside on the busy pedestrianized shopping street. *Rua de Santa Catarina 112, tel. 02/23887. No credit cards. Closed Sun. Inexpensive.*

O Castico da Sé. Above a bar on a steep old-town street close to the cathedral, this tiny upstairs dining room does a roaring lunchtime trade. Make a stab at the indecipherable handwritten menu, and you'll be rewarded with huge portions of grilled and stewed meat and fish, which come complete with salad and vegetables. The clientele is mostly local business people, who know a bargain when they see one. The stone walls, beams, and lanterns provide atmosphere, while the fine food is dispensed with little ceremony. Be prepared to wait in line at lunchtime. *Rua da Bainharia 18, no tel. No credit cards. Inexpensive.*

Pedro dos Frangos. In an area full of budget restaurants, the popular Pedro dos Frangos stands out for the quality of its barbecued chicken, which grills temptingly in the window. If you're in a hurry, sit at the bar, though it's more comfortable upstairs in the plain dining room, where ordering a *mei* *frango* gets you a sublime half chicken and fries. *Rua do Bonjardim 219–223, tel. 02/200–8522. No credit cards. Closed Tues. Inexpensive.*

Lodging **Infante de Sagres.** This, Oporto's first luxury hotel built after
★ World War II, is named after the city's most famous son, Prince Henry the Navigator, and does indeed provide formal, princely service. Visiting royalty have been happy to stay here for years, and you'll be pleased by its very central location, close to Avenida dos Aliados. Public rooms are very impressively turned out, in a style closer to the 1890s than the 1990s, with a lot of carved wood. Guest rooms have less character, though all are supremely comfortable and have good marble bathrooms. *Praça D. Filipa de Lencastre 62, 4000, tel. 02/200–8101, fax 02/ 314937. 83 rooms with bath. Facilities: restaurant, bar, garden, solarium. AE, DC, MC, V. Very Expensive.*

Dom Henrique. The Dom Henrique attracts business travelers who want a central base; its elegant rooms and amenities are spread throughout the 22 floors of an octagonal downtown tower. The spacious guest rooms are extremely well-apppointed, and many have superb city views—as does the main restaurant and bar. While perhaps not the place for a leisurely vacation, the hotel is ideal if you require more than just the basic comforts. *Rua Guedesa Azevedo 179, 4000, tel. 02/200–5755, fax 02/ 201–9451. 112 rooms with bath. Facilities: restaurant, grill, bar, shops. AE, DC, MC, V. Expensive.*

★ **Tivoli Porto Atlântico.** This hotel lies west of the city center, off Avenida da Boavista, in a residential suburb near the Museum of Modern Art. Part of the Lisbon-based Tivoli group, it's a quiet, relaxed, and suprisingly small base from which to tour the city and the surrounding area. The comfortable interior is unobtrusively modern. Guest rooms share a terrace and provide every little service, down to a shoe-shine kit; bathrooms are marble clad and luxurious. Other facilities are good, including two pools (one indoor, one outdoor). A fine buffet breakfast is the only meal served, but there's an excellent French-style restaurant, the Foco, associated with and adjacent to the hotel. *Rua Afonso Lopes Vieira 66, 4100, tel. 02/694941, fax 02/ 667452. 58 rooms with bath. Facilities: restaurant, bar, 2 pools, shops, parking. AE, DC, MC, V. Expensive.*

Grande Hotel do Porto. Once Oporto's finest hotel, the Grande offers a touch of old-fashioned style at reasonable prices. It's located on the city's best shopping street, and visitors are immediately impressed with its turn-of-the-century public rooms and restaurant and its efficient staff. Guest rooms aren't as polished as they were in the hotel's heyday, but the lived-in feel is half the attraction. Some rooms feature intriguing decor and lighting, which take you back through the decades. *Rua de Santa Catarina 197, 4000, tel. 02/200–8176, fax 02/311061. 100 rooms with bath. Facilities: restaurant, bar, parking. AE, DC, MC, V. Moderate.*

Hotel Peninsular. Centrally located between São Bento Station and Praça da Liberdade, this popular small hotel has an impressive tiled entrance hall, spick-and-span rooms with TV, and a modern—if slightly cheerless—bar. *Rua Sá da Bandeira 21, 4000, tel. 02/200–3012, fax 02/384984. 57 rooms with bath. Facilities: bar. AE, MC, V. Inexpensive.*

Pensão Estoril. The Estoril has been renovated in recent years and now offers compact but smart rooms at reasonable rates. It's in a quiet location near the city center and has a terrace and small garden, a bar, and parking nearby. Ask for a room with a balcony. *Rua de Cedofeita 193, 4000, tel. 02/200–2751. 17 rooms with bath. Facilities: bar, terrace, garden. No credit cards. Inexpensive.*

Ponte de Lima
Dining

Restaurante Encanada. Close to the old town and market, the Encanada is adjacent to the tree-lined avenue along the riverfront. A terrace provides river views. The menu is limited, but you can count on good local cooking, with dishes that depend on what's available at the market. Homemade fish cakes, with rice and salad, make a tasty, light lunch. *Praça Municipal, tel. 058/ 941189. MC, V. Closed Thurs. Moderate.*

Lodging

Turismo de Habitação. The Ponte de Lima region is well known for its Manor House Tourism program; the organizing body, Turihab, has its central reservations office in town (*see* the Lodging introduction, *above*). There are 26 properties in the area, mostly concentrated on the north bank of the Ria Lima. All have a limited number of rooms and have to be booked through Turihab. Ask about the early 18th-century Paço de Calheiros, which has lovely gardens; the 17th-century Casa de Pomarchão (closed Dec.–Jan.); the Moinho de Estorãos, a converted water mill by an old Roman bridge (open May–Sept.); and the 18th-century manor house Casa do Outeiro. All these are 1 kilometer–7 kilometers (⅗ mile–4 miles) from Ponte de Lima. *Facilities: usually minimal; houses may have communal lounge, bar, pool or local swimming facilities, fishing, gardens; lunch and dinner may be available on request. No credit cards. Inexpensive–Moderate.*

Viana do Castelo
Dining

Os Tres Arcos. This locally renowned seafood restaurant, facing the town gardens and river, is always a good bet. Sole, trout, and eel are especially recommended, and while the selection of shellfish changes according to the season, what there is sits temptingly in the window. You can eat at the bar or, more expensively, in the arched interior (the name means "The Three Arches"). *Largo João Tomás da Costa 25, tel. 058/24014. MC, V. Closed Mon. Moderate.*

Os Tres Potes. The cellarlike dining room, converted from a 16th-century bakery, gets very busy in summer as people crowd in to eat to the accompaniment of the weekend folksinging and dancing sessions. Sitting at tables under stone arches, you can choose from a fine range of regional dishes. Start with the *aperitivos regionais* (a selection of ham, spicy sausage, cheese, and olives), and move on to the house-style bacalhau. There's a good wine list, too. *Beco dos Fornos 7, off Praça da República, tel. 058/23432. Reservations required for Fri. and Sat. dinner; advised other times. MC, V. Closed Mon. Moderate.*

Lodging
★

Hotel Santa Luzia. Majestically situated on a wooded, rocky outcrop behind the basilica, the government-owned Santa Luzia overlooks the town and coast. A large white country mansion, it was recently renovated in sumptuous 1930s style, and the grand public rooms are a delight, as are the private gardens and terrace. There's an outdoor pool, too. Guest rooms are spacious and well equipped, and some have a beautiful view of the sea. For location and solitude, the Santa Luzia can't be beat, but note that it's 4 kilometers (2½ miles) from the center of Viana. *Monte de Santa Luzia, 4900, tel. 058/828889 or 058/ 828890, fax 058/828892. 48 rooms with bath. Facilities: resta-*

rant, bar, garden, pool, tennis courts, parking. *AE, DC, MC, V. Expensive.*

Vila Nova de
Cerveira
Dining and Lodging

Pousada de Dom Dinis. The pousada in Vila Nova de Cerveira makes a superb first- or last-night stop in Portugal, just 13 kilometers (8 miles) from the Spanish border at Valença. Opened in 1982, it was built inside the town's 14th-century fortified castle walls, which face the Rio Minho. Ancient, mottled buildings within the ramparts now house the guest rooms, which have been enhanced by lovely reproductions of traditional Minho furniture. Some rooms have private patios. The modern restaurant features local Minho dishes, including the popular river fish. In season, lamprey is a particular favorite. *Praça da Liberdade, 4920, tel. 051/795601. 29 rooms with bath. Facilities: restaurant, bar. AE, DC, MC, V. Expensive.*

Vila Real
Dining

O Aldeão. A popular local restaurant, the Aldeão piles its plates high with Portuguese specialties, which include a full range of meat grills. The steak comes with a bit of everything and satisfies even the largest of appetites. Service is friendly, the surroundings straightforward, and the prices unbeatable for this quality and quantity of food. *Rua Dom Pedro de Castro 70, tel. 059/24794. MC, V. Inexpensive.*

Lodging

Miracorgo. This hotel is a rather unattractive modern block in the center of town, but its exterior can be forgiven once you've secured a valley-facing room, with views of the dramatic stepped terraces of the Rio Corgo below. The handsome reception area, bright guest rooms, and good service add to the hotel's attractions. *Av. 1 de Maio 76–78, 5000, tel. 059/25001. 76 rooms with bath. Facilities: bar, indoor pool, health club, shops, garage. AE, DC, MC, V. Moderate.*

The Arts and Nightlife

The Arts

Oporto is the center of the arts in the North. Outside the city there's little in the way of concerts and artistic events to appeal to visitors, but, the annual festivals of northern Portugal are vibrant and colorful affairs, perhaps more so than in any other region. Many date back hundreds of years, and the local populations display an infectious enthusiasm for the celebrations that most visitors will find hard to resist. If at all possible, try to have your trip coincide with at least one of the events noted below.

The Minho
At Easter, Braga has the country's most impressive *Semana Santa* (Holy Week) festivities—including eerie torchlit processions of hooded participants—which reach their climax on Good Friday. In June, as part of the city's *Festas de São João* (Feast of Saint John) celebration, there's a costumed procession of King David and the Shepherds and a traditional fair.

In Guimarães, the first week in July marks the *Festas de São Torcato*, when there's a fair and procession to the nearby village of São Torcato. The biggest celebration is the following month: The first Sunday in August sees the *Festas Gualterianas* (Festival of Saint Walter), a boisterous festival and fair that dates back to the 15th century. Barcelos hosts the colorful *Festas das Cruzes* (Festival of the Cross) in the first week of

May, when the town is lit up by bright lights and the river illuminated by a grand fireworks display.

The most spectacular Minho festival is the *Romaria de Nossa Senhora da Agonia* (Procession and Fair of Our Lady of Sorrows), held in Viana do Castelo in August (over the weekend closest to the 20th) and attracting thousands of pilgrims. In addition to religious parades, there are floats, fireworks displays, traditional dancing, and music. At Esposende and Ponte da Barca, the *Festas de São Bartolomeu do Mar* (Festivals of Saint Bartholomew of the Sea) fall in the same month, August, as does Caminha's *Festas de Santa Rita de Cassia* (Festival of Saint Rita of Cassia), which features the usual processions, dancing, and fireworks. In mid-June, Monção celebrates the *Festa do Corpo de Deus* (Festival of Corpus Christi), which includes a symbolic battle between good and evil.

Inland, Ponte de Lima's highly enjoyable *Feiras Novas* (New Fair), dating back to the 12th century, is held in mid-September. It includes an enjoyable fair, a religious procession, fireworks, music, and various traditional entertainments.

Oporto and the Douro
Oporto is the place to find the more traditional arts. For concerts and recitals consult the tourist office, whose staff will advise you of events worth attending. Noted as a center for modern art, Oporto enjoys regular exhibitions at the Museum of Modern Art (*see* Off the Beaten Track, *above*), as well as at a variety of galleries, some of which are on the main Avenida da Boavista. Films in Oporto are shown in their original language; check local newspapers for current listings.

The region also has its share of festivals. Oporto's major celebration is the *Festas de São João* held on June 23–24 every year. The whole city erupts with bonfires and barbecues, and people gather to eat the traditional roast kid, washing it down with vinho verde. The local population roams the streets all night, hitting passers-by on the head with, among other things, leeks and plastic hammers. There are similar, but less extensive, revels at Vila do Conde at the same time.

On the first weekend in June, Amarante hosts the *Festa de São Gonçalo* (Festival of Saint Gonçalo), when the saint is commemorated by the baking of phallus-shaped cakes, which are exchanged between unmarried men and women. Other celebrations include a fair, folk dancing, and traditional singing. The town's art museum also hosts regular exhibitions of modern art.

The pilgrimage to the shrine at Lamego is the centerpiece of the *Festas de Nossa Senhora dos Remedios* (Festival of Our Lady of Cures). The main religious procession, in which many pilgrims climb the staircase on their knees, is on September 8 but the festivities start at the end of August and include concerts, dancing, parades, a fair, and torchlit processions.

Trás-os-Montes
Vila Real, like many towns, has festivals in June for the "popular saints," Anthony and Peter, with fairs, music, and fireworks. Chaves hosts the *Feira dos Santos* at the beginning of November. It is a winter fair that emphasizes the region's rural character and attracts people from miles around. Miranda holds the *Festa de São Tiago* (Festival of Saint James) at the end of July; it includes traditional dancing, games, and fireworks

SONY

PACK WISELY.

Given a choice, the seasoned traveler always carries less.
Case in point: Sony Handycam® camcorders, America's most
popular. They record up to 2½ hours on a single tape.
VHS-C tapes record only 30 minutes.* And why carry five tapes
when you can record everything on one? Which brings us
to the first rule of traveling: pack a Sony Handycam camcorder.

SONY
R STEREO L

8x
Hi-Fi Stereo

POWER ZOOM LENS/AUTO FOCUS

video Hi8
Handycam AUTO LOCK

AF
PRECISION
CCD

150

FADER

Over 1500 Great Weekend Escapes...

in Six Fabulous Fodor's Guides to
Bed & Breakfasts, Country Inns, Cottages,
and Other Weekend Pleasures!

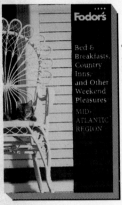

The Mid-Atlantic Region

The South

New England

The West Coast

England and Wales

Canada

Fodor's
Where the best memories begin

over the river. In August, Bragança celebrates its annual festival in similar style.

Nightlife

Outside Oporto, nightlife in the region is fairly restricted. The liveliest places are Braga and the coastal Minho resorts, including Viana do Castelo, which have numerous bars and discos.

Amarante Every Saturday night from July through September, the gardens of the **Casa da Calçada,** near the bridge in town, host a festival with traditional music and dancing. It starts at 8 PM, and the entrance price includes as much barbecued and buffet food as you can eat.

Braga Braga has a surprisingly active nightlife for such a conservative, religious city. Its central café-bars, such as **Café Vianna** and **Café Astoria,** both in the arcaded Praça da República, are good places for a drink and are lively at any time of the day or night. **O Nosso Café** (Av. da Liberdade) is a popular bar with a late-night disco. Along the same avenue, Braga's youth also converge upon the notorious disco under the **Hotel Turismo** (Praceta João XXI). Others frequent the less trendy but enjoyable **Salsa** (Rua de Diu), a little farther down the avenue.

Oporto The nicest places for an evening drink are the old-style cafés: either the **Brasileira** (Rua Sá da Bandeira 61), the **Majestic** (Rua de Santa Catarina 112), or the **Imperial** (Praça da Liberdade), all of which are open daily until around 10 PM. For a restful glass of port, the best place is the **Solar do Vinho do Porto** (Jardim do Palácio do Cristal), which is open until midnight every day except Sunday (*see* Tour 1, *above*). Livelier is **Postigo do Carvão** (Rua Fonte Taurina 26), a former warehouse in the Ribeira district converted into a fashionable bar. The **Mal Cozinhado** (Rua do Outeirinho 13, tel. 02/381319; closed Sun.) is a lively restaurant hosting traditional music and dancing, including *fado* (traditional folk music), during the summer.

Oporto has a number of good discos—all very young and fashionable—west of the city center in the new commercial developments. In the *Centro Comercial Brasileira* (Av. da Boavista), try **Griffon's** and **Swing,** which are open until 4 AM. For a more sophisticated evening's entertainment, there are two casinos within reach of Oporto, at Espinho to the south and Póvoa de Varzim to the north (*see* Tour 2, *above*). Both are open daily throughout the year 3 PM–3 AM and feature dining, dancing, and cabaret in addition to the gaming tables. Foreign visitors must take their passports.

Viana do Castelo The center of Viana do Castelo is lively in the summer, and several bars and cafés cater to the mostly Portuguese tourists. The young crowd hangs out at the **Ministerio** (Rua do Tourinho 41), a fun bar with loud music. On the town beach, Praia da Cabedelo, the **Luziamar** bar and disco are popular.

9 Madeira

By Deborah
Luhrman

Born in the United
States and
educated in
California,
Deborah Luhrman
was an award-
winning television
producer in Los
Angeles before
moving to Madrid,
where she writes
on Spanish
business, food,
and wine and on
Portugal.

Madeira is a mountainous, subtropical island blanketed with colorful flowers and overflowing with waterfalls that attract nearly half a million visitors each year. The small island's other big appeal is its temperate climate: It's warmed by Atlantic currents in winter (making swimming possible on sunny winter days), and it's cooled by trade winds in summer. Located 900 kilometers (560 miles) southwest of Lisbon, Madeira has roughly the same latitude as Casablanca. In the middle of the island is a backbone of high, rocky peaks and the crater of a now-extinct volcano. Steep-sided green ravines fan out from the center like the spokes of a wheel. Although Madeira is only 57 kilometers (35 miles) long and 22 kilometers (13 miles) wide, the distances seem much greater, as the roads climb and descend precipitously from one ravine to the next. The other islands that are grouped with Madeira include: tiny Porto Santo, which has a popular sandy beach and only 5,000 inhabitants; the Ilhas Desertas, a chain of waterless and unpopulated islands south of Madeira; and the Ilhas Selvagens, located farther south, near the Canary Islands, and also uninhabited.

Madeira was discovered and claimed for the Portuguese in 1419 by explorer João Gonçalves Zarco, whose statue you can see in the main intersection of the capital, Funchal. Because the uninhabited island was at that time covered with a nearly impenetrable forest, Zarco named it *Madeira*, which means "wood" in Portuguese. Eventually the island became more populated and by around the 15th and 16th centuries the colony had grown rich from sugar plantations. Even after alternative sources of sugar were developed, in the New World, Madeira's wine industry sustained the island's growth. Later, banana plantations prospered, and more recently tourism—which now accounts for 20% of the economy—has become big business.

Madeira displays an unmistakable air of British colonialism that dates to the 1650s and the marriage of Portuguese princess Catherine of Bragança to England's King Charles II. Charles gave Madeira an exclusive franchise to sell wine to England and all its colonies, and he granted Madeirans the same free-trade rights as English captains. The wine sales created a business boom on the island and that prosperity lured many British families to live in Funchal.

Today the British still flock to Madeira, although nowadays—because it's cheaper—most visitors arrive with large tour groups; it's also a popular holiday destination for Germans and Scandinavians. And though the island has lots of sports and entertainment, it's best loved by a reserved crowd that likes to wander through gardens and sip afternoon tea. Young people seeking an action-packed vacation may be unfulfilled in Madeira. Traditionally Madeira has been a winter resort, but that has begun to change—even though the best (and most crowded) time to visit is still during Christmas week, when every tree in Funchal is decorated with lights and the main boulevard becomes an open-air folk "museum." Traditional pastimes, from making bread and pressing sugarcane to basketry and weaving, are demonstrated throughout the week. On New Year's Eve cruise ships from all over the world pull into the harbor for an incomparable fireworks display exploding from the hilltops surrounding Funchal. In April the Flower Festival capitalizes on Madeira's best natural resource; and in

September there's the Fiesta Nossa Senhora do Monte, which commemorates the patron saint of the island.

Essential Information

Important Addresses and Numbers

Tourist Information The busy tourist office of **Madeira** (Av. Arriaga 18, Funchal, tel. 91/29057 or 91/25658), open daily 9–8, dispenses maps, brochures, and up-to-date information on the constantly changing bus schedules. On the island of **Porto Santo**, a tiny tourist office (Av. Henrique Vieira de Castro, Vila Baleira, tel. 91/98-23-61, ext. 203) with a helpful staff, attends to visitors weekdays 9–5:30 and weekends and holidays 9:30–12:30.

Consulates **United States** (Av. Luis Camõbes, Block D, Apt. B, Funchal, tel. 91/47429), **Great Britain** (Av. Zarco 2, 4th floor, Funchal, tel. 91/21221).

Emergencies In the event of an emergency in Madeira you can dial the nationwide number **115**, or in Funchal call the **police** (tel. 91/22022), **fire department** (tel. 91/22122), **Red Cross** (tel. 91/41115) for ambulances. For **medical emergencies**, you can also dial 91/20000.

Late-Night Pharmacies Pharmacies are open at night and on Sunday according to a rotating schedule. Dial **166** for information.

Arriving and Departing by Plane

Airport and Airlines There is no longer any regularly scheduled passenger-boat service to Madeira, so visitors must arrive by plane at the **Aeroporto Santa Catarina** (tel. 91/522941 or 91/522972), situated east of Funchal in Santa Cruz and about 35 minutes away by car. (Numerous charter flights link Funchal with most northern European capitals.) The island is also served by **TAP Air Portugal** (Av. Comunidades Madeirenses 8–10, Funchal, tel. 91/30151; Aeroporto Santa Catarina, tel. 91/522864), which makes six flights daily from Lisbon (in one hour, 45 minutes) and at least four trips daily from London (four hours away), and **Gibraltar Airways** (Av. Zarco 2, tel. 91/29113 or 91/20161) has also begun nonstop service between London and Funchal, several times a week. A local charter carrier called **Air Columbus** (Aeroporto Santa Catarina, tel. 91/523001) and its Canadian affiliate **Ultra Mar Charter Corporation** (347 College St., Suite 205, Toronto, Canada M5T 1S5, tel. 416/921–9191, fax 416/921–3443) offer flights twice a month along the Toronto–Montréal–Azores–Funchal route.

Between Madeira and Porto Santo
By Plane The interisland flight to Porto Santo from Madeira provides spectacular low-altitude views of Machico and São Lorenço peninsula. **TAP** shuttles an 18-seat Dornier turboprop plane on the 15-minute flight between the islands four times daily. Tickets cost 10,800$00 round-trip, and children 2–12 pay half-fare. Reservations should be made in advance, especially for July and August.

By Boat The ***Independencia***, a sleek, 244-passenger catamaran, plies between Funchal and Porto Santo daily June through September, and every day except Tuesday October through May. The boat sails from the Funchal harbor at 8 AM for the 1½-hour voyage and heads back from Porto Santo at 5, making this a popular day trip. A round-trip ticket costs 6,400$00; children 4–12 pay half-fare. Tickets may be purchased in advance at the Funchal marina (tel. 91/27020), which is open weekdays 9–12:30 and 2–5:30 and Saturday 9–12:30, or at the dock before the boat departs. For sailings on summer weekends, it's a good idea to buy tickets in advance.

Getting Around

By Car The best way to explore Madeira is by car. Although it's a small island, the terrain is steep, so bear in mind that driving can be torturously slow. For example, the drive from Funchal to Porto Moniz on the western end is only 156 kilometers (93 miles) round-trip but takes all day, as the roads twist and turn up the mountains and along terraced ravines.

Porto Santo roads are easier to handle, but the 10-kilometer-long (6-mile-long) island is so small that most visitors get around on foot or by taxi.

Car Rentals Most major agencies have rental offices at the Madeira airport and in Funchal, including **Hertz** (R. Ivens 12, tel. 91/26026), **Avis** (Largo António Nobre 164, tel. 91/763495 or 91/764546), **Budget** (Hotel Duas Torres, Estrada Monumental, tel. 91/25619 or 91/36508), and **Europcar** (Estrada Monumental 306, tel. 91/28116 or 91/28176).

Car rentals on Porto Santo are handled by **Moinho** (Hotel Praia Dourada, Rua Estevādo D'Alencastre, tel. 91/982403 or 91/982780) and **Atlantic** (Av. Vieira de Castro, tel. 91/98-46-83).

By Bus Madeira has two extensive bus systems that are frequently used by visitors and islanders alike. Yellow buses serve Funchal and its surrounding neighborhoods: Nos. 1 and 3 run west from the city, and make stops along Estrada Monumental, where most of the hotels are located. Beige-and-red buses fan out to other points on the island. Both systems leave from an outdoor terminal at the end of Avenida do Mar, near the old town. Generally several buses a day travel to each village on the island, but schedules change constantly, so inquire at your hotel or the tourist office for departure times.

Guided Tours

Orientation Travel agencies specializing in island tours abound in Funchal. Visits usually include multilingual motorcoach tours to Cabo Girādo, the inland peaks, Porto Moniz, the village of Santana; and meals or snacks in typical island restaurants. The best operators are **InterVisa** (Av. Arriaga 30, 3rd floor, tel. 91/25641 or 91/25642), **CAT Tours** (Av. Arriaga 52, tel. 91/25294 or 91/23379), and **Panorama Travel** (Dr. Joādo B. Cāmara 3–A, tel. 91/29097 or 91/29036).

Special-Interest Nature lovers may want to consider a combination sightseeing-and-hiking tour among the central peaks of Madeira, offered by **Windsor Travel** (Estrada Monumental 252, tel. 91/31056 or 91/31057) and **Blandy Travel** (Av. Comunidades Madeirenses 1, tel. 91/20161 or 91/32065).

The Madeira tourism office also offers afternoon boat excursions up and down the coast from Funchal on the 130-passenger *Pirata Azul* (*Blue Pirate*). Tickets cost 3,500$00 and are available in advance at the marina boat office (tel. 91/32258 or 91/32258). Ask at the tourist office for schedules.

Exploring Madeira

Orientation

Madeira is a small island that receives nearly half a million tourists per year, so its attractions are heavily visited and easily accessible. The following exploring tours cover the capital city of Funchal, its environs, the western end of Madeira, the mountains, and the neighboring island of Porto Santo. Each tour begins in Funchal and can be completed in one day, although visitors who have more time may want to divide their sightseeing into smaller portions. For example, a drive to Câmara de Lobos or Ribeira Brava—stops that appear in Tour 3—for lunch make satisfying afternoon excursions from Funchal, which is covered in Tour 1. Be sure to allow plenty of time when driving around the island. Destinations often appear close on the map but take a long time to reach, due to winding mountain roads and slow-moving trucks.

Highlights for First-Time Visitors

Beach at Porto Santo (*see* Tour 5)
Botanical Gardens (*see* Tour 2)
Flower and Fruit Market (*see* Tour 1)
Levada walk (*see* Tour 4)
Madeira Wine Tour (*see* Tour 1)
Pico de Arieiro and Pico Riuvo (*see* Tour 4)
Sled ride from Monte (*see* Tour 2)
Waterfalls on the road to Porto Moniz (*see* Tour 3)

Tour 1: Funchal

Numbers in the margin correspond to points of interest on the Madeira and Funchal maps.

When the first colonists arrived in Madeira in July 1419, the valley they were about to settle was a mass of bright yellow fennel, or *funchal* in Portuguese. Today the bucolic fields ❶ are gone, and the city of **Funchal** is the bustling business-and-political center of the island. Although a number of historic buildings can be toured, the best way to get to know Funchal is to observe the activities at the waterfront, market, and city squares, daily haunts of the islanders.

❷ Our exploring tour starts at **Parque Santa Catarina,** which overlooks the harbor and Avenida Arriaga, the main street of Funchal. In spring the street is ablaze with the bright purple blossoms of the jacaranda trees that line both sides; flowers bloom in the park year-round. At the top of the gardens is a pink mansion called **Quinta Vigia,** the residence of the president of Madeira. In the center of the park rests the tiny **Capela de Santa Catarina** (Santa Catarina Chapel), built by Zarco in 1425 and one of the oldest buildings on the island.

❸ From here, descend to the **docka** (dock), where the big container ships—mostly from northern Europe—unload. Luxury cruise ships also moor here for day visits to the island. Walk

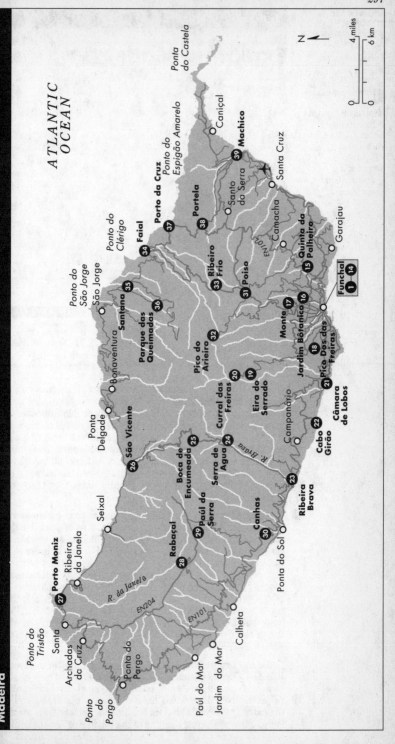

Madeira

ATLANTIC
OCEAN

Ponta
do Castela

Ponta do Espigão Amarelo

Porto da Cruz

Caniçal

Machico **39**

Santa Cruz

Portela **38**

Santo
da Serra

Ponta do Clérigo

Faial **37**

34

Camacha

**Ribeiro
Frio** **33**

Poiso **31**

Quinta da
Palheiro

Ponta do São Jorge

São Jorge

35

Santana

Garajau

15

Funchal **1** — **14**

Bonaventura

**Parque das
Queimadas**

36

Monte **17**

16

Ponta Delgada

**Pico do
Arieiro** **32**

Jardim Botânico **18**

São Vicente

20

19

**Pico Dos das
Freiras** **21**

26

**Boca de
Encumeada** **25**

**Curral das
Freiras**

**Eira do
Serrado**

Campanário

**Cabo
Girão** **22**

Seixal

**Serra de
Agua** **24**

R. Brava

**Câmara
de Lobos**

**Paúl da
Serra** **29**

23

**Ribeira
Brava**

Rabaçal **28**

Canhas **30**

R. da Janela

Ponta do Tristão

Porto Moniz **27**

Ribeira
da Janela

Santa

EN204

Ponta do Sol

Archadas
da Cruz

EN101

Calheta

Ponta
do
Pargo

Ponta do Pargo

Paúl do Mar

Jardim do Mar

N

0   4 miles
0   6 km

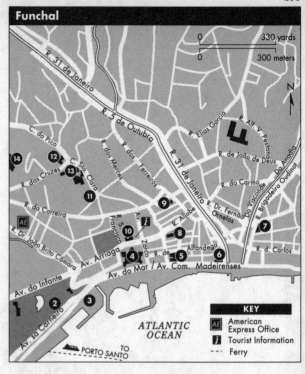

Funchal

KEY

AE American
Express Office

i Tourist Information

--- Ferry

east on Avenida Comunidades Madeirenses (commonly known
as Avenida do Mar), the seafront boulevard. Across the street
4 from the yacht harbor you'll pass **Pálacio de São Lourenço** (St.
Lawrence Palace), built in the 17th century as Madeira's first
fortress and still used as a military headquarters. One more
5 block east will bring you to the **parlamento** (parliment), which
6 is housed in the restored 16th-century **Antigua Alfândega** (Old
Customs House). From here deputies govern the island, which
is part of Portugal but enjoys greater autonomy than other
mainland provinces.

7 At the traffic circle head up Rua Profetas to the **Mercado dos
Lavradores** (Workers' Market). Orchids, bird-of-paradise flowers, anthuriums, and other less-exotic blooms are sold in the
center patio by women who are required by law to dress in the
native costume of Madeira—a full, homespun skirt with yellow, red, and black vertical stripes and an embroidered white
blouse. Pyramids of tropical fruits and stalks of bananas are
sold at produce stands, and the downstairs seafood market features rows of fierce-looking *espada* (a soft whitefish). Their
huge bulging eyes are caused by the change in pressure between their deep-water habitat and the sea level. *Open Sat.–
Thurs. 7–2, Fri. 7 AM–8 PM.*

Cross the bridge and walk back toward the center of town on
Rua Dr. Fernão Omelas, the main commercial street of Funchal, which changes into Avenida Arriaga at the 15th-century
8 Sé (cathedral). Renowned for its intricate mozarabic ceiling,
the cathedral reveals an Arabic influence throughout, particularly in the geometric designs of the inlaid ivory in the ceiling.

Be sure to have a look at the carved choir-stalls in the the side entrance and in the chancel, which depict the prophets and the apostles, and the antique tilework at the side entrance in the belfry. *Av. Arriaga, no tel. Open daily 9–1 and 3–6.*

From the square in front, go up Rua João Tavira and turn right at Rua do Bispo to the **Museu de Arte Sacra** (Museum of Sacred Art), located in the old bishop's house. The museum contains Flemish paintings, polychrome wood statues, and other religious treasures gathered from the island's churches. Most of the paintings were commissioned by the first merchants of Madeira, many of whom came from Brugge, Belgium. For example, the *Adoration of the Magi* was painted in 1518 for a rich merchant from Machico and paid for not in gold but in sugar. You can tell how important sugar was to the island by examining the coat of arms of Funchal, which depicts five loaves of sugar in the shape of a cross. *Rua do Bispo 21, tel. 91/28900. Admission: 100$00. Open Tues.–Sat. 10–12:30 and 2:30–6:00, Sun. 10–1.*

Time Out A good place to stop for coffee, afternoon tea, or a light lunch is **O Patio** (Rua da Carreira 43), a cool, tiled open-air patio. At the same address you can find Livraria Inglesa, Funchal's only English-language bookstore, where magazines, novels, and books about Portugal are sold.

Back on Avenida Arriaga be sure to tour the **São Francisco Adega du Vinho** (wine lodge), where you can see a demonstration of how wine barrels are made, visit cellars where the wine is stored, and hear historical tales about the Madeira vintage. The wineries, themselves, however, are located outside town and are closed to visitors. One legend has it that when the bloodthirsty duke of Clarence in 1478 was sentenced to death for plotting against King Edward IV, he was given his choice of execution methods, since he was the king's brother. He decided to be drowned in a barrel of the drink! There is plenty of time for tasting at the end of the visit. *Av. Arriaga 28, tel. 91/20121. Admission: 500$00. Tours weekdays 10:30 and 3:30.*

Next head uphill and north three blocks on Rua São Francisco and Calçada Santa Clara. Naturalists will want to stop in at the **Museu Municipal** (City Museum) for its displays of animals found on Madeira and in its seas—including a ferocious collection of stuffed sharks. Attached is a small aquarium, where you may watch the graceful movements of an octopus and view a family of sea turtles. *Rua Mouraria 31, tel 91/29761. Admission: 65$00. Open Tues.–Fri. 10–8, weekends noon–6.*

Continue to climb Calçada Santa Clara to **Quinta das Cruzes,** a museum housed in a gracious mansion that was once the home of Zarco. The building itself is impressive, as is the collection of antique furniture inside: Of special interest are the *palanquins*—lounge chairs that were once used to carry the grand ladies of colonial Madeira around town. Outside the Quinta is a botanical garden filled with stone columns and tombstones. *Calçada do Pico 1, tel. 91/22382. Admission: 100$00. Open Tues.–Sat. 10–12:30 and 2:30–5:30, Sun. 10–1.*

As you leave the gate, follow the wall of the Quinta to the front for a great view of Funchal. The big pink building on the left is the **Convento de Santa Clara** (Santa Clara Convent), where Zarco is buried. Inside the church, walls are lined with ceramic tiles, giving the sanctuary an Arabic look. You can also see the

14 old walls of the **Fort do Pico** (Pico fort), which was built in the late 1500s to protect the settlement against pirate attacks. One of the worst raids on Funchal was made in the 16th century by the pirating nobleman Bertrand de Montluc, who sacked the churches and stole barrels of Madeira. He resold the wine to his noble friends and unwittingly helped spread the reputation of the island's drink.

Tour 2: The Funchal Environs

Although buses stop at most attractions on this tour, exploring is much easier if you drive: You won't have to return to Funchal after each sight, and you'll be able to stop at the lookouts to enjoy spectacular views along the way.

Head out of Funchal on EN–101, the road to the airport. At the fork take a left on to EN–102 and follow signs toward Camacha.

15 **Quinta da Palheiro,** also known as the Blandy Gardens, is on the right, 5 kilometers (3 miles) outside the city. Here you may stroll the 30-acre estate owned by the Blandy wine family. Garden enthusiasts come here for the famous collection of camelia trees that bloom between December and April and for the formal gardens with flowering perennials. Unfortunately, visitors are not invited to tour the big white house, in which the family lives. *Follow signs to Camacha. Admission: 450$00. Open weekdays 9:30–12:30.*

16 Even more impressive is the **Jardim Botânico** (Botanical Garden), which you can reach by backtracking toward Funchal and turning uphill on Caminho do Meio. The garden, with wonderful views of the town, was opened by the government in 1960 on the grounds of the old plantation Quinta do Bom Sucesso and includes well-labeled subtropical plants from Asia, Africa, South America, and Australia; anthurium, bird-of-paradise plants, and a large cactus collection are just some examples. Be sure not to miss the petrified trunk of an ancient heather tree that was found near Curral das Freiras: It's been dated 10 million years old. A house on the grounds serves as a simple natural-history museum. *Caminho do Meio. Admission: 300$00 adults, 100$00 children. Open daily 10–6.*

17 Go back to Funchal and turn up Rua 31 de Janeiro to get to the village of **Monte** (6 kilometers/4 miles), home of one of Madeira's oddest attractions: the snowless sled ride. Before taking the plunge, stop at the white-stucco church **Nossa Senhora do Monte** (Our Lady of the Mountain). The tiny statue above the altar was found by a shepherdess in the nearby town of Terreira da Luta in the 15th century and has become the patron saint of Madeira. The small church also contains the tomb of Emperor Charles I of Austria, the last Habsburg monarch who died here from tuberculosis in 1922 after being sent to the beneficial climate of Madeira.

Time Out If you need refreshment before you take part in the traditional sled ride back to Funchal, stop at the **Bar Catanha,** just uphill from the church. While sipping your beer, notice the old photos of sleds and drivers. Not much has changed over the years.

You'll recognize the sled drivers because they'll be lined up on the street where the church is and adorned in white pants, white shirt, and goatskin boots soled with rubber tires. The sleds look like big wicker baskets on wood runners and have flowered cushions for passengers to sit on. Running alongside the sleds are two drivers, who control the vehicle with ropes as it careens over the slippery cobblestones for the 20-minute ride back to Funchal. The sled's runners are greased with lard, but if the basket starts going too fast the drivers jump on the back to slow it down; if it stalls, they push and pull until it gets going again. The life span of the sleds is only about two years, since they were first created to carry only supplies from Monte to Funchal; later, passenger sleighs were developed that could haul as many as 10 people at a time and required six drivers. Nowadays people generally take the bus or a taxi to Monte, and the sled ride back down is purely a joyride. If you've driven to Monte, however, and want to take the sled down, taxis and buses are available from Funchal.

(18) Next, head west out of Funchal on Rua Dr. Pita and go 6 kilometers (3½ miles) to a miradouro (lookout) at **Pico Dos das Freiras;** this is a fine spot from which to take pictures of the city. Continue on EN–105 and then EN–107, and follow signs **(19)** to the village of Curral das Freiras. At **Eira do Serrado,** 16 kilometers (9½ miles) from town, park the car and walk to the viewpoint that looks over the Grande Curral—the crater of a long-extinct volcano in the center of the island. From here Pico Riuvo and the craggy summits of central Madeira look like a granite city shimmering in the sunlight or shrouded in mist. Island legend says the peaks are the castle fortress of a virgin princess, who can be seen sleeping peacefully in the rocha da cara (rock face). It's said that she wanted to live in the sky like the clouds and the moon, and she was so unhappy at being earthbound that the princess's father—the volcano god—caused an earthquake that pushed the rocky cliffs high into the sky so she could live near the heavens.

(20) Back on the road you'll pass through a series of switchbacks and two tunnels leading down to the village of **Curral das Freiras** (Nuns' Shelter). The sisters of the Convent of Santa Clara took refuge here from bands of marauding pirates. Nearly the geographic center of Madeira, the valley sits in the middle of a circle of extinct volcanoes that long ago pushed the island up from the bottom of the sea.

Tour 3: Western Madeira

The tour of the western part of Madeira includes the greenest and lushest part of the island: In some places you can see a dozen waterfalls spilling into a cool pine forest. The route follows the dramatic north coast, where a narrow highway clings to the cliff face, and passes under and through several more waterfalls. You can't avoid getting your car wet as you drive through the cascades.

(21) Begin this tour by heading west from Funchal along the coast on EN–101. You'll drive past banana plantations en route to **Câmara de Lobos,** 20 kilometers (12 miles) from the city. This impoverished fishing village was made famous by Winston Churchill, who, during a visit to Madeira in the 1950s, painted pictures of the multicolored boats and the fishermen's tiny homes. The boats are still here, pulled up onto the rocky beach during the day. You will also see women doing the wash in public fountains and bare-bellied children running riot in the narrow streets. A crumbling promenade, which protrudes from the main plaza, offers views west to Cabo Girádo.

Back on the tour the uphill road reveals houses of all sizes, all of whose grounds are landscaped with flowers. It's easy to see why Madeira is called "a floating garden in the Atlantic." Ten-foot-tall poinsettias, scarlett hibiscus, bougainvillea, rhododendron, aloe, geraniums, hydrangeas, roses, sunflowers, and bird-of-paradise plants thrive in this subtropical climate, where flowers bloom year-round.

22 Continue west to **Cabo Giráo.** At 1,900 feet, it's one of the highest sea cliffs in the world. From here you can see ribbons of terraces carved out of even the steepest slopes and farmers daringly cultivating grapes or garden vegetables. Neither machines nor animals are used on Madeiran farms because the plots are so small and difficult to reach. Not long ago, farmers blew into conch shells as a means of communication with neighbors across the deep ravines.

The route skirts eucalyptus and pine forests as you travel to-
23 ward the town of **Ribeira Brava**, a pleasant village with a pebbly beach and a seafront fruit market and one of the sunniest spots on the island. At the town, turn right on EN–104, where the road snakes through a sheer-sided canyon. In every direction you look you can see high waterfalls tumbling down canyon walls and into a pine forest. Straight ahead there are cloud-
24 shrouded peaks. At **Serra de Agua,** 7 kilometers (4 miles) away you may notice a stone *pousada* (a state-run inn) surrounded by moss-green rocks, ferns, and more waterfalls. The road contin-
25 ues to climb 41 kilometers (25 miles) until it reaches the **Boca de Encumeada** (Mouth of the Heights), where there are good views of the north coast. Many hiking trails begin here. (*See* Hiking in Sports and Outdoor Activities, *below.*)

26 At the town of **Sáo Vicente,** the road joins the one-lane north-coast highway that is chiseled out of the cliff face and is said to be one of the most expensive road projects, per mile, ever undertaken. At the beginning of the century, workers in baskets were suspended by rope so they could carve out ledges and tunnels along the planned route. Proceed with caution and make sure to tap your horn when going around blind curves. Large tour buses constantly use this narrow road; if you happen to meet a coach, you may be forced to back up to a turnout.

As you wind along the coast there are a number of waterfalls ahead: At one point the road passes behind a falls, and there's another delightful falls cascading right onto the road so you have to drive through it. Stop at one of the viewpoints and notice the windbreaks, made of thick mats of purple heather, that protect the terraced vineyards.

27 **Porto Moniz,** with its natural pools formed by ancient lava, is the destination of nearly all visitors to this part of the island, 16 kilometers (11 miles) from Sáo Vicente. Even though the town is such a popular place, there's not much to do except splash around the pools (no changing facilities), eat, and sunbathe: It's getting here that's fun. Several large restaurants are situated along the coast and cater to tourists.

As you drive along the winding uphill road to the viewpoint at **Santa,** be sure to look back and see the patterns made by the heather windbreaks in the village of Porto Moniz. At the fork, turn left on EN–204, a road that crosses through Madeira's widest valley and provides a unique perspective of both sides of the island. If you have time, take a short detour to **Rabaçal,** a water wonderland. Madeirans love to come here in summer to picnic alongside the cascades and quiet pools.

Past Rabaçal the road heads into a moorland called **Paúl da Serra,** where sheep graze and sea gulls spiral above the marshes. This is the closest thing to flatland in Madeira, and it looks strangely out of place. Turn right on EN–208, and follow signs to the town of **Canhas.** The twisting road passes more terraced farms and houses outshone by their bright flowering gardens and in 20 kilometers (12 miles) joins the southern coastal road EN–101 that returns you to Funchal.

Tour 4: Central Peaks and the Village of Santana

The barren high peaks of central Madeira offer spectacular views of the island and ample opportunity for hiking. Included in this tour is the much-photographed village of Santana with its thatch-roof, A-frame houses.

Head out of Funchal on Rua 31 da Janeiro, which turns into EN–103 as it passes the village of Monte. The road twists and climbs through eucalyptus groves and pine forests before it reaches a crossroads at the town of **Poiso,** where you should turn left and follow signs to Pico do Arieiro. This stretch travels over a barren plain above the tree line: Watch for errant sheep and goats wandering across the pavement on their way to graze stubbly gorse and bilberry.

Pico do Arieiro, at 5,963 feet, is Madeira's third-highest mountain; stop in the parking lot of the pousada and make the short climb to the lookout, where you can scan the rocky central peaks. There are views of the clouds below, and to the southeast is the Curral das Freiras crater. Look in the other direction, and try to spot the huge **Penha D'Aguia rock,** that stretches up like a monolith on the north coast. The trail from the lookout that crosses the narrow ridge leads to Pico Ruivo (6,104 feet), the highest point on the island (*see* Hiking in Sports and Outdoor Activities, *below*). Winter days can be chilly at these heights, so there is usually an inviting fire blazing in the bar of the strategically placed pousada here.

Head back to Poiso and continue the scenic drive north to **Ribeiro Frio.** The landscape grows more lush on this side of the island, and the road is full of waterfalls that splash the passing cars. At Ribeiro Frio there's a **trout hatchery,** the starting point for an interesting 40-minute *levada* walk to the lookout of Balcões (*see* Hiking in Sports and Outdoor Activities, *below*). *Levadas* are a network of irrigation canals that crisscross the island and often flow through tunnels, bringing valuable water from the mountains to the tiny terraced farms. Some levadas were hand-chiseled in stone hundreds of years ago; they're still being built today, with the aid of modern machinery.

Time Out   If you need some refreshment after your hike, stop at **Victor's,** in Ribeiro Frio. Inside the rustic wood-and-glass building is a welcoming fireplace, and you can get a beer or afternoon tea and the best *bolo de mel* (spice cake) on the island.

④ Continue north on EN–103 and follow signs to **Faial;** expect the road to descend in a series of switchbacks into a deep ravine. The tiny A-frame huts that dot the terraces along the steep sides are used as a barn for cows, which are never allowed to graze freely on Madeira. The prohibition was made, first, because there is not enough land for the animals to graze, and, second, because the animals could easily fall off a ledge.

⑤ At Faial turn left toward **Santana,** a village famous for its A-frame, thatch-roof cottages painted in bright colors. Most of these are upscale versions of traditional Madeiran homes. Sadly, this style has been replaced elsewhere on the island by nondescript concrete-block houses. A road from Santana leads to ⑥ **Parque dus Queimadas,** where you can stop to picnic or pick up another hiking trail that approaches Pico Ruivo from a different angle.

Backtrack to Faial on EN–103, and from there continue east to ⑦ **Porto da Cruz,** on the road that skirts the back of the landmark **Penha D'Aguia rock** (Eagle Rock), whose sheer cliffs tower over the village. Positioned in a fertile valley filled with tiny farms and gardens, the town is as pretty as any on Madeira, with its little bay and cliffs.

⑧ Climb again on EN–101 to **Portela,** where the view looks south over the gentler valley of Machico. From here it's an easy drive through banana plantations and sugarcane fields and into the ⑨ village of **Machico.**

Local folklore says the bay of Machico was discovered in 1346 by two English lovers, Robert Machin and Anne d'Arfet, who set sail from Bristol for France to escape Anne's disapproving parents. The couple's boat was thrown off course by a storm and was wrecked in this bay. After becoming ill, Anne died a few days later, and Robert then died of a broken heart. But their crew, according to legend, escaped on a raft, and news of the island made its way back to the court of the Portuguese king, who sent Zarco to investigate. When the explorer arrived he found a wood cross with the lovers' sad story, and he named the place in memory of Machin.

Explore the village church, and wander through the fishermen's quarter. From the seafront you can capture clear views of the **Ponta São Lourenço peninsula,** which sticks out into the ocean to the east. From here you can head back past the airport at Santa Cruz and return to Funchal on EN–101.

Tour 5: Porto Santo

Beachcombers may want to head directly from Madeira to **Porto Santo,** some 50 kilometers (30 miles) northeast. The tiny island is very dry and measures only 11 kilometers (6½ miles) by 6 kilometers (3½ miles), and its wide, sandy beach runs along the entire south coast—perfect for long walks in the surf. The rest of the island has little to offer, however, and remains refreshingly underdeveloped. The island once supported many farms, but a severe drought in the 1970s killed vineyards and drove most farmers out of business. Fields now lay barren, and residents have either moved away or switched to tourism-related jobs.

Porto Santo's main village, **Vila Baleira,** is a sleepy town with cobblestone streets and whitewashed buildings. A flower-filled park extends from the center to a fishing pier that is flanked on both sides by endless beach. The park contains an idealized statue of Christopher Columbus, the most important personage in Porto Santo's history. Columbus married Isabela Moniz, daughter of Bartolomeu Perestrelo, the first governor of the island. This was before Columbus was famous, when he sailed for Portuguese merchants and simply dreamed of a shortcut to the Indies. The young couple never lived on the island, but they spent some time in Funchal.

The **Casa de Cristóvão Colombo** (Columbus Museum and House) is located in the old governor's 15th-century home. Inside, lithographs illustrate the life of Columbus, and there are copies of 15 portraits of the discoverer, which prove that nobody really knows what he looked like. Ask to see the restored kitchen and bedroom in the upper part of the house. *Rua Cristóvão Colombo 12. Admission free. Open Mon.–Sat. 10– noon and 2–5:30.*

Traveling counterclockwise around the island you should stop first at the scenic **Portela** viewpoint, which overlooks the harbor, the town, and the long ribbon of beach. Move on to **Serra de Foca,** where a dirt track passes old salt flats before winding down to a rocky beach popular with divers. As you continue around the island you may have to dodge goats grazing along the edges of the road.

Along the road is **Pico do Castelo,** a favorite picnic spot named in memory of the castle that once stood here to protect the town from pirates. All that remains, however, is one of the castle's four cannons. The young pine trees covering the slopes were planted by the government to help retain moisture; they're a special variety that will never grow taller than 9 feet, so the views will not be lost. From here it's an easy walk to **Pico do Facho** (1,552 feet), the highest point on the island.

A little more than 2 kilometers (1¼ miles) farther is the **Fonte da Areia** (Spring in the Sand), a spring that flows out of a sandstone cliff. Women used to come here to do their washing, but they don't now, since the water is piped into town. As you head to the southern tip of the island you'll pass several windmills in disrepair, which were once used for grinding wheat.

The next sight—**Pico dos Flores**, another lookout—is worth a trip down the bumpy dirt roads. From here you can enjoy long-distance views of Madeira and the rocky, uninhabited island south of Porto Santo called Ilhéu de Baixo. Back on the road that runs along the beach, encroaching development due to tourism becomes apparent: A handful of high-rise apartment blocks is a sign. Since there is no longer any agriculture, islanders seem anxious to sell their property. But it could be that Porto Santo's remote location will help protect it from uncontrolled growth.

What to See and Do with Children

Younger visitors to Madeira will be enthralled by the **sled rides** down cobblestone streets from Monte (*see* Tour 2, *above*) to Funchal.

There is also an exotic-bird park just downhill from the Botanical Gardens called **Jardim dos Loiros**, where kids and their parents can see colorful tropical species from Asia, Africa, South

America, and Australia. *Quinta Bom Sucesso, Funchal, tel. 91/26035. Admission: 300$00 adults, 100$00 children 6–14. Open daily 8–6.*

An imaginative playground with wood climbing-equipment at the gardens of **Quinta Magnolia** is perfect for taking a break from the sightseeing circuit. *Rua Dr. Pita, Funchal, tel. 91/ 764598. Admission free. Open daily 9–dusk.*

Shopping

Not many visitors to Madeira escape without purchasing some of the local products. In addition to wine (*see* Tour 1, *above*), is-land merchants specialize in embroidered table linens, needle-point, basketry, and tropical flowers.

Basketry

The wickerwork industry of Madeira is centered in the village of Camacha, where there's a large cooperative shop on the main square that sells every imaginable type of basket as well as some wicker furniture. Most of the work is done in individual homes, and on many rural roads it's common to see men carry-ing huge bundles of willow branches to be used for basketry. *Open daily 10–8:30.*

Embroidery

Thousands of local women spend their days stitching intricate flowered patterns on organdy, Irish linen, cambric, and French silks. Their handiwork decorates tablecloths, place mats, and napkins, all of which are expensive and highly prized by north-ern Europeans. When buying embroidery, make sure it has a lead seal attached to certify that it was made on the island and not imported from elsewhere. One of the most popular shops is **Patricio & Gouveia** (Rua do Visconde de Anadia 33, tel. 91/ 22928), where you can visit the upstairs factory and see the white-uniformed employees stencil patterns and check produc-tion; the actual embroidery is done by an army of women in their homes. Some of the most beautiful work can be found at the **Casa do Turista** (José S. Ribeiro 2, tel. 91/24907), near the Funchal marina.

Needlepoint

Needlepoint and tapestry-making were introduced to Madeira in the early part of this century by a German family. You can visit their factory, **Kiekeben Tapestries** (Rua da Carreira 194, tel. 91/22073), and buy pieces at their shop, **Bazar Maria Kiekeben** (Av. do Infante 2, tel. 91/27857).

Sports and Outdoor Activities

Fishing

Madeira and Porto Santo are meccas for those hoping to reel in huge blue marlin, yellowfin tuna, albacore, swordfish, and dorado. The European marlin record (1,212 pounds) was set here. Fishing excursions can be arranged at the Funchal harbor through **Turipesca** (tel. 91/31063 or 91/42468) and in Porto Santo through **The Dive Center** (Rua J. G. Zarco 5, tel. 91/982162) or **Anguilla** (tel. 91/983573).

Golf

Madeira's one and only golf course has recently been expanded to 27 holes. The **Campo de Golfe da Madeira** (Hwy. EN–102, tel. 91/552345 or 91/552356), open to the public, is near the airport in Santo da Serra.

Hiking

Walking is a favorite outdoor activity in Madeira, and you can do it among the mountain peaks or alongside the levadas (*see* Tour 3 in Exploring Madeira, *above*). The tourist office provides a booklet listing 45 hikes of varying lengths and difficulties.

The most popular hike on the island is an 8-kilometer (5-mile) trek that departs from behind the pousada at **Pico de Arieiro** and winds along a ridge top to the island's highest peak, Pico Ruivo. The four-hour hike is of medium difficulty and provides great views of the entire island.

An easy excursion that will give you a taste of Madeira footpaths begins just north of the trout hatchery, in **Ribeiro Frio.** Follow signs to Balcões: The route includes 2 kilometers (1¼ miles) of mossy forest along the path of an old levada. From the viewpoint at Balcões the jagged peaks of central Madeira tower behind you, and there are views of villages along the north coast. The round-trip hike should take about 40 minutes.

Horseback Riding

Horses were once a common means of transportation on Madeira, but now they're used only for pleasure. Horse rentals are available through the **Riding Club of Choupana** (tel. 91/31015 or 91/30131), in Madeira, and the **Quinta dos Profetas** (tel. 91/98-31–65), in Porto Santo.

Scuba Diving

Madeira is too far north for colorful tropical fish, but divers enjoy the clear, still seas of summer and report lots of interesting marine life and coral formations. A diving center at the **Carlton Hotel** (Largo António Nobre, tel. 91/31031) rents scuba gear, as does the **British Diving Club** (Rua Gorgulho, no tel.) at the Lido swimming complex. **The Dive Center** (Rua J. G. Zarco 5, tel. 91/982162) organizes underwater excursions in Porto Santo.

Swimming

Although Madeira has no sandy beaches, sea swimming is possible from access points at three hotels: the **Carlton** (*see* Lodging, *below*), the **Savoy** (Rua Imperatriz Dona Amelia 108, tel. 91/25301), and **Reid's** (*see* Lodging, *below*). Also available are two public swimming pools and sea access, slightly west of Funchal, at the **Lido Swimming Complex** (Rua Gorgulho; 170$00 adults, 50$00 children 11–17; open summer, daily 9–7, and winter, daily 9–6) and **Quinta Magnolia** (Rua Dr. Pita, tel. 91/764598, 135$00 adults, 55$00 children). The onetime British Country Club, now a public park, with beautiful views of Funchal, is open daily 9–4 and includes acres of gardens and lawns, as well as a jogging-and-fitness course and tennis courts available by reservation.

In **Porto Moniz** cement pools have been built around the rocky coastline for delightful summer wading.

Beaches

When Madeirans want to swim they head for the beach on the neighboring island of **Porto Santo.** It is an idyllic, undeveloped strand of soft, golden sand that stretches 9 kilometers (5½ miles) along the entire southern coast of the island. Although Porto Santo beach has a tendency to get crowded close to town in summer, it is so long that there are always empty stretches and quiet sand dunes. The warm ocean currents make swimming possible on sunny winter days.

Dining and Lodging

Dining There are a number of restaurants on Madeira that specialize in island cuisine, and most typical meals revolve around a deep-sea fish known as *espada*. Although *espada* means "swordfish" on mainland Portugal, in Madeira it refers to a softer whitefish that's like scabbard or cutlass fish. It's served everywhere and prepared dozens of ways, from poached à la Provençal to fried with bananas. Seafood gourmets will also want to try the Portuguese version of bouillabaisse, called *caldeirada de peixes variados*, a slowly simmered combination of fish, shellfish, potatoes, onions, and olive oil. The other popular fish plate is *bife de atum*, a hearty tuna steak. Those with adventurous tastes should search out *polvo com vinagre*—a tangy octopus salad.

A favorite meal of tourists and locals alike is *espetada*, a beef shish kebab seasoned with bay leaves and butter. Traditionally it was a party dish prepared in the country over open fires, and the meat was skewered on laurel branches. Nowadays, the delicacy is served on iron skewers, but it still makes a fun meal: The kebabs are hung vertically from special stands placed in the center of each table for the food to be shared by all diners. Also worth trying is *milho frito* (fried cubes of savory corn pudding), a side dish native to Madeira.

Typically, dessert menus include delicious tropical fruits, such as bananas, papaya, and *anona* (custard-filled apples); and *maracujá* (passion fruit). Those with a sweet tooth will also enjoy *bolo de mel*, a spicy Christmas cake made with molasses and served with a glass of Madeira.

Madeira's wines have been enjoyed for more than 500 years and were especially popular in bygone eras, when they graced the tables of Napoleon, the Russian czars, and even George Washington. It is a fortified wine served as an aperitif or with dessert, depending on its sweetness. Unlike other wines, Madeira is heated to produce its distinctive mellow flavor—a process that supposedly developed after thirsty sailors sampled the Madeira that had been shipped through equatorial heat. They discovered that it actually tasted better that way. There are four varieties of Madeira. From driest to sweetest, they are: *sercial, verdelho, boal,* and malmsey. For a tasty nonalcoholic drink, try *Brisa maracuja*, a sparkling passion-fruit drink.

Funchal has a variety of dining places and two restaurant rows: One is in the Old Town on Largo do Corpo Santo, and the other is between the Carlton and Casino Park hotels, on Rua Imperatriz Dona Amelia. Eating out in Funchal is a fairly formal activity, especially in hotel restaurants, where men are expected to wear suits, and reservations are always required. Village restaurants in other parts of the island are informal and generally serve huge plates of fish and vegetables at bargain prices.

Restaurant ratings correspond to Lisbon's dining chart, in Chapter 3. Highly recommended restaurants are indicated by a star ★.

Lodging Nearly all visitors to Madeira stay in Funchal, where a strip of hotels begins at the casino and extends westward along the sea for miles. As a general rule, the hotels closest to the casino are most expensive.

Madeiran hotels cater to package-tour operators, who offer better prices and reserve huge blocks of rooms during peak holiday-travel periods. This may be one place where normally do-it-yourself travelers are better off going through an agency. Christmas and New Year's is the busiest season to visit Madeira, and reservations must be made far in advance. Summer can also be crowded, especially during August, when the Portuguese take vacations.

Highly recommended lodgings are indicated by a star ★.

Category	Cost*
Very Expensive	over 20,000$00
Expensive	15,000$00–20,000$00
Moderate	10,000$00–15,000$00
Inexpensive	under 10,000$00

All prices are for a standard double room for two, including tax, except during Christmas week, when rates are substantially higher.

Câmara de Lobos
Dining

Coral Bar. Ignore the pleasant tables on the plaza and head upstairs to the simple rooftop terrace, where you can look out onto the spectacular cliffs of Cabo Girão, Madeira's most famous fishing village. The day's catch is unloaded about a block away and served here in big earthenware bowls. Try the *peixe* *mista* (mixed seafood) in spicy tomato-and-mushroom sauce or the espada with fried bananas. *Largo República 2, tel. 91/ 942469. No reservations. Dress: casual. AE, DC, MC, V. Inexpensive.*

Funchal Dining

Les Faunes. Named for the series of Picasso lithographs that adorns the walls, Les Faunes is the reincarnation of the famous Reid's Grill, which for decades was the epitome of Madeira dining. In 1991 the Reid's Hotel (*see* Lodging, *below*) refurbished its crowning jewel with a sophisticated blue-gray decor and placed tables on two tiers so all diners can enjoy the stunning view of Funchal at night. A pianist plays romantic background music during your meal. The French menu changes daily, but expect to find such dishes as carpaccio of beef with caviar, galantine of scallops in grapefruit sauce, and pheasant with figs and port. *Reid's Hotel, Estrada Monumental 139, tel. 91/ 23001. Reservations required. Jacket and tie required. AE, DC, MC, V. No lunch. Very Expensive.*

Carochinha. Amber Victorian lamps, candlelight, and lace tablecloths create the romantic atmosphere of this English-style restaurant beside the municipal gardens, in the center of town. Salads are available at lunch, as well as traditional British fare such as roast beef and Yorkshire pudding. Evening diners usually go for specialties with French accents, such as duck in orange sauce and coq au vin. Afternoon tea is served weekdays 3:30–5:30. *Rua São Francisco 2A, tel. 91/23695. Reservations advised for dinner. Jacket advised. AE, DC, MC, V. Closed Sun. Expensive.*

★ **Solar do F.** The emphasis here is on high-quality Portuguese dishes in an upscale atmosphere with impeccable service. Choose your dining area: a stone chamber that looks like a wine cellar, an elegant French-provincial dining room. The restaurant, one block uphill from the Madeira Carlton hotel, is perched at the edge of an overgrown ravine, and in good weather tables are placed outside in the garden. Try the avocados stuffed with shrimp or the espada served Madeiran style, with mushrooms in a spicy tomato sauce. *Av. Luís Camões 19, tel. 91/20212. Reservations advised. Jacket and tie advised. AE, DC, MC, V. Moderate–Expensive.*

★ **A Seta.** It's tacky, and the parking area is crammed with tour buses, but this hilltop restaurant situated high above Funchal serves the best espetada on the island. You'll share long narrow tables with other diners, while high-energy waiters dodge in and out among folk dancers and *fado* (traditional Portuguese folk music) singers. The meat is cooked over a charcoal fire in the dining-room fireplace, then the skewers are suspended from ingenious wrought-iron hooks at each table. It's a messy meal but lots of fun. *Estrada do Livramento 80, tel. 91/47643. Reservations advised. Jacket advised. AE, DC, MC, V. Closed Wed. Moderate.*

Gavina's. Beyond the Lido swimming complex, at the edge of the sea, is this unadorned seafood house with a long tradition of providing Funchal with the freshest fish and shellfish. The grim concrete exterior may be off-putting, but once inside you can choose your dinner from the seafood tank then settle down in front of long picture windows that look out over the waves. Free transportation to and from most hotels is provided on request. *Rua do Gorgulho (Praia), tel. 91/62918. No reservations. Dress: casual. AE, DC, MC, V. Moderate.*

★ **Golfinho.** Owner Virgilio Gavina, a former championship swimmer and water-skier, has a passion for the sea, and it shows in his old town restaurant. Resembling the inside of a submarine, the dining area includes an eclectic collection of old scuba gear and brass ship-fittings, in a beautifully polished wood interior. Gavina owns a fleet of three fishing boats and goes fishing whenever possible to bring his customers a wide selection of fresh seafood. In addition to the ubiquitous espada, there are usually three or four varieties of fish on the menu, often *dourada* (sea bass), red mullet, and turbot. Meat dishes are also served, including a tasty espetada. Don't miss the house special, *espedarte* (an appetizer of smoked swordfish). *Largo do Corpo Santo 21, tel. 91/26774. No reservations. Jacket advised. AE, DC, MC, V. Closed Sun. Moderate.*

Le Jardin. Dine in the glass-enclosed sidewalk café or in the plant-filled dining room decorated with wrought-iron furniture. This old town restaurant is a favorite with Scandinavian visitors, who appreciate the international cuisine cooked tableside and served with panache. Pepper steak is popular, as are the bananas flambé. *Rua Don Carlos, tel. 91/22864. Reservations advised. Dress: casual. AE, MC, V. Moderate.*

Churrascaria Gavião. Located on a busy corner in the middle of old town, this stand-up chicken-and-steak place is the Portuguese equivalent of a fast-food joint. Place mats are laid out around a circular bar that has a charcoal grill in the middle. When a slot opens up, simply step forward and order what looks good. *Rua Don Carlos 64, tel. 91/24821. No reservations. Dress: casual. No credit cards. Inexpensive.*

Combatentes. This large plain dining room situated behind the municipal gardens is where Funchal's businesspeople go for inexpensive daily lunch specials. You can get big portions of simple Madeiran cooking such as espada, grilled sardines, turkey, or lamb. Dinner is also served. *Rua Ivens 1, tel. 91/21388. No reservations. Dress: casual. MC, V. Inexpensive.*

O Arco. Located in Funchal's shopping district, this simple tiled dining room is a good place to try typical Madeiran dishes such as espetada and grilled fish. Two stone arches are the only decoration in this spotless restaurant, and no English is spoken, but the staff is friendly, the food fresh, and the place always filled with diners. *Rua da Carreira 63A, tel. 91/20134. No reservations. Dress: casual. No credit cards. Inexpensive.*

Xaramba. When young Madeirans want a break from seafood they usually head for this lively pizza place tucked behind the church in the old section of town. Individual-size pies are prepared behind a long bar as hungry customers watch. The ovens stay hot until 3 AM, and the tiny restaurant fills up late at night, so come early or be prepared to wait for a table. *Rua Fontes São Tiago 11, tel. 91/29785. No reservations. Dress: casual. No credit cards. No lunch. Inexpensive.*

Lodging **Casino Park.** Part of the casino complex designed by Oscar Niemeyer, the architect of Brasilia (capital of Brazil), this hotel is a rather drab, gray, concrete building that sits next to what looks like a nuclear reactor but is actually the casino. Inside, the public rooms are much more pleasant and are flooded with natural light from floor-to-ceiling windows that overlook the gardens and sea. A bright orange-and-beige color scheme pervades the guest rooms. The hotel has convention facilities. *Quinta da Vigia, 9000, tel. 91/33111, fax 91/32076. 400 rooms with bath. Facilities: 2 restaurants, 2 bars, coffee shop, salt-*

water pool, tennis court, fitness center, sauna, Jacuzzi, satellite TV. AE, DC, MC, V. Very Expensive.

Madeira Carlton. A top-notch staff adds warmth to this 18-story beachfront high-rise 10 minutes from central Funchal on foot. Many of the guests at this hotel (once a member of the Sheraton chain) are repeat visitors who have come here every season since the hotel opened, in 1971, and are still attracted by friendly service and a range of sports facilities. The Carlton has a bustling lobby furnished in '70s-modern style and large bedrooms with terraces that provide sweeping views of the ocean or mountains. Ask for a room on one of the renovated floors, where carpets, drapes, and spreads are coordinated in an airy pastel color scheme and baths have been refurbished with Portuguese tile. *Largo António Nobre, 9000, tel. 91/31031, fax 91/27284. 374 rooms with bath. Facilities: 4 restaurants, 3 bars, disco, 2 saltwater pools, children's pool, tennis court, miniature golf, sailboarding, scuba diving school, hairdresser, satellite TV. AE, DC, MC, V. Very Expensive.*

★ **Reid's.** It's a marvelously old-fashioned and decadently luxurious hotel, with corridors that smell of furniture wax, bathwater that comes out tinted blue (from water softeners), and a bellhop who plays a chime to announce dinner each evening. For more than 100 years Reid's has been an exclusive British resort, where aristocrats and business tycoons get away from it all. Situated on a rocky point a 15-minute walk from the center of town, the hotel is surrounded by 10 acres of gardens filled with flowering plants. Rooms are large, with wainscoting and pastel bargello bedspreads, and all have wide balconies with sea views. Baths include towel warmers. Cruise-ship visitors to Funchal and those staying in other hotels often stop by for afternoon tea on the terrace or a nightcap in the bar. Formal wear is advised in the dining room. *Estrada Monumental 139, 9000, tel. 91/23000, fax 91/30499. 173 rooms with bath. Facilities: 2 restaurants, bar, 2 saltwater pools, 2 tennis courts, sailboarding, waterskiing, sauna, massage. AE, MC, V. Very Expensive.*

Baia Azul. A gleaming white-marble lobby decorated with sleek burgundy furniture sets the mood at this multilevel hotel, which opened in 1991. Located on the outskirts of Funchal about a 30-minute walk west of the center of town, the accommodation offers ocean views from 75% of the rooms, and the pool area is fringed by an old banana plantation. Bedrooms are cheerfully decorated with pink carpets and flowered chintz. *Estrada Monumental, 9000, tel. 91/766260, fax 91/764245. 21 rooms with bath. Facilities: restaurant, coffee shop, 2 bars, saltwater pool, children's pool, squash court, fitness room, sauna, Jacuzzi, game room, hairdresser, satellite TV. AE, MC, V. Expensive.*

Eden Mar. This seven-story inn up the street from the Lido swimming complex is one of the newest hotels to capitalize on the package-tour trade. It's a favorite with families, who settle in for long stays and appreciate the kitchenettes in each unit. The lobby is white marble, but the rest of the hotel has a homey floral-print decor. All rooms have sea views. *Rua do Gorgulho 2, 9000, tel. 91/762221, fax 91/761966. 68 two-room suites and 37 studios, all with kitchenette and bath. Facilities: restaurant, coffee shop, bar, saltwater pool, gym, sauna, squash court. AE, MC, V. Expensive.*

Quinta da Penha França. Located in an unbeatable area—just above Funchal harbor—this is the place for those who prefer their resorts casual rather than glitzy. The homey, four-story white house with green shutters is surrounded by gardens and a sunny pool. Every room is slightly different, and the furnishings border on the antique. *Rua da Penha França 2, 9000, tel. 91/29087. 41 rooms with bath. Facilities: swimming pool. AE, MC, V. Moderate–Expensive.*

★ **Quinta do Bela Vista.** Formerly the mansion of the rich Doctor Roberto Monteiro, this hotel provides elegance and hospitality that will make you feel like you're visiting a well-to-do family friend. The Quinta, which opened in 1991, is located in the hills above Funchal and offers only four guest rooms in the original home; the downstairs has been converted into a gourmet restaurant. The other rooms are arranged in two new buildings, constructed in the same elegant colonial style as the main house. All guest quarters are classically decorated with mahogany furniture, four-poster beds, and French doors that open onto the gardens. *Caminho do Avista Navios 4, 9000, tel. 91/764144, fax 91/765090. 72 rooms with bath. Facilities: restaurant, bar, pool, tennis court, gym, sauna, Jacuzzi. AE, DC, MC, V. Moderate.*

Estrelicia. Named for Madeira's exotic bird-of-paradise flower, the Estrelicia is topmost of three high-rise towers built uphill from the hotel strip. Perhaps because of its somewhat inconvenient location, the hotel is an especially good value. This Best Western accommodation has a lively waterfall in its lobby and gold bedspreads and brown-leather chairs in its large, carpeted guest rooms. *Caminho Velho da Ajuda, 9000, tel. 91/30131, fax 91/61044. 148 rooms with bath. Facilities: restaurant, 2 bars, disco, saltwater pool, children's pool, tennis court, hairdresser. AE, MC, V. Inexpensive.*

Hotel Madeira. This hotel situated on a quiet street in central Funchal has a pleasant marble lobby and tiny rooftop pool. Rooms are basic but carpeted, and each has a balcony—some overlook the municipal gardens. *Rua Ivens 21, 9009, tel. 91/30071. 30 rooms with bath. Facilities: restaurant, bar, pool. AE, MC, V. Inexpensive.*

Machico
Lodging

Atlantis. This 16-story luxury hotel not far from the airport and close to a golf course is a small world unto itself, and guests seldom venture off the grounds. The resort offers the only indoor pool in Madeira and an elegant tawny-marble lobby. Rooms are small, but all have balconies with views of Zarco Bay or the mountains. *Agua de Pena, 9200, tel. 91/965811, fax 91/965859. 322 rooms with bath. Facilities: 3 restaurants, 2 bars, nightclub, indoor and outdoor pools, tennis courts, bridge club. AE, MC, V. Moderate.*

Pico Do Arieira
Dining and Lodging

Pousada do Arieiro. Designed for visitors who would rather hike than sunbathe, this state-owned inn is located among Madeira's rocky peaks, high above the tree line. The exterior of the white-stucco building is bleak, but inside you'll find cozy rooms with chintz curtains and bedspreads. The dining room has spectacular views of the island and serves traditional island cooking, including good soups and espada. In winter there is usually a welcoming fire blazing in the bar. *Mailing address: Apart. 478, 9006 Funchal, tel. 91/30131, fax 91/28611. 21 rooms with bath. Facilities: restaurant. AE, MC, V. Moderate.*

Porto Moniz
Dining

Restaurant Orca. This is the place to go for espada caught fresh and prepared in every way imaginable. Try it fried with orange, banana, kiwi, or passion fruit. All meals come with big servings of vegetables and rice and are served in the large, fern-filled dining room with long picture windows that overlook the rocky swimming area at the far end of Madeira. *By rocks at end of rd., tel. 91/852359. No reservations. Dress: casual. AE, MC, V. Inexpensive.*

Porto Santo Dining

Arsénios. Red-and-white-check tablecloths are your clue that this is the place for pizza, spaghetti, and lasagna. Portuguese specialties are also served in a rustic, comfortable dining room. *Av. Dr. Manuel Pestana Jr., tel. 91/982348. No reservations. Dress: casual. AE, MC, V. Inexpensive.*

Bainai. A covered patio serves as a combination sidewalk café and town meeting-place, as just about everybody seems to wander by in the morning for a cup of coffee. Bainai also serves sandwiches, *feijãoda* (bean stew), and *carne vinho e alho* (pork marinated in wine and garlic). *Rua Dr. Nuno S. Teixeira, tel. 91/982649. No reservations. Dress: casual. No credit cards. Closes at 5. Inexpensive.*

Esplanada da Praia. Located pier-side in a boxy white building with green shutters, this restaurant serves hearty Portuguese dishes featuring shrimp, squid, and fish fresh off the hook. *Av. Infante D. Henrique, tel. 91/983230. No reservations. Dress: casual. V. Inexpensive.*

Pôr do Sol. At the far end of the beach, near Ponta da Calheta, an island housewife makes sandwiches and fries burgers and fresh seafood in a primitive kitchen. The dining room is gleaming white and spotless, and there's a wide terrace at the beach's edge. This place has tables on the terrace and has the feel of a beach-picnic take-out restaurant but is not. *Ponta da Calheta, tel. 91/982380. No reservations. Dress: casual. No credit cards. Inexpensive.*

Teodorico. In this farmhouse restaurant, authentic espetada is the one and only dish available, but it can be washed down with carafes of the dry red wine that's produced on the island and served here. In warm weather you can eat outdoors on tables and chairs made from tree stumps; indoors you'll sit in a tiny tiled dining room with four tables and a wood-burning oven at one end. *Sera de Fora, tel. 91/982257. Reservations necessary. Dress: casual. No credit cards. No lunch. Inexpensive.*

Lodging
★

Hotel Porto Santo. Located on the beach and about a 15-minute walk from town, this hotel—a member of the Trusthouse Forte chain—is a beachcomber's dream come true. Aside from the seemingly endless stretches of golden sand, there's a country-club atmosphere, numerous sports activities, and a library-lounge that resembles a comfortable living room. Rooms overlook the countryside instead of the beach and are heavily booked throughout August, but during spring and fall you may have the place to yourself. *Porto Santo, 9400, tel. 91/982381 fax 91/982611. 102 rooms with bath. Facilities: restaurant, bar saltwater pool, tennis court, sailboarding, bicycle rentals ping-pong, darts, minigolf. AE, MC, V. Moderate.*

Praia Dourada. This comfortable white-stucco hotel in the middle of the village is a five-minute walk from the beach and is popular with budget-minded German and Portuguese travelers. Inside, the corridors are dark, but the carpeted rooms are bright, and there's a small pool with a sun deck. *Rua L Estevão D'Alencastre, 9400, tel. 91/982315, fax 91/982487. 3 rooms with bath. Facilities: saltwater pool. AE, MC, V. Inexpensive–Moderate.*

Ribeira Brava
Dining

Agua Mar. This restaurant, with sun umbrellas and bright blue tablecloths has a popular beachfront setting and is frequented on the weekend by large families who drive out from Funchal to lunch here. Just about all the classic Portuguese specialties are served; the house favorite is the fresh fish and *peixe com arroz* (seafood rice). *Tel. 91/951148. No reservations. Dress: casual. MC, V. Moderate.*

Ribeiro Frio
Dining

Victor's Bar. This rustic, pinewood-and-glass restaurant a few steps from the trout hatchery in the central Madeiran mountains makes the best of the local product. Trout soup, smoked trout, and grilled trout are served, and in the background is the sound of a rushing river that passes by outside the dining room. *Tel. 91/782898. No reservations. Dress: casual. No credit cards. Moderate.*

Serra de Agua
Dining and Lodging

Pousada dos Vinháticos. This tiny stone lodge perched on the edge of a pine forest provides accommodations for nature lovers, most of whom swear this is the most beautiful part of Madeira. Although Vinháticos is state-operated, the friendly staff gives it the feel of a private home. The interior features wood paneling and exposed stone. Madeira specialties espetada and carne vinho e alho are featured in the restaurant. *Hwy. EN–104 between Brava and Encumeada Pass on western part of island, 9350, tel. 91/952344, fax 91/952540. 12 rooms with bath. Facilities: restaurant. AE, MC, V. Moderate.*

The Arts and Nightlife

The Arts

Festivals Madeira proudly makes the most of its folkloric traditions. No matter when you visit, there's a good chance you will see folk dances performed at a restaurant or hotel. Costumed dancers whirl to the music of a small guitarlike instrument called a *machête*, the forerunner of the ukelele. Musicians also shake a colorful pole decorated with tiny folk-dancer dolls that jangle like a tambourine. Special occasions include the weekend before Lent, when **Carnival** is celebrated throughout Funchal with processions and costume parades; the **Flower Festival,** in the last week of April, which brightens the downtown with a flower carpet, a parade, and lots of music; August 14 and 15, when the **Festival of Nossa Senhora do Monte,** the patron saint of Madeira, attracts pilgrims from all corners of the island; the last week of September, when the **Wine Harvest Festival** takes place, and features plenty of singing, dancing, and wine tasting; and **New Year's Eve,** with demonstrations of traditional crafts, bands of strolling dancers and singers, thousands of lights, and spectacular fireworks launched from the hillsides surrounding Funchal.

Theater The **Teatro Municipal Baltazar Diaz** (Av. Arriaga, tel. 91/20416), in Funchal, offers occasional concerts and plays. The local newspaper carries listings, but the easiest way to find out the schedule is to check posters outside the theater. Tickets can be purchased at the box office.

Nightlife

Evening entertainment in Funchal is sedate and centers around the big hotels, which offer Las Vegas–style floor shows and bands for cheek-to-cheek dancing.

Bars If you're looking to meet someone or simply to have a quiet chat against a backdrop of live jazz, the current "in" spot is the terrace-bar **Salsa Latina** (Rua Imperatriz D. Amélia 101, tel. 91/25182). For a more unusual evening's entertainment try the Japanese-style **Karioki Bar** (Hotel do Mar, Estrada Monumental, tel. 91/31001), where would-be singing stars from the audience have a chance to show their stuff.

Cabaret Young entertainers perform nightly dinner shows at the **Madeira Carlton Hotel** (Largo António Nobre, tel. 91/31031) and the **Casino Park Hotel** (Quinta da Vigia, tel. 91/33111).

Casino Gamblers will want to try their luck in the **Casino da Madeira** (Av. do Infante, tel. 91/31121), which opens nightly at 8 and is housed in a modern building that resembles a roulette wheel.

Discos Funchal's elegant younger set gravitates to **Baccará** (Av. do Infante, tel. 91/31121), a postmodern disco beneath the casino. Here green laser lights bounce off the concrete walls and the pounding beat never wanes. The over-30 crowd sometimes prefers the huge **O Farol** (Largo António Nobre, tel. 91/31031), at the Madeira Carlton Hotel, where hits from the '70s and '80s are mixed in with contemporary disco tunes.

Fado A steady stream of tourists fills the tables of Funchal's fado club, **Marcelino Pao y Vinho** (Travessa da Torre 22–A, tel. 91/30834). In the center of the old town, the club attracts aficionados as well as the just plain curious, who come to hear Portugal's soulful national music played each night from 9:30 until about 2.

10 Excursion to the Azores

By David Ing

Originally from Oxford, England, David Ing has settled in Madrid, Spain, where he writes about travel, food, and wine.

Touring the Azores will not be a cosmopolitan experience: There are no big cities to lure you with big-city glitz and endless itineraries of must-see attractions. When you visit the Azores you can expect to find restful islands that lack the familiar stress of many destinations, but offer year-round natural beauty and a poised calm. The essence of the islands is reflected not only in the startling flora such as the ubiquitous hydrangea hedges with their pink, white, and blue bursts in summer, but in the friendly, sincere nature of the people who live on the islands.

Reputed to be the lost land of Atlantis, the Azores—anchored in the mid-Atlantic and straddling an imaginary line between New York and Lisbon—are a chain of nine volcanic islands at the meeting point of the American and European plates. Throughout their history the Azores have experienced major eruptions and earthquakes, which have devastated some towns and left gaping craters, and have created barren areas resembling the surface of the moon. But don't imagine that the islands are deserts of lava and rock; most of the landscape is colorful and lush, due to frequent storms (especially January through March) that feed myriad streams and lakes. The archipelago enjoys waters warmed by the Gulf Stream and mild temperatures that rarely exceed 73°F in August and 55°F in February.

The Azores are divided into three groups. São Miguel, the most popular island, and the little island of Santa Maria comprise the eastern group. São Miguel—the biggest and most accessible of the chain—offers a good cross-section of all the islands, both in its nature and architecture. If you have time, try to stay on at least one of the smaller islands (particularly Faial, Pico, or São Jorge), which, along with Terceira and Graciosa, form the central group. Tiny Flores—a favorite of many people—and even tinier Corvo comprise the western isles.

Aside from their enticing beauty, the Azores have historic appeal, too. Reputedly, the islands were discovered by Phoenicians, who are believed to have come across the chain before Christ's time, although there is no evidence to confirm that they actually settled here. History records that Portuguese mariners, in their haste to find a westward route to the Orient initially ignored the islands, and it wasn't until about 1427 when they landed.

When the Portuguese throne was absorbed by Spain's Philip I in 1580, the Azores at first demonstrated a strong resistance to the occupation: In one conflict, the invaders were driven back to sea by islanders from Terceira who stampeded cattle into the troops. But in time, under Spanish rule, the Azores began to thrive: Angra, the then-largest town in the group, enjoyed golden age as the major hub of shippping routes between the Old and New worlds, although it suffered frequent attacks by pirates such as Francis Drake and Walter Raleigh. Even after Portugal regained independence in 1640, the the Azores' peaceful existence was occasionally shattered by raiding French and North African corsairs.

Although the islands were remote, they were important in the 18th and 19th centuries. In the late 1700s the island of Pico, and to a lesser extent, Faial, attracted foreigners, especially New England whalers who set up hunting bases on the islands.

century later Faial became the main link in the first trans-Atlantic telegraph network, because the island was considered a midway point in the Atlantic. In its role, Faial was responsible for transcontinental communications and for conveying weather conditions for ocean traffic. Unfortunately, successive governments in Lisbon failed to invest in the distant islands, causing widescale emigration and decline. Even after the 1974 Carnation Revolution, which brought a return to deocracy in Portugal after years of dictatorship, the islands were still regarded as the most backward region of a backward country.

But since Portugal joined the Economic Community (EC) in 1986, the standard of living has risen considerably: The Azores have received aid packages for their main industries—agriculture and fishing—and for new roads and building projects. Thousands of emigrants who left to find work in the United States and Canada have returned to take advantage of new opportunities, and are breathing life into the community. Given the strong ties that so many Azoreans have with North America, you should have no problem finding someone who speaks English.

About 70% of those who visit the Azores are from the "Continent" (the islanders' name for mainland Portugal); fewer than 40,000 tourists are foreigners. This region, where tourism is still in its infancy, attracts mostly "over 40s" travelers, probably because there's not much in the way of nightlife, organized sporting events, or entertainment. But if you're looking for unpolluted air and water and a quiet, easy-going lifestyle, this destination is ideal. There's no rule as to how much time you should spend here, but a quick trip should be no fewer than four or five days, which should give you enough time to get a fairly solid impression of the Azores.

Most people visit the Azores in summer, the driest season, but in November and December (also fairly dry months) the crowds are gone and you'll have virtually the entire island group to yourself. Regardless of when you visit, flowers will always be in bloom: Azaleas follow camellias, which are replaced by hydrangeas. Even the wild ginger lily—called a weed—produces a riot of orange through autumn and into winter.

Essential Information

Important Addresses and Numbers

Tourist Information The main tourist office for the Azores is the **Direção Regional de Turismo** (Rua Marcelino de Lima, Horta, Faial, tel. 092/23801). There are also offices in São Miguel (Av. Infante Dom Henrique, Ponta Delgada, tel. 096/25743), Terceira (Rua Rio de Janeiro 47–A, Angra do Heroísmo, tel. 095/23393), Faial (Rua Vasco da Gama, Horta, tel. 092/22237), and Pico (Hotel Caravelas (Rua Conselheiro Terra Pinheiro, Madelena, tel. 092/92500). All offices are open June–September, Monday–Saturday 9–12:30 and 2–5:30; during off-peak months hours vary. Small offices, called *postos de turismo*, are open June–September, and can be found in São Jorge (Rua Roque Afonso, Velas, tel. 095/42214), Santa Maria (Aeroporto, Vila do Porto, tel. 096/53140), and Graçiosa (Praça Fontes Pereira de Melo, Santa Cruz, tel. 095/72125).

Consulates **United States** (Av. Infante Dom Henrique, Ponta Delgada, tel. 096/22216), **United Kingdom** (Largo Vasco Bensaúde 13, Ponta Delgada, tel. 096/22201).

Emergencies The national emergency number is 115.

Hospitals **Hospital de Ponte Delgada** (Praça 5 de Outubro, Ponta Delgada, São Miguel, tel. 096/22322), **Hospital de Angra** (Rua do Varreiro, Angra do Heroísmo, Terceira, tel. 095/22122), **Hospital Distrital da Horta** (Rua Príncipe Alberto de Mónaco, Horta, Faial, tel. 05/22121).

Arriving and Departing by Plane

The only way to get to the Azores is by plane: **TAP Air Portugal** (1 Exeter Plaza, 7th floor, Boston, MA 02116, tel. 617/262-8585) offers flights from Boston via Lisbon that stop at Terceira on Thursday night and at São Miguel on Friday night. Planes from Lisbon to Boston fly on the same days and make the same stops. A free stopover to the islands is not officially offered when you purchase a Boston–Lisbon return fare, but sometimes the airline honors such requests, depending on how full the flight is. Ask for a double ticket (free voucher) before you pay an additional fare to the islands.

At press time, only TAP flies from Europe to Lisbon and Madeira, although with deregulation in the EC this may soon change. There are two flights daily to São Miguel in summer (one in winter) and one flight daily to Terceira and Faial (three weekly in winter to Faial) from Lisbon. TAP flies Monday and Saturday between Madeira and São Miguel.

In summer, **SATA, Azores Express** (227 S. Main St., Fall River, MA 02721, tel. 508/677–0555; 221 Dufferin St., suite 106A, Box 18, Toronto, Ontario M6K 1Y9, tel. 416/588–4499) flies weekly charters direct from Boston (5½ hours) and two charters a month direct from Toronto (6 hours) to São Miguel.

Lawson Tours (Rua Lisboa 16A, Ponta Delgada, São Miguel, tel. 096/24540; 2 Carlton St., Suite 620, Toronto, Ontario M5B 1JT, tel. 416/977–3000) flies weekly from Toronto to Ponta Delgada, on São Miguel in summer; certain flights call at Terceira on the way. **Air Colombus** links the islands with Canada and Madeira (see Arriving and Departing in Madeira, Chapter 8).

Between the Islands

By Plane SATA serves the main islands with regular flights, the longest of which is between Faial and Flores, and takes about 55 minutes; to reach some smaller islands you may have to change planes. SATA's main regional offices are on São Miguel (Av. Infante Dom Henrique 55, Ponta Delgada, tel. 096/27221), Terceira (Rua Dr. Eduardo Abreu 2, Angra do Heroísmo, tel. 095/22013), and Faial (Rua Sera Pinta, Horta, tel. 092/23911). Flights sometimes depart early, so make sure you get to the airport on time. If you can book in advance a route that takes in several islands, you may get a discount. You can then change the dates of your flights but not the route. For all summer flights you will need to make advance reservations.

By Boat Small, modern ferries connect the five islands in the central group—Faial, Pico, São Jorge, Terceira, and Graciosa. From May to September there are at least four half-hour crossings daily from Faial to Pico and at least one per day (except Sunday) from São Jorge to either Pico (one hour) or Faial (two hours). There are sailings alternate weekdays between Terceira and Graciosa (four hours). From October through April, crossings are less frequent. Traveling by boat is cheaper than flying, and also offers good views of the islands. Tickets can be purchased from **Transmaçor** (Rua Nova 29, Horta, Faial, tel. 092/23334; Av. Alvaro Martins Homen, Angra, Terceira, tel. 095/25104).

By Car All the islands except Corvo have car-rental agencies, most with a limited number of automobiles. You can book in advance through Avis's local agency, **Ilha Verde** (Praça 5 de Outubro 19, Ponta Delgada, São Miguel, tel. 096/25200), which has subagents on the other islands.

Road Conditions The road surfaces are generally good, and distances on the islands are relatively short: Even São Miguel can be toured in less than a day.

By Taxi Many visitors to the smaller islands hire cabs for the day, by the hour, or for a specific route. Drivers allow time for stops and charge preset tariffs for typical sightseeing journeys.

Guided Tours

Travel agencies on most of the islands organize sightseeing tours. Among the agencies are: **Ornelas** (Av. Infante Don

Henrique, Ponta Delgada, São Miguel, tel. 096/22236) and **Agência Açoreana de Viagens** (Lado Sul-Matriz 69, Ponta Delgada, São Miguel, tel. 096/25396). These agencies have branches or sub-agencies on the other islands, as well.

Exploring the Azores

São Miguel

The most-visited and largest island in the Azores is São Miguel, 65 kilometers (40 miles) long, with 759 square kilometers (296 square miles), or a third of the island group's total landmass. Most of the 125,000 residents (more than half the Azores' population) live in the central strip between the capital city of Ponta Delgada on the south coast and Ribeira Grande, on the north.

The western part of the island is mainly pasture, and the east is more wooded, mostly with Japanese cedar. In between grow exotic crops such as pineapple and passion fruit. The island also contains the only tea plantations in Europe.

Ponta Delgada Ponta Delgada, with a population of 35,000, is the largest city in the Azores and is the islands' main port. There is an interesting museum and some churches here—enough to keep you occupied for half a day. A good place to start is the Praça de Gonçalo Velha, where behind the arches of the 18th-century city gates is the **São Sebastião parish church** with a Manueline and Baroque entrance, embellished with carved cedar and tropical woods. Inside is a collection of 14th-century English religious garments and silver chalices.

Nossa Senhora da Esperança (Our Lady of Hope), a convent and chapel on Praça 5 de Outobro, is a four-minute walk from the western end of the harbor. Displayed inside the chapel is an image of Christ, said to have been given to the nuns here in the 16th century by Pope Paul III. A number of miracles have been attributed to the image, which has taken on a cult following and is celebrated during the Senhor Santo Cristo festival, which begins on the fifth Sunday after Easter and lasts for six days. The mixture of piety and pleasure features fireworks displays, music, and colorful processions through streets carpeted in flower petals. The image is now swamped in jewels that have been offered by faithful followers over the years.

Turn left up Rua da Esperança and left at the town theater for the former monastery of Santo André, now the **Carlos Machado town museum.** In addition to an art collection that includes 16th-century painted panels, there's an interesting ethnological display depicting Azorean life through the centuries; natural history and geological exhibits; and a toy collection. *Rua João Moreira, no tel. Admission free. Open weekdays 9–noon and 2–5.*

In the suburb of Faja de Baixa, about 7 kilometers (4 miles) from the center of the city, you can tour the **pineapple plantations** and see how fruit ripens in the greenhouses, a system unique to the Azores. Pineapple liqueur is offered for tasting. *Plantações Augusto Arruda, Rua da Abilheira, tel. 096/31126. Admission free. Open daily 9–8.*

Just 3 kilometers (2 miles) away is **Quinta da Bela Vista,** a 18th-century mansion housing an eclectic collection that in cludes armor, vintage Jaguar sports cars, and horse-drawn carriages. The house sits in peaceful gardens with walkways through lush shrubs. Visits are by appointment only. *Bom Fim Adelheira, Faja de Baixa, tel. 096/31317. Admission: 1,000$00.*

Crater Lakes at Sete Cidades and the West The road to the crater at the small village of **Sete Cidades** promises several good viewpoints, and from these you can glimpse the diversity of São Miguel's terrain. In less than an hour's drive from Ponta Delgada you'll reach the giant hollow—once a volcano—that is now almost filled by the twin lakes of **Lagoa Verde** (Green Lake) and **Lago Azul** (Blue Lake), both framed by the forested rim. The best view is from Vista do Rei (King's View) on the south side.

Drive into the crater and across the causeway that divides the two lakes, and pick up the road that leads to **Ribeira Grande.** The novel attraction here is the **Da Silva plant,** where Maracuja do Ezequiel liqueur is made from locally grown passion fruit. Visitors are welcome on weekdays, although there are no formal tours or set hours of operation. *Rua Condes da Ribeira Grande, tel. 096/472352. Admission free.*

Stay on the road and head for **Lagoa do Fogo** (Fire Lake), another crater lake—without the trees, but with a beach lapped by clear waters. On the way you'll pass **Caldeira Velha,** a plunging waterfall with a natural swimming pool below. As the road climbs there are more sweeeping views of both coasts, before it drops back down to Ponta Delgada.

Furnas and the East The eastern part of the island offers a number of natural attractions including dramatic gorges overgrown with semi-tropical vegetation; cedar forests that sweep to the sea below the Miradouro Tronqueira viewpoint; and the imposing Pico de Vara, which, at 3,510 feet, is the highest peak on São Miguel.

On the eastern edge of the tiny spa town of **Furnas** are the caldeiras: boiling geysers, some that spew clouds of sulphurous smoke, and mini craters that gurgle hot mud. All this action is a natural "exhaust system" that has inhibited volcanic eruptions since the 17th century. There are two springs within a few feet of each another at the foot of the caldeiras: One releases sparkling cold water, while the other is soothingly warm. Nearby is the original 19th-century spa hospital that has been recently refurbished and is open to the public as a spa.

On the other side of the Italianate town of Furnas, with its pastel-colored houses and twin-tower church, is **Terra Nostra Park.** On the grounds is a 1770 house (now part of the adjoining Terra Nostra Hotel) founded by Thomas Hickling, a Bostonian who made his fortune shipping oranges from the islands. The mass of exotic trees on the property were brought in from all corners of the world. In front is a thermal swimming pool that's open to the public every day except Sunday, when it's reserved for hotel guests. The water, which has turned brown, is not dirty, but discolored from the high iron content. *Rua Padre José Jacinto Botelho, tel. 096/54304. Admission to park and pool: 250$00.*

Located 3 kilometers (2 miles) from Terra Nostra Park, on the road to Povoação, is the **Lagoa da Furnas,** a lake fringed by azaleas and other flowering shrubs that change with the season. To explore the lake you can rent pedal boats on the shore. Along the lake's north side is a lane that leads to more geysers. Locals use the shafts set in the hot earth to cook *cozido*, a fish, meat, or vegetable stew prepared in earthenware pots that are lowered into the ground by wire.

Looming above Lagoa da Furnas is the **Pico de Ferro** (Iron Peak), from where you can see an Alpine-like vista of rolling hills and woods that stretch out out from the lake. To get there take the Ribeira Grande road and turn left at the golf course.

The other main attraction in the eastern part of the island is the **Ilheu de Vila Franca,** a flooded crater that provides a perfect natural swimming pool, and has a small beach. The crater, which is located on the south coast, 25 kilometers (15 miles) from Ponta Delgada, is most easily reached by small boats that ply the waters from the fishing village of Franco do Campo— the first capital of the island and known for its long tradition of pottery-making.

Terceira

Although it's the second most-populated of the islands, Terceira has a mostly uninhabited interior, where bush and rough pasture intermingle. Nearly all the settlements are dotted along the coast. The eastern side has many stone-walled pastures, with more rugged landscapes concentrated in the center, around two extinct craters. The island is less spectacular scenically than the others, although **Angra,** it's capital, is the most historically interesting town on the island chain.

The strong folkloric tradition of Terceira is the driving force behind the Espirito Santo (Holy Ghost) festivals held throughout the islands from May to September. Colorful street festivities, where an elected "emperor" hands out sweets and delicacies, are repeated all over the islands between Whitsun and late summer. The sweets represent the food that was formerly handed out to the poor from tiny *imperios* (chapels). These often gaily-colored buildings can be picked out by the white dove of the Holy Ghost or the crown on their roofs.

Terceira is also the best island to see the *tourada a corda* (bullfight on a cord), a 16th-century tradition. In this event, the bull is allowed to run the street on a rope held by a gang of *mascarados* (masked men), while bravadoes try to get as close to the padded horns as they dare. Some bullfights end up with the bull and taunters splashing into the sea, but the animal is never killed. A good time to see this peculiar happening is around St. John's Day (June 24), although the touradas are held throughout the summer in many villages on the island. The tourist office has a calendar of fights.

Angra do Heroísmo Because of its sheltered position on the southern coast of Terceira, Angra do Heroísmo—first city of the Azores—became the hub for trading between the Old and New Worlds and the Orient, especially during the Spanish occupation from 1583 to 1640. Much gold and silver passed through this important city, thus making it the target of many raids, mostly by the English. A number of the town's buildings feature fine architectural details; you'll need about six hours to see a sampling.

One of the most notable structures is the **Castelo de São João Baptista** (St. John the Baptist fort), which has a smaller sister fortress, the **Castelo de São Sebastião** (St. Sebastion fort), across the mouth of the *angra* (bay). Both were constructed during the Spanish occupation to guard the entrance to the harbor. You can climb on to the turreted walls to a wooded promontory overlooking the town from the road that leads to Monte Brasil. A good excursion is to take a 3-kilometer (2-mile) taxi ride up to the summit, where there are picnic tables and barbeques among the trees; then walk down the serpentine road (one-way traffic) to the fort.

In the town, one of the most striking buildings is the twin-towered 16th-century **Cathedral do São Salvador** (also Santa Sé do Salvador). Its high walls are noticeably bare inside, as most of the building's treasures were destroyed during the 1980 earthquake and a later fire. The graceful columns are testimony to the rebuilding work that has gone on since.

Immediately behind the cathedral is the 17th-century **Bettencourt Palace**, a baroque building with impressive cedar paneling, which is now a public library. During opening hours the public is invited to wander in and look around. *Rua da Rosa, tel. 095/22697. Admission free. Open Oct.–May, weekdays 9–8 and Sat. 9–3; June–Sept., weekdays 9–5 and Sat. 9–3.*

Also in town is the city museum, housed in the **Convento de São Francisco** (Convent of St. Francis)—a former monastery. Although the convent is currently closed for repairs, it is scheduled to reopen in early 1993. Highlights are an armory and exhibition rooms that feature Flemish paintings, statues, furniture, and musical instruments. *Ladeiro de São Francisco, tel. 095/25121. Admission free. Open weekdays 9–noon and 2–5.*

Thoughtfully situated in the center of town, the **Jardim Publico** (Public Gardens), with its colorful trees and flowers, provides visitors with an opportunity to take in some of the town's natural beauty. A zigzag path leads to the Alta da Memoría, a giant obelisk that marks the visit of King Pedro IV in the 1830s. *Ladeira de São Francisco. Admission free. Open daily dawn–dusk.*

Around the Island A drive along the west coast road takes you to the often misty and mysterious **Mata de Serreta forest park,** on the slopes of Caldeira de Santa Barbara, where the smell of eucalyptus leaves fills the air. On the north side of the island is the tiny village of **Biscoitos,** named for the small, biscuit-size chunks of lava that have formed on the island and have created an especially fertile environment for vegetation. The **Adega Brum wine museum** here demonstrates how vines are grown in tiny circles in the volcanic stone, which traps moisture and heat for the plants. You can also walk around the traditional winery and view the collection of old tools and documents assembled by the Brum family, as well as sample the wines. *Canada do Caldeiro, tel. 095/98904. Admission free. Open June–Sept., Mon.–Sat. 9–7; Oct.–May, Mon.–Sat. 10–4.*

From Angra take the road to Golfo, but continue straight until you see signs for Caldeira. **Caldeira de Guilherme Moniz,** at 15 kilometers (10 miles) in diameter, is the largest crater on the archipelago. On its northern edge is the well-marked **Algar do Carvão cave,** where a tunnel leads 330 feet down to a series of underground caverns, whose walls are covered with fancifully-shaped stalactites and stalagmites. There is a lake at the bottom. *Tel. 095/22992. Admission: 200$00. Open daily 2–4.*

Faial

Turtle-shaped Faial is the most westerly island of the central group and is separated from neighboring Pico by about 8 kilometers (5 miles) of sea. Much of the interior of the 173-square-kilometer (68-square-mile) island is rollling pasture, divided in summer by thick hedges of predominately blue hydrangeas that give Faial its nickname, the Blue Island. To the west is woodland and virgin bush that slopes down from the 2,890-foot-high crater rim of Cabeço Gordo.

Ponta dos Capelinhos A striking contrast to tranquil scenery is the Ponta dos Capelinhos, located in the district of Capelo, in Faial's southeastern corner. This stark, ash-covered point was created by a series of underwater eruptions that began on September 16, 1957. After a year of seismic "fireworks" that were accompanied by hundreds of tremors, what started as an island became the sombrero-shaped promotory you see today. Since its birth, more than half the point has been washed away by the unrelenting sea, but there are still places below the old lighthouse where you can literally tread new ground across a thick carpet of long-cooled volcanic ash. The **exhibition center,** opposite the lane that leads down to the lighthouse, explains the history of the point through stunning photo displays. *Open Tues.–Sun. 10–1 and 2–6:30.*

In nearby villages you can still see remains of buildings that were devastated by the earthquake. A popular exploration is to take a taxi to the Cabeço Gordo crater, where you can begin an easy-going two-and-a-half-hour stroll along a marked trail that leads down to a forest park at Capelo, the small village on the western end of the island. Here you can prepare your own barbeque on grills made from chunks of lava, among the beech trees that give the island its name, before walking the last 4 kilometers (2½ miles) that will return you to the Ponta dos Capelinhos.

Horta Serene Horta, about 23 kilometers (13 miles) away at the other end of the island, is Faial's capital and only town. Set between two bays and with a background of green hills dotted with windmills, it offers a soothing balance to the unforgiving landscape at Ponta dos Capeinhos. Sacked twice by the British during the Spanish occupation, Horta was also the scene of the last—and one of the bloodiest—naval actions between Britain and the United States, when in 1814 the American privateer, *General Armstrong,* was set on fire after putting up a brave battle. The Bay of Horta was reported to be full of weapons and pieces of broken fighting ships and to be tinted red from sailors' blood.

Today it is a lively meeting place for yachters, many of whom use the island as a trans-American stopover. Their favorite haunt, the unassuming **Café Sport,** a pub overlooking the harbor, was voted one of the 10 most famous bars in the world by *Time* magazine. The walls and ceilings are smothered with nautical memorabilia and drawings, paintings, and carvings by some of the hundreds of sailors who have dropped anchor here. Daytime visitors can view the priceless scrimshaw collection kept upstairs. The bar really comes to life in the summer, when sailors stop here to collect mail and provisions and exchange money. Many celebrate the Week of the Sea Festival (1st and 2nd Sundays in August), which includes regattas, windsurfing and swimming competitions, and children's games. Evidence of skippers who have passed through Horta can be seen on the harbor walls, where they have painted their boats' colors—a tradition that is supposed to ensure a safe journey.

Full of 18th- and 19th-century homes that retain their original bay windows and verandas, the town also has two interesting museums. The **Museu de Arte Sacra** (Sacred Art Museum) features a collection of rare 15th-century Flemish sculptures brought from the Low Countries (now Holland and Belgium) by early settlers. *Rua Conselheiro Medeiros, tel. 092/22090. Admission free. Open Tues.–Sun. 9:30–12:30 and 2–5.*

The **Museu Municipal** (Municipal Museum) has an unusual permanent collection of ships, buildings, and figures made out of fig-tree pith. A recent temporary exhibit featured photographs that documented the islands' days as a major aviation hub in the '30s, when trans-Atlantic "flying boats" used the harbor to refuel. *Largo Duque de Avila Bolama, tel. 092/23348. Admission free. Open Tues.–Sun. 9:30–12:30 and 2–5.*

A 3-kilometer (2-mile) walk or drive from town, along the back of the harbor to the Monte da Guia promontory reveals great views of the town, of neighboring Pico, and of the foaming waters of the Caldeira do Inferno (Hell's Crater), below. At the foot of the hill on the same road is a turn-of-the-century whaling station (closed to the public), the sole reminder of the once-thriving 19th-century industry.

Toward the end of that same century, Faial became the major hub of world telegraphic communications. Cables that had been layed to Europe to warn the continent of brewing storms were soon hooked up to the United States, forming a trans-Atlantic link that was to become obsolete by the 1950s. History buffs will enjoy viewing the last remnants of the 17th-century fortifications—the stone gateway and fort near Porto Prim beach. Nature-lovers should follow the road that leads to Flamengos for 3 kilometers (2 miles) to reach Faial's **Jardim Botânico** (Botanical Gardens). Some 90 specimens of native island plants can be seen here. *Take rd. marked Vale Flamengos–Quinta São Lourenço, tel. 092/31119. Admission free. Open weekdays 9–12:30 and 2–5:30.*

Pico

Named after its towering volcanic peak, which reaches a height of 7,640 feet, Pico is the most rugged and primitive island in the central group: Several natural arches remaining from old lava flows can still be seen on the north coast. However, the 48-kilometer-long (30-mile-long) island, which was once a whaling center, has its gentler side, too, with miles of woodland, flowering shrubs, and upland pastures. Pico is among the best places on the Azores to see craftspeople—weavers, distillers, and boat-builders—at work. Pico, with its tiny settlements, is a good day trip from the larger Horta (*see* Between the Islands by Boat in Essential Information, *above*).

Madalena **Madalena** is little more than a scattering of houses around its port and parish church. What's most interesting about the town lies in its fields, which man has toiled for centuries to make fit for farming. The *currais* are small plots divided by lava walls, and are square-shaped for growing vines and semi-circular for fig trees; *moroicos* are the vast pyramid-shape mounds of rocks heaped high to clear a way to soil below. Other sights, such as the thicket-covered lava fields on the road east of Santa Luzia (also found on Terceira and Faial) were provided courtesy of Mother Nature.

Pico's "longitudinal" road runs the entire length of the island (about 20 kilometers, or 12 miles), from Madalena, up to a frequently wind-swept plateau dotted with lakes. A side road (marked "Montanha") takes you another 8 kilometers (5 miles) to an altitude of nearly 6,000 feet. It might look easy to climb to the top, but the tourist office advises using a guide (the office will provide lists), as there are many deep fissures on the flanks. Pico's volcanic peak makes a dramatic photo-op, but it isn't so easy to see, as it often gathers storm clouds. The best times to see the summit are dawn and dusk.

About 5 kilometers (3 miles) back down to Madalena is the **Furna de Frei Matias,** the most accessible of many similar caves on Pico that were formed by lava flows whose upper crust solidified to form a tunnel of rock. Take a flashlight and you can walk for several hundred yards inside.

Pico, with its strong tradition of whaling, still celebrates the coming of the leviathans during its annual festival held the last week in August in the village of Lages do Pico. Year-round you can visit the **Museu dos Baleeiros** (Whalers' Museum), situated on the waterfront at Lajes, for a taste of what life was like for the crews on the exhibitions. An audio-visual show tells the story in English. The well-laid out museum features giant jaw bones, vicious-looking harpoons, and the ubiquitous scrimshaw—the whalebone on which crewmen etched fanciful scenes while they awaited the next catch. *Rua dos Baleeiros, 096/672276. Admission free. Open daily 9:30–12:30 and 2–5.*

Lages More evidence of the whaling industry can be seen on the way east from Lages to **Calheta de Nesquim,** a village huddled below the clifftop main road. Here whalers (the traditional streamlined boats used for hunts) are lined along the slipway in front of the church to remind people of the old whaling days. On the road you'll see white towers that, until the 1980s when the hunts were banned, were used as lookout points. Sentinels posted in the towers would watch for whale sightings, then fire rockets to alert their colleagues at sea. Then they would guide the crew to their targets by moving sheets in the appropriate direction.

Sports and Outdoor Activities

Fishing

Fishing enthusiasts can hook up with fast motor boats based in São Miguel, Terceira, and Faial. For charter boats, contact the **Horta Marina** (tel. 092/31693), **Pescatur** (Rua João Francisco Cabral 49D, Ponta Delgada, telex 096/85570), or **Turatlântica**

(Rua do Galo 21, Angra, fax 095/29333). Several world and European records have been set in the Azores, with tuna, swordfish, and marlin among the game. Freshwater anglers can try their hand at fly-fishing on São Miguel and Flores, but must first obtain a fishing license from the tourist office. Apart from trout in the streams, there are also pike, perch, and carp in São Miguel's lakes.

Hiking/Climbing

These are two of the most popular pastimes for visitors to the islands, and there are plenty of tracks and quiet roads to explore. Tourist offices stock a booklet that describes the best island paths. Terceira's climbing club, **Os Montanheiros** (tel. 095/22992), explores some of the island's caves and can provide information about rental equipment.

Swimming

You'll find clean, but small sandy stretches of beach on São Miguel, Terceira, Faial, and Santa Maria. All the islands have swimmable areas, either off rocks or in pools created by solidified lava flows that have run into the sea. Some pools have little more than steps and a concrete path built for easy access; others have changing rooms, toilets, sunbathing areas, and bars. You can also swim in the big lakes on São Miguel.

Water Sports

A few hotels rent scuba-diving, snorkeling, and sailboarding equipment to guests, and when available, nonguests may rent as well. However, the best places to rent and take lessons are: on São Miguel, **Clube Navale** (Av. Copk, Ponta Delgada, tel. 096/23005); on Terceira, **Clube Naval da Praia da Vitória** (Av. Beira Mar, Praia, tel. 095/52993) or **Clube Nautico de Angra do Heroísmo** (Av. 28 de Maio, Angra, tel. 095/23300); and on Faial, **Clube Navale da Horta** (Rua T. Valadim, Horta, tel. 092/22331).

Dining and Lodging

Dining Most restaurants in the Azores have fairly unsophisticated cuisine, which usually includes grilled fish and steaks. Although there are few creative sauces, and vegetables and salads may be hard to come by, the home-style food is invariably good, even in the humblest of places. Prices are generally low, but the check will add up if you indulge in a lot of seafood and shellfish.

Soup, often watercress or *caldo do nabo* (turnip), is a typical appetizer. Among the specialties from the sea are *polvo guisado em vinho* (octopus stewed in wine), *bife de atum* (tuna), *caldeiradas de peixe* (fish stew), and *arroz de lapas* (limpets with rice). The main seafoods are lobster, crab, and *perce bes*, or goose barnacles (grey tentacles with a tasty, pinkish flesh inside). Meat dishes include *morcela* (black blood sausage), sometimes eaten with pineapple; *linguiça con inhames* (pork-fillet sausages with yams); *sopa de Espirito* (a substantial broth containing thick chunks of beef); and *alcatra* (spicy beef stew).

You'll find a variety of pastries and sweetmeats, including *queijadas* (cheesecakes) and *especiés* (cakes flavored with cinnamon and other spices). Sugar cookies are molded into shapes of flowers, birds, and animals, especially during the Espirito Santo festivities. When a cook wants to give thanks for a cured ailment, sweetmeats often take on the form of the affected body part—such as a breast or leg.

The typical island wine is *verdelho*, a dry, brownish-white, which was once exported to Europe, North America, and the Russian czars. For most people it's an acquired taste. There are also lighter, fruity whites, some of which come from Graciosa. The red *vinho de cheiro* can still be ordered in restaurants, although the EC banned the traditional grape used because the fruit is said to have been the cause of headaches and blindness. Given the edict, winegrowers are experimenting with other grapes.

Plenty of fruit is grown on the islands, from pineapples to bananas, and you can finish your meal with a pineapple or passion-fruit liqueur produced on São Miguel. Various brandies, including fig, loquat, and blackberry, are still produced here—especially on Pico—in ancient copper stills.

In the moderately priced restaurants, reservations are advised during festivals and in the summer. Unless otherwise noted, dress is casual.

Restaurant ratings correspond to Lisbon's dining chart, in Chapter 3. Highly recommended restaurants are indicated by a star ★.

Lodging Only São Miguel offers a variety of hotels, including everything from historic to imaginatively designed modern accommodations. On the other islands, hotels are mostly modern and functional in design. If you're looking for budget accommodations, contact the tourist office for lists of private homes, which offer self-catering apartments or bed-and-breakfast plans. With an eye to tourism, the islands' government is encouraging several new lodging projects, among them, a campaign on São Miguel to turn historic homes into guest houses. Reservations are advised in summer. Ratings are based on prices quoted during high season.

Highly recommended lodgings are indicated by a star ★.

Category	Cost*
Expensive	15,000$00–20,000$00
Moderate	10,000$00–15,000$00
Inexpensive	under 10,000$00

Prices are for a double room, including tax.

Faial **O Barão.** Despite the flashy decor, which includes diamond-
Dining shape mirrors everywhere, this is the smartest restaurant in
★ town. Try the stewed tuna or regional beef stew, followed by an orange- or almond-flavor *pudin* (pudding). *Alameda Barão de Roches 21, Horta, tel. 092/22124. DC, MC, V. Moderate.*
O Biraca. This tiny place is a bit difficult to find but worth the effort: Walk along the seafront to the creek, then go 3 blocks inland. The green-and-white color scheme and pine fittings

promote the cheery atmosphere you'll find here. Try the spicy black blood sausage, or the tangy octopus salad, steeped in onions and peppers. *Rua Conceição 2, Horta, tel. 092/22655. No credit cards. Inexpensive.*

Vista da Baia Varadouro. A side road just before Capelo leads down to this terrace restaurant that overlooks the bay for which it's named. The views are pleasant, especially if you come for lunch or an early dinner. Owners Frank Varga and his California-born wife, Mary, serve monster-size helpings of grilled fish and meats, accompanied by home-grown salads. *Varadoura, tel. 092/95140. No credit cards. Closed Wed. and holidays. Inexpensive.*

Lodging **Estalagem Santa Cruz.** Built inside a 16th-century fort that
★ was captured by Sir Walter Raleigh, this modernized harborside hotel has a place in local history and once belonged to Raymond Burr, the star of TV's "Perry Mason." Today it is tastefully decorated in the Iberian style, with antiques in the corridors, lots of dark wood, and quarry tiles. *Rua Vasco da Gama, 9900 Horta, tel. 092/23021. 25 rooms with bath. Facilities: restaurant, bar, entertainment. AE, MC, V. Moderate.*

Hotel Fayál. A five-minute walk up the hill from the harbor brings you to this hotel, which was built around the former quarters of the Western Union Telegraph Company. Apartments grouped around a lawn at the back once housed the workmen who lay the trans-Atlantic cables. Rooms in the new section have small terraces that look out over the harbor toward Pico. *Rua Cônsul Dabney, 9900 Horta, tel. 092/22181. 123 rooms with bath. Facilities: restaurant, bar, disco, outdoor pool, tennis courts, boutique, beauty salon. AE, DC, MC, V. Moderate.*

Pico **Residencial Pico.** Although this restaurant is decidedly mod-
Dining est, with farming implements lining the walls, the fare is good and dependable. Ramblers come by here and often stay in the rooms available for overnight stays, but we don't recommend the Residencial as a lodging accommodation at this time, because it's in the throes of remodeling. *Rua dos Biscoitos, Madalena, tel. 092/622292. MC, V. Inexpensive.*

Restaurant Lagoa. The plain, modern facade of this restaurant—the only place to eat out in town—is uninviting, but inside you'll find the Lagoa is clean and efficiently run. Try some cuts of conger eel or fillet pork sausages with yams. *Praça de São Pedro, Lajes, tel. 092/9797272. MC, V. Inexpensive.*

Lodging **Hotel Caravelas.** The angular terraces of this modern L-shaped hotel overlook the harbor and the tuna-fishing fleet. Rooms have dark wood fittings that contrast with the beige and grey decor. One wing is made up of apartments, most of which have kitchenettes. *Rua Cons. Terra Pinheiro, 9950 Madalena, tel. 092/92500. 67 rooms with bath. Facilities: restaurant, gym, sauna. AE, DC, MC, V. Moderate.*

Residencial Açor. Tucked away in the narrow streets of the old town, this pension—with simple but clean rooms—offers delightful views of the sea and mountains. *Rua D. João Paulino, 9930 Lajes, tel. 092/97438. 13 rooms with bath. MC, V. Inexpensive.*

Residencial Montanha. Built in 1986 on the hills over São Roque harbor, this modern pension with a comfortable lounge and bright, airy rooms is one of the best budget stops on the islands. A terrace, running all the way around the building, overlooks the gardens on which the Montanha is situated. Only breakfast is served, but there's a small restaurant nearby. *Rua do Capitão Mor, 9940 São Roque, tel. 092/642699. 16 rooms with bath. Facilities: bar. No credit cards. Inexpensive.*

São Jorge

Dining

Borges. Conveniently located for people traveling to the airport (it's on the same road), and less than 10 minutes' drive from Velas, the Borges is the place to come for the mostly basic but tasty old stand-bys such as roast chicken and pork chops. The surroundings are pleasant, too, with plain but tasteful interior decor and views of the forested cliff the restaurant faces. *Queimada, Velas, tel. 095/42128. No credit cards. Inexpensive.*

Velense. One of the only restaurants in town that stays open year-round, this place—situated opposite the Residencial Neto (*see below*)—has a steady clientele that comes for the local cheese-with-figs appetizer, the *abobora* (pumpkin soup), and the almond pie. *Rua Dr. José Pereira, Velas, tel. 095/42160. No credit cards. Inexpensive.*

Lodging

Estalagem das Velas. The uncompromising concrete facade hides a cozy, modern inn situated on the slopes above the port of Velas. From here you'll get magnificent views of Pico. Reproduction antique maps of the Azores adorn the walls of the basic, but comfortable, brown-and-beige bedrooms. *Av. da Conceicão, 9800 Velas, tel. 095/42632. 24 rooms with bath. Facilities: bar, tennis. MC, V. Inexpensive.*

Residencial Neto. This old two-story black-stone and white-washed house backs the harbor, provding nice views from the terrace at the rear. The Neto is a clean and homey budget pension, and there's a seawater-filled pool in the back. *Rua Dr José Pereira, 9800 Velas, tel. 095/42403. 16 rooms with bath Facilities: bar, pool. No credit cards. Inexpensive.*

São Miguel

Dining

★

A Pedra. The name, which means "stone" in Portuguese, refers to the lava-face walls and arches inside this east-side restaurant. The 18th-century French period-style bar adds to the distinctive ambience. *Rua João de Melo Abreu 33A, Ponta Delgada, tel. 096/628284. Reservations required. Jacket and tie required. No credit cards. Moderate.*

Coliseu. This restaurant, with a spacious dining room and clean, white walls, is a favorite of locals. You can watch your food being prepared in the open kitchen, and the service is particularly good. Baked octopus is a specialty. *Av. Roberto Ivens, Ponta Delgada, tel. 096/27120. MC, V. Moderate.*

O Retiro. A part of the well-situated Terra Furnas Hotel, this dining spot enjoys a view of the grassy square belonging to the hotel. O Retiro offers an à la carte menu that in the summer includes cozido, cooked on the baks of Lagoa das Furnas. *Rua Padre José Jacinto Botelho, Furnas, tel. 096/54304. Reservations required. Jacket and tie required. AE, DC, MC, V. Moderate.*

Arturus. The tasteless bright green strips that border the front window and the restaurant's difficult location, on a back road behind the hospital, are off-putting, but any local will tell you Arturus is *the* place for grilled fish. *Rua João Francisco Cabral 49, Ponta Delgada, tel. 096/24990. No credit cards. Inexpensive.*

★

Cavalo Branco. The unique taste of the food served in this tavern—whose name means "white horse"—can be attributed to the kitchen's stone oven, the only one on the island. The owner-chef makes her own sausages and wine. In summer there's folk music and dancing. *Rua do Meio Meio 23, Santa Bárbara, tel. 096/98365. No credit cards. Inexpensive.*

Marisqueira Regional. This restaurant that sits behind a waterside church, is the best fish-and-seafood spot in a town known for these specialties. To reach the entrance you have to pass under a tunnel of overhanging trees—one of the pleasant surprises when you come here. *Av. Gaspar Fructuoso, Lagoa, tel. 096/92138. MC, V. Inexpensive.*

Lodging **Açores Atlântico.** The top hotel in town is centrally located and offers great views of the sea. Despite its imposing modern architecture, this seven-story hotel maintains a human touch and features a cozy piano bar frequented by local businesspeople. *Av. Infante Dom Henrique, 9500 Ponta Delgada, tel. 096/ 35196. 140 rooms with bath. Facilities: restaurant, bar, indoor pool, sauna, gym, hairdresser, gift shop. AE, DC, MC, V. Expensive.*

Bahia Palace. Situated on the southern coast road on the way to Furnas, this modern, six-story hotel offers excellent views of Água d'Alto Bay and a short strip of sandy beach. The Bahia Palace is set in its own gardens and has a spacious, comfortable feel. *Água d'Alto, 9600 Vila Franca do Campo, tel. 096/52228. 101 rooms with bath. Facilities: restaurant, bar, pool, gym, sauna, tennis courts, sailboarding. AE, DC, MC, V. Expensive.*

★ **Caloura.** Though just 16 kilometers (10 miles) from Ponta Delgada by car, the Caloura is as secluded as any hotel on the island. The L-shape modern building has terraces that overlook the pool and are divided by lava buttresses. From the restaurant you get wonderful views of the rocky coastline. *Água de Pau, 9560 Lagoa, tel. 096/93240. 20 rooms with bath. Facilities: restaurant, bar, pool, sauna, gym, tennis, scuba-diving courses, horseback riding, sailboarding. No credit cards. Moderate.*

São Pedro. This early 19th-century town house was owned and designed by Thomas Hickling, who created Terra Nostra Park. The best rooms are in the back and overlook a walled garden and the waterfront. Full of creaking floorboards and antique furnishings, the São Pedro would make an ideal setting for an Agatha Christie novel. Stop into the bar, even if the somewhat gloomy interior doesn't entice you to stay the night. *Largo Almirante Dunn, 9500 Ponta Delgada, tel. 096/22223. 26 rooms with bath. Facilities: bar. AE, DC, MC, V. Moderate.*

★ **Solar do Conde.** This 150-year-old manor house with its own courtyard and gardens has a collection of one-story self-catering apartments faithfully copied from the original estate cottage. All accommodations are decorated with 19th-century furniture. The stone-walled cellars of the main house, riddled with nooks and crannies, have been converted into an intimate dining room. *Rua do Rosário 36, 9545 Capelas, tel. 096/98887. 27 rooms with bath. Facilities: restaurant, bar, pool. AE, DC, MC, V. Moderate.*

★ **Terra Nostra.** From the outside this hotel, built in 1937, is not impressive; the high ceilings and massive staircase inside create the look of a country mansion. A new wing was added recently. Some rooms overlook the park of the same name. *Rua Padre José Jacinto Botelho, 9675 Furnas, tel. 096/54104. 79 rooms with bath. Facilities: restaurant, bar, tennis courts, indoor and outdoor pools. AE, DC, MC, V. Inexpensive–Moderate.*

Sete Cidades. The reception area at this good budget choice is not inviting, but the rooms are clean and comfortable and the staff friendly. *Rua do Contador 20, 9500 Ponta Delgada, tel. 096/27344. 32 rooms with bath. Facilities: bar. MC, V. Inexpensive.*

Terceira
Dining
★ **Casa Roda.** An international cuisine includes many fish selections, but don't overlook the meat specialties: *porco con ervas aromaticas* (pork cooked in herbs) and tender filet mignon. There's a terrace for dining outdoors. This newly refurbished restaurant overlooking Angra Bay is on the site of a former children's home. Desperate mothers without the means to support their children would push them through the *roda* (swinging door) to the nuns on the other side. *Rua Principe do Mónaco 64, Angra, tel. 095/22110. AE, MC, V. Moderate.*

★ **O Pescador.** Considered by locals to be the best restaurant in the beach town of Priai, O Pescador is renowned for its fresh seafood dishes: Chefs use the *cataplana* technique from the Algarve, in which the food is steamed in pans. *Rua Constantino José Cardoso, Priai, tel. 095/53495. MC, V. Moderate.*

★ **Quinta do Martelo.** This former *quinta* (farmhouse), about 6 kilometers (4 miles) out of Angra, behind São Mateus, is now a restaurant that serves ample helpings of traditional Azorean food. Before or after a meal guests can wander around the gardens. *Canada do Martelo 24, Cantinho, tel. 095/31842. No credit cards. Inexpensive.*

Lodging **Albergaria Cruzeiro.** The unattractive facade hides a bright, modern interior. This can be a good family accommodation, especially if you stay in one of the five bedrooms set up as comfortable minisuites, with refrigerator and sitting area. *Praça Dr. Sousa Júnior, 9700 Angra do Heroísmo, tel. 095/24071. 47 rooms with bath. Facilities: restaurant, bar, car rental. AE, DC, MC, V. Moderate.*

Hotel Angra. This hotel gets high marks in at least two areas: it's the most comfortable choice in town and is located in the central plaza. When you tire of looking at eclectic decor, you can gaze out at the peaceful public gardens. *Praça Velha, 9702 Angra do Heroísmo, tel. 095/24041. 82 rooms with bath. Facilities: restaurant, bar. AE, DC, MC, V. Moderate.*

Monte Brasil. A spacious entrance hall leads up a pink-marble staircase to the bedrooms and an attic breakfast room/bar from where you'll get broad views of the town and coast. Its bright, airy bedrooms and fine location—just five minutes from the town center—make this nice-sized inn a good-value choice. *Alto das Covas 8, 9700 Angra do Heroísmo, tel. 095/22440. 29 rooms with bath. Facilities: bar. AE, DC, MC, V. Inexpensive.*

Residencial Salles. A best bet for those who want to stay near the beach or airport, this pension is comfortable, modern, and has terraces that overlook the town square and coast. *Praça Francisco Ornelas da Câmara 2, 9760 Praia da Vitória, tel. 095/53541. 24 rooms with bath. Facilities: bar. AE, DC, MC, V. Inexpensive.*

Portuguese Vocabulary

If you have reading knowledge of Spanish and/or French, you will find Portuguese easy to read. However, Portuguese pronunciation can be somewhat tricky. Despite obvious similarities in Spanish and Portuguese spelling and syntax, the Portuguese sounds are a far cry—almost literally so—from their ostensible Spanish equivalents. Some of the main peculiarities of Portuguese phonetics are the following.

Nasalized vowels: if you have some idea of French pronunciation, these shouldn't give you too much trouble. The closest approach is that of the French *accent du Midi,* as spoken by people in Marseille and in the Provence area, or perhaps an American Midwest twang will help. Try pronouncing *"an," "am," "en," "em," "in," "om," "un,"* etc., with a sustained *"ng"* sound (e.g. *"bom"-"bong,"* etc.).

Another aspect of Portuguese phonetics is the vowels and diphthongs written with the tilde: *ã, ão, ães.* The Portuguese word for *"wool," "lã,"* sounds roughly like the French word *"lin,"* with the *"-in"* resembling the *"an"* in the English word *"any,"* but nasalized. The suffix *"-tion"* on such English words as "information" becomes in Portuguese spelling *"ção,"* pronounced *"-sa-on,"* with the *"-on"* nasalized: *"Informação,"* for example. These words form their plurals by changing the suffix to *çoes,* which sounds like *"-son-ech"* (the *"ch"* here resembling a cross between the English *"sh"* and the German *"ch":* hence *"informaçoes"*).

The cedilla occurring under the *"c"* serves exactly the same purpose as in French: it transforms the *"c"* into an *"ss"* sound in front of the three so-called "hard" vowels ("a," "o," and "u"): e.g. *graça, Açores, açúcar.* The letter "c" occurring without a cedilla in front of these three vowels automatically has the sound of "k": pico, mercado, curto. The letter "c" followed by "e" or "i" is always "ss," and hence needs no cedilla: nacional, Graciosa, Terceira.

The letter "j" sounds like the "s" in the English word "pleasure." So does "g" except when the latter is followed by one of the "hard" vowels: hence, generoso, gigantesco, Jerónimo, azulejos, Jorge, etc.

The spelling *"nh"* is rendered like the *"ny"* in *"canyon":* cf. *"senhora."*

The spelling *"lh"* is somewhere in between the *"l"* and the *"y"* sounds in *"million":* cf. *"Batalha."*

In the matter of syllabic stress, Portuguese obeys the two basic Spanish principles: 1) in words ending in a vowel, or in "n" or "s" the tonic accent falls on the next-to-the-last syllable: fado, mercado, azulejos; 2) in words ending in consonants other than "n" or "s," the stress falls on the last syllable: *favor, nacional.* Words in which the syllabic stress does not conform to the two above rules must be written with an acute accent to indicate the proper pronunciation: sábado, república, politécnico.

Numbers

1	um, uma
2	dois, duas
3	três
4	quatro
5	cinco
6	seis
7	sete
8	oito
9	nove
10	dez
11	onze
12	doze
13	treze
14	catorze
15	quinze
16	dezaseis
17	dezasete
18	dezoito
19	dezanove
20	vinte
21	vinte e um
22	vinte e dois
30	trinta
40	quarenta
50	cinquenta
60	sessenta
70	setenta
80	oitenta
90	noventa
100	cem
110	cento e dez
200	duzentos
1,000	mil
1,500	mil e quinhentos

Days of the Week

Monday	Segunda-feira
Tuesday	Terça-feira
Wednesday	Quarta-feira
Thursday	Quinta-feira
Friday	Sexta-feira
Saturday	Sábado
Sunday	Domingo

Months

January	Janeiro
February	Fevereiro
March	Março
April	Abril
May	Maio
June	Junho
July	Julho
August	Agosto
September	Setembro
October	Outubro

| November | Novembro |
| December | Dezembro |

Useful Phrases

Do you speak English?	Fala Inglês?
yes	sim
no	não
please	por favor
thank you	obrigado
thank you very much	muito obrigado
excuse me, sorry	com licença, desculpe
I'm sorry	desculpe-me
Good morning or good day	Bom dia
Good afternoon	Boa tarde
Good evening or good night	Boa noite
Goodbye	Adeus
How are you?	Como está?
How do you say in Portuguese?	Como se diz em Português?
Tourist Office	Turismo
Fine	Optimo
Very good	Muito bem (muito bom)
It's all right	Está bem
Good luck	Felicidades (boa sorte)
Hello	Olá
Come back soon	Até breve
Where is the hotel?	Onde é o hotel?
How much does this cost?	Quanto custa?
How do you feel?	Como se sente?
How goes it?	Que tal?
Pleased to meet you	Muito prazer em o (a) conhecer
The pleasure is mine	O prazer é meu
I have the pleasure of introducing Mr. . . .	Tenho o prazer de lhe apresentar o senhor. . . .
I like it very much	Gosto muito
I don't like it	Não gosto
Many thanks	Muito obrigado
Don't mention it	De nada
Pardon me	Desculpe-me (Perdão)
Are you ready?	Está pronto?
I am ready	Estou pronto
Welcome	Seja benvindo
A am very sorry	Desculpe (Lastimo muito)
What time is it?	Que horas são?
I am glad to see you	Muito prazer em o (a) ver
I don't understand	Não entendo
Please speak slowly	Fale lentamente por favor

I understand (or) It is clear	Compreendo (or) Está claro
Whenever you please	Quando quizer
Please wait toilet	Faça favor de esperar casa de banho
I will be a little late	Chegarei um pouco atrasado
I don't know	Não sei
Is this seat free?	Está vago este lugar?
Would you please direct me to . . . ?	Por favor indique-me . . . ?
Where is the station, museum . . . ?	Onde é a estação, museu . . . ?
I am American, British	Eu sou Americano, Inglês
It's very kind of you	É muito amavel
Please sit down	Por favor sente-se

Sundries

cigar, cigarette	charuto, cigarro
matches	fosforos
dictionary	dicionário
key	chave
razor blades	laminas de barbear
shaving cream	creme de barbear
soap	sobonete
map	mapa
tampons	tampões
sanitary pads	pensos higiénicos
newspaper	jornal
magazine	revista
telephone	telefone
envelopes	envelopes
writing paper	papel de carta
airmail writing paper	papel de carta de avião
post card	postal
stamps	selos

Merchants

bakery	padaria
bookshop	livraria
butcher's	talho
delicatessen	charcutaria
dry cleaner's	limpeza a seco
grocery	mercearia
hairdresser, barber	cabeleireiro, barbeiro
laundry	lavandaria
shoemaker	sapateiro
supermarket	supermercado

Emergencies/Medical

ill, sick	doente
I am ill	estou doente
My wife/husband/child is ill	Minha mulher/marido/criança está doente
doctor	doutor/medico
nurse	enfermeira/o
prescription	receita
pharmacist/chemist	farmacia
Please fetch/call a doctor	Por favor, chame o doutor/medico
accident	acidente
road accident	acidente na estrada
Where is the nearest hospital?	Onde é o hospital mais proximo?
Where is the American/British Hospital?	Onde é o Hospital Americano/Britanico?
dentist	dentista
X-ray	Raios-X
pain-killer	analgésico
bandage	ligadura
ointment for bites/stings	pomada para picadas
cough mixture	xarope para a tosse
laxative	laxativo
thermometer	termómetro

On the Move

plane	avião
train	comboio
boat	barco
taxi	taxi
car	carro/automovel
bus	autocarro
seat	assento/lugar
reservation	reserva
smoking/non-smoking compartment	compartimento para fumadores/não fumadores
rail station	estação caminho de ferro
subway station	estação do Metropolitano
airport	aéroporto
harbor	estação martima
town terminal	estação/terminal
shuttle bus/train	autocarro/comboio com ligação constante
sleeper	cama
couchette	beliche
porter	bagageiro
baggage/luggage	bagagem
baggage trolley	carrinho de bagagem
single ticket	bilhete de ida
return ticket	bilhete de ida e volta
first class	primeira classe
second class	segunda classe
When does the train leave?	A que horas sai o comboio?

| What time does the train arrive at . . . ? | A que horas chega o comboio a . . . ? |
| When does the first/last train leave? | Quando parte o primeiro/ultimo comboio? |

Hotels

room	quarto
bed	cama
bathroom	casa de banho
bathtub	banheira
shower	duche
toilet/Men/Women	toilete/Homens/Senhores
toilet paper	papel higiénico
pillow	almofada
blanket	cobertor
chambermaid	criada/empregada de quarto
breakfast	pequeno almoço
lunch	almoço
dinner	jantar
Do you have a single/double/twin-bedded room?	Tem um quarto individual/duplo/com duas camas?
I'd like a quiet room	Eu gostave de um quarto sossegado
I'd like some pillows/blankets	Gostava de mais almofadas/cobertores
What time is breakfast?	A que horas é o pequeno almoço?
Is it served in the room?	Éi servido no quarto?
Come in!	Entre!
Are there any messages for me?	Há algum recado para mim?
Would you please call me a taxi?	Por favor chama-me um taxi?
Please take our bags to our room	Por favor leve as nossas malas para o nosso quarto

Dining Out

menu	carta
fixed-price menu	preço fixo
wine list	carta de vinhos
house wine	vinho da casa
waiter	criado/empregado
Waiter!	Faz favor!
bill/check	conta

Index

Personal Itinerary

Departure *Date*

Time

Transportation

Arrival *Date*   *Time*

Departure *Date*   *Time*

Transportation

Accommodations

Arrival *Date*   *Time*

Departure *Date*   *Time*

Transportation

Accommodations

Arrival *Date*   *Time*

Departure *Date*   *Time*

Transportation

Accommodations

Fodor's Travel Guides

U.S. Guides

Alaska

Arizona

Boston

California

Cape Cod, Martha's
Vineyard, Nantucket

The Carolinas & the
Georgia Coast

Chicago

Disney World & the
Orlando Area

Florida

Hawaii

Las Vegas, Reno,
Tahoe

Los Angeles

Maine, Vermont,
New Hampshire

Maui

Miami & the Keys

New England

New Orleans

New York City

Pacific North Coast

Philadelphia & the
Pennsylvania Dutch
Country

San Diego

San Francisco

Santa Fe, Taos,
Albuquerque

Seattle & Vancouver

The South

The U.S. & British
Virgin Islands

The Upper Great
Lakes Region

USA

Vacations in New York
State

Vacations on the
Jersey Shore

Virginia & Maryland

Waikiki

Washington, D.C.

Foreign Guides

Acapulco, Ixtapa,
Zihuatanejo

Australia & New
Zealand

Austria

The Bahamas

Baja & Mexico's
Pacific Coast Resorts

Barbados

Berlin

Bermuda

Brazil

Budapest

Budget Europe

Canada

Cancun, Cozumel,
Yucatan Peninsula

Caribbean

Central America

China

Costa Rica, Belize,
Guatemala

Czechoslovakia

Eastern Europe

Egypt

Euro Disney

Europe

Europe's Great Cities

France

Germany

Great Britain

Greece

The Himalayan
Countries

Hong Kong

India

Ireland

Israel

Italy

Italy's Great Cities

Japan

Kenya & Tanzania

Korea

London

Madrid & Barcelona

Mexico

Montreal &
Quebec City

Morocco

The Netherlands
Belgium &
Luxembourg

New Zealand

Norway

Nova Scotia, Prince
Edward Island &
New Brunswick

Paris

Portugal

Rome

Russia & the Baltic
Countries

Scandinavia

Scotland

Singapore

South America

Southeast Asia

South Pacific

Spain

Sweden

Switzerland

Thailand

Tokyo

Toronto

Turkey

Vienna & the Danube
Valley

Yugoslavia

Special Series

Fodor's Affordables

Affordable Europe

Affordable France

Affordable Germany

Affordable Great
Britain

Affordable Italy

**Fodor's Bed &
Breakfast and
Country Inns Guides**

California

Mid-Atlantic Region

New England

The Pacific Northwest

The South

The West Coast

The Upper Great
Lakes Region

Canada's Great
Country Inns

Cottages, B&Bs and
Country Inns of
England and Wales

The Berkeley Guides

On the Loose in
California

On the Loose in
Eastern Europe

On the Loose in
Mexico

On the Loose in the
Pacific Northwest &
Alaska

**Fodor's Exploring
Guides**

Exploring California

Exploring Florida

Exploring France

Exploring Germany

Exploring Paris

Exploring Rome

Exploring Spain

Exploring Thailand

Fodor's Flashmaps

New York

Washington, D.C.

Fodor's Pocket Guides

Pocket Bahamas

Pocket Jamaica

Pocket London

Pocket New York
City

Pocket Paris

Pocket Puerto Rico

Pocket San Francisco

Pocket Washington,
D.C.

Fodor's Sports

Cycling

Hiking

Running

Sailing

The Insider's Guide
to the Best Canadian
Skiing

**Fodor's Three-In-Ones
(guidebook, language
cassette, and phrase
book)**

France

Germany

Italy

Mexico

Spain

**Fodor's
Special-Interest
Guides**

Cruises and Ports
of Call

Disney World & the
Orlando Area

Euro Disney

Healthy Escapes

London Companion

Skiing in the USA
& Canada

Sunday in New York

**Fodor's Touring
Guides**

Touring Europe

Touring USA:
Eastern Edition

Touring USA:
Western Edition

**Fodor's Vacation
Planners**

Great American
Vacations

National Parks of the
West

**The Wall Street
Journal Guides to
Business Travel**

Europe

International Cities

Pacific Rim

USA & Canada

WHEREVER YOU TRAVEL, *H*ELP IS NEVER FAR AWAY.

From planning your trip to providing travel assistance along the way, American Express® Travel Service Offices* are always there to help.

Portugal

LISBON
Top Tours
Av. Duque De Loule 108
(1) 315 5885

MADEIRA
Top Tours
Rua Brigadeiro
Couceiro 28
Funchal
(91) 742 611

PORTIMÃO
Top Tours
Estrada Da Rocha
Praia Da Rocha
(82) 417 552

PÔRTO
Top Tours
Rua Alferes Malheiro 96
(2) 208 2785

QUARTEIRA
Top Tours
Avenida Infante De Sagres 73
(89) 302 726